Using Microcomputers

A Complete Introduction

Using Microcomputers

A Complete Introduction

H. L. Capron
Ralph E. Duffy

The Benjamin/Cummings Publishing Company, Inc.
Redwood City, California ● Fort Collins, Colorado
Menlo Park, California ● Reading, Massachusetts ● New York
Don Mills, Ontario ● Wokingham, U.K. ● Amsterdam ● Bonn
Sydney ● Singapore ● Tokyo ● Madrid ● San Juan

Editorial Director: Sally D. Elliott
Sponsoring Editor: David B. Jackson
Developmental Editor: Margy Kuntz
Production Supervisor: Laura Kenney
Production Editor: Judith Hibbard
Text Design: Seventeenth Street Studios
Cover Design: Victoria Philp
Cover Illustration: Computer graphic created by Melvin L. Prueitt, © Los Alamos National
Laboratory
Photo Researcher: Sarah Bendersky
Photo Editor: Wendy Earl
Copy Editor: Toni Murray
Illustrator: George Samuelson
Composition and Technical Art: Graphic Typesetting Service

Production and manufacturing management by The Compage Company, San Francisco

Library of Congress Cataloging-in-Publication Data

Capron, H. L.
   Using microcomputers: a complete introduction / H.L. Capron,
Ralph E. Duffy.
     p.   cm.
   Includes index.
   ISBN 0-8053-0461-4
   1. Microcomputers.   I. Duffy, Ralph E.   II. Title.
QA76.5.C364   1989
004—dc19   88-38531
                                    CIP

Software version: ISBN 0-8053-0461-4   Non-software version: ISBN 0-8053-0466-5

CDEFGHIJ-VH-93210

The Benjamin/Cummings Publishing Company, Inc.
390 Bridge Parkway
Redwood City, California 94065

For Jamison and Jason
         HLC

For Mary Jo Cashman, Bill Wills, and Muhammad Husami
         RED

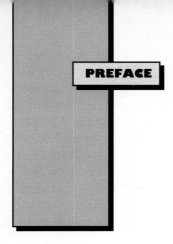

PREFACE

Why Adopt This Book?

Using Microcomputers: A Complete Introduction offers both a general and a hands-on introduction to microcomputers in a manner that students can readily follow and will even enjoy. The broad-based coverage of principal microcomputer concepts gives students a solid background in hardware, software, and computer issues. The hands-on applications chapters, which cover three market-leading commercial software packages, let students apply microcomputer techniques and keystrokes as they read. As an instructor you will find this text useful for both beginning students and those with some computer knowledge. Moreover, this text has all the elements you have been asking for, including accompanying software and a complete supplements package.

A Complete Introduction

Using Microcomputers: A Complete Introduction covers all the topics needed for an introductory course in microcomputers. In addition, we have specific, hands-on instruction in four major areas: word processing, spreadsheets, database management systems, and business graphics. Other features of this text include a friendly writing style, up-to-date coverage, a colorful art and photo program, and extensive student learning aids.

The book is divided into three parts. Part I, "Microcomputer Orientation," begins with a discussion about computers in today's society to provide students with a context for the use of software. The book then outlines the major hardware and software components of a microcomputer system. Part II, "Hands-On Applications Packages," provides thorough, hands-on coverage of four primary microcomputer applications—word processing, spreadsheets, database management, and graphics—using software that a majority of schools have elected to teach: WordPerfect, Lotus 1-2-3, and dBASE III PLUS. This section includes both introductory and advanced topics. These chapters are the heart of the book, giving students practical knowledge they can use in and out of the classroom. Part III, "Beyond the Basic Applications," includes chapters on data communications, desktop publishing, advanced microcomputer applications, and microcomputer trends. The text ends with four appendixes: a quick reference to directories and subdirectories, a brief explanation of the use of Lotus 1-2-3 as a database, a preview of dBASE IV, and an overview of IBM's new PS/2 and OS/2.

Our purpose has been to construct as *flexible* a textbook as possible, because we recognize that courses on microcomputer applications vary widely from school to school. For example, some instructors may choose to cover only Part II, spending all the classtime teaching applications in a microcomputer laboratory and assigning other elements of the text as outside reading. Instructors with limited class- or lab time may cover only the introductory chapters for each application, giving students a chance to learn the basic skills necessary for using each package. Other instructors may wish to emphasize the general nature of the text, assigning the hands-on exercises as optional class work. Whatever the goals and thrust of your course, we hope you find our coverage tailor-made to your needs.

Features

In addition to the many practical examples woven into each chapter, we have included a variety of pedagogical elements and features to enhance students' interest and maximize their comprehension. We will now look at each of these features.

Exercises. The exercise section in each applications chapter contains a set of generic exercises that can be used with any program. The exercises range from easy to complex and help students reinforce their newfound skills. The optional lab manual extends these chapter-end exercises.

Color-Coded Computer Screens. Computer-screen illustrations, which show exactly what students will see when they run a program, are used extensively throughout the applications chapters. These screens have been color-coded to help students locate their place easily in a lab setting.

Keystrokes Only Boxes. Each chapter in Part II includes these handy reference boxes, which contain the sequence of keystrokes used in the text examples. After they read the example, students can refer to these boxes to duplicate the results of the example or to generate their own work.

Random Bits Boxes. Random Bits boxes provide students with helpful bits of information. Topics range from practical how-to information to unique computer applications.

Real World Pages. Found at the end of each chapter, the Real World pages illustrate a broad range of microcomputer usage by presenting examples of how people and businesses use microcomputers in their daily lives.

Buyer's Guide. This special 16-page section explains how to evaluate and purchase a microcomputer system and software.

Ready Reference Guide. This unique section lists the main keystrokes alphabetically by function for WordPerfect, Lotus 1-2-3, and dBASE III PLUS. Students should find this section helpful long after they have completed the course.

Additional Features. We have included a variety of additional pedagogical features: key terms boldfaced in the text, extensive summaries with key terms boldfaced, review questions, informative margin notes, a thorough glossary, and a complete index.

The Software Packages

With this text, Benjamin/Cummings offers both educational versions of commercial software and software to assist the instructor. You can provide the educational version of WordPerfect 4.2 and the limited-use version of dBASE III PLUS to your students in one of two ways: your students can purchase the version of the text with the software included or you can obtain master diskettes from Benjamin/Cummings which you can copy for your lab. If you elect to use our software, please note the licensing agreements and special WordPerfect order form at the end of the text. If you have any questions or need any further information about our software offerings, please contact your local Benjamin/Cummings representative or call toll free: (800) 950-BOOK.

WordPerfect Enhanced Version 4.2. This educational version of Word-Perfect contains all the features of the full-function version with the following exceptions: saved document size is limited to approximately 50,000 characters, "WPC" is printed randomly at the ends of paragraphs, advanced printing features are not accessible, and the HELP function is not active.

dBASE III PLUS Limited Use Version. The accompanying educational version of dBASE III PLUS is fully functional. The only restriction is that each database may contain a maximum of 31 records.

University Gradebook. This is complete class record-keeping software developed by Professor David Herrick of the University of Oregon. Available for the IBM-PC and compatibles, University Gradebook calculates student grades using an instructor-defined weighting system.

The Supplements Package

The ancillary materials that accompany *Using Microcomputers: A Complete Introduction* have been carefully crafted to augment the text's effectiveness and to help you teach and manage your classroom or lab.

Lab Manual. Written by Mary Allyn Webster of the University of Florida, the lab manual extends the end-of-chapter exercises by providing additional hands-on practice in the form of advanced exercises and mini-cases. These exercises have been carefully crafted to match the level and tone of the exercises in the text.

Instructor's Guide. The instructor's guide, written by author Ralph Duffy, provides objectives, outlines, key words and concepts, review-question answers, and teaching tips for each chapter in the text. The instructor's guide is available on disk, and you may obtain a separate data disk that provides sample documents in WordPerfect, sample worksheets in Lotus 1-2-3, and sample databases in dBASE III PLUS.

Test Item File. The test item file was prepared by Barbara McCormick of North Seattle Community College. It contains approximately 1700 test questions, presented in several test formats and with answers included for the instructor. The test item file is also available on MicroTest, Benjamin/Cummings's microcomputer test generator.

Related Titles. Benjamin/Cummings offers other related texts that you and your students may find valuable, depending on the level and duration of your course. These include:

Student Edition of Lotus 1-2-3 by T. J. O'Leary (50176).

Hands-On MS-DOS, WordPerfect, dBASE III PLUS, Lotus 1-2-3 by Lawrence Metzelaar and Marianne Fox. This text is available in two versions: as an instructional manual alone (32051) or as a manual with educational versions of WordPerfect and dBASE III PLUS included (32052).

Special Note to the Student

We have tried to present the applications in this book by using examples that are similar to situations you might encounter at home or on the job. We think this book will give you needed tools and knowledge, broaden your background, and raise your confidence level.

We welcome your reactions to this book. Any comments, favorable or otherwise, will be read with care. Write to us in care of the Computer Information Systems Editor, Benjamin/Cummings Publishing Co., 390 Bridge Parkway, Redwood City, CA 94065. All letters with a return address will be answered.

Acknowledgments

We are grateful to the many teachers of microcomputer applications courses who took pains to tell us how to make the book suitable for their needs. These committed instructors helped us accomplish the goal of writing a comprehensive but readable text, and we thank them for their contributions. We list their names below.

Joyce Abler, Central Michigan University
Gary Armstrong, Shippensburg State University
Christopher Bell, Illinois State University
Warren J. Boe, University of Iowa
Don R. Brown, Antelope Valley College
James H. Cooper, Solano Community College
Francis Dunston, Casper College
Henry Estrada, Evergreen Valley College
Richard Fleming, North Lake College
Linda Gammill, Weber State College
Robert Gillan, Northwestern State University of Louisiana
Jean Gonzalez, Cypress College
Tom Harris, Ball State University
Harold Hartman, Iowa State University
John Hays, San Joaquin College
Harry Hoffman, Miami-Dade Community College
Russell C. Hollingsworth, Tarrant County Community College
Cary Hughes, North Texas State University
William Jackson, Metropolitan State University
Usha Jindall, Washtenaw Community College
Ronald G. Kapper, College of DuPage
Kevin Kreitman, San Jose State University
Rose M. Laird, Northern Virginia Community College at Annandale

Doug Meyers, Des Moines Area Community College
Kathleen Middleswart, North Seattle Community College
Douglas Robertson, University of Minnesota
Leonard Schwab, California State University
Peter Simus, Fresno State University
Karen Stalworth, Western Illinois University
David F. Stephan, Baruch College–City University of New York
Douglas A. Troy, Miami University
Thomas Van Valley, Western Michigan University
George Vlahakis, Evergreen Valley College
Karen Watterson, Shoreline Community College
Nancy Webb, Skyline College
Mary Allyn Webster, University of Florida at Gainesville

The employees of Benjamin/Cummings have contributed to the success of this book. We would like to thank sponsoring editor David Jackson, developmental editor Margy Kuntz, and production editor Laura Kenney for their hard work and patience. In addition, Judith Hibbard and Wendy Earl deserve special recognition for their extra-special efforts.

H. L. Capron
Ralph E. Duffy

BRIEF CONTENTS

Part I
Microcomputer
Orientation   1

Chapter 2 continues ▶

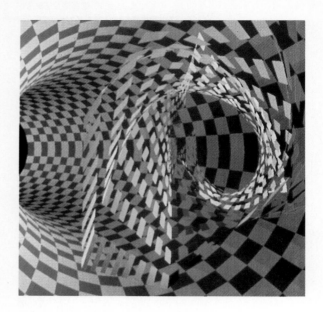

Chapter 5 continues ▶

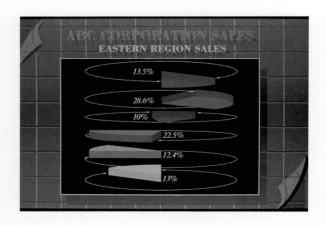

Ready Reference Guide
follows page 383

Part III
Beyond the Basic
Applications   385

Chapter 11
Data Communications   387

Microcomputer Orientation

Microcomputers were first a curiosity, then a toy, and finally a tool. Now that prices have tumbled and capability has increased by leaps and bounds, microcomputers are widely used in homes, schools, and businesses. We begin this section with a look at how people are using microcomputers in everyday life, then turn to the subject of computer hardware. In the final chapter of this section, we examine the operating system, the special instructions that are the gateway to using the microcomputer for particular applications. We will talk about these applications in detail later.

The Microcomputer Revolution

Chapter Objectives

After reading this chapter you should be able to

- Describe the difference between raw data and computer-processed information

- Differentiate hardware, software, and data

- Classify computers by size and type

- Describe, generally, the different parts of micro-computer hardware

- Describe packaged software and applications software

- Explain how data is organized for processing

- List several general advantages of computers

- Describe several uses of computers

- Discuss how computers are used for problem solving

When Dan Hoyt registered for his first term at the University of Washington, among the classes he chose were Introduction to Business, Business Law, and English. For his second term he decided to include a hands-on computer class so he could be an active participant in learning about computers. Dan thought this was a practical approach because he knew that, in any subject, doing is the quickest way to understanding. And, he thought, a hands-on approach to computers was particularly appropriate because a computer is a medium of doing.

Enough of Dan. Why are *you* taking this course? To get your hands on a computer? To get the skills you need for success in business? To fulfill a course requirement? To just find out what it's all about? Any of these is a good and sufficient reason.

Or perhaps you understand the choices coming your way. With the amount of data doubling approximately every two years, businesspeople have two choices—to be overwhelmed with data or to learn to use a computer to translate data into valuable information.

Although the focus of this book is on how to use microcomputers to solve problems, let us pause to consider computers in general and their impact.

Overview of a Computer System

What is a computer, anyway? A six-year-old called a computer "radio, movies, and television combined!" A ten-year-old described a computer as "a television set you can talk to." That's getting closer, but it still does not recognize the computer as a machine that has the power to make changes. A **computer** is a machine that accepts data (input) and processes it into useful information (output). **Data** is raw material that can be processed by a computer. Such material can be letters, symbols such as $ or +, numbers, or facts. Examples of facts that can serve as data are grades in a class, baseball batting averages, or light and dark areas in a photograph. Processed data becomes **information**—data that is organized, meaningful, and useful.

Data that is uninteresting to one person may become very interesting information to another. The raw facts of births, eating habits, and growth rates of calves, for instance, may mean nothing to most people. But when revealed with the help of a computer, the relationships among feed, growth, and beef quality are critical information to a cattle breeder.

The computer itself, and associated equipment, is called **hardware.** The instructions that tell a computer what you want it to do are called **software,** or **programs.** To be more specific, a program is a set of step-by-step instructions that directs the computer to do the tasks you want it to do. A **computer programmer** is a person who writes programs.

But most of us do not write programs. Instead, we use programs written by someone else. This means we are **users**— people who purchase and use computer software. In business, users are often called **end-users** because they are at the end of the "computer" line, actually making use of the computer's information (Figure 1-1).

*Figure 1-1 **End-users.** End-users are people who use computer software to produce information. Today, people are using software to solve problems in areas such as education, business, manufacturing, and science.*

As we continue this section, we will first examine the different types of computers, then hardware, software, and data. What follows is an overview, a look at the "big picture" of a computer system. Thus, many of the terms introduced in this section are defined only briefly. In later chapters we will discuss the different parts of a computer system in greater detail.

Computers: Big and Small

Computers range from tiny to monstrous, in both size and power. The type of computer that a person or an organization needs depends on that person's or organization's computing requirements. Clearly, the National Weather Service, which keeps watch on the weather fronts of many continents, has requirements different from a car dealer's service department, which keeps track of parts inventory. And the requirements of both these organizations are different from those of a salesperson using a small portable computer to record client orders on a field trip.

Mainframes and Supercomputers. Large computers are called **mainframes** (Figure 1-2a). Mainframes are capable of processing data at very fast speeds—millions of instructions per second. They can also store large amounts of data. Because they process vast amounts of data so quickly, some of the principal users of mainframes are large banks, insurance companies, and manufacturers.

The mightiest of the mainframes—and, of course, the most expensive—are known as **supercomputers** (Figure 1-2b). Supercomputers process *billions* of instructions per second. They are used principally for such mammoth data tasks as worldwide weather forecasting and oil exploration. They are also used by the military for weapons research and analyzing surveillance data.

Minicomputers. The next step down from mainframes are **minicomputers** (Figure 1-2c). Minicomputers are slower and less powerful than mainframes. They are also less costly, which makes them affordable for small businesses. The term **supermini** has been coined to describe minis at the top of the size and price scale. Minicomputers are widely used by retail businesses, colleges, and state and city agencies.

Microcomputers. The smallest computers, such as personal or home computers, are called **microcomputers** (Figure

COMPUTERS TO GO
Small but powerful. Portable, lightweight, convenient. All of these things and more, a laptop computer is functionally equivalent to a full stay-in-place microcomputer but smaller than a conventional microcomputer. Most laptops can operate on a battery pack, making them ideal for people working in the field, such as traveling salespeople and newspaper reporters.

From a hardware point of view, a laptop differs from a standard microcomputer mainly in that the laptop is smaller and has a less readable screen. Laptops vary greatly from each other, just as other microcomputers do. Laptops can weigh from 10 to 20 pounds, they can use various forms of storage (5¼- or 3½-inch diskettes or hard disks), and they can come with a variety of accessories. One point they do have in common: Small does not mean cheap—a laptop can cost as much or more than a desktop microcomputer.

Figure 1-2 Computer classifications. *Computers come in many different shapes and sizes. Shown here are (a) a mainframe computer, (b) a supercomputer, (c) a minicomputer, and (d) a microcomputer.*

1-2d). For many years the computer industry was on a quest for the biggest and most powerful computer. But it was by thinking small that the computer industry was able to reach the greatest number of people, both in business and in the home.

Unfortunately, the definitions of *mainframe, minicomputer,* and *microcomputer* are not fixed, because computer technology is changing so rapidly. One observer noted that looking at these three different types of computers is like trying to take a picture of three melting ice cubes. However, since these categories are still used throughout the industry, they are worth keeping in mind.

Hardware: A Tour of the Machine

A computer system consists of four main types of hardware that work together to manipulate data. These hardware devices let you input, process, output, and store data. The devices operate as follows (Figure 1-3).

■ **Input devices** take data in machine-readable form—that is, some form the computer can understand—and send it to the processing unit.

■ The **processor,** more formally known as the **central processing unit** (**CPU**), has the electronic circuitry that manipulates input data into the information wanted. The CPU actually executes computer instructions. **Memory** is the electronic circuitry that temporarily holds the input data and computer instructions (software) needed by the CPU.

Figure 1-3 The four main hardware devices. This diagram shows the relationships among the input devices, the central processing unit, the output devices, and the secondary storage devices.

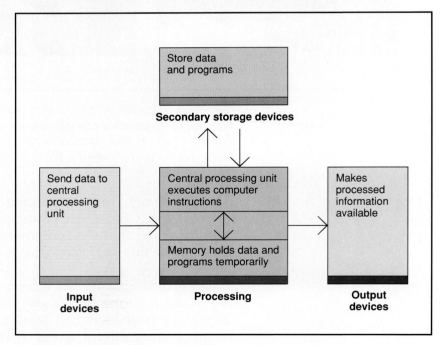

- **Output devices** show people the processed data—information—in some form they can use easily. For example, information often is displayed on the computer's screen or printed on paper.

- **Secondary storage devices** are separate hardware devices that can store additional data and programs. These devices supplement memory.

Now let us briefly consider the equipment for input, processing, output, and storage that you would find on a microcomputer.

Suppose you want to do word processing on a microcomputer. *Word processing* software lets you input, save, revise, and print text such as a report or memo. We will refer to word processing software to show how it relates to typical microcomputer hardware (Figure 1-4, on the next page). The *input* device is a keyboard. You use the keyboard to type, or key in, the text material and also to make changes to the text. The microcomputer's *central processing unit* is a **microprocessor**—a silicon chip etched with logic circuitry. The microprocessor resides within the microcomputer housing. The CPU uses the word processing software to accept and process the data you input. The typical *output* devices are the screen and the printer. As you enter the text on the keyboard, the text appears on the screen in front of you. After you examine the text on the screen, make changes, and determine that it is acceptable, you can print the text on a printer. The *secondary storage* device is disk, a magnetic medium that stores the document until it is needed again. There are several types of disks: **floppy disks,** which are 5¼ inches in diameter, look something like a 45 rpm record and are somewhat flexible; 3½-inch diskettes, which are not flexible; and **hard disks.** All of these components will be discussed in detail in the next chapter. Let us now move on to software.

Software: Telling the Machine What to Do

When most people think about computers, they think about the equipment. However, it is really the software—the step-by-step instructions required to turn data into information—that makes a computer useful.

As we have noted, many people use prewritten software.

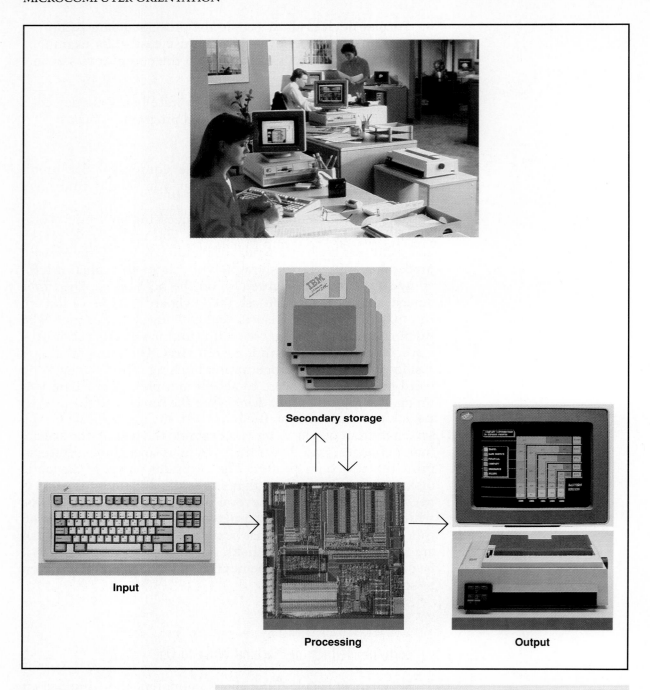

Secondary storage

Input

Processing

Output

Figure 1-4 A microcomputer system. *In this IBM PS/2 microcomputer system, the input device is a keyboard, which feeds data to the central processing unit. The central processing unit is an array of electronic circuitry on pieces of silicon in the computer housing. The two output devices in this example are the monitor and the printer. The secondary storage device is 3½-inch diskette. These components of the system operate together to make the computer work for you.*

The term **packaged software** refers to prewritten software that is literally packaged in a container of some sort—usually a box or folder—and is sold in stores. Packaged software for microcomputers usually includes a software diskette and an instruction manual, known as **documentation.** There is a great variety of packaged software, including software for writing papers, preparing budgets, drawing graphs, and playing games. Much of this software is **user friendly;** that is, it is fairly easy for someone with little or no training to use. You simply insert the diskette in the disk drive, type a specified instruction on the keyboard, and the software begins to run.

In this book we are particularly concerned with microcomputer **applications software.** Most packaged software is applications software, software that is *applied*—or put to use—to solve a particular problem (Figure 1-5). For example, if you want to use a microcomputer to write a memo, then you need word processing applications software. Or if you want to use a microcomputer to practice your French verbs, you need language-drill applications software.

Figure 1-5 *Packaged applications software.* *A variety of software is available for business users to help them solve different problems.*

Although applications software is general enough to be sold to a large number of people, it is possible to "customize" the program by personalizing the data you give it. For example, one personal applications program called Personal Fitness helps you design a fitness program. It is advertised as follows: *Talk about easy to use! Each day you'll spend less time at the keyboard than you do on a coffee break. With no computer jargon ... just simple, sensible English.* Well. Sounds easy enough. When you start the program, questions appear on the screen. The responses you type on the keyboard also show on the screen, so the computer/person dialogue is in front of you. If you indicate that this is the first time you have used the software, you will be asked questions about your age, weight, exercise habits, food intake, and so forth (Figure 1-6). The Personal Fitness program will analyze this data and then make recommendations for a "new and healthier lifestyle." As you

---

RANDOM BITS

High Points in Microcomputer History

1975 His business about to go bankrupt, Ed Roberts takes one last gasp and invents the MITS Altair, a microcomputer kit he advertises in *Popular Electronics.* The overwhelming positive response sends the microcomputer industry on its way and propels Harvard undergrad Bill Gates toward Albuquerque to be near the action at MITS. The first stirrings of Gates' company, Microsoft, are heard.

1977 Apple Computer founders Steve Jobs and Steve Wozniak develop the Apple II personal computer in a garage, financed by the sale of an old VW bus. Apple Computer makes the *Fortune* 500 roster in five years; something no company has ever done in such a short time.

1978 Dan Bricklin and Bob Frankston invent VisiCalc, the electronic spreadsheet software that introduces the Apple II to business users.

1981 The IBM personal computer is announced, along with Microsoft's MS-DOS, which becomes an operating-system standard. IBM produces the first microcomputer with an 80-column screen, a keyboard with upper- and lowercase letters, useful function keys, and open architecture (hardware that can accept add-on equipment).

1983 Lotus 1-2-3, created by Mitch Kapor, replaces VisiCalc as the reigning spreadsheet software and catapults the IBM PC into the premier business microcomputer position.

1984 Steve Jobs introduces the computer he calls "insanely great": the Apple Macintosh. The early Mac does have outstanding graphics ability and an attractive learning curve, but initially it lacks significant business software. As the software picture changes, especially with the development of desktop publishing software, the Macintosh makes more inroads into the business community.

There have been many important events since, including new chips; large and small microcomputers; and microcomputer stores, magazines, and networks. But none has had the impact on the microcomputer as these signal events.

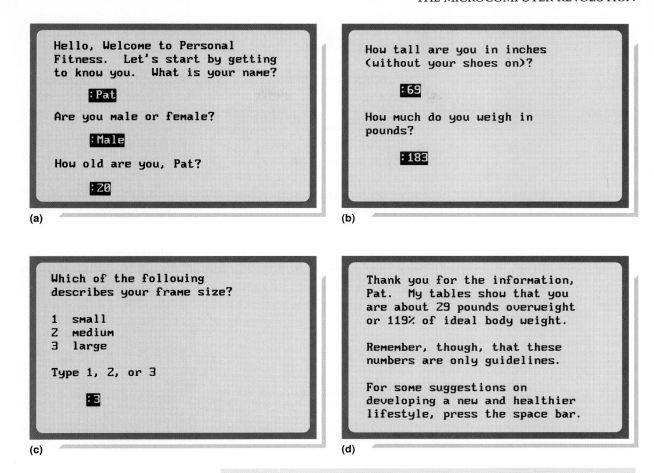

Figure 1-6 Personal Fitness software screens. *These screens show the Personal Fitness program at work.*

continue to use the software over time, you will report (that is, key in) items such as caloric intake, pulse rate, or miles walked. The software will produce charts and graphs showing weight loss, pulse pattern, and so on, to help you monitor your progress. Note the input-process-output sequence here. The *input* to the program consists of your own habits (in number form) and personal statistics. The *processing* is the analysis of that data by the software. The *output* is the set of recommendations and the charts and graphs.

Although business applications software is not quite that easy to use, it works on the same principles as this personal applications package. For example, one type of software package helps businesses keep track of and pay their bills. A business provides input in the form of invoice numbers, vendor names, and amounts owed. The computer processes this data and produces output in the form of computer-generated checks and various reports that help track expenses.

Data: Just the Facts

Up to this point we have been considering data in a general sense as unorganized information. Now let us take a closer look.

To be processed by the computer, raw data must be organized into characters, fields, records, and files (Figure 1-7). We start with the smallest element, the character.

- A **character** is a letter, digit, or special symbol (such as $, ?, or *). One or more related characters constitute a field.

- A **field** contains a set of related characters. For example, suppose a health club is making address labels for a mailing. For each person on the mailing list, the club might have a member-number field, a date-joined field, a name field, a street address field, a city field, a state field, a zip code field, and a phone number field.

Figure 1-7 How data is organized. In this picture of a disk file, data is organized into characters, fields, and records. A file is a collection of related records. Data is stored on a disk in files.

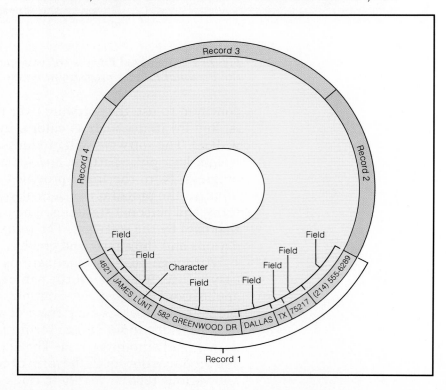

- A **record** is a collection of related fields. Thus, on the health club list, one person's member number, date joined, name, address, city, state, zip code, and phone number constitute a record.

- A **file** is a collection of related records. All of the member records for the health club constitute a file. When data is stored on a disk, it is stored in files. Each file on a disk is given a name by the user.

Now that we have taken a quick look at what computers are all about, let us look at their impact on our lives.

Computers in Today's World

It seems that everywhere you turn these days, there is a computer—in stores, cars, homes, offices, hospitals, banks. Why have computers become an everyday sight? What are some of the traits of computers that make them so useful?

The Nature of Computers

The computer is a workhorse. It is generally capable of laboring 24 hours a day, does not ask for raises or coffee breaks, and will do the ten-thousandth task exactly the same way it did the first one—without complaining of boredom.

There are at least six reasons why computers have become an indispensable part of our lives:

- **Speed.** By now it is human nature to be resentful if service is not fast. But it is "computer nature" that provides that fast service. Thus, unless we are prepared to do a lot more waiting—for paychecks, grades, telephone calls, travel reservations, bank balances, and many other things—we need the split-second processing of the computer. The speed of the computer also makes it ideal for processing large amounts of data, as in accounting systems and scientific applications.

- **Reliability.** Computers are extremely reliable. Of course, you might not think this from the way stories about "computer mistakes" are handled in the press. Unfortunately, what is almost never brought out in these stories is that the mistakes are not the fault of the computers themselves. True, there are sometimes equipment failures, but most errors supposedly made by computers are really human errors.

- **Storage capability.** Computer systems are able to store tremendous amounts of data, which can then be retrieved quickly and efficiently. This storage capability is especially important in an information age.

- **Productivity.** Computers are able to perform boring, dangerous, or highly sensitive jobs that people should not perform or in some cases cannot perform, such as working with nuclear fuel rods. Computers also free human beings for other kinds of productivity.

- **Decision making.** Because of expanding technology, communications, and the interdependency of people, we suffer from an information deluge. Although this is in part brought on by the computer, it is also the computer that will help solve it. To make essential business and governmental decisions, managers need to take into account a variety of financial, geographical, and logistical factors. The computer helps the managers sort "wheat from chaff" and make better choices.

- **Reduction in costs.** Finally, for all of these reasons, the computer helps reduce waste and hold down the cost of labor, energy, and paperwork. Thus, computers increase productivity and reduce the costs of goods and services.

With all these wonderful traits to its credit, it is no wonder that the computer has made its way into almost every facet of our lives. Let us look at some of the ways computers are being used to make our workdays more productive and our personal lives more rewarding.

The Uses of Computers

The uses of computers are as varied as we can imagine, but the following are some of the principal uses:

- **Paperwork.** There is no doubt that our society runs on paper, and computers have revolutionized the way paperwork is handled. Computers are used to prepare manuals, documents, letters, memos, and other types of written communication. Computerized bookkeeping, record

keeping, and document sending have also made paperwork more efficient.

- **Money.** Computers have brought us the age of do-it-your-
self banking, with automatic teller machines available
for simple transactions. Computers have also helped fuel
the cashless economy, enabling the widespread use of
credit cards and instant credit checks by banks, department stores, and other retailers. Some oil companies are
using credit card–activated, self-service gasoline pumps
(Figure 1-8).

- **Commerce.** Products from meats to magazines are now
packaged with zebra-striped symbols, the Universal Product Code, that can be read by computer scanners at
supermarket checkout stands to determine the price of
the products. The Universal Product Code is one of the
highly visible uses of computers in commerce; however,
there are numerous others. Modern-day warehousing and
inventory management could not exist without computers. Take your copy of this book, for instance. From
printer to warehouse to bookstore, its movement was
tracked with the help of computers.

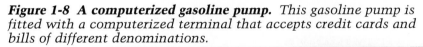

Figure 1-8 A computerized gasoline pump. *This gasoline pump is
fitted with a computerized terminal that accepts credit cards and
bills of different denominations.*

Figure 1-9 Computer-assisted transportation. *Air traffic controllers rely on computers to display and track the positions of aircraft on a large round screen, as shown here. Each controller is responsible for a certain geographical area and "passes" aircraft to another controller as the plane moves into another territory.*

COMPUTERS: WHO IS IN CHARGE?

Computers are given a lot of credit these days. If you believe what you read in the papers, computers can run our factories, mine the ocean depths, explore space, teach in schools, and tend our cows. Can computers really do all that? Yes, computers can do all that and much more. But perhaps the computer's ability is not the main issue. The key question is this: Do we truly want to turn computers loose in such a fashion? Probably not. We need to remember who is in control. People have the ultimate control over what computers can do.

- **Energy.** Energy companies use computers to locate oil, coal, natural gas, and uranium. Electric companies use computers to monitor their vast power networks. In addition, meter readers use handheld computers to record how much energy is used each month in homes and in businesses.

- **Transportation.** Computers are used to help run rapid transit systems, load container ships, keep track of railroad cars, fly and land airplanes and keep them from colliding, and schedule airline reservations (Figure 1-9). They are also used in cars and motorcycles to monitor fluid levels, temperatures, and electrical systems and to improve fuel mileage.

- **Government.** The federal government is the largest single user of computers. The Social Security Administration, for example, produces 36 million benefit checks a month with the help of computers. Computers are also used for forecasting weather, for servicing parks, for processing immigrants, for meting out justice, and—yes—for collecting taxes.

- **Agriculture.** Are we ready for high tech down on the farm? Absolutely. Farming is a business, after all, and a small computer—which can be a lot cheaper than a tractor—can help with billing, crop information, cost per acre, fertilizer combinations, and so on. As farming becomes less profitable, wise management—which can be aided by computers—becomes increasingly important.

- **Education.** Computers have been used behind the scenes for years in colleges and school districts for record-keeping and accounting purposes. Now, of course, they are in the classroom—elementary, secondary, and college. Many parents and teachers—and students—feel that computer education is a necessity, not a novelty.

- **Training.** Computers are being used as training devices in industry and government. It is much cheaper and safer, for instance, to teach aspiring pilots to fly in computerized "training cockpits," or simulators, than in real airplanes.

- **Health and medicine.** Computers have been used on the business side of medicine for some time; but, in addition, they are being used in the healing process itself. For instance, computers are used to produce cross-sectional x-ray views of the body, to provide ultrasound pictures, to help pharmacists test patients' medications for drug compatibility, and to help physicians make diagnoses (Figure 1-10). Computers are also being used for health maintenance, in everything from weight-loss programs to recording heart rates.

Figure 1-10 Computer model of a virus. Three-dimensional computer models of molecules help researchers study the structure of molecules, aiding in drug design, cancer research, and much more. This colorful graphic shows the structure of a virus that causes respiratory diseases.

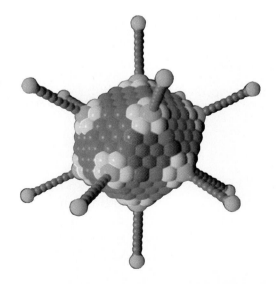

Figure 1-11 Voyager photo of Saturn. *This color-enhanced image of Saturn is computer-generated. Voyager spacecraft photos are sent to Earth in the form of dots; computers then reassemble and interpret the photos.*

- **The sciences.** As you might imagine, computers are used extensively in the sciences to process research data. In many projects, however, scientists are using computers during the research phase as well. Consider, for example, a Food and Drug Administration computer program that simulates the way a mouse's digestive system reacts to suspected toxins. Computers are also used to generate models of DNA, the molecule that houses the genetic instructions that determine the specific characteristics of organisms. On another front entirely, the National Aeronautics and Space Administration has developed a computerized system for use in Arecibo, Puerto Rico, to scan the heavens and listen in on eight million narrow-band radio frequencies in an attempt to find signs of communication from alien beings in outer space. (So far, no takers.)

- **Graphics.** There is no better place to get a sense of the computer's impact than in the area of design and graphics. For example, breathtaking photographs of the rings of Saturn are beamed back to Earth over nearly a billion miles of space (Figure 1-11). Technically, however, these transmissions from space are not photographs at all. Rather, they are all electronic impulses assembled by computers. Closer to home, the computer as artist is used by biochemists to examine the structure of molecules, by architects to give clients a computer-animated graphics walkthrough of proposed buildings, and by aircraft designers to create experimental aircraft and put them through simulated practice flights. Business executives play artist, making bar graphs and pie charts out of tedious figures and using color to convey trends with far more impact than numbers alone can do. Finally, a whole new kind of artist has emerged, who uses computers to create cartoon animation, landscapes, television logos, and still-life drawings (Figure 1-12).

- **The home.** Are you willing to welcome the computer into your home? Many people already have, usually as an educational tool for their children. But that is only the beginning. Adults often keep records and write letters and memos on their computers. The more adventurous hook up the family computer to control heating and air conditioning, answer telephone calls, and so on. The question about whether you *need* a home computer remains open to debate, but there is no question that it can make your life easier and more entertaining.

Figure 1-12 Computer-generated art. *Computers give artists a new creative tool. Although this field of grass looks like a photograph, it is really a complex computer-generated image.*

The End-User Perspective

There are over 20 million microcomputers already at work in businesses, and their numbers are increasing steadily. Most of these computers are not being used by computer experts. Instead, they are used by people who view computers as a tool to do a job.

In fact, microcomputers have brought a whole new class of users to computing—the *end-users.* These people use computer-processed data to do such jobs as monitoring real estate sales, checking factory materials, looking up legal precedents, and tracking ocean currents. End-users are usually less interested in what they can do with a computer than in what a computer can do for them.

The Computer as a Tool

When most people think of tools, they think of hand tools such as hammers and saws, or perhaps lug wrenches and screwdrivers. But think of a tool in a broader sense, as something used to do a job. This broadens the horizon to include stethoscopes, baseball bats, kettles, typewriters, and—yes—computers.

The computer is a sophisticated tool, but a tool nonetheless. But who would use such a tool? Would you buy a stethoscope if you had no medical plans, or a baseball bat if you had no intention of hitting a ball? Probably not. You probably would not purchase a computer either, or learn how to use it, unless you had some use in mind. Businesspeople are not interested in buying useless tools. Businesses purchase computers because they have a problem—or perhaps a set of problems—to solve.

The bulk of this book is about solving problems by using a microcomputer. We are going to show you, chapter by chapter, how to do this. But, in this section, we want to give you an overview of problem solving using a microcomputer. In particular, we want to show you the kinds of problems that lend themselves to a microcomputer solution.

Problem Solving with Microcomputers

Given a new tool, people think of new ways to use it. So it is with the computer. The people with the greatest incentive for dreaming up new uses for the computer are the people who write and sell software. It is in their interest to develop and promote new software solutions. They have done this successfully for years. Even so, the collective set of business problems is limited, and the number of ways to solve these problems is limited too. Thus, the problems and the software solutions fall, for the most part, into just a few categories.

These categories of problems and their solutions can be found in most business environments. We begin with the categories often called, because of their widespread use, the Big Five: word processing, spreadsheets, database management, graphics, and communications. We will also examine desktop publishing, an important but somewhat less universal category.

As we present a brief description of each category, remember that this is just an overview and that you do not need to understand everything just yet.

Word Processing. The most widely used microcomputer software is **word processing** software. This software lets you create, edit, format, store, and print text. In this definition the word that makes word processing different from plain typing is the word "store." A computer can store, or remember, everything you key in. Since you can store the memo or document you type, you can retrieve it another time, change it, reprint it, or do whatever you like with it. The timesaving factor is that the unchanged parts of the saved document do not need to be retyped, and the whole thing can be reprinted as if new. Contrast this with the days of cutting and pasting (not to mention using whiteout) and you begin to appreciate why old-fashioned typewriters are gathering dust.

Spreadsheets. Used to organize business data, a **spreadsheet** is a worksheet divided into columns and rows. For example, the simple expense spreadsheet in Figure 1-13 shows time periods (quarters of the year) as columns and various categories (rent, phone, and so forth) as rows. Notice that figures in the right-hand column and in the bottom row are the result of calculations. Manual spreadsheets have been used as business tools for centuries. But a spreadsheet can be tedious to prepare, and when there are changes, a considerable amount of work may need to be redone. In a complicated spreadsheet, for example, a single number change can cause a ripple effect of many changes. An **electronic spreadsheet** is still a spreadsheet, but the computer does the work. In particular, spreadsheet software automatically recalculates the results when a number is changed. This capability lets businesses try different combinations of numbers; the experimentation is often called playing "What if . . ." games. With a computer results are obtained quickly. Businesses use electronic spreadsheets (hereafter just called spreadsheets) for everything from budgeting and forecasting to income tax preparation and property management. We will discuss spreadsheets in much more detail in Chapters 6 and 7. For now, we will just say that if calculations are called for, a spreadsheet probably is too.

Figure 1-13 A simple expense spreadsheet. This expense sheet is a typical spreadsheet of rows and columns. Note the calculations needed to generate the values in the rightmost column and the bottom row.

EXPENSES	JAN. - MAR.	APR. - JUN.	JUL. - SEPT.	OCT. - DEC.	TOTAL
RENT	425.00	425.00	425.00	425.00	1700.00
PHONE	22.50	31.25	17.00	35.75	106.50
CLOTHES	110.00	135.00	156.00	91.00	492.00
FOOD	280.00	250.00	250.00	300.00	1080.00
HEAT	80.00	50.00	24.00	95.00	249.00
ELECTRICITY	35.75	40.50	45.00	36.50	157.75
WATER	10.00	11.00	11.00	10.50	42.50
CAR INSURANCE	75.00	75.00	75.00	75.00	300.00
ENTERTAINMENT	150.00	125.00	140.00	175.00	590.00
TOTAL	1188.25	1142.75	1143.00	1243.75	4717.75

Database Management. Software used for **database management**—the management of a collection of interrelated files—handles data in several ways. The software can store data, update it, manipulate it, and report it in a variety of forms. By the time the data is in the reporting stage—given to a user in a useful form—it has become information. A concert promoter, for example, can store and change data about upcoming concert dates, seating, ticket prices, and sales. After this is done the promoter can use the software to retrieve information, such as the number of tickets sold in each price range or the percentage of tickets sold the day before the concert. Database software can be useful for anyone who must keep track of a great amount of information.

Graphics. It might seem wasteful to show businesspeople computer **graphics,** or numbers rendered as pictures, when it would be less expensive to use the numbers in standard computer printouts. However, maps, charts, and other forms of graphics can help people compare data and spot trends more

Figure 1-14 Business graphics. *These colorful computer-generated graphics can help people compare data and spot trends.*

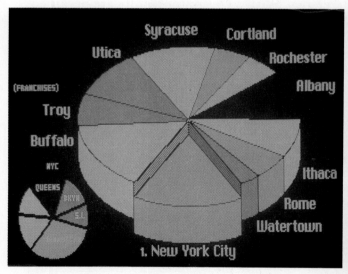

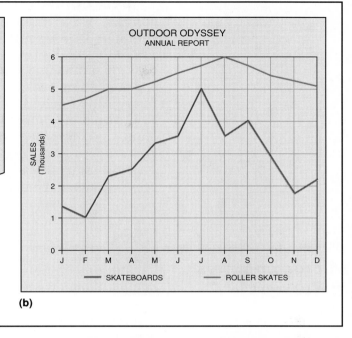

OUTDOOR ODYSSEY ANNUAL REPORT

Here are the figures for skateboards and roller skates at Outdoor Odyssey. In January, 1300 skateboards were sold and 4500 roller skates were sold. In February, skateboard sales dropped slightly to 1000, while roller skate sales increased slightly to 4700. In March, skateboard sales increased greatly to 2300, while roller skate sales continued to increase slightly to 5000. In April, skateboard sales increased to 2500.

(a)

(b)

Figure 1-15 Words versus pictures. *Compare the time it takes to read the paragraph (a) with the time it takes to understand the graph (b). With graphics, information can be conveyed more quickly and in less space.*

easily and make decisions more quickly (Figure 1-14). Pages of confusing text can be made into an easily read chart that anyone can pick up and understand. Note the comparison of words and pictures in Figure 1-15.

The use of color also has an impact that helps people "get the picture." Finally, although color graphs and charts have been used in business for years—usually to make presentations to higher management or outside clients—the computer now allows computer users to render graphics quickly and fairly inexpensively.

Communications. The process of exchanging data by using communications facilities, such as the telephone, is called **data communications.** In simplest terms, data communications allows you to hook up a phone to your computer and access data stored in someone else's computer in another location. The ability to communicate from one computer to another greatly expands the reach of computer technology.

Desktop Publishing. Since publishing in one form or another typically consumes up to 10% of a company's gross revenues, **desktop publishing** has been given a warm welcome by business. The two key elements of desktop publishing are desktop publishing software and high-quality printers. Desktop publishing packages let businesses use a computer to produce printed materials that combine graphics with text. The resulting professional-looking newsletters, reports, and brochures can improve communication and help organizations make a better impression on the outside world.

Now let us consider how these applications software packages have changed the business world.

Microcomputers in Business

Microcomputers, as personal productivity tools, can help people write, organize, plan, manage, and communicate more effectively. Although there are still more wonders just around the corner, microcomputers are already a big success story.

In just the past few years, microcomputers have evolved from obscure kits that only stouthearted hobbyists could understand to useful machines that are changing the course of business. Microcomputers first entered the world of business in small numbers. However, as their usefulness became apparent, microcomputers were purchased in quantity for many office workers. Now microcomputers are found in almost every type of business—large and small.

The greatest number of microcomputers can be found in engineering and architecture offices, where half the employees have a computer. Other enterprises that rely heavily on microcomputers are insurance, real estate, accounting, legal services, financial institutions, communications, government services, and education.

The Microcomputer Advantage

Why have so many organizations turned to microcomputers? Benefits fall into these general categories:

- **Decentralization.** Microcomputers have brought computing power directly to the people who need it. There was a time when all computer processing was done in a centralized location by large computer systems managed by computer professionals. There is now a freer flow of information—and power.

- **Access to data.** Businesspeople can access data faster and more accurately by using a microcomputer. As one manager explained, "I can get sales data faster from the computer than by asking one of my staff. The net effect on the company is that we have increased sales without increasing staff."

- **Decision making.** Alternative solutions to a problem can be explored quickly with a microcomputer. Software packages can support the whole decision process: gathering data, analyzing it, putting it together in different combinations, and communicating the results to others. A manager considering a new product, for example, may need to consider the prices and availability of raw materials, labor costs, consumer needs, and a variety of other data. With a computer, various scenarios can be played out, leading the manager to better results than the "educated hunch" of the past (Figure 1-16).

Figure 1-16 Educated decision making. *With computers, business-people can "try out" different scenarios without investing a great deal of time and money. This helps managers make better and more educated decisions.*

- **News sharing.** Linked company microcomputers can spread the word more rapidly and to more people than conventional memos are able to. In addition to shuffling less paper, employees are better informed and better educated about their companies. Even computer-stored calendars and schedules can be shared and compared.

- **Information gathering.** Microcomputer users can obtain information from outside information services, from a mainframe computer, or from each other. In addition to the advantages of shared information, users can often avoid rekeying data, thus saving time and reducing the chance of error.

- **Presentations.** No matter how information is formally presented, microcomputers can help. For example, graphics can be presented in a variety of forms, and affordable high-quality printers let people print their own brochures right in the office.

- **Competition.** Companies that use the computer to help analyze and compare various business scenarios usually make fewer mistakes and generally make better business decisions. This approach is starting to make major changes in the competitive environment. Perhaps the company that computes better also competes better.

- **Group productivity.** Today, many microcomputers are islands unto themselves. But in offices where computers are connected together, it is easier for workers to share information, thus improving productivity.

BUT I'M WORKING AS FAST AS I CAN

Not all workers see the computer as their new friend. Employees who work directly on the computer all day are often monitored by the machine itself. The computer can keep track of the number of keystrokes per minute, length of breaks, and general productivity. The unkindest cut of all is the message used by some computer systems: "You're not working as fast as the worker next to you."

A Few Troubling Problems

Not everything is roses and productivity, however. As the number of computers and users expands, so do the problems. The first problem to emerge was incompatibility. In the first heady days of business microcomputers, there was a hodgepodge of hardware and software. Software that worked well on one machine did not necessarily work on another. This led to confusion and duplicate efforts in communication, training, and software-purchasing decisions. That problem has been solved largely by managers who insist on standards for hardware and software. A company may decide, for example, that a particular microcomputer is the company standard; users in the company should use only those machines or machines that are compatible.

Other troublesome problems remain. Some are related to the users themselves. Elated with early accomplishments, some users never get past the simple tasks. Others are inefficient users, lacking the training to use software appropriately. Still others are computer junkies, spending alarming amounts of time fixated on the machine.

But the most treacherous problems are related to data. Managers fret in particular about data transferred to the users' microcomputers from corporate mainframe computers. What happens when users get the data? Might they keep it so long that it is out of date? Will they make reports that do not match the data in other reports? Will there be duplicate—and expensive—data spread around the company?

The problems are serious but not impossible to solve. Many users have few such problems and are able to make uninhibited use of computers. Their success is often directly related to the service of computer professionals.

The essence of end-user computing is service. The user is the revenue producer in the company, so the role of the computer and of computer professionals is to serve the user.

Service is provided in a variety of ways. A common approach is the **information center,** which provides direct user support. The information center is focused on the end-user and usually can provide immediate assistance. Typical services include hardware and software selection, formal training, technical assistance, and—the tough one—access to data.

Service, as you might expect, adds to the cost of using microcomputers.

The Bottom Line

In the early days, with missionary zeal, companies wooed their own employees to become computer users by promising free service. But users who get free service have little incentive to be efficient. Many companies now use the more traditional chargeback method, charging users according to the amount of service used.

But consider a more general question: Are microcomputers in business earning their keep? No one denies that microcomputers have made a significant impact on business. But some brave managers are actually asking business-like questions about microcomputers: Where did they all come from? What are they doing here? And, most puzzling: Are they paying their way? No scientific method has yet been devised to measure the true economic benefits of personal computers.

On to Hardware

The purpose of our journey is to learn to use a microcomputer to solve different types of problems. In this chapter we have provided a rationale for using a computer and examined the categories of software that businesspeople use. Now that we have seen an overview of microcomputer software, we must take a closer look at the hardware that runs it. The upcoming chapter is devoted exclusively to hardware—the computer itself.

Summary and Key Terms

- A **computer** is a machine that accepts **data** (input) and processes it into useful **information** (output).

- The computer itself, and its associated equipment, is called **hardware.** The instructions that tell a computer what to do are called **software,** also referred to as programs. A **program,** which is written by a **computer programmer,** is a set of step-by-step instructions that directs the computer to do certain tasks.

- People who buy and use computer software are referred to as **users,** or **end-users.**

- Computers range in size and computing capability. Large computers are called **mainframes** and are capable of processing data at very fast speeds—millions of instructions per second—and of storing great amounts of data. The largest mainframe computers, **supercomputers,** process billions of instructions per second. **Minicomputers** are slower and less powerful than mainframes. The term **supermini** refers to the most expensive and powerful of the minicomputers. The smallest computers are **microcomputers.**

- Computer hardware includes **input devices;** the **processor,** or **central processing unit** (CPU); **output devices;** and **secondary storage devices. Memory** temporarily holds data and software instructions needed by the CPU.

- An input device on a microcomputer is a keyboard. The microcomputer's CPU is a **microprocessor,** a silicon chip etched with logic circuitry. Common output devices on a microcomputer are the screen and the printer. Secondary storage devices for a microcomputer are diskettes or **hard disks.** Diskettes may be 5¼-inch flexible disks (also called **floppy disks**) or 3½-inch inflexible disks.

- **Packaged software** for microcomputers usually includes a diskette and an instruction manual, called **documentation.** Some software is **user friendly,** which means it is fairly easy for someone with little or no training to use. Most packaged software is **applications software,** software that is applied to solve a particular problem.

- To be processed by the computer, raw data must be organized into characters, fields, records, and files. A **character** is a letter, number, or symbol. One or more related characters constitute a **field.** A **record** is a collection of related fields, and a **file** is a collection of related records.

- Computers have become an indispensable part of our lives because they process information very quickly, they are reliable, and they store tremendous amounts of data. People use computers to evaluate facts and make better decisions. Computers perform boring, dangerous, or sensitive tasks and free people for other types of productive work. Because computers increase productivity, they reduce the costs of goods and services.

- Computers are now incorporated in many places in our lives, including energy industries, transportation, agriculture, education, training, health and medicine, the sciences, graphics, and many homes.

■ Five important categories of microcomputer applications are word processing, spreadsheets, database management, graphics, and communications. **Word processing** allows the user to create, edit, format, store, and print text. An **electronic spreadsheet (spreadsheet** for short) is a worksheet divided into columns and rows and is used for calculations. Software used for **database management**—the management of a collection of interrelated files—can store data, update it, manipulate it, and report it. **Graphics** programs help the user prepare maps, charts, graphs, and illustrations. **Data communications** is the process of exchanging data by using communications facilities.

■ Another important but less universal microcomputer applications category is **desktop publishing,** which is used to produce high-quality text and graphics.

■ Business advantages of microcomputers include decentralization; rapid data access; more effective decision making, news sharing, and information gathering;

improved presentations, sharper competition, and increased group productivity.

■ Problems that still trouble microcomputer users include incompatibility of equipment and software, insufficient training, and the consequences of sending data from corporate mainframes. These problems are solvable and are not experienced by all users.

■ The essence of effective end-user computing is service. A common approach to service is the **information center,** which provides direct user support.

Review Questions

1. What is the difference between data and information?

2. Define *hardware* and *software.*

3. Define *end-user.*

4. List and describe computers by their classifications.

5. Consider how a microcomputer would be used in a specific environment, such as a retail store or a computer lab. Describe the devices for input, output, and storage that would be appropriate for it.

6. How are the CPU and memory related?

7. What is documentation?

8. When people call software "user friendly," what do they mean?

9. What is applications software?

10. Describe how data is organized for processing.

11. List five areas in which computers are used.

12. Why do businesspeople view computers as a tool?

13. What are the "Big Five" microcomputer software applications categories? Do you know some common brand names for each category?

FROM THE REAL WORLD

Campbell Soup and Computers

It is a big company, really big: $4 *billion* in annual revenue, rank 100 in the *Fortune* 500, and owner of two mainframe computer systems. Would a company like Campbell Soup also need microcomputers? Yes. A great many microcomputers? Yes. Campbell Soup has, in fact, over 800 microcomputers. The collection consists mostly of IBM microcomputers (70%); the remainder are Wang PCs and COMPAQ computers.

As is often the case, microcomputers entered the Campbell Soup environment in a rather haphazard way. They first were introduced by some market analysts who brought in Apple II computers. Soon the use of microcomputers spread to other departments. These early acquisitions were not formally planned nor were purchases standardized in any way. However, as the benefits of microcomputers became clear, a cohesive plan was formed to purchase microcomputer hardware and software. The rapidly growing use of microcomputers at Campbell Soup is now actively supported by top management. A staff of microcomputer specialists provides consultation, support, and

training for microcomputer users in all departments.

One benefit of microcomputers at Campbell is that planners can use spreadsheets to analyze production and sales data. Spreadsheet data helps users spot trends, uncover opportunities for new products, identify untapped markets, and determine where advertising dollars should go. For example, microcomputer-monitored field tests of freezing equipment led to a decision to purchase less expensive freezers for Le Menu frozen dinners, yielding a $5 million saving.

Another benefit is that hundreds of Campbell employees can use word processing programs to write letters, memos, and

reports. The documents are stored on disk, so if any changes are needed, the document can be quickly edited and reprinted. No retyping means more time for other tasks.

The key vision at Campbell is to link the large numbers of microcomputers together to support far-flung company operations and customers. The system will tie together all company operations, from the fields (where Campbell grows its vegetables and contracts for its meat) through manufacturing, packaging, and sales, to the grocery store chains. The final link in the chain is the customer, whose varied—and changing—regional and ethnic tastes Campbell wishes to serve.

2

Microcomputer Hardware

Chapter Objectives

After reading this chapter
you should be able to

- Appreciate the need to
  know something about
  computer hardware
  before studying software

- Identify the basic components of microcomputer
  hardware

- Understand how the cen-
  tral processing unit turns
  data into information

- Understand the basics of
  data representation

- Describe a variety of
  input and output devices

- Explain the function of
  secondary storage

- Identify various secondary storage devices

- Appreciate the need for
  data communications
  hardware

Do you already have a personal computer? Or do you plan to buy a personal computer? Do you expect to use personal computers only at school or on the job? Any of these situations are possibilities, but circumstances can change. Consider the case of Martha Carrier.

Martha took several computer courses as she studied for her degree in communications. By the time she graduated, she felt confident using a variety of software packages and was eager to try her computer skills in her first job. She was hired as an assistant public relations representative and soon had the opportunity to use word processing software on a micro-computer at the office. It was not long, however, before she wanted to do a little office work at home. Although she thought that this reason alone justified the purchase of her own computer, she also relished the thought of writing letters and keeping personal records on a computer.

Martha wanted a computer that she could add on to later; she knew her first computer would have to be modest—just the basics. In addition to the microprocessor and memory inside the computer, the computer system she chose included a keyboard, a monitor, a disk drive for storage, and a printer.

In this chapter we will examine these components in depth. We will also look at the add-ons that Martha can use to expand the capabilities of her computer. But let us begin our hardware discussion with an overview.

The Basic Components

 he basic components of microcomputer hardware are

- A microprocessor
- Memory
- A keyboard
- A monitor
- A printer
- Secondary storage

If you opened up a personal computer, you would find an impressive array of electronics gear, as shown in Figure 2-1. (Caution: Some manufacturers are *not* interested in having you peer under the hood, and doing so will void your warranty.

Figure 2-1 Inside a micro-computer. *This photo shows what you would see if you removed the cover from an IBM PS/2.*

Check your documentation first.) Most of what you see is related to the *central processing unit—CPU—*and *memory.*

Both the CPU and memory are on silicon chips, which are smaller than thumbtacks. A miniaturized CPU can be etched on a single chip, so it is often called a "computer on a chip." A central processing unit on a chip is a *microprocessor* (Figure 2-2, on the next page). It is the heart of the microcomputer; it controls and coordinates many of the computer's functions.

In addition to the microprocessor chip, a personal computer has two kinds of *memory* chips—RAM and ROM. **RAM** stands for random-access memory. This type of memory temporarily holds the program instructions and data used by the CPU. RAM is also the computer's scratch pad; for example, it holds the intermediate results of calculations. **ROM** stands for read-only memory. The contents of ROM are programmed into the chip by the microcomputer manufacturer. Both the CPU and memory chips are mounted on a single circuit board, called the **motherboard.**

You can interact with the computer by using an input device such as a keyboard. A **monitor** is needed to display both input and output. A **printer** is used to produce computer output on paper. A *secondary storage device* is needed to store data. A common secondary storage device is a *disk drive,* which reads and writes data on diskettes. *Hard disks* are also available as an option for many personal computers.

Now let us examine each component in depth, beginning with the central processing unit.

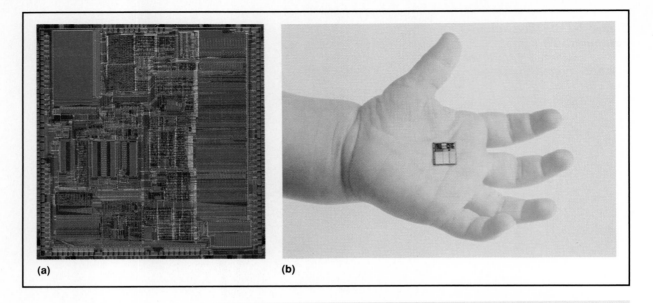

(a) (b)

Figure 2-2 A microprocessor. *(a) Wiring and hundreds of thousands of electrical components can be imprinted on a single microprocessor. (b) Microprocessors are small enough to fit on the palm of a baby's hand—with room to spare.*

The Central Processing Unit

The casual personal computer user does not have to delve into the depths of central processing unit technology and terminology. However, there are rewards for the user who chooses to do so. Knowledge of how the computer works can enhance your own use of the computer. Furthermore, familiarity with the hardware could help you make more informed choices about selecting options for a new computer system.

People input data to the computer and use the information that it outputs, but it is the *central processing unit (CPU)* that actually transforms the raw data into processed information. The central processing unit consists of electronic circuits that interpret and execute program instructions and communicate with the input, output, and storage devices. As Figure 2-3 shows, the CPU consists of two parts:

- The control unit, which directs the computer system

- The arithmetic/logic unit, which controls arithmetic and logical operations

Let us consider each of these.

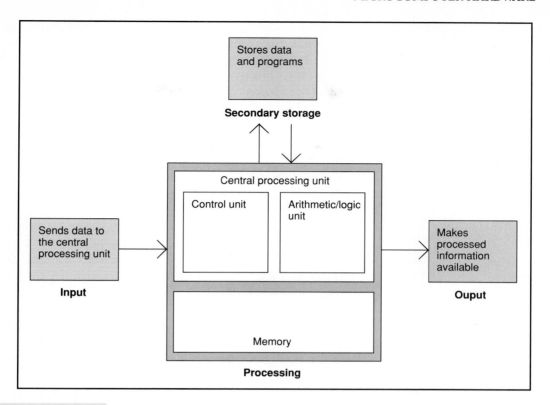

Figure 2-3 The central processing unit. *The two parts of the CPU are the control unit and the arithmetic/logic unit. The CPU interacts closely with memory, referring to it for instructions and data.*

The Control Unit

The **control unit** directs and coordinates the entire computer system. It contains circuitry that uses electronic signals to carry out, or execute, stored program instructions. Like an orchestra leader, the control unit does not execute the instructions itself; rather, it directs the arithmetic/logic unit to do so.

The control unit must communicate with the arithmetic/logic unit, memory, and the input and output devices. These connections are usually made through a collection of electrical pathways called a **bus line,** or **data bus.** A bus line allows data to be passed among the components of the system.

The Arithmetic/Logic Unit

The **arithmetic/logic unit** (**ALU**) contains the electronic circuitry that executes all arithmetic operations and logical operations. Logical operations are comparing operations. The arithmetic/logic unit is able to compare numbers, letters, or special characters and take various courses of action. The ALU, for example, can examine two numbers and decide whether the first is greater than, less than, or equal to the second number. It is by comparing that a computer is able to tell, for instance, whether charge-card customers have exceeded their credit limits and whether one political candidate has more votes than another.

The Memory Connection

The CPU interacts closely with memory, referring to it for both instructions and data. Instructions tell the computer what to do; data is used according to the instructions. Both instructions and data are in memory. For example, data might be an employee's hourly rate and hours worked, and the instructions would tell the computer to multiply those two data items together to get the employee's salary. Memory holds the data after it is input to the system and before it is processed. It also holds the data after it has been processed but before it has been released to the output device. Memory consists of electronic circuits, just as the CPU does. Let us look at memory in more detail.

Memory: RAM and ROM

As we noted, the two basic types of memory chips in every computer are popularly known as RAM (random-access memory) and ROM (read-only memory).

RAM chips can store programs and data temporarily. Program instructions can use data stored on RAM chips or place new data on the chips. RAM is usually known simply as *memory*, the place where instructions and data are kept while your program is running. The main advantage of RAM is that data can be accessed quickly and easily. However, RAM is usually **volatile;** that is, the stored data is lost once the power is shut off. This is one of the reasons why we need secondary storage. The more RAM in your computer, the more powerful the programs you can run. In recent years the amount of RAM storage in a personal computer has increased dramatically.

ROM contains programs and data that are recorded into chips at the factory. The contents of ROM can be used, but they cannot be changed by the user. ROMs, often called **firmware,** are used to store programs that will not be altered. For example, a pocket calculator might have a program for calculating square roots stored in ROM. You can use the square root program and read the results, but you cannot alter or erase the program. Unlike RAM, ROM is **nonvolatile;** that is, turning the computer off has no effect on ROM chips.

Data Representation: "On/Off"

Before the central processing unit can use data, the data must be presented in a way the computer can understand. People are accustomed to thinking of computers as complex mechanisms, but in fact these machines recognize only two things: a symbol for "off" and a symbol for "on." To a computer, the numeral 0 means "off" and the numeral 1 means "on." This two-state system is called the **binary system.** By using only the two states—which represent electrical currents turned on or off—sophisticated ways of representing data are constructed. That is, all data used by the computer can be represented by combinations of 0s and 1s.

Bits and Bytes

Each 0 or 1 in the binary system is called a **bit** (for *binary* dig*it*). The bit is the basic unit for storing data in memory. To be useful, a computer must be able to store and process numbers, letters, and special characters (such as $ and ?). To do this, the bits are put together in groups, usually groups of 7 or 8, called **bytes.** Each byte (pronounced "bite") usually represents a single character of data, such as the letter *A* or the number 4.

The ASCII Data-Coding Scheme

As we said, a byte—a group of bits—represents a character of data. But how does the computer know which set of bits is equivalent to which character? In theory, we could each make up our own definitions, declaring certain bit patterns to represent certain characters. But this would be about as practical as each of us speaking our own special language. Since we need to communicate with the computer and with each other, it is

Figure 2-4 The ASCII code. *Shown are binary representations for capital letters and numbers.*

Character	ASCII		Character	ASCII
A	100 0001		T	101 0100
B	100 0010		U	101 0101
C	100 0011		V	101 0110
D	100 0100		W	101 0111
E	100 0101		X	101 1000
F	100 0110		Y	101 1001
G	100 0111		Z	101 1010
H	100 1000			
I	100 1001		0	011 0000
J	100 1010		1	011 0001
K	100 1011		2	011 0010
L	100 1100		3	011 0011
M	100 1101		4	011 0100
N	100 1110		5	011 0101
O	100 1111		6	011 0110
P	101 0000		7	011 0111
Q	101 0001		8	011 1000
R	101 0010		9	011 1001
S	101 0011			

appropriate that we use a common scheme for data representation. That is, we must agree on which groups of bits represent which characters.

The coding scheme for representing numbers, letters, and special characters on microcomputers is called **ASCII** (pronounced "AS-key"), which stands for American Standard Code for Information Interchange. ASCII uses 7 bits for each character. The ASCII representation has been adopted as a standard by the United States government. Figure 2-4 shows the ASCII code.

Memory Size

Bytes are also used to describe the size of a computer's memory. Computer manufacturers express the capacity of a computer's memory in terms of K. **K** represents the number 2 to the tenth power, which is 1024. A **kilobyte** is K bytes—that is, 1024 bytes. A common personal computer memory size is 640K, an abbreviation for 640 kilobytes, or approximately 655,000 bytes of memory. One **megabyte** of memory is 1,000,000—1 million—bytes. The letter **M** is used to represent *megabyte*; 2M, for example, means 2 megabytes.

The Keyboard and Other Input Devices

As you know, **input** is the data that you give to the computer system for processing. Sometimes the input—such as a memo or insurance claim figures or salary data—originates with you. In other cases, the computer could offer choices or ask questions on the screen; the selections you make and answers you give are also input. *Input devices* include the *keyboard, mouse, joy stick,* and a variety of other devices. Since the keyboard is the most common input device, we begin there.

The Keyboard

As Figure 2-5 shows, a **keyboard** is similar to a typewriter. A keyboard is connected to the computer by a cable. Although keyboards come in a variety of sizes and styles, they usually have many features in common. For example, all keyboards have character keys in the center section of the keyboard. These keys are arranged like the traditional QWERTY keyboard found on typewriters. When a key is pressed, two things happen: The corresponding character is sent to the computer's memory and the character also appears on the monitor screen. That is, the activity on the screen is a visual confirmation of the data your fingers are sending to memory. The **cursor,** a flashing square or dash on the screen, moves on the screen as you type to indicate where the next character will be inserted.

Most keyboards also include a numeric keypad, cursor movement keys, and a set of function keys (Figure 2-6, on page 43). The **numeric keypad** resembles a 10-key calculator and is convenient for entering numeric data. **Cursor movement keys** control the movement of the cursor over the screen. Some-

Figure 2-5 A typewriter-style keyboard. Most keyboards follow the standard QWERTY layout of typewriters and are connected to the computer by a cable.

Finding Your Way around a Keyboard

The main section of an IBM keyboard includes the familiar keys found on a typewriter keyboard, as well as some special command keys. These keys can have different uses depending on the software. Some of the common uses are described in this box.

Special Keys on Main Keyboard

 The Escape key, Esc, allows you to escape to the previous screen of the program.

The Tab key, Tab, allows you to tab across the screen and set tab stops as you would on a typewriter.

 The Control key, Ctrl, is used in combination with another key to initiate a command.

 The Alternate key, Alt, is used along with another key to initiate a command.

 The Backspace key moves the cursor to the left to correct a keying error.

 The Enter, or Return, key words like a carriage return.

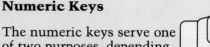 The Shift key produces uppercase letters.

The Caps Lock key controls the entry of lowercase or uppercase letters.

Numeric Keys

The numeric keys serve one of two purposes, depending on the status of the Num Lock key. When the computer is in the Num Lock mode, these keys can be used to enter numeric data; otherwise, they move the cursor.

 The End key moves the cursor to the end of the line.

This key moves the cursor down.

 The Page Down key, PgDn, advances one full screen while the cursor remains in the same position.

This key moves the cursor to the left.

This key moves the cursor to the right.

 The Home key moves the cursor to the top left-hand corner of the screen.

 This key moves the cursor up.

The Page Up key, PgUp, backs up the previous screen while the cursor remains in the same position.

 The Insert key, Ins, can be used to insert additional characters within a line. It can also be used to type over characters in a line.

 The Delete key, Del, deletes a character or space.

The Print Screen key, PrtSc, when pressed with the Shift key, causes the screen display to be printed.

The Minus key enters a minus sign on the screen when the computer is in Num Lock mode. Otherwise, it moves the cursor to the top of the screen.

 The Plus key enters a plus sign on the screen when the computer is in Num Lock mode. Otherwise, it moves the cursor to the bottom of the screen.

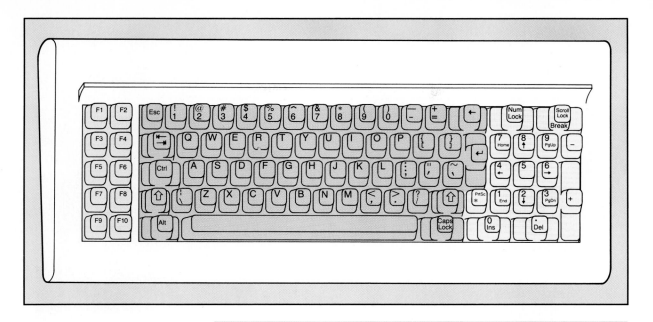

Figure 2-6 An IBM keyboard. *This style of keyboard has three main parts: The function keys on the left, the character keys in the center, and the numeric keyboard on the right. The numeric keys can also be used to move the cursor.*

times these keys are part of the numeric keypad and are designated by arrows indicating direction. **Function keys** are used to give certain commands to the computer. They let you perform tasks that would be tedious if you had to key them using the "typewriter" part of the keyboard. For example, if you were using a word processing program and wanted to underline a certain part of the text, you could press a designated function key to indicate this to the program. The particular job a function key performs varies with the software used.

Other Input Devices

There are other ways to interact with microcomputers. A discussion of some of the most common follows.

Mouse. A **mouse** is a computer input device that actually looks a little bit like a mouse (Figure 2-7a, on the next page). The mouse has a ball on its underside. Rolling the mouse across a flat surface, such as a desktop, causes a corresponding move-

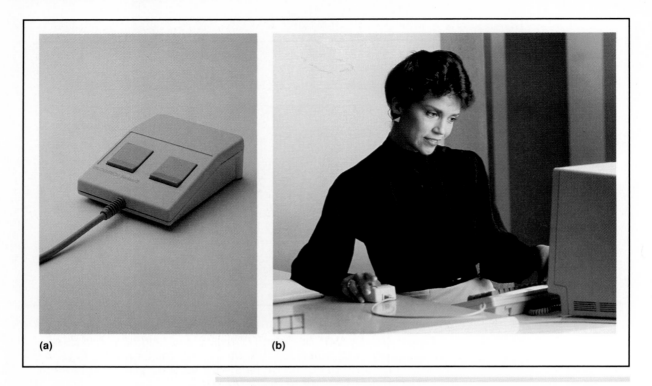

(a)   **(b)**

Figure 2-7 A mouse. *(a) The mouse is an inexpensive input device. (b) Rolling the mouse across a surface controls the movement of the cursor on the screen. Clicking the buttons on the mouse lets you communicate with the computer.*

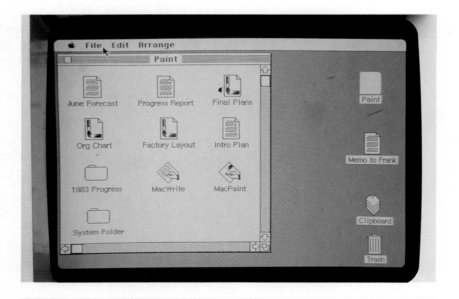

Figure 2-8 Icons. *This Macintosh software uses pictures, or icons, to represent different files.*

ment of the cursor on the computer screen. You communicate with the computer by clicking a button on top of the mouse (Figure 2-7b).

Some people who write software for personal computers have made the mouse an important part of using the software. For example, some software displays pictorial symbols called **icons** (Figure 2-8). One icon might be a picture of a sheet of paper, used to represent a memo you have stored. If you want to retrieve the memo, roll the mouse on the desk surface until the cursor is over the picture of the paper. Then signal the computer that you wish to open the file by rapidly clicking the mouse button twice. These actions replace typing commands in words on the keyboard.

Light Pen. For direct interaction with your computer screen, few devices beat a light pen (Figure 2-9). Resembling a ballpoint pen, a **light pen** has a light-sensitive cell at the end.

Figure 2-9 Light pen. When the light-sensitive cell of this input device is placed against the screen, it closes a circuit and enables the computer to identify a point on the screen.

Figure 2-10 A digitizer. *This woman is using a digitizer to input data from her diagram to the computer. Note the results of the digitized input on the computer screen.*

When this end of the light pen is placed against the screen, it closes a photoelectric circuit, pinpointing the place on the screen where pictures or data on the screen are entered or modified. A light pen is versatile enough to modify screen graphics or allow you to select from a list of activity choices on the screen.

Digitizer. A **digitizer** is a device used to input pictures to a computer. A computer screen is made up of a series of dots called **pixels** (from *pic*ture *el*ements). Each pixel on the screen can be illuminated individually. An image—whether a drawing or a photo—can be considered a series of tiny rectangles; each rectangle corresponds to a pixel on the screen. The image can be scanned by a digitizer (Figure 2-10), which converts each rectangle of the image into digital data that the computer can accept and represent as pixels on the screen.

Joy Stick. A well-known input device, the joy stick is that gadget dear to the hearts of video game players. A **joy stick** is a handheld device with a knob or lever that allows fingertip control of objects on a computer screen. When you move the lever in a certain direction, the screen figure moves in the same direction.

Voice Input Devices. Have you talked to your computer lately? This is possible with current technology, even though there are some limitations. What could be more direct than speaking to a computer?

Voice input devices, more formally known as **speech recognition devices,** let you speak to the computer to input data (Figure 2-11). Voice input is about twice as fast as keyboard input by a skilled typist. When you speak into a microphone, the voice input device converts your speech into digital code that can be understood by the computer. Voice input is more commonly used with large computers, and employees speak commands that tell them to sort packages or report bank balances. However, there are microcomputer applications too. For example, voice input devices for microcomputers are particularly valuable to physically disabled users.

Figure 2-11 Voice input. With a voice input device you can input data by speaking to your computer. This system in an interior design store accepts voice input data about textile goods.

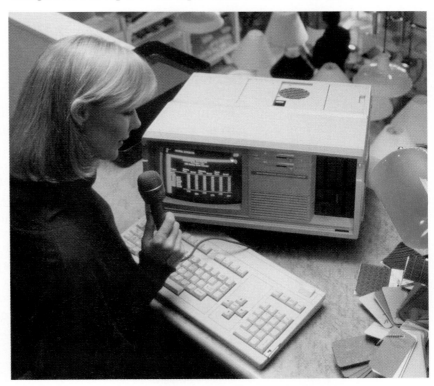

The Monitor

The **monitor** is an important part of every computer system. It not only reflects your input, it also works as an output device, showing the computer's response to your input. Monitors come in many different sizes, shapes, and colors (Figure 2-12). The most common type of monitor screen is the **cathode ray tube** or (**CRT**). These are the same type of screens that are found on televisions. Other types of screens are **liquid crystal display** (**LCD**) and **light emitting diode** (**LED**), flat display screens found on laptop computers. These screens are smaller and lighter than CRTs, but the quality usually suffers. **Monochrome** screens display only one color—usually green or amber—which appears on a black background. Color monitors can display many different colors and are widely used in graphics.

Screen Resolution. As we mentioned earlier, monitor screens show images as collections of dots called pixels. The **resolution** of the screen—its clarity—is directly related to the number of pixels on the screen: The more pixels, the finer the resolution. If you think of the screen as a rectangular grid of pixels, resolution can be defined as the number of pixel rows by the number of pixel columns. There are three common resolution levels:

- Medium—200 rows by 320 columns of pixels
- High—200 rows by 640 columns of pixels
- Super-high—1024 rows by 1024 columns of pixels

If you have a special use for very clear, precise images or need to do very fancy or detailed graphics, you would want to use a higher resolution screen.

Graphics Cards. As they come from the factory, some personal computers can display only text on their screens; to display graphics, each of these computers must have a **graphics card** (also called a **graphics adapter board**) added. To display color graphics, you need both a color monitor and color graphics circuitry, either built in or on a graphics card. These cards will be discussed in more detail in Chapter 10.

As important as the computer screen is as an output device, most users also need a printer to communicate on paper. Let us take a closer look at printers and other output devices.

Figure 2-12 Different monitor screens. *(a) Studies show that amber monitor screens reduce eyestrain. (b) This high-resolution brilliance is available only on color CRT monitors. (c) Laptop computers often use liquid crystal display (LCD) technology for their small lightweight screens.*

(a)

(b)

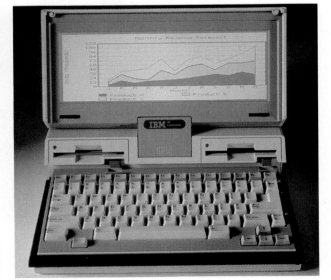

(c)

Printers and Other Output Devices

As you might already suspect, a principal device used to produce computer output is the printer.

A **printer** is a device that produces printed paper output—known as **hard copy** because it is tangible and permanent (unlike "soft copy," which is displayed on a screen). We begin by distinguishing impact and nonimpact printers.

Impact Printers

Impact printers form images on paper as typewriters do, by striking a character against a ribbon, which makes an image on the paper. Impact printers for microcomputers are **character printers**—that is, they print character by character across the page from one margin to the other. A typical impact printer is

Figure 2-13 Daisy wheel printer. *The daisy wheel (inset) consists of a set of spokes, and each spoke carries a raised character. A printer can have several interchangeable daisy wheels, each with a different type style. When printing, the daisy wheel rotates to the spoke with the appropriate character. A hammer strikes against the ribbon, which then strikes the paper and leaves an imprint.*

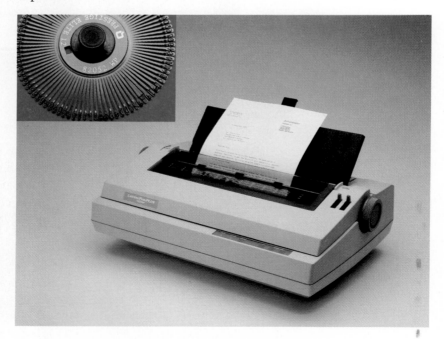

the daisy wheel; many dot-matrix printers are also impact printers. Let us consider these two types of printers.

The **daisy wheel printer** contains a removable wheel with a set of spokes; each spoke contains a raised character (Figure 2-13). The wheel rotates to align the appropriate character over the ribbon. The spoke is then struck by a hammerlike device, which pushes the character against the ribbon, leaving an imprint of the character on the page. You can change the type style by simply changing the wheel. Noted for its high-quality printing, this kind of printer is useful for word processing and professional correspondence. For this reason, daisy wheel printers are also called **letter-quality printers.** It should be noted that the daisy wheel printer is the only type of printer that cannot print graphics.

Dot-matrix printers construct a character by using a movable print head of tiny pins that are pushed against the ribbon to print dots. The character is formed column by column, following the principle of lights on a basketball scoreboard, to produce the shape of the character. Figure 2-14 (on the next page) shows how this works. A typical matrix is 5 × 7, that is, five dots wide and seven dots high. Other matrices have 7 × 9 dots or even more; the more dots, the better the quality of the letter produced. In fact, some newer models have a 24-pin print head—that is, 24 pins per column. These print heads eliminate the polka-dotted look of models with fewer dots. Because of the improved results they produce, printers with 24-pin heads are sometimes called **near-letter-quality printers** (Figure 2-15, on the next page).

Nonimpact Printers

Nonimpact printers form characters by using heat, ink spray, or lasers. With these types of printers, there is no physical contact between the printer and the paper when the characters are being formed. There are many advantages of nonimpact printers, but the key reasons for their growing popularity are that they are faster and quieter because they have no type elements or hammers physically moving around. The three major types of nonimpact printers are thermal, ink jet, and laser. All of these use the dot-matrix concept to form characters.

Figure 2-14 Forming dot-matrix characters. *(a) This art shows the letter* G *being printed as a 5 × 7 dot-matrix character. The moving matrix head has seven pins stacked vertically, which move sideways to form each letter. (b) Letters, numbers, and special characters formed as 5 × 7 dot-matrix characters.*

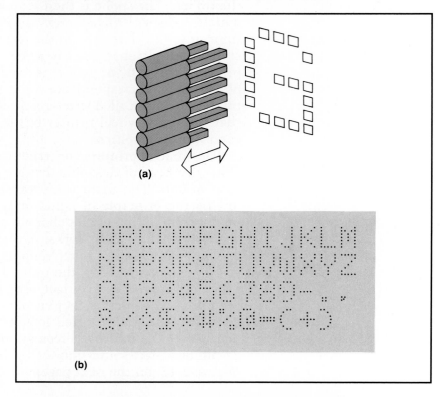

Figure 2-15 Output from two dot-matrix printers. *Note the difference in quality between (a) output from a 9-pin dot-matrix printer and (b) output from a 24-pin dot-matrix printer.*

The number of pins in a
dot-matrix printer affects
the quality of the type.

The number of pins in a
dot-matrix printer affects
the quality of the type.

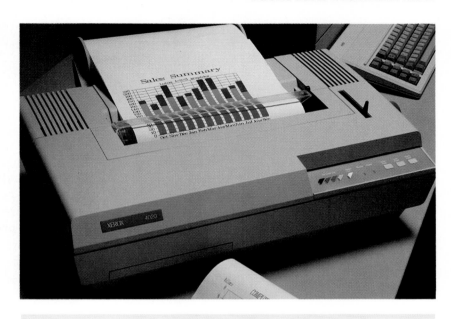

*Figure 2-16 **Ink-jet printer.*** *Although relatively slow, ink-jet printers can produce text and graphics in color. Output produced by ink-jet printers usually is higher quality than output produced by dot-matrix printers.*

Thermal. Thermal printers produce characters by heating the pins in the print head. Although thermal printers are inexpensive and quiet, their need for special paper and their low quality are serious disadvantages.

Ink Jets. Spraying ink from tiny nozzles, **ink-jet printers** are up to ten times faster than impact printers. The ink passes through an electric field; the field deflects the ink to produce a character. Ink-jet printers can use multiple nozzles to print in several different colors (Figure 2-16).

Laser. To transfer images to paper, **laser printers** use a laser beam to write the characters onto the surface of a rotating metal drum that contains the full range of characters. Then inklike toner is deposited on the drum; the ink adheres where the letters were written and is pressed on the paper. The result is extremely high-quality images, printed at record-breaking speeds.

A laser printer is a key ingredient in *desktop publishing*. Laser printers let users combine high-quality text and graphics, an appropriate blend for newsletters and other types of reports. Unfortunately, the high quality produced by a laser printer is matched by its high price tag. Typical prices range from $1000 to $3000.

Serial versus Parallel Printers

There are two standard methods of interfacing a printer to a computer. The first method is called a serial interface, and printers that use this method are called **serial printers.** Serial printers receive data a bit at a time. The second method is called parallel interface. **Parallel printers** receive data faster, usually 8 bits (1 byte) at a time. The important point to remember is that a serial printer cannot be connected to a computer that has only a parallel interface and vice versa.

Other Output Devices

Although printers and screens are the principal output devices, there are other output devices that are important for certain applications.

Plotters. Under control of the computer, plotters (Figure 2-17) draw hard-copy output in the form of maps, bar charts, engineering drawings, and even two- or three-dimensional illustrations. Plotters move one or more pens, under the control of the computer, over a paper surface.

Plotters are not commonly used with microcomputers, mostly because fine pictorial output has taken a back seat to the numbers and letters generated by word processing and spreadsheet software. However, if you balk at primitive dot-matrix output drawings but do not have a quality graphics printer, you might want to consider a plotter.

Voice Output. We have already examined voice input. Speech recognition is actually more difficult than **speech synthesis**—the process of enabling machines to talk to people. In fact, computers are frequently like people in the sense that they find it easier to talk than to listen. Spoken computer messages are not, of course, real human voices. Rather, they are the product of **voice synthesizers** (also called **voice output devices** or **audio-response units**), which convert data to sounds understandable to humans.

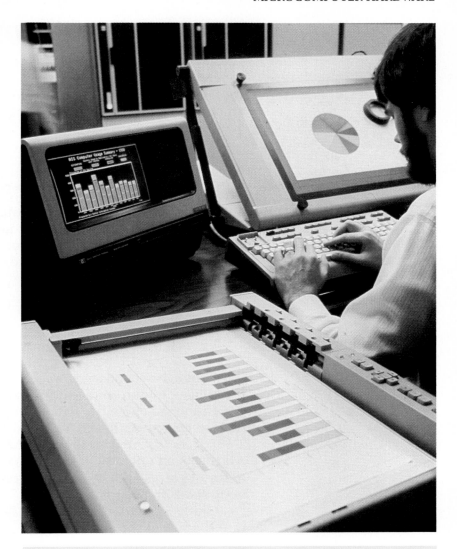

Figure 2-17 A plotter. *Designers of circuit boards, street maps, schematic drawings, graphs, and similar applications can work in fine detail on a computer screen and then print the results on a plotter.*

Voice synthesizers can be relatively inexpensive ($200 or so) and connect to almost any computer. Many synthesizers plug into the computer where the printer does, but they speak the output rather than print it. Other synthesizers are built into the computer. Voice output applications can be found in schools and businesses. For example, a student can hear information being displayed on a screen to reinforce the learning process, or a customer's keyed-in microcomputer inquiry can be sent over the phone to obtain a spoken bank balance from the bank's computer.

So far, we have discussed getting data in and out of the computer. However, you may wish to store the data you have used or the information you have derived from processing. Since data in memory is used only temporarily, a computer needs secondary storage.

Secondary Storage Devices

Secondary storage for computers provides the ability to store data in extremely compressed form, and it is unquestionably one of the computer's most valuable assets. Secondary storage lets you store data economically, reliably, and conveniently.

Diskettes

Although secondary storage devices are always evolving, the most common storage device is still the **disk drive.** A disk drive can read and write data onto a **diskette,** a round, plastic surface coated with magnetically sensitive material (Figure 2-18). Data is stored on the disk surface in areas called tracks. All tracks on one disk are concentric; that is, they are circles of various sizes with the same center. Data is recorded as magnetic spots on the tracks.

The disk drive works like this: First you insert the diskette into the slot in the disk drive (Figure 2-19). This activates the drive spindle, which clamps the diskette so that the diskette can spin without slipping.

The disk drive rotates the diskette at about 300 revolutions per minute. As the diskette is rotating, the disk drive moves its **access arm,** positioning the attached **read/write heads** over the disk surface, to transfer data back and forth between the diskette and memory. Most disk drives are **double sided,** meaning that they have two read/write heads, one for each side of the diskette.

Each track on a diskette is divided into **sectors,** which hold a specific number of characters of data (Figure 2-20, on page 58). Data on the track is accessed by referring to the track number and the sector number where the data is stored. Most microcomputers use **soft-sectored diskettes,** meaning that the

Figure 2-18 Parts of a disk-ette. (a) *This cutaway view shows the different parts of a 5¼-inch floppy diskette.* (b) *This figure shows the cutaway view of 3½-inch diskette.*

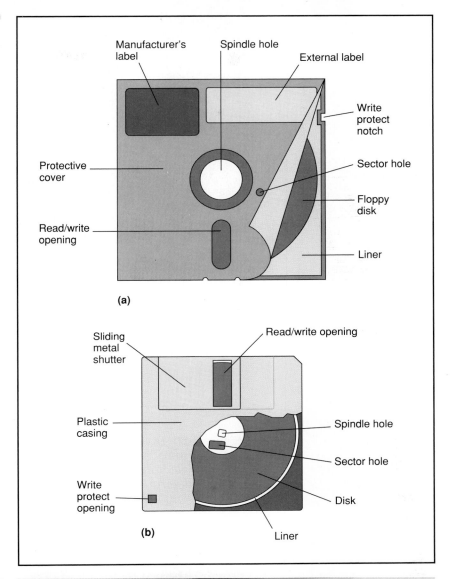

(a)

(b)

Figure 2-19 Disk drives. *Computers read and write data on diskettes inserted in disk drives. To use a diskette you must first insert it into the slot in the front of the disk drive.*

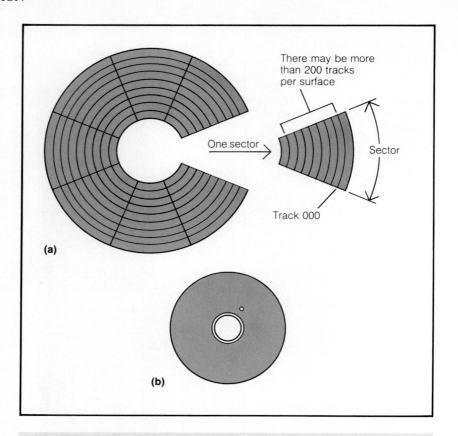

Figure 2-20 Disk sectors. *(a) Data on a diskette is identified by its track number and sector number. (b) A soft-sectored diskette has a single hole to identify the start of the first sector. The sectors are determined by the software.*

disk sectors are determined by the software. A soft-sectored disk has a single hole to mark the beginning of the track.

Diskettes must be handled with care. Figure 2-21 shows proper care and handling of diskettes.

Hard Disks

Hard disks are sealed modules that contain one or more rigid disks and the access arms and read/write heads (Figure 2-22, on page 60). Hard disks are expensive, although many are now under $1000. However, with storage capacities of 20, 30, 40 or more megabytes, they may be worth the price. (Some diskettes have a storage capacity of up to 1.5 megabytes.) Also, hard disks are extremely reliable, since they are sealed against contamination by airborne dust and human hands.

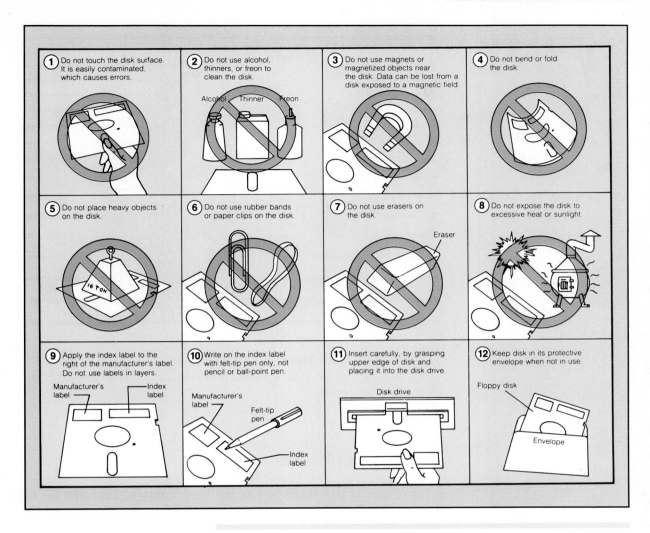

Figure 2-21 Caring for diskettes. *Although 3½-inch nonflexible diskettes are less fragile than floppy diskettes because of their plastic jacket, all diskettes require special handling. These pictures illustrate a few of the rules for taking care of diskettes.*

Hard disks can save you time as well as space. It is much faster to use a file on a hard disk, and you do not have the inconvenience of shuffling diskettes in and out of the disk drive. Most microcomputers for business are now sold with hard-disk drives.

Unlike a diskette, however, a hard disk cannot be transported from one computer to another. For that reason, a hard-disk system needs one diskette drive to provide users with software portability—that is, the ability to move software and

Figure 2-22 Innards of a hard disk. *This hard disk can store about 20 million characters on a pair of 3½-inch metal disks.*

data conveniently from one place to another. Also, hard-disk files should be backed up—copied—to diskettes regularly as a security measure.

Backup: Data Insurance

No one really likes to pay for insurance, but no one likes to get caught without it, either. Consider what happened at Norward Community College. Norward has a campuswide computer system that hooks small department computers to a central computer with a shared hard disk. Secretaries were in the habit of keeping their data files on the hard disk. They were supposed to keep copies of their files on their own diskettes. And they did—or at least some of them did, some of the time. As sometimes happens, the hard disk crashed—physically malfunctioned so that data was destroyed. One department lost three years of files. Secretaries from another department had faithfully backed up their files until two months before, when, they declared, they were "just too busy." The price of insurance was their time, and, unfortunately, they had not paid.

Just how important is backup, anyway? It is as important as your files. The absolute best backup procedure is to make a duplicate copy of each file as soon as it is made. But backing up on diskettes is time-intensive. Fortunately, dealers are offering a variety of tape- or disk-based backup systems that are relatively inexpensive and easy to use. The price of one of these systems may save you the cost of lost data in the future.

Modems

Many organizations find that their needs are best served by a **network** of microcomputers that can operate independently for their individual users or in cooperation with other computers—micros, minis, or mainframes—to exchange data and share resources. This subject is intimately tied to *data communications*, the process by which computers exchange data over communications facilities—in particular, the telephone.

The extra hardware needed for these processes varies according to the communications scheme adopted. If the computers in a network are geographically distant from one another, modems are needed. A **modem** (Figure 2-23) is used to convert data generated by the sending computer to a form that can be passed through a communications link such as the telephone system. Another modem at the other end reconverts the data

Figure 2-23 Modems. Modems convert computer-produced data into signals that can travel over telephone wires and vice versa. (a) This external modem rests under the telephone that hooks the computer to the outside world. (b) This internal modem slips into an expansion slot inside the computer. The phone cord plugs into a jack in the back of the computer.

(a)

(b)

for use by the receiving computer. As shown in Figure 2-23, a modem can be internal or external. The subject of data communications is so important that we will examine it in detail in Chapter 11.

The Goodies: Add-Ons and Supplies

You probably have seen people buy every kind of gadget for their boat or car or camper. For computer users, the story is no different. In this discussion, *add-ons* refers loosely to any semi-permanent device that attaches to the computer so that it can be directly affected by computer processing; an example is an extra disk drive. *Supplies*, on the other hand, are necessary or not-so-necessary tools such as printer ribbons or dust covers.

Does the computer have open or closed architecture? This is the heart of the architecture—and add-on—discussion. **Open architecture** means that the computer is designed so that you can buy additional circuit boards that fit in slots called **expansion slots** inside the computer (Figure 2-24). These circuit boards let you expand the capabilities of your computer with numerous add-ons. **Closed architecture** computers can support only add-ons that are plugged into the back of the computer. What

Figure 2-24 Expansion boards. *This circuit board slips into an expansion slot inside the computer to expand the capabilities of the computer.*

kinds of add-on items might you want for your own microcomputer? There are several possibilities. Assuming you already have a full keyboard, a classy printer, and a color monitor, you might consider add-ons such as more memory, an extra disk drive, a hard disk, a modem, a video camera, a plotter, and input devices such as a joy stick, light pen, or mouse.

But perhaps you want even more sophistication. Would you like a computer that can talk and hear? All manner of products are available to give your computer the gift of gab and ears to hear. Adventurous consumers can even find speech-activated video games.

A wide variety of supplies, from serious to silly, are readily available through catalogs and computer stores. In addition to standard items such as print wheels, printer ribbons, diskettes, and paper, you might want to consider these sample goods: locking rolltop diskette trays, disk drive head-cleaning kits, diskette markers, complete micro-cleaning kits, keyboard drawers (to slide the keyboard under the computer when not in use), CRT stands that swivel and tilt, dust covers, antiglare CRT screen shields, hanging CRT racks, wrist supports (to hold your wrists over the keyboard), copyholders, lockup cables, security alarms, surge protectors (to prevent electric surges from hurting your files), every conceivable printer form (including letterhead stationery, invoice forms, paycheck forms, address labels, Rolodex cards, and so on), ergonomic footrests, antistatic mats, "sound barrier" printer covers, and—finally—complete emergency power systems.

But you need not buy one item at a time; in fact, vendors encourage the purchase of the complete computer work center, which includes furniture—desk, cabinets, shelves, adjustable chair—and almost everything else, with a price to match.

Onward

We leave this chapter with these thoughts: Although it is necessary to have a firm grasp of hardware concepts, this is not a hardware world. It is an applications world. Few people want to linger fondly over RAM and ROM or contemplate the wonder of printers. People buy computers so they can run software applications. They want to apply word processing and spreadsheet and database software to their office problems. To do this, people must first understand the underlying software of a computer system, the operating system. To which we turn in Chapter 3.

Summary and Key Terms

- The basic hardware components of a microcomputer system are the microprocessor, memory, keyboard, monitor, printer, and secondary storage.

- The central processing unit (CPU) and memory are etched on silicon chips mounted on the **motherboard.** A microcomputer has a microprocessor chip and two kinds of memory chips—RAM (random-access memory) and ROM (read-only memory).

- The central processing unit (CPU) transforms raw data into processed information. The CPU is a set of electronic circuits that interpret and execute program instructions and communicate with the input, output, and storage devices. The CPU consists of two parts: the **control unit,** which directs and coordinates the computer system, and the **arithmetic/logic unit** (**ALU**), which contains the electronic circuitry that executes all arithmetic and logical operations. A **bus line,** or **data bus,** allows data to be passed among the components of the computer system.

- **RAM,** usually known as memory, stores instructions and data while the program is running. RAM is usually **volatile;** the stored data is lost once the power is shut off. **ROM,** often called **firmware,** stores programs and data that will not be altered or erased. ROM is **nonvolatile.**

- All data used by the computer can be represented by combinations of 0s (which mean electric current is off) and 1s (which mean current is on). This two-state system is called the **binary system.** Each 0 or 1 is a **bit,** a basic unit for storing data in memory. To process and store characters, the bits are grouped into **bytes.** A byte, usually 7 or 8 bits, represents a character of data.

- **ASCII,** a commonly used coding scheme for representing characters on microcomputers, uses 7 bits for each character.

- Bytes are also used to describe the size of a computer's memory. A **kilobyte** is **K** bytes, or 1024 bytes. A **megabyte,** represented by **M,** is 1 million bytes.

- **Input** is the data that you give to the computer system for processing.

- **Keyboards** are the most common type of input device. Most keyboards include a **numeric keypad** for entering numeric data, **cursor movement keys** to control the movement of the cursor, and **function keys,** which give certain commands to the computer.

- A **cursor** is a flashing indicator on a screen that shows where the next character will be inserted.

- Other common input devices for the microcomputer include the **mouse,** the **light pen,** the **digitizer,** the **joy stick,** and **voice input devices.**

- An **icon** is a small picture that represents a computer command or activity.

- The **monitor** is an output device that reflects the user's input. The most common type of monitor screen is the **cathode ray tube** (**CRT**). Other types of screens are **liquid crystal display** (**LCD**) and **light emitting diode** (**LED**).

- **Monochrome** screens display only one color; color screens can display many different colors.

- An image on the computer screen is created by a series of tiny dots, or **pixels.** The greater the number of pixels, the greater the **resolution,** or clarity, of the screen.

- To display graphics, some computers must have built-in graphics capability or a **graphics card** or **graphics adapter board** added.

- A **printer** is an output device that produces printed paper, known as **hard copy.** Some printers are **impact printers,** which form characters by physically striking the paper. Other printers are **nonimpact printers,** which use a noncontact printing method.

- Impact printers are usually **character printers** because they print character by character across the page. Two types of impact printers are the **daisy wheel printer** and the **dot-matrix printer.** Daisy wheel printers are **letter-quality printers,** producing solid characters. Dot-matrix printers form letters of tiny dots based on a specific matrix. **Near-letter-quality printers** have 24-pin print heads.

■ Nonimpact printers—which include **thermal, ink-jet,** and **laser printers**—are faster and quieter than impact printers. The high-quality laser printer is a key ingredient in desktop publishing.

■ There are two standard methods of interfacing a printer to a computer. Printers that use a serial interface method are **serial printers** and receive data a bit at a time. Those using a parallel interface method are **parallel printers,** which receive data several bits at a time.

■ Plotters draw hard-copy output in the form of maps and charts. **Voice synthesizers** (also known as **voice-output devices** or **audio-response units**) convert data to sounds. **Speech synthesis** is easier to achieve in computers than **speech recognition.**

■ **Secondary storage** is necessary because memory, or primary storage, can be used only temporarily. A common storage device is the **disk drive** that reads and writes data onto a **diskette.** As the diskette rotates, the disk drive's **access arm** moves to position the **read/write heads** over the disk surface to transfer data between the diskette and memory. A **double-sided** disk drive has two read/write heads. Each track on a diskette is divided into **sectors,** which hold a specific number of characters of data. Most microcomputers use **soft-sectored** diskettes.

■ **Hard disks** are sealed modules that contain one or more rigid disks.

■ A **network** is a group of computers that can operate independently or in cooperation with each other to exchange data and share resources. **Data communications** is the process by which computers exchange data over communications facilities. A **modem** is a device that converts data from the sending computer to a form that can be passed through a communications link such as the telephone; another modem at the receiving end reconverts the data.

■ The term *add-ons* refers to any semi-permanent devices that attach to the computer. Computers with **open architecture** are designed so that additional circuit boards will fit in **expansion slots** inside the computers. Computers with **closed architecture** do not have expansion slots.

Review Questions

1. List the basic components of a microcomputer system.

2. What is the difference between RAM and ROM?

3. Describe how data is represented in bits and bytes.

4. Describe how these input devices work: mouse, light pen, digitizer, joy stick.

5. Describe the relationship between the number of pixels on a screen and screen resolution.

6. What are the differences between impact and nonimpact printers?

7. Discuss the features of a laser printer and its appropriate uses.

8. What are the advantages of a hard disk over diskettes?

9. Why are backup files important?

10. If money is not a concern, what personal computer add-ons seem appealing to you?

FROM THE REAL WORLD

Computers Make Computers at IBM

We know that computers are used in offices and factories, but have we really reached the point where computers are cloning themselves? Can we accurately use the phrase *self-made personal computers*? Not quite, because the machines ultimately depend on their human masters for direction. But consider this: The first human hands to touch the IBM Personal System/2 computer may be your own.

The scene is in a manufacturing plant nestled in the rolling hills of Austin, Texas. The "hands-off" process involves computer-controlled robots in the manufacturing operation, from the receiving dock to the loading dock. The nine-step process includes receiving, parts staging, removal of materials from pallets, materials distribution, robotic assembly, testing, serial-number imprinting, packaging, and finished-goods storage.

Each computer-in-the-making is carried through the automated process on a yellow carrier called a tote. The tote cycles endlessly, ferrying a computer through the automated process. The journey begins at gravity-fed racks that adjoin the parts staging area. Computer-bearing totes move along a conveyor from the racks to where the robots work.

Equipped with vision and hand-like grippers, robots assemble the pieces: They insert memory boards, mount disk drives, attach keyboards and screens, and mount power supplies. The robots produce at the rate of one computer a minute. Human intervention is needed only when a machine signals that it cannot fix itself.

But the automation process is not limited to robots: The entire grand scheme of robots building computers is orchestrated by more IBM personal computers. Microcomputers are involved in product testing, process control, and materials distribution. And, while they run the show, microcomputers are in constant communication with each other through a network.

Microcomputers also communicate with the robots, querying them constantly for performance statistics: How many parts did you handle this last hour? How many average tries to get it right? How many times did a human have to assist you? Are your statistics up to the norm? And so on. Even robots are accountable. However, robots need not be laid off if computer sales lag; production is simply reduced to fewer hours. In fact, a factory line of robots can be adjusted easily to match market fluctuations.

3

The Disk Operating System

Chapter Objectives

After reading this chapter
you should be able to

- Explain why an operating
  system is needed

- Describe the difference
  between internal and
  external DOS commands

- Explain how the disk
  drive name, and particularly the default drive,
  are used in operating system commands

- Load the DOS operating
  system

- List all the files on a disk

- Prepare new diskettes for
  use

- Name, copy, and erase
  files

- Transfer and use the
  operating system com-
  mands needed for appli-
  cations programs

When Bill Fitzgerald first used his microcomputer, he was intrigued by the variety of packaged software games available for it. In each case Bill inserted the software applications disk, turned on the machine, and let the software take over from there. This procedure immediately brought easy instructions to the screen, often accompanied by vivid graphics and even music. Bill did not realize, however, that the disk the software came on also carried another kind of software called an operating system, which is often hidden from the user.

An **operating system** is a set of *programs* that lets the computer system control resources, execute programs, and manage data. All applications programs need to interact with an operating system to run. Today, Bill wants to use a software package that does not contain the operating system, so he will have to interact directly with the operating system to get the software going. Before Bill can use his applications software, he must load an operating system into the computer. Once he loads the operating system, Bill sees the following symbol on the screen:

A>

That is, he sees the letter "A" followed by the mathematical symbol for greater than. A> is called A greater, or—more often—the A prompt. At this point Bill must give some instruction, and the computer is willing to wait all day until he does. Perhaps all Bill needs to do is insert his packaged software disk and then type a certain word to make the software package take the lead again. But it could be more complicated than that because A> is actually the signal for direct communication between the user and the operating system. Bill is no longer shielded from the operating system, and he must take some responsibility for understanding it.

As we have indicated, just about anyone can quickly learn to use certain types of packaged software, the kind that interacts with the operating system in a way that is not noticeable to the user. But many people want to know more so they can take full advantage of computer resources. Understanding operating systems is an important step in that direction.

In this chapter we will study the IBM Personal Computer's operating system, called **MS-DOS** (for **Microsoft Disk Operating System**). You may hear MS-DOS called PC-DOS (PC stands for *Personal Computer*); the differences are not significant. We will call the operating system simply **DOS** (rhymes with *boss*). There are several versions of DOS. The differences among them (for our purposes) are small, as long as you are using any version numbered 2.0 through 3.3. First we will discuss what DOS is, then examine the hardware you need to use DOS, and—finally—show you how to use DOS on your computer.

The Operating System: Power Software in the Background

The emphasis in this text is on applications programs for word processing, spreadsheets, and databases. Before you use these programs, however, you need to understand some basics about DOS, since you will be using DOS whenever you use your computer. As we said before, an operating system is a set of programs that lets the computer manage its own resources: the CPU, memory, secondary storage devices, and various input/output devices. In a broader sense resources also include data and programs. Figure 3-1 gives a conceptual picture of operating system software as a cushion between the hardware and applications programs.

Figure 3-1 A conceptual diagram of an operating system. Next to the outer rim, closest to the user, are applications programs—software that helps a user compute a payroll or play a game or calculate the trajectory of a rocket. The operating system is the set of programs necessary between the applications programs and the hardware.

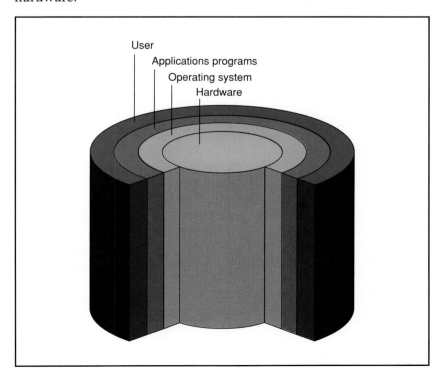

DOS programs are stored on one or more diskettes, which were probably purchased with the computer. These programs are executed by issuing a **command,** a name that invokes the correct program. Whole books have been written about DOS commands, but we will consider only the commands you need to use an applications program. These commands let you

- Access DOS files by using DOS commands

- Prepare (format) new diskettes for use

- List the names of the files you have on your disk

- Name new files on disk and change the names of old files

- Copy files from one disk to another

- Erase files from a disk

This is a rather short list, and, as you will see, most of the commands are straightforward.

Internal DOS Commands

Although you may not use all DOS commands, certain programs invoked by DOS commands must be in your computer's memory before you can use DOS or an applications program such as Lotus 1-2-3. These essential DOS programs are accessed using commands referred to as the **internal DOS commands.** The internal DOS programs must be loaded— placed—into your computer's memory when you first turn on your computer. Once the internal DOS programs are in memory, you can remove the DOS disk but still use the internal DOS programs. However, internal DOS sometimes must be reloaded when you stop using one applications program and wish to use a different applications program. And, of course, since the computer loses whatever is in its memory when you turn off the machine, you must reload internal DOS into memory whenever you turn the computer on to use an applications program. All the applications packages discussed in this book use internal DOS programs and need them in memory in order to work properly.

When you want to use an internal DOS program, tell DOS to execute the program by typing in the appropriate command name. Internal DOS commands execute immediately because the internal DOS programs are loaded into the computer when

THE NORTON UTILITIES

DOS is not prepared for every circumstance you may encounter. Supplemental programs like the Norton Utilities may take up the slack. Typically, such programs improve on or add to DOS's normal file-handling programs. For example, one brief command can sort all file names, so they show up in order when you use the DIR command. Another handy feature is the ability to map space usage for the entire disk—that is, to display where files are stored on disk.

Other useful Norton Utilities features allow you to change screen foreground and background colors (white on blue is one combination), test disks to verify that they are readable, and get system information about your own computer (memory size, operating system version, and more).

But the Norton Utilities are most famous for the UnErase command, which may be able to reclaim a file that has been deleted accidentally. How is this possible? When a file is deleted, the data is not actually gone—it is still on the disk. However, the space no longer belongs to that file and may be overwritten by a new file. The trick is to use the UnErase process before a new file can be written on the disk over the file you are trying to save.

it is booted. (In contrast, *external DOS programs*, which we will discuss shortly, reside on disk as program files and must be read from disk before they can be executed.) Two important internal DOS commands are the *COPY command*, which lets you make copies of files, and the *DIR command*, which lets you list the names of files you have stored on a disk.

External DOS Commands

Most applications programs require a lot of the computer's memory to run. Therefore, only the internal DOS programs, which are necessary to support the work of applications programs, are loaded into memory when the computer is booted. The other DOS programs, which reside in files on the DOS disk, are accessed using commands referred to as the **external DOS commands.** One of the most important external commands is the *FORMAT command*, which prepares a disk so that it is capable of storing files.

The point of this discussion is that you must have access to the external DOS programs before you can use them. Therefore, you must have the DOS disk in the proper disk drive before you can use the external commands. Usually, however, all you will need are the internal DOS commands.

Now let us consider the hardware you will need to run DOS.

A Brief Hardware Discussion

As you know from your earlier reading, a computer has several distinct pieces of hardware. The *central processing unit* executes the instructions in a computer program. The computer's memory contains program instructions and data. Internal DOS programs are loaded into memory. Secondary storage is needed, usually one or more disk drives. Since many DOS commands involve files on disk, we are particularly concerned about disk drives in this chapter.

Disk Drive Configuration. There are two kinds of disk drives: diskette drives and hard-disk drives, or hard drives. If you have two diskette drives, they are called drives A and B. A hard drive is called drive C. (Occasionally, there is a second hard drive, called drive D.) Configurations vary, but the three most common are shown in Figure 3-2. The first has diskette drive A on the left and diskette drive B on the right. The second has diskette drive A on the left and hard-drive C on the right. The third has diskette drives A and B stacked on the left (A on top, B on the bottom) and hard-drive C on the right.

From now on, to make your reading a little easier, we will use the word *disk* to refer to both diskettes and hard disks. When it is necessary to distinguish between these two storage devices, we will use the terms *diskette* and *hard disk*.

Figure 3-2 Disk drive configurations. *As you use different computers, you may see several types of disk drive combinations. The following are the most common: (a) Diskette drive A on the left, diskette drive B on the right. (b) Diskette drive A on the left, hard-drive C on the right. (c) Diskette drives A and B stacked on the left, hard-drive C on the right.*

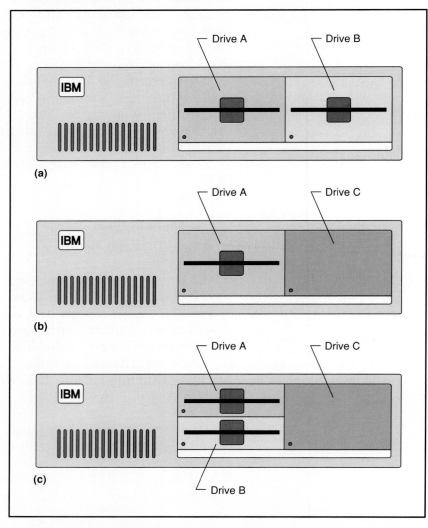

The Default Drive. Since some DOS commands refer to disk files, which store programs and data, we need to pause for a moment to consider where those files are. For example, the DIR command displays a list of files, but how does DOS know which drive contains the disk that the files are stored on? Although DOS commands let you specify a particular drive, it is easier to omit a drive specification, thus permitting DOS to use the default drive.

The **default drive,** also called the **current drive,** is the drive that the computer is currently using. If your computer does not have a hard disk, DOS will always start with drive A as the default drive. If you do have a hard disk, drive C is usually the default drive. DOS will always remind you which drive is currently the default drive by means of the prompt. If you see A>, then the default drive is A. Similarly, B> means the default drive is B, and C> means the default drive is C.

You can change to another default drive if you wish: Type the letter of the desired drive, followed by a colon, and then press Enter. Suppose, for example, that the default drive is currently drive A, but you want to access files on the disk that you have in drive B. To change the default drive to B, type:

```
B:
```

and then press Enter. (You can, by the way, type an upper- or lowercase B. DOS recognizes either.) Now the screen shows a B>.

Only one disk drive at a time can be the default drive. If you ask DOS to retrieve a file for you and DOS replies that it cannot find the file, perhaps the file is not on the disk in the default drive. You may need to change the default drive or place another disk in the current default drive.

Types of Diskettes. As we discuss the DOS commands, we will refer to different types of diskettes. The three types of diskettes you will use are (1) DOS disks, (2) applications software disks, and (3) data disks. What do these three have in common? All contain files. DOS disk files contain the operating system programs. Applications software disks contain the applications software. Data disk files contain the data that is related to applications software.

When are these three types of disks used? The DOS disk is used to start the computer system and, as you proceed, to provide services and control of software and files. Applications software disks are used after the internal DOS programs are loaded into memory. (Sometimes, as you will see later, internal DOS and applications software are on the same disk.) Data disks are used concurrently with applications software, either to supply input data or, more likely, to store the files you create.

Data disks are different from DOS and applications software disks. To begin with, the DOS and applications software may belong to your school or company and may be used by several people. Data disks, however, are usually purchased by you, belong to you, are used only by you, and contain data created by you. When you first purchase a data disk, it contains no files; that is, the disk is empty. To prepare a disk to receive

RANDOM BITS

DOS Command Sampler

This sampler assumes that your system has two diskette drives. If you have a one-drive system, you can still use the commands, but you can refer only to drive A. Also, when you use the COPY command with only one drive, you must supply a new name for the new file, since two files with the same name and extension cannot exist on the same disk. If you have a hard disk in your computer, you will probably refer to the single diskette drive as drive A and the hard-disk drive as drive C.

Make these assumptions when using the sampler:

- A is the default (current) drive, and A> is the prompt on your screen.

- FN stands for a file name. EX stands for extension.

- All commands must be followed by pressing Enter.

- Wherever, for space reasons, the command appears here on two lines, type the command all on one line.

Internal DOS Commands

YOU WANT THE COMPUTER TO	TYPE
Change the default drive to B	B:

YOU WANT THE COMPUTER TO	TYPE
Change the default drive to A	A:
Let the computer know the date (February 2, 1991), so it is recorded on the disk with files you create or alter that day	DATE 2-2-91
Let the computer know the time (11:00 A.M.) so that it will be recorded with the files you use	TIME 11:00
Use military time to express 2:15 P.M.	TIME 14:15
List the files on drive A	DIR
List the files on drive B	DIR B:
List files on drive A in abbreviated form	DIR/W
List files on drive B in abbreviated form	DIR B:/W

YOU WANT THE COMPUTER TO	TYPE
Print the files on drive A	DIR >PRN
Print the files on drive B	DIR B:>PRN
Copy a file named FN1.EX from the disk in A onto the disk in B	COPY A:FN1.EX B:
Copy FN1.EX to B with the new name FN2.EX2	COPY A:FN1.EX B:FN2.EX2
Copy all the files with extension EX1 from A to B	COPY A:*.EX1 B:
Copy all the files with file name FN1 from A to B	COPY A:FN1.* B:
Copy all the files from A to B without overwriting any files on B	COPY A:*.* B:
Erase (delete) the file FN1.EX from the disk in A	DEL FN1.EX
Erase (delete) the file FN1.EX from the disk in B	DEL B:FN1.EX
Erase all files with the extension EX1 from A	DEL *.EX1
Erase all files with the file name FN1 from A	DEL FN1.*
Erase all the files from A (Warning: You lose everything on the disk when you do this)	DEL *.*.
Erase file FN1.EX from A (produces the effect as DEL)	ERASE FN1.EX
Change the name of file FN1.EX1 on A to FN2.EX2	RENAME FN1.EX1 FN2.EX2
Change the name of file FN1.EX1 on B to FN2.EX2	RENAME B:FN1.EX1 FN2.EX2
Change the extension name of all files with the extention EX1 to EX2	RENAME *.EX1 *EX2

External Dos Commands

YOU WANT THE COMPUTER TO	TYPE
Format (prepare for use) the blank disk in drive A	FORMAT A:
Format the blank disk in B	FORMAT B:
Format the blank disk in B and transfer internal DOS to the disk	FORMAT B:/S
Format the blank disk in B and write a label on the disk	FORMAT B:/V
Format a disk in drive B to include internal DOS and a label	FORMAT B:/S/V
Make an exact copy of the disk in drive A on the disk in drive B (will overwrite files on B, if any)	DISKCOPY A: B:

the files you will create, you must use the FORMAT command. We will show you how to do this later in this chapter.
(In contrast, DOS and applications software disks, which already
have files on them, have been formatted and should not be
formatted again.)

When you create files for your data disk, you choose a name
for the file. When there are several files on the disk, you may
want to see a list of all the files. You may want to copy files
from one data disk to another so you can have a backup copy.
You may want to erase files you no longer need. To do these
things, you need to know how to use the appropriate DOS
commands. But first we must begin at the beginning—getting
DOS into memory.

Loading DOS into Memory

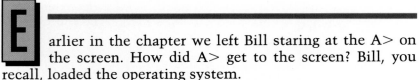

arlier in the chapter we left Bill staring at the A> on
the screen. How did A> get to the screen? Bill, you
recall, loaded the operating system.

These are the steps to load DOS if you are *not* using hard
disk drive C:

- Place the DOS disk in drive A and close the drive latch.

- Turn on the computer and monitor.

- Type in the date and time when they are requested. If
  you do not wish to change the date and time, press the
  Enter key twice.

Now the A> prompt appears on the screen, indicating that the
operating system is loaded and awaits further instruction. Here
is how it works. Whenever you turn the computer on, it attempts
to load the *internal* DOS programs into memory. The computer expects to find these programs in files on a disk in drive
A. If the DOS disk is there, then the internal DOS programs
are automatically loaded into memory. This process is known
as a **cold boot.**

You may be wondering why the word *boot* is used to describe
the DOS loading process. Why such an odd word? It makes
sense to computer makers because the computer uses instructions embedded in the hardware to load DOS. Since DOS gives
the computer more power, the computer is said to be "pulling
itself up by its own bootstraps" when you boot it.

If the computer is already on and you want to run a different applications program, you may need to reload internal DOS.

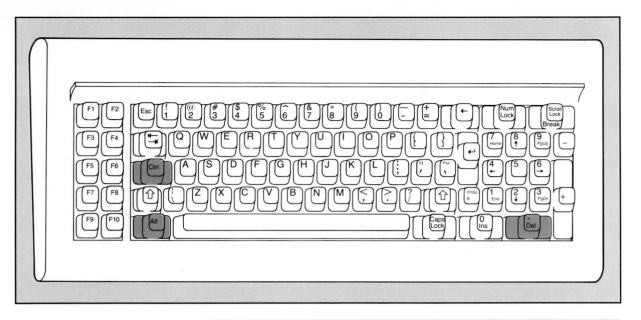

Figure 3-3 A warm boot. *If your computer is already on and you want to reboot—restart—the system, press the Ctrl, Alt, and Del keys simultaneously. But be careful; when you do this, you clear everything out of memory.*

First make sure that a DOS disk is in drive A. Then press the Ctrl, Alt, and Del keys simultaneously (Figure 3-3). (When keys are to be pressed at the same time, instructions often join the key names with hyphens. For example, Ctrl-Alt-Del tells you to press the three keys simultaneously.) When you press these three keys and there is a DOS disk in drive A, you clear everything out of memory and then load DOS. Pressing Ctrl-Alt-Del is called doing a **system reset** or, more commonly, a **warm boot.** A warm boot is faster than a cold boot. This is because during a cold boot, DOS takes a few moments to check the computer's memory. If you are using a hard disk and do not insert a disk in drive A, your computer will boot from the hard disk.

After you place the DOS disk in drive A and boot the computer, you will be asked by DOS to type in the date and time. You can skip this step if you want—just press Enter twice (Figure 3-4a, on the next page). However, date and time are stored with the file name when a file is created or updated. You may find that knowing the date and time is important when you look at your files in the future. If you wish to enter the date and time, type each of them carefully, following the directions shown on the screen. Figure 3-4b shows what the screen looks like after you have typed in date and time.

***Figure 3-4 Starting
DOS.*** *(a) When you load
DOS, it will ask you for the
current date and time. (b)
Enter the date and time by
using the format shown on
the screen. If you prefer,
you may simply press the
Enter key twice instead of
entering the date and time.*

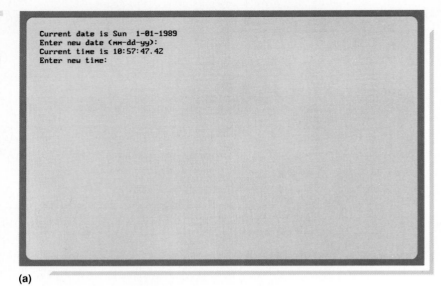

```
Current date is Sun  1-01-1989
Enter new date (mm-dd-yy):
Current time is 10:57:47.42
Enter new time:
```

(a)

```
Current date is Sun  1-01-1989
Enter new date (mm-dd-yy): 7-10-90
Current time is 10:59:43.42
Enter new time: 3:15


The IBM Personal Computer DOS
Version 3.30 (C)Copyright International Business Machines Corp 1981, 1987
               (C)Copyright Microsoft Corp 1981, 1986

A>
```

(b)

Once you have completed these steps, DOS sends a signal
to the computer screen to display A>. A>, as we have noted,
is a signal that the computer is waiting for you to do something. In fact, A> (or C> if you are using a hard disk) is usually
referred to as a **system prompt** because it is a prompt for DOS,
or Disk Operating *System.* When you see the system prompt,
you can use an internal DOS command or load and execute
an applications program. If the DOS disk is in the disk drive,
you can also use an external command.

Now let us consider some DOS commands in detail.

The DIR Command: Where the Files Are

One of the most useful internal DOS commands is the **DIR command.** DIR is short for *directory*. The command is easy to use and provides a lot of information. DOS keeps a record of all the files stored on a disk in the **disk directory.** The DIR command displays this directory for you on your computer's screen.

Executing this command is very simple: When you see a system prompt, such as A>, type:

```
DIR
```

Then press Enter. You can type the DIR command (and all other DOS commands) in either upper- or lowercase. The DIR command tells DOS to list the names of the files on the disk in the default drive. When you press Enter, DOS executes the command and lists the file names on your screen. Assuming that you have the DOS disk in the A drive, the external DOS programs, shown in Figure 3-5 (on the next page), are displayed. (Note: The number of files in your DOS directory may vary, depending on the version of DOS you have and the number of additional files on the DOS disk.)

The DIR Display Line

Now examine Figure 3-5 more closely. Each line displayed represents one file on the DOS disk. The file name is shown in the two leftmost columns on the screen. The middle column shows the number of bytes of disk space occupied by the file. (Recall that a byte is equivalent to a character of data.) The two rightmost columns show the date and time the file was created.

File Names

Since many files can be stored on one disk, DOS requires that each file on a disk be given a unique name to distinguish it from all the other files stored on the same disk. Each file has a **complete name** consisting of two parts, the **file name** and the **file extension.** It is the complete name—file name plus extension—that must be unique. Referring again to Figure 3-5, column 1 on the DIR display contains the file name, and

```
     Volume in drive A has no label
     Directory of A:\

     COMMAND   COM    23210     3-07-85     1:43p
     ANSI      SYS     1651     3-07-85     1:43p
     ASSIGN    COM     1509     3-07-85     1:43p
     ATTRIB    EXE    15091     3-07-85     1:43p
     BACKUP    COM     5577     3-07-85     1:43p
     BASIC     COM    17792     3-07-85     1:43p
     BASICA    COM    27520     3-07-85     1:43p
     CHKDSK    COM     9435     3-07-85     1:43p
     COMP      COM     3664     3-07-85     1:43p
     DISKCOMP  COM     4073     3-07-85     1:43p
     DISKCOPY  COM     4329     3-07-85     1:43p
     EDLIN     COM     7261     3-07-85     1:43p
     FDISK     COM     8173     3-07-85     1:43p
     FIND      EXE     6403     3-07-85     1:43p
     FORMAT    COM     9398     3-07-85     1:43p
     GRAFTABL  COM     1169     3-07-85     1:43p
     GRAPHICS  COM     3111     3-07-85     1:43p
     JOIN      EXE    15971     3-07-85     1:43p
     KEYBFR    COM     2473     4-12-85     4:22p
     KEYBGR    COM     2418     4-12-85     4:23p
     KEYBIT    COM     2361     4-12-85     4:25p
     KEYBSP    COM     2451     4-12-85     4:24p
     KEYBUK    COM     2348     4-12-85     4:26p
     LABEL     COM     1826     3-07-85     1:43p
     MODE      COM     5295     3-07-85     1:43p
     MORE      COM      282     3-07-85     1:43p
     PRINT     COM     8291     3-07-85     1:43p
     RECOVER   COM     4050     3-07-85     1:43p
     RESTORE   COM     5410     3-07-85     1:43p
     SELECT    COM     2084     3-07-85     1:43p
     SHARE     EXE     8304     3-07-85     1:43p
     SORT      EXE     1664     3-07-85     1:43p
     SUBST     EXE    16611     3-07-85     1:43p
     SYS       COM     3727     3-07-85     1:43p
     TREE      COM     2831     3-07-85     1:43p
     VDISK     SYS     3307     3-07-85     1:43p
     ART       BAS     1879     3-07-85     1:43p
     BALL      BAS     1966     3-07-85     1:43p
     BASIC     PIF      369     3-07-85     1:43p
     BASICA    PIF      369     3-07-85     1:43p
     CIRCLE    BAS     1647     3-07-85     1:43p
     COLORBAR  BAS     1427     3-07-85     1:43p
     COMM      BAS     4254     3-07-85     1:43p
     DEBUG     COM    15552     3-07-85     1:43p
     DONKEY    BAS     3572     3-07-85     1:43p
     EXE2BIN   EXE     2816     3-07-85     1:43p
     MORTGAGE  BAS     6178     3-07-85     1:43p
     CONFIG    SYS       22     8-25-87    12:02a
          48 File(s)        14336 bytes free
```

Figure 3-5 The contents of a DOS directory. *When you use the
DIR command to list the DOS directory, you will see a list similar to the example shown. Note that the two left-hand columns
contain the complete file name, the middle column contains the
number of bytes the files takes up on the disk, and the two right-
hand columns show the date and time the file was created.*

column 2 contains the extension. For example, in line 15 of the file listing in Figure 3-5, the file name is FORMAT and the extension is COM; the complete name is written FORMAT.COM. Notice that the file name and the extension are separated by a period, referred to as a dot. The dot is used to refer to a file, even though it does not appear when you use the DIR command. Also notice line 18 of the directory in Figure 3-5; it shows JOIN in the leftmost column and EXE in the second column. JOIN is the file name and EXE is the extension. JOIN.EXE is the complete file name.

A file name can be from one to eight characters long. Letters and numbers can be used within a file name. (Caution: A common error is to try to include a blank space as part of the file name; this is not allowed.) The extension is always three characters (letters and numbers) or less.

DOS identifies a file by its complete name and the letter of the drive—A, B, or C—that contains the disk on which the file is stored. The drive letter followed by a colon and the complete name is called a **file specification.** For example, if the DOS disk is in drive A, refer to the file for the JOIN command as

`A:JOIN.EXE`

With some applications programs, such as Lotus 1-2-3, you usually do not have to worry about placing the letter of a drive before the file name because the applications program automatically stores—saves—your file on drive B. You need to provide drive letters with file names only when you want to store or retrieve a file on a disk that is not in the default drive.

Your Own Files

When you use an applications program such as Word-Perfect, Lotus 1-2-3, or dBASE III PLUS, you will want the program to store your files on your own diskette, often called a **data disk.** You may have other diskettes containing DOS or WordPerfect or some other applications program, but the diskette or diskettes for your own files are separate. This diskette starts out without any files; it is up to you to place files on it as you see fit. In the next chapter you will start to learn how to use applications programs to make files.

Since DOS or some applications program diskette is usually in drive A, your data disk is usually in drive B. Each applications program adds its own special extension to the name of the files that you store on your data disk. This means that you will simply give your file a file name and let the applications program worry about the extension. When you execute the DIR command for your data disk (remember to switch the default drive to B first), the extensions tell you which applications package you used to create each file.

Disk Space

At the bottom of the DIR screen display are two very important pieces of information—the number of files stored on the disk and the approximate amount of unused space on the disk. In Figure 3-6 you can see that there are 48 files on the disk and 14,336 bytes available for the storage of additional files. You can use the DIR command to see how full your disks are getting as you store files on them. Most diskettes can store no more than 112 files in a directory, although higher-capacity diskettes can store up to 224 files and hard disks can store up to 512 files. You will probably run out of free bytes before you exceed the number of files the disk can hold.

To get a feel for the size of a file, use the DIR command to see how much disk space—in bytes—a newly created file occupies. As a general rule, when you have less than 20,000 bytes free on a diskette, you should either delete some files or start a new diskette. If you try to save or copy a file that is larger than the remaining disk space, DOS does not save or

Figure 3-6 The DIR display line. The DIR display shows the number of files in the directory and the number of bytes still available on the disk.

The DIR display line ⎯⎯⎯

```
PRINT     COM     8291    3-07-85    1:43p
RECOVER   COM     4050    3-07-85    1:43p
RESTORE   COM     5410    3-07-85    1:43p
SELECT    COM     2084    3-07-85    1:43p
SHARE     EXE     8304    3-07-85    1:43p
SORT      EXE     1664    3-07-85    1:43p
SUBST     EXE    16611    3-07-85    1:43p
SYS       COM     3727    3-07-85    1:43p
TREE      COM     2831    3-07-85    1:43p
UDISK     SYS     3307    3-07-85    1:43p
ART       BAS     1879    3-07-85    1:43p
BALL      BAS     1966    3-07-85    1:43p
BASIC     PIF      369    3-07-85    1:43p
BASICA    PIF      369    3-07-85    1:43p
CIRCLE    BAS     1647    3-07-85    1:43p
COLORBAR  BAS     1427    3-07-85    1:43p
COMM      BAS     4254    3-07-85    1:43p
DEBUG     COM    15552    3-07-85    1:43p
DONKEY    BAS     3572    3-07-85    1:43p
EXE2BIN   EXE     2816    3-07-85    1:43p
MORTGAGE  BAS     6178    3-07-85    1:43p
CONFIG    SYS       22    8-25-87   12:02a
       48 File(s)      14336 bytes free

A>
```

copy the file; instead it produces a message that says "Insufficient Disk Space." If you are using a hard disk, you will have much more space available for file storage. But even hard disks can be filled, so use DIR to check the amount of unused space occasionally.

DIR Variations

If you use the DIR command and there are more than 23 files on the disk, not all the file names will fit on one screen. If you simply use the DIR command, the first files will move by quickly and disappear off the top of the screen. When the action stops, only the last 23 files show on the screen. The DIR command has two variations to get around this problem. The first packs in more files per screen by displaying only the file names and extensions in columns on the screen. To use this variation, type

```
DIR/W
```

and press Enter. Figure 3-7 shows the result of a DIR/W command. Notice that up to five columns of file names can be displayed. DIR/W displays the file names faster than DIR. You can print the list of file names on paper. To do this, type

```
DIR/W >PRN
```

Then press Enter. This prints the file names in the abbreviated form.

Figure 3-7 The DIR/W command. This screen shows the result of using the DIR/W command to display an abbreviated version of the DOS directory.

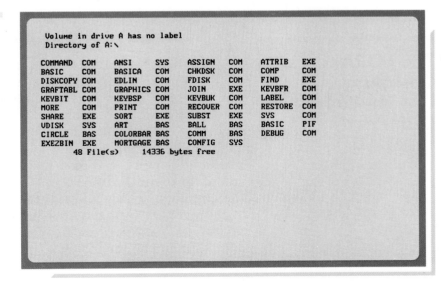

```
Volume in drive A has no label
Directory of A:\

COMMAND  COM    ANSI     SYS    ASSIGN   COM    ATTRIB   EXE
BASIC    COM    BASICA   COM    CHKDSK   COM    COMP     COM
DISKCOPY COM    EDLIN    COM    FDISK    COM    FIND     EXE
GRAFTABL COM    GRAPHICS COM    JOIN     EXE    KEYBFR   COM
KEYBIT   COM    KEYBSP   COM    KEYBUK   COM    LABEL    COM
MORE     COM    PRINT    COM    RECOVER  COM    RESTORE  COM
SHARE    EXE    SORT     EXE    SUBST    EXE    SYS      COM
VDISK    SYS    ART      BAS    BALL     BAS    BASIC    PIF
CIRCLE   BAS    COLORBAR BAS    COMM     BAS    DEBUG    COM
EXE2BIN  EXE    MORTGAGE BAS    CONFIG   SYS
       48 File(s)     14336 bytes free
```

Figure 3-8 The DIR/P command. *This screen shows the result of using the DIR/P command to display the DOS directory screen by screen.*

```
Volume in drive A has no label
Directory of A:\

COMMAND  COM    23210    3-07-85    1:43p
ANSI     SYS     1651    3-07-85    1:43p
ASSIGN   COM     1509    3-07-85    1:43p
ATTRIB   EXE    15091    3-07-85    1:43p
BACKUP   COM     5577    3-07-85    1:43p
BASIC    COM    17792    3-07-85    1:43p
BASICA   COM    27520    3-07-85    1:43p
CHKDSK   COM     9435    3-07-85    1:43p
COMP     COM     3664    3-07-85    1:43p
DISKCOMP COM     4073    3-07-85    1:43p
DISKCOPY COM     4329    3-07-85    1:43p
EDLIN    COM     7261    3-07-85    1:43p
FDISK    COM     8173    3-07-85    1:43p
FIND     EXE     6403    3-07-85    1:43p
FORMAT   COM     9398    3-07-85    1:43p
GRAFTABL COM     1169    3-07-85    1:43p
GRAPHICS COM     3111    3-07-85    1:43p
JOIN     EXE    15971    3-07-85    1:43p
KEYBFR   COM     2473    4-12-85    4:22p
KEYBGR   COM     2418    4-12-85    4:23p
Strike a key when ready . . .
```

Another approach to the too-many-files-for-the-screen problem is to request one screen at a time. To do this, type

DIR/P

and press Enter. The resulting screen display (Figure 3-8) is not in shorthand notation. It looks just like the original DIR display except that the final line of each screen says "Strike a key when ready." This variation of the DIR command displays one screen of file information at a time and moves on to the next screen at your discretion.

We have given a lot of space to the DIR command. Our next DOS command, FORMAT, is just as important.

The FORMAT Command: Getting Your New Disk Ready

Perhaps the most important external DOS command, if you are using diskettes, is the FORMAT command. The FORMAT program is stored on the DOS disk. When you buy a new blank diskette, the **FORMAT command** must be used to prepare the diskette before files can be stored on it. The formatting process sets up a directory for the new disk, marks off sectors, and tests tracks to make sure data can be stored on them (Figure 3-9). (A list of bad tracks is placed in the directory so they will not be used.)

You need to format a new disk only once. (*Caution: If you reformat a disk that has files stored on it, all the files will be lost.*) Remember, the FORMAT program is not part of internal

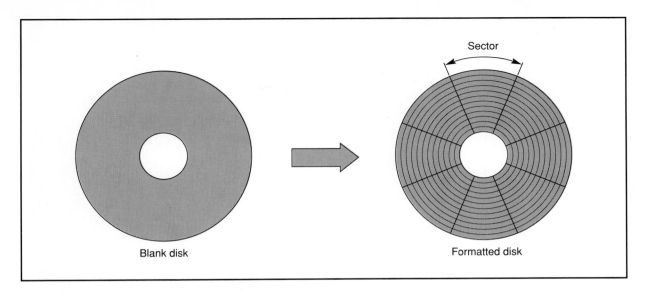

Sector

Blank disk

Formatted disk

*Figure 3-9 **Formatting a
disk.*** *The formatting
process sets up a directory
for the new disk, marks off
sectors, and tests tracks to
make sure data can be
stored on them. You must
format a blank disk before
you can store files on it.*

DOS, so you need the DOS disk in drive A. (Note to hard-disk
users: External commands are stored with internal commands
on hard disks; therefore, you can use FORMAT without placing the DOS disk in a drive.)

To use the FORMAT command, place the DOS disk in the
A drive and your blank disk in drive B. Then type

`FORMAT B:`

and press Enter. You will be reminded to insert your new disk
in drive B and then told to press "any key" or Enter (depending
on your version of DOS). Make sure that the new disk is in B
and the drive door is closed. Then press Enter. It will take
about one minute for DOS to prepare your disk. When the
formatting is completed, you will see a message similar the
one shown in Figure 3-10a (on the next page).

If the FORMAT program finds any bad sectors on the disk,
you will see a message similar to the one shown in Figure 3-
10b. Try repeating the formatting process. If you still have
some bad sectors, you may want to return the disk for a
replacement or a refund.

The FORMAT program then asks, "Format another (Y/N)?"
You can continue to format new disks by typing Y and pressing
Enter. When you want to stop formatting, just type N and press
Enter; this causes the system prompt to appear again.

It is also possible to format a diskette with a single drive
system. After you type the command

`FORMAT A:`

*Figure 3-10 The FORMAT
command.* *(a) This screen
shows the message you will
see after formatting is completed. (b) If there are any
bad sectors on the disk,
DOS lets you know how
many bytes are in those
sectors.*

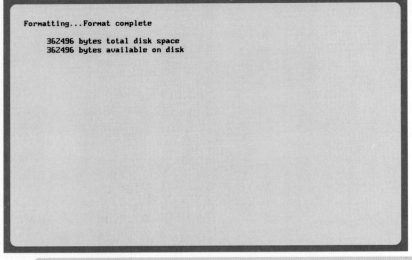

```
Formatting...Format complete

      362496 bytes total disk space
      362496 bytes available on disk
```

(a)

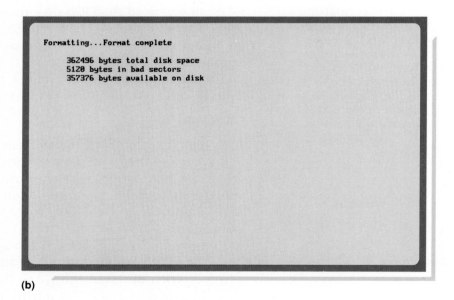

```
Formatting...Format complete

      362496 bytes total disk space
        5120 bytes in bad sectors
      357376 bytes available on disk
```

(b)

and press Enter, remove the DOS disk from drive A and replace
it with the disk you want to format. Then proceed as before.

If you have a hard drive, be aware that the command FOR-
MAT C: reformats the entire hard disk, destroying all your
hard-disk files in the process.

There are several options that can be used with the FOR-
MAT command. We will discuss two of these options: placing
the operating system on the new disk and labeling the new
disk.

Including the Operating System on the New Disk

When using the FORMAT command, you have the option of copying part of the operating system onto your new disk. That is, the internal DOS programs can be placed on the formatted disk. Putting DOS on your diskette lets you boot directly from your own disk without shuffling disks around. However, be aware that DOS takes up some of the diskette's usable space. To put DOS on an unformatted disk, type

```
FORMAT B:/S
```

and press Enter, instead of FORMAT B:. The formatting process is the same, but after it has been completed, you will see the message "system transferred" on the screen. Since only the internal DOS programs are copied onto your disk, you now have what is called a **system disk,** as opposed to the DOS disk, which contains both internal and external DOS programs.

Labeling a New Disk

You can place labels on the outside of your disk. You can also use the FORMAT command to label the disk internally. The length of the label can be from 1 to 11 characters, and the label is displayed whenever you use the DIR command for that disk. You might use your name or a short description of the contents of the disk as a label. Either of these could make the DIR display more meaningful to you. To use this option, type

```
FORMAT B:/V
```

and press Enter. After DOS formats the disk, it will ask you for a **volume label.** If your name is Garcia, for example, you can type GARCIA and press Enter. When you use the DIR command for this disk, the label "GARCIA" will be displayed at the top of the directory, as shown in Figure 3-11 (on the next page).

If you want to use both the system transfer option and the disk-labeling option, type

```
FORMAT B:/S/V
```

and press Enter.

Now that a blank disk is formatted, it is ready to receive files. One way to get files on the formatted disk is to use the COPY command.

Figure 3-11 Internal disk labels. *You can use a variation of the FORMAT command to create an internal label for a disk directory. In this screen the label is "GARCIA."*

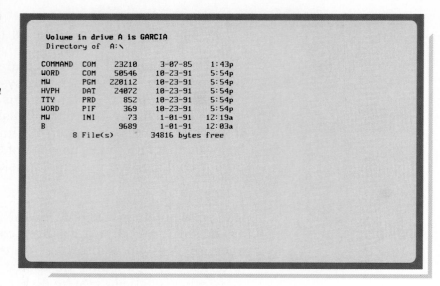

```
Volume in drive A is GARCIA
  Directory of  A:\

COMMAND  COM     23210     3-07-85     1:43p
WORD     COM     50546    10-23-91     5:54p
MW       PGM    220112    10-23-91     5:54p
HYPH     DAT     24072    10-23-91     5:54p
TTY      PRD       852    10-23-91     5:54p
WORD     PIF       369    10-23-91     5:54p
MW       INI        73     1-01-91    12:19a
B                 9689     1-01-91    12:03a
        8 File(s)         34816 bytes free
```

The COPY Command: Backing Up Files

The **COPY command** lets you copy one, some, or all of your disk files to another disk. There are several reasons for wanting another copy of a disk file. You may want a copy at work and another at home, or you may need to send a copy to a colleague in another office or city. The most common reason for using the COPY command, however, is the need for backup copies of your files.

Think about it. Suppose you keep all your word processing files, spreadsheets, and databases on one disk; you really do have "all your eggs in one basket." Diskettes are vulnerable. Even hard-disk files can be destroyed. You must keep two copies of each important file, preferably on separate disks.

This is how the COPY command works. Assume that you have the A> prompt and that you have a file named COMMAND.COM on the disk in the A drive. Put a formatted disk (your backup disk) in drive B and type

```
COPY A:COMMAND.COM B:
```

Make sure your spacing is correct. Then press Enter. When the copying process is completed, you will see the message "1 File(s) copied." This means an exact copy of COMMAND.COM has been written on the disk in drive B. Your original file is still stored on the disk in drive A.

If you need to copy several files, there are some shortcuts you can use. For example, when you use the COPY command, you can replace the file name or the extension name with an asterisk (*). DOS recognizes the asterisk as a **global character**—a character that represents any string of characters, similar to a "wild card" in some card games. Therefore, using * as either a file name or an extension in the COPY command lets you copy several files with a single command. The easiest way to understand this concept is to follow an example.

Suppose that you have several files with the extension COM on a disk, and you want to copy all these files from the disk in drive A to the disk in drive B. To do this, type

```
COPY A:*.COM B:
```

Make sure that there are no spaces among the characters A:*.COM, then press Enter. The * in this example has been used in place of the file name. Therefore, DOS copies any file—regardless of the file name—with a COM extension onto the disk in drive B. DOS stores these files with the same file name that they had on drive A.

As another example, consider copying several files that have the same file name—LETTER—but different extensions. To do this, type:

```
COPY A:LETTER.* B:
```

and press Enter.

You can also use COPY to make a backup copy of an entire disk—that is, to copy all the files from one disk onto another. To copy all the files from the disk in drive A to the backup disk in drive B, type

```
COPY A:*.* B:
```

Figure 3-12 Copying files. *The COPY command copies files from one disk to another, one file at a time. In this example all the files on the disk in drive A are being copied to the disk in drive B. Each file is listed as it is copied. The asterisks in the command tell the program to copy all file names and all file extensions.*

```
A>copy A:*.* B:
COMMAND.COM
ANSI.SYS
FORMAT.COM
CHKDSK.COM
SYS.COM
DISKCOPY.COM
DISKCOMP.COM
COMP.COM
EDLIN.COM
MODE.COM
FDISK.COM
BACKUP.COM
RESTORE.COM
PRINT.COM
RECOVER.COM
ASSIGN.COM
TREE.COM
GRAPHICS.COM
SORT.EXE
FIND.EXE
MORE.COM
BASIC.COM
```

The asterisks tell DOS to make a copy of any file name and any extension. DOS displays on the screen the actual name and extension of each file as it is copied (Figure 3-12, on the previous page).

This command is so important that it needs extra emphasis. Remember how vulnerable disk files are. Remember how important your files are. Remember the COPY command and use it to make backup disks.

The DISKCOPY Command: Copying All the Files

Like the COPY *.* command, the DISKCOPY command copies all the files from one disk, called the **source disk,** onto another disk, called the **target disk.** But there are two important differences: (1) DISKCOPY writes over any existing files on the target disk, and (2) DISKCOPY formats new disks before copying the files. (*Caution: Since DISKCOPY destroys all existing files on the target disk, the target disk should not contain any files you want to keep.*) Therefore, if you want two disks that are identical (contain the same files) or if you want to copy files onto an unformatted disk, use DISKCOPY. One further caution: DISKCOPY makes an exact clone of the disk being copied, bad tracks and all. For this reason, some people prefer to use the COPY *.* command.

DISKCOPY is an external command, so the DOS disk must be in drive A before you can use it. To use the DISKCOPY command, type

```
DISKCOPY A: B:
```

and press Enter. The DISKCOPY program loads into memory and begins running. DOS then asks you to insert the disk you want to copy—the source disk—in drive A and the disk you are going to copy to—the target disk—in drive B. Remember, unless you want to copy the DOS disk, remove it from drive A and replace it with the appropriate source disk. When the source and target disks are in place, press Enter to begin copying.

We have already mentioned the importance of making backup copies of files. DISKCOPY is convenient when you want an exact copy of all files on a given disk.

This concludes our detailed discussion of specific DOS commands. Many of the other commands you will use on a regular basis, such as ERASE and RENAME, can be found in the box called "Random Bits: DOS Command Sampler." You can use the sampler as a reference guide.

RANDOM BITS

DOS for the Power User

Isn't it enough to know how to format a disk and to list and copy files? For some people, the least line of resistance is indeed enough. But if you are serious about being in control of your personal computing, then you will want to know some of the extra DOS features.

ASSIGN Sometimes programs expect to use certain disk drives, perhaps one you do not have. For example, you may have diskette drive A and hard-disk C, but the program wants to use drive B. Use the ASSIGN command to send all files destined for drive B to drive C by typing

```
ASSIGN B=C
```

AUTOEXEC.BAT This special file is activated by DOS when you turn the computer on. A typical AUTO-EXEC.BAT file lets you go directly to your applications software. If, for example, you usually want to set the date and then use Word-Perfect, then the AUTO-EXEC.BAT could contain

the two lines DATE and then WP.

CHKDSK If you type CHKDSK, the screen displays a disk and memory status report, which contains information such as how many bytes are free.

COPY CON You do not always have to copy from one disk file to another; you can copy a short file directly from the keyboard to the disk file XFILE by using the command COPY CON XFILE (CON stands for console). After you enter the command, type in your file. Signal the end of the file by pressing the F6 key. COPY CON is often used to make AUTOEXEC.BAT files.

Directories Directory commands are especially useful if you create hard-disk files. Rather than having all your files together, you can establish a directory for each category of files. A detailed explanation of directories can be found in Appendix A.

TYPE Use the TYPE command with a file name, say TEMPO, to cause the contents of that file to appear on the screen. To execute this command, type

```
TYPE TEMPO
```

Caution: Special characters in the file may not be readable.

Wild-card characters The wild-card characters let you manipulate groups of files with a single command. A question mark is used for a single variable character and an asterisk (∗) for a file name or extension. If, for example, you want to delete files named TEMP1, TEMP2, and TEMP3, use the ? in a single command:

```
DEL TEMP?
```

If you want to list all files with the extension BAK, use

```
DIR *.BAK
```

Using DOS with Applications Programs

The internal DOS commands are usually the only commands that an applications program needs when it runs. When you purchase a new applications package, you must configure the applications disks before you can use the software. **Configure** is a general term that means preparing the applications disks so they can run on your particular computer system. The program may need to know, for example, about your printer or monitor. In this chapter, however, we are concerned only with the DOS component of the configuration process.

When you get an applications package, you may want to copy the internal DOS commands onto the applications disk so your computer can boot right from this disk. If internal DOS is not on the applications disk, then you will first have to boot your computer by using a DOS disk and then replace the DOS disk with the applications disk. However you load DOS, the applications program works in the same way. The point is that, one way or another, you must begin with the operating system. If a copy of DOS is already on the applications disk you want to use, then you do not need a separate DOS disk or the extra disk shuffling that goes with it.

There is another problem you can avoid if you have internal DOS commands right on the applications disk. When you finish using an applications program, the computer may immediately attempt to read the internal DOS files from the disk currently in drive A. If the disk in drive A does not contain the internal DOS files, then you will see the following message displayed in the upper-left corner of your screen:

```
Non-System disk or disk error
Replace and strike any key when ready
```

If you wish to stop working, you usually can just turn off the computer and leave. But if you wish to continue working with the computer, then you must insert a disk that contains the internal DOS commands in drive A and press any key.

If you want to place internal DOS commands and an applications program on the same disk, do the following:

1. Format a new disk (not the applications disk) to include the internal DOS files. That is, assuming the new disk is in drive B, type

    ```
    FORMAT B:/S
    ```

2. Now copy all applications program files to the new disk. Place the applications disk in drive A and the newly formatted disk in drive B. Type

    ```
    COPY A:*.* B:
    ```

    (Caution: Do not use DISKCOPY, since this command would delete the DOS files you just included.)

Some applications programs on disk are **copy-protected;** that is, you cannot copy these files onto another disk. In this case you must use the DOS disk before you can run the applications program.

A note of caution: Students sometimes think that the COMMAND.COM file is sufficient to provide the internal DOS commands. This is not true. If, instead of the procedure above, you simply copy COMMAND.COM onto your applications disk, you will be missing the hidden files. There are three **hidden files:** the volume label and the DOS system files IBMBIO.COM and IBMDOS.COM. These files are so hidden, in fact, that even when present they do not show up on a directory listing. It is beyond the scope of this discussion to describe these files. The point is that you must use the FORMAT B:/S command, as described, to get both COMMAND.COM and the hidden files.

If you are using a hard disk, then your operating system is already on the hard disk. There is no need to transfer a copy of DOS to the applications disk because the applications programs will be placed on the hard disk also.

There is one final consideration: Sometimes applications programs require so much disk space that there is no room to add the operating system. In this case, if you are using diskettes, you must use the DOS disk to boot the system before you can run the applications program.

Note for Users of DOS Version 3.3

DOS version 3.3 is on two separate diskettes. The **start-up diskette** contains the internal DOS commands. You need to be sure that the start-up disk is in drive A whenever you boot your computer. The start-up disk also contains many other files; the most important is the FORMAT file. You must have the start-up disk in drive A when you use the FORMAT B:/S command.

All the other external commands are stored on the second diskette, called the **operating diskette.** To use these commands, you must remove the start-up disk from drive A after you have booted your computer and replace it with the operating diskette. You cannot boot the computer from the operating diskette. The FORMAT program is also on the operating diskette and can be used if you do not wish to transfer the internal DOS files to the newly formatted disk. The DISKCOPY program is found only on the operating disk.

On to Applications

The operating system itself serves no specific purpose; its function is to support applications programs. Now that you know enough about operating system software to use applications programs, it is time to learn about these programs. We begin with the most universal application—the one everyone wants to learn—word processing.

Exercises

3-1

1. Place your DOS disk in drive A. Make sure that the drive door is closed. Turn on your computer. (If you have a color monitor, you will need to turn it on too: Turn the top dial clockwise.) If your computer is already on, press Ctrl-Alt-Del. When the internal DOS commands are read into memory, you will be asked for the time and date. Press Enter in response to both questions. You should see the A> prompt in the upper-left corner of the screen. Turn the knobs on the right side of the display screen to see what they do.

    Check to see that your display is turned on. If your screen seems to be blank even though you have booted the computer, check to see that the brightness knob is set properly.

    If you do not get the A> prompt, make sure that your DOS disk is inserted correctly in the A drive and that the drive door is properly closed. Then try to boot the system again.

2. After you have the A> prompt, type DIR and press Enter. How many files are listed when you type DIR? How much storage space is left on the disk?

3. What do you see in the lower-left corner of the screen after the DIR program is finished?

4. Type B: and press Enter. Now what do you see in the lower-left corner? What happens when you type DIR and press Enter? Type A and press Enter.

3-2

1. Place a DOS disk with the FORMAT.COM file in drive A. Use the DIR command to make sure that you have the proper disk in drive A.

2. Type FORMAT A: and press Enter. Then follow the directions on the screen. *Make sure you replace the DOS diskette with a blank diskette before you press the appropriate key.*

3. After the FORMAT program has finished, type N to indicate that you are finished formatting disks. You should see the A> prompt.
4. Now type DIR and press Enter. What message do you see?

3-3

1. Place the DOS disk in drive A. Place a formatted disk in drive B. The disk in drive B will be your data disk.
2. Type

    ```
    COPY A:FORMAT.COM B:
    ```

    Then press Enter.
3. When you see the A> prompt again, type

    ```
    DIR B:
    ```

    and press Enter. What files are on the new disk now? How much storage space is left on your data disk?
4. Type

    ```
    COPY A:CHKDSK.COM B:
    ```

    Then press Enter. When you see the A> prompt again, type DIR B: and press Enter.
5. How many files are there on your data disk now? How much storage space is available on the disk?
6. Type

    ```
    COPY A:*.EXE B:
    ```

    and press Enter. Now type

    ```
    DIR B:
    ```

    How many files were just copied onto the disk? What do these files have in common?

3-4

1. With the A> prompt on your screen and your data disk in drive B, type B: and press Enter. Which drive is now the default drive?
2. Type

    ```
    RENAME CHKDSK.COM WXYZ.ABC
    ```

    then press Enter.
3. Type DIR and press Enter. What happened to the CHKDSK.COM file?

4. Type A: and press Enter to return to the A> prompt.

3-5

1. With your data disk in drive B and the A> prompt on the screen, type B: and press Enter. What prompt do you see now?
2. Type

   ```
   DEL WXYZ.ABC
   ```

   and then press Enter. Type DIR and press Enter. What has happened?
3. Type

   ```
   DEL FORMAT.COM
   ```

   and press Enter. Now type DIR. How many files are left?
4. Type

   ```
   DEL *.EXE
   ```

   and press Enter. Type DIR. Now what message do you get?

3-6

1. Place the DOS disk in drive A and your data disk in drive B. You will format your data disk again (no files there to lose now). Then you will copy internal DOS to your data disk. Finally, you will create an internal label on your data disk to identify it.
2. Make sure that you have an A> prompt. Then type

   ```
   FORMAT B:/S/V
   ```

   and press Enter. Watch the screen for information.
3. When you are asked for a volume label, type your name (or the first 11 characters of your name). Then press Enter.
4. When you see "Format another? (Y/N)?" type N and press Enter.
5. Type

   ```
   DIR B:
   ```

   What is the first line printed on the screen? Now your data disk is a system disk. Why is a system disk helpful?
6. Use the COPY command to copy the FORMAT.COM file onto your data disk. Now you have the ability to format new disks

by placing your data disk in drive A and issuing the FORMAT command.

7. Remove your disks from drives A and B.
8. Turn off the computer and the monitor if you have a color monitor.
9. Place both disks in their proper places and treat them carefully.

Summary and Key Terms

- An **operating system** is a set of programs that lets the computer system control resources (CPU, memory, secondary storage devices, and input/output devices), execute programs (software), and manage data.

- The operating system for the IBM Personal Computer is called **Microsoft Disk Operating System, MS-DOS,** or simply **DOS.**

- DOS programs, which are stored on one or more diskettes, are executed by issuing a **command,** a name that invokes the correct program.

- **Internal DOS programs** are loaded from the disk into memory and can be accessed after the DOS diskette has been removed from the disk drive. **External DOS programs** may be accessed only when the DOS diskette is in the disk drive.

- If you have two diskette drives, they are called drives A and B. A hard drive is called drive C. The **default drive,** also called the **current drive,** is the drive that the computer is currently using.

- The three types of diskettes are DOS disks, applications software disks, and data disks. DOS disk files contain the operating system programs. Applications software disks contain the applications software programs. **Data disk** files contain the data you create.

- Booting the system is the process of loading the operating system into memory. If you boot the system when the computer is not already booted, this process is known as a **cold boot.** If the computer is already booted, this process is known as a **system reset,** or **warm boot.** A **system prompt** signals the user when the process is complete and the operating system is ready for a command.

- The **DIR command** displays the **disk directory,** a record of all files stored on a disk.

- Each file on a disk must have a unique name to distinguish it from all other files on that disk. Each file has a **complete name** that consists of two parts, the **file name** and the **file extension.** These two parts are separated by a period, referred to as a dot. The dot is used as part of the file name, even though the dot does not appear when you use the DIR command. A file name may be from one to eight characters long. The extension must be three characters or fewer.

- The drive letter followed by a colon and the complete name is called a **file specification.**

- DOS includes three **hidden files:** the volume label. IBMBIO.COM, and IBMDOS.COM. Your computer must have access to these files to perform some functions.

- Across the bottom of the DIR screen, the computer displays the number of files stored on the disk and the approximate amount of unused space on the disk.

- DIR/W abbreviates the directory information, displaying only the file names and extensions in columns. DIR/P lists all the information but displays one screen of listings at a time.

- The **FORMAT** program, an important external DOS program, must be used to prepare new diskettes before files can be stored on them. The formatting process sets up a directory for the new disk, marks off sectors, and tests tracks.

- Use FORMAT B:/S to create a **system disk,** which contains a copy of the internal DOS programs. Use FORMAT B:/V to create a **volume label** for the disk.

- The **COPY program,** an internal program, lets you copy one, some, or all of your disk files to another disk. The most common reason for using the COPY program is to make backup files. There are some short-cuts to use when copying several files. DOS recognizes the asterisk as a **global character,** which is like a "wild card." Using * as either a file name or an extension in the COPY command lets you copy several files with a single command.

- The **source disk** is the disk you copy from. The **target disk** is the disk you copy to.

- DISKCOPY is an external DOS program. Like the COPY *.* program, DISK-COPY copies all the files from one disk onto another disk. However, DISKCOPY writes over any existing files on the target disk and formats a new disk before copying the files.

- You must **configure** new applications software disks before you can use the software on your computer. The configuration process prepares the applications disk to run on your particular computer system.

- You will not be able to copy files from a **copy-protected** disk onto another disk.

- DOS version 3.3 is on two separate diskettes. The **start-up diskette** contains internal DOS commands and some other files; all other external commands are stored on the **operating diskette.** To use these other external commands, you must remove the start-up disk from drive A after you have booted the computer and replace that disk with the operating diskette.

Review Questions

1. In which disk drive does the computer expect to find the DOS disk when you boot the computer?

2. What are the two methods of booting the computer?

3. Which part of DOS is read into the computer's memory and stays there while you are using the computer?

4. What is meant by the term *default drive*?

For the remaining questions, assume that you have the A> prompt on your computer's screen. As part of your answer, indicate whether the command you use is an internal or an external DOS command.

5. If drive A is the current drive, which DOS command would you type to make drive B the current drive?

6. Which command would you enter to see a list of the files on a disk in drive A?

7. Which command would you enter to copy a file named FNAME1.EX1 from drive A to drive B? The file should have the same name on the disk in drive B.

8. How would you copy all the files with the extension XYZ to a disk in drive B?

9. Which command would you give to remove a file named WORK.SUM from the disk in drive A? What if the file were on the disk in drive B?

10. How would you change the name of a file named ACCT.REC to ACCT.PAY?

11. Which command would you enter to prepare a new disk in drive B for use by the computer? What would you type if you wanted the internal DOS programs to be copied to the new disk? What disk would have to be in drive A when you gave this command?

12. If you had only one disk drive (drive A) in your computer and you wanted to format a new disk, which command would you enter?

13. What DOS command lets you write an internal label on your new disk?

14. How is the DISKCOPY command different from the COPY command?

15. What is the complete file name (file specification) for a file on a disk in drive B, with the file name ACCT and the extension REC?

FROM THE REAL WORLD

Computer Training at Bethlehem Steel

Sheets of steel do not meander leisurely through the production line at Bethlehem Steel—they zoom by at 30 miles an hour. At that speed it is easy to make an expensive mistake. Incorrect gauge settings for pressure, tension, or temperature can ruin tons of steel in a matter of minutes.

Steel workers need training to keep up with the technology of the workplace. But Bethlehem Steel is not thinking of placing its workers in classrooms or sending them to the library. Instead, the company purchased software that lets users interact with a computer right at the factory site. The Bethlehem factories operate 24 hours a day, so the training must be available around the clock. By using computers, the training is as available to the night crew as it is to the day shift.

The interactive software runs on IBM PCs or compatibles. The programs access prerecorded video images stored on video disks. This provides an effective combination of video, audio, and motion. Since headphones can be attached, workers can use the system on the factory floor. There are also systems in training areas. Analysts estimate that the software cuts training time down from months to weeks.

The bulk of the computer-based curriculum is about Bethlehem's methods for rolling steel. However, vocational topics—such as electrical skills and theory, preventive maintenance, hand tools and measuring instruments, and rigging and pipe fitting—are also available. A separate software package presents a course on computer literacy.

When computer training was first introduced, a systems analyst encountered a shop steward planted in front of the color screen, his arms folded across his chest. Two workers came and sat down, and the steward asked one to touch the screen. The prospective student agreed readily enough. "Where's the game?" he said. "I want to make it 'bang.'" This anecdote demonstrates that the new generation of workers has been around computers and also that entertaining courses see more action than dull ones.

The broad goal is to upgrade the workforce. Although the union is nervous about the ultimate ramifications of more training—will fewer workers be needed?—the workers themselves have accepted it readily. As one put it, "I know layoffs are coming. I'm trying to survive."

How to Buy Your Own Personal Computer

Owning a personal computer is not like owning a toaster or a television set, nor is buying one like buying a suit off the rack. There is a lot to learn about the new technology and the ways in which it might help you.

We cannot pick your new computer system for you any more than we could pick a new car for you. But we can tell you what to look for. We do not mean that we can lead you to a particular brand and model—so many new products are introduced into this area every month that doing so would be impossible. If you are just starting out, however, we can help you define your needs and ask the right questions.

Where Do You Start?

Maybe you have already done some thinking and have decided that a personal computer offers advantages. Now what?

Who Needs It?

Here are some common home applications for personal computers:

- Education for children
- Filing and retrieving records

- Word processing
- Business "homework"
- Entertainment, games
- Running a home business
- Personal finance

- Desktop publishing
- Access to remote information
- Learning programming
- Shopping and banking from home

You can start by talking to other personal computer owners about how they got started and how to avoid pitfalls. (Plan on a long conversation. Personal computer owners are notoriously talkative on this subject.) Or you can read some computer magazines, especially ones with evaluations and ratings, to get a feel for what is available. Next visit several dealers. Don't be afraid to ask questions. You are considering a major purchase, so plan to shop around.

Analyze Your Wants and Needs

You may want to narrow your computer search by determining what price range you are in. But it might make more sense to begin with a needs/wants analysis. Why do you want a computer? Be

Shopping for software and hardware. *There is a wide range of useful products available today. Many users spend more on software than they did on the original equipment.*

realistic: Will it probably wind up being used for games most of the time or for business applications? People use personal computers for a variety of applications, as noted in the box called "Who Needs It?" Prioritize your needs; don't plan to do everything at once. At some point you will have to establish a budget ceiling. After you have examined your needs, you can select the best hardware/software combinations for the money. Before we look at hardware and software in detail, pause to consider whether you want to buy now or buy later.

Buy Now or Buy Later?

People who are interested in buying a computer may delay their purchases because the price is too high or because they think more sophisticated computers are coming soon. Prices are certainly variable, and it is quite true that you may get a bargain by waiting. And it is also true that something will no doubt come along in a year or two (or even sooner) that will make present equipment seem inadequate in some way. Improvements usually take the form of (1) the same kind of equipment becoming available at a lower price; (2) new models or competing equipment offering more power (more speed, more memory), easier handling, or a wider range of better-designed software; or (3) the quality of the new models is better for a lower price.

Yet, clearly, the longer you wait to buy, the longer you miss out on acquiring experience and expertise with personal computers. And, of course, you miss out on the usefulness and fun. Certainly, if you want a machine for word processing or for business-related purposes, there is no point in waiting. If you want something that is easier to use than the equipment you see now, however, you may be advised to put it off for at least a year.

What to Look For in Hardware

The basic microcomputer system consists of a central processing unit (CPU) and memory, a monitor, a keyboard, a storage device (diskette or hard-disk drive), and a printer. Unless you know someone who can help you out with technical expertise, you are probably best advised to look for a packaged system— that is, one in which the above components (with the possible exception of the printer) are assembled and packaged by the same manufacturer. This gives you some assurance that the various components will work together.

Let us now take a quick look at the various parts of the system: CPU, memory, monitor, keyboard, secondary storage, printers, and other hardware options. Then we will consider portability and some hardware options.

Central Processing Unit

Personal computers started out with what is known as an 8-bit processor, but now most manufacturers make machines with 16-bit or 32-bit processors. More bits mean more power, faster processing, more memory, and a larger and more complex instruction set.

Memory

Memory is measured in bytes. The amount of memory you need in your computer is determined by the amount of

The complete microcomputer system. *You may not need fine oak furniture right away, but to have a complete microcomputer system you will need a central processing unit and memory, monitor, keyboard, storage device, and printer.*

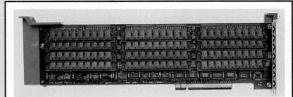

Adding memory. *This add-on memory board gives an IBM PS/2 an additional 12 million bytes of memory.*

memory required by the applications programs (like word processing or spreadsheets) that you want to use. A minimum of 640K bytes is suggested for personal computers used for business applications. You may be able to get by with less, however, if you buy a home computer primarily for games or word processing. Most machines have expandable memory, so you can add more later if you need it. If you plan to use the IBM OS/2 operating system, you will need 2MB to run the applications programs written for OS/2.

Monitor

Sometimes called a video display screen, the monitor is a very important part of your computer system—you will spend all your time looking at it. Before you buy any monitor, you should test it by attaching it to the computer you intend to purchase and running some of the applications programs you intend to use. This is the only way to be sure that you will not be disappointed when you take your computer home.

Discussion of some of the factors you should consider when selecting a monitor follows.

Monitor displays. (Top) Color monitors let you see your graphic displays and text in a multitude of colors. (Bottom) High-resolution monochrome monitors are highly readable.

Screen Width. Although some Macintosh computers have a 9-inch screen, most monitors have a screen display of between 12 and 14 inches. Generally, a larger screen provides a display that is easier to read, so you will probably want at least a 12-inch screen. Some monitors called Full-Page monitors can display a complete $8\frac{1}{2}$-by-11-inch page of text on the screen. These monitors are especially useful for desktop publishing applications. For most other purposes, a screen that displays 25 lines of 80 characters each is the standard.

Screen Readability. As you shop for your monitor, be sure to compare the readability of different monitors. First, make sure that the screen is bright and has minimum flicker. Next, check the shape of the characters. Some screens are difficult to read because they chop off the descenders—the tails that fall below the line—of the lowercase letters *g*, *p*, *q*, and *y*. In addition, look to see whether the characters appear crowded on the screen—that is, jammed together to a degree that makes them difficult to read. Glare is another major consideration: Nearby harsh lighting can cause glare to bounce off the screen, and some screens seem more susceptible to glare than others. Check to see whether a glare-reducing screen is available for the monitor.

A key factor affecting screen quality is resolution, a measure of the number of dots, or pixels, that can appear on the screen. The higher the resolution—that

Color or Monochrome. Monochrome (green, amber, or white on a black background) monitors are best when a computer will be heavily used for word processing applications. If you want to create graphics on your screen or if you plan to run entertainment programs on your computer, you will probably want to buy a color monitor. Color monitors are sometimes called RGB (for Red, Green, Blue) monitors. RGBI (for Red, Green, Blue with Intensity adjustability) monitors are more modern than RGB monitors. Many programs are written to be run solely on computers with color monitors. Some color monitors have a text switch on the front; pressing the switch changes a color monitor into a monochrome monitor for word processing applications.

is, the more dots—the more solid text characters appear. For graphics, more pixels means sharper images. But do not be tempted to pay a higher price for the best resolution unless your applications need it.

Graphics Adapter Boards. If you want to use an applications program that displays graphics and the computer you are considering does not come with the ability display them, you will have to buy a graphics adapter board (sometimes called a graphics card) to insert in the computer. There are several different standards for graphics adapter boards. Monitors designed for use with one type of card may not be capable of understanding the signals from a different type. Multiscan monitors, also called multimode monitors, are designed to work with a variety of graphics adapter boards. Check carefully to be sure that you have the right monitor/graphics board combination.

Ergonomic Considerations. Look to see whether the monitor can swivel and tilt, since this will remove the need to sit in one position for a long period of time. The ability to adjust the position of the monitor becomes an important consideration if there are different users for the same computer. Another possibility is to purchase add-on equipment that will perform these functions. If you need a portable computer to haul back and forth to different places, however, a screen that is attached to the keyboard will be easier for you to handle and less likely to be damaged in transit.

Keyboard

Keyboards vary a lot in quality. The best way to know what suits you is to sit down in the store and type for a while. Consider how the keys feel; the color, slope, and layout of the keyboard; and whether it is detachable.

Keyboard Feel. You will find that there are real differences in the feel of keyboards. Find a keyboard that lets you know through your sense of touch when you have engaged a key and released it. Make sure the keys are not cramped together; you will find that your typing is error-prone if your fingers are constantly overlapping more than one key. This is especially of concern if you have large hands, chubby fingers, or long fingernails.

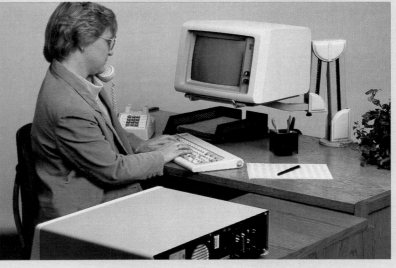

Ergonomic considerations. (Left) By placing a glare shield over your CRT monitor, you decrease glare and increase the clarity of the characters. (Right) This monitor stand tilts and swivels so that your neck does not have to.

Typewriter-style keyboard. *Many keyboards now have 12 function keys along the top of the board, a numeric keyboard on the right, plus an extra cursor movement pad.*

Secondary storage. *(Top) $3\frac{1}{2}$-inch diskette drives are the standard on IBM PS/2 and Macintosh computers. The $3\frac{1}{2}$-inch diskette is enclosed in a plastic case, which helps protect the disk. $5\frac{1}{4}$-inch floppy diskettes are widely used on the IBM personal computer line and its compatibles. (Bottom) The inside of this hard disk drive shows the access arm hovering over the disk.*

Keyboard Color. Ideally, keys should be gray with a matte finish. The dull finish reduces glare.

Keyboard Slope. If you plan to use your keyboard for many hours at a time, its slope will be very important to you. A keyboard slope should be a minimum of 7 degrees and a maximum of 15 degrees. Slopes outside this range can cause discomfort in the wrist and, consequently, high error rates. Some personal computer keyboards have adjustable slopes.

Keyboard Layout. Besides evaluating keyboard feel, look at the layout of the keyboard. Most follow the standard QWERTY layout of typewriter keyboards. However, some also have a separate numeric keypad to the right of the character keys. You may find this useful if you enter a lot of numbers. In addition, some keyboards have separate function keys. The IBM Personal System/2, for instance, has 12 function keys in a row above the regular keys. These keys are used to move things around on the screen, delete, and so on. To accomplish these tasks with computers without function keys, you must hold down a pair of keys (not labeled as to function) simultaneously. This is less convenient.

Detachable Keyboard. Although you may be used to typing on a typewriter, where the keyboard is not separate from the rest of the machine, you may find a computer with a detachable keyboard—one that can be held on your lap, for example—desirable. You can move a detachable keyboard around to suit your comfort. This feature becomes indispensable when a computer is used by people of different sizes, such as large adults and small children.

Secondary Storage

You will need one or more disk drives to read programs into your computer and to store any programs or data that you wish to keep.

Diskettes. Most personal computer software today comes on diskettes. Floppy disks, used with many older personal computers, are $5\frac{1}{4}$ inches in diameter. New diskettes are only $3\frac{1}{2}$ inches across and have become the modern standard. Because $3\frac{1}{2}$-inch diskettes are smaller and protected inside a plastic case, they fit in convenient places, such as a purse or a pocket. Their drives take up less space in the computer, and they can hold more data.

On most systems at least one disk drive is built right into the computer. Although not always necessary, you may find it helpful to have two (dual) disk drives to facilitate copying of disks for safekeeping. If your system has only one built-in drive, you may purchase another drive as a separate component.

Hard Disks. Most hard disks (also called *fixed disks*) are 5-inch or $3\frac{1}{2}$-inch Winchester disks. Although more expensive than diskette drives, hard disks are fast and reliable and hold more data. These features have made the hard disk an increasingly attractive option for personal computer buyers. Many personal computers come with a built-in hard-disk drive with a storage capacity of at least 20 million bytes—characters—of data; greater capacities are available if you can pay for them. A hard disk can also be bought separately.

Printers

A printer is probably the most expensive piece of peripheral equipment you will buy. Although some inexpensive printers are available, most likely you will find that those costing $400 and up are the ones most useful to you.

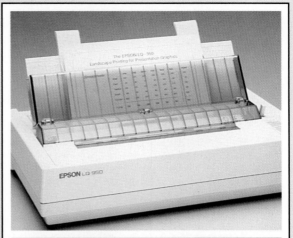

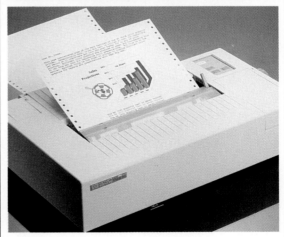

Printers. *(Top) 24-pin dot-matrix printers, such as this one, can produce results of near letter quality. (Middle) Laser printers are often used with desktop publishing software. (Bottom) Ink-jet printers can produce colorful graphic output.*

When choosing a printer, you will want to consider speed, quality, and cost. Also verify whether a printer will work with the applications software you intend to use. For example, will it print graphs created with Lotus 1-2-3? If you plan to use your personal computer for desktop publishing, you want a printer with an established page description language such as PostScript.

Dot-Matrix Printers. For "everyday" printing, a dot-matrix printer, costing about $500, will do very nicely. A dot-matrix printer can print as many as 250 characters per second, forming each character out of a grid of pins or dots much like the lights on a bank temperature sign or stadium scoreboard. The appearance of the characters is not as good as those you would get from, say, an electric typewriter. This is why they are not considered "letter-quality" printers—that is, adequate for office correspondence. Some dot-matrix printers, however, can make a second pass at the characters or use a more dense array of dots and make the letters more fully formed; the result is called near letter quality. Dot-matrix printers can also be used for printing computer-generated graphics.

Letter-Quality Printers. A letter-quality printer produces the sharp characters that are a must for business correspondence. Most letter-quality printers use a daisy wheel, a device that can be removed, like a typewriter element, and replaced with another wheel with a different type font on it. The disadvantage of the daisy wheel printer is that it is relatively slow—it often produces only 55 characters per second or less. A letter-quality printer typically costs between $500 and $3000. Daisy wheel printers cannot print computer-generated graphics.

```
A dot-matrix printer in draft
mode can print fast. However,
the type is less readable than
output from other printers or
from a dot-matrix printer in
near letter quality mode.


This is an example of near
letter quality output. A dot-
matrix printer prints each
character twice or uses a more
dense array of dots for
improved quality.
```

Letter-quality printers with a daisy wheel are relatively slow. However, as shown here, they produce fully-formed characters that rival output from the finest typewriters. This makes them desirable for business correspondence.

Laser printers are fast and they produce high quality output, as shown here. They are useful for desktop publishing, which often combines text and graphics in one document. Generally, laser printers are more expensive than most other printers.

Examples of output from various printers.

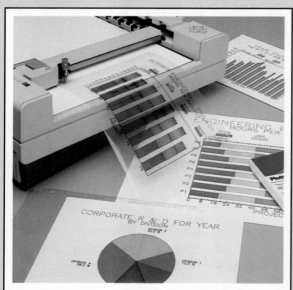

A plotter. *Plotters for personal computers can produce high-quality graphic output.*

Ink-Jet Printers. Although relatively slow, ink-jet printers can produce text and graphics whose color range and density usually surpass the color graphics of dot-matrix printers. The price spectrum is from $300 to several thousand dollars.

Laser Printers. These printers are top of the line in print quality and speed. They are also the most expensive, starting at about $2000. Laser printers are used by desktop publishers to produce text and graphics on the same page.

Plotters. Plotters draw hard-copy graphics output in the form of maps, bar charts, engineering drawings, overhead transparencies, and even two- or three-dimensional illustrations. Plotters often come with a set of six pens in six different colors.

Printer Covers. Although quiet printers are available, most dot-matrix and letter-quality printers are noisy. An unmuffled printer generates about 80 decibels of sound, somewhere between a typewriter (70 decibels) and an outboard motor (90 decibels). If you will be working in an enclosed environment with your printer, the noise may become irritating. To reduce the problem, consider inexpensive, sound-absorbing pads to go under the printer. If the problem is extreme, plastic printer covers are available that will reduce the noise to the level of a quiet conversation.

Portability

Do you plan to let your computer grow roots after you install it, or will you be moving it around? Do you want a large video display or will the smaller versions on portable computers do? Portable computers have found a significant niche in the market, mainly because they are

A laptop computer. *These small computers, which often include built-in software, are an attractive option for users who travel.*

packaged to travel easily. The ultimate in portability is the laptop computer, which is lightweight (often under 10 pounds) and small enough to fit in a briefcase. There are trade-offs, however, such as screen readability and the amount of internal power available. Consider all aspects carefully.

Other Hardware Options

There are a great many hardware variations; we will mention a few here.

Communications Connections. If you wish to connect your computer via telephone lines to electronic bulletin boards, mainframe computers, or information utilities such as CompuServe or The Source, you will need a modem. This device converts computer data into signals that can be transmitted over telephone lines. The Hayes Smartmodem family of products has become the industry standard; most new modems claim some degree of Hayes compatibility. A modem with a speed of 1200 or 2400 bits per second is sufficient for most uses, although modems with speeds up to 9600 bits per second are available.

A modem. *This external modem can be used with a variety of computers and can be moved from one machine to another.*

Color slide–producing equipment. *Data from the computer screen is transferred to the screen of the Polaroid Palette, where it can be photographed and developed quickly into color prints, slides, or overheads.*

Other Input Devices. If you are interested in games, you may wish to acquire a joy stick, which looks sort of like the stick shift on a car. A joy stick allows you to manipulate a cursor on the screen.

A more sophisticated device is a mouse, a gadget that you roll on a tabletop to move the cursor on the screen to make menu selections. Many software packages and operating systems are designed to let you work most efficiently if your computer has a mouse attached. If you are planning to use your computer for desktop publishing, a mouse is essential.

A scanner or digitizer is very useful if you need to store pictures and typed documents in your computer. Scanners are frequently purchased by people who want to use their computers to do desktop publishing.

There are several other input devices available. Ask your dealer about the equipment that follows.

Color Slide–Producing Equipment. If you plan to use your computer primarily to produce text and graphics slides for presentations, consider purchasing one of the devices designed to produce 35mm color slides from computer images.

Surge Protectors. These devices, sometimes called power protectors, protect against the electrical ups and downs that can affect the operation of your computer. Some of the more expensive models provide up to 10 minutes of full power to your computer if the electric power in your home or office is knocked out. This gives you time to save your work to disk (so that it won't be lost as the power fails) or to print out a report you need immediately. If lightning storms or power fluctuations occur in your area, you would be well advised to purchase a surge protector if one is not supplied with your computer.

Interface Boards and Cabling.

All the hardware components of your system need to be connected with the proper cables. Sometimes these cables and any of the interface boards they require are sold as separate components. Check to be sure that you have all the necessary boards and cables when you buy your system. If you ask a dealer for a printer, you will get a printer; do not forget to add that you need the proper cable and any additional hardware required to connect it to your computer.

Sound. Be sure to check out sound effects, particularly if you are interested in games. Make sure there are different tones, that they are not unpleasant, and that you have control over starting and stopping them. Many systems also have packaged software that allows you to produce computer-generated music.

What to Look For in Software

There was a time when standardization of personal computers was non-existent; each type of personal computer had its own operating system. Software that ran on one computer did not necessarily run on another. This is still true to some extent, but great strides have been made.

In a nutshell, the current standard is MS-DOS, made popular by IBM. Most personal computers today are compatible with the established IBM standard. Another new standard from IBM, called OS/2, is beginning to emerge. Applications programs that will do what you want to do are available for your use if you purchase a computer that uses one of

---

> **System Requirements**
> **Operating Systems:**
> PC-DOS (2.0 or higher for single user)
> **Hardware Requirements:**
> IBM PC, XT, AT and compatibles.
> Hard disk required.
> **Main Memory:**
> Minimum of 640K bytes of RAM required.
> **Printer:**
> Any IBM PC compatible printer.

Read the directions. Make sure your hardware works with the software you are buying by reading the fine print carefully.

---

these two operating systems. There are also many excellent programs written to run on the Apple Macintosh.

We have noted the main categories of software in the list in the box called "Who Needs It?" Now let us consider hardware requirements, brand names, demonstrations, and languages.

Hardware Requirements for Software

When you look at a software package in a store, be sure to read what kind of hardware it requires. For example, you may read "This package requires two disk drives, an 80-character display screen and printer, 256K of memory and MS-DOS." You would hate to get home with your new software package and find you need to spend more for a joy stick or a few hundred dollars for a special circuit board that goes inside the computer. Usually, the salesperson can advise you on hardware requirements for any particular software you might want to buy.

Brand Names

In general, publishers of brand-name software usually offer better support than smaller, less well-known companies. Support may be in the form of tutorials, classes by the vendor or others, and the all-important hotline assistance. Support may be crucial. In addition, brand-name publishers usually produce superior documentation and offer upgrades to new and better versions of the software.

Software Demonstrations

Wherever you can, ask to have the software demonstrated. You should not buy anything until you see that it works.

Despite this admonition, we must acknowledge that approximately half of the software purchased for personal computers is ordered through the mail from advertisements in computer magazines. In some cases, you may rely on the reputation of the software manufacturer or a recommendation from a friend. Other useful aids are the detailed software reviews found in trade publications such as *InfoWorld* or *PC Magazine*.

Languages

You may purchase languages on disk if you wish to write your own applications programs. BASIC is the most popular language for personal computers, but some personal computers can use FORTRAN, Pascal, C, and other languages.

Shopping Around: Where to Buy

Where you buy is important, and usually the trade-off is between price and service—but not necessarily.

The Dealer

The important point to remember is that you are buying a relationship with a dealer at the same time you are buying your computer. In a sense, you are also paying for your dealer's expertise. Answers to your questions, both now and in the future, may be the single most important part of your purchase. Vendors like IBM, Hewlett-Packard, and Apple have established a nationwide organization of authorized dealers. A vendor-authorized dealer is usually a well-established business with recognized expertise in the product they sell.

You can also buy a personal computer in a computer store such as Computer-Land. You can buy one from a discount house or a bookstore. You can buy one

Dealer support. *Some dealers provide software demonstrations so you can try before you buy.*

from the manufacturer's own retail outlets; Tandy-Radio Shack has its own stores.

Of course, you can buy a personal computer or peripheral by mail or from an individual. But we don't recommend this unless you have a lot of experience, because such a sale is usually without dealer support. Furthermore, you need to be absolutely certain that the software and the equipment you are buying—processing unit, monitor, printer, and any other peripherals—will work together as a unit.

If you work for a large company or educational institution, check to see whether your employer has made an employee purchase arrangement with a vendor. Substantial discounts are often available under such programs.

Questions to Ask the Salesperson at the Computer Store

- How many units of this machine do you sell in a month?

- Is the machine popular enough to have a user's group in my area?

- Is there anyone I can call about problems?

- Does the store offer classes on how to use this computer and software?

- Do you offer a maintenance contract for this machine?

- Does someone in your store fix the machines?

- Can I expand the capabilities of the machine later?

Financing

One advantage of going to a dealer is that the seller may help you finance your purchase by either carrying the loan or making arrangements with a financial institution.

Service and Support

Perhaps the biggest single argument for buying at a specialized computer store is service and support. Who is going to help you through the rough spots? Computer-store salespeople may be qualified to demonstrate different equipment and software and to make sure everything works before it leaves the store. Some computer stores will help you over the

Repair. *If your computer breaks down, you will probably need to take it to a repair center.*

phone with any glitches you encounter at home. You will have to be your own judge about how much help to expect, however. There is a great deal of turnover of computer-store personnel; equipment and software change rapidly, and you may find, in fact, that the personnel are not as knowledgeable and helpful as you had hoped.

Many stores offer training classes (free or for a price). Many will replace your computer, if there is a warranty to that effect. Some offer a loaner while your computer is being repaired.

Maintenance Contract

When buying a computer, you may wish to consider a maintenance contract, which should cover both parts and labor. Such a contract has five basic levels of comprehensiveness:

- The most comprehensive type of contract offers a repair person who will fix your system on-site within a certain number of hours. This option is usually available only for significant business customers.

- The next best is a courier pickup and delivery repair service. This usually costs 25% less than on-site repair.

- Carry-in service allows you to bring your machine in for repairs. With courier or carry-in service, the store may provide you with a loaner while they fix your hardware.

- Another type of contract provides a hot line you can call. The person at the other end will help you trouble-shoot. Clearly, this service resolves only basic problems; you should not get inside the machine with tools.

- The least convenient maintenance contract requires you to mail the machine in for repair.

Used Computers

Used-car lots are common enough. Could used-computer stores become a staple in society? Probably not, because there is too little profit for dealers, and they do not want to warrant the goods. But it may be possible to pick up a bargain from an individual. Check the ads in your local newspaper.

But be careful. There is no way, for instance, for you to know what kind of workout the secondhand computer has had. Did the owner just play with it from time to time? Or was it the office work-horse every day for two years? Try out everything you can. Try each key on the keyboard and test all the disk drives.

Another angle, and this may be a psychological one, is that the seller may

Documentation. *Clear, easy-to-follow documentation is one of the most important features of a software package.*

want to charge you a price that is related to the original price. Perhaps the seller paid $5000 for the system and thinks that $3000 is a fair price for the used equipment. But new comparable equipment may now cost less than $3000. Always compare the cost of a used computer system with today's prices.

Despite these reservations, there certainly may be some real bargains available in used equipment. Shop carefully.

Now That You Have It, Will You Be Able to Use It?

Once the proud moment has come and your computer system is at home or in the office with you, what do you do with it?

Documentation

Nothing is as important as documentation, the written manuals and instructions that accompany hardware and software. Unfortunately, some of it is inadequate. The weakest link in personal computer systems is the documentation. Ask to see the documentation when you buy. See if you can perform one of the procedures described in the documentation on a machine in the store. The instructions should be simple to understand and contain very little jargon.

Documentation should include simple instructions so you can perform basic tasks in short order. Some documentation goes on for many pages about a particular activity; it gives you all the variations for all the options, when all you really need to get started is the simplest form of the activity. The frills can come later.

Visual clarity is another characteristic of effective documentation. Sections in a manual should be separated with durable tabbed pages. There should be lots of white space, pictures, demonstrations, and examples so that you have no trouble following what is happening. The documentation should also have attractive, practical packaging, it should not be just a collection of typewritten sheets. Effective packaging alone, of course, does not guarantee good documentation.

Training

Can you teach yourself? Besides the documentation that comes with your computer and with software packages you may buy, there are numerous books on the market that can teach you about various software packages and programming. There are several books on the popular Lotus 1-2-3 package, for example, and hundreds on the BASIC language. Magazines can also help you, and several have columns to answer questions from readers.

As mentioned, some computer stores offer classes in the use of computers. Private parties do too, although the fees are often substantial. Many local colleges offer courses, although you may want to get in line early for sign-ups. It may also be possible to get private lessons. Although this may be the most expensive method, it might be very effective.

Some computer manufacturers and software vendors provide self-teaching material on diskettes that can teach you through hands-on participation right on your own computer. These lessons, called tutorials, may be the most effective teaching method of all.

Training. *Hardware and software purchases, especially in business, sometimes include classes provided by the dealer.*

that the most technologically advanced or the most powerful is automatically the best, but great power is of real importance in only a few applications. Why buy features that you will never need?

For businesspeople, what often matters most is compatibility—that is, assurance that the machine will run the software used at the office. It may be that for you, the "best" computer is one just like the one you will use at work or in school. For the uninitiated, support may be more important than any other single factor: Just who is going to answer your questions, once you bring all the boxes home?

The Very Best?

Best is a relative term. Clearly, each computer has its own strengths and weaknesses, and an expert will recommend different computers for different users and applications. Some people think

Survey for the Prospective Buyer

With this background we hope you are now in a position to answer some questions about the kind of computer you want. Take a copy of the filled-in survey with you when you shop.

Survey for the Prospective Buyer

1. **Price Range.** I can spend
   ____ under $1000
   ____ up to $1500
   ____ up to $2500
   ____ up to $3500
   ____ up to $4500
   ____ more

2. **Uses for Computer.** Rank the uses that follow in order of importance. I wish to use the computer for

   ____ Playing video games

   ____ Adult education (foreign-language drill, learning programming, and so forth)

   ____ Children's education (teaching arithmetic, typing, programming, and so forth)

   ____ Word processing (writing papers, reports, memos, letters)

   ____ Business applications (financial spreadsheets, database management, accounting, scheduling)

   ____ Business "homework"

   ____ Mailing lists

   ____ Personal record keeping (address lists, list of insured possessions, appointment calendar, fitness progress, and so forth)

   ____ Personal finance (taxes, managing expenses, tracking stock market, and so forth)

   ____ Programming

   ____ Information retrieval (from services such as CompuServe, The Source, or more specific information sources)

   ____ Producing graphics presentations

   ____ Other:

   _____

3. **Hardware Features Wanted.** I want the following features on my computer:

   ____ MS-DOS compatible or
   ____ OS/2 compatible

   ____ 16-bit processor or
   ____ 32-bit processor

   ____ 256K bytes of memory or
   ____ 640K bytes of memory or
   ____ 1MB memory or
   ____ 2MB or more memory

   ____ 80-column screen

   ____ Extra-large screen

   ____ Excellent screen readability

   ____ Monochrome screen or
   ____ color screen

   ____ Screen that can tilt and swivel

   ____ Multiscan monitor

   ____ Color graphics capability

   ____ EGA graphics standard or
   ____ VGA graphics standard or
   ____ other graphics standard

   ____ Detachable keyboard

   ____ Numeric keypad

   ____ Function keys

   ____ Single disk drive or
   ____ dual disk drive

   ____ $5\frac{1}{4}$-inch disk drives

   ____ $3\frac{1}{2}$-inch disk drives

   ____ Hard-disk drives

   ____ Dot-matrix printer

   ____ Letter-quality printer

   ____ Ink-jet printer

   ____ Laser printer

   ____ Printer cover

   ____ Modem

_____ Joy stick

_____ Mouse

_____ Portability

_____ Sound

_____ Other:

_____

_____

**_Business soft-
ware._** _A vari-
ety of software
is available for
business users._

4. Software Wanted. I want
the following software:

___ Games and recreation
software

___ Word processing

___ Spreadsheets

___ Database management

___ Graphics

___ Information services

Games. _Soft-
ware for games
often comes in
colorful
packages._

___ Desktop publishing

___ Education packages

___ Home business
packages

___ BASIC

___ Pascal

___ FORTRAN

___ COBOL

___ C

___ Other:

_____

5. Other Features Wanted.
The following are impor-
tant to me:

___ Manufacturer's
reputation

___ Dealer's
reputation

___ Dealer
financing

___ Local service and
support

___ Training

___ Documentation quality

___ Maintenance contract

___ Other:

_____

Hands-On Applications Packages

Now it is time to learn to write reports, plan budgets, store and retrieve data, and draw graphs—all with some wonderful help from the computer. For these are the hands-on applications chapters, the chapters that tell you how to use applications software for word processing, spreadsheets, database management, and graphics. This software is the key attraction of microcomputers.

4 Introducing Word Processing

Chapter Objectives

After reading this chapter you should be able to

- Define word processing

- Describe the main functions of word processing

- Describe the advantages of using a word processing program

- Load a word processing package

- Create, save, edit, and print a document by using word processing

- Change the appearance of a document by using different word processing commands

Have you ever left a sentence out of a typed term paper? And what about misspelled words or just plain typos? As a tool, the typewriter has its shortcomings. The basic problem with a typewriter is that you are producing a permanent mark whenever you press a key. Therefore, if you make a mistake, it is hard to correct without a lot of extra work.

Things get even worse if you must add or delete several sentences. At best, the whole page must be retyped. But the altered document may be longer or shorter than the original text, so the new version may not fit on one page anymore. Now you have to retype the pages that follow it, too.

Or, like many of us, you might reluctantly turn to the whiteout or to cutting and pasting, reconciling yourself to the smudged and mutilated results. You do this because you do not have the time to type it all again.

You may be able to hand in a less-than-perfect term paper, but this is not acceptable in the workplace. The appearance of a document or letter is crucial to the image of a business. And beyond image, there may be exacting legal demands. Documents submitted in a court of law, for example, must be originals (not copies), and there may be no corrections made on the document. If the same legal document needs to be sent to different people or offices, one document must be typed perfectly again and again. If an attorney notices that a required sentence or clause has been omitted, at least one page of all the documents must be redone.

For you as a student, careful typing is required when you seek employment. A poorly typed resume makes a bad impression. If you pay to have your resume typed, you may have to pay again to add more courses and experience. A customized resume for a particular position might require partial or even complete retyping of your original resume. There is a better way: word processing.

Word Processing as a Tool

Word processing is the creation, editing, formatting, storing, and printing of a text document. Let us examine each part of the definition. First, a *text document* is anything that can be keyed in, such as a letter. *Creation* is the original composing and keying of the document. *Editing* is making changes to the document to fix errors or improve its content—for example, deleting a sentence, correcting a misspelled name, or moving a paragraph. *Formatting* refers to

SOME MAXIMS FOR BEGINNERS IN WORD PROCESSING

■ *Try before you buy.* In a way, word processing programs are like cars. Each one is a little different, and there are some that just seem to "fit" you. Try to "test drive" several packages by entering, saving, and printing a short letter with each one before you decide on the one you want to buy.

■ *Now is better than later.* Using a satisfactory program now is better than waiting for that one perfect package to come along later.

■ *Keep it simple.* After you have selected a package, learn how to use it to do the essential tasks of word processing, such as creating, modifying, saving, and printing documents. Practice the commands needed to perform these tasks until you know them well. When you actually use word processing, you will accomplish 95% of your work by using only 5% of the available commands. Learn basic commands and worry about the frills later, when you actually need them.

adjusting the appearance of the document to make it look appropriate and attractive. For example, you might want to center a heading, make wider margins, or use double spacing. *Storing* the document means saving it on a data disk. *Printing* is producing the document on paper, using a printer connected to the computer.

Some people think of word processing as just glorified typing. And, in a way, it is. But consider the advantages of word processing over typing. Word processing stores your typed words in the computer's memory, lets you see what you type on the screen before printing, remembers what you type and lets you change it, and prints the typed document at your request.

There are two notable differences between using a word processing program and using a typewriter. The first difference is the separation of typing from printing: When you use word processing, typing the document and printing the document do not occur at the same time; you print the document on paper whenever you like. Perhaps you want to print an intermediate draft, just to see how it looks, and then continue making changes. Or you may choose to commit your work to paper only in the final version.

The second difference between word processing programs and typewriters is related to the first: When you use a word processing package you can make changes as you go along, or even at some later time, and print out a revised—and perfect—copy. The key here is that only the changes themselves are retyped, not the entire document.

Although word processing can be readily distinguished from old-fashioned typing, this is just part of the story. A word processing package is a sophisticated tool with many options. Many of the options will be covered in this chapter and the next. We begin with an overview of how word processing works. This is followed by an easy-to-follow example, where you can see how different word processing features are used.

An Overview: How Word Processing Works

Think of the computer's screen as a page of typing paper. On the screen the word processing program indicates the top of the page and the left and right edges (margins) of the typed material. When you type you can see the line of text you are typing on the screen—it looks just like a line of typing on paper. Remember that you are not really typing on the screen; the screen merely displays what you are entering into memory. As you type, the program displays a *cursor* to show where the

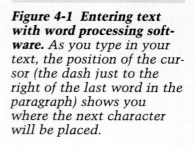

A word processing program lets you use the computer's keyboard to
enter text into the computer's internal memory. You can see what
you are entering on the screen and make modifications to the
text. Then the program lets you save the text._

Doc 1 Pg 1 Ln 4   Pos 56

***Figure 4-1 Entering text
with word processing software.*** *As you type in your
text, the position of the cursor (the dash just to the
right of the last word in the
paragraph) shows you
where the next character
will be placed.*

Cursor

next character you type will appear on the screen (Figure 4-1).
The cursor is usually a blinking dash or rectangle that you can
easily see.

You can also move the cursor around on the screen by using
special *cursor control keys* on the right side of the keyboard
(Figure 4-2). The up and down cursor movement keys move
the cursor up or down one line at a time. The *PgUp* and *PgDn*
keys let you move the cursor up or down a whole page at a
time.

Scrolling

A word processing program lets you type page after page of
material. Most programs show a line of dashes on the screen
to mark where one printed page will end and another will
begin; this line is not printed when you print your document.
Most word processing programs also display the line number
and the page number on which you are currently typing.

A screen can only display about 24 lines of text. Although
the screen display size is limited, your document size is not.
As you continue to type new lines, the earlier lines you typed
move up the screen as each new line is added at the bottom
of the screen. Eventually, the first line you typed disappears
off the top of the screen. But the line has not disappeared from
the computer's memory.

To see a line that has disappeared from the top of the screen,
use your cursor movement keys to move the cursor up to the

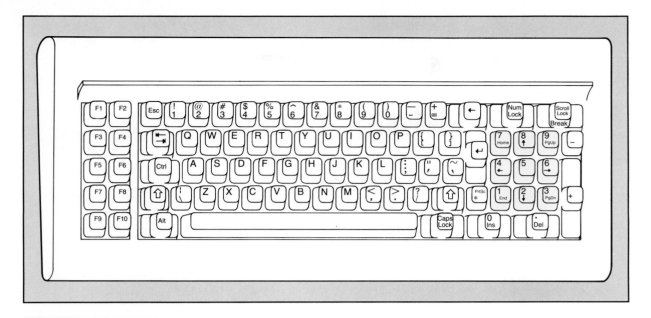

Figure 4-2 Getting around.
The cursor movement keys, located on the right side of the keyboard, let you move the cursor around on the screen.

top of the screen. As you continue to press the up cursor movement key, the line that had disappeared drops back down onto the screen. The program treats the text you are typing as if it were all on a long roll of paper like a roll of paper towels or a scroll. You "roll the scroll" up or down on the screen by moving the cursor. This process, called **scrolling,** lets you see any part of the document on the screen—but only 24 or so lines at a time (Figure 4-3, on the next page).

No Need to Worry about the Right Side

When you start to type the first line of a document, you will eventually get to the right side of the screen. The word processing program watches to see how close you are to the edge of the "paper" (the right margin). If there is not enough room at the end of a line to complete the word you are typing, the program automatically starts that word at the left margin of the next line down. You never have to worry about running out of space on a line; the word processor plans ahead for you. This feature is called **word wrap.** You also do not have to push a carriage return key at the end of each line as you would with a typewriter; in fact, you *should not* use a carriage return at the end of a line, or word wrap will not work properly. However, you can use a carriage return—that is, you can press Enter—to provide a blank line or to signal the end of a paragraph.

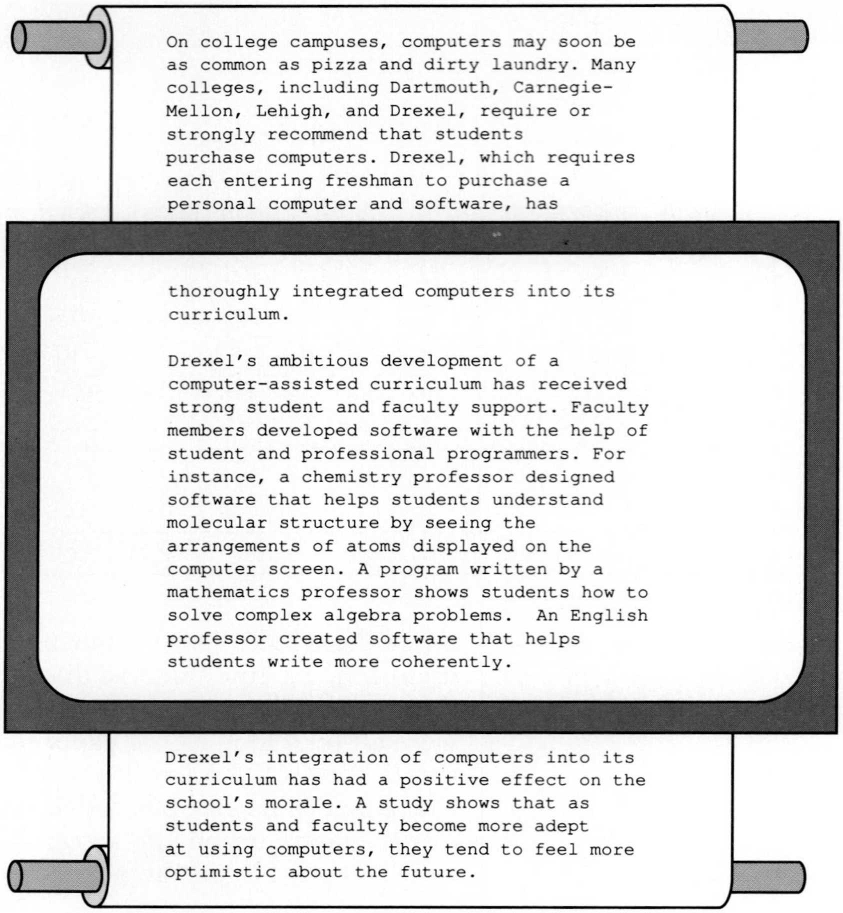

On college campuses, computers may soon be
as common as pizza and dirty laundry. Many
colleges, including Dartmouth, Carnegie-
Mellon, Lehigh, and Drexel, require or
strongly recommend that students
purchase computers. Drexel, which requires
each entering freshman to purchase a
personal computer and software, has

thoroughly integrated computers into its
curriculum.

Drexel's ambitious development of a
computer-assisted curriculum has received
strong student and faculty support. Faculty
members developed software with the help of
student and professional programmers. For
instance, a chemistry professor designed
software that helps students understand
molecular structure by seeing the
arrangements of atoms displayed on the
computer screen. A program written by a
mathematics professor shows students how to
solve complex algebra problems. An English
professor created software that helps
students write more coherently.

Drexel's integration of computers into its
curriculum has had a positive effect on the
school's morale. A study shows that as
students and faculty become more adept
at using computers, they tend to feel more
optimistic about the future.

Figure 4-3 Scrolling through a document. Although most documents contain many lines of text, the screen can display only about 24 lines at one time. You can use the cursor movement keys to scroll up and down through the document.

Easy Corrections

What if you make a mistake while you are typing? No problem: Move the cursor to the position of the error and make the correction. Word processing programs let you delete characters or whole words or lines that you have already typed, and they close up the resulting spaces automatically.

You can also insert new characters in the middle of a line or a word without typing over (and erasing) the characters that are already there. The program nudges existing characters to the right of the insertion as you type the new characters. However, if you wish, the word processing program also lets you *overtype* (replace) characters you typed before. We will discuss these correction techniques in more detail later.

Function Keys: Making It Easy

As we mentioned in Chapter 2, the *function keys* on a keyboard can save you a lot of time. Most word processing packages let you use the function keys, but the result of pressing each function key differs according to each applications program. For example, if you are using one word processing program and you want to underline a word in a report, you can press F8. But if you are using another program, you might have to press another function key or even a combination of keys to do the same task.

Figure 4-4 A function-key template. *This template helps you remember which function keys perform which tasks. Without the template you would have to memorize numerous key combinations.*

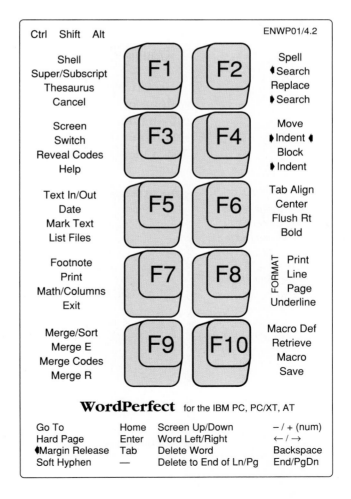

To help people remember which function key performs which task, software manufacturers often provide a sheet of plastic or paper that describes the use of each key. This sheet, called a **template,** fits over the function keys (Figure 4-4, on the previous page).

Now you are ready to see how these concepts work in a word processing package.

Getting Started: Using a Word Processing Package

Carl Wade has just graduated with a business degree and is looking for an entry-level job in an advertising firm. Carl already has a resume, but he wants to use a word processing package to prepare a cover letter. Carl chooses WordPerfect, the word processing package that dominates both businesses and college campuses. (Note: When it is necessary to be specific in this example, we will use WordPerfect commands.)

Loading the Program

As always, Carl begins by booting the computer. (This can be done by first using a Disk Operating System—DOS—disk or by using the word processing disk itself if the internal DOS files have been transferred onto it. Refer to Chapter 3, "The Disk Operating System," if you need help doing this.) After

Figure 4-5 Getting started with WordPerfect. *When Carl first loads WordPerfect, the screen is almost as blank as a fresh sheet of paper. The information at the bottom of the screen includes the page number, the line number, and the position of the cursor. Note the cursor in the upper left corner.*

Status line

Doc 1   Pg 1   Ln 1   Pos 10

Carl boots the computer, he makes sure he has his word processing disk in drive A and his formatted data disk in drive B.

At this point, with the A> prompt on the screen, Carl needs to type a command to get the word processing program started. The command varies with the program; examples are WS for WordStar, WORD for Microsoft Word, and WP for WordPerfect. When the appropriate command is typed, the word processing program is loaded from the disk in drive A into the computer's memory. Depending on the word processing program used, a set of choices, called a **menu,** may appear on the screen. However, WordPerfect, the program Carl is using, immediately displays an almost blank screen to represent a blank sheet of typing paper (Figure 4-5).

Creating the Cover Letter

The following steps describe, in a general way, how Carl creates (enters), saves, and prints his letter. Although the specific keystroke instructions refer to WordPerfect, the general

RANDOM BITS

Changing the Default Drive

When saving a file with an applications program, the file is saved on the disk in the default drive. If you have two diskette drives, the default drive is usually drive A. If you are using a hard-disk drive, the default drive is usually drive C. Sometimes, however, you may not want to save your file on the disk in the default drive. For example, if you have your applications disk in drive A and your data disk in drive B, you probably will want to save the file on your data disk, not the applications disk.

To save a file on a disk in a drive other than the default drive, you have two options. The first is to type the letter of the drive, followed by a colon, before the name of the file you wish to save. For example, if you want to save a file named REPORT on the disk in drive B, type B:REPORT. This tells the computer to save REPORT on the disk in drive B. When you retrieve the file, you also have to type the B: before the name of the file. Otherwise, the computer will look for the file on the disk in drive A. The second option is to change the

default drive after you load the applications program. If you change the default drive to B, for example, the computer automatically stores your files on the disk in drive B. You do not have to tell the computer which drive you want to use. All of the programs discussed in this book let you do this; however, the way you change the drive varies with the program. If you wish to use this option, read the documentation that comes with the program to find out how to change the default drive for the program you are using.

approach fits any word processing package. (An abbreviated version of the discussion that follows can be found in the box "Keystrokes Only: The Cover Letter Example.") Once Carl has loaded the word processing program, he proceeds as follows.

Entering the Letter. Carl starts by typing the letter (Figure 4-6) on the computer's keyboard. He uses the keyboard as he would a typewriter. He can see the results of his keystrokes on the screen. If he needs to make corrections, he can use the Backspace key or the Del key. Carl knows the letter is being stored in memory as he types, so as he continues to use the word processing package, he can continue to make changes to any part of the letter.

Figure 4-6 The first draft of Carl's cover letter. Carl can enter this draft and use WordPerfect to make the changes described in the text.

```
                                              18 Leroy Street
                                              Binghamton, NY  10037
                                              July 13, 1992


Ms. Louise Graham
Director of Personnel
Charnley Advertising, Inc.
1900 Corporate Lane
Baltimore, Maryland 21200


Dear Ms. Graham:

I am writing to inquire about the possibility of a position in
Charnley's accounts department.

I recently graduated from Pennsylvania State University with a BA
in business.  My area of interest was marketing.

I became acquainted with your company through my intern work at
the Dunhill Agency in New York.  I have always hoped to combine
my background in business and my interest in marketing.  Charnley
Advertising seems to offer the best opportunity for doing this.

I will be in Baltimore on July 28 and 29.  Would it be possible
for us to meet to discuss this further?  I can be reached at 600-
623-4667.  I look forward to hearing from you.

Sincerely,


Carl Wade
```

Saving the Letter. When Carl has finished keying in the letter and has corrected his mistakes, he stores—saves—the letter in a file on his data disk. (Recall that memory keeps data only temporarily; you must save your typed documents on disk if you want to keep them.) To save the letter on disk, Carl presses the F10 function key. WordPerfect now asks him to name the file before it is saved. A file name lets DOS keep track of the file's location on a disk so the file can be found when requested in the future. Carl names his file B:CLETTER— the B: tells the program which disk to store the file on, and CLETTER is the name of the file. Carl then presses Enter. By storing the letter on his data disk, Carl has made sure that he will always have a copy of the letter if he needs it again.

KEYSTROKES ONLY

The Cover Letter Example

These instructions are for creating Carl Wade's cover letter, as described in the text. The WordPerfect keystrokes that follow can also be used to create your own text.

Entering the Letter

1. Load WordPerfect.

2. Type the letter.

Saving the Letter

1. Press the F10 key.

2. When asked, type the document name (B:CLETTER, for example).

Printing the Letter

1. Turn on the printer.

2. Press the Shift key and the F7 key together.

3. Press 1 to print the full document.

Exiting the Program

1. Press F7.

2. WordPerfect asks, "Save Document? (Y/N)." Press the appropriate key. (If you have not already saved the file, press Y.)

3. Press Y to exit the program.

Retrieving the Letter

1. If the word processing program is not already loaded, load the program.

2. Press the Shift key and the F10 key together.

3. Type the complete name of the file (B:CLETTER in this example). Press Enter.

Editing the Letter

To use the insert mode:

1. Position the cursor where you wish to insert text.

2. Type the new text.

To use the typeover mode:

1. Press the Ins key to turn on the typeover mode.

2. Position the cursor under the first letter of the word (or words) you wish to type over.

3. Type the new text.

4. Turn off the typeover mode by pressing the Ins key again.

To add new paragraphs:

1. Position the cursor at the insert point. Press Enter.

2. Type the insertion. Press Enter.

Saving the Corrected Letter

1. Press F10 followed by The document name. Press Enter.

**WORD PROCESSING
AND YOUR
POLITICIAN**

Political speech writers seem to know a good thing when they see it. The good thing, in this case, is word processing. During a campaign perhaps ten or more slightly different versions of a speech must be prepared for a candidate each day. Sometimes a speech must be modified at the last minute to include comments about late-breaking world or local news or perhaps a juicy scandal in the opponent's campaign.

Speech writers use word processing programs to provide speed and flexibility in producing a speech. With such programs a speech writer can store the basic political positions of a candidate in separate files on a disk. When a speech is required for a group, the writers can combine the appropriate positions in one document. A few new paragraphs can be added to the speech to customize it for the particular group who will hear it. Then the finished speech can be printed for the candidate.

The writers can even save a separate file of stories and jokes to be used as "ice breakers" at the beginning of the speech. One or two of these can be inserted at the beginning of the speech if the candidate wants to establish an informal atmosphere.

Printing the Letter. Carl decides he wants to see a printed copy of what he has written so far. He turns on the printer and prints the letter by holding down the Shift key while pressing the F7 function key. WordPerfect asks him whether he wants to print the whole document (choice 1) or only one page at a time (choice 2). Because he has only a one-page letter, it really makes no difference which he chooses. He presses 1 for choice 1. This activates the printer, and his letter is printed.

Exiting the Program. Once Carl has finished using the program, he gives the command to exit the program: He presses the F7 function key. Then, in response to WordPerfect's questions, he types N (do not save the file, since it is already saved), then Y (do exit). This leads him back to the A> prompt. If Carl wanted to start a new file without leaving the program, he could clear the screen by typing N in response to the second question.

Editing the Letter

As we said, a significant payoff of word processing is the ease of making corrections to existing documents. Suppose Carl decides, for example, that his cover letter would be more effective if he made several changes. Consider for a moment what Carl would have to do if the letter had been prepared on a typewriter. He would, of course, have to retype the entire letter. Now follow the word processing approach to making changes.

Since Carl is not already using the word processing program, he places the word processing disk and his data disk in the appropriate drives and loads WordPerfect into memory, as before.

Retrieving the Letter. Carl presses the Shift key and the F10 function key together to retrieve the file. When WordPerfect asks for the name of the document to retrieve, he types B:CLETTER, as illustrated in Figure 4-7. The current version of his letter, just as he last saved it on his data disk, is loaded into memory and then displayed on the screen.

Making the Changes. We have already described how existing text can be moved over to allow new text to be inserted. When on-screen copy acts this way, the computer is in the

Figure 4-7 Retrieving the letter. *To retrieve a document, Carl must type in the name of the file he wants. B: tells the computer the drive that holds the diskette with the file; CLETTER tells the computer the name of the file that holds the document.*

Document to be Retrieved: B:CLETTER_

insert mode. This mode is the standard way of inserting corrections when you are using word processing. For example, suppose Carl wants to add the word "express" before the word "interest" in the second paragraph. All he has to do is move the cursor so it is below the "i" in "interest" and then type the word "express" and press the Spacebar. This automatically adds the word to the sentence (Figure 4-8a, on the next page).

Another correction option is to type right over the existing text. This feature, called **typeover mode,** replaces the existing text with the new text. If Carl wants to replace the word "express" with the word "special" he presses the insert key, (Ins), moves the cursor under the "e" in "express" and types "special" (Figure 4-8b). Then he presses Ins again to turn off the typeover mode. It may seem odd that Carl presses the Ins key to enter the typeover mode. This occurs because the program starts with the insert mode as the default mode, and the Ins key acts as a **toggle switch,** allowing you to switch between the insert mode and the typeover mode.

Carl also wants to add several sentences that explain his experience. He decides to insert the sentences between the third and fourth paragraphs. To insert the new sentences, Carl uses the cursor movement keys to position the cursor at the point where he wishes to add the new sentences. Then he types the sentences. He may, of course, make any other changes he wishes at this time. When he is finished, he presses Enter to provide the proper spacing at the end of the new paragraph. Compare the final version (Figure 4-9, page 117) with the original version (Figure 4-6).

Figure 4-8 Editing the letter. Carl uses the flexibility of word processing to edit his letter. (a) First he uses the insert mode to add the word "express" in the middle of a line. He positions the cursor and types in the word. (b) Carl decides to use the typeover mode to change "express" to "special." As Carl keys in the word "special," he types over the word he wants to replace.

```
                                    18 Leroy Street
                                    Binghamton, NY  10037
                                    July 13, 1992


        Ms. Louise Graham
        Director of Personnel
        Charnley Advertising, Inc.
        1900 Corporate Lane
        Baltimore, Maryland 21200


        Dear Ms. Graham:

        I am writing to inquire about the possibility of a position in
        Charnley's accounts department.

        I recently graduated from Pennsylvania State University with a BA
        in business.  My area of express interest was marketing.

        I became acquainted with your company through my intern work at
        the Dunhill Agency in New York.  I have always hoped to combine
B:\CLETTER                                    Doc 1 Pg 1 Ln 21     Pos 43
```

(a)

```
                                    18 Leroy Street
                                    Binghamton, NY  10037
                                    July 13, 1992


        Ms. Louise Graham
        Director of Personnel
        Charnley Advertising, Inc.
        1900 Corporate Lane
        Baltimore, Maryland 21200


        Dear Ms. Graham:

        I am writing to inquire about the possibility of a position in
        Charnley's accounts department.

        I recently graduated from Pennsylvania State University with a BA
        in business.  My area of specess interest was marketing.

        I became acquainted with your company through my intern work at
        the Dunhill Agency in New York.  I have always hoped to combine
Typeover                                      Doc 1 Pg 1 Ln 21     Pos 39
```

(b)

Saving the Corrected Letter. As before, Carl presses the F10 key to save the letter on his disk. WordPerfect asks if Carl wants to replace the earlier version of the letter with the new version. Carl types Y for *yes,* and the letter is again saved in a file named B:CLETTER. Carl could have also told WordPerfect to use a different name when it asked what document to save.

After you have practiced a bit, you will see that making changes with word processing is swift and efficient, even for a short document such as a letter. Considering the volume of correspondence—or any kind of typing—in an office, the labor savings is significant.

Figure 4-9 The corrected letter. Carl prints out the corrected letter, knowing he can make further changes later if he wishes.

```
                                           18 Leroy Street
                                           Binghamton, NY  10037
                                           July 13, 1992



         Ms. Louise Graham
         Director of Personnel
         Charnley Advertising, Inc.
         1900 Corporate Lane
         Baltimore, Maryland 21200


         Dear Ms. Graham:

         I am writing to inquire about the possibility of a position in
         Charnley's accounts department.

         I recently graduated from Pennsylvania State University with a BA
         in business.  My area of special interest was marketing.

         I became acquainted with your company through my intern work at
         the Dunhill Agency in New York.  I have always hoped to combine
         my background in business and my interest in marketing.  Charnley
         Advertising seems to offer the best opportunity for doing this.

         While I was in school, I prepared and monitored advertising
         campaigns and tracked account budgets.  I am also familiar with
         several types of computers and computer systems.

         I will be in Baltimore on July 28 and 29.  Would it be possible
         for us to meet to discuss this further?  I can be reached at 600-
         623-4667.  I look forward to hearing from you.

         Sincerely,


         Carl Wade
```

Formatting: Making It Look Nice

Now that you know the basics of creating text with a word processing program, you can turn your attention to the appearance, or **format,** of the document. This is not a trivial matter. In fact, one of the most appealing aspects of word processing is the ability it gives you to adjust the appearance of a document. You can use this capability to present your company—or yourself—attractively on paper.

Image is important. A multimillion-dollar company that relies on public opinion certainly wants to appear at its best on paper. So do little companies that do not have money to spend on fancy typesetting and printing. All of these companies, big and small, can afford word processing.

Figure 4-10 Formatting considerations. *Word processing software lets you change the look of your document. For example, you can change the margins or center a page with just a few keystrokes. You can also alter the indentations, use double spacing, or make dozens of other style changes in a matter of seconds.*

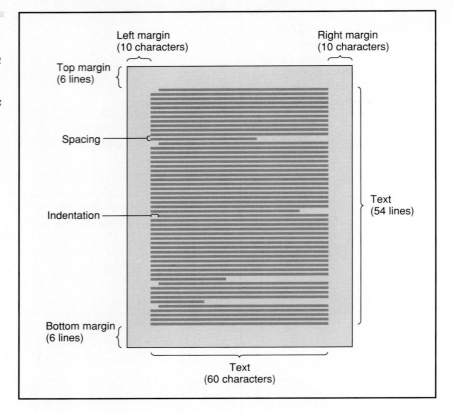

The format of a document is the way the document appears on the page. *Format* refers to the size of the margins, the organization of text, the space between the lines, and all the other factors that affect appearance. Figure 4-10 shows some format considerations. Word processing software offers many features to control and vary the format of a document.

To show you how formatting works, we return to Carl Wade.

The Resume Example

Once Carl finishes his cover letter, he takes another look at his resume (Figure 4-11). He sees at a glance that it can use some improvement: The resume is bunched up at the top of the page, giving it a short, squatty look. Carl wonders if the name and address lines would look better if they were centered. And he sees that the text runs together, making it hard to read. As Carl ponders various ways to fix the resume, he loads the original version from the disk and studies it on the screen.

```
CARL WADE
18 LEROY STREET
BINGHAMTON, NY  10037
600-623-4667


CAREER OBJECTIVE
Challenging position with an advertising agency as an entry-level
account representative.  Seeking the experience that leads to a
career as an accounts manager.

EDUCATION
College: The Pennsylvania State University
Degree: Bachelor of Arts
Major: Business
Specialization: Marketing
GPA: 3.8

HONORS AND ACTIVITIES
Lloyd B. Trennon Honor Scholarship (2 years)
Kiwanis Achievement Scholarship (3 years)
Class Treasurer (Junior year)
President, Computer Club (Senior year)

EMPLOYMENT HISTORY
Junior Intern.  The Dunhill Agency, Binghamton, NY.  Earned one
of three student internships.  Assisted in preparing and
monitoring advertising campaigns.  Used Lotus 1-2-3 to track
account budgets.  (Full time for two summers, part time senior
year.)

Receptionist.  Martin Lumber Company, Binghamton, NY.
Responsibilities included greeting customers, coordinating
calendars and appointments, and taking community groups on
company tours.  (Summer job.)

REFERENCES
Available on request.
```

Figure 4-11 The first draft of Carl's resume. This is Carl's first draft of his resume. It is a good start, but he can make it much better. If Carl had to rely on a typewriter to make the corrections described in the text, he would have to retype the entire page.

Carl decides to try several format changes to make the resume longer and more attractive. These changes are (1) adding a space after each major heading, (2) centering the name and address lines, (3) centering the text vertically on the page, (4) widening the width of the margins, (5) evening up the right-hand margin, and (6) using boldface and underlining to highlight certain words. (An abbreviated version of the discussion that follows can be found in the box "Keystrokes Only: The Resume Example.")

Adding Blank Lines

The first change is easy enough: Carl positions the cursor at the end of each major heading (for example, the heading "CAREER OBJECTIVE") and pushes Enter once. This moves the cursor one line down and adds a blank line in the text.

Centering Lines

To center the name and address lines between the left and right sides of the page, Carl positions the cursor under the leftmost character of a line, presses the Shift key and the F6 key simultaneously, and then presses the down cursor key. This automatically centers the line of text. He repeats this process for each of the next three lines. Figure 4-12 shows the results.

Vertical Centering

Carl's next improvement is to center the resume on the page, a process called vertical centering. **Vertical centering** adjusts the top and bottom margins so the text is centered

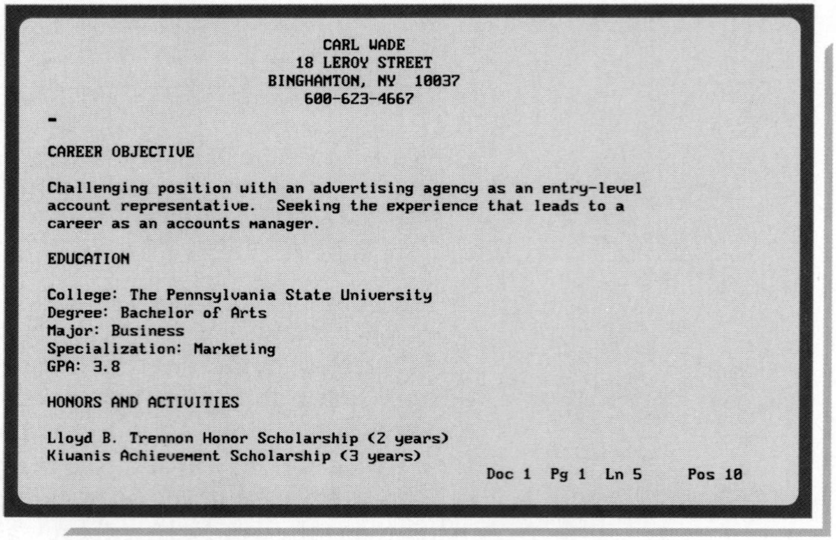

Figure 4-12 Easy centering.
Carl can center the top four lines without the risk of introducing typing errors.

```
                      CARL WADE
                   18 LEROY STREET
                 BINGHAMTON, NY  10037
                    600-623-4667
 -

 CAREER OBJECTIVE

 Challenging position with an advertising agency as an entry-level
 account representative.  Seeking the experience that leads to a
 career as an accounts manager.

 EDUCATION

 College: The Pennsylvania State University
 Degree: Bachelor of Arts
 Major: Business
 Specialization: Marketing
 GPA: 3.8

 HONORS AND ACTIVITIES

 Lloyd B. Trennon Honor Scholarship (2 years)
 Kiwanis Achievement Scholarship (3 years)
                                    Doc 1  Pg 1  Ln 5     Pos 10
```

vertically on the printed page. This eliminates the need to calculate the exact number of lines to leave at the top and bottom of a page, a necessary process if centering vertically using a typewriter.

To center the whole page vertically, the cursor must be at the top of the page. After Carl moves the cursor, he presses the Alt key and the F8 key at the same time. Then he types 3 to choose the vertical centering option and presses Enter.

Changing Margins

When Carl first typed his resume, he left the margins—left and right, top and bottom—on their original settings. The original settings are called **default settings**—settings used by the word processing package unless these settings are deliberately changed by the user. Both the default left and right margins are usually 1 inch (ten characters) wide, leaving room for about 64 characters per line of text. The default top and bottom margins are also usually 1 inch each; these settings allow about 55 lines of text per page.

Documents are often typed using the default margin settings. However, if the document would look better with narrower or wider margins, the margin settings can be changed accordingly. Most packages even allow several different margin settings in various parts of the same document. Carl wants to widen the left and right margins for the entire resume by ½ inch, or five characters, on each side. To do this, he must change the left margin from its default position of 10 to position 15 and change the right margin from its default position of 74 to position 69. He presses the Shift key and F8 at the same time, presses 3 for the margin option, and gets the message "Set 10 74 to Left =." He types 15 after the equals sign and presses the Enter key to change the left margin. Then he sees the message, "Right =" and types 69 to move the right margin. Finally, he presses Enter again. The result is shown in Figure 4-13 (on page 123).

When the margin settings are changed, most word processing software automatically adjusts the text to fit the new margins. This is called **automatic reformatting.** Notice in Figure 4-13 how WordPerfect automatically reformatted the resume so the text now fits in the new margin widths. With some word processing packages, you may have to press special keys to initiate the reformatting.

KEYSTROKES ONLY

The Resume Example

These instructions are for creating Carl Wade's resume, as described in the text. The WordPerfect keystrokes that follow can also be used to create your own text.

Adding Blank Lines

1. Position the cursor at the end of the line where you want to add a blank line. Press Enter.

Centering Lines

1. Position the cursor under the leftmost character of the word or words you want to center.

2. Press the Shift key and the F6 key together.

3. Move the cursor down one line by pressing the down cursor key.

Vertical Centering

1. Place the cursor at the top of the document.

2. Press the Alt key and the F8 key simultaneously.

3. Press 3 to choose the vertical centering option. Press Enter.

Changing Margins

1. To widen the margins by ½ inch, press the Shift key and F8 at the same time.

2. Press 3 to choose the margin option.

3. When you see the message "Set 10 74 to Left =," type 15. Press Enter.

4. When you see the message "Right =," type 69. Press Enter.

Justifying the Right Margin

1. In WordPerfect the right is justified automatically when the document is printed. However, the text looks ragged right on the screen.

2. To switch to ragged-right margins, move the cursor to the top of the page and press the Ctrl and F8 keys together. Then type 3 to select the ragged-right option.

Adding Boldface and Underlining

To boldface existing text:

1. Press the Alt and F4 keys simultaneously.

2. Move the cursor to highlight the word or words you want to boldface.

3. Press the F6 key.

To boldface as you type:

1. Press F6, then type the word or words to be boldface.

2. Press F6 again to signal the end of the boldface text.

To underline existing text:

1. Press the Alt and F4 keys simultaneously.

2. Move the cursor to highlight the word or words you want to underline.

3. Press the F8 key.

To underline as you type:

1. Press F8, then type the word or words to be underlined.

2. Press F8 again to signal the end of the underlined text.

Figure 4-13 Changing the margins. *When Carl widened the margins, Word-Perfect automatically shifted the text to fit into the narrower space. Notice how the CAREER OBJECTIVE paragraph now takes up four lines rather than three.*

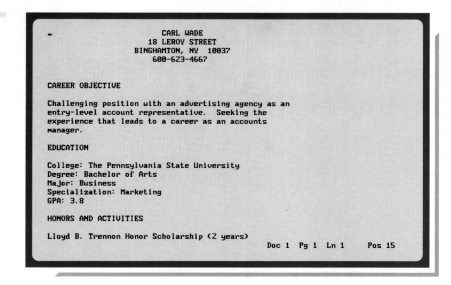

Justifying the Right Margin

Carl now wants to even up the right-hand margin. Notice in Figure 4-11 that the left side of the resume is neatly lined up, but the right side is uneven, or ragged. **Ragged-right margin** means that the end of each line does not end in the same position on the right side of the document. But Carl wants his right margin to be **justified,** that is, to line up neatly on the right-hand side.

Some word processing software assumes right justification as the default setting, meaning that the right margin is automatically justified unless a user specifically requests a ragged-right edge. Many word processing packages, such as Word-Perfect, automatically justify the right margin when the document is printed, even though the right margin appears ragged on the screen. The advantage of this approach is that inadvertent blanks between words can be seen and removed before the document is printed. In Figure 4-14 (on the next page) Carl's resume has been printed. Notice that WordPerfect has justified the right margin by spreading each line of text from margin to margin, leaving some gaps in the middle of the line.

If Carl wanted to print his resume with a ragged-right margin, he would first move the cursor to the top of the page. Next, he would press the Ctrl and F8 keys at the same time. Carl would then type 3 and press Enter, to turn the justification off.

Figure 4-14 Justified margins. *When Carl prints out his resume, WordPerfect justifies, or evens up, the right-hand margin.*

```
                              CARL WADE
                          18 LEROY STREET
                       BINGHAMTON, NY  10037
                          600-623-4667


        CAREER OBJECTIVE

        Challenging position  with an  advertising agency as an
        entry-level  account  representative.      Seeking  the
        experience  that  leads  to  a  career  as  an accounts
        manager.

        EDUCATION

        College: The Pennsylvania State University
        Degree: Bachelor of Arts
        Major: Business
        Specialization: Marketing
        GPA: 3.8

        HONORS AND ACTIVITIES

        Lloyd B. Trennon Honor Scholarship (2 years)
        Kiwanis Achievement Scholarship (3 years)
        Class Treasurer (Junior year)
        President, Computer Club (Senior year)

        EMPLOYMENT HISTORY

        Junior Intern.   The  Dunhill  Agency,  Binghamton, NY.
        Earned one  of three  student internships.  Assisted in
        preparing and  monitoring advertising  campaigns.  Used
        Lotus 1-2-3 to track  account budgets.  (Full time for
        two summers, part time senior year.)

        Receptionist.   Martin Lumber  Company, Binghamton, NY.
        Responsibilities    included    greeting    customers,
        coordinating  calendars  and  appointments,  and taking
        community groups on company tours.  (Summer job.)

        REFERENCES

        Available on request.
```

Adding Boldface and Underlining

Finally, Carl decides to add a few special touches to his resume. He wants to use darker text, or **boldface** text, for the address and name lines and the major headings, and he wants to underline his job titles to emphasize them. To boldface words, he positions the cursor at the beginning of the word and presses the Alt key and the F4 key together. Then he moves the cursor to the end of the word. This highlights the word (Figure 4-15a).

Figure 4-15 Marking text.
(a) Carl marks—or high-lights—the text he wants in boldface. (b) When Carl presses F6 to boldface the text, the marked text appears brighter than the surrounding text.

CARL WADE
18 LEROY STREET
BINGHAMTON, NY 10037
600-623-4667

CAREER OBJECTIVE

Challenging position with an advertising agency as an
entry-level account representative. Seeking the
experience that leads to a career as an accounts
manager.

EDUCATION

College: The Pennsylvania State University
Degree: Bachelor of Arts
Major: Business
Specialization: Marketing
GPA: 3.8

HONORS AND ACTIVITIES

Lloyd B. Trennon Honor Scholarship (2 years)
Block on   Doc 1 Pg 1 Ln 7   Pos 31

(a)

CARL WADE
18 LEROY STREET
BINGHAMTON, NY 10037
600-623-4667

CAREER OBJECTIVE

Challenging position with an advertising agency as an
entry-level account representative. Seeking the
experience that leads to a career as an accounts
manager.

EDUCATION

College: The Pennsylvania State University
Degree: Bachelor of Arts
Major: Business
Specialization: Marketing
GPA: 3.8

HONORS AND ACTIVITIES

Lloyd B. Trennon Honor Scholarship (2 years)
                                        Doc 1 Pg 1 Ln 7   Pos 31

(b)

continued ▶

Next Carl presses F6. The words that will be printed in bold-face appear brighter, dimmer, or a different color than the surrounding words on the screen, depending on the word processing package (Figure 4-15b). When the resume is printed, the marked words will appear darker than the rest of the text. If Carl wants to enter the command to boldface text as he types a document, he can press F6 before he starts to type the word or words he wants to be bold and then press F6 again after he has finished typing.

Figure 4-15 Marking text (continued). (c) Carl uses the F8 key to underline key words in his resume.

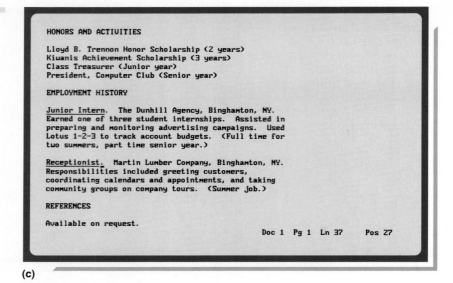

```
HONORS AND ACTIVITIES

Lloyd B. Trennon Honor Scholarship (2 years)
Kiwanis Achievement Scholarship (3 years)
Class Treasurer (Junior year)
President, Computer Club (Senior year)

EMPLOYMENT HISTORY

Junior Intern.  The Dunhill Agency, Binghamton, NY.
Earned one of three student internships.  Assisted in
preparing and monitoring advertising campaigns.  Used
Lotus 1-2-3 to track account budgets.  (Full time for
two summers, part time senior year.)

Receptionist.  Martin Lumber Company, Binghamton, NY.
Responsibilities included greeting customers,
coordinating calendars and appointments, and taking
community groups on company tours.  (Summer job.)

REFERENCES

Available on request.
                              Doc 1  Pg 1  Ln 37    Pos 27
```

(c)

Underlining is also easy. To underline already typed text, Carl needs to position the cursor at the beginning of the section he wants to underline. Next he presses the Alt key and F4 together. He then uses the cursor movement keys to highlight the text to underlined. After he has done this, he presses F8. The text will be underlined on the screen (Figure 4-15c). If Carl wants to underline text while he is typing, he presses F8 to start the underlining command and then presses F8 again when he wants to stop the underlining.

Carl's final version of his resume is shown in Figure 4-16. As you can see, the resume is much more attractive and readable than the original version. As before, Carl saves his resume on the data disk, so he has the option of making more changes in the future. The changes can be format changes or even changes to the substance of his resume; he can, for example, add job experience as he gains it.

An Important Point to Remember

When you first use a computer, you may be afraid that you will do something stupid and the computer will start to smoke. That will not happen. But you may do something foolish that will make *you* burn with frustration. The most likely scenario is that you lose a document you have been working on, because you forgot to save it on disk before turning the computer off.

Only you can prevent "frustration fires" by being careful

Figure 4-16 The final draft.
Compare this version of Carl's resume to his first draft in Figure 4-11.

```
                        CARL WADE
                     18 LEROY STREET
                  BINGHAMTON, NY  10037
                      600-623-4667


CAREER OBJECTIVE

Challenging position  with an  advertising agency as an
entry-level  account  representative.      Seeking  the
experience  that  leads  to  a  career  as  an accounts
manager.

EDUCATION

College: The Pennsylvania State University
Degree: Bachelor of Arts
Major: Business
Specialization: Marketing
GPA: 3.8

HONORS AND ACTIVITIES

Lloyd B. Trennon Honor Scholarship (2 years)
Kiwanis Achievement Scholarship (3 years)
Class Treasurer (Junior year)
President, Computer Club (Senior year)

EMPLOYMENT HISTORY

Junior Intern.   The  Dunhill  Agency,  Binghamton, NY.
Earned one  of three  student internships.  Assisted in
preparing and  monitoring advertising  campaigns.  Used
Lotus 1-2-3 to track  account budgets.  (Full time for
two summers, part time senior year.)

Receptionist.   Martin Lumber  Company, Binghamton, NY.
Responsibilities    included    greeting    customers,
coordinating  calendars  and  appointments,  and taking
community groups on company tours.  (Summer job.)

REFERENCES

Available on request.
```

to save your documents on disk. As we mentioned in Chapter 3, it is also a good idea to copy your data disk onto a backup disk at regular intervals, perhaps once a day. You can use the DOS DISKCOPY command for this purpose. The copying procedure takes only a few minutes. You may never need the backup disk. However, the one time you are in a hurry and neglect to make a backup is the one time you will need it.

Beyond the Basics

You can use the basic commands introduced in this chapter to create all types of text documents—letters, memos, reports, resumes, and so on. Many people use only these simple functions. But there is more—much more. In the next chapter we will show you sophisticated commands that let you take full advantage of word processing programs.

Exercises

4-1

1. Load your word processing program and insert a formatted data disk in drive B. Then enter the letter shown in Figure 4-17, making corrections, when needed, as you type. Do not worry if the lines on your screen do not look exactly like the sample—your word processing program may allow a different number of characters per line.

Figure 4-17

NATIONAL COMPUTER SUPPLIES COMPANY
200 WICKER DRIVE
CHICAGO, IL 60680

Ms. Jane Ejde
Wholesale Manager
Computer Supply, Inc.
1220 Oak Street
Oklahoma City, OK 40712

Dear Ms. Ejde:

Your order of May 10 for 400 boxes of 3½-inch diskettes was shipped to you on May 12 via Southwest Trucking. They have promised delivery no later than May 18.

Enclosed is our recent catalog. In addition to exciting new products, we offer competitive pricing on our standard line of computer supplies. We will continue to send you our new catalogs as they become available.

We appreciate your business. We'll do everything we can to make sure that our products and services keep you a satisfied customer.

Sincerely,

Paul Hernandez
Regional Manager

PH/rd

Enclosure: NCS Catalog

2. Save the letter on your data disk. The file name should be EX4-1.
3. Print the letter.
4. Exit the word processing program.

4-2

1. Load or enter the word processing program.
2. Retrieve the EX4-1 file. Review it on the screen. Is it still the same document?
3. Make the following changes to the letter:
   - Change "Ms. Jane Ejde" to "Mr. Jake Warde"
   - Change "Dear Ms. Ejde" to "Dear Mr. Warde"
   - Change "400 boxes" to "800 boxes"
   - Add the word "most" before the word "recent" in the second paragraph
   - Add the following sentence between the first and second paragraphs: Please note on the enclosed invoice that you qualify for a 5% discount because you are a new customer.
4. Save the revised letter as EX4-2.
5. Print the revised letter.
6. Without exiting the word processing program, use the appropriate commands for your package to clear the screen. (Note for WordPerfect users: You need to press F7, then N (for do not save file), then N (for do not exit program).)

4-3

1. Enter the text shown in Figure 4-18 (on the next page), using word wrap. Note: your margins will not be the same as in Figure 4-18. Save the file as EX4-3.
2. Now change the margins to 20 on the left and 62 on the right.
3. Center the heading "JOHN FITZGERALD KENNEDY" on the line. Then center the dates "1917–1963."
4. Boldface the two lines you centered.
5. Center the body of the text vertically on the page.
6. Underline the following lines:
   - "Inaugural Address (January 1961)"
   - "Address, White House dinner honoring Nobel Prize winners (April 1962)"
   - "Address at the Berlin Wall (June 1963)"
7. Save the revised document as EX4-3A.
8. Print the revised document twice; once with a justified right margin and once with a ragged-right margin.
9. Use the appropriate commands to clear the screen.

```
JOHN FITZGERALD KENNEDY
1917-1963


And so, my fellow Americans, ask not what
your country can do for you; ask what you
can do for your country.
Inaugural Address (January 1961)

I think this is the most extraordinary
collection of talent, of human knowledge,
that has ever been gathered together at the
White House, with the possible exception of
when Thomas Jefferson dined alone.
Address, White House dinner honoring Nobel
Prize winners (April 1962)

All free men, wherever they may live, are
citizens of Berlin. And therefore, as a
free man, I take pride in the words "Ich
bin ein Berliner."
Address at the Berlin Wall (June 1963)
```

Figure 4-18

4-4

1. Write a letter to a friend by using a word processing program.
    The letter should have the following format:
    - 1½-inch margins on each side.
    - A blank line between each paragraph
    - A right-justified margin
    - At least one underlined word
    - At least one boldface word
2. Save the letter as EX4-4.
3. Print the letter.

4-5

1. Enter the document shown in Figure 4-19.
2. Save the document as EX4-5. Print EX4-5.
3. Center the document vertically on the page. Create a right-justified margin, and then print the document.
4. Change the margin settings so there are 2-inch margins on each side. Make sure the copy is still centered vertically and that the lines are still right-justified. Save this revised document as EX4-5A.
5. Print EX4-5A. How many lines longer is the printed version of EX4-5A than the printed version of EX4-5?

Figure 4-19

```
                        TO GIVE UP HALFWAY


        During the "Warring States" period of China, there was a man
    by the name of Yue Yang who went to another state for further
    studies. He returned home a year later.  At that time, his wife
    was weaving on the loom. When she saw him return so suddenly, she
    felt very strange and asked, "Have you completed your study?"

        In reply, Yue Yang said, "No, but I decided to return home
    because I missed you."

        On hearing this, his wife said nothing.  She took a pair of
    scissors and cut the silk threads on the loom.  Having done this,
    she said, "The loom wove the silk thread by thread, inch by inch,
    and foot by foot before it made a piece of cloth.  Now that I have
    cut it, all the effort and time spent have been wasted. When you
    went elsewhere for further study, you had to learn continuously
    day by day.  If you should give up halfway, would it not be the
    same as cutting the cloth on the loom?"

        Yue Yang was very much moved after seeing what his wife had
    done and hearing what she had said.  He left home again for
    another state to complete his study.  This time, he stayed for
    seven years until he had successfully completed his study.
```

**AROUND-THE-WORLD TOURS
SUMMER SCHEDULE**

LOCATION	DATES
London-Paris-Rome	6/20-7/7
Rome-Athens	6/20-7/7
The Orient	6/25-7/25
Amsterdam-Berlin	6/25-7/25
Napal	6/30-7/14
Acapulco-Cozumel	7/3-7/24
Trinidad	7/3-7/24
Australia-New Zealand	7/15-8/15

Figure 4-20 (a)

4-6

1. Enter the document shown in Figure 4-20a. Format the document exactly as it is shown in the figure.
2. Save the document as EX4-6.
3. Make the changes shown in Figure 4-20b. Align the columns as they were in Figure 4-20a.
4. Save the revised document as EX4-6A.
5. Print EX4-6 and EX4-6A.

AROUND-THE-WORLD TOURS
SUMMER SCHEDULE

LOCATION	DATES
London-Paris-Rome	6/20-7/7
Rome-Athens	6/20-7/7
~~Geneva - Zurich~~	6/25 - 7/15
~~The Orient~~	~~6/25-7/25~~
Hong Kong - Bangkok	6/25 - 7/25
~~Amsterdam-Berlin~~	~~6/25-7/25~~
	7/1 - 7/30
Nepal	~~6/30-7/14~~
Acapulco-Cozumel	7/3-7/24
~~Trinidad~~	~~7/3-7/24~~
Australia-New Zealand	7/15-8/15
Kenya	7/30 - 8/20
Hawaii - Fiji	8/1 - 8/20

Figure 4-20 (b)

4-7

1. Enter the class information sheet shown in Figure 4-21 (on the next page). The heading should be centered and underlined. The words on the left-hand side of the sheet (such as "OFFICE:" and "OFFICE HOURS:") should be in boldface. Try to line up the information on the sheet exactly as it is shown.
2. Save the information sheet as EX4-7.
3. Print the information sheet.
4. Exit the word processing program.

Figure 4-21

CSS 110 WINTER 1990

OFFICE:	2316A
OFFICE HOURS:	10:00-10:50 AM
MATERIALS:	<u>Learning About Computers</u>
	by Andrew Cashman
	Computer Lab Access Card
	Two 3½-inch Disks

GRADING:

5 Quizzes	@	6 pts =	30
5 Exercises	@	3 pts =	15
3 Tests	@	10 pts =	30
1 Final	@	20 pts =	20
Participation	@	5 pts =	5

Total   = 100

```
92 - 100 = A
82 -  91 = B
70 -  81 = C
60 -  69 = D
 0 -  59 = F
```

NOTES:

1. Class attendance is required.

2. Don't be late to class.

3. Don't miss tests or quizzes; no make-ups will be given.

4. No incompletes will be given in this class.

5. There are no "extra credit" assignments in this class.

Summary and Key Terms

■ Word processing is the creation, editing, formatting, storing, and printing of a text document. The advantages of word processing over typing are that you can store your document, which makes it easier to incorporate changes, and you can see what you type before printing it.

■ As you type, the screen displays a cursor to show where the next character you type will appear. You can move the cursor around on the screen by using cursor movement keys on the right side of the keyboard. The PgUp and PgDn keys let you move the cursor up or down a whole page at a time.

■ Word processing programs treat the text you type as if it were on a long roll of paper, or scroll. You "roll the scroll" up or down on the screen by moving the cursor. This process, called **scrolling**, lets you see any part of the document on the screen.

- When a word that you type at the end of a line cannot fit on that line, the word processing program automatically starts that word on the next line. This feature is known as **word wrap.** Do not use the carriage return (that is, do not press Enter) at the end of a line unless you want to signal the end of a paragraph or provide a blank line.

- Word processing programs let you delete characters, words, or lines and close up spaces automatically; you can also insert text by typing new characters or replace old text by typing new text over the old.

- The use of each function key differs according to each applications program. A paper or plastic **template,** which fits over the function keys, briefly describes the use of each key.

- To load the word processing program, type a command at the A> prompt. A set of choices, called a **menu,** may appear on the screen.

- To enter text, use the keyboard as you would a typewriter. After completing the document and making corrections, save the document on a data disk.

- To edit a document, you must first retrieve it from the disk. The **insert mode** is the standard way of inserting corrections when using word processing. **Typeover mode** replaces the existing text with the new text. Switch between the two modes by pressing Ins, a toggle switch. Each press of a **toggle switch** changes from one of two settings to another.

- The **format** of a document is the way the document appears on the page: the organization of text, margin width, line spacing, use of boldface and underlining, and so on.

- The phrase *centering text* usually refers to centering text on a line. **Vertical centering,** however, adjusts the top and bottom margins so the text is centered vertically on the page.

- The original margin settings are called the **default settings.** Both the default left and right margins are usually 1 inch (or 10 characters) wide, leaving room for about 64 characters per line of text. The default top and bottom margins are also usually 1 inch each, allowing about 55 lines of text per page. When the margin settings are changed, most word processing software automatically adjusts the text to fit the new margins. This is called **automatic reformatting.**

- **Ragged-right margin** means that the end of each line does not end in the same position on the right side of the document. **Justified** text lines up neatly on the right-hand side, creating an even margin.

- **Boldface** words appear brighter, dimmer, or a different color than the surrounding words on the screen, depending on the word processing package. When the document is printed, the marked words will appear darker than the rest of the text. Underlined words on the screen are underscored when printed.

Review Questions

1. What are the basic functions of word processing?

2. How is word processing different from typing?

3. What is the cursor?

4. What is meant by the term *word wrap*?

5. What is meant by the term *scrolling*? How do you use scrolling when you are viewing a long document on the screen?

6. What is the difference between the insert mode and the typeover mode when using word processing? How do you get into insert mode?

7. When should Enter be used when entering text? Why?

8. How do you move the cursor up and down a line? How do you move the cursor from left to right?

9. If, after completing a document, you saw that a word in the middle of the document was misspelled, what steps would you take to correct the spelling?

10. How do you delete a character?

11. How do you separate paragraphs when using word processing?

12. What happens to an unsaved file when you turn the computer off?

13. What is meant by the term *boldface*?

14. What is the format of a document? What is reformatting?

15. How is vertical centering different from centering?

Using Word Processing at the Wall Street Journal

You can have the *Wall Street Journal* delivered to your doorstep each morning, whether you live in Seattle or Phoenix or Detroit. This modern miracle is due to a sophisticated electronic delivery system: The copy is sent by satellite to printing plants around the country. It would seem that the *Wall Street Journal* represents just about the latest word in technology.

This was not always the case. Until recently, the reporters' equipment was not on a technological par with the delivery systems. Their tools? Manual typewriters. But now reporters from New York to London are trading in their typewriters for personal computers. And their favorite software is, of course, word processing.

Wall Street Journal reporters initially were trained on dedicated word processors. But these machines had insufficient storage capacity and, worse, could function only as word processors. It soon became clear that the entire organization needed to move to a PC-based system.

The move to PCs was studied carefully. Reporters were included in the decision process, and they had their own ideas. They insisted on amber screen monitors—amber letters on a black background— because these screens have proved to be easiest on the eyes. They also preferred keyboards with a large number of function keys, to take advantage of software that uses function keys to reduce the number of key-

strokes. The final hardware package included an IBM PC clone, the AST Premium 286, with hard disk, graphics card, and internal modem.

The reporters use a commercial word processing package called XyWrite. They also use a custom-made communications program that lets them make selections from an on-screen menu to access the news wire service. This lets reporters track important related stories in a matter of seconds instead of hours, so the reporters are becoming better informed. The reporters can use the system to access stock prices and to peruse electronically stored old *Wall Street Journal* stories that might supply useful background material for a current story. Reporters also have immediate access to spelling checkers and thesaurus programs. These tools give reporters better access to information, ease of writing and revising, and—most importantly—a head start at beating the filing deadline.

5 Advanced Word Processing

Chapter Objectives

After reading this chapter you should be able to

- Mark a section—block—of text

- Move, copy, delete, save, retrieve, search, and replace blocks of text

- Explain advanced page-formatting features such as tabs, spacing, and headers and footers

- Describe the following word processing features: subscripts, superscripts, footnotes, and endnotes.

- Use various printer options

- Describe word processing–related software, such as spelling checkers and thesaurus programs

- Name and manage disk files

Now that you are familiar with the basics of word processing, it is time to examine some of the more sophisticated features. Many of these features—such as the ability to move a block of words anywhere in a document—are important time-savers for people who must rework papers or memos on tight schedules.

In this chapter we will show you how to manipulate large amounts of text, called text blocks; advanced page-formatting techniques; different printing options; and some special "added" attractions, such as spelling checker programs.

Text Blocks

A **text block** is a unit of text in a document. It can consist of one or more words, phrases, sentences, paragraphs, or even pages. Text blocks can be moved, deleted, copied, saved, and inserted. You can manipulate text blocks by using just a few keystrokes. To appreciate the power of these commands, imagine trying to move a paragraph to another place in a paper if your only tool is a typewriter.

A Survey Example

Barbara Crim is taking her first sociology course at California College. Halfway through the term, she is asked to write a survey that evaluates people's eating and exercising habits. After class Barbara goes to the school's computer lab, checks out WordPerfect, and sits down to write the survey.

After reading the first draft of her survey (Figure 5-1), Barbara decides that it needs some changes. She wants to reverse the order of questions 4 and 5 so all of the eating-habit questions will be together. She also wants to eliminate question 9, since it deals with hobbies rather than eating or exercising. And finally, she needs to type the Never-Always scale for questions 2 through 8. Before Barbara can do any of these tasks, however, she must first define—or **mark**—the blocks she wants to manipulate. (An abbreviated version of the discussion that follows can be found in the box called "Keystrokes Only: The Survey Example.")

Figure 5-1 The first draft of Barbara's survey. Barbara enters this draft of her survey.

Newspapers, magazines, and TV shows are filled with stories on health and fitness. But just how healthy are people today? An introductory sociology course at California College is conducting a survey to evaluate community attitudes and activities. We would appreciate your helping us by answering the following questions. Please circle the number that corresponds to the answer that best describes your behavior.

1. Do you eat a variety of foods from each of the four food groups each day?
   Never   1   2   3   4   5   Always

2. Do you limit the amount of fat and cholesterol you eat?

3. Do you limit the amount of salt you eat?

4. Do you maintain your desired weight--being neither overweight nor underweight?

5. Do you limit the amount of sugar you eat?

6. Do you exercise vigorously for 15-30 minutes at least 3 times a week?

7. Do you walk to nearby locations rather than driving your car?

8. Do you take part in leisure activities that increase your level of fitness?

9. Do you participate in group activities or hobbies that you enjoy?

10. What is your age?
    a. under 18   b. 18-21   c. 22-35   d. 36-50   e. over 50

11. What is your sex?
    a. male   b. female

12. What is your marital status?
    a. single   b. married   c. divorced

Marking a Block

Marking a block of text is done in different ways with different word processing software. In general, you move the cursor to the beginning of the chunk of text that constitutes the block. Then you either press a function key or use the keys to place block markers there. You do the same thing at the end of the block. Once the block is marked, it can be subject to a variety of block commands.

Since Barbara is using WordPerfect, she positions the cursor at the beginning of question 4 (just under the "4"), and presses Alt and F4 at the same time. This turns on the Block command. WordPerfect reminds Barbara that the command is

Figure 5-2 Marking a block of text. *Barbara uses the Alt and F4 keys to mark question 4.*

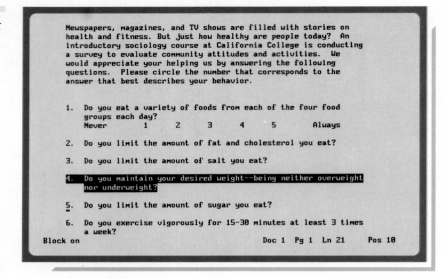

```
Newspapers, magazines, and TV shows are filled with stories on
health and fitness. But just how healthy are people today?  An
introductory sociology course at California College is conducting
a survey to evaluate community attitudes and activities.  We
would appreciate your helping us by answering the following
questions.  Please circle the number that corresponds to the
answer that best describes your behavior.


1.  Do you eat a variety of foods from each of the four food
    groups each day?
    Never         1       2       3       4       5         Always

2.  Do you limit the amount of fat and cholesterol you eat?

3.  Do you limit the amount of salt you eat?

4.  Do you maintain your desired weight--being neither overweight
    nor underweight?

5.  Do you limit the amount of sugar you eat?

6.  Do you exercise vigorously for 15-30 minutes at least 3 times
    a week?
Block on                               Doc 1  Pg 1  Ln 21     Pos 10
```

on by flashing the words "Block on" in the lower-left corner of the screen. Next Barbara moves the cursor until the entire question is highlighted. Now the block is marked (Figure 5-2).

Notice that the marked block stands out on the screen. Many word processing programs present marked blocks in **reverse video.** In other words, the print in the marked area is the color of the normal background and the background is the color of the normal print. If, for example, the screen normally has white letters on a black background, the marked portion of the text shows black letters on a white background.

Moving a Block

Once the block is marked, Barbara can use the Block Move command. The **Block Move command** removes a block of text from its original location and places it in a second location—the block still occurs only once in the document. Moving a block from one location to another is also called *cutting and pasting*, a reference to what literally would have to be done if you were using a typewriter.

Different word processing packages move text blocks in different ways. Some packages require only that you move the cursor to the new location; then, when you press a certain key or keys, the block disappears from its old location and is inserted at the location of the cursor. However, other word processing packages, such as WordPerfect, have separate commands: one that means "cut"—or delete the block from the old location—and another that means "paste"—or insert the block in the new location.

To move question 4 under question 5, Barbara has marked question 4—the block she wants to move. Now she presses the Ctrl key and F4 simultaneously to select the Block command options (Figure 5-3a). Next she presses 1 to cut the question from the survey. The question disappears from the screen (Figure 5-3b). Barbara now moves the cursor to the position

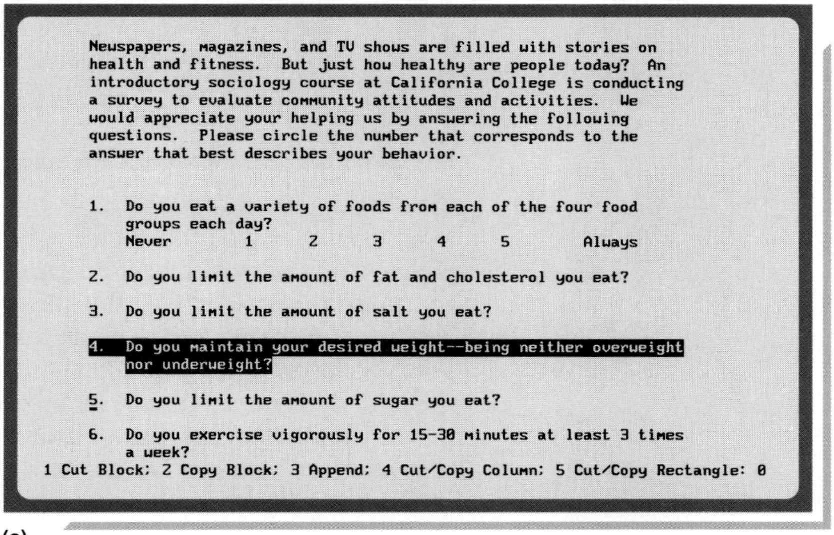

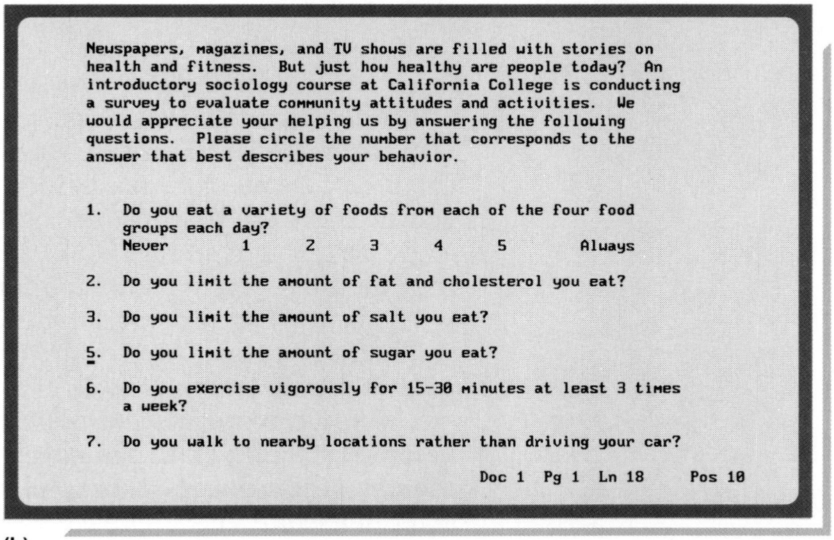

Figure 5-3 Easy moves. (a) *After Barbara marks the text she wants to move, she accesses the Block command options by pressing Ctrl-F4. (b) Barbara selects 1 and the text disappears from the screen.*

(a)

(b)

continued ▶

Figure 5-3 Easy moves (continued). (c) *Barbara then moves the cursor to the spot where she wants to insert the question. When she selects 5 from the Block command options, the text appears in its new location.*

Newspapers, magazines, and TV shows are filled with stories on health and fitness. But just how healthy are people today? An introductory sociology course at California College is conducting a survey to evaluate community attitudes and activities. We would appreciate your helping us by answering the following questions. Please circle the number that corresponds to the answer that best describes your behavior.

1. Do you eat a variety of foods from each of the four food
    groups each day?
    Never   1   2   3   4   5   Always

2. Do you limit the amount of fat and cholesterol you eat?

3. Do you limit the amount of salt you eat?

5. Do you limit the amount of sugar you eat?

4. Do you maintain your desired weight--being neither overweight
    nor underweight?

6. Do you exercise vigorously for 15-30 minutes at least 3 times
    a week?

                                        Doc 1 Pg 1 Ln 20   Pos 10

(c)

where she wants to insert question 4—under question 5. Once again she presses Ctrl-F4 to select the Block command options. She types 5 to "paste" the cut text in the new position. Figure 5-3c shows the survey after the question has been moved. Notice that, in addition to inserting the question in the new location, the old location has been "sewed up"—there is no gap where the question used to be. Barbara then changes the numbering so the order is correct.

Deleting a Block

Barbara is not done yet; she must get rid of question 9. One way to do this is to mark the question as a block and then use the **Block Delete command.** In WordPerfect the Block Delete command is the first half of the Block Move command—the "cut" part of "cut and paste." Other word processing programs may have a separate command for deleting blocks.

As before, Barbara marks the block—in this case question 9. Then she presses Ctrl and F4 simultaneously. Finally, she presses 1 to delete the block.

As you can see, the Block Delete command makes it easy to remove chunks of unwanted text from a document. Although the same thing could be accomplished with character-by-character deletions, this approach is not very efficient for a large amount of text.

Copying a Block

Now Barbara wants to add the Never-Always scales. Since they will all be the same, she can do this easily by using the Block Copy command. The Block Copy command is similar to the Block Move command. The **Block Copy command** copies the block of text into a new location. However, the block also stays in its original location—that is, the same text appears twice (or more) in the document. The Block Copy command comes in handy when similar material is needed repeatedly in the same document, since you only have to key in the text once.

Figure 5-4 The final draft. Barbara has made all the changes she wants at this time, so she prints the final draft of her survey.

Newspapers, magazines, and TV shows are filled with stories on health and fitness. But just how healthy are people today? An introductory sociology course at California College is conducting a survey to evaluate community attitudes and activities. We would appreciate your helping us by answering the following questions. Please circle the number that corresponds to the answer that best describes your behavior.

1. Do you eat a variety of foods from each of the four food
    groups each day?
    Never   1   2   3   4   5   Always

2. Do you limit the amount of fat and cholesterol you eat?
    Never   1   2   3   4   5   Always

3. Do you limit the amount of salt you eat?
    Never   1   2   3   4   5   Always

4. Do you limit the amount of sugar you eat?
    Never   1   2   3   4   5   Always

5. Do you maintain your desired weight--being neither overweight
    nor underweight?
    Never   1   2   3   4   5   Always

6. Do you exercise vigorously for 15-30 minutes at least 3 times
    a week?
    Never   1   2   3   4   5   Always

7. Do you walk to nearby locations rather than driving your car?
    Never   1   2   3   4   5   Always

8. Do you take part in leisure activities that increase your
    level of fitness?
    Never   1   2   3   4   5   Always

9. What is your age?
    a. under 18   b. 18-21   c. 22-35   d. 36-50   e. over 50

10. What is your sex?
    a. male   b. female

11. What is your marital status?
    a. single   b. married   c. divorced

Barbara types the scale once, as shown in Figure 5-1. Then she marks the block of text and presses Ctrl-F4. She types 2 to select the copy function, then she moves the cursor to the position where she wants to insert the text—under question 2. She presses Ctrl-F4 again and types 5 to copy the text. She repeats these steps to copy the answer line under each question. The final survey is shown in Figure 5-4 (on the previous page).

Saving and Retrieving a Block of Text

Barbara has another block command at her fingertips—she can save a block of text from the survey as a separate file on her disk. This is a useful function, since it lets you save part of an existing document and retrieve it later to use in another document. Since word processing software lets you insert text from a disk file into a document you are currently working on, you can quickly build a new document from parts of earlier documents. This process is known as **boilerplating.** Boiler-plating can be a real labor saver. For example, Barbara decides to save the questions about age, sex, and marital status from her existing survey, since these are common survey questions. She knows the next time she writes a survey she can simply insert this block of text into the new document.

To save the questions, Barbara marks the text (Figure 5-5). Then, with text still marked, she presses F10—the Save function key. When she gets the message "Block name:," she types

Figure 5-5 Saving a block of text. Barbara marks the block of text she wants to save. Then she uses the Save function key to save the block as a separate file on her disk.

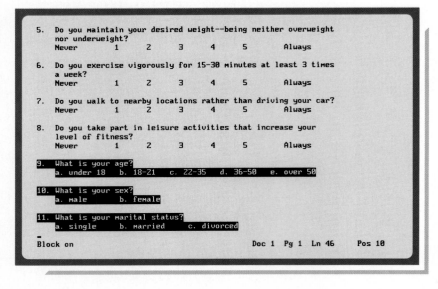

B:SQUEST for *survey questions*, then presses Enter. Word-Perfect saves the block as a separate file on Barbara's disk.

Later, when Barbara wants to retrieve the file, she places the cursor at the point where she wants to insert the stored text (Figure 5-6a). Then, without exiting the current file, she presses the Shift key and F10 key together. This activates the retrieve function. When she types in the name of her file with the stored information, the software reads the text from the disk and instantly inserts it in the new document (Figure 5-6b).

Figure 5-6 Retrieving a block of text. *(a) To retrieve a block of text and insert it in a new document, Barbara moves the cursor to the position where she wants to insert the text. (b) Then, without leaving the current file, she uses the retrieve function to retrieve the block of text.*

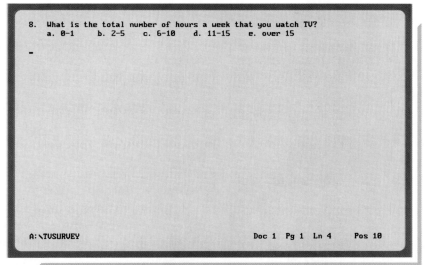

(a)

(b)

Even though it has taken us several pages to describe block commands, they are quite easy to use once you learn how. The ability to move blocks of text is a real boon if you have writing tasks. Perhaps the biggest advantage is that you can key in your thoughts as they come to you and rearrange them later—without retyping.

KEYSTROKES ONLY

The Survey Example

These instructions are for creating Barbara Crim's survey, as described in the text. The WordPerfect keystrokes that follow can also be used to create and edit your own text.

Marking a Block

1. Position the cursor under the first character of the text block you want to mark.

2. Press the Alt key and the F4 key together. Note the flashing "Block on" message in the lower-left corner.

3. Move the cursor to the end of the text block you want to mark. The text block should now be highlighted in reverse video.

4. To turn off the Block command, press Alt-F4 again. The "Block on" message should disappear.

Moving a Block

1. Mark the block you want to move.

2. Press the Ctrl and F4 keys at the same time.

3. Press 1 to cut the marked block—the block disappears.

4. Move the cursor to the location in which you want to insert the text.

5. Press Ctrl-F4 again. Then press 5 to retrieve the cut text.

Deleting a Block

1. Mark the block you want to delete.

2. Press the Ctrl and F4 keys at the same time.

3. Press 1 to delete the marked text.

Copying a Block

1. Mark the block you want to copy.

2. Press the Ctrl and F4 keys simultaneously. Press 2 to activate the Block Copy command.

3. Move the cursor to the location where you want to insert the copied text.

4. Press Ctrl-F4 again. Then press 5 to insert a copy of the marked text.

5. Repeat steps 3 and 4 if you wish to copy the text in more than one location.

Saving and Retrieving a Block

To save a block:

1. Mark the text you want to save. The block function should still be on.

2. Without exiting the current file, press the Shift key and the F10 key at the same time. WordPerfect asks you for a block name.

3. Type the block name. Press Enter. The block will be saved as a separate file on your data disk.

To retrieve a block:

1. Position the cursor in the location where you want to insert the saved block of text.

2. Press the Shift key and the F10 key at the same time. The message "Document to be retrieved:" appears.

3. Type in the name of the block you want to retrieve. Press Enter. The saved block of text is inserted automatically.

More Page Formatting

We mentioned some basic aspects of formatting in Chapter 4: setting margins, vertical centering, and so forth. But there are many other formatting options. The following are some options that can sometimes be very helpful. (For specific WordPerfect keystrokes for the sections that follow, see the box called "Keystrokes Only: Special WordPerfect Features.")

Spacing

Most of the time you will want your documents—letters, memos, reports—to be single spaced. But there are occasions when it is convenient or necessary to double space or even triple space a document. Word processing lets you do this with ease. In fact, a word processing program lets you switch back and forth from one type of spacing to another, just by pressing a few keys. A writer, for example, can print one copy of a new chapter single spaced for ease of reading. Then the same document can be double spaced and printed for the editor, who will appreciate the space to make changes.

Tabs

In many texts and documents, the first line of each paragraph is indented. Indenting paragraphs is a common feature, and word processing software provides a tab function for this purpose. **Tabs** (or **tab stops**), which you may have used on a typewriter, are points along the text line to which the cursor moves when the Tab key is pressed. Word processing packages have **default tab settings**—places where the cursor will automatically go when the Tab key is pressed. These are usually at every fifth character position along a line. One press of the Tab key moves the cursor to position 5, a second press moves the cursor to position 10, and so on.

If the default tab settings are not appropriate for your document, you can change them to suit your needs. For example, you can change the settings so you have tab stops in positions 3, 7, and 18 if you wish. You can also change the tab settings at any point in a document, so the first half of the document might have tab stops at positions 5 and 10, while the second half of the document might have tab stops at 8 and 16.

Figure 5-7 Two-column text. *Two-column text is often used in newsletters and brochures to give the document a professional look. Many word processing packages can produce two or more columns on one page.*

RUSHING RIVER TOURS

North Yuba

Our favorite spring river, the Yuba, sparkles and romps through a beautiful forested canyon. The Yuba is ideal for active first timers and has sections for experienced rafters looking for Class V thrills.
Class IV or V, 2-4 days

South Fork American

The most popular whitewater rafting river in the West. Exciting and lots of fun, with many memorable rapids. The river flows through the green and gold foothills of California's Gold Rush Country. The South Fork has served as an introduction to river rafting for countless beginners and continues to lure veterans back year after year.
Class III, 2 days

Middle Fork American

A wilderness alternative to South Fork American. The Middle Fork offers excellent isolated camping, good fishing, and gold panning in addition to an exciting and beautiful river run. This is the longest wilderness run available in California during the summer months. The 26-mile trip takes us through Tahoe National Forest and Auburn State Recreation Area.
Class III+, 2-3 days

North Fork American

The North Fork American is the most intimate and romantic run in the Sierra. This clear, free-flowing aqua jewel of the California Wild and Scenic River system makes rafting an inspiration.
Class IV, 1 day

Middle Fork Stanislaus

The Middle Fork of the Stanislaus has to be the cutting edge of whitewater adventure in California. Previously known to only a few of the state's best

Text Columns

Text columns are often used in newsletters and advertising copy. Many word processing programs let you have one or more columns of text on a page. For instance, if you were creating a newsletter or brochure, it would be easier to read and look more professional if it had two columns of text on a page. Figure 5-7 shows a sample brochure with this format.

Page Headers and Footers

Another useful formatting option provides page headers and footers. These are single lines of text that are printed on

*Figure 5-8 Headers and
footers.* Another useful formatting option provides
page headers and footers.
With many word processing
programs, you can create
these single lines of text,
which are automatically
printed on each page of a
document.

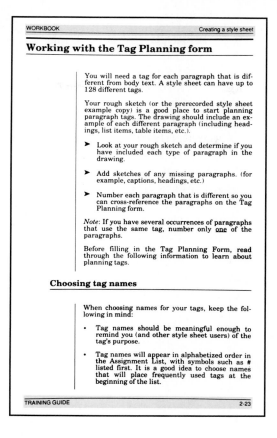

each page of a document. **Page headers** are printed in the top
margin of each page, and **page footers** are printed in the bottom
margin of each page. Word processing makes including these
features easy: You simply choose the header and/or footer option,
then type your line of text once. The program automatically
prints the text on each page.

In publishing, a typical header is a running chapter header—
a line of text at the top of each page that tells you the chapter
name and number. In published technical journals, a typical
footer contains the revision number. In business, the document title or a security warning may appear as a header or
footer (Figure 5-8).

Other Special Features

In addition to letting you format documents easily, word
processing programs let you do things that are hard or
impossible to do on a typewriter. We will consider these features in this section: subscripts and superscripts, footnotes
and endnotes, and the search and replace function.

Subscripts and Superscripts

Subscripts and superscripts are often used in research papers and technical articles. A **subscript** is a letter or numeral printed slightly below the rest of the line. Chemical and mathematical formulas often contain subscripts. For example, the formula for water is H_2O. Notice that the 2 is just below the line. In this formula the 2 is a subscript. A **superscript** is a letter or number printed slightly above the rest of the text in a line. An example is the famous formula $E = MC^2$. The 2 in this case is a superscript—it shows that the value of C is squared. Footnotes are usually indicated in text by superscripts. Word processing packages allow you to mark a character as a subscript or a superscript quickly and easily.

Figure 5-9 A footnote. *Remembering to leave space at the bottom of a page for a footnote can be an exasperating chore. With a word processing package, the software automatically saves the room and prints and numbers the footnotes for you.*

125

organisms as phototrophs or chemotrophs. **Phototrophs** use light as their primary energy source, whereas **chemothrophs** depend on oxidation-reduction reactions for energy. For a principal carbon source, **autotrophs** (self-feeders) use carbon dioxide and **heterotrophs** (feeders on others) require an organic carbon source.[1]

If we combine the energy and carbon sources, we derive the following nutritional classifications for organisms: **photoautotrophs, photoheterotrophs, chemoautotrophs,** and **chemoheterotrophs**. The nutritional classification of microbes is summarized in Table 5-3. Almost all of the medically important microorganisms discussed in this book are chemoheterotrophs.

Photoautotrophs

Photoautotrophs use light as a source of energy, and carbon dioxide as their chief source of carbon. They include photosynthetic bacteria (green sulfur and purple sulfur bacteria, and cyanobacteria), algae, and green plants. The process by which photoautotrophs transform carbon dioxide and water

[1]Autotrophs may also be referred to as *lithotrophs* (rock eating), and heterotrophs may also be referred to as *organotrophs*.

Footnotes and Endnotes

If you have ever typed a report for school, you probably have had to create **footnotes**—copy printed at the bottom of a particular page that pertains to the topic referenced by a mark in text (Figure 5-9). Footnotes are inconvenient when you are using a typewriter, because you have to plan ahead and leave enough room at the bottom of the page for them.

Endnotes present a slightly different problem. Like footnotes, **endnotes** are additional points about topics in text. However, the actual notes are collected at the end of the report instead of being printed on the same page as the topic. Word processing software eliminates the headaches associated with footnotes and endnotes.

For example, after you type in a quotation or article that you need to reference, a word processing package lets you press a function key to indicate that a footnote or endnote is required for this text. Then you type in the text of the footnote or endnote. When you print your report, the software automatically numbers all the notes. If you need footnotes, the software places them at the bottom of the required pages. If you signaled that you wanted endnotes, then the program collects all the endnotes and prints them on the last page or pages of your document.

Search and Replace

Suppose you type a long report in which you repeatedly spell the name of a client as "Mr. Nuyan." After you submit the report to your boss, she sends it back to you with this note: "Our client's name is Nguyan, not Nuyan. Please fix this error and send me a corrected copy of the report."

You could scroll through the whole report, looking for "Nuyan" and replacing it with "Nguyan." Then you could save and reprint the report. There is, however, a more efficient way— the **search and replace function.** This function can search through a document quickly, finding each instance of a certain word or phase and replacing it with another word or phase as desired. Note that you make the request just once, but the replacement is done over and over. Most word processing programs offer **conditional replace,** which asks you to verify each replacement. In other instances, the search function can be used by itself to find a particular item in a document.

RANDOM BITS

A Word Processing Glossary

Word processing has its own jargon. In addition to standard terms such as *word wrap* and *cut and paste*, there are phrases to describe the more sophisticated features. Most word processing packages include these features:

Hard space. A hard space is a space linking two words as an unbreakable unit, so they cannot be broken at the end of a line. For example, T. S. Eliot is correct, but if T. comes at the end of a line, the effect is confusing.

Linked paragraphs. Some word processors automatically make sure that a heading is printed on the same page as the paragraphs to which it refers.

Orphan. An orphan occurs when the first line of a paragraph appears alone at the foot of a page or column, while the rest of the paragraph appears in the next one. If the orphan option is invoked, the software prevents orphans by forcing a page or column change before the paragraph begins.

Printer offset. A larger left-hand margin on right-hand pages and a larger right-hand margin on left-hand pages allows extra space for binding or punched holes.

Snaking columns. Also called newspaper-style columns. When the text of the first column reaches the foot of the page, it continues ("snakes") to the top of the second column on the same page.

Soft hyphen. Right-justified printing looks best when long words can be hyphenated to avoid too much space on a line of type. A word processing package lets you insert hyphens that will appear in print only if the word has to be broken at the end of the line.

Widow. A widow occurs when the last line of a paragraph appears alone on the top of a page or column, while the rest of the paragraph appears on the preceding page. If the widow option is invoked, the software prevents widows by forcing a page or column change before only one line remains in a paragraph.

---

past 20 years, computer programmers have been improving the software that turns computers into chess players. With their processing speed and memory capacity, computers can scan thousands of possible moves per second. In fact, supercomputers can scan over 100,000 moves per second—a clear advantage over human players. However, what happens when computers play each other?

In one computer chess match,

the world computer chess champion, a $14 million Cray supercomputer, faced a challenger, a $20,000 Sun microcomputer— and lost. This clash revealed the most important factor in computer chess: the strategy provided by the software. Quite simply, the minicomputer's software was more effective. For Hans Berliner, one of the designers of the winning software, this was just a warm-up match. His ultimate goal is the Fredkin Prize, a $100,000

Orphan

---

you are likely to lose. For the past 20 years, computer programmers have been improving the software that turns computers into chess players. With their processing speed and memory capacity, computers can scan thousands of possible moves per second. In fact, supercomputers can scan over 100,000 moves per second—a clear advantage over human players. However, what happens when computers play each

other?

In one computer chess match, the world computer chess champion, a $14 million Cray supercomputer, faced a challenger, a $20,000 Sun microcomputer— and lost. This clash revealed the most important factor in computer chess: the strategy provided by the software. Quite simply, the minicomputer's software was more effective. For Hans Berliner, one of the designers of the winning soft-

Widow

Printing Options

Printing is fundamental to word processing; no one wants to keep fascinating prose hidden away on disk. We described the WordPerfect printing command in the last chapter. Now it is time to consider some common printing options that you can use when you print a document.

Page Numbering

If you have a multiple-page document, you probably will want each page to be numbered. Many word processing packages automatically number the pages for you. They also let you choose the location—top or bottom of the page—and position—center, flush left, or flush right—of the page number. If you have a one-page document, such as a short letter, then you can indicate that you do not want the page to be numbered.

You can always tell which page you are on by looking at the **status line** on the screen. Usually, this line of information not only lists the page number, it also states the line number and the character position of the cursor. The software displays the status line at the top or bottom of the screen.

Printer Typing Styles

Many printers can change the way the typed words look on a page. For example, you can often choose between various

Figure 5-10 Fonts. One way to change the look of your document is to change the typestyle, or font. This figure shows some of the common fonts available as printer options.

Upper- and lowercase	ALL CAPS
Venice	*VENICE*
New York	NEW YORK
Monaco	MONACO
Times	TIMES
Bookman	BOOKMAN
Zapf Chancery	*ZAPF CHANCERY*
Helvetica	HELVETICA
Chicago	**CHICAGO**
Avant Garde	AVANT GARDE
Park Avenue	*PARK AVENUE*

```
With monospace printing,
each letter takes up the
same amount of space:
ABCDEFGHIJKLMNOPQRSTUVWXYZ
```
(a)

```
With proportional printing,
each letter takes up a
different amount of space:
ABCDEFGHIJKLMNOPQRSTUVWXYZ
```
(b)

Figure 5-11 Proportional versus monospace printing. (a) With the monospace printing option, each character has the same width. (b) With the proportional printing option, character widths differ.

settings for **pitch** (the number of characters per inch), **font** (the style of type), and **lines per inch** (the number of lines printed in an inch). Your word processing software has default settings for these three options. However, most packages let you change one or more of these options before you print a document. For example, you may find that changing the font improves the appearance of some documents. (Figure 5-10, on the previous page, shows some of the different fonts available.) The appearance of the document usually will not change on the screen, but it will look different when it is printed.

Most printers produce characters that are the same width. This type of printing is called **monospace printing.** Some printers can also produce what is known as proportional printing. **Proportional printing** (also called **proportional spacing**) means that wide characters (such as *H* and *M*) occupy more space on the paper than thin characters (such as *i* and *l*), as Figure 5-11 shows. Proportional printing is often used in typeset books and magazines. When used, proportional printing gives your document a professional appearance. If your printer can produce this type of text, then your word processing package will probably let you request the proportional printing option.

Figure 5-12 Continuous fanfold paper. Using continuous fanfold paper is an efficient way to print form letters and long documents.

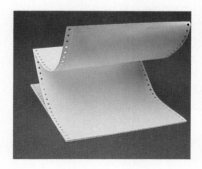

Printing Multiple Copies

Word processing software is often used to create documents that must be seen by more than one person. Examples of this are memos or minutes of meetings that are sent to all the members of a committee. If a copy machine is not available or if photocopies are not desirable, most word processing packages can automatically print any number of copies you request.

Printing on Single Sheets

Most printing is done on **continuous fanfold paper** (Figure 5-12). The software's default setting assumes that your printer is using this paper. Some printers, however, have an option that lets you use single sheets. This is useful when the final version of a document must be printed on letterhead stationery or on especially high-quality or colored paper. After the first page is printed, the software pauses to let you remove the printed sheet and insert a new sheet of paper.

Pressing a key on your keyboard signals the word processing software to begin printing the second page of the document. Then the software pauses before printing the third page, and so on until the end of the document. When you are finished printing, you can return to the default setting and reload the printer with continuous fanfold paper.

Extra Added Attractions

The popularity of word processing programs has encouraged the development of some very helpful programs that are used in conjunction with word processing software. These programs analyze text that has already been entered. Some of the most widely used programs of this type can check spelling, provide a thesaurus, monitor grammar and style, write form letters, and generate tables of contents and indexes. If your reports are riddled with spelling errors and typos, then you might find a spelling checker especially helpful.

Spelling Checker Programs

A **spelling checker program** will find any spelling errors you may have made when typing a document. The program compares each word in your document to the words it has in its "dictionary." A spelling checker's dictionary is a list of from 20,000 to 100,000 correctly spelled words. If, while looking through your document, the spelling checker program finds a word that is not on its list, it assumes that you have misspelled or mistyped that word. Some spelling checkers place a special mark (such as the @ symbol) next to the offending word. Others highlight the suspect word by making it brighter or a different color. When the checker program is finished, you use your word processing program to look through your document for any marked words. Spelling checkers often do not recognize proper names, such as Ms. Gillen, or acronyms, such as NASA. So you must decide if the word is actually misspelled. If the word is misspelled, you can correct it easily with the word

Figure 5-13 Spelling checker. *The highlighted word "conjusion" is a misspelling, so the spelling checker offers some alternatives in the area below the dashed lines. In this case, pressing A replaces the misspelled word with the correct spelling.*

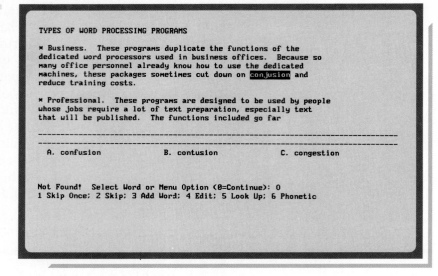

```
TYPES OF WORD PROCESSING PROGRAMS

× Business.  These programs duplicate the functions of the
dedicated word processors used in business offices.  Because so
many office personnel already know how to use the dedicated
machines, these packages sometimes cut down on conjusion and
reduce training costs.

× Professional.  These programs are designed to be used by people
whose jobs require a lot of text preparation, especially text
that will be published.  The functions included go far

--------------------------------------------------------------
--------------------------------------------------------------

  A. confusion            B. contusion          C. congestion


Not Found!  Select Word or Menu Option <0=Continue>: 0
1 Skip Once; 2 Skip; 3 Add Word; 4 Edit; 5 Look Up; 6 Phonetic
```

processing software. If the word is correct, then you delete the mark.

A more sophisticated type of spelling checker program highlights a word that it believes is misspelled. Then it displays all the words from its dictionary that are close in spelling or sound to the word you typed. In other words, the program tries to help you out by displaying all the words that it thinks you may be trying to spell (Figure 5-13). If you recognize the correct spelling of the word in the list you are given, you can replace the incorrect word with the correct word from the list. If the word the program thought was misspelled is correct, you just leave it unchanged and signal the spelling checker to continue searching through your document. Some spelling checkers even check your spelling as you are typing. As soon as you type a word that the checker does not recognize, it causes the computer to sound a beep to catch your attention. Then it offers suggestions in the usual way. (Some people do not like machines beeping at them. They prefer to turn this feature off and find their errors later.)

The best spelling checkers let you create your own auxiliary dictionaries. If a word in your document is not in the spelling checker's main dictionary, the program then searches through your special dictionaries. This can be very useful. Suppose, for example, that you often write to a client named Mr. Mitchell and use computer jargon such as *byte* and *mainframe.* An ordinary dictionary would flag the words "Mitchell," "byte," and "mainframe" as misspelled. If you add these terms, which are correct in your environment, to your auxiliary dictionary, they will be considered correct in the future.

If you have this type of spelling checker, you should add to your auxiliary dictionary the names of your friends and business associates and words that are often used in your job or field of study. Some spelling checkers come with special dictionaries for the medical, legal, or computer professions. You can even buy dictionaries that include words from a foreign language.

Many word processing programs include their own spelling checkers as part of the word processing package; that is, the spelling checkers are built in. This makes the checkers very easy to use. Once you have entered your text by using the word processing software, all you have to do to check your spelling is press a key.

Thesaurus Programs

Have you ever chewed on the end of your pencil trying to think of just the right word—a better word than the bland one that immediately comes to mind? Perhaps you were energetic enough to haul down a thesaurus and look the word up. A **thesaurus** is a book that gives synonyms (words with the same meaning) and antonyms (words with the opposite meaning) for common words. But never mind the big books. Now you can have a great vocabulary at your fingertips—electronically, of course. Your access to this word supply is via a **thesaurus program** (Figure 5-14), which may be part of your word processing program or a separate disk used in conjunction with the program.

Figure 5-14 A thesaurus program. *The words labeled A through K are synonyms for the highlighted word "remove."*

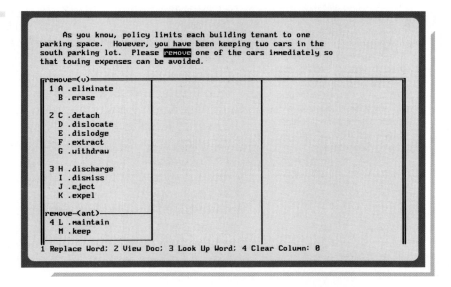

Suppose you find a word in your document that you have used too frequently or that just does not quite seem to fit. Place the cursor on the word. Then press the appropriate key to activate the thesaurus program. The program immediately provides a list of synonyms for the word you want to replace. You can then replace the old word in your document with the synonym you prefer. It is easy, and it is even painlessly educational.

If your word processing software does not have built-in spelling checker or thesaurus programs, you can purchase them as separate packages. But be sure that they are designed to work with your particular software. These separate programs can be loaded into memory and executed. The first thing the program will ask you for is the name of the file containing the document that is supposed to be checked. Once you supply the file name, the checking or replacing operations occur in the same way as with the built-in programs.

GETTYSBURG REVISITED

Some people are worried that the style and grammar programs will remove true originality and give all prose an unattractive sameness. Consider the ringing words of Abraham Lincoln at Gettysburg: "Fourscore and seven years ago our fathers brought forth upon this continent a new nation, conceived in liberty, and dedicated to the proposition that all men are created equal."

When rewritten by a style program, this Gettysburg line became "Eighty-seven years ago our ancestors started a free country here, where people are equal." Not exactly inspiring. Obviously, we need not always take a computer's advice.

Grammar and Style Programs

A computer program cannot offer creativity, inspiration, class, elegance, or ingenuity. In short, no program will make you the next Shakespeare or Hemingway. But there are programs that can improve your writing: They are called **grammar and style programs.** When you write using a word processing program, these extra programs can identify some of your grammatical or stylistic flaws. Let us consider some specific features.

A grammar and style program—sometimes called an editing program—can identify unnecessary words or wordy phrases that appear in your writing. To help you eliminate repetition, it can check to see if particular patterns of words appear again and again. It can also check for sentences that seem too long (run-on sentences) and indicate that you should break them up into several short sentences for clearer writing.

Grammar and style programs can also identify spelling errors that a spelling checker program cannot pick up. For example, the word "four" is a correctly spelled word and would not be flagged by a spelling checker. However, "four example" is an incorrect use of the word *four*, and thus a spelling error. Editing programs identify this kind of problem. Consider another error that most spelling checkers do not notice: correctly spelled double-typed words. For example, if you inadvertently type "on the the table," many spelling checkers would pass right over the two occurrences of the word "the." Editing programs spot such errors for you. Most grammar and style programs do not try to correct grammatical errors—they just point them out and you take it from there. Even if you are not the next great American novelist, you can use these programs to produce correct and clear English.

Form Letter Programs

A form letter used to be rather primitive, with your name typed—often in a different font—as an afterthought. No more. Now **form letter programs**—sometimes called mail-merge programs—can be used to send out masses of "personalized" letters that cannot be distinguished from a letter produced on a fine typewriter. These programs have been a boon to fundraising and political groups and a bane to the weary citizens who are tired of mounds of junk mail in their mailboxes. But, junk or not, these mailings are effective and, therefore, here to stay. In fact, you can join in and use them for your own group or organization. Here is how form letter programs work.

■ First you create and store the form letter by using your word processing program. Instead of actually typing a person's name and address, you type some predefined symbols in the appropriate places in the letter (Figure 5-15a).

Figure 5-15 A form letter program. *A form letter program works in conjunction with your word processing program. With them you combine (a) text with (b) names and addresses to create (c) good-looking individualized letters.*

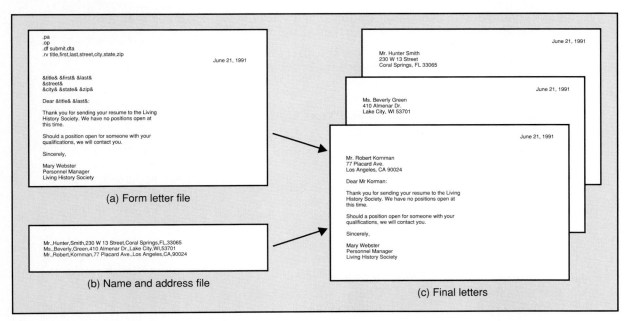

(a) Form letter file

(b) Name and address file

(c) Final letters

- You then store all the individual names and addresses in a second file (Figure 5-15b) by using your word processing program.

- Your last step is to ask the form letter program to print, on your printer, as many form letters as you have names in your second file (Figure 5-15c).

Each time the program prints a letter, it replaces the symbols with a new name and address from the second file. The form letter program automatically adjusts the form letter for differences in the length of each person's name and address. Each one of the letters looks as if it has been typed especially for the addressee. This is the "personal touch" in the electronic age.

KEYSTROKES ONLY

Special WordPerfect Features

These instructions are for using many of the formatting options, printing options, and other special features described in this chapter. For most of these commands, you need to use the function keys. The plastic template that fits over the function keys is a helpful reminder.

Changing the Spacing

1. To change the spacing for the whole document, move the cursor to the top of the document.

2. Press the Shift key and F4 together. Then select 4 to access the spacing options.

3. Enter the number of line spaces you want between each line of text—1 is one line space, 2 is two line spaces, and 3 is three line spaces. Then press Enter.

Changing the Tab Stops

1. Press the Shift key and F8 together. Then select 2 to access the tab option.

2. Follow the directions on the screen to set the new tab stops.

Creating Text Columns

1. Press the Alt and F7 keys to access the column options.

2. Choose 4 to define the columns you want to have. Follow the instructions on the screen to define the columns. Press Enter. WordPerfect returns you to the column options.

3. Choose 3 to turn the column option on.

Creating Page Headers and Footers

1. Press the Alt key and F8 together.

2. Select the header/footer option by typing 6.

3. Follow the directions on the screen to create your header and/or footer.

Creating Subscripts and Superscripts

1. To mark a subscript or superscript, press Shift-F1 just before the character you want to mark as a subscript or a superscript. Then select from the options offered on the screen.

2. A lowercase "s" in the lower left of the screen lets you know that the next character will be a subscript. An uppercase "S"

Table of Contents and Index Generator Programs

Most students never need to use a table of contents program or an index generator. But authors of lengthy and formal writing, such as books or scholarly tomes, usually benefit from these programs. To use **a table of contents program,** the author presses a designated **key** to place special marks by chapter headings as he or she **writes.** When the author is finished, the table of contents **generator** notes the page numbers on which the marked headings **occur** and generates a table of contents for the book. This **table** lists the headings and the pages on which the headings **occur.**

An **index generator program** works in a similar way. The author marks important terms in the text by pressing appropriate keys. Then he or she runs the index generator. The program sorts and then prints all the marked terms in alphabet-

---

tells you that the next character will be a superscript. Type the character. The subscript or superscript will appear above or below the line only when the document is printed.

Creating Footnotes and Endnotes

1. Press the Ctrl key and the F7 key together.

2. Select from the footnote and endnote options displayed on the screen.

Using the Search and Replace Functions

To use the search function:

1. Press F2. The message "Srch:" appears. Type in a word, phrase, or character, then press F2 again. The search will progress from the cursor location to the end of the document.

2. To search backwards from the cursor location to the beginning of the document, press the Shift key and F2 together.

To use the search and replace function:

1. Press Alt and F2 together. The message "w/ Confirm?(Y/N) N" appears. Type Y to verify each replacement individually.

2. The message "Srch:" appears. Type in the word or characters you wish to replace, then press F2.

3. Next the message "Replace with:" appears. Type in the substitution, then press F2 again.

Creating Page Numbers

1. Press the Alt and F8 keys. Then press 1 to select the page number option.

2. Select the appropriate position for the number.

Using the Spelling Checker

Note: To use the spelling checker, you must have the checker program on your WordPerfect disk or on another disk. If you do not have the program, you cannot use this option.

1. Press Ctrl and F2 simultaneously. Then press 3 if you want the entire document to be checked.

Using the Thesaurus

Note: To use the thesaurus program, you must have it on your WordPerfect disk or on another disk. If you do not have the program, you cannot use this option.

1. Place the cursor under the word you want to look up.

2. Press Alt and F1 simultaneously.

ical order. After each term the program also prints the pages in the book on which the term is used or explained. As you can imagine, the table of contents and index generator programs are great labor savers.

Managing Disk Files

As the number of files on a diskette or hard disk grows, you will realize the need to organize file storage. Word processing software can help you keep track of the names and contents of your files.

What's in a File Name?

It is time to name the new file. What will the name be? Well, of course, it must fall within the DOS file name guidelines that we mentioned in Chapter 3—it can consist of up to eight characters (letters and numbers). It must also be unique. That is, a new file name must be different from every other file name on the same disk.

The eight-character limit on file names presents a problem to many people: How can you describe the contents of a file in eight characters? Even if you pick a meaningful name, you may not remember your naming technique later. The solution does not involve any particular command or function key: Many people solve this problem by keeping a special file that describes all the other files.

The idea is simple enough. Pick an easy-to-remember file name like CONTENTS. In CONTENTS, enter the file name and a short description of each document (Figure 5-16). For information on the contents of any file on your disk, retrieve CONTENTS and scroll through it as you would a table of contents. Your word processing software makes it easy to add and delete entries in this document whenever you add or delete files from the disk.

Uniqueness is another important factor in file naming. Suppose you ignore the uniqueness requirement and choose a name that already exists. Your word processing package will not give up the existing file easily. If the software needs a file name before it can open, or start, a file and you give the name of an existing file, the software will assume that you want to look at the existing file. If you try to name the file once it has been written, and you offer an existing name, the software tells

Figure 5-16 A sample contents file. You can use a file like the one shown here to keep a list of each file name and the contents of the documents.

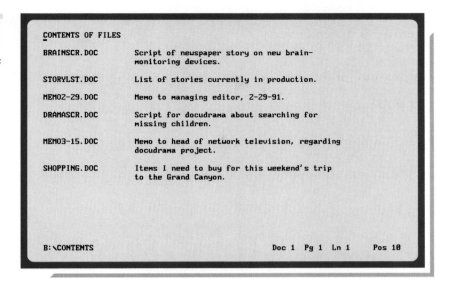

```
CONTENTS OF FILES

BRAINSCR.DOC      Script of newspaper story on new brain-
                  monitoring devices.

STORYLST.DOC      List of stories currently in production.

MEMO2-29.DOC      Memo to managing editor, 2-29-91.

DRAMASCR.DOC      Script for docudrama about searching for
                  missing children.

MEMO3-15.DOC      Memo to head of network television, regarding
                  docudrama project.

SHOPPING.DOC      Items I need to buy for this weekend's trip
                  to the Grand Canyon.




B:\CONTENTS                                Doc 1  Pg 1  Ln 1      Pos 10
```

you about the duplication and asks if you really want to overwrite—replace—the existing file with the new file. In fact, many word processing packages are so busy protecting you from yourself that it can get a little tiresome. *Are you sure you want to do that?* is a common theme. One way to make sure your file name is unique is to use the software's list function, a command that is similar to the DIR command in DOS.

Listing File Names

Remember the DIR command in DOS? The DIR command lists all the file names on a disk. But if you want to use it when you are using a word processing program, you must first exit the word processing software and load DOS. The problem is that your document must be named and saved before you exit the word processing program. Also, switching back and forth between your word processing software and DOS is time-consuming.

A better alternative is the DIR-like commands that are part of word processing software and can be used while you are working on a document. These commands let you check the names of the files you have on your data disk without leaving the word processing program. Some word processing software displays a list of the files on your data disk whenever you start to create a document. With other word processing software, you display the names of your disk files by pressing a function key. This will not disturb the document you are working on: The screen is momentarily filled with file names, but your

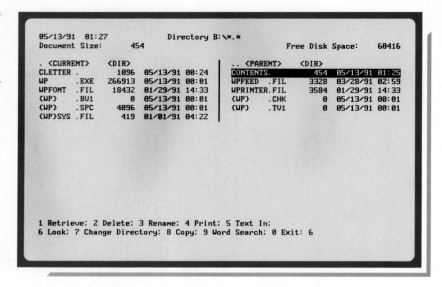

Figure 5-17 A WordPerfect directory list. *The DIR-like commands that are often part of word-processing software let you see a list of all the files on a disk without having to exit the program first.*

document returns at the press of a key. When you want to name and save a document, press the key to see the list of files. Then select a unique file name and save the document (Figure 5-17).

The ability to see a list of the file names you have on your disk is also useful when you cannot recall the name of a file you want to retrieve from the disk. To refresh your memory, just press the function key to list the names of your existing files.

When the Disk Gets Full

If you store a number of large documents on a disk, you eventually run out of storage space on that disk. When this happens, your request to save a document will be met with the message, "Disk Full." Don't worry—your document is not lost; it is still in memory. But you need to place a different formatted disk in drive B and make the save request again.

As alternative to saving the file on a different disk is to use the **delete file function.** This frees space on the disk so that a new save request will be successful. When you use the delete file function, you will be asked for the name of the file you want to delete. Delete any files you no longer need. Then save the current file. As we mentioned in Chapter 3, it is a good idea to use the DOS DIR command to see how many free bytes remain on your data disk. When it starts to get full, use a new data disk.

We Hope You Are Convinced

We hope you are convinced that word processing is a great time-saver. We hope you are convinced that word processing is easy to learn. We hope you are convinced that word processing is the best software tool—well, one of the best tools—for microcomputers. And, most of all, we hope you are convinced that word processing is essential for your career, no matter what it is.

Word processing, however, is not the only important software tool. Some people, in fact, are much more interested in software that works with numbers rather than words. We are talking, of course, about spreadsheet software. This important topic is the subject of our next chapter.

Exercises

5-1

1. Load your word processing program and insert a formatted disk in drive B. Then enter the letter shown in Figure 5-18 (on the next page), making corrections, when needed, as you type. Use the Tab key to begin each paragraph at the first tab stop. Do not worry if the lines on your screen do not look exactly like the sample—your word processing program may allow a different number of characters per line.
2. Save the letter on your data disk. The file name should be EX5-1.
3. Call EX5-1 to your screen and mark the second paragraph (including blank lines) as a block.
4. Use your word processing software's Block Move command to move the marked paragraph below the third paragraph.
5. Save the revised letter as EX5-1A.
6. Print the letter with a ragged-right margin.
7. Exit the word processing program.

5-2

1. Reload the word processing program. Retrieve the EX5-1A file.
2. Mark the last sentence of the second paragraph as a block.
3. Use the Block Delete command to delete the block.
4. Save the new file as EX5-2.
5. Without exiting the word processing program, use the appropriate commands for your package to clear the screen.

Figure 5-18

Mr. Louis Stern
STA International
333 Homewood Avenue
Durham, NC 27702

Dear Mr. Stern:

I am writing to inquire about any openings that STA International may have in technical writing.

I have just graduated from the University of North Carolina, Chapel Hill, with a B.A. in writing and a minor in physics. My course work also included math, chemistry, and biology.

As my resume shows, I have already had some experience as a free-lance editor of computer manuals. I have also been involved in other forms of editing and writing for the past two years. I have had experience in many aspects of publication, including copy writing, proofreading, layout, pasteup, and typesetting.

Would it be possible for us to meet to discuss this further? I can be reached by phone at 919-967-0000.

Sincerely,

Maria Simone

5-3

1. Retrieve the EX5-2 file.
2. Mark the first six lines (address, date, and salutation lines) as a block.
3. Use the Block Save command to save the block as a file named EX5-3. Then use the Block Delete command to delete the block from the letter. Notice that you now have a standard form letter. Save the letter in a file named EX5-3A.
4. Position the cursor at the upper left of the letter on your screen. Then use the retrieve function to insert the file EX5-3 in the letter. Where is the new text inserted?
5. Save the revised letter as EX5-3B.
6. Print two copies of EX5-3B.
7. Exit the word processing program.

Figure 5-19

$$E = MC^2$$

$$Y_2 = B_0 + B_1X_1 + B_2X_2 + B_3X_3$$

$$H_2O$$

$$H_2SO_4 + 2KOH \text{ ---> } K_2SO_4 + 2H_2O$$

$$16x^2 - 9y^3 + 4x^3 - 5y^8 - A_k = B_k{}^4$$

5-4

1. Load your word processing program. Use the subscript and superscript feature to enter the formulas shown in Figure 5-19. Do the subscripts and superscripts appear as such on your screen? If not, is there a way you can see which characters are stored as subscripts and superscripts?
2. Save the formulas in a file named EX5-4.
3. Print the formulas. Are the subscripts and superscripts printed as you want them?
4. Clear the screen.

5-5

1. Enter the text shown in Figure 5-20 and save the file as EX5-5. Make a list of all the incorrect spellings and incorrect usages of correctly spelled words that you find.
2. Use the appropriate keystrokes to run your software's spelling checker program. Correct the misspellings identified by the spelling checker. Does your spelling checker point out that the spelling of "Male" in "Express Male" is incorrect and that the correct spelling is *Mail*? Why or why not?
3. Correct the spellings of the incorrectly used words.
4. Save the revised file as EX5-5A.
5. If you have a thesaurus program, use it to provide alternative words for the word "large" in the last sentence of the paragraph. Select one of the alternative words that the program suggests. Replace the word "large" with the new word you choose.

Figure 5-20 Misspelled words.

Messemger survices opperate only withina city and its sububs. Messinger survices in city usually costs les then Express Male a iss much fastur. Sum large offices empploy there own messingers to pick up and deleaver dokuments.

6. Save the file as EX5-5B.
7. Print the file.
8. Clear the screen.

5-6

1. Enter the report shown in Figure 5-21. Format the report exactly as it is shown in the figure.
2. Use your program's search and replace feature to change "Water" to "water" throughout the page.
3. Save the file as EX5-6.
4. Print the report.
5. Use the appropriate keystrokes to change the single spacing to double spacing.
6. Save the file as EX5-6A.
7. Print the revised report.
8. Now use the page-numbering feature to include a page number at the bottom of the report. The page number should appear centered on the page. Print the report.
9. Use the page-numbering feature again to move the page number to the upper-right corner of the page. Print the report again.

Figure 5-21

WATER ON EARTH

If we could cruise the universe in quest of life, we would do well to search for worlds with Water (H2O). We might not recognize life on dry planets even if it existed. All organisms familiar to us are made mostly of Water and live in a world where Water dominates.

Life probably began in Water, and it has been inextricably tied to Water ever since. Most of the cells in organisms are surrounded by Water; in fact, the cells contain from about 70 percent to 95 percent Water.1 Earth's surface is also wet, with Water covering three-fourths of our planet.

This abundance of Water is a major reason Earth is habitable. In a book many biologists consider a classic, The Fitness of the Environment (1913), Lawrence Henderson highlights the importance of Water to life. While acknowledging that life adapts to its environment through natural selection, Henderson emphasizes that for life to exist at all, the environment must first be a suitable abode.

10. Save the revised file as EX5-6B.
11. Clear the screen.

5-7

1. Enter the material shown in Figure 5-22. Change the spacing so the material is double spaced.

Figure 5-22

ARTS AND DESIGN

Art History
Art Studio
Dramatic Art
Graphic Design
Interior Design
Photography

BUSINESS AND MANAGEMENT

Accounting
Business Law
Computers and Information Systems
Economics
Finance
General Business
International Business
Marketing
Small Business/Entrepreneurship

BIOLOGY

Anatomy
Bioethics
Biotechnology
Ecology
Immunology
Zoology

ENGINEERING

Artificial Intelligence
Civil Engineering
Computer Science
General Electronics
Microelectronics
Semiconductor Devices
Signal Processing
Telecommunications

HUMANITIES

History
Languages
Literature
Writing
Political Science

2. Save the file as EX5-7.
3. Use a spelling checker program to check for any misspelled words. Save the revised file as EX5-7A.
4. Use your program's text column feature to give the material a two-column format. Save the revised file as EX5-7B.
5. Print the listing.
6. Now use the Block Move command to move the Biology course section before the Business and Management section. Save the revised file as EX5-7C.
7. Print the revised listing.
8. Clear the screen.

5-8

Assume that you are working for a real estate office. You need to prepare informational letters for potential home buyers. Some of these buyers qualify for one or more of the many mortgage insurance programs offered by the federal government. Your supervisor asks you to type up letters that contain the appropriate information for two prospective buyers. She also wants you to store the information on the different mortgage programs. To do so, follow these steps:

1. Set your left margin to 12 and your right margin to 68. Set your first tab stop to 26.
2. Enter in all the information shown in Figure 5-23 except the information that appears in brackets at the end of each paragraph. Format the entries exactly as shown in the figure.
3. Use the appropriate commands to mark and then store each individual mortgage program (each paragraph). Use the names that appear in the brackets at the end of each section as the file name for that section.
4. Create the two letters shown in Figure 5-24, using the retrieve function to insert the appropriate sections as you type. The margin settings for the first and last paragraphs of the letters should be left = 10 and right = 74. The margin settings for the portion of the letter that contains the mortgage descriptions should be left = 12 and right = 68.
5. Save the letter to the Smiths as EX-8A. Save the letter to Ms. Wilcox as EX-8B.
6. Use the search function to search for the word "mortgage" in one of the letters. How many times does the word appear?
7. Print the letter to the Smiths with double-spaced lines and a ragged-right margin.
8. Print the letter to Ms. Wilcox with single-spaced lines, vertically centered on the page, and a right-justified margin.
9. Exit the program.

Figure 5-23

Section 100. Insurance for loans granted for home improvements, alterations, and repairs. These loans are usually limited to $5,000.00. [EX5-100]

Section 110. Insurance for loans granted for constructing or buying a home or for refinancing an existing mortgage debt. The home must be an individual's principal residence. [EX5-110]

Section 203. Mortgage insurance for one- to four-family homes at the FHA-prescribed interest rate. [EX5-203]

Section 213. Mortgage insurance for new seasonal homes that meet Title 10 requirements. [EX5-213]

Section 221. Mortgage insurance for one- to four-family dwellings for persons displaced by urban renewal or eminent domain. [EX5-221]

Section 232. Mortgage insurance for dwellings of members of the armed forces, including the Coast Guard. [EX5-232]

Section 240. Mortgage insurance for implementing the construction of experimental housing using new materials or new designs. [EX5-240]

Section 255. Home ownership assistance program for low- and moderate-income families. [EX5-225]

Figure 5-24

July 12, 1990

Dear Mr. and Mrs. Smith:

The Park Forest Realty Co. has determined that you are eligible for the following federal home buyers assistance programs:

Section 203. Mortgage insurance for one- to four-family homes at the FHA-prescribed interest rate.

Section 221. Mortgage insurance for one- to four-family dwellings for persons displaced by urban renewal or eminent domain.

Section 240. Mortgage insurance for implementing the construction of experimental housing using new materials or new designs.

We would be pleased to assist you in applying for the above assistance at one of our convenient neighborhood offices.

Yours truly,

Jose Hernandes

(a)

continued ▶

Figure 5-24 (continued)

July 14, 1990

Dear Ms. Wilcox:

The Park Forest Realty Co. has determined that you are eligible for the following federal home buyers assistance programs:

Section 110. Insurance for loans granted for constructing or buying a home or for refinancing an existing mortgage debt. The home must be an individual's principal residence.

Section 221. Mortgage insurance for one- to four-family dwellings for persons displaced by urban renewal or eminent domain.

Section 232. Mortgage insurance for dwellings of members of the armed forces, including the Coast Guard.

Section 255. Home ownership assistance program for low- and moderate-income families.

We would be pleased to assist you in applying for the above assistance at one of our convenient neighborhood offices.

Yours truly,

Jose Hernandes

(b)

Summary and Key Terms

- A **text block** is a unit of text—one or more words, phrases, sentences, paragraphs, or even pages. Text blocks can be moved, deleted, copied, saved, and inserted. To manipulate a block of text, you must first define, or **mark,** the block. The marked block often stands out in **reverse video** on the screen.

- Use the **Block Move command** to move the text to a different location; this process is also known as cutting and pasting. The **Block Delete command** lets you delete a block of text. The **Block Copy command** copies the block of text into a new location, leaving the text in its original location.

- Word processing programs let you create a document from parts of documents that have been previously saved in another disk file. This process is known as **boilerplating.**

- Word processing programs offer many formatting options. You can change the line spacing of a document. You can change the preset, or **default, tab settings** to change the **tab,** the place where the cursor automatically goes when the Tab key is pressed. Also, you can create **page headers** and **page footers,** lines of text that are automatically printed on each page of a document.

■ Other features, such as **subscripts** and **superscripts** and the automatic setting of **footnotes** and **endnotes** are offered by most word processing programs. Another feature, the **search and replace function,** quickly searches through a document to find each instance of a certain word or phrase and replaces it with another word or phrase. Most programs offer **conditional replace,** which asks you to verify each replacement.

■ Word processing packages usually have a number of printing options, including automatic page numbering and different page number positions.

■ The **status line,** which is displayed at the top or bottom of the screen, states the page number, line number, and character position of the cursor.

■ Many printers can change the way the printed pages look: You can often choose between various settings for **pitch, font,** and **lines per inch.** Most printers offer only **monospace printing.** Some printers also offer **proportional printing,** or **proportional spacing.** Most word processing programs

can automatically print multiple copies of a document. Another printing option is to print on single sheets of paper rather than on **continuous fanfold paper.**

■ A number of special programs work in conjunction with the word processing software, analyzing text that has been entered already. These programs include a **spelling checker program,** which includes a built-in dictionary, and a **thesaurus program,** which includes a built-in **thesaurus,** a reference that supplies synonyms and antonyms. **Grammar and style programs,** sometimes called editing programs, identify wordy phrases, repetition, run-on sentences, and spelling errors that cannot be identified by a spelling checker. **Form letter programs**—sometimes called mail-merge programs— allow you to create "personalized" form letters automatically. With a **table of contents program,** you easily set up a table of contents, and an **index generator program** helps people create indexes.

Review Questions

1. What is meant by the term *text block*?

2. Name five operations that can be performed on a block of text.

3. What is the difference between a Block Move and a Block Copy operation?

4. What is boilerplating?

5. Without using keystrokes, describe the steps needed to save and retrieve a block of text.

6. What are page headers? Page footers?

7. What are tab stops?

8. Give an example of a superscript. Give an example of a subscript.

9. What does the search and replace function allow you to do?

10. What is the function of a thesaurus program?

11. What is the meaning of pitch? Font?

12. What is proportional printing?

13. How does a spelling checker recognize spelling errors in a document?

14. When using word processing, how can you list the names of the files on your data disk?

15. What steps can you take if you get a "disk full" message when you try to save a document?

FROM THE REAL WORLD

Generation Gap at the Office

At a time when most corporate executives are recognizing the utility of personal computers, many members of the legal profession are reluctant to go near a keyboard. Part of the problem seems to be due to cultural factors. Many law offices, for example, are organized so that the attorneys have secretaries who do all their typing. In fact, many senior attorneys do not know how to type and do not necessarily think it is appropriate for them to do so. As one senior attorney put it, "Lawyers aren't typists." It seems unlikely that they will give up what one worker called "their antiquated manual systems."

Young lawyers, on the other hand, tend to be computer literate and to know how to use word processing software to prepare legal reports. In fact, savvy attorneys are using computers as a legitimate tool to address many of their day-to-day chores, including looking up legal precedents stored in computer files.

Many offices are split between attorneys who are adamantly opposed to bringing technology into the office and those who feel that it is long overdue. The split can be dramatic, emphasizing a clear and sometimes stressful generation gap in the law office.

There are three groups involved in the office struggle. At the top are the law office executives. They lean toward technology because they need the management tools that a personal computer provides. The young attorneys also want computers because they know that personal computers can make them more efficient. And in the middle are the bulk of attorneys who have no wish to change their way of doing business.

Who will win this battle of wills? It might seem that the "techies" must eventually triumph, but that is not a foregone conclusion. On one hand there is the money issue. Can senior partners be persuaded that a $4000 computer system is really of significantly greater value than a $400 typewriter? On the other hand, some law offices have offered a personal computer to any attorney who wants one and have found few takers. In a worst-case scenario one law office actually dissolved over the computerization issue. Several partners would not accept the advantages of technology; their adversaries disdainfully referred to them as the "quill pen set."

One young attorney makes a convincing case for personal computers by noting that everything is a function of time. "If you are going to continue to operate the way you did 20 years ago, you're going to be left behind, because I can beat you at every turn."

6 Introducing Spreadsheets

Chapter Objectives

After reading this chapter you should be able to

- Describe the difference between a manual spreadsheet and an electronic spreadsheet

- Describe how businesses can use spreadsheets

- Explain the different parts of the spreadsheet screen

- Explain automatic recalculation

- Create a simple spreadsheet

- Use several spreadsheet commands

Do you remember Bob Cratchit in Charles Dickens's *A Christmas Carol*? He spent his time shivering in Scrooge's business office, copying figures into ledger books. The pages in such books, ruled into rows and columns, are called worksheets or **spreadsheets** (Figure 6-1a). The manually constructed spreadsheet has been used as a business tool for centuries. Spreadsheets can be used to organize and present business data, thus aiding managerial decisionmaking. But spreadsheets are not limited to businesses. Personal and family budgets, for example, are often organized on spreadsheets.

Unfortunately, the work involved in manually creating a large spreadsheet is time-consuming and tedious, even when using a calculator or copying results from a computer printout. Another problem with manual spreadsheets is that it is too easy to make a mistake. You may not discover the mistakes, and this could have serious consequences for the business and possibly your job. If you do discover the mistake after the spreadsheet is finished, you must manually redo the calculations that used the wrong number.

Electronic Spreadsheets

An **electronic spreadsheet** is a computerized version of a manual spreadsheet (Figure 6-1b). Working with a spreadsheet on a computer eliminates most of the drudgery of setting up a manual spreadsheet. In general, it works like this: You enter the data you want in your spreadsheet and then key in the types of calculations you need. The electronic spreadsheet program automatically does all the calculations for you and produces the results. The program does not make any calculation errors, and if you want a printed copy of the worksheet, it can be produced quickly. Also, you can store your electronic spreadsheet on your disk so that it can be used again. But the greatest labor-saving aspect of the electronic spreadsheet is that when you change one value or formula in your worksheet, all the rest of the values on the spreadsheet are recalculated automatically to reflect the change.

Spreadsheet programs are very versatile. Let us pause for just a moment to list some specific business applications.

- **Budget management.** You can use a spreadsheet to list anticipated expenses for your business and all the anticipated sources of income. Then use the spreadsheet to analyze your expenditures. In addition, you can analyze

Figure 6-1 Manual versus electronic spreadsheets. (a) This manual spreadsheet is a typical spreadsheet consisting of rows and columns. (b) The same spreadsheet created with a spreadsheet program.

	JAN.	FEB.	MAR.	APR.	TOTAL	MIN	MAX
SALES	1750	1501	1519	1430	6200	1430	1750
COST OF GOODS SOLD	964	980	932	943	3819	932	980
GROSS MARGIN	786	521	587	487	2381	487	786
NET EXPENSE	98	93	82	110	383	82	110
ADM EXPENSE	77	79	69	88	313	69	88
MISC EXPENSE	28	45	31	31	135	28	45
TOTAL EXPENSES	203	217	182	229	831	182	229
AVERAGE EXPENSE	68	72	61	76	277	61	76
NET BEFORE TAXES	583	304	405	258	1550	258	583
FEDERAL TAXES	303	158	211	134	806	134	303
NET AFTER TAX	280	146	194	124	744	124	280

(a)

(b)

expenditures by categories such as labor, office rent, and loan interest. When things change, you can easily see the effect. Suppose, for example, you hire more workers or increase the price of a product. You can quickly check the effect of your move on anticipated profits.

■ **Competitive bidding.** Many industries use spreadsheet software to prepare a bid to compete for a contract. In the construction industry, for example, you can enter in the spreadsheet materials and other resources needed to complete the project. Then you can explore "What if . . ." scenarios by changing types and costs of materials, delivery dates, equipment rentals, number and types of workers, and so forth. This is the way business people determine what combination produces the best—and possibly lowest—bid.

■ **Investments.** In the finance and investment industries, spreadsheets are used to analyze the costs of borrowing money and the profits anticipated from lending money. Spreadsheets are used to analyze investment portfolios by keeping track of dividends and increases or decreases in the value of individual investments. By using spreadsheets to play out various stock-market and economic scenarios, the crucial question—"Do I buy more now or do I sell now?"—is more easily answered. The spreadsheet program gives you the tools to rapidly analyze masses of complex economic data accurately and quickly.

The tasks just described would be tedious and time-consuming if done with a calculator. Electronic spreadsheet programs remove drudgery from the jobs of accountants, marketing managers, stockbrokers, contractors, and others who work with the flow of cash in a business.

RANDOM BITS

No More Erasers

In 1977 Daniel Bricklin was a student in the Harvard School of Business. He spent most of his evenings working on case studies for his classes. This work required the preparation of manual spreadsheets to do cash-flow analyses, profit projections, and other types of financial models. To make decisions about the way the businesses in his case studies should be run, Bricklin had to prepare separate spreadsheets analyzing each alternative available to him as a manager. He often made errors and had to spend hours erasing and redoing his calculations. He, like other students and business managers around the world, was spending too much time doing and redo-

ing arithmetic with a paper, pencil, and calculator. This left less time to study and understand the results of the calculations and to consider what they meant for business.

But what was the alternative? Dan toyed with the idea of doing the calculations for each case on the computer. However, each case study was so different that it would require a new computer program to analyze each case. Using a computer was just not possible. During the winter of 1978, Bricklin and Robert Frankston, a programmer friend, worked to develop a general-purpose program that could be used to solve any spreadsheet problem. This program evolved into

the first electronic spreadsheet, called VisiCalc for *Visible Calculator.*

When VisiCalc was modified to run on the inexpensive Apple II personal computer, a combination was formed that was eagerly accepted by students, businesspeople, and professionals who used numbers in their work. In fact, VisiCalc is credited with being a major factor in making the Apple computer a success. For several years VisiCalc was the best-selling software for a personal computer. Since the introduction of VisiCalc, other companies have produced dozens of different spreadsheet programs.

Spreadsheet Fundamentals

Before we can show you how to use a spreadsheet, we must first discuss some basic spreadsheet features. The characteristics and definitions that follow are common to all spreadsheet programs.

Cells and Cell Addresses

Figure 6-2 shows one type of spreadsheet—a teacher's grade sheet. Notice that the spreadsheet is divided into rows and columns, each labeled with a number or a letter. The rows have *numeric labels* and the columns have *alphabetic labels*. There are actually more rows and columns than you can see on the screen; some spreadsheets have 8192 rows and 256 columns—more than you may ever need to use.

The intersection of a row and column forms a cell. **Cells** are the storage areas in a spreadsheet. When referring to a cell, you use the letter and number of the intersecting column and row. For example, in Figure 6-2, Cell B7 is the intersection of

Figure 6-2 Anatomy of a spreadsheet screen. This screen shows a typical spreadsheet—a teacher's grade sheet. It provides space for 20 rows numbered down the side and 8 columns labeled A through H. The intersection of a row and column forms a cell. When the cursor is on a cell, that cell is known as the active cell.

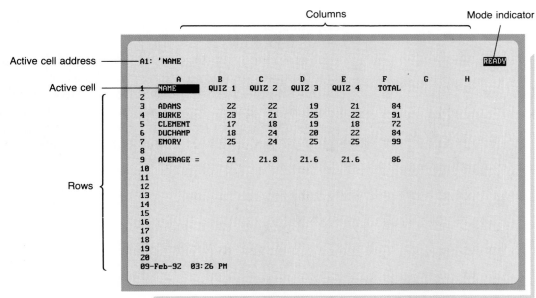

column B and row 7. This reference name is known as the **cell address.**

On a spreadsheet there is always one cell known as the **active cell,** or **current cell.** When a cell is active, you can enter data or edit the cell's contents. The active cell is marked by a highlighted bar—the spreadsheet's cursor. The spreadsheet cursor is also called a **pointer.** The upper-left corner of the screen will display the active cell address. The active cell in Figure 6-2 is Cell A1.

Contents of Cells: Labels, Values, Formulas, and Functions

Each cell can contain one of four types of information: a label, a value, a formula, or a function. A **label** provides descriptive information about entries in the spreadsheet. A cell that contains a label cannot be used to perform mathematical calculations. For example, in Figure 6-2, Cells A1, A9, and F1 contain labels.

A **value** is an actual number entered into a cell to be used in calculations. Values can also be the result of a calculation. In Figure 6-2, for example, Cell B3 contains a value.

A **formula** is an instruction to the program to calculate a number. A formula generally contains cell values and one or more arithmetic operators: a plus sign (+) to add, a minus sign (−) to subtract, an asterisk (*) to multiply, and a slash (/) to divide. When you use a formula rather than entering the calculated result, the software can automatically recalculate the result if any of the values change. Formulas must be entered without spaces between the characters. Figure 6-3 shows some common formulas.

A **function** is a preprogrammed formula. Functions let you perform complicated calculations with a few keystrokes. Two common functions are the @SUM function, which calculates sums, and the @AVG function, which calculates averages. Most spreadsheet programs contain a number of different functions. Figure 6-4 (on page 182) shows some common functions.

Ranges

Sometimes it is necessary to specify a range of cells to build a formula or perform a function. A **range** is a group of one or

Figure 6-3 Some spreadsheet formulas. *Spreadsheet formulas use arithmetic operators to perform calculations.*

FORMULA	MEANING
(A1+A2) or +A1+A2	The contents of cell A1 plus the contents of cell A2
(A2-A1) or +A2-A1	The contents of cell A2 minus the contents of cell A1
(A1*A2) or +A1*A2	The contents of cell A1 times the contents of cell A2
(A2/A1) or +A2/A1	The contents of cell A2 divided by the contents of cell A1
+A1+A2*2	The contents of cell A2 times the number 2 plus the contents of cell A1
(A1+A2)*2	The sum of the contents of cells A1 and A2 times 2
+A1+A2/4	The contents of cell A2 divided by the number 4 plus the contents of cell A1
(A1+A2)/4	The sum of the contents of cells A1 and A2 divided by 4
(A2-A1)*B1	The difference of the contents of cells A1 and A2 times the contents of cell B1
(A2-A1)/B1	The difference of the contents of cells A1 and A2 divided by the contents of cell B1

more cells arranged in a block shape that the program treats as a unit during an operation. Figure 6-5 (on page 183) shows some ranges. To define a range, you must indicate the upper-left and lower-right cells of the block. The cell addresses need to be separated by one period. For example, in Figure 6-2, the QUIZ 1 range is referenced as B3.B9, and the ADAMS range is referenced as B3.F3. In the function @SUM(A4.G8), A4.G8 is the range.

Moving the Cursor

To place data in a cell, you must first move the cursor to that cell. You can use the cursor movement keys to move the cursor one row or column at a time. You can also use the cursor movement keys to scroll through the spreadsheet both vertically and horizontally.

However, moving around a large spreadsheet via the cursor keys can be tedious at times. Most programs let you zip around the spreadsheet by pressing predefined keys and function keys.

For example, if you press the Home key, the cursor moves "home" to Cell A1. Or you can go directly to a cell by pressing a designated **GoTo function key,** also known as the **Jump-To function key.** When you press this key, the software asks you for the desired cell address. You type in the address—for example, D7—and press Enter. The cursor immediately moves to Cell D7. Depending on the current location of the cursor, using the GoTo function key may be the fastest way to get to a cell.

Figure 6-4 Some Lotus 1-2-3 functions. This figure shows some of the built-in functions available in Lotus 1-2-3. These functions let you perform difficult or repetitive calculations with just a few keystrokes.

FUNCTION	MEANING
@SUM(range)	Calculates the sum of a group of numbers specified in an entire range. For example, the formula @SUM(A1..A10) calculates the sum of all numbers in cells A1 through A10.
@AVG(range)	Calculates the average of a group of numbers. For example, the formula @AVG(A1..A10) calculates the average of all the numbers in cells A1 through A10.
@SQRT(y)	Calculates the square root of a number. For example, @SQRT(A2) calculates the square root of the value contained in A2.
@COUNT(range)	Counts the number of *filled* cells in a range and displays the total number of cells containing a value. For example, the formula @COUNT(B1..B5) counts the number of cells in that range that contain values. If there are five of these cells in the range, the function will display the number 5.
@MIN(range)	Calculates and displays the smallest value contained in a range of values.
@MAX(range)	Calculates and displays the largest value contained in a range of values.
@PMT(principal,interest,term)	Calculates the individual payments on a loan with known principal, interest rate, and term. For example, the formula @PMT(A1,B1,C1) calculates the monthly payment by using the contents of A1 as the principal, the contents of B1 as the interest rate, and the contents of C1 as the term of the loan.
@IF(cond,x,y)	Determines whether a condition is true or false by using logical operators to compare numbers. Logical operators include equals (=), less than (<), greater than (>), less than or equal to (<=), and greater than or equal to (>=). The program then processes the data in a certain way, depending on whether the condition is true or false.
@COS(y)	Calculates the cosine of the value y.
@SIN(y)	Calculates the sine of the value y.
@TAN(y)	Calculates the tangent of the value y.

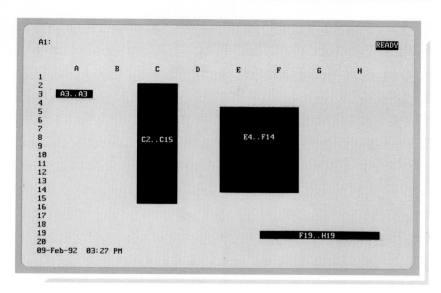

Figure 6-5 Ranges. *A range is a group of one or more cells arranged in a rectangle. You can name a range or refer to it by using the addresses of the upper-left and lower-right cells in the group.*

Operating Modes

A **mode** is the condition or state in which the program is currently functioning, such as waiting for a command or selecting a menu item. Most spreadsheets have three main operating modes: the READY mode, the ENTRY mode, and the MENU mode. The Lotus 1-2-3 spreadsheet screen displays a **mode indicator**—a message that tells you what mode of operation the spreadsheet is currently in—in the upper-right corner of the screen (Figure 6-2, on page 179).

The READY Mode. Most spreadsheets are in the READY mode as soon as they are loaded into the system and the spreadsheet appears on the screen. The **READY mode** indicates that the program is ready for whatever action you want to take, such as moving the cursor, entering data, or issuing a command. As you begin entering data into a cell, you automatically leave the READY mode and enter the ENTRY mode.

The ENTRY Mode. When you are in the **ENTRY mode,** you can enter data into the cells. When a label is being entered, the word "LABEL" appears in the mode indicator; a label is

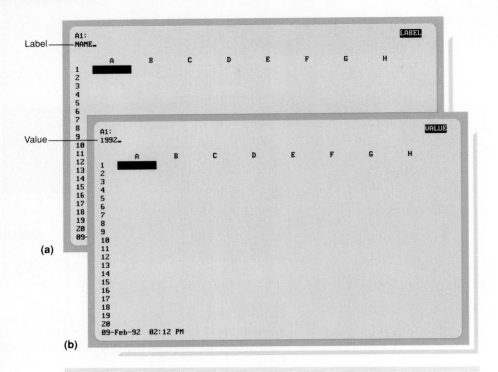

Figure 6-6 The ENTRY mode. *When you are in the ENTRY mode, you can enter data into the cells. (a) When a label is being entered, the word "LABEL" appears in the mode indicator. (b) When a value is being entered, the word "VALUE" appears in the mode indicator.*

recognized by a beginning alphabetic character (Figure 6-6a). The word "VALUE" appears in the mode indicator when a number or formula is being entered into a cell (Figure 6-6b). After you key in the data and press Enter, the information is stored in the cell and the program returns to the READY mode.

When you are in the ENTRY mode, the program does not let you jump or scroll around the spreadsheet—you can only create new cells or make changes to filled cells. The ENTRY mode lets you work on only one cell at a time. But sooner or later you will need to work on a whole group of cells. To do this, you need to enter the MENU, or command, mode.

The MENU Mode. The **MENU mode** lets you use commands to manipulate a large number of cells at one time. Programs display commands in a **command menu,** which is shown near the top of the screen (Figure 6-7). The command menu contains a list, or menu, of different options, such as File and Move. The commands are very important, and we will discuss

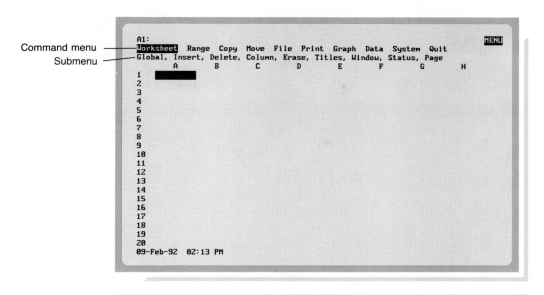

Command menu
Submenu

Figure 6-7 The MENU mode. *When you are in the MENU mode, a command menu appears near the top of the screen.*

them in more detail later in the chapter. For now, all you need to know is that to enter the MENU mode, you press the slash (/) key.

The Control Panel

Spreadsheets can get complicated. To help you keep track of what you are doing, most spreadsheet programs show a **control panel** in the top of the screen. The spreadsheet's control panel usually consists of three lines.

The First Line. The first line of the control panel is a status line. This line tells you the cursor location (the cell address) and the contents of that cell. At times the status line will also show the format—appearance—of the value or label in the cell and the width of the cell. (We will discuss these options in Chapter 7.)

To the far right of the status line is the mode indicator. As we mentioned earlier, this indicator tells you the spreadsheet's current mode of operation.

The Second Line. The second line of the control panel is used in a variety of ways, depending on the operating mode. If you are in the ENTRY mode, the line displays the data you

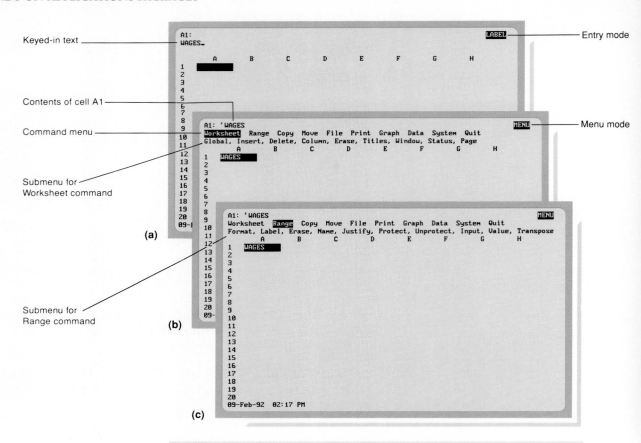

Keyed-in text

Contents of cell A1

Command menu

Submenu for
Worksheet command

Submenu for
Range command

Entry mode

Menu mode

(a)

(b)

(c)

Figure 6-8 The Lotus 1-2-3 control panel. *The first line of the control panel shows you the cursor location and the contents of that cell. (a) When you are in ENTRY mode, the second line of the panel displays the data you are typing in before it is entered into the cell. (b) When you are in the MENU mode, the second line of the panel shows the current menu options, and the third line shows the submenu for the command that the cursor is on. (c) When you move the cursor to another command, the submenu changes.*

are typing in before it is actually entered into the cell (Figure 6-8a). This lets you make changes and corrections before entering the data. If you are in the MENU mode, the line shows the current menu options (Figure 6-8b). This line is also occasionally used for prompts—that is, questions to prompt you for further information needed by the program.

The Third Line. The control panel's third line appears only when the program is in the MENU mode and you have placed the cursor over one of the options. This line shows a **submenu,** a list of options for the command you are choosing (Figure 6-8b).

Let us look at menus and submenus in more detail.

Menus and Submenus

We have already mentioned that you can select spreadsheet commands by choosing from the command menu. Sometimes selecting a command from the menu does not cause a command to be executed; instead, you will see a submenu. This is an additional set of options that refer to the command you selected from the command menu. For example, in Figure 6-8b, the second menu row shows the subcommands—Global, Insert, Delete, Column, and so forth—for the major command Worksheet. Moving the cursor to another major command in the menu causes a different set of commands to appear (Figure 6-8c).

Submenus let you pick only the options that pertain to a particular command. Some of the choices on submenus have options of their own that are displayed on yet another submenu. This layering of menus and submenus lets you first give the computer the big picture with a general command, such as "print a spreadsheet," and then select a particular option for the general command, such as "print the first page."

Now that we have covered the basics of spreadsheets, let us pull this information together and see how you can use spreadsheet software for a practical application.

Creating a Simple Spreadsheet

Learning to use an electronic spreadsheet program requires time. It might be a good idea to read the manual that comes with the program and spend some time experimenting with the program. Electronic spreadsheet programs have much greater capabilities than the average user will ever need. To explain an electronic spreadsheet program completely would require an entire book. However, you can understand how such programs work by studying some examples. The examples we will present use Lotus 1-2-3. (Although primarily known as a popular electronic spreadsheet program, Lotus can also be used as a database program and a graphics program. We will look at the graphics aspects of the program in Chapter 10. Appendix B discusses using Lotus as a database.) Lotus has established a standard approach to electronic spreadsheets; most popular spreadsheet programs work in a similar manner.

Lotus refers to the collection of data keyed into the program as a **worksheet.** Lotus emphasizes the worksheet terminology by saving spreadsheet files with the file name extension

WK1 or WKE. We will use the terms *worksheet* and *spreadsheet* interchangeably.

The Expense Sheet Example

Lyle Mayes teaches a biology course at Wilson High School. He recently bought the Lotus 1-2-3 program and uses it to keep track of his class's grades. Now he wants to use the program to keep track of his expenses. His expense sheet for the months of January through April is shown in Figure 6-9. Notice that each type of expense appears in a separate row of the expense sheet and each column is labeled with the name of a month. The amount of money spent on each item is entered in the cell at the intersection of the appropriate row and column.

The rightmost column of the spreadsheet contains the total amount spent on each item and the total income for the four-month period. At the bottom of each month column, Lyle enters the total amount spent and the balance of his account—the total amount of income minus the total amount of the expenses. As you can see, creating an expense sheet can be a time-consuming chore, and if a mistake is made, a number of recalculations must be done.

Now let us follow the steps that Lyle takes to create this spreadsheet with Lotus 1-2-3. (An abbreviated version of the discussion that follows can be found in the box called "Keystrokes Only: The Expense Sheet Example.")

Figure 6-9 Lyle's expense worksheet. *This is Lyle's handwritten expense sheet. Notice that if he makes any changes to one of the values—for example, the March food expense—he has to do numerous recalculations.*

	JAN.	FEB.	MAR.	APR.	TOTAL
INCOME	2300	2300	2300	2300	9200
EXPENSES					
Rent	525	525	525	525	2100
Food	140	150	150	150	590
Phone	50	64	37	23	174
Heat	80	50	24	20	174
Insurance	75	75	75	75	300
Car	200	200	200	200	800
Leisure	105	120	95	125	445
TOTAL EXPENSES	1175	1184	1106	1118	4583
BALANCE	1125	1116	1194	1182	4617

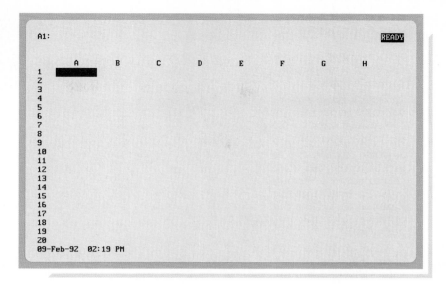

Figure 6-10 A blank spreadsheet. *The blank display indicates that Lotus 1-2-3 is loaded and ready to accept data.*

Loading the Program

To start his work, Lyle first boots the system. Then he places his formatted data disk in drive B and the Lotus 1-2-3 disk in drive A. He types the command to execute the program—either LOTUS or 123, depending on his version of the program. Then he responds to the program prompts until he sees an empty spreadsheet with the cursor positioned in Cell A1 (Figure 6-10). Because a personal computer's screen can display only about 24 lines on a screen with 80 characters per line, the screen display shows only part of all the rows and columns that are available in the computer's memory. An electronic spreadsheet is like a piece of paper; you use only as much as you need. For the expense sheet, Lyle needs to use only columns A through F and rows 1 through 17.

Entering the Labels and Values

Since Lyle already knows what he wants to type into the spreadsheet, he starts by entering the labels—the names of the months and the types of expense. Starting with Cell A3, Lyle types the word INCOME. As he types, the mode indicator display changes from READY to LABEL. When Lyle finishes typing, the second line of the control panel displays the text, "INCOME." Lyle then presses Enter to store his entry in the cell (Figure 6-11, on the next page). When he does this, the mode indicator immediately returns to READY.

PLANNING YOUR SPREADSHEET

1. Determine the results you want to display on your spreadsheet.

2. Determine the data you have to put into your spreadsheet to calculate the results you want.

3. Write down the rules for converting the spreadsheet's inputs to its outputs. These are usually formulas that relate the input values to the output values.

4. Write down the names of the input and output values that you will use in your spreadsheet and the equations you will use. Record the exact forms in which they will be entered in your spreadsheet. Then double check this information to make sure that it is completely correct.

5. Create the electronic spreadsheet by typing in the necessary information. Test your spreadsheet with a range of test values. Check the results produced by the spreadsheet against your own calculations that use the test data. If the results differ, go through your spreadsheet to find your mistake.

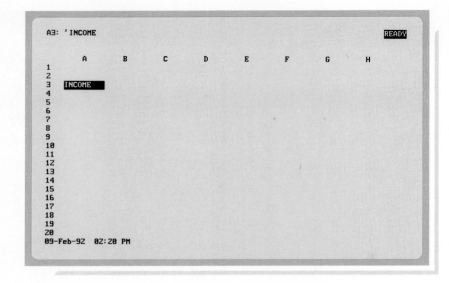

Figure 6-11 Entering labels. *Lyle begins to set up his spreadsheet by entering the labels. When he presses Enter, the label is stored in the cell.*

To enter the rest of the labels and numbers, Lyle follows the same procedure, moving the cursor from cell to cell by using the cursor movement keys. If he makes a mistake as he is typing, he can use the Backspace key to make the correction before moving from the cell. Remember that the cursor must be on a cell to store data in the cell. Figure 6-12 shows Lyle's spreadsheet with all the labels and numbers entered in their cells.

Entering the Formulas and Functions

Lyle must enter the total income for the four months in Cell F3. Lyle could retype each value contained in row 3 (2300 + 2300 + 2300 + 2300) into Cell F3 and then press Enter—the spreadsheet would calculate the total for him and enter the result in F3. But if any of the values in the equation changed, Lyle would have to retype the entry. Instead, Lyle uses a formula that will add the contents of each of the four cells, regardless of their value. The formula he uses is (B3 + C3 + D3 + E3). This formula tells the program to add the values that appear in the cells B3, C3, D3, and E3. Note that all formulas must be enclosed in parentheses or begin with an operation symbol;

Figure 6-12 Entering values. *This screen shows Lyle's spreadsheet with all the labels and numbers entered.*

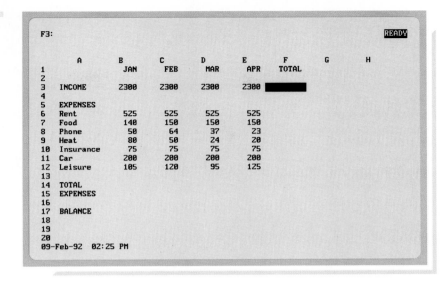

```
F3:                                                                    READY

            A         B         C         D         E         F         G         H
  1                   JAN       FEB       MAR       APR       TOTAL
  2
  3    INCOME         2300      2300      2300      2300    ████████
  4
  5    EXPENSES
  6    Rent           525       525       525       525
  7    Food           140       150       150       150
  8    Phone          50        64        37        23
  9    Heat           80        50        24        20
 10    Insurance      75        75        75        75
 11    Car            200       200       200       200
 12    Leisure        105       120       95        125
 13
 14    TOTAL
 15    EXPENSES
 16
 17    BALANCE
 18
 19
 20
 09-Feb-92   02:25 PM
```

Cell contents

Figure 6-13 Entering formulas. *Lyle has entered the formula (B3 + C3 + D3 + E3) into Cell F3. Notice that the displayed value of the cell is the result of the calculation—9200. When the cursor is on Cell F3, you can see the actual contents of the cell in the upper-left corner of the screen.*

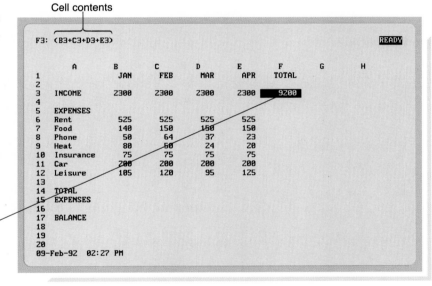

```
F3: (B3+C3+D3+E3)                                                      READY

            A         B         C         D         E         F         G         H
  1                   JAN       FEB       MAR       APR       TOTAL
  2
  3    INCOME         2300      2300      2300      2300     9200
  4
  5    EXPENSES
  6    Rent           525       525       525       525
  7    Food           140       150       150       150
  8    Phone          50        64        37        23
  9    Heat           80        50        24        20
 10    Insurance      75        75        75        75
 11    Car            200       200       200       200
 12    Leisure        105       120       95        125
 13
 14    TOTAL
 15    EXPENSES
 16
 17    BALANCE
 18
 19
 20
 09-Feb-92   02:27 PM
```

Displayed value

otherwise, the program will read the formula as a label. Lyle keys in the formula and presses Enter to store it in Cell F3.

If you look at Figure 6-13, you will see that Cell F3 does not show the formula—instead it shows the *result* of the formula. If the cursor is on the cell, then the formula appears in the upper-left corner of the screen. The result of the formula is the **displayed value** of the cell. The formula itself is the actual **cell contents.** This is an important distinction to remember. Displayed values change if other values in the spreadsheet change. Formulas can be changed only if new information is entered into the cell.

SUM function

***Figure 6-14 Entering func-
tions.*** *Lyle has entered the
Lotus 1-2-3 function
@SUM(F6..F12) in Cell F15.
In this function (F6..F12) is
the range. As with formulas
the cell shows the result of
the calculation, and the
function is shown in the
first line of the control
panel.*

```
F15: @SUM(F6..F12)                                              READY

           A        B        C        D        E        F        G        H
 1                  JAN      FEB      MAR      APR      TOTAL
 2
 3       INCOME     2300     2300     2300     2300     9200
 4
 5       EXPENSES
 6       Rent       525      525      525      525      2100
 7       Food       140      150      150      150      590
 8       Phone      50       64       37       23       174
 9       Heat       80       50       24       20       174
10       Insurance  75       75       75       75       300
11       Car        200      200      200      200      800
12       Leisure    105      120      95       125      445
13
14       TOTAL
15       EXPENSES   1175     1184     1106     1118     4583
16
17       BALANCE
18
19
20
09-Feb-92  02:33 PM
```

Balance formula

***Figure 6-15 A complete
spreadsheet.*** *This screen
shows Lyle's spreadsheet
with all the labels, values,
formulas, and functions in
place.*

```
F17: (F3-F15)                                                   READY

           A        B        C        D        E        F        G        H
 1                  JAN      FEB      MAR      APR      TOTAL
 2
 3       INCOME     2300     2300     2300     2300     9200
 4
 5       EXPENSES
 6       Rent       525      525      525      525      2100
 7       Food       140      150      150      150      590
 8       Phone      50       64       37       23       174
 9       Heat       80       50       24       20       174
10       Insurance  75       75       75       75       300
11       Car        200      200      200      200      800
12       Leisure    105      120      95       125      445
13
14       TOTAL
15       EXPENSES   1175     1184     1106     1118     4583
16
17       BALANCE    1125     1116     1194     1182     4617
18
19
20
09-Feb-92  02:38 PM
```

To calculate the totals in the other rows, Lyle could enter
the formula (B6 + C6 + D6 + E6) for row 6, and so on, for each
of the Cells F6 to F12. However, Lotus provides a simpler way
of summing columns or across rows—the @SUM function.
For example, Lyle can key in @SUM(B6.E6) in Cell F6. This
tells Lotus 1-2-3 to add up the contents of Cells B6 through
E6. The @ symbol tells Lotus that you are entering a function.
The (B6.E6) part of the function is a range; recall that a range
is a group of one or more cells arranged in a block. Lyle uses
the @SUM function with the appropriate ranges for Cells F6

through F12 and Cells B15 through F15. Figure 6-14 shows the result.

Finally, Lyle needs to use a formula to compute the monthly balance. Remember, the monthly balance is the monthly income minus the monthly total expenses. So, for January, Lyle places the formula (B3 − B15) in Cell B17. This tells Lotus to take the value of Cell B15 and subtract it from the value of Cell B3. Lyle then fills in the rest of the balance row. Figure 6-15 shows the resulting spreadsheet.

Making Corrections

Suppose that Lyle realizes that he made a mistake in his January food expense (the correct amount is 150). He also made

---

KEYSTROKES ONLY

The Expense Sheet Example

These instructions are for creating Lyle Mayes's expense sheet, as described in the text. The Lotus 1-2-3 keystrokes that follow can also be used to create your own spreadsheets.

Loading the Program

1. Place Lotus 1-2-3 in drive A and a formatted data disk in drive B.

2. Type LOTUS or 123 followed by Enter. (Note: The command required to load Lotus varies by version. If one command does not work, try the other.)

3. Follow the instructions on the screen. Lotus has been loaded when you see a blank worksheet.

Entering Labels and Values

1. To enter a label or value, move the cursor to the desired cell.

2. Type the label or value. Your entry appears on the second line of the control panel. Use the Backspace key to make corrections.

3. Press Enter. The data appears in the cell.

Entering Formulas and Functions

1. To enter a formula or function, move the cursor to the desired cell.

2. If you are entering a formula, remember that it must be enclosed in parentheses or start with an operator.

3. If you are entering a function, remember that it must start with the @ symbol. You must also define a range for the function. To

do this, look for the starting and ending cells of the range you wish to use, for example, Cells B6 and E6. Then type in the starting cell address, a period, and the ending cell address. The range for cells B6 through E6 would be written B6.E6.

4. Press Enter. The calculated value appears in the cell. To see the formula or function, move the cursor onto the cell and look at the second line of the control panel.

Making Corrections

1. To correct an already filled cell, move the cursor to that cell.

2. Type in the new data.

3. Press Enter. The new data appears in the cell. Any calculations based on that cell are automatically recalculated.

a mistake in his April leisure expense (the correct amount is 123). Since the incorrect cells are already filled, Lyle needs to position the cursor on the filled cell and type in the new data; the keyed-in changes appear in the second line of the control panel. Then Lyle presses Enter and the old data in the cell is replaced by the new data. Lyle moves the cursor over Cell B7, types in 150, and presses Enter. Then he moves the cursor to Cell E12, types in 123, and presses Enter.

If the expense sheet were done manually, Lyle would also have to recalculate the totals for row 7 and row 12 and the total expenses and balances for columns B, E, and F. But since the expense sheet is now entered as an electronic spreadsheet, the spreadsheet program instantly recalculates these values. Figure 6-16 shows the result of typing only the two changed values. Nothing else had to be changed in the worksheet—it automatically adjusted all contents to reflect the changed values.

Automatic recalculation of the whole worksheet usually takes only several seconds. This ability to recalculate a spreadsheet at the touch of a button is what has revolutionized the processes of budgeting and financial modeling. Now people who work with numbers can spend their time analyzing their spreadsheets rather than doing arithmetic.

Now that Lyle has entered his worksheet, he can use the command menu to save, retrieve, and print it.

Figure 6-16 Automatic recalculation. *Lyle enters in the changes for January's food expense and April's leisure expense. Lotus 1-2-3 automatically recalculates the affected totals and balances.*

	A	B	C	D	E	F	G	H
		JAN	FEB	MAR	APR	TOTAL		
1								
2								
3	INCOME	2300	2300	2300	2300	9200		
4								
5	EXPENSES							
6	Rent	525	525	525	525	2100		
7	Food	150	150	150	150	**600**		
8	Phone	50	64	37	23	174		
9	Heat	80	50	24	20	174		
10	Insurance	75	75	75	75	300		
11	Car	200	200	200	200	800		
12	Leisure	105	120	95	**123**	**443**		
13								
14	TOTAL							
15	EXPENSES	**1185**	1184	1106	**1116**	**4591**		
16								
17	BALANCE	**1115**	1116	1194	**1184**	**4609**		
18								
19								
20								

E12: 123   READY

09-Feb-92 02:39 PM

Using Spreadsheet Commands

Using the layered command menu can be a little tricky at first. To help make choosing the proper menus and submenus easier, you can create a command tree. A **command tree,** which looks somewhat like an upside-down tree, shows choices from the main command menu and choices from associated submenus (Figure 6-17). The main command menu line at the top forms the trunk of the tree. Making a command choice from this menu leads you down on a submenu branch. Some of the branches are short and simple, like the one for the Insert command. Others, like Worksheet and Range, have many branches. Each successive branch is reached by selecting from the chain of submenus that appears on the screen.

To take some action—execute an instruction—on your spreadsheet, you must work your way out toward the tip of a branch. The commands along the way, as you go through the layers of menus, are merely vehicles for getting you to the instruction that will take the action you want. You must choose the right options from the submenus to get there. If you make a false step (get into the wrong submenu), you can get back to the next higher menu by pressing the Esc key. In fact, you can get out of the MENU mode completely by continuing to press

Figure 6-17 A command tree. This command tree shows all the submenus associated with the Worksheet command. Notice that if you follow the Worksheet-Erase path there are no additional submenus. However, if you follow the Worksheet-Global path, there are many different choices you can make.

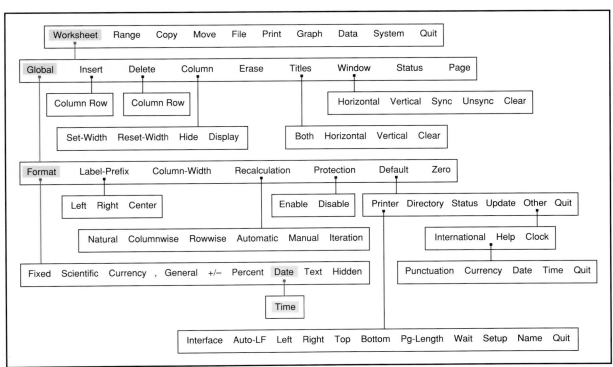

the Esc key until you see READY in the mode indicator. Remember that you work your way down through the levels of submenus by moving the menu cursor to a selection and pressing Enter. You can undo a selection and work your way back up to a previous menu by pressing the Esc key.

Now let us show you the steps Lyle takes to use several of the important commands on the main menu. (An abbreviated version of the discussion that follows can be found in the box called "Keystrokes Only: Using Spreadsheet Commands.")

The File Command

The File command lets you manipulate the Lotus files on your data disk. You can use the File command to perform such tasks as saving files, retrieving files, erasing files, and listing files. Figure 6-18 shows the command tree for the File command. We will look at how to use the File command to save, retrieve, and list files.

Saving a File. Since Lyle is finished with his spreadsheet, he can save it on his data disk by using the File command. To use this command, Lyle must press the / key to obtain the command menu. Next he moves the menu cursor to the word "File" (Figure 6-19a). Notice that Save is one of the choices on the File submenu. With the cursor on File, Lyle presses Enter to access the File submenu. Now the submenu is the active menu. Lyle moves the cursor to Save. When he does, the bottom line of the control panel shows a description of the Save option (Figure 6-19b). Lyle presses Enter to select Save, and

Figure 6-18 The File command. *This figure shows the command tree for the File command.*

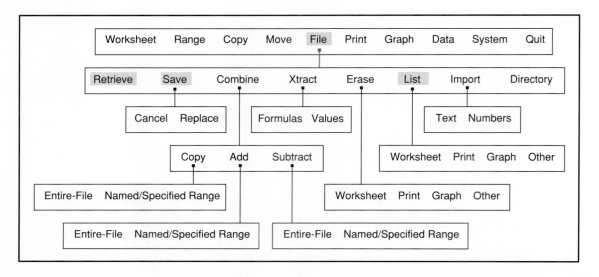

***Figure 6-19 Saving a
file.*** *(a) To select the File
command, Lyle moves the
cursor to the word "File."
Note the submenu now
shows options for the File
command. Then Lyle
presses Enter. (b) Now the
submenu becomes the
active menu. Lyle moves
the cursor to the word
"Save" and presses Enter.
(c) Lotus 1-2-3 then asks
him to enter a file name.*

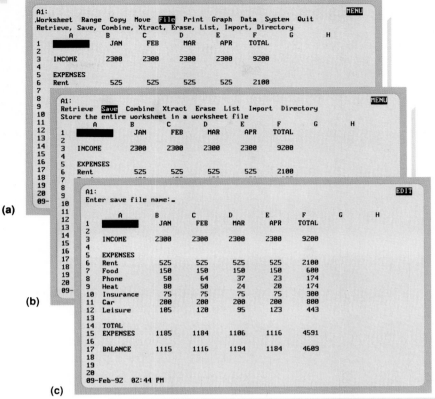

(a)

(b)

(c)

Lotus 1-2-3 prompts him for the file name he wishes to use
(Figure 6-19c). Remember that file names can be up to eight
characters long. Spreadsheet file names can contain letters,
numbers, hyphens, and the underscore character. Lyle chooses
the name B:EXPENSES, types it in, and presses Enter. (Lotus
automatically adds an extension.) Since this is a new file, it is
saved immediately.

There is another, faster, way to make these types of menu
choices: Just type the first letter of the option you want to use,
rather than moving the cursor. For example, Lyle can save his
file more quickly by typing / (to access the MENU mode), then
F (for file), S (for save), followed by the file name. So Lyle could
type:

`/FSB:EXPENSES`

and press Enter to save his file. The shortcut method can be
used for any of the menu commands.

Retrieving a File. Like the Save command, the Retrieve
command is a File subcommand. If Lyle wants to retrieve
the EXPENSES file, he needs to press the / key to obtain the

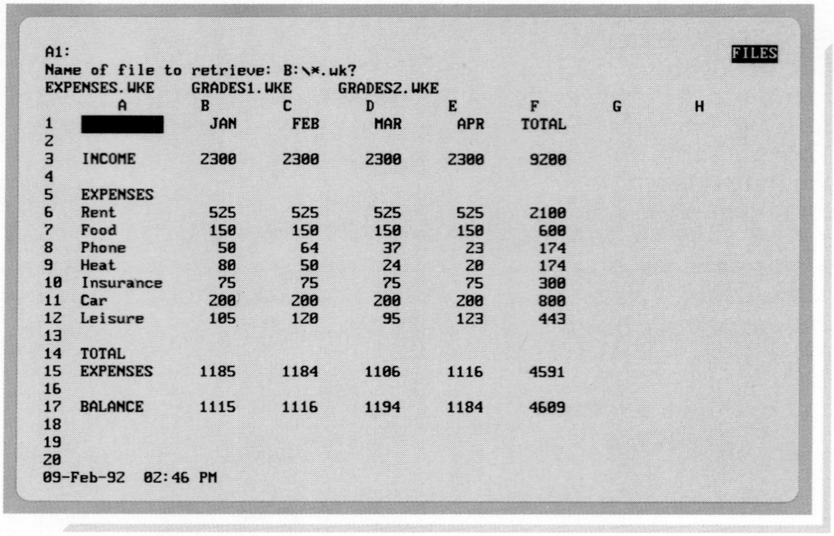

*Figure 6-20 Retrieving a
file.* When Lyle wants to
retrieve a file, Lotus 1-2-3
displays a list of the worksheet files stored on Lyle's
disk.

```
A1:                                                          FILES
Name of file to retrieve: B:\*.wk?
EXPENSES.WKE    GRADES1.WKE      GRADES2.WKE
                A       B       C       D       E       F       G       H
1                       JAN     FEB     MAR     APR     TOTAL
2
3       INCOME          2300    2300    2300    2300    9200
4
5       EXPENSES
6       Rent            525     525     525     525     2100
7       Food            150     150     150     150     600
8       Phone           50      64      37      23      174
9       Heat            80      50      24      20      174
10      Insurance       75      75      75      75      300
11      Car             200     200     200     200     800
12      Leisure         105     120     95      123     443
13
14      TOTAL
15      EXPENSES        1185    1184    1106    1116    4591
16
17      BALANCE         1115    1116    1194    1184    4609
18
19
20
09-Feb-92   02:46 PM
```

command menu. Then he selects the File command and the Retrieve subcommand. Selecting the Retrieve command erases
the current worksheet (if there happens to be one in memory) and then loads and displays the requested worksheet.

Lotus 1-2-3 then prompts Lyle for the name of the file he
wants to retrieve. The program will jog Lyle's memory by listing the names of his stored files on the bottom line of the
control panel (Figure 6-20). Lyle can either type in the name
of one of the listed files and press Enter, or he can move the
cursor to that file name and press Enter.

After Lyle enters the name of the file, the mode indicator
flashes the word "WAIT"—this indicates that Lotus is loading
the worksheet. When the worksheet appears on the screen,
the mode indicator displays the word "READY."

Listing Files. If Lyle wants to check to see what worksheet files he has on his data disk, he can use the List subcommand. To do this, he types / and selects the File option. Then
he selects List from the first submenu and Worksheet from the
second submenu. Lotus then displays a list of the worksheet
files on the screen. When Lyle wants to return to the worksheet, he presses Enter.

The Print Command

Spreadsheet programs generally let you print a copy of
the spreadsheet at any time during the session. The Print

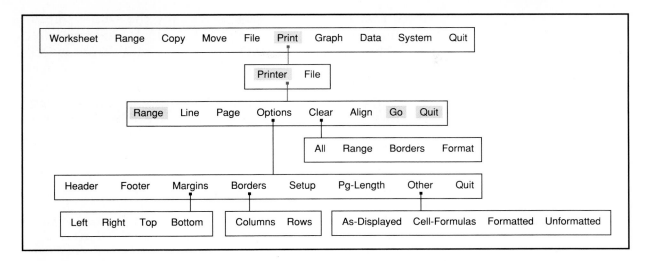

Figure 6-21 The Print command. *This figure shows the command tree for the Print command.*

command provides options for printing all or part of a spread sheet on paper. Figure 6-21 shows the command tree for the Print command.

Lyle wants to print a copy of his spreadsheet. To do this, he must tell Lotus 1-2-3 what part of the spreadsheet he wants to print and whether he wants the spreadsheet printed on paper or stored on a disk.

Lyle begins by selecting the Print option from the menu. Then he selects Printer from the first submenu because he wants to have a printed copy of the spreadsheet. When Lyle selects Printer, another submenu appears (Figure 6-22).

Now Lyle must tell Lotus how much of the spreadsheet he wants to print. Notice that there is a Range command in the second submenu. To tell Lotus which part of the spreadsheet he wants to print, Lyle must define the range he wants to print.

Figure 6-22 Printing a worksheet. *After Lyle chooses the Print option from the menu and the Printer option from the first submenu, another submenu appears. This submenu lets Lyle describe the range he wishes to print, start the printing process, and leave the Print menu.*

```
A1:                                                                    MENU
Range  Line  Page  Options  Clear  Align  Go  Quit
Specify a range to print
          A        B       C       D       E       F       G       H
                   JAN     FEB     MAR     APR     TOTAL
 1
 2
 3    INCOME      2300    2300    2300    2300    9200
 4
 5    EXPENSES
 6    Rent         525     525     525     525    2100
 7    Food         150     150     150     150     600
 8    Phone         50      64      37      23     174
 9    Heat          80      50      24      20     174
10    Insurance     75      75      75      75     300
11    Car          200     200     200     200     800
12    Leisure      105     120      95     123     443
13
14    TOTAL
15    EXPENSES    1185    1184    1106    1116    4591
16
17    BALANCE     1115    1116    1194    1184    4609
18
19
20
09-Feb-92  02:47 PM
```

Notice that Lyle's work does not occupy the whole spread-sheet. Rather, it is clustered in a small block. The upper-left corner of the block is Cell A1. The lower-right corner is Cell F17. The two cell addresses define the range of the worksheet that needs to be printed.

To tell Lotus the range, Lyle selects the Range command. Then he types A1 (the cell in the upper left of his worksheet) followed by a period and F17 (the cell in the lower right of his worksheet). Lyle then presses Enter. This returns him to the

Figure 6-23 The printed worksheet. *For Lyle, getting a printed spreadsheet that shows his revisions takes only a few keystrokes. If he had been working with a handwritten ledger, making revisions would have been tedious and the result less attractive than this printed spreadsheet.*

	JAN	FEB	MAR	APR	TOTAL
INCOME	2300	2300	2300	2300	9200
EXPENSES					
Rent	525	525	525	525	2100
Food	150	150	150	150	600
Phone	50	64	37	23	174
Heat	80	50	24	20	174
Insurance	75	75	75	75	300
Car	200	200	200	200	800
Leisure	105	120	95	123	443
TOTAL					
EXPENSES	1185	1184	1106	1116	4591
BALANCE	1115	1116	1194	1184	4609

TRY LYING ON YOUR SIDE

When you are displaying your spreadsheet on your computer's screen, you can move along a row to see all the columns of data in that row. Even if your screen can display only 80 characters on a line, you can still scroll sideways along a line by moving the cursor. However, when a wide spreadsheet is printed, the columns that will not fit across the page appear on a separate page. This means that you will have to cut and paste—literally—your printed copy of the spreadsheet.

Most printers usually print 80 characters per line. When printing in compressed mode, they can print 132 characters per line. If this is still not sufficient to print all of the columns in your spreadsheet, you can purchase software that will turn your spreadsheet sideways, printing the spreadsheet along the length of the printer paper. With the output from your spreadsheet in this form, you will have all the rows running continuously on the same piece of fanfold paper. This makes the printed spreadsheet much easier to read.

menu he just left. Next Lyle makes sure that his printer is on and ready to print. Then he selects Go from the second submenu to begin the printing. Figure 6-23 shows the final printed spreadsheet.

When the printing is completed, the second submenu is still the active menu. To return to the READY mode, Lyle must select the Quit command from the submenu.

Like the other commands we have discussed, the commands involved in the printing task can be entered quickly by typing:

```
/PPRA1.F17
```

pressing Enter, and then typing G. When you want to leave the PRINT mode, type Q.

The Worksheet Erase Command

If Lyle wants to start another worksheet without leaving and reentering the Lotus 1-2-3 program, he can use the Worksheet Erase command. This command clears the worksheet in the computer's memory of any information that has been entered, and an empty worksheet appears on the screen. The Worksheet Erase command does not erase any worksheets saved on a disk.

To use the Worksheet Erase command, Lyle presses the / key. Then he selects Worksheet from the menu and Erase from the submenu. When Lotus asks if he really wants to erase the worksheet, Lyle types Y for yes. The new worksheet appears on the screen.

The Quit Command

To leave the spreadsheet program and return to DOS, you must use the Quit command from the command menu. Many spreadsheet programs do not automatically save your file when you use the Quit command, so always remember to save before you quit.

Since Lyle has already saved his file, he selects the Quit command. Lotus 1-2-3 asks him to confirm the command with a Y (yes, leave the program) or an N (no, do not leave the program). Lyle presses Y, and the DOS prompt appears.

Using Spreadsheet Commands

These instructions are a summary of the text under "Using Spreadsheet Commands." The Lotus 1-2-3 keystrokes can also be used with your own spreadsheet.

Saving a File

1. Press the / key to enter the MENU mode.

2. Select the File command by moving the cursor to File and pressing Enter. A submenu appears.

3. Select the Save command by moving the cursor to Save and pressing Enter.

4. When asked, type the file name (B:EXPENSES in this example) and press Enter. Lotus executes the command and returns you to the READY mode.

Retrieving a File

1. Press the / key to enter the MENU mode.

2. Select the File command by moving the cursor to File and pressing Enter. A submenu appears.

3. Select the Retrieve command. (Caution: Selecting Retrieve erases your current spreadsheet—make sure you have saved it before using this command.)

4. Lotus displays the list of files you have on disk. Either type in the name of the file (B:EXPENSES in this example) or move the cursor over the name of the

file you wish to retrieve. Then press Enter.

5. The retrieved file appears on the screen, and Lotus returns you to READY mode.

Listing Files

1. Press the / key to enter the MENU mode.

2. Select the File command by moving the cursor to File and pressing Enter. A submenu appears.

3. Select the List command. Another submenu appears.

4. Select the Worksheet command. On the screen Lotus displays a list of your spreadsheet files.

5. To return to the current spreadsheet, press Enter.

Printing a Spreadsheet

1. Press the / key to enter the MENU mode.

2. Select the Print command by moving the cursor to Print and pressing Enter. A submenu appears.

3. Select the Printer command. Another submenu appears.

4. Select the Range command. Lotus asks you to define the range you want to print.

5. Type in the range in the correct form. Then press Enter. Lotus returns to the second submenu.

6. Make sure your printer is turned on. Then select the Go command from the displayed submenu.

7. To return to the READY mode after the spreadsheet is printed, select Quit from the displayed submenu.

Erasing the Worksheet

1. Press the / key to enter the MENU mode.

2. Select the Worksheet command by moving the cursor to Worksheet and pressing Enter. A submenu appears.

3. Select the Erase command. Lotus asks you to confirm the command. Type Y for yes. (Caution: Remember to save your worksheet before using this command.)

Exiting the Program

1. Press the / key to enter the MENU mode.

2. To leave Lotus 1-2-3 and return to DOS, select the Quit command. (Caution: Lotus 1-2-3 does not save your files before exiting— always remember to save your file first!)

3. When Lotus asks you to confirm the command, press the appropriate key. The DOS prompt appears.

Help!

The wide assortment of commands can be bewildering to the novice user. In fact, command choices can be confusing to an experienced user, too. But help is as close as your computer. When you are lost or confused, press the **Help key** (F1). Pressing the Help key places you in the HELP mode. You can press the Help key anytime, even in the middle of a command.

The HELP mode is useful in two ways. First, it is **context sensitive**—that is, it offers helpful information related to the command you are using when you press the Help key. Second, you can select the **help index,** which—for all practical purposes—gives you access to a reference manual right on your screen. Use the help index to select a topic, and the spreadsheet program supplies aid on that topic. It is easy to get out of the HELP mode: Press the Esc key once.

Only the Beginning

In this chapter we only brushed the surface of spreadsheet software. But you should have some idea of why spreadsheets are needed and how to go about setting one up and making changes. In the next chapter we will build on this base and tackle more complicated spreadsheet topics.

Exercises

6-1

1. Place your spreadsheet program disk in drive A and your data disk in drive B. Load your spreadsheet program.
2. In which cell is the cursor? Press the right arrow key five times. In which cell is the cursor? Press the down arrow key five times. In which cell is the cursor? Press the up arrow key two times. In which cell is the cursor?
3. Move the cursor to the following locations:
   - A8
   - F15
   - B4
   - AA60
   - Home

	A	B	C	D	E	F
1	NAME	QUIZ 1	QUIZ 2	QUIZ 3	QUIZ 4	TOTAL
2						
3	ALDISS	22	22	19	21	
4	BENKE	23	21	25	22	
5	CHANG	24	18	20	22	
6	DERRING	18	24	25	22	
7						
8						
9						
10						
11						
12						
13						
14						
15						
16						
17						
18						
19						

Figure 6-24

4. Move the cursor to the bottom row of the spreadsheet. In which cell is the cursor? Move the cursor to the farthest right column of the spreadsheet. In which cell is the cursor?
5. Enter the MENU mode. Exit the MENU mode.
6. Exit from the spreadsheet program and return to DOS.

6-2

1. Load your spreadsheet program.
2. Enter the worksheet shown in Figure 6-24.
3. Save the worksheet on your data disk as EX6-2.
4. Exit the spreadsheet program.

6-3

1. Load the spreadsheet program and retrieve EX6-2.
2. Enter the following formulas to calculate the total points for each student:

In Cell F3: $(B3 + C3 + D3 + E3)$
In Cell F4: $(B4 + C4 + D4 + E4)$
In Cell F5: $+B5 + C5 + D5 + E5$
In Cell F6: $(18 + 24 + 25 + 22)$

Does the formula in F5 produce the same type of result as the formula in F3? If not, how are they different?

3. Save the revised spreadsheet as EX6-3.
4. Increase Aldiss's grade in Cell B3 by 2 points. What happens to the total in Cell F3? Move the cursor to F3. Has the formula changed?
5. Decrease Derring's grade in Cell D6 by 5 points. What happens to the total in Cell F6? Move the cursor to F6. Has the formula changed?
6. Change the formula in F6 to:

   +B6+C6+D6+E6

   Now what happens to the total in Cell F6? Increase Derring's grade in Cell D6 by 8 points. What happens to the total in Cell F6?
7. Save the revised spreadsheet as EX6-3A.

6-4

1. Retrieve EX6-3. Enter the following functions to calculate the average for each test and the average total points:

   In Cell B8: @AVG(B3.B6)
   In Cell C8: @AVG(C3.C6)
   In Cell D8: @AVG(D3.D6)
   In Cell E8: @AVG(E3.E6)
   In Cell F8: @AVG(F3.F6)

2. Change the 18 in Cell C5 to 20. Do any changes occur in the spreadsheet? If so, what are they and where do they occur?
3. Change the 21 in Cell E3 to 25. Do any changes occur in the spreadsheet? If so, what are they and where do they occur?
4. Save the revised spreadsheet as EX6-4.
5. Print the spreadsheet.

6-5

1. Use the Worksheet Erase command to clear the spreadsheet on the screen. Then use the File List command. How many files are listed?
2. Return to the blank worksheet.
3. Enter the spreadsheet shown in Figure 6-25 (on the next page).

Figure 6-25

```
          A         B         C          D         E          F
1                            TOTAL      AVERAGE
2                            DOLLARS    DOLLARS
3       PLAYER     MATCHES   EARNED     PER MATCH
4       ---------------------------------------------------------------
5       CARVER       20      91147
6       COLES        27      40602
7       DANIELS      25      20026
8       HANES        10      27000
9       KING         22      70170
10      LOPEZ        24      89736
11      OKAMOTO      13      55941
12      SEALLY        6      10200
13      SMITH        21      91477
14      THOMPSON     27      67403
15      WILLS        23      75100
16      WHITE        17      45183
17
18      TOTAL
19
```

4. Use the @SUM function to calculate the total number of matches (Cell B18) and the total dollars earned (Cell C18).
5. In column D calculate the average dollars per match for each player.
6. Save the spreadsheet as EX6-5.
7. Print the spreadsheet.
8. Clear the spreadsheet to get a blank worksheet.

6-6

1. Retrieve EX6-5.
2. Enter the changes that follow. After you make each change, note changes that occur in any other cells.

    In Cell B5: 25
    In Cell C7: 20000
    In Cell B12: 10
    In Cell A15: WILLIS
    In Cell C16: 55183

3. Save the revised spreadsheet as EX6-6.
4. Print the spreadsheet.
5. Exit the program.

6-7

1. Load your spreadsheet program. Enter the spreadsheet shown in Figure 6-26.

ITEM	UNITS SOLD	UNIT COST	UNIT PRICE	TOTAL COST	TOTAL SALES	PROFIT
BINDER	500	4	7			
BOOKBAG	350	5	10			
CALENDAR	300	3	8			
NOTEBOOK	400	1	2			
SHIRT	800	4	8			
SCHEDULE	675	1	2			

Figure 6-26

2. Create formulas that calculate each item's total cost. (The total cost for each item equals the number of units sold multiplied by the cost of each unit.) Enter the formulas in the appropriate column.
3. Create formulas that calculate each item's total sales. (The total sales for each item equals the number of units sold multiplied by the price of each unit.) Enter the formulas in the appropriate column.
4. Create formulas that calculate the profit made on each item. Enter the formulas in the appropriate cells.
5. Save the spreadsheet as EX6-7.
6. Print the worksheet.
7. Erase the worksheet.

6-8

1. Retrieve EX6-7.
2. Make the following changes to the worksheet:
    - Decrease the number of units sold of each item by 50
    - Increase the unit cost of each item by 5
    - Increase the unit price of each item by 10
3. Save the spreadsheet as EX6-8.
4. At the bottom of the TOTAL COST, TOTAL SALES, and PROFIT columns, place the appropriate formulas or functions that will calculate the totals for each column. Enter a label that reads TOTAL in Cell A12.
5. Save the spreadsheet as EX6-8A.
6. Print the spreadsheet.
7. Exit the program.

Summary and Key Terms

- Forms that are used to organize data into rows and columns are called **spreadsheets.** An **electronic spreadsheet** is a computerized version of a manual spreadsheet. The electronic spreadsheet program quickly and automatically performs calculations to reflect changes in values or formulas.

- The intersection of a row and column forms a cell. **Cells** are the storage areas in a spreadsheet. When referring to a cell, you use the letter and number of the intersecting column and row. This reference name is the **cell address.**

- There is one cell known as the **active cell,** or **current cell.** The active cell is marked by the spreadsheet's cursor, also called a **pointer.**

- Each cell can contain one of four types of information. A **label** provides descriptive information about entries in the spreadsheet. A **value** is an actual number entered into a cell. A **formula** is an instruction to the program to perform a calculation. A **function** is a preprogrammed formula. Sometimes you must specify a **range** of cells to build a formula or perform a function.

- You can use the cursor movement keys to scroll through the spreadsheet horizontally or vertically. You may also use a **GoTo function key,** also known as the **Jump-To function key.**

- A **mode** is the condition or state in which the program is currently functioning. Most spreadsheets have three main operating modes: the **READY mode,** the **ENTRY mode,** and the **MENU mode.** The spreadsheet screen displays a **mode indicator,** which tells you the current mode.

- Spreadsheet programs display commands in a **command menu** shown near the top of the screen. The command menu contains a list, or menu, of different options.

- Most spreadsheet programs display a **control panel** to help you keep track of what you input. The control panel usually consists of three lines. The first line is the status line; the second line is used in a variety of ways; and the third line shows a **submenu,** which lists options for the command you are choosing.

- A **command tree** shows all the choices from the main command menu and all the choices from associated submenus.

- To create a spreadsheet, you enter labels, values, formulas, and functions into the cells. Formulas and functions do not appear in the cells; instead, the cell shows the result of the formula or function. The result is called the **displayed value** of the cell. The formula or function is the **cell contents** of the cell. To make corrections to data in a cell, you must move the cursor to that cell.

- The File command lets you manipulate the Lotus files on your data disk. You can use the File command to save, retrieve, list, and erase files.

- The Print command provides options for printing all or part of a spreadsheet on paper. It also lets you store a "printed" spreadsheet on disk.

- The Worksheet Erase command clears the current worksheet out of memory, providing you with a blank worksheet. This command will not affect already saved worksheets.

- To leave the spreadsheet program and return to DOS, you must use the Quit command from the command menu. Always save your file before you quit, since many spreadsheet programs do not automatically save files.

- The **Help key** places you in the HELP mode. This mode is **context sensitive**—that is, it offers helpful information related to the command you were using when you pressed the Help key. While in HELP mode, you can select the **help index,** which gives you access to an on-screen reference manual.

Review Questions

1. In a spreadsheet, what is the intersection of a row and column called?

2. Where are the entries in a spreadsheet stored?

3. How are individual columns and rows identified on an electronic spreadsheet?

4. What is meant by the formula @AVG(B1..B10)? Where will the result of this formula be displayed on the screen?

5. What is another way to write the formula +A1+A2+A3+A4+A5?

6. What is a range?

7. Regardless of the cursor's location in the spreadsheet, what are three ways in which you can move the cursor to Cell A1?

8. What are three of the modes in which Lotus 1-2-3 operates?

9. What mode must you be in to make an entry in a cell? Can you make an entry in a cell when you see the command menu on the screen?

10. What key do you press to access the command menu?

11. What is displayed in the mode indicator when you start to enter a value in a cell? What is displayed in the mode indicator when you start to enter a label in a cell?

12. What are some of the commands available in the command menu?

13. What is a submenu? How do you access a submenu? How do you make a choice from a submenu?

14. What is automatic recalculation?

15. What command in Lotus 1-2-3 lets you store, retrieve, list, or erase your worksheet files?

FROM THE REAL WORLD

All the Gold in California

Going prospecting for gold? Do not forget the essential tools. Pickax. Pan. Boots. Computer. Better include some spreadsheet software if you are really serious. You can call yourself serious if you hope to make a profit on gold. It is not a simple matter.

The precious metal called gold is a barometer of the economy: Its price soars rapidly during economic turmoil and descends just as fast when the economy is fat and placid. But no matter what the state of the economy and the related price gold can command, the costs of finding gold remain high. It is not difficult to run a profitable operation when the price of gold is high; it is very difficult when gold prices tumble. Enter the computer, the tool to smooth the bumps introduced by the bobbling economy.

The computer can help pinpoint likely gold veins, sparing companies from spending time and effort on unlikely exploration sites. The problem with mining gold is that gold fragments in the earth cannot be seen with the naked eye. Methods for detecting the invisible gold were discovered in the 1930s, but they were not economically attractive until the advent of today's computer technology.

Consider the case of Homestake Mining of California, the largest gold-mining company in the world outside of South Africa. Homestake's gold ventures are centered around the personal computer. At Homestake prospecting by computer starts with a mountain of data. The data represents the analyzed results of core samples dug from the mine site. The samples are tested for gold and other minerals. The data about the samples is placed into a three-dimensional spreadsheet containing 5000 cells, each corresponding to a specific block of earth and containing information about its mineral content. The spreadsheet is then used to locate probable areas of gold.

Even as drilling is going on, Homestake continues to add data to the initial computer study. As more data is fed into the computer, the locations of recoverable deposits can be more precisely defined. The computer helps engineers decide which locations will pay off. Although the operation was originally on Homestake's mainframe computer, now on-site personal computers run the program. This saves the mining engineers the time and trouble of sending data to and receiving data from a remote location.

The computer system answers two basic questions: Does a given block of earth contain gold? And, if so, is it cost-effective to mine the gold? Dare we ask a third: Is the computer worth its weight in gold?

7 Advanced Spreadsheets

Chapter Objectives

After reading this chapter you should be able to

- Plan and use a spreadsheet

- Develop and enter labels

- Format values

- Develop and enter formulas

- Use a variety of spreadsheet commands

- Define the terms *template* and *macro*

- Create simple macros

In the previous chapter we introduced the concept of an electronic spreadsheet and showed some common spreadsheet features. Spreadsheets have a large number of capabilities and a great deal of flexibility. Therefore, they can be applied to a wide range of problems. In this chapter we will present one example—creating a loan-analysis worksheet—to show you some of the additional capabilities that spreadsheets have. Using this example, we will show you how the spreadsheet is created, how to enter labels, how to derive and enter formulas, how to make changes to the spreadsheet, and how to use the completed spreadsheet.

Figure 7-1 A loan-repayment schedule. Ted determines what each customer will have to pay per month and gives a running balance of the interest paid and the remaining balance.

TED NUNEZ
FINANCIAL CONSULTANT

PRICE OF CAR = $10,000
INTEREST RATE = 10%
TERM OF LOAN = 12 MONTHS
TOTAL OWED = $10,549.91
MONTHLY PAYMENT = $879.16

MONTH	INTEREST PAID	REMAINING BALANCE
0	$0.00	$10000.00
1	$83.00	$9204.17
2	$76.70	$8401.72
3	$70.01	$7592.57
4	$63.27	$6776.69
5	$56.47	$5954.00
6	$49.62	$5124.46
7	$42.70	$4288.00
8	$35.73	$3444.58
9	$28.70	$2594.12
10	$21.62	$1736.58
11	$14.47	$871.89
12	$7.27	$0.00

A Loan-Analysis Example

Ted Nunez is an entrepreneur who advises people who want to purchase a new automobile. Most of Ted's clients need to borrow the money to purchase a car—and they need to know how much a new car is actually going to cost. Ted gives them a complete breakdown of the financial aspects of the purchase: the size of the monthly payments, the total amount owed, the amount charged for interest, and a running balance of the amount borrowed that still needs to be repaid—also known as the principal (Figure 7-1). This type of breakdown is known as a loan-repayment schedule.

One service that Ted's clients would appreciate is the ability to see the impact of different interest rates, different amounts borrowed, and different terms—lengths of time—for repaying the loan. Ted wants to demonstrate a client's options by showing the effects of these various changes. He needs to be able to produce these different possibilities quickly, and he wants to be able to give clients a printed copy of each scenario, so they can study it at their leisure.

Since Ted took a class in microcomputer applications, he knows that he can use an electronic spreadsheet program to produce the different loan-repayment schedules. Any of the popular spreadsheet programs would work, but Ted is familiar with Lotus 1-2-3, so that is the program he uses.

Before Ted can use the program, however, he needs to design his spreadsheet. Ted wants to design a general worksheet that contains labels and formulas but no data. After he enters this worksheet into Lotus, he can use the spreadsheet over and over again, filling in the appropriate data for each client.

To design the worksheet, Ted must first decide what information he wants in it, what labels, values, and formulas he is going to need, and what he wants the spreadsheet to look like overall. Ted decides that he needs to show the following information:

- The price of the car (in dollars)

- The interest rate on the loan (as a percentage)

- The term of the loan (in months)

- The client's monthly payment (in dollars)

- The running monthly balance, showing the interest paid off and the balance remaining for each month (in dollars)

Ted then sketches, on paper, how he wants the spreadsheet to look (Figure 7-2, on the next page). He notes that he will need specific formulas to calculate the amount to repay, the monthly

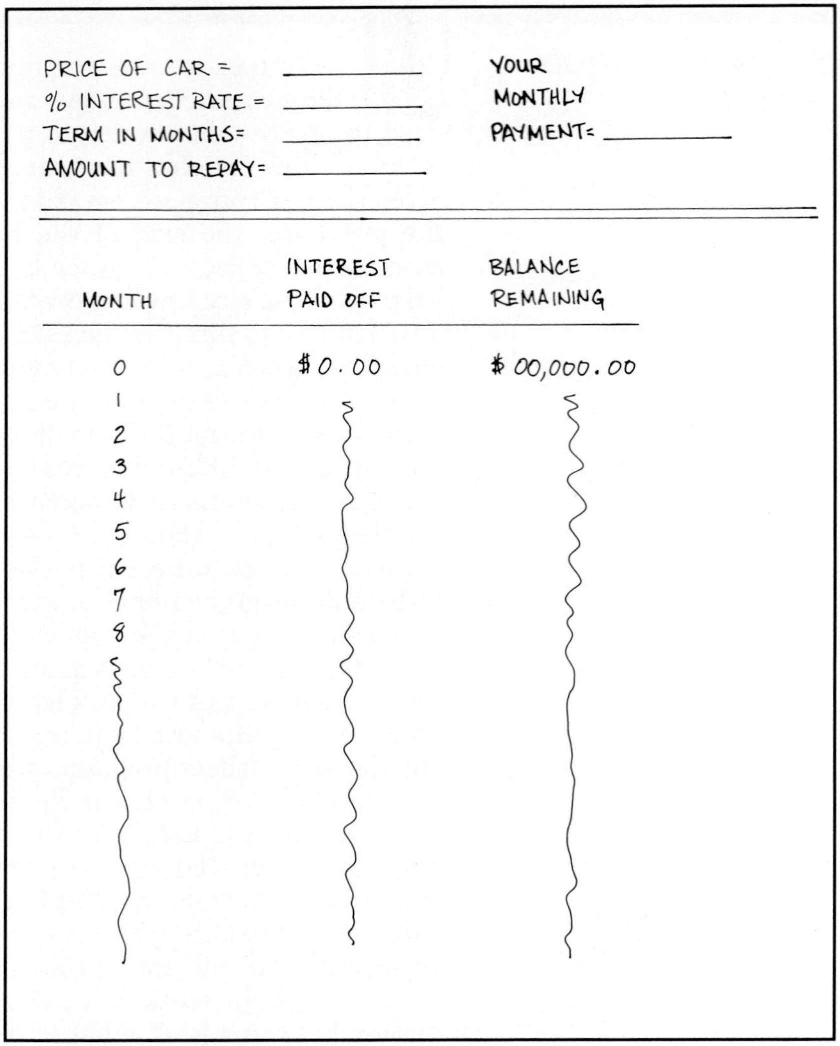

Figure 7-2 Designing the spreadsheet. *Ted sketches how he will set up his electronic spreadsheet.*

payment, the interest paid, and the remaining balance. Now Ted is ready to start entering the information into a computer. (An abbreviated version of the discussion that follows can be found in the box called "Keystrokes Only: The Loan-Analysis Example.")

Planning and Entering Labels

Recall from Chapter 6 that a label is a descriptive element in a spreadsheet—it is not used in calculations. The labels in Ted's worksheet include the headings and the lines he uses to separate different parts of the worksheet.

Ted begins to enter the first label by moving the cursor to Cell A2, and typing PRICE OF CAR =. Then he presses Enter

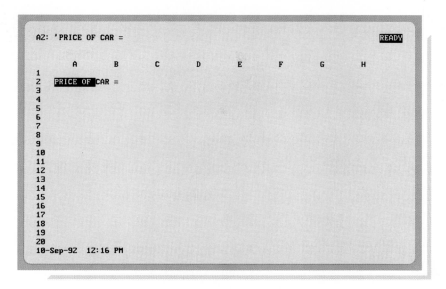

```
A2: 'PRICE OF CAR =                                                    READY

         A       B       C       D       E       F       G       H
   1
   2  PRICE OF CAR =
   3
   4
   5
   6
   7
   8
   9
  10
  11
  12
  13
  14
  15
  16
  17
  18
  19
  20
  10-Sep-92  12:16 PM
```

Figure 7-3 The default setting for column width. *The default col-umn-width setting for Lotus 1-2-3 is 9 characters. Here Ted has entered a label that is 14 characters wide—the extra characters spill into the next column.*

to enter the label into the cell. When he does this, he notices that only the first 9 characters appear in the cell. The rest of the characters appear in Cell B2 (Figure 7-3). The problem is that the default setting for the cell width is only 9 characters, and the label is 14 characters wide. (Recall that default settings are the settings that the computer automatically uses.) Ted wants the cell to show more than 9 characters, so he needs to change the column-width setting.

Changing the Column Width

It is not possible to change the column width of only one or two cells in a column—all of the cells in the column must be the same width. This means that you must set the width of the column to the width of the widest cell needed for that column.

Ted looks over the labels he is going to use in column A and finds that the longest label is 17 characters wide, so he decides to add one space and make the column 18 characters wide. To change the width of column A, Ted must use one of the Lotus 1-2-3 commands—the Worksheet command. To do this, he first moves the cursor to the column he wants to change—column A. Then he presses the / key to enter the

MENU mode. Next he selects the Worksheet option by pressing Enter. Notice in Figure 7-4a that a submenu appears that contains the Column command. Ted selects this command and gets another submenu (Figure 7-4b). Since he wants to set the column width, he selects Set-Width and, when prompted, types in 18 to change the column width to 18. Then he presses

Figure 7-4 Changing the column-width settings. *Ted enters the MENU mode and selects the Worksheet command. Next he selects (a) the Column command and then (b) the Set-Width command.*

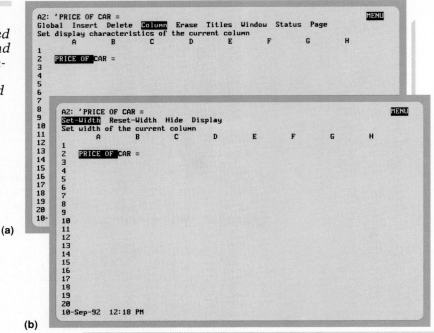

Figure 7-5 The new column width. *Now Ted's label in Cell A2 fits into the cell. The "[W15]" next to the D2 cell address reminds Ted that the column D is now 15 characters wide.*

Cell width indicator

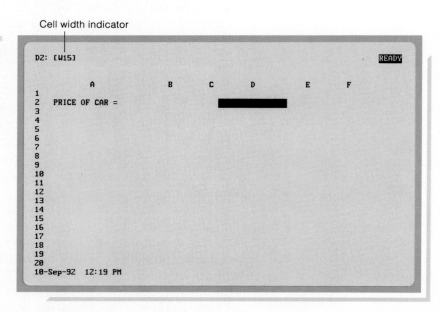

Enter. The cell width in column A automatically changes.

Ted also changes the column widths of the other columns: columns B and D to 15, and column C to 3 so that column F will fit on the screen. Figure 7-5 shows the result. Notice how "[W15]" appears after the cell address in the control panel. The "W" stands for Width and the "15" is the number of characters. This notation tells you that the column is now 15 characters wide.

Formatting Labels

Now that column A is wide enough, Ted enters the four labels in Cells A3 to A5 and the YOUR MONTHLY PAYMENT = label in cells E2 through E4. When a label is entered in a cell, it is displayed on the screen in a certain way. This is called the label's **format.** The **default format** for labels is **left justification.** This means that the first character of the label is displayed starting at the left-hand side of the cell. Most spreadsheet programs let you change the format for labels to **right justification,** where the label is displayed with the last character in the label at the very right of the cell. You can also **center** a label in a cell. The differences among these formats is apparent only if the label you enter is shorter than the width of the cell.

You can override the default format for a given cell by typing a **prefix**—a character typed just before you type the actual label in the cell. In Lotus 1-2-3 an apostrophe (') indicates left justification, a double quotation mark (") means right justification, and a **caret** (^) means that the label is to be centered in the cell (Figure 7-6).

Figure 7-6 Label formats. Labels can be formatted in one of three ways—left-justified, centered, or right-justified.

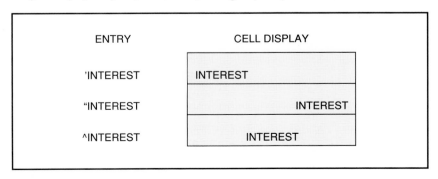

You can ask the spreadsheet program to supply the prefix for you automatically when you enter a label; this is called setting the **default label prefix.** For example, if you set the default label prefix to center, the program supplies a caret prefix for each label you type and centers each label in its cell. There are two different ways to set default label prefixes—one way uses the Global command and the other the Range command. The **Global command** sets the label format for *all* the unfilled cells in the spreadsheet. The **Range command** changes the settings for a specified *range* of filled cells in the spreadsheet.

Ted decides he wants to right justify the remaining labels. Since the current default setting for the labels is left justification, Ted needs to change the format for all the cells that will contain labels. To do this, Ted uses the Global command.

Global Label Changes. To use the Global command, Ted presses / to enter the MENU mode. He selects the Worksheet command. Then he selects the Global command. Next Ted chooses the Label-Prefix command. He can then choose which format he wants to have—in this case, Right. He selects Right and presses Enter. From now on, when Ted types in a label, it will be right-justified within the cell.

Ted now enters the labels for Cells A9, B8 and B9, and D8 and D9 (Figure 7-7a). Note that labels that have already been entered are not affected by the Global command—only the labels you enter *after* changing the default format show the new format.

Range Label Changes. After looking at his spreadsheet, Ted decides that he really wants to center the BALANCE REMAINING label after all. To do this he uses the Range command. To set the range label prefix for Cells D8 through D9, Ted presses / and selects Range, Label-Prefix, and Center from the menus. Then he defines the range as D8.D9. The result is shown in Figure 7-7b.

The Label Repeat Command

Notice in Figure 7-2 (on page 214) that Ted wants to mark off sections of his worksheet with dashed lines. He wants row 6 to be set off by a line of equals signs (=) and row 10 to be set off by a line of dashes (-). Instead of typing in the equals signs and dashes numerous times, Ted can use the **Label Repeat command.** This command tells Lotus 1-2-3 to repeat the character you enter as many times as needed to fill a cell. To use

Label prefix

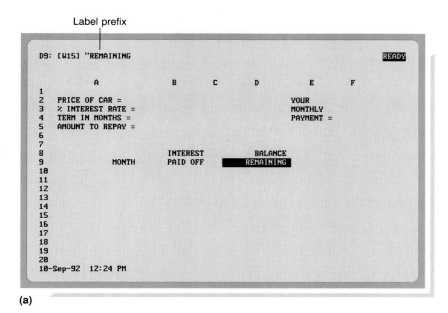

(a)

Label prefix

Figure 7-7 Changing the label format. *Ted has entered in his text labels. (a) Notice that the labels in the ranges A2 to A5 and E2 to E4 are left-justified and the labels in the range A8 to D9 are right-justified. (b) Ted uses the Range command to center the labels in Cells D8 and D9.*

this command, Ted places the cursor in Cell A6 and presses the Backslash key (\). (Do not confuse this with the Slash key (/) used to enter the MENU mode.) Next Ted presses the Equals

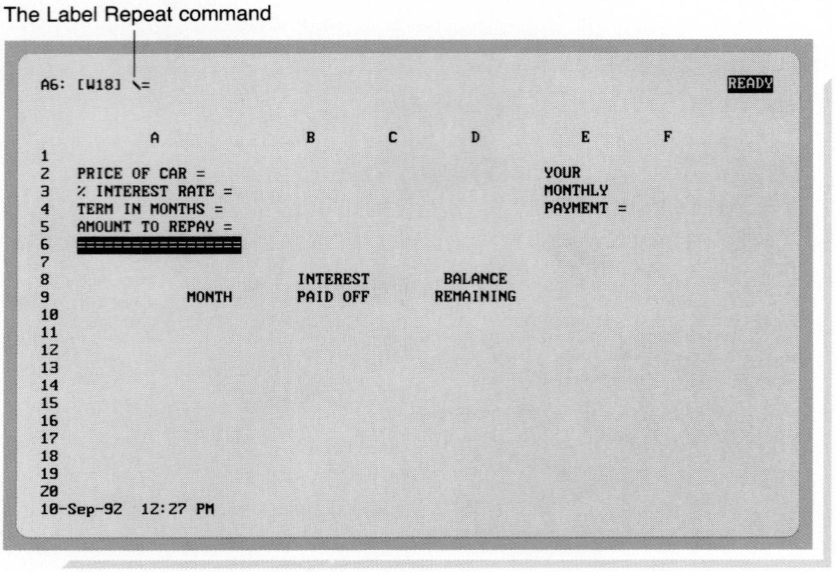

The Label Repeat command

```
A6: [W18] \=                                                    READY

             A              B        C        D        E        F
 1
 2   PRICE OF CAR =                                     YOUR
 3   % INTEREST RATE =                                  MONTHLY
 4   TERM IN MONTHS =                                   PAYMENT =
 5   AMOUNT TO REPAY =
 6   =================
 7
 8                     INTEREST      BALANCE
 9           MONTH     PAID OFF      REMAINING
10
11
12
13
14
15
16
17
18
19
20
10-Sep-92  12:27 PM
```

Figure 7-8 The Label Repeat command. *The Label Repeat command lets Ted use only two keystrokes to fill a cell with equals signs.*

key (=) once. Then he presses Enter. Lotus automatically fills the cell with equals signs (Figure 7-8). Ted could use this method to fill the rest of the cells in the row, but there is a more efficient method: the Copy command.

Copying Labels

The **Copy command** lets you duplicate the contents of one or more cells in a range. Although any cell can be copied, we will show how Ted uses the Copy command to duplicate a label. The Copy command may seem confusing at first, but after a little practice you will find it easy.

The cell or cells you wish to copy are referred to as the **copy from range.** In the example the copy from range is Cell A6. The cell or cells you wish to copy to are referred to as the **copy to range,** in this case Cells B6 through F6.

The placement of the cursor in the worksheet is important when you issue the Copy command. When you issue the command, most spreadsheet programs assume that the copy from range is the current active cell. So be sure to place the cursor in the cell you want to copy before you issue the command.

Figure 7-9 Using the Copy command. When Ted selects the Copy command, Lotus 1-2-3 asks him to enter (a) the copy from range and (b) the copy to range. (c) This screen shows the result of the command.

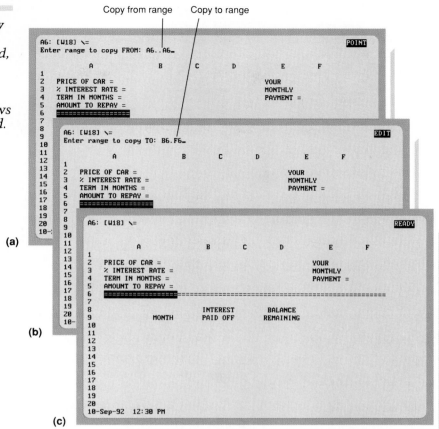

(a)

(b)

(c)

Ted makes sure the cursor is on A6. Then he presses the / key to enter the MENU mode and selects Copy. In response, Lotus 1-2-3 displays the message "Enter range to copy FROM" and gives the current range—A6..A6 (Figure 7-9a). (Do not be confused by this notation. It says that the upper-left corner of the range is Cell A6 and the lower-right corner of the range is A6—in other words, the range is a single cell, A6.) Ted could change the range if he wished by typing in a new range, but since A6 is the cell he wants to copy, he simply presses Enter.

Now that the program knows what it is supposed to copy, it needs to know where to put the copied material. The program prompts Ted with the message "Enter range to copy TO." Ted responds by typing in B6.F6, since B6 is the starting cell of the range and F6 is the ending cell of the range (Figure 7-9b). Ted then presses Enter, and Lotus 1-2-3 fills the cells in the specified range with equals signs (Figure 7-9c). Ted repeats this procedure to make a line of dashes under the MONTH, INTEREST PAID OFF, and BALANCE REMAINING labels. Figure 7-10 shows the spreadsheet with all the labels filled in.

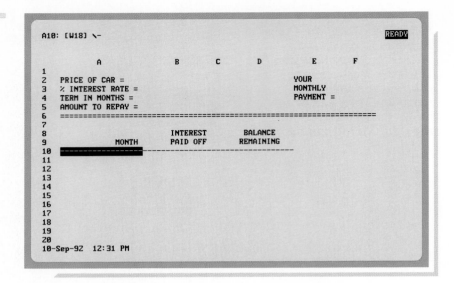

Figure 7-10 The entered labels. Ted has now entered in all his labels.

Formatting Values

Now Ted needs to determine how he wants to present the numbers produced by the spreadsheet—in other words, how to format the information the client is going to see.

Unlike labels, values are always displayed right-justified in a cell. However, most spreadsheet programs can display a value in a variety of different formats. Currency ($00.00), percent (00%), and date (00-00-00) formats are common formats for values. Figure 7-11 shows some of the other possible formats. The default format for a value is a regular number. When you format a value, the value stored in memory remains the same; the value just looks different on the screen. Lotus 1-2-3 uses an indicator after the cell address to show you the format changes you have made. Figure 7-12 shows and describes some common indicators. As with labels, you can use the Global command to set the format for all the values in the spreadsheet and the Range command to change the format for a range of existing values in the spreadsheet.

Ted wants to have the total loan amount, as well as all other values that represent dollars, displayed in a currency format. However, he wants to keep the format of the interest rate (Cell B3), the loan term (Cell B4), and the month numbers (Cells A11 through A35) as regular numbers. Therefore, Ted decides to use the Range command to change the format for the values to be shown as currency.

Figure 7-11 Value formats. *Values can be formatted in several different ways. This figure describes some of the common formats—however, different spreadsheet programs may have different formats.*

FORMAT	DESCRIPTION	EXAMPLE
Fixed	A fixed number of decimal positions can be set (in this example, three decimal places)	7654.321
Scientific	Values expressed in scientific notation	765E+21
Currency	Values displayed as dollars and cents, with a dollar sign in front and commas between 1000 units; two decimal places fixed; may display negative values in parentheses or after a minus sign	$7,654.32
, (comma)	Values displayed as in currency format with dollar sign omitted, comma between 1000 units; with two decimal places	7,654.32
General	Values displayed the same way as they are entered; zeros after decimal point not displayed	7654.321
% (percent)	Displays value of cell, multiplied by 100, followed by a percent sign; two decimal places displayed	765432.10%
Date	Displays serial dates; day–month–year, day–month, or month–year format	25–March–45
Text	Formulas displayed as entered; values displayed in general format	7654.321

Figure 7-12 Common format indicators. *Format indicators are displayed after the cell address in the first line of the control panel when a formatting change has been made.*

WHAT YOU SEE	WHAT IT MEANS
A1: [W10] 1234	Cell A1; column width set to 10; cell contains value 1234
A1: (D3) 1234	Cell A1; date format 3; cell contains value 1234
A1: (C2) 1234	Cell A1; currency format with two decimal places; cell contains value 1234
A1: (P2) 1234	Cell A1; percent format with two decimal places; cell contains value 1234
A1: (T) [W5] 1234	Cell A1; text format; column width set to 5; cell contains value 1234
A1: (C1) [W15] 1234	Cell A1; currency format with one decimal place; column width set to 15; cell contains value 1234

Range Value Changes. Ted begins by placing the cursor on Cell B2. Then he presses / to enter the MENU mode and selects the Range command. Next Ted selects the Format command and then the Currency command from the Format submenu. Lotus 1-2-3 asks him how many decimal positions he wants to show. Often Lotus shows the number 2 as a decimal-place default. Since currency has only two decimal places, Ted presses Enter. When Lotus asks him to define the range for the changes, Ted simply presses Enter again because he wants to change only Cell B2. Ted repeats this procedure for Cells B5 and F4. Notice in Figure 7-13 that you now see a "(C2)" next to the cell address in the control panel.

Next Ted formats the INTEREST PAID OFF and BALANCE REMAINING columns. He places the cursor on B11, presses /, selects Range, Format, Currency, and types in 2 as before. Then when Lotus asks him for the range to format, Ted enters B11.B35 and presses Enter. Ted then repeats this procedure for column D. Now when the values are entered, all of the formatted cells in columns B and D will be displayed in the currency format.

Global Value Changes. Since Ted is using different value formats in his worksheet, he does not want to use the Global command, which would change the format of all the cells, including the ones Ted wants to leave in the default format. However, if Ted had wanted to change the format of the whole worksheet, he could have used the Global command as he did with the labels. To use the Global command to format values,

Figure 7-13 Changing the value format. Notice "(C2)" next to the cell address in the top line of the control panel. It means that the value in Cell F5 is displayed as currency with 2 decimal places.

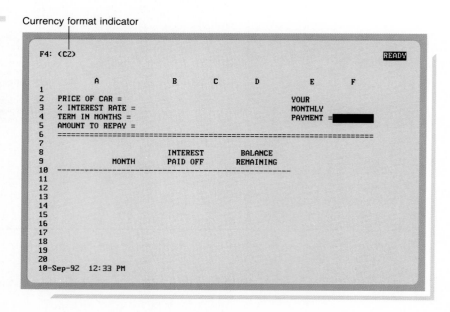

Currency format indicator

press / to enter the MENU mode, select Worksheet, Global, Format, and then select the format you wish to use.

Developing and Entering the Formulas

ow Ted is ready to work on the formulas that he will use in the spreadsheet.

Deriving the Formulas

As we mentioned earlier, Ted needs to develop formulas for the amount to repay, the monthly payment, the interest paid, and the remaining balance. Let us take a closer look at how Ted derives each formula.

Amount to Repay. The total amount the clients need to repay is the amount borrowed—the principal—plus the interest. Figuring out the total payment and the monthly payments is complicated, but Lotus 1-2-3 makes it easy by automatically calculating the monthly payments in Cell F4. The total amount to repay is then just the number of monthly payments (Cell B4) multiplied by the amount of the monthly payment (Cell F4). This formula is written (B4*F4) or +B4*F4. Note that the formula must begin with a left parenthesis or a plus sign. Otherwise, Lotus will read the entry as a label.

Monthly Payment. Lotus has a function exclusively for calculating monthly payments—the **@PMT function.** To use this function, Ted must supply Lotus with three pieces of information: (1) the amount borrowed (Cell B2), (2) the monthly interest rate, and (3) the term of the loan (Cell B4). To get the monthly interest rate, Ted will divide the interest rate (Cell B3) by 100 so it represents a percentage. Then he will divide the result by 12 (the number of months in a year). So the formula he will use for the monthly interest rate is (B3/100)/12.

Each monthly payment consists of two parts: repayment of interest and repayment of principal. Ted needs to know how much of the monthly payment is going to each part.

Interest Paid. To calculate the interest paid for a particular month, Ted needs to multiply the monthly interest rate by the previous month's remaining balance. For example, the amount of interest paid in month 1 would be the monthly interest rate—(B3/100)/12—multiplied by the balance remaining when you first get the loan (month 0). On his spreadsheet in Cell B12, Ted decides to use the formula ((B3/100)/12)*D11. When the spreadsheet is completed, the result of this formula will be displayed in Cell B12.

Remaining Balance. To calculate the remaining balance, Ted first needs to calculate how much of the monthly payment went to paying back the principal. Ted does this by subtracting the amount of the interest paid from the monthly payment (Cell F4). Then he subtracts this result from the previous month's remaining balance. To do this for month 1, Ted uses the formula (D11 − (F4 − B12)).

Entering the Formulas

Once Ted has developed his formulas, he can enter them into the worksheet. Ted begins by entering the amount to repay in Cell B5. He types in (B4*F4) and presses Enter. Notice in Figure 7-14a that $0.00 appears in Cell B5. This occurs because no amounts have been entered for B4 and F4.

Next Ted wants to enter the @PMT function in Cell F4. But let us pause a minute here. Notice that the monthly payment and the interest paid formulas both are based on the monthly interest rate. Instead of typing in the formula for this—(B3/100)/12—each time he wants to use the value in another formula, Ted decides to enter the formula in an unused cell. That way, each time he wants to use the formula for monthly interest rate, he can simply reference the cell that contains that formula.

Ted moves his cursor to Cell C1 (which is currently not being used) and types in (B3/100)/12. Then he presses Enter. Now each time Ted wants to use the monthly interest rate, he can simply type in the address of Cell C1.

Next he moves the cursor to F4 and types @PMT(B2,C1,B4). This tells Lotus 1-2-3 to use the values in B2, C1, and B4 to calculate the monthly payment. The order of the cells is very important—Lotus reads the first value, or cell address, as the amount borrowed; the second value, or cell address, as the monthly interest rate; and the third value, or cell address, as the term of the loan. If the values are in the wrong order, the calculation will be wrong. After Ted presses Enter, an **ERR message** appears (Figure 7-14b). This occurs because there are no values as of yet in Cells B2, C1, and B4, so Lotus cannot calculate the monthly payment. Once these values are entered, the ERR will be replaced with the result of the formula.

Now Ted starts to enter the formulas for interest paid and balance remaining. Remember that the interest paid is based on the data from the previous month, so Ted sets up the spreadsheet so the first month listed is month 0—the month before any payments are made. Before any payments are made, the interest paid is always 0. So Ted enters this amount in Cell B11. The balance remaining for month 0 will be the original

Figure 7-14 Entering the formulas for amount to repay and the monthly payment. Ted enters the formulas for (a) amount to repay and (b) monthly interest rate and monthly payment. The ERR message appears because there are no values as of yet in Cells B2, C1, and B4.

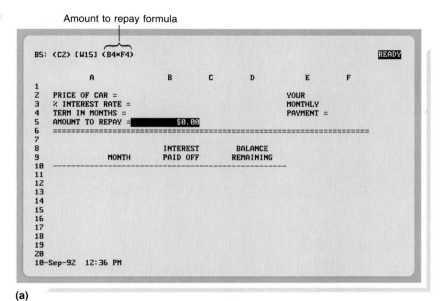

amount of the loan. When Ted uses the worksheet, he will enter this amount in Cell B2. Therefore, Ted types in (B2) in Cell D11. This tells Lotus to enter the amount from B2 into D11. Notice that the spreadsheet shows the entries as $0.00 (Figure 7-15a).

Ted then enters the formula for interest paid in the first month in Cell B12. Remember that this is calculated by multiplying the monthly interest rate (Cell C1) by the previous month's remaining balance (Cell D11). Since Ted entered the monthly interest formula in Cell C1, he can type in (C1*D11), instead of ((B3/100)/12)*D11 (Figure 7-15b). He also enters the

*Figure 7-15 Entering the formulas for interest paid off and the remaining balance. (a) For the first month (month 0), Ted enters a 0 for the interest paid and (B2) for the balance remaining. For the second month, Ted enters (b) (C1*D11) for the interest paid.*

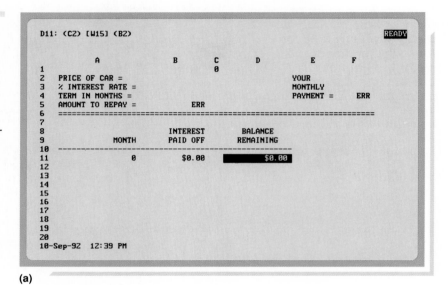

(a)

(b)

continued ▶

Balance remaining formula

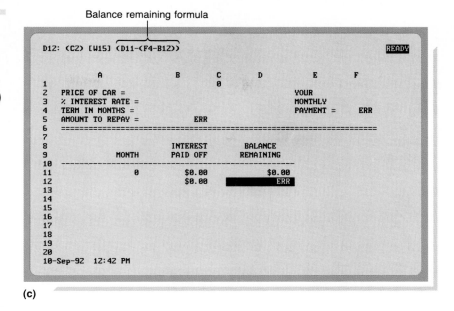

Figure 7-15 Entering the formulas for interest paid off and the remaining balance (continued). *For the second month, Ted also enters (c) (D11 − (F4 − B12)) for the balance remaining.*

(c)

balance remaining formula, $(D11 − (F4 − B12))$, in Cell D12 (Figure 7-15c).

Ted could continue to enter the formulas, changing the appropriate cell addresses each time, but there is an easier way. Ted can use the Copy command to copy the formulas. We introduced the Copy command earlier in this chapter. This command is straightforward with labels and numbers, but there are some added twists when you copy formulas. So let us take another look at the Copy command.

Copying Formulas

When you copy formulas, it is unlikely that you will want to use the identical formula in different parts of the spreadsheet. For example, let us say you had the formula $(A1 + 1)$ in Cell A2. In Cell A3 you would probably want to see the formula $(A2 + 1)$. When you use the Copy command, the spreadsheet makes these changes for you. If you copy a formula down a column, the row numbers used in the formula will change—in each successive cell they will increase by 1 (Figure 7-16a, on the next page). If you copy a formula along a row, the column letters in the formula will change—in each successive cell they will advance by a letter (Figure 7-16b). In spreadsheet terms we say that the cell addresses (such as A1 or A2) are **relative.** This means that they will change in a predictable way as the formula is copied.

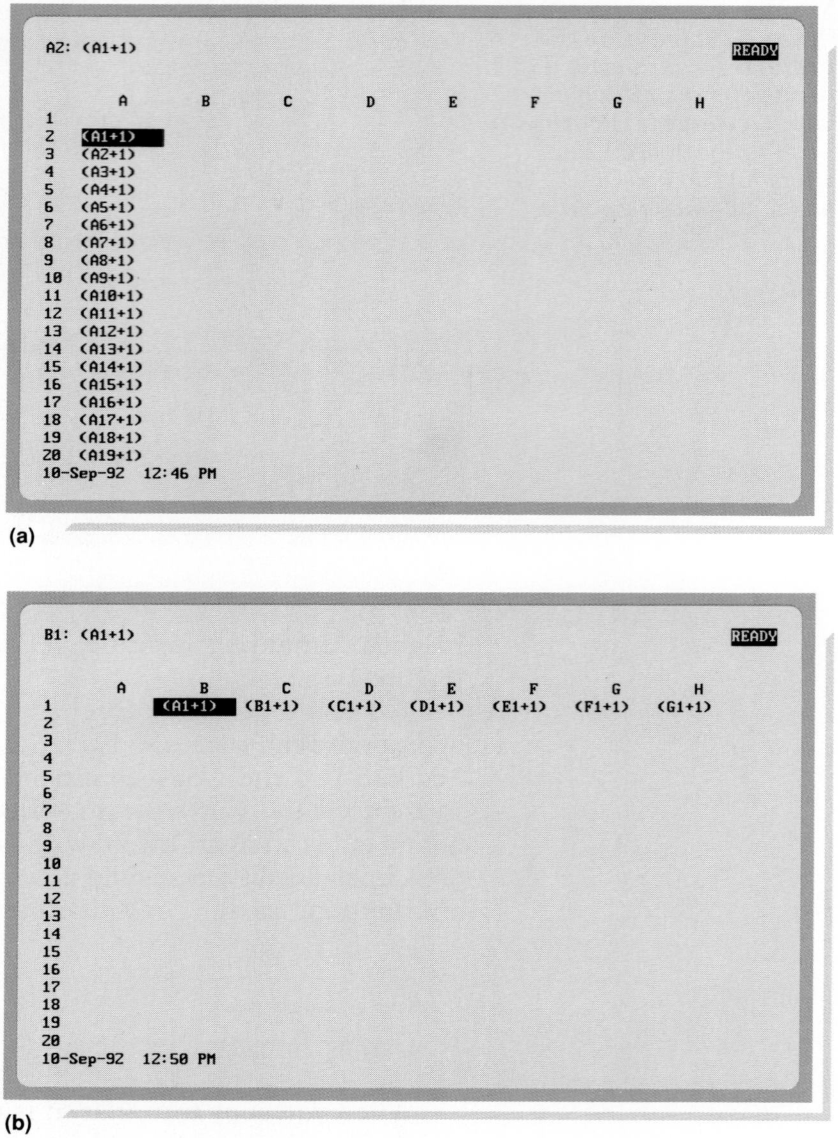

Figure 7-16 Copying formulas. *(a) When the formula in Cell A2 is copied to Cells A3 through A20, the row numbers change but the column letters stay the same. (b) When the formula in Cell B1 is copied to Cells C1 through H1, the column letters change but the row numbers stay the same.*

(a)

(b)

However, there may be situations when you do not want your program to assume that cell addresses are relative. In these cases you can instruct the program to reference absolute cell addresses. **Absolute addresses** are cell addresses that are *not* changed when a formula is copied from one location to another. For example, in the formula for interest paid that Ted wants to use, the reference to Cell C1 needs to remain constant each time the formula is copied. Ted can make this cell reference an absolute address by placing a dollar sign before both the column and the row of the cell address. That is, Ted can write the formula as (C1*D11). This formula tells Lotus

1-2-3 to keep the C1 reference the same every time the formula is copied.

You can also use mixed cell references in a formula. **Mixed cell references** are a combination of relative and absolute addresses. For example, if Ted wrote the formula ($C1*D11), Lotus would keep the column reference C the same but change the row reference by 1 each time the formula was copied.

As we mentioned, to copy the formula for the interest paid, Ted must make the C1 reference an absolute address. First he needs to replace the formula in Cell B12 with the formula (C1*D11). To enter the formula, he moves the cursor to B12; then he enters (C1*D11) and presses Enter. Next he presses the / key and selects the Copy command from the menu. As before, he enters the copy from range—in this case B12—and the copy to range, B13.B35. This means the formula will appear 24 times—the number of months Ted wants to see. Then he presses Enter again. Figure 7-17a shows what you actually see on the screen. Figure 7-17b shows the copied formula. Notice that the C1 reference stays the same and the D11 reference becomes D12, D13, D14, and so on down to 35.

Figure 7-17 Copying the formula for interest paid. *When Ted copies the formula for interest paid off, (a) he sees an ERR message in Cell B13 and $0.00 entered in every other cell in the column. (b) If Ted checked the contents of the cells in the column, he would see the formulas shown.*

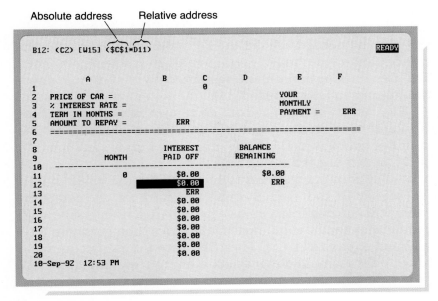

Absolute address   Relative address

(a)

(b)

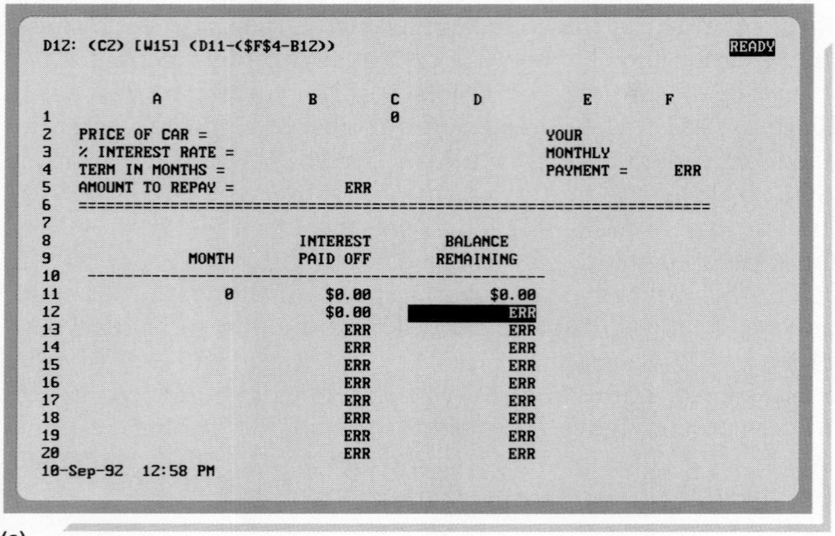

(a)

```
       BALANCE
      REMAINING
-----------------------
            $0.00
(D11-($F$4-B12))
(D12-($F$4-B13))
(D13-($F$4-B14))
(D14-($F$4-B15))
(D15-($F$4-B16))
(D16-($F$4-B17))
(D17-($F$4-B18))
(D18-($F$4-B19))
(D19-($F$4-B20))
(D20-($F$4-B21))
(D21-($F$4-B22))
(D22-($F$4-B23))
(D23-($F$4-B24))
(D24-($F$4-B25))
(D25-($F$4-B26))
(D26-($F$4-B27))
(D27-($F$4-B28))
(D28-($F$4-B29))
(D29-($F$4-B30))
(D30-($F$4-B31))
(D31-($F$4-B32))
(D32-($F$4-B33))
(D33-($F$4-B34))
(D34-($F$4-B35))
```

(b)

Figure 7-18 Copying the formula for balance remaining. *When Ted copies the formula for balance remaining, (a) he sees a column of ERR messages on the screen. (b) This figure shows the actual formulas contained in each cell in the column.*

To copy the formula for remaining balance, Ted moves the cursor to Cell D12 and enters the formula for balance remaining. He takes a look at his formula, (D11 – (F4 – B12)), and realizes that he needs to make the F4 reference an absolute reference. So he types in (D11 – (F4 – B12)) and enters it. Then Ted uses the Copy command again to copy the formula down the column to D35 (Figure 7-18).

The last thing Ted needs to do to complete all his entries is to enter the month numbers in column A. He can do this in one of two ways: (1) He can enter each number in each cell, or (2) he can use the formula (A11 + 1) and copy it down the cells. The formula tells Lotus 1-2-3 to take the value of Cell A11 and add 1 to it. If Ted copies this formula, the cell references will automatically change by one in each successive cell. Ted decides to use the formula. He moves the cursor to Cell A12 and enters (A11 + 1). Then Ted uses the Copy command to copy the formula down the column to row 35. Figure 7-19 shows the calculated results.

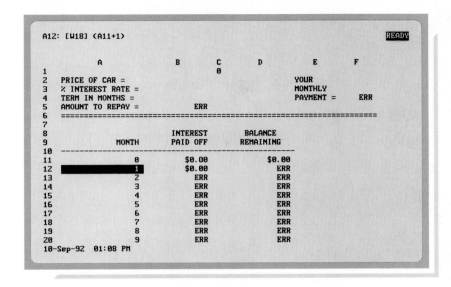

```
A12: [W18] (A11+1)                                              READY

              A            B        C        D           E        F
   1                                         0
   2   PRICE OF CAR =                                  YOUR
   3   % INTEREST RATE =                               MONTHLY
   4   TERM IN MONTHS =                                PAYMENT =    ERR
   5   AMOUNT TO REPAY =            ERR
   6   =====================================================================
   7
   8                            INTEREST      BALANCE
   9               MONTH        PAID OFF      REMAINING
  10   ---------------------------------------------------------------------
  11                 0          $0.00         $0.00
  12                 1          $0.00         ERR
  13                 2          ERR           ERR
  14                 3          ERR           ERR
  15                 4          ERR           ERR
  16                 5          ERR           ERR
  17                 6          ERR           ERR
  18                 7          ERR           ERR
  19                 8          ERR           ERR
  20                 9          ERR           ERR
  10-Sep-92   01:08 PM
```

Figure 7-19 Entering the month numbers. *Ted uses the formula (A11 + 1) in Cell A12 and then copies the formula into Cells A13 through A35.*

Editing the Spreadsheet

Now that Ted has entered all the formulas and labels, he wants to double check to make sure all his entries are correct, make changes if necessary, and make some cosmetic alterations to the spreadsheet. Lotus 1-2-3 has some simple commands to help him with these tasks.

Suppose Ted made a mistake. Perhaps he put the wrong information in a cell or range, or maybe he wants to insert or delete a row or column. Let us take a look at the commands used in Lotus to fix these mistakes.

Editing a Cell

Most spreadsheets have an **EDIT mode,** which lets you edit the entered label, value, or formula without retyping the whole entry. To use this command, Ted would move the cursor to the cell he wants to fix and press the F2 function key. This automatically places him in the EDIT mode. Now he can move the cursor back and forth through the entry, correcting as he goes. When he has made his corrections, he presses Enter—the new entry is placed in the cell and Lotus 1-2-3 returns him to the READY mode.

Erasing a Cell or Range

To erase a cell, Ted would move the cursor to the offending cell. Then he would access the command menu and select the Range option. Next Ted would select the Erase command. When the message "Enter range to erase" appears, Ted types in the appropriate range and presses Enter. The cells specified by the range are immediately erased.

Moving a Cell or Range

If Ted accidentally typed data in the wrong cell or range and he wanted to move the data to another cell or range, he could use the Move command. The Move command takes the contents of a range and transfers it to a different location. The contents are erased from the original cell. When this command is executed, the program automatically adjusts any formulas that depend on the moved cell entries. To use this command, Ted presses / to enter the MENU mode. Then he selects the Move command. The Move command requests the user to first identify a *move from* range and then a *move to* range. Ted types in the appropriate ranges and presses Enter.

Inserting a Row or Column

The Insert command allows Ted to add new blank rows or columns with a minimum of effort. This command does not replace any existing row or columns; instead, it pushes rows down and columns over to make room. When inserting a row or column, the position of the cursor determines where the new material will be placed. New rows are inserted just above the cursor, and new columns are inserted just to the left of the cursor.

Suppose Ted decides to insert a row between rows 5 and 6. He moves the cursor to row 6 and then selects the command sequence Worksheet, Insert, and Row. When Lotus 1-2-3 asks for the row range, Ted presses Enter. A blank row is inserted just above row 6. To add a column, Ted would select Column instead of Row.

Deleting a Row or Column

Now Ted wants to remove the row he just added. Once again he positions the cursor in row 6 and selects the Worksheet command. Then he selects the Delete command, rather than the Insert command. He selects Row and presses Enter at the range prompt. The added row disappears. To delete a column, Ted would select Column instead of Row.

Hiding Cells

Ted wants to make a cosmetic change to his worksheet by suppressing, or hiding, the display shown in Cell C1. Remember that this was the cell in which we placed the formula for calculating the monthly interest rate—something that Ted does not need to show his clients. Hiding the cell contents means that the value or formula in the cell is not displayed on the screen nor on a printed copy of the worksheet—it is still used in calculations, however. To hide a cell, Ted uses the Hidden command. This command is used to suppress the display of one or more cells in a worksheet. Ted moves his cursor to Cell C1. He uses the menus and submenus to select Range, Format, and Hidden. This suppresses the display of the contents of Cell C1. Now the worksheet appears as shown in Figure 7-20.

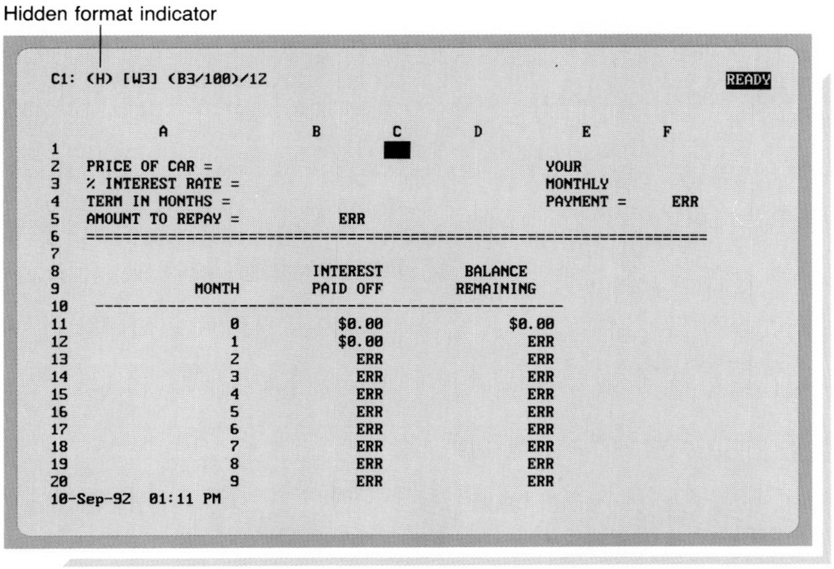

Figure 7-20 Hiding a cell. *Ted uses the Hidden command to hide the contents of Cell C1. Note that the cell no longer displays a 0. However, the formula entered into the cell is still used in calculations.*

Hidden format indicator

KEYSTROKES ONLY

The Loan-Analysis Example

These instructions are for creating Ted Nunez's spreadsheet, as described in the text. The Lotus 1-2-3 keystrokes that follow can also be used to create your own spreadsheets. (Note: Material introduced in Chapter 6 is not covered in this discussion.)

Changing the Column Width

1. Position the cursor in the column you wish to change.

2. Press the / key to enter the MENU mode.

3. Select the Worksheet option by pressing Enter.

4. Select the Column command by moving the cursor to Column and pressing Enter.

5. Select the Set-Width command.

6. Type in the desired column width and press Enter.

Formatting Labels

To format labels by using the Global command:

1. Press the / key to enter the MENU mode.

2. Select the Worksheet command.

3. Select the Global command.

4. Select the Label-Prefix command.

5. Select the desired label format.

To format labels by using the Range command:

1. Press the / key to enter the MENU mode.

2. Select the Range command.

3. Select the Label command.

4. Select the desired label format. Lotus asks you to define the range you wish to format.

5. Type in the range in the correct form. Then press Enter.

Copying Labels

1. Position the cursor in the cell to be copied.

2. Press the / key to enter the MENU mode.

3. Select the Copy command. Lotus asks you to enter the *copy from* range and displays the active cell range.

4. Press Enter to select this range. Lotus asks you to enter the *copy to* range.

5. Type in the range in the correct form. Then press Enter.

Formatting Values

To format values by using the Range command:

1. Press the / key to enter the MENU mode.

2. Select the Range command.

3. Select the Format command.

4. Select the desired value format. Lotus asks you to define the range you wish to format.

5. Type in the range in the correct form. Then press Enter.

To format values by using the Global command:

1. Press the / key to enter the MENU mode.

2. Select the Worksheet command.

3. Select the Global command.

4. Select the Format command.

5. Select the desired value format.

Copying the Formulas

1. Make sure that any absolute and/or mixed cells have been referenced with the $ symbol.

2. Position the cursor on the cell you wish to copy.

3. Press the / key to enter the MENU mode.

4. Select the Copy command. Lotus asks you to enter the *copy from* range and displays the active cell range.

5. Press Enter to select this range. Lotus then asks you to enter the *copy to* range.

6. Type in the range in the correct form. Then press Enter.

Editing a Cell

1. To edit the data in a cell, position the cursor on that cell.

2. Press F2 to enter the EDIT mode.

3. Use the cursor movement keys to move the cursor to the desired location.

4. Make the correction and press Enter. The correction appears in the cell.

Erasing a Cell or Range

1. Position the cursor on the cell you wish to erase.

2. Press the / key to enter the MENU mode.

3. Select the Range command.

4. Select the Erase command. Lotus asks you to enter the range you wish to erase.

5. If you are erasing a single cell, press Enter. If you are erasing a range, type in the range in the correct form. Then press Enter.

Moving a Cell or Range

1. Position the cursor on the cell you wish to move.

2. Press the / key to enter the MENU mode.

3. Select the Move command. Lotus asks you to enter a *move from* range and displays the active cell range.

4. Press Enter to select this range. Lotus then asks you to enter the *move to* range.

5. Type in the range in the correct form. Then press Enter.

Inserting a Row or Column

To insert a row:

1. Position the cursor in the cell below the place where you wish to insert the new row.

2. Press the / key to enter the MENU mode.

3. Select the Worksheet command.

4. Select the Insert command.

5. Select the Row command. Lotus asks you to enter the range of rows to be inserted. Press Enter to select the displayed range.

To insert a column:

1. Position the cursor in the cell to the right of the place where you wish to insert the new column.

2. Press the / key to enter the MENU mode.

3. Select the Worksheet command.

4. Select the Insert command.

5. Select the Column command. Lotus asks you to enter the range of columns to be inserted. Press Enter to select the displayed range.

Deleting a Row or Column

To delete a row:

1. Position the cursor in the first cell in the row to be deleted.

2. Press the / key to enter the MENU mode.

3. Select the Worksheet command.

4. Select the Delete command.

5. Select the Row command. Press Enter.

To delete a column:

1. Position the cursor in the first cell in the column to be deleted.

2. Press the / key to enter the MENU mode.

3. Select the Worksheet command.

4. Select the Delete command.

5. Select the Column command. Press Enter.

Hiding Cells

1. Position the cursor on the cell you wish to hide.

2. Press the / key to enter the MENU mode.

3. Select the Range command.

4. Select the Format command.

5. Select the Hidden command.

6. Press Enter.

Using the Completed Worksheet

To test the completed worksheet, Ted enters 11000 for the price of the car, 10 for the annual interest rate, and 18 months for the term. The spreadsheet automatically calculates all the results (Figure 7-21). Then Ted prints out the resulting payment schedule and checks the results with his calculator to verify that they are correct. To show the efficiency of electronic spreadsheets, Ted enters a new value for annual interest rate, 7. Notice how all the calculations are automatically recalculated in Figure 7-22.

But there is one aspect of the worksheet with which Ted

Figure 7-21 Using the completed worksheet. Ted enters in the values for the car price, the interest rate, and the term of the loan. Lotus 1-2-3 automatically does all the calculations for him. The values displayed in parentheses are negative values.

```
PRICE OF CAR =        $11,000.00              YOUR
% INTEREST RATE =             10              MONTHLY
TERM IN MONTHS =              18              PAYMENT = $660.63
AMOUNT TO REPAY =     $11,891.30
=======================================================================

                      INTEREST      BALANCE
             MONTH    PAID OFF       REMAINING
-----------------------------------------------------------------------
              0        $0.00        $11,000.00
              1       $91.67        $10,431.04
              2       $86.93         $9,857.34
              3       $82.14         $9,278.85
              4       $77.32         $8,695.55
              5       $72.46         $8,107.38
              6       $67.56         $7,514.32
              7       $62.62         $6,916.31
              8       $57.64         $6,313.32
              9       $52.61         $5,705.30
             10       $47.54         $5,092.22
             11       $42.44         $4,474.02
             12       $37.28         $3,850.68
             13       $32.09         $3,222.14
             14       $26.85         $2,588.36
             15       $21.57         $1,949.31
             16       $16.24         $1,304.92
             17       $10.87           $655.17
             18        $5.46             $0.00
             19        $0.00         ($660.63)
             20       ($5.51)      ($1,326.76)
             21      ($11.06)      ($1,998.45)
             22      ($16.65)      ($2,675.73)
             23      ($22.30)      ($3,358.65)
             24      ($27.99)      ($4,047.27)
```

is not satisfied. He notices that after the last month of the term of the loan (month 18 in this case), the balance remaining figures are not zero. Instead, the spreadsheet shows negative values (Lotus 1-2-3 displays them inside parentheses). This occurs because Lotus continues to calculate the formulas for all 24 months, even though the length of the term is only 18 months. Rather than make a complicated redesign of his worksheet, Ted decides to use another one of the Lotus functions, the @IF function.

Here is how the **@IF function** works: You give Lotus a condition to test. If the condition is true, you tell Lotus what to do; then you tell Lotus what to do if the condition is false.

Figure 7-22 Automatic recalculation. When Ted changes one of the values, in this case the interest rate, the program automatically redoes all the calculations.

```
PRICE OF CAR =          $11,000.00              YOUR
% INTEREST RATE =                7              MONTHLY
TERM IN MONTHS =                18              PAYMENT = $645.53
AMOUNT TO REPAY =       $11,619.63
=================================================================================

                            INTEREST        BALANCE
                MONTH       PAID OFF         REMAINING
        ----------------------------------------------------------------
                  0           $0.00         $11,000.00
                  1          $64.17         $10,418.63
                  2          $60.78          $9,833.87
                  3          $57.36          $9,245.70
                  4          $53.93          $8,654.10
                  5          $50.48          $8,059.05
                  6          $47.01          $7,460.52
                  7          $43.52          $6,858.51
                  8          $40.01          $6,252.98
                  9          $36.48          $5,643.92
                 10          $32.92          $5,031.31
                 11          $29.35          $4,415.13
                 12          $25.75          $3,795.35
                 13          $22.14          $3,171.95
                 14          $18.50          $2,544.92
                 15          $14.85          $1,914.23
                 16          $11.17          $1,279.86
                 17           $7.47            $641.79
                 18           $3.74           ($0.00)
                 19          ($0.00)         ($645.53)
                 20          ($3.77)       ($1,294.84)
                 21          ($7.55)       ($1,947.92)
                 22         ($11.36)       ($2,604.82)
                 23         ($15.19)       ($3,265.55)
                 24         ($19.05)       ($3,930.13)
```

Figure 7-23 The @IF function. *(a) Ted uses the @IF function to test whether the balance remaining for each month is greater or less than 0. If the balance for the month is greater than 0, Ted wants the balance to be displayed. If the balance for the month is less than 0, Ted wants $0.00 to be displayed. (b) The result of using the @IF function.*

```
                                        BALANCE
                                        REMAINING
        ------------------------------------------------------------------
        (B2)
        @IF((D11-($F$4-B12))>0,(D11-($F$4-B12)),0)
        @IF((D12-($F$4-B13))>0,(D12-($F$4-B13)),0)
        @IF((D13-($F$4-B14))>0,(D13-($F$4-B14)),0)
        @IF((D14-($F$4-B15))>0,(D14-($F$4-B15)),0)
        @IF((D15-($F$4-B16))>0,(D15-($F$4-B16)),0)
        @IF((D16-($F$4-B17))>0,(D16-($F$4-B17)),0)
        @IF((D17-($F$4-B18))>0,(D17-($F$4-B18)),0)
        @IF((D18-($F$4-B19))>0,(D18-($F$4-B19)),0)
        @IF((D19-($F$4-B20))>0,(D19-($F$4-B20)),0)
        @IF((D20-($F$4-B21))>0,(D20-($F$4-B21)),0)
        @IF((D21-($F$4-B22))>0,(D21-($F$4-B22)),0)
        @IF((D22-($F$4-B23))>0,(D22-($F$4-B23)),0)
        @IF((D23-($F$4-B24))>0,(D23-($F$4-B24)),0)
        @IF((D24-($F$4-B25))>0,(D24-($F$4-B25)),0)
        @IF((D25-($F$4-B26))>0,(D25-($F$4-B26)),0)
        @IF((D26-($F$4-B27))>0,(D26-($F$4-B27)),0)
        @IF((D27-($F$4-B28))>0,(D27-($F$4-B28)),0)
        @IF((D28-($F$4-B29))>0,(D28-($F$4-B29)),0)
        @IF((D29-($F$4-B30))>0,(D29-($F$4-B30)),0)
        @IF((D30-($F$4-B31))>0,(D30-($F$4-B31)),0)
        @IF((D31-($F$4-B32))>0,(D31-($F$4-B32)),0)
        @IF((D32-($F$4-B33))>0,(D32-($F$4-B33)),0)
        @IF((D33-($F$4-B34))>0,(D33-($F$4-B34)),0)
        @IF((D34-($F$4-B35))>0,(D34-($F$4-B35)),0)
```

(a)

```
PRICE OF CAR =          $11,000.00              YOUR
% INTEREST RATE =                7              MONTHLY
TERM IN MONTHS =                18              PAYMENT = $645.53
AMOUNT TO REPAY =       $11,619.63
==================================================================================

                        INTEREST        BALANCE
                MONTH   PAID OFF         REMAINING
        ----------------------------------------------------------------------
                0       $0.00           $11,000.00
                1       $64.17          $10,418.63
                2       $60.78          $9,833.87
                3       $57.36          $9,245.70
                4       $53.93          $8,654.10
                5       $50.48          $8,059.05
                6       $47.01          $7,460.52
                7       $43.52          $6,858.51
                8       $40.01          $6,252.98
                9       $36.48          $5,643.92
                10      $32.92          $5,031.31
                11      $29.35          $4,415.13
                12      $25.75          $3,795.35
                13      $22.14          $3,171.95
                14      $18.50          $2,544.92
                15      $14.85          $1,914.23
                16      $11.17          $1,279.86
                17      $7.47           $641.79
                18      $3.74           $0.00
                19      $0.00           $0.00
                20      $0.00           $0.00
                21      $0.00           $0.00
                22      $0.00           $0.00
                23      $0.00           $0.00
                24      $0.00           $0.00
```

(b)

The condition Ted wants to test is whether the balance remaining for each month is greater or less than 0. If the balance remaining in a particular cell is greater than 0, then Ted wants the result of the formula to be displayed. If the balance is not greater than 0, Ted wants a 0 displayed.

In this worksheet the formula for balance remaining for the first month is (D11 − (F4 − B12)). So the first half of the formula is

```
(D11-($F$4-B12))>0
```

(Remember that > means greater than.)

If it is *true* that the result of the calculation (in other words, the balance remaining) is greater than 0, then the program should display the result of the calculation in the cell. If the condition is *false*, then the program should show a 0, which Lotus will display in currency format. So the second half of the formula is

```
(D11-($F$4-B12)),0
```

Therefore, Ted makes the following entry in Cell D12:

```
@IF((D11-($F$4-B12))>0,(D11-($F$4-B12)),0)
```

Ted can then use the Copy command to replace the old formula in the cells in column D. Now the formula for balance remaining appears in his worksheet as shown in Figure 7-23a. The worksheet with the actual values displayed as they would be seen by a customer is shown in Figure 7-23b.

Now that Ted has completed his worksheet, he saves it for future use.

Spreadsheet Templates

As we mentioned, Ted wanted to create a spreadsheet he could use over and over again. This type of spreadsheet is known as a template. The term **template,** when it applies to worksheets, refers to a worksheet that has already been designed for the solution of a specific problem. All the necessary labels and formulas have been entered in the appropriate areas. Column widths and the formats for cells have already been specified. The user simply enters the numbers for his or her particular problem, and the worksheet performs the required calculations.

Like Ted, you can design a general-purpose worksheet of your own that contains titles, formulas, and formatting information but no data. You might do this for your personal monthly budget. Such a worksheet can be stored on disk and used as the basis for a template. At the beginning of each month, you load the template into the computer's memory and then fill in your monthly income and expenses as they occur.

You can also purchase templates on diskettes, ready to be loaded into memory and filled with your specific data. Prepackaged templates are available for a variety of purposes. Packages

```
A2:  'PRICE OF CAR =
A3:  '%INTEREST RATE =
A4:  'TERM IN MONTHS =
A5:  'AMOUNT TO REPAY =
B5:  (B4*F4)
C1:  (B3/100)/12
E2:  'YOUR
E3:  'MONTHLY
E4:  'PAYMENT
F4:  @PMT(B2,C1,B4)
A6:  ================
B6:  ==============
C6:  ===
D6:  ==============
E6:  =========
F6:  =========
A9:  ''MONTH
B8:  ''INTEREST
B9:  ''PAID OFF
D8:  ^BALANCE
D9:  ^REMAINING
A10: ---------------
B10: --------------
C10: ---
D10: --------------
E10: ---------
F10: ---------
A11: 0
A12: (A11+1)
A13: (A12+1)
A14: (A13+1)
A15: (A14+1)
A16: (A15+1)
A17: (A16+1)
A18: (A17+1)
A19: (A18+1)
A20: (A19+1)
A21: (A20+1)
A22: (A21+1)
A23: (A22+1)
B11: (C2) 0
B12: ($C$1*D11)
B13: ($C$1*D12)
B14: ($C$1*D13)
B15: ($C$1*D14)
B16: ($C$1*D15)
B17: ($C$1*D16)
B18: ($C$1*D17)
B19: ($C$1*D18)
B20: ($C$1*D19)
B21: ($C$1*D20)
B22: ($C$1*D21)
B23: ($C$1*D22)
D11: (C2) (B2)
D12: @IF((D11-($F$4-B12))>0,(D11-($F$4-B12)),0)
D13: @IF((D12-($F$4-B13))>0,(D12-($F$4-B13)),0)
D14: @IF((D13-($F$4-B14))>0,(D13-($F$4-B14)),0)
D15: @IF((D14-($F$4-B15))>0,(D14-($F$4-B15)),0)
D16: @IF((D15-($F$4-B16))>0,(D15-($F$4-B16)),0)
D17: @IF((D16-($F$4-B17))>0,(D16-($F$4-B17)),0)
D18: @IF((D17-($F$4-B18))>0,(D17-($F$4-B18)),0)
D19: @IF((D18-($F$4-B19))>0,(D18-($F$4-B19)),0)
D20: @IF((D19-($F$4-B20))>0,(D19-($F$4-B20)),0)
D21: @IF((D20-($F$4-B21))>0,(D20-($F$4-B21)),0)
D22: @IF((D21-($F$4-B22))>0,(D21-($F$4-B22)),0)
D23: @IF((D22-($F$4-B23))>0,(D22-($F$4-B23)),0)
```

Figure 7-24 A template for Ted's worksheet. *If you carefully enter the information in this list, you will create Ted's car-loan analysis worksheet for terms of 12 months or less.*

for individual use perform income tax preparation, stock-port-folio analysis, family budgets, and financial planning. Templates available for use in business include worksheets for payroll, general ledger entries, and project planning.

Some computer books and magazines often give templates in the form of lists that contain the cell addresses and the labels, numbers, and formulas needed to create a worksheet. We have shown Ted's worksheet in this form in Figure 7-24. The cell locations are given at the left of the table. The commands, or entries, that must be typed at that location are listed following the address of the cell. Move your cursor to the cell location given at the left of the table and then type the entries. If you do this carefully, you will get a working template for the first year of a car loan.

RANDOM BITS

Five Companies

Spreadsheets are not just for keeping track of budgets. The examples that follow illustrate some other ways spreadsheets are used in businesses.

Aviation West handles cargo for airlines flying out of Seattle. Customers deliver their own freight, which Aviation West loads onto cargo planes. Aviation West bills the airlines according to the weight of the freight. Supervisor Sandra Shaw uses spreadsheet software to keep track of the weight of each load, in pounds. This data fits nicely into a spreadsheet format, with the flight numbers as columns and the flight dates as rows.

In the financial service business, the brokerage giants have long been computer-sophisticated. Raymond James & Associates, based in Florida, stays in

the game by providing Sun Belt retirees with microcomputer-generated analyses of their finances. The brokers use spreadsheet programs to perform sophisticated "What if . . ." calculations on individual customer accounts. For example, a broker might use the program to consider "what if" this customer converts some current stocks into municipal bonds, thereby collecting lower revenues but eliminating taxes on the gains.

The Great Harvest Bread Company uses spreadsheets to keep an eye on the profit margin. The company uses the software to help choose vendors. The costs of ingredients vary from vendor to vendor, and a certain vendor may offer bargain prices on one or two items. The spreadsheet program tallies

the total costs based on ingredients used, thus pointing to the most economical vendor overall. In addition, these totals can be recalculated automatically if some of the costs change.

American Lunch, a cafeteria in Atlanta, uses spreadsheet software to calculate profit margins for different menu items and to monitor the effect of changes in the price of ingredients. Otherwise, the restaurant might be selling a dish for $5 that cost $6 to make.

Sales representatives in Chevron's fertilizer division travel with laptop computers. The salespeople use spreadsheet software to analyze farmers' needs. After entering in data on soil type and planned yield, the salespeople can print the report right on the spot.

Macros

S ometimes you need to enter repetitive sequences of keystrokes to communicate commands to your spreadsheet program. Two examples are the keystrokes needed to save a worksheet to disk or the keystrokes to print a worksheet at the printer.

Macro Advantages

Whenever you find that you are repeatedly using the same set of spreadsheet keystrokes, you should think about creating a macro. A **macro** is a sequence of commands (and sometimes formulas and data) stored as a label in a separate area of the worksheet. The macro is given a name, usually one or two keystrokes. When you push the keys representing the name of the macro, the spreadsheet program executes the keystrokes for the macro commands exactly as if you were typing them in on your keyboard.

Using a macro also reduces the number of keystroke errors that you make. You enter the command keystrokes carefully in the macro. Then you proofread the macro, try it out, and eliminate any errors. From that point on, this particular sequence of commands will be entered flawlessly each time you use the macro.

In addition to helping you by storing keystrokes in memory, macros let you use commands that cannot be executed directly from the keyboard. These commands must first be stored in a macro before they can be executed by the spreadsheet program. Lotus provides **Advanced Macro Commands** (sometimes called the Lotus 1-2-3 Command Language) that can be used in macros to give the user a powerful programming language. These are beyond the scope of this book, so we will not describe them here. However, sophisticated Lotus users find that these commands expand the power of Lotus tremendously. Just as templates for worksheets are available on disk, in books, and in magazines, hundreds of useful macros are available on disks and in books. Many spreadsheet users maintain libraries of their own macros, which they insert in their worksheets whenever the macros will be time-savers.

Some of the keystrokes that you enter from the keyboard must be stored in a different form in a macro. Figure 7-25 shows the keystrokes that you enter from the keyboard and their macro equivalents.

Keystroke	Macro equivalent	Function	Keystroke	Macro equivalent	Function
↵	~	Enter	(Del key)	{del}	Del key (Use only in EDIT mode)
↓	{down}	Moves cursor down	Esc	{esc}	Esc key
↑	{up}	Moves cursor up	F2	{edit}	Presses F2
→	{right}	Moves cursor right	F3	{name}	Presses F3
←	{left}	Moves cursor left	F4	{abs}	Presses F4
Home	{home}	Moves cursor to Cell A1	F5	{goto}	Presses F5
End	{end}	Moves cursor to end	F6	{window}	Presses F6
PgUp	{pgup}	Moves cursor one page up	F7	{query}	Presses F7
PgDn	{pgdn}	Moves cursor one page down	F8	{table}	Presses F8
Ctrl →	{bigright}	Moves cursor one page right	F9	{calc}	Presses F9
Ctrl ←	{bigleft}	Moves cursor one page left	F10	{graph}	Presses F10
←	{backspace}	Backspace key		{?}	Waits for keyboard entry

Figure 7-25 Special macro commands. *You can enter most keystrokes in a macro simply by typing the appropriate key. This figure shows some additional keystrokes.*

A Simple Macro

Since Ted frequently prints out the loan-analysis worksheet for his clients, he decides to create a simple macro to let him print a copy of a completed worksheet quickly. To do this, he first loads his worksheet into memory. Then he reviews the commands used to print a worksheet and enters them from his keyboard:

/P	Ted signals Lotus 1-2-3 that he wants to print the worksheet.
P	Ted indicates that he wants the output sent to the printer.
R	He signals that he is going to tell what range (part) of the worksheet he wants to have printed.
A1.F35 (Enter)	The range of the worksheet that contains client information is in the rectangle whose upper-left corner is Cell A1 and whose lower-right corner is Cell F35. Ted types this range and then presses Enter.
G	Ted types G (for Go) and Lotus starts printing.
Q	When the printing is finished, Ted types Q (for Quit) to return to the READY mode.

A shorthand version of this command is

`/PPRA1.F35`

followed by Enter, and then

`GQ`

(no Enter needed).

Now that he has verified the exact sequence of commands needed to print the worksheet, Ted is ready to store the commands as a macro. Ted wants his macro to be stored in an area of his worksheet that will not clutter up his loan-analysis results. He decides to store the macro in Cell H1 because column H will not show on the screen when he is using his spreadsheet.

He can enter the series of commands just as he did at the keyboard, with two important differences. First, he must enter an apostrophe (') to signal that he is beginning a label before he starts typing his macro. (Otherwise, when he presses the Slash key (/), he will be placed in the MENU mode and will be unable to enter the macro in his worksheet.) Second, the action of pressing Enter on the keyboard has to be stored in a macro by using a symbol, the **tilde** (~), pronounced "til'dah." Ted types in the macro as shown in Figure 7-26.

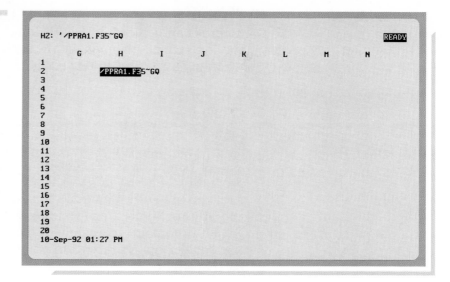

Figure 7-26 *Ted's macro.*
This macro allows Ted to print his spreadsheet by ressing the Alt and P keys at the same time.

The next step is giving the macro a unique name so that Lotus 1-2-3 can find the macro when Ted signals that he wants to execute it. Macros in Lotus must be named according to the following rule: The name must consist of a backslash (\) followed by a letter of the alphabet. Since there are only 26 letters in the alphabet, you can have a maximum of only 26 macros in a spreadsheet. Because the macro executes the Print command, Ted decides to name his macro \P.

Here is exactly how Ted implements his macro:

- Ted places the cursor on Cell H1, which will hold the macro.

- He then types

  `'/PPRA1.F35~GQ`

  and presses Enter.

- He then types the / to enter the MENU mode and selects Range, Name, and Create. When asked for the macro name, Ted types \P and presses Enter. Then he presses Enter again to enter the range.

Lotus now knows the name and the location (range) of the macro and will store this information with the worksheet. Since he wants his template to contain the macro, Ted saves the new version of his worksheet on his data disk.

Now Ted is ready to test his macro. He turns on his printer. Then he signals Lotus to execute the \P macro by pressing the Alt key and the letter in the macro name—in this case, the P key—together. Lotus executes the macro and prints his worksheet.

Ted's macro is a simple one, but it will save him time. Macros can be complex, with long strings of commands. But the steps we have shown are the same ones that you will follow when constructing advanced macros.

Just the Facts

Now that you have worked with both words and numbers, it is time to explore another type of applications program—one that lets you work with facts. Regardless of the data you are working with—for example, the prices of tickets, the titles of books, or the names of ball players—data is useful only if it is easily accessible. A database management system, the subject of the next two chapters, can help you get your facts straight.

Exercises

7-1

1. Load your spreadsheet program. Set the column width at 12 for columns A through E. Then enter the labels shown in Figure 7-27 for Cells A1 through E1 and Cells A2 through A7.
2. Use the Range command to center the labels in Cells A1 through A7. Use the Range command to right justify the labels in Cells B1 through E1. Notice that the labels in Cells B1 through E1 should be right justified.
3. Set the range format to fixed for Cells B2 through B7. The number of decimal places should be set at 0. Enter the data shown in the figure for those cells. Position the cursor in Cell B3. What is displayed next to the cell address indicator in the upper-left corner of the screen?
4. Enter the data shown in the figure for Cells C2 through C7 and Cells E2 through E7. Set the range format to currency with two decimal places for those cells. Position the cursor in Cell C3. What is displayed next to the cell address indicator in the upper-left corner of the screen?

Figure 7-27

	A	B	C	D	E
1	STOCK	SHARES	PRICE	DATE BOUGHT	DIVIDENDS
2	AT&T	20	27	05-Jul-93	1.2
3	APPLE	100	40	13-Oct-93	0.5
4	COMPAQ	50	53	21-Jan-94	0
5	IBM	150	111	23-Apr-94	4.4
6	ASHTON-TATE	90	25	09-Aug-94	0
7	MICROSOFT	200	56	17-Nov-94	0

5. Enter the data shown in the figure for Cells D2 through D7.
    Do you need to enter the information as a value or as a label?
6. Save the spreadsheet as EX7-1.
7. Exit the program.

7-2

1. Load your spreadsheet program and enter the worksheet shown
    in Figure 7-28. As you are entering the information, center the
    words in Cells B1, C1, and D1. Save the worksheet as EX7-2.
    Notice that the labels in Cells B1 through E1 should be right
    justified.
2. Enter the @SUM function in Cell E7 to calculate the totals for
    Cells B7 through D7. Use the Copy command to copy this
    function into Cells E8 through E12 so that the monthly totals
    are calculated.
3. Enter the @SUM function in Cell B14 to calculate the totals
    for Cells B7 through B12. Use the Copy command to copy this
    function into Cells C14, D14, and E14.
4. Enter the @AVG function in Cell B15 to calculate the average
    sales for B7 through B12. Use the Copy command to copy this
    function into Cells C15, D15, and E15.
5. Save the worksheet as EX7-2A.
6. Exit the program.

7-3

1. Load the program and retrieve EX7-2A.
2. Change the format of the values in the range B7..E12 to the
    currency format. The number of decimal places should be set
    at 2. What happens to the values in those cells?

Figure 7-28

	A	B	C	D	E
1		FIRST	HALF	SALES	
2					
3					
4	MONTH	CARS	TRUCKS	VANS	TOTAL
5	==
6					
7	JANUARY	100000	50000	30000	
8	FEBRUARY	120000	40000	40000	
9	MARCH	100000	60000	50000	
10	APRIL	130000	70000	50000	
11	MAY	200000	90000	70000	
12	JUNE	270000	130000	110000	
13					
14	TOTAL =				
15	AVERAGE =				

3. Change the column width to 15 for columns B, C, D, and E. Now what happens to the values in those cells?
4. Change the format of the values in the range B14.E14 to the currency format. The number of decimal places should be set at 2.
5. Change the format of the values in the range B15.E15 to the fixed number format. The number of decimal places should be set at 2.
6. Save the revised spreadsheet as EX7-3.
7. Print the worksheet.
8. Erase the worksheet from the screen.

7-4

1. Retrieve EX7-3.
2. Use the Worksheet Insert Column command to add a column between column D and column E. What happens to the data in column D? In column E?
3. Enter the information that follows into the new column. (Note: You will have to set the width of the column and format it so that the dollar values can be displayed as shown).

Row 4: "CYCLES"
Row 5: = = = = = = = = =
Row 7: $70,000.00
Row 8: $50,000.00
Row 9: $50,000.00
Row 10: $60,000.00
Row 11: $80,000.00
Row 12: $130,000.00

Did the totals in column F change when you entered this data? If not, change the formulas so those amounts reflect the new data you entered.
4. Are the totals and average amounts for the CYCLES column calculated? Why or why not? If not, make the necessary changes so those amounts are calculated.
5. Save the worksheet as EX7-4.
6. Print the worksheet.

7-5

1. Enter the worksheet shown in Figure 7-29. Format the worksheet exactly as it is shown—you will have to determine the proper column widths and format. Also enter the formulas for the balances in column H and totals for columns F, G, and H.
2. Save the spreadsheet as EX7-5.

INVOICE NO.	INVOICE DATE	CUST. NO.	COMPANY	DATE DUE	TOTAL DUE	TOTAL PAYMENTS	BALANCE
1520	09/01/90	86	CLARK & REYNOLDS	10/02/90	$743.56	$375.00	
1521	09/01/90	12	HARPER MANUFACTURING	10/02/90	$409.86	$0.00	
1522	09/02/90	15	PG & E	10/03/90	$557.64	$557.64	
1523	09/02/90	36	BARDEL & ANDREWS	10/03/90	$344.05	$300.00	
1524	09/02/90	20	GARDEN MANUFACTURING	10/03/90	$119.62	$119.62	
1526	09/03/90	123	MAXWELL & SONS	10/04/90	$682.45	$0.00	
1527	09/03/90	22	MASON'S SUPPLIES	10/04/90	$705.91	$700.00	
1528	09/04/90	12	HARPER MANUFACTURING	10/04/90	$359.44	$350.00	
				TOTAL			

Figure 7-29

3. Make the following changes to the spreadsheet:
   - Change 743.56 in Cell F4 to 375.00
   - Change 119.62 in Cell F8 to 478.92
   - Change 557.64 in Cell G3 to 400.15
   - Change 0.00 in Cell G6 to 682.45
4. Print the worksheet.
5. Save the revised spreadsheet as EX7-5A.

7-6

A mortgage is a loan used to buy real estate, such as a house. The mortgage is paid off in equal monthly installments for a certain number of years, usually 15, 25, or 30. In this exercise you will be developing a template that calculates the monthly payment on a mortgage.

1. Begin with a blank spreadsheet on your screen. Set the column width for A and B to 12.
2. Enter the following labels:

   A1:   ^INTEREST
   A2:   ^TERM (YRS)
   A4:   ^AMOUNT
   A5:   ^BORROWED
   B4:   ^MONTHLY
   B5:   ^PAYMENT
   A6:   ---------
   B6:   ---------

3. Set the format to percent for Cell B1. There should be 2 decimal places.
4. Set the format to currency for the range A7.B20. There should be 2 decimal places.
5. Enter the following values and formulas in their respective cells:

   A7:   100000
   A8:   (A7 + 10000)

```
                    INTEREST          10.00%
                    TERM  (YRS)          20

                    AMOUNT          MONTHLY
                    BORROWED        PAYMENT
             -------------------------------------------
                    $100,000.00        $965.02
                    $110,000.00      $1,061.52
                    $120,000.00      $1,158.03
                    $130,000.00      $1,254.53
                    $140,000.00      $1,351.03
                    $150,000.00      $1,447.53
                    $160,000.00      $1,544.03
                    $170,000.00      $1,640.54
                    $180,000.00      $1,737.04
                    $190,000.00      $1,833.54
                    $200,000.00      $1,930.04
                    $210,000.00      $2,026.55
                    $220,000.00      $2,123.05
                    $230,000.00      $2,219.55
```

Figure 7-30

6. Use the Copy command to copy the formula in A8 to Cells A9 through A20.
7. Use the @PMT function to calculate the monthly payment in Cells B7 through B20. The monthly interest is the interest (Cell B1) divided by 12. The monthly term is the term in years (Cell B2) multiplied by 12.
8. Save the template as EX7-6.
9. Enter .1 for the interest in Cell B1 (the interest should appear as 10.00% in the cell) and 20 years for the term in Cell B2. Your spreadsheet should be similar to the one shown in Figure 7-30. If it is not, double check your entries.
10. Save the worksheet as EX7-6A.
11. Change the interest rate to 15% and the term to 25 years.
12. Save the worksheet as EX7-6B.
13. Print the worksheet.

7-7

1. Retrieve EX7-6A.
2. Create a macro that will print the worksheet. Place the macro in Cell C1 with the name \P.
3. Create a macro that will save the worksheet as EX7-7. Place the macro in Cell C2 with the name \S.
4. Use the \P macro to print the worksheet.
5. Hide the contents of Cells C1 and C2.
6. Use the \S macro to save the worksheet.
7. Erase the worksheet from the screen.

7-8

1. Use the @IF function to create a formula that has the value 0 if A1 is positive and the value 1 if A1 is negative. Place the formula in Cell B1. Use your spreadsheet to see what this function will display in Cell B1 if A1 equals the following:

    - -120
    - 50
    - 200
    - -7

2. Use the @IF function to create a formula that has the value 0 if A2 is less than B2, and the value 1 if A2 is greater than or equal to B2. Place the formula in Cell C2. Use your spreadsheet to test this function if A2 and B2 contain the following values:

A2	B2
100	50
50	100
-100	-50
-50	-100

3. Use the @IF function to create a formula that has the value 0 if (A3 ∗ B3) is less than or equal to 0 and displays the result of the calculation if (A3 ∗ B3) is greater than 0. For example, if A3 = 5 and B3 = 2, then Cell C3 would display the result of multiplying 5 by 2, or 10. Place the formula in Cell C3. Use your spreadsheet to evaluate this function if A3 and B3 contain the following values:

A3	B3
2	2
-2	5
-3	-10
15	0

4. Save the worksheet as EX7-8.

7-9

1. Assume you work for a company that sells art supplies. The company gives customers a 10% discount off the list price of a product if the customer buys 100 or more units of that product. If the customer buys less than 100 units of a product,

there is a 5% discount. Using your spreadsheet program, construct a worksheet in which the list prices of the items are stored in column A, the quantities ordered of the items are stored in column B, and the total amounts that the customer owes are displayed in column C.

2. Enter the following values for column A:

       100
        50
       150
       200
        20

3. Enter the following values for column B:

       150
       100
        50
       200
        75

4. Save the spreadsheet as EX7-9.
5. Print the spreadsheet.
6. Exit the program.

Summary and Key Terms

- To design a worksheet by using a spreadsheet program, you must decide what information you want to include; what labels, values, and formulas you will need; and what you want the spreadsheet to look like overall.

- When a label is entered in a cell, it is displayed on the screen in a certain way. This is called the label's **format.** The **default format** for labels is **left justification.** You can override the default format by typing a **default label prefix** just before typing the actual label in the cell. In Lotus 1-2-3 an apostrophe indicates left justification, a double quotation mark indicates **right justification,** and a **caret** indicates that you want to **center** the label.

- The **Global command** changes the format for all unfilled cells; the **Range command** changes the settings for a specified range of cells.

- The **Label Repeat command** tells Lotus to repeat the character you enter as many times as needed to fill a cell.

- The **Copy command** lets you duplicate the contents of one or more cells in a range. The cell or cells you wish to copy are referred to as the **copy from range.** The cell or cells you wish to copy to are referred to as the **copy to range.**

- Unlike labels, values are always displayed right-justified in a cell. However, most spreadsheet programs can display a value in a variety of different formats. Some common formats are currency, percent, scientific, and date formats.

- Lotus has a special function for calculating monthly payments—the **@PMT function.** To use this function, you must supply information on the amount borrowed, the monthly interest rate, and the term of the loan.

- An **ERR message** tells you that no values have been entered, so Lotus cannot make the calculation requested in the cell in which the message appears. Once values are entered, the ERR message will be replaced with the result of the formula.

- You can use the Copy command to copy the formulas entered. The cell addresses are **relative**—that is, they will change in a predictable way as the formula is copied. You may, however, instruct the program to reference **absolute addresses.**

You can also use **mixed** cell references, which combine relative and absolute addresses.

- Most spreadsheets have an **EDIT mode,** which lets you edit an already entered label, value, or formula without retyping the whole entry.

- With the Erase command, you can erase a cell or range. The Move command transfers the contents of a range to a different location. The Insert command allows you to add new blank rows or columns. The Delete command allows you to delete rows or columns. The Hidden command suppresses the display of one or more cells in a worksheet.

- The **@IF function** allows you to test conditions related to the cells in the worksheet.

- A **template** is a worksheet that has already been designed for the solution of a specific problem. All the necessary labels and formulas have been entered in the appropriate areas, and the column widths and formats for cells have been specified.

- A **macro** is a sequence of commands (and sometimes formulas and data) stored as a label in a separate area of the worksheet. Lotus provides **Advanced Macro Commands** that can be used in macros to give the user a powerful programming language. The action of pressing Enter is represented in a macro by the **tilde.** Macro names consist of a \ followed by a letter of the alphabet.

Review Questions

1. What do you need to do before you enter a worksheet by using a spreadsheet program?

2. What is meant by the term *default column width?* How can you change the default column width?

3. What is meant by the term *default label prefix?*

4. How do you change the format of a label?

5. What is the difference between the Global Format command and the Range Format command?

6. What does the Label Repeat command do?

7. What is the copy to range? What is the copy from range?

8. What information does the @ PMT function provide? What three pieces of information must be supplied when you use this function?

9. What is a relative cell address in a formula? What is an absolute cell address? What is a mixed cell reference?

10. What is meant by the formula +H11*(D33−G13)? Explain this generally, not with reference to Ted's worksheet.

11. What does it mean to hide a cell in a worksheet? What command in Lotus 1-2-3 is used to hide a cell?

12. Explain what is meant by this cell entry:

    `@IF(L11=L22,M10,M15)`

13. What is a template? Why is a template useful?

14. What is a macro? Why are macros used in a worksheet?

15. How do you name a macro? How do you execute a macro?

Keeping Track of People at RKO

RKO is a large and diverse company that includes 12 radio stations, 2 TV stations, a bottling division, 2 hotels, and sales from RKO Pictures film classics like *King Kong*. These enterprises employ about 2800 people around the country; Robert Del Guidice, vice president of human resources, keeps track of them.

Mr. Del Guidice oversees hiring, labor relations, employee benefits, and affirmative action with the help of a computer. His key software tool is Lotus 1-2-3, which he uses for a variety of purposes. He uses his modem to send Lotus spreadsheet files containing bonus recommendations for executives. He knows how to download the company's daily stock-closing price into a spreadsheet, execute a Lotus macro he wrote to compute the stock's value,

and tell a colleague how much an individual stock incentive plan is worth at the moment. He finds Lotus to be very helpful when he has to take into consideration accrued vacation and sick leave to design an employee severance plan.

Del Guidice also does his entire budget by using Lotus. The year he translated his spreadsheets to pie charts was the first year that his budget was approved without anything being changed at all. He observes that the graphics may seem like bells and whistles, but they present a picture that helps the audience understand.

Despite this rather long list of applications on the personal computer, Del Guidice considers his computer use to be modest. "I don't think we're the ultimate computer users by any stretch of the imagination. I

feel we've reached a plateau and my gut tells me there's a level of sophistication out there that we have not yet achieved, and maybe someday we'll get there."

His computer is on all day, and Del Guidice estimates he is at the keyboard 15 to 20% of the workday. He cannot conceive of doing the work he does today without computers. A logical conclusion might be that *computer skills* are part of the job description for his department. Although he notes that everyone on his staff has computer skills, he is reluctant to say that these skills are an absolute job requirement. But what about the job description for the manager? Del Guidice hedges there too—his answer is "Probably not." But then he adds that it is a skill he would like the manager to have. He also notes that people are quick to indicate any computer experience on resumes. Typically, in a section titled "Other interests," they mention that they are comfortable with Lotus 1-2-3 or another program. He also notes that the people in his own organization would be more valuable on the job market because of their computer skills.

Del Guidice cannot imagine doing his work today without computers. "Everybody says the same thing," he says. "How did we live without these things?"

8 Database Management Systems

Chapter Objectives

After reading this chapter you should be able to

- Define *database* and *database management systems*

- Explain the differences among fields, records, and files

- Describe the advantages of using database programs

- Load and exit dBASE III PLUS software

- Use dBASE III PLUS commands to create a database file, input records, and list records and fields

- Use dBASE III PLUS commands to add, delete, and modify records

Storing and using data is absolutely vital in today's society. A **database** is an organized collection of related data. In a loose sense you are using a database when you use a phone book, look in a library's card catalog, or take a file out of a file cabinet. Unfortunately, as the amount of data increases, creating, storing, changing, sorting, and retrieving data become overwhelming tasks. For example, suppose you had a collection of names and addresses, each on a separate index card stored in a box (Figure 8-1). If you had only 25 cards, putting the cards in alphabetical order or even finding all the people who have the same zip code would be fairly easy. But what if you had 100, or 1000, or 10,000 cards? What if you had several different boxes, one organized by names, one by city, and one by zip codes? What if you had different people adding more cards each day, not knowing if they are duplicating other cards in the file? And what if you had another set of people trying to update the data on the cards? As you can see, things might get out of hand. Enter computers and database management software.

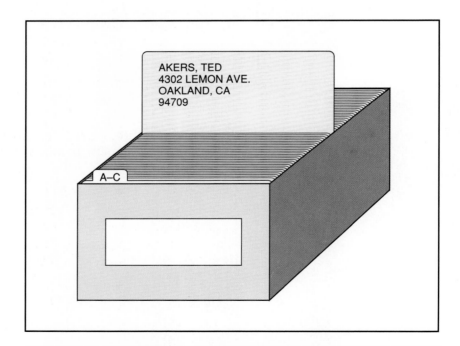

Figure 8-1 An index-card database. *Each card in this index-card file contains one person's name and address. The cards are arranged alphabetically by last name.*

Getting It Together: Database Programs

A database management system (DBMS) is software that helps you organize data in a way that allows fast and easy access to the data. In essence, the program acts as a very efficient and elaborate file system. With a database program you can create, modify, store, and retrieve data in a variety of ways. Some benefits of database management system software are

- **Integrated files.** Using a database, separate files can be joined together. For example, consider two file drawers, one for customers and one for sales representatives. Suppose you needed data—perhaps the address of a sales rep who helped a particular customer. You would have to look first in the customer drawer to find the name of the sales rep and then in the sales rep drawer to find the sales rep's address. Database programs smooth the way for these types of searches by storing the relationships needed to combine data from different files stored on disk.

- **Reduced redundancy.** When businesses have many different files, the same data is often stored in several different places. In a database, data is usually stored in just one place. This reduces the amount of duplicate data in the system. In addition, updating can be done quickly and efficiently, without having to track down the repeated data.

- **Shared data.** Data in files can be shared by different people. Separate files for each department or function are unnecessary. Data can be stored once and accessed by authorized people using computers.

- **Centralized security.** When data is all in one place, you have better control over access to it. Scattered files are more difficult to protect. Security is particularly important for personnel files, restricted product information, customer credit ratings, marketing plans, and similar sensitive data.

In this chapter we will show you how to create and modify a database. Then, in the next chapter, we will show you how to locate and manipulate data in a database. But first we need to discuss some of the general terms used with databases.

Using a Database Management System

There are a large number of DBMS programs on the market today. Covering all the operations, features, and functions of every individual package would be impossible. Therefore, throughout this chapter and the next, we will discuss the characteristics and features of one of the most popular database programs—dBASE III PLUS, which we will call dBASE for short. This program has many features in common with other database software packages.

Database Organization

In a file system, data is stored in segregated files. A file system cannot store information about how data in one file is related to data in another file. A database, however, can store data relationships, so files can be integrated. Data stored in integrated files can be combined. The way the database organizes data depends on the type, or **model,** of the database.

Figure 8-2 A relational database. In this example the address list in (a) is organized as a relational database in (b). Note that the data is laid out in rows and columns; each field is equivalent to a vertical column and each record is equivalent to a horizontal row.

Akers, Ted
4302 Lemon Ave.
Oakland, CA 94709

Brown, Ann
345 Willow Rd.
Palo Alto, CA 94025

Chandler, Joy
4572 College Ave.
Berkeley, CA 94705

James, Susan
822 York St.
San Francisco, CA 94103

Mead, Ken
8 Rocklyn Ave.
Tiburon, CA 94903

(a)

Field

LAST NAME	FIRST NAME	STREET	CITY	STATE	ZIPCODE
AKERS	TED	4302 LEMON AVE.	OAKLAND	CA	94709
BROWN	ANN	345 WILLOW RD.	PALO ALTO	CA	94025
CHANDLER	JOY	4572 COLLEGE AVE.	BERKELEY	CA	94705
JAMES	SUSAN	822 YORK ST.	SAN FRANCISCO	CA	94103
MEAD	KEN	8 ROCKLYN AVE.	TIBURON	CA	94903

← Record

(b)

There are three database models—hierarchical, network, and relational. Each type structures, organizes, and uses data differently. Hierarchical and network databases are usually found on mainframes and minicomputers, so we will not discuss them here. On personal computers, however, relational databases are usually used.

A **relational database** organizes data in a table format consisting of related rows and columns. Figure 8-2a shows an address list; in Figure 8-2b, this data is laid out as a table. In a relational system, data in one file can be related to data in another, allowing you to tie together data from several files.

Fields, Records, and Files

In a relational database a table is called a **relation.** Notice in Figure 8-2b that each box in the table contains a piece of data, known as a **data item.** Each column of the table represents a **field,** or **attribute.** The specific data items in a field may vary, but each field contains the same type of data—for example, first names or zip codes. In a given relation there is a fixed number of fields. All the data in any given row is called a **record,** or **tuple.** Each record has a fixed number of fields, but there can be a variable number of records in a given relation. Figure 8-2b shows five records—one for each person. A relation—a table—is also called a **file.** Furthermore, a database file can be considered a collection of records. Although we have introduced the formal terms *attribute, tuple,* and *relation* in this discussion, we shall be referring to them by their more common names: *field, record,* and *file,* respectively.

Database File Structure

There are two steps to creating a database file: designing the structure of the file and entering the data into the file. To create the file structure, you must choose meaningful fields. The fields you choose should be based on the data you will want to retrieve from the database. For example, if you are creating a list of addresses, you might define fields for name, street address, city, state, and zip code. After you load the program and tell the software that you want to create a file structure, you will see a structure input form on the screen. The form is similar to Figure 8-3 (on the next page). Notice that the program asks for several types of information. Let us take a look at each one.

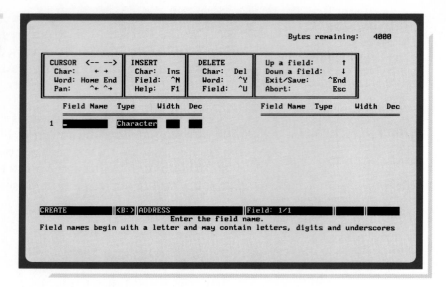

Figure 8-3 Building the file structure. *When you create a file structure, you must fill in information about the field name, field type, and field width for each field in your database.*

Field Names. **Field names** are the names of the data you want to use. For example, a field called PHONE might contain a phone number, and a field called NAME might contain a name. They can be up to ten characters long, must begin with a letter, and cannot contain a space or any punctuation. Letters, numbers, and underscores are permitted.

Field Types. There are four commonly used types of fields: character fields, numeric fields, date fields, and logical fields. **Character fields** contain descriptive data such as names, addresses, and telephone numbers. **Numeric fields** contain numbers used for calculations. When you enter a numeric field, you must specify the number of decimal places you wish to use. **Date fields** are automatically limited to eight characters, including the slashes used to separate the month, day, and year. **Logical fields** accept only single characters. Logical fields are used to keep track of true and false conditions. For example, if you want to keep track of whether a bill has been paid, you could use a logical field and enter Y for *yes* or N for *no*.

Field Widths. The **field width** determines the maximum number of characters or digits to be contained in the field, including decimal points. Most database programs let you enter up to 128 fields in each record, and each character type field can be up to 254 characters.

Telling the Program What to Do

The dBASE program gives you two options for entering commands: You can either use a menu—called the **Assistant menu**—or type in commands directly by using the **COMMAND mode.** Either method gets the job done.

The Assistant Menu. When you first access dBASE, the Assistant menu appears on the screen, as shown in Figure 8-4a. This menu offers a set of choices. Each selection on the top line of the menu has an associated **selection bar** that appears

Figure 8-4 Telling dBASE III PLUS what to do. *The dBASE program gives you two options for entering commands: (a) The Assistant menu offers you a series of choices. You can use the cursor movement keys and Enter to make your selections. (b) When you are in the COMMAND mode, you see a dot—called the dot prompt—near the lower left of your screen. With the limited-use version of dBASE III PLUS, the prompt is a dot followed by the word (DEMO). In this mode you simply type in the command you want to use and then press Enter.*

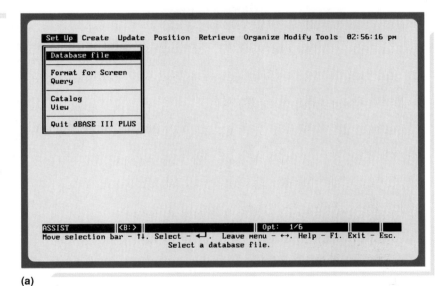

(a)

Dot prompt

(b)

THINKING IT THROUGH

Here are some points to consider if you are thinking about using a database on a personal computer.

■ Think about why you want to use a DBMS. What data do you want to store in your database files?

■ How do you want to input the data you want to store?

■ How do you want the DBMS to retrieve and present the stored data to you?

■ Will you want to be able to retrieve certain records, based on certain data values—such as all records with a certain zip code?

■ Will you want periodic reports made by the DBMS from your database?

■ How many fields do you need to store on a record?

■ What is the maximum number of records you need to store in a file?

■ What common fields are included in each file you wish to relate? Most relational DBMS programs for personal computers require specific conditions if you want to link two files together. Often, "joined" files must contain a common field.

■ If a particular DBMS seems appropriate, look at the documentation for it. Can you understand it? If not, are there helpful guides available in bookstores?

when the main selection is highlighted by the cursor. In Figure 8-4a, for example, the cursor rests on Set Up; the associated selection bar offers the choices Database file, Format for Screen, Query, Catalog, View, and Quit dBASE III PLUS. You can use the right and left cursor keys to move the cursor back and forth across the menu choices on the top line. When you wish to select an option, highlight that option with the cursor and press Enter.

The COMMAND Mode. If you want to issue commands directly to dBASE, you need to dismiss the Assistant menu and enter the COMMAND mode. To do this, press the Esc (Escape) key once. The menu screen disappears and a dot, called the **dot prompt,** appears near the lower left of your screen (Figure 8-4b). When you see the dot prompt, the program is ready for you to type a command. It is similar to the A> prompt that signals that the operating system is ready for a DOS command. After typing each command, press Enter. You can return to the Assistant menu any time by typing ASSIST after the dot prompt and then pressing Enter. In fact, you can switch back and forth between the Assistant menu and the dot prompt any time you want to; as noted, Esc takes you from the menu to the dot prompt, and ASSIST takes you from the dot prompt to the Assistant menu.

Relational Operators

At times, you will need to use a command called a **relational operator** when making comparisons or when entering instructions. The following relational operators are commonly used:

COMMAND	EXPLANATION
<	Less than
>	Greater than
=	Equal to
<=	Less than or equal to
>=	Greater than or equal to
<>	Not equal to

These operators are particularly useful when you want to locate specific data items. For example, to instruct a program to search through an address database and find the records of all the people who live in Wisconsin, you would enter the command

```
LIST FOR STATE = "WI"
```

This tells the program to look for the characters WI in the state field.

Now that we have reviewed the basics of database programs, let us move on to the most critical part of using a DBMS—the design and creation of a database.

Building a Database

Rita Chung works as an intern for a public television station in the San Francisco area. One of her jobs is to keep track of the people who have pledged to donate money to the station. Currently, each person's name, city, and phone number is kept on a separate card, along with the amount pledged and the date the pledge was made. Rita wants to place this data into a computer by using dBASE. She also wants to add another column of data that tells whether each person has actually paid the amount he or she pledged.

First Rita sketches on paper the structure of the database—what data she wants in each row and column (Figure 8-5, on the next page). Her next step is to enter this structure into the computer. (An abbreviated version of the discussion that follows appears in the box called "Keystrokes Only: Building a Database.")

Loading the Program

To use dBASE, Rita must first boot the system. Once she sees the A> on the screen, she places dBASE Disk #1 in drive A and her formatted data disk in drive B. Then she types DBASE and presses Enter. When the program has been loaded, dBASE displays a copyright notice and asks Rita to press Enter to start the program. Then dBASE displays the instruction "Insert System Disk 2 and press Enter, or press Ctrl-C to abort."

Rita removes Disk #1 and places Disk #2 in drive A. Then she presses Enter again, which causes the Assistant menu to appear on the screen.

Throughout the rest of this chapter, we will be using dot prompt commands. However, when appropriate, the instructions for using both the dot prompt commands and the Assistant menu can be found in the "Keystrokes Only" box.

Figure 8-5 Designing the
file structure. Rita quickly
sketches how she wants to
set up her database. Note
that she has seven fields—
LNAME, FNAME, CITY,
PHONE, AMOUNT, DATE,
and PAID.

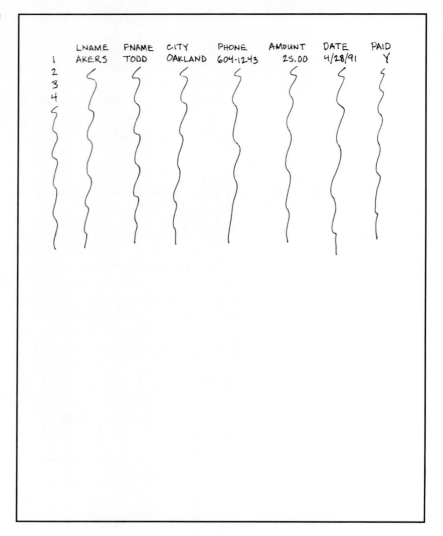

Creating the File Structure

As we mentioned earlier, before Rita can enter data into
her database, she needs to create the file structure for her files.
She starts by pressing the Esc key to leave the ASSISTANT
mode. The dot prompt appears in her screen's lower-left corner.
This means that the program is ready for Rita to enter a command. To create a file structure, she types CREATE and presses
Enter. dBASE responds by asking for the name of the file she
wishes to create (Figure 8-6a). Because Rita wants to store the
data file on her data disk in drive B, she types in B:PLEDGES
and presses Enter. When she does this, a Create screen appears,

Figure 8-6 Creating the file structure. *(a) Once Rita is in the COMMAND mode, she types in CREATE after the dot prompt and presses Enter. dBASE then asks her to name the new file.*
(b) After Rita enters the name B:PLEDGES, a Create screen appears. The lower highlighted line on the screen tells Rita several pieces of information (from left to right): the mode she is in (CREATE), the disk drive where her file will be stored (B), the name of her file (PLEDGES), and the number of fields currently in the file (1/1). The program uses the last two lines to prompt Rita regarding her next step.

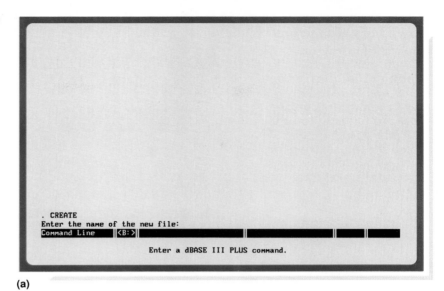

(a)

(b)

and a cursor flashes under the Field Name heading (Figure 8-6b). Notice that "CREATE" appears in the lower-left corner of the screen. dBASE uses this space to tell you what command you are currently using. Under the lower highlighted bar, the program prompts Rita regarding her next step. In this case, dBASE prompts her to enter a field name and also defines the guidelines for doing so.

Now Rita fills in the blanks for each field in her database. She types in LNAME for *last name* (remember, dBASE does not accept spaces in field names) and presses Enter. The cursor

Figure 8-7 Entering fields into the file structure.
(a) Rita starts to fill in the definitions for the first field in her file. When she presses Enter, the cursor moves to the next column. (b) When Rita has completed the information for one field, the cursor moves down to the next line.

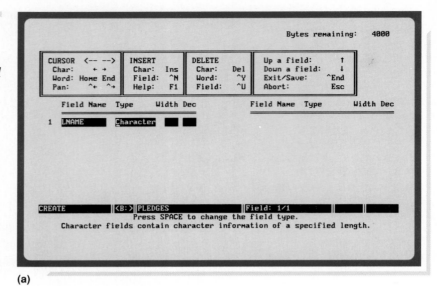

(a)

(b)

moves to the Type column. In Figure 8-7a notice the word "Character" under the Type column. If Rita wanted to enter another type of field, she could press Spacebar until the appropriate field type appeared in the column. However, LNAME is a character field, so she simply presses Enter and the cursor moves on to the Width column. Rita wants the width of the LNAME field to be ten characters wide, so she types 10. After she presses Enter, the cursor moves down to the next line (Figure 8-7b). Note that the decimal place column (Dec) was ignored, since LNAME is not a numeric field.

Rita continues to enter the fields. The completed field

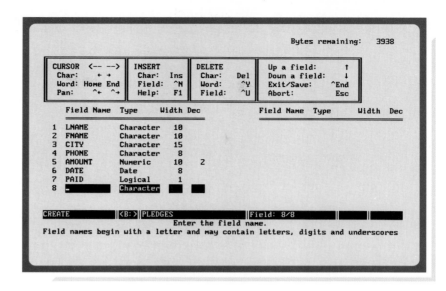

Figure 8-8 The completed file structure. Rita has filled in all the
information on the file structure. To save this structure and return
to the dot prompt, Rita can press Enter or Ctrl-End.

structure is shown in Figure 8-8. Notice that she defined the
PHONE field as a character field. Although a phone number
contains numbers, it is not used in calculations and is therefore considered a character field. Note also that Rita does not
have to define a width for the DATE field or the PAID field,
since the widths for date fields and logical fields are entered
automatically when the field types are defined.

Once Rita has finished creating the file structure, she signals dBASE that she is done by pressing Enter without filling
in any data. The program asks her to confirm her action by
pressing Enter again. When she does, dBASE responds with the
prompt "Input Data Records Now? (Y/N)." Rita wants to double-check her file structure before she enters the data, so she
types N. This returns her to the COMMAND mode.

Viewing the Structure

Rita can view the completed file structure by using the
List Structure command. At the dot prompt she types in LIST
STRUCTURE and presses Enter. dBASE responds by displaying the screen shown in Figure 8-9 (on the next page). Notice
that the number of data records shown is 0. When Rita enters
the data, this number will change to show the total number
of records she has entered.

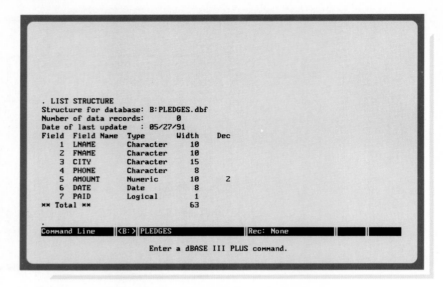

```
. LIST STRUCTURE
Structure for database: B:PLEDGES.dbf
Number of data records:        0
Date of last update   : 05/27/91
Field  Field Name  Type        Width   Dec
    1   LNAME       Character      10
    2   FNAME       Character      10
    3   CITY        Character      15
    4   PHONE       Character       8
    5   AMOUNT      Numeric        10     2
    6   DATE        Date            8
    7   PAID        Logical         1
** Total **                       63
.

Command Line      |<B:>| PLEDGES                     |Rec: None

                Enter a dBASE III PLUS command.
```

Figure 8-9 Viewing the structure. *Rita uses the List Structure command to look at the structure of her data file. Notice that the total number of characters for this file is one more than the sum of the numbers in the Width column. The reason for this is that dBASE automatically adds a one-character field at the beginning of each record to make room for special symbols.*

Entering the Data

To enter records into the database, Rita uses the Append command. When she sees the dot prompt, she types APPEND and presses Enter. dBASE uses the database structure—the field definitions she just typed in—to provide an input form, as shown in Figure 8-10. The designated width for each field is highlighted.

Using the input form is easy—all Rita has to do is fill in the blanks. Each time Rita finishes typing in an entry, she presses Enter to move to the next field. However, if the width of the entry is exactly the size of the field, the program automatically advances to the next field. If Rita tries to enter too much data into the field, the system beeps or displays an error message. If Rita makes a mistake while she is typing, she can use the Backspace key to make corrections. Once Rita has filled in all the data for the first record (Figure 8-11), dBASE displays another blank input form, so Rita can enter the data items for the fields in the second record. She continues in this manner until all the data records are entered. Then she presses

Enter or holds down the Ctrl key while pressing the End key. All the created records are stored automatically, and dBASE returns to the dot prompt.

Figure 8-10 The data input form. *Rita uses the Append command to access a data input form for her file. The highlighted areas show the designated field width for each field.*

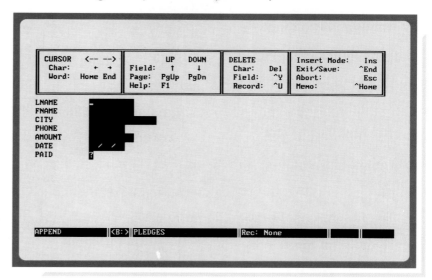

Figure 8-11 Entering the data. *Rita fills in the data for the first record.*

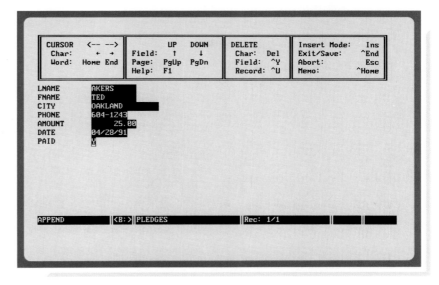

KEYSTROKES ONLY

Building a Database

These instructions are for creating Rita Chung's database, as described in the text. The following dBASE III PLUS keystrokes can also be used to create your own databases.

Loading the Program

1. Load DOS.

2. Place dBASE III PLUS Disk #1 in drive A and a formatted data disk in drive B.

3. Type dBASE and then press Enter.

4. Follow the instructions on the screen. dBASE has been loaded when you see the Assistant menu.

Creating the File Structure

Using the COMMAND mode:

1. Enter the COMMAND mode by pressing the Esc key. When you see the dot prompt, type CREATE and press Enter. dBASE prompts you for the name of the file.

2. Type in your file name, for example, B:PLEDGES, and press Enter. The file structure form appears on the screen.

3. Enter the appropriate characteristics for each field. After you have entered the information in one column, press Enter to move the cursor to the next column. You can use the Backspace key and Del key

to make corrections as you type.

4. Once all the fields have been defined, press Enter or press Ctrl-End to save the file structure. Then press Enter to confirm the action. When dBASE displays the message "Input Data Records Now? (Y/N)," type the appropriate answer.

Using the Assistant menu:

1. If you are in COMMAND mode, enter the ASSISTANT mode by typing ASSIST. The Assistant menu appears on the screen.

2. Move the cursor to the Create option. Then select the Database file option from the Create submenu by moving the cursor to the option and pressing Enter.

3. Select the disk drive you want to use to store your files. Then, in response to the prompt "Enter the name of the file," type in the file name you wish to use and press Enter. The file structure form appears on the screen.

4. Enter the appropriate characteristics for each field. After you have entered the information in one column, press Enter to move the cursor to the next column. You can use the Backspace key and Del key to make corrections as you type.

5. Once all the fields have been defined, press Enter or press Ctrl-End to save the

file structure. Then press Enter to confirm the action. When dBASE displays the message "Input Data Records Now? (Y/N)," type the appropriate answer.

Viewing the Structure

Using the COMMAND mode:

1. Type LIST STRUCTURE and press Enter. The display automatically appears.

Using the Assistant menu:

1. Select the Tools option from the main menu. Then select the List Structure option from the submenu.

2. Type N when you see the message "Direct the output to the printer? (Y/N)." The display appears on your screen.

3. Press any key to return to the main menu.

Entering the Data

Using the COMMAND mode:

1. Type APPEND and press Enter. A data-entry form appears on the screen.

2. Enter the data for the first record field. Each time you press Enter, the cursor moves to a new field in the current record. If you have filled in the last field in the record, pressing Enter displays a new record. Continue to add new records and data as needed.

3. When you have finished entering all the data, press Enter or Ctrl-End. dBASE automatically stores the records and returns you to the dot prompt.

Using the Assistant menu:

1. Select Update from the main menu and Append from the Update menu. A data-entry form appears on the screen.

2. Enter the data for the first record field. Each time you press Enter, the cursor moves to a new field in the current record. If you have filled in the last field in the record, pressing Enter displays a new record. Continue to add new records and data as needed.

3. When you have finished entering all the data, press Enter or Ctrl-End. dBASE automatically stores the records and returns you to the menu.

Listing the Records

Using the COMMAND mode:

1. Type LIST and press Enter. A list of the records appears on the screen.

Using the Assistant menu:

1. Select the Retrieve option from the main menu and the List option from the Retrieve menu.

2. Select the Execute the Command option. Type N when you see the message "Direct output to printer? (Y/N)" A list of the records appears on the screen.

3. Press any key to return to the main menu.

Listing Specific Fields

Using the COMMAND mode:

1. Type LIST followed by the field names you wish to list, in the order in which you wish to list them. (For example, typing LIST LNAME, PAID, PHONE lists only the LNAME, PAID, and PHONE fields, in that order.)

2. Press Enter. The listing appears on the screen.

Using the Assistant menu:

1. Select the Retrieve option from the main menu and the Display option from the Retrieve menu.

2. Select the Construct a Field List option. A submenu appears on the left, listing all the fields of the record.

3. Select the fields you wish to view in the order you wish to view them. Then press either the left or right cursor movement key to return to the Display submenu.

4. Select the Specify a Scope option. Then select All as your scope. dBASE returns to the Display submenu.

5. Select Execute the Command. The listing appears on the screen.

6. Press any key to return to the main menu.

Closing the Files and Exiting the Database Program

Using the COMMAND mode:

1. To close the files, type USE and press Enter.

2. To exit the database program, type EXIT and press Enter.

Using the Assistant menu:

1. Select Set Up from the main menu.

2. Select Quit dBASE III PLUS from the Set Up menu. This automatically closes all open files and returns you to DOS.

Listing the Records

The entry screens are adequate for entering data, but it is hard to go through them to look for errors—especially if the database is very large. dBASE has a handy command for viewing the contents of a file—the List command. To see a list of all the records she just typed in, Rita types LIST and presses Enter. A list of the records, as shown in Figure 8-12a, appears on the screen. Notice that under the PAID column a "T" (true) or an "F" (false) appears, although Y or N had been entered. Since the PAID column is a logical field, dBASE automatically translates the Y and N into T and F, respectively. After the listing appears, dBASE returns to the dot prompt.

Figure 8-12 Listing records. (a) Rita uses the List command to look at the records she has entered into the PLEDGES file. (b) Rita can use a variation of the List command to view data in specific fields. In this case she wants to see the data contained in the LNAME, PAID, and PHONE fields.

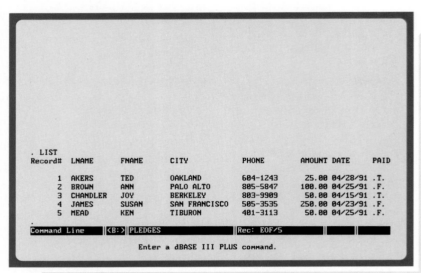

(a)

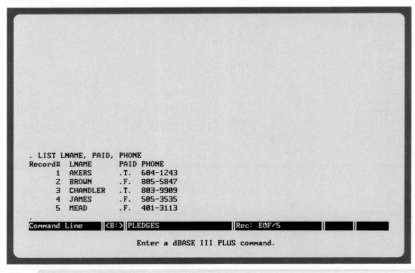

(b)

Listing Specific Fields

Suppose Rita wants to see only some of the fields in the database. She can use a variation of the List command to do this. At the dot prompt, she types LIST followed by the fields she wants to see in the order she wants to see them. For example, Rita decides she wants to see a list that shows just the LNAME, PAID, and PHONE fields, in that order. To do this, she types

```
LIST LNAME, PAID, PHONE
```

and presses Enter. dBASE then displays the list shown in Figure 8-12b.

Closing the File and Exiting the Program

To close the file without leaving dBASE, Rita types in USE at the dot prompt and presses Enter. The current file closes and the dot prompt reappears. Rita can either reopen the file by typing USE again or create another database file by using the Create command.

Now Rita wants to exit the program and return to DOS. She does this by typing QUIT. The Quit command closes all the files and returns Rita to DOS.

Getting Help

If Rita needs help when using dBASE III PLUS, she can use the F1 function key to access a help program. If she has the Assistant menu on her screen, she can get information on each choice by using the cursor movement keys to highlight a choice on the menu. Then she presses the F1 key. A help screen for that choice appears. She presses the Escape key to leave the help screen and resume her work.

When she is using dot prompt commands, she can get help by typing HELP followed by a space and then the command name. For example, if she wants help with the List command, she types

```
HELP LIST
```

and presses Enter (Figure 8-13, on the next page).

Figure 8-13 A help screen. The dBASE help feature provides an on-line user's guide. In this example Rita has asked for information about the List command by typing HELP LIST at the dot prompt.

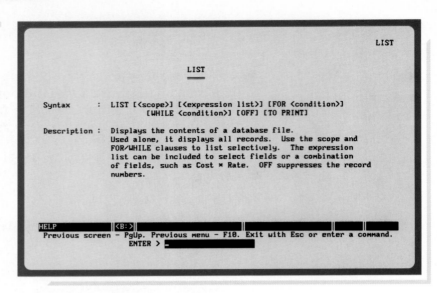

Changing the Database

Once a database file exists, it is unlikely to stay the same for very long. Over a period of time, new records will be added, and others will be changed or even deleted. Changes can be made to every record in the database, selected records, or one specific record. Most database programs provide a variety of commands that let you maintain data. The main editing commands in dBASE are Edit, Browse, Append, and Delete. Let us return to Rita Chung to see how these different commands work. (An abbreviated version of the discussion that follows can be found in the box called "Keystrokes Only: Changing the Database.")

Opening Files

To add, edit, or delete data in a file, it is necessary to tell dBASE which file it needs to use. The Use command, followed by a file name, opens the desired file. Rita presses the Esc key to access the dot prompt mode. Then she types USE B:PLEDGES, which tells dBASE to open the file called PLEDGES—that is, to make PLEDGES available for use. Then Rita presses Enter. When a database file is open, the name of the file will be displayed at the bottom of your screen.

Modifying Existing Records

When one of Rita's coworkers hands her a list of pledge activity, she notices that one of her existing records, Record 1, needs to be updated—Ted Akers has a new phone number. She also notices that Ann Brown has paid, so Rita needs to record the payment in Record 2. To modify these records, Rita can use one of two commands: the Edit command or the Browse command. We will use the Edit command to change one record and then use Browse to change the other.

Figure 8-14 Modifying records with the Edit command. *(a) Rita uses the Edit command to make changes to Record 1. (b) As she types in the changes, the new data is written over the old.*

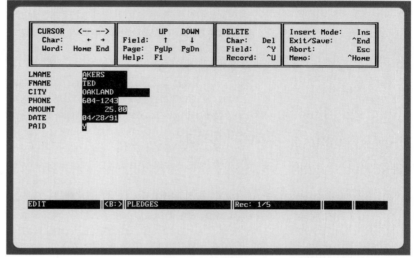

(a)

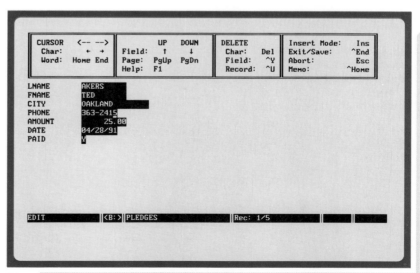

(b)

Using the Edit Command. The Edit command allows editing of data in an individual record. Therefore, to use it, Rita must tell DBASE which record she wants to see. To edit Record 1, Rita types EDIT 1 and then presses Enter. Record 1 appears on the screen (Figure 8-14a). Rita moves the cursor to the PHONE field, then types in the new phone number. (If necessary, she can also use the Ins and Del keys to make additional changes to the data.) Notice in Figure 8-14b that the new data is written over the old data. To store the changed record in the database and return to the dot prompt, Rita presses Ctrl-End.

Once Rita has used the Edit command to access a particular record, she can edit previous or succeeding records in the file by pressing the PgUp or PgDn key. The PgUp key moves her to a previous record; the PgDn key moves her to the next record.

Using the Browse Command. The Browse command provides the same editing capabilities as the Edit command. However, Browse displays all the records in the database. The program displays only as much data as will fit on the screen—usually about 12 records. To see records not shown on the screen, you can scroll up or down by using the PgUp and PgDn keys. If there are a number of fields in a record, you may have to **pan**—move horizontally across the screen—to the left or right by using the Ctrl key and the left or right cursor key.

To use the Browse command, Rita types in BROWSE and then presses Enter. Since there are currently only five records in her file, the screen displays all the records (Figure 8-15). To update Record 2, Rita moves the cursor down to Record 2 and

Figure 8-15 The Browse screen. Rita can use the Browse command to view and modify the records in her database.

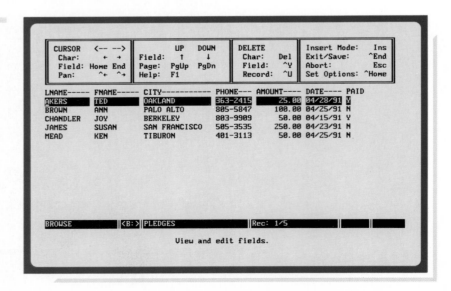

over to the PAID field. Then she types Y. After she has made the change, she presses Ctrl-End to save the data and return to the dot prompt.

Adding Records

When Rita wants to add new records to her database, she can use either the Append command or the Browse command. Suppose Rita receives data on two new subscribers—Mary Schwartz and Ted Greenlee—to add to the database. Let us examine how she will use each command.

Adding Records with Append. To add the first new record—Mary Schwartz—Rita types APPEND and presses Enter. A blank data-entry form for the PLEDGES file, just like the one used to add the original records, appears on the screen. Rita types in the data on Mary Schwartz, pressing Enter after typing data into each field. The completed screen is shown in Figure 8-16.

Before Rita stores the data in the database, she wants to check to make sure everything is correct. Since the program automatically moved to the next record when Rita filled in the PAID field, she has to use the PgUp key to return to Mary's record. After Rita has checked over the data, she presses Enter, and a blank input screen appears. Rita can continue adding records to the database in this manner. When she is finished, she presses Ctrl-End. The dot prompt reappears.

Figure 8-16 Adding records with Append. Rita uses the Append command to add Mary Schwartz's record.

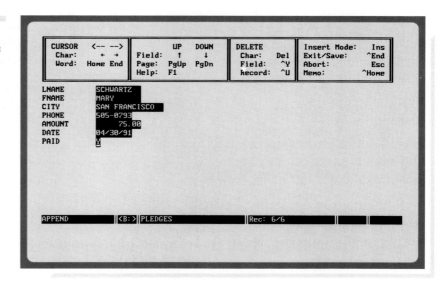

KEYSTROKES ONLY

Changing a Database

These instructions summarize the text discussion of changing a database. The dBASE III PLUS keystrokes that follow can also be used with your own databases.

Opening Files

Using the COMMAND mode:

1. Type USE and the name of the files you wish to open, for example, B:PLEDGES.

2. Press Enter. The file is now open and ready for use.

Using the Assistant menu:

1. Select Set Up from the main menu. Then select Database file from the Set Up menu.

2. Select the disk drive in which your file is stored. A list of your files on the disk in that disk drive appears on the screen.

3. Select the name of the file you wish to open. When dBASE prompts, "Is the file indexed? (Y/N)," type N. The file is now open and ready for use.

Modifying Existing Records

Using the COMMAND mode:
To use the Edit command:

1. Type EDIT followed by the number of the record you wish to edit. Then press Enter. The record appears on the screen.

2. Move the cursor to the field you wish to change and type in the new data. You can also use the Ins and Del keys to make changes.

3. To store the changed record in the database and return to the dot prompt, press Ctrl-End.

To use the Browse command:

1. Type BROWSE, then press Enter. The records in the file appear on the screen.

2. Move the cursor to the field you wish to change and type in the new data. You can also use the Ins and Del keys to make changes.

3. To store the changed record in the database and return to the dot prompt, press Ctrl-End.

Using the Assistant menu:
To use the Edit command:

1. Select Position from the main menu, GoTo Record from the Position submenu, and Record from the GoTo Record submenu.

2. Type in the number of the record you wish to edit, then press Enter.

3. Next select Update from the main menu and Edit from the Update menu. The record appears on the screen.

4. Move the cursor to the field you wish to change and type in the new data. You can also use the Ins and Del keys to make changes.

5. To store the changed record in the database and return to the main menu, press Ctrl-End.

To use the Browse command:

1. Select Update from the main menu and Browse from the Update menu. The records in the file appear on the screen.

2. Move the cursor to the field you wish to change and type in the new data. You can also use the Ins and Del keys to make changes.

3. To store the changed record in the database and return to the main menu, press Ctrl-End.

Adding Records

Using the COMMAND mode:
To use the Append command:

1. Type APPEND and press Enter. A blank entry form appears on the screen.

2. Enter the data. Then press Ctrl-End to store the data and return to the dot prompt.

To use the Browse command:

1. Type BROWSE and press Enter.

2. Move the cursor to the last record in the file. Then press the down cursor key to move beyond that record.

3. When dBASE asks if you want to add new records, type Y. A blank record appears on the screen.

4. Enter the data. Then press Ctrl-End to store the data and return to the dot prompt.

Using the Assistant menu:
To use the Append command:

1. Select Update from the main menu and Append from the Update menu. A blank entry form appears on the screen.

2. Enter the data. Then press Ctrl-End to store the data and return to the main menu.

To use the Browse command:

1. Select Update from the main menu and Browse from the Update menu.

2. Move the cursor to the last record in the file. Then press the down cursor key to move beyond that record.

3. When dBASE asks if you want to add new records, type Y. A blank record appears on the screen.

4. Enter the data. Then press Ctrl-End to store the data and return to the main menu.

Deleting Records

Using the COMMAND mode:
To use the Browse command:

1. Type BROWSE and press Enter.

2. Move the cursor to the record you wish to delete and press Ctrl-U. The word "Del" appears in the lower-right corner of the screen. (To remove the deletion mark, press Ctrl-U again.) If you want to delete more than one record, repeat this step until all the records you want to remove are marked for deletion.

3. Exit the BROWSE mode by pressing Ctrl-End.

4. Use the List command to make sure the correct records are marked. An asterisk appears next to records marked for deletion.

5. Type PACK and press Enter. The marked records are deleted from the file.

To use the Delete command:

1. Type DELETE FOR followed by the field name, an equals sign, and a value in the field that identifies the record you want to delete. Values in character fields must be contained in quotation marks. For example, to delete a record that contains the name MEAD in the LNAME field, you would type

`DELETE FOR LNAME="MEAD"`

If you want to delete more than one record, repeat this step until all the records you want to remove are marked for deletion.

2. Press Enter. You will see a message "records deleted" preceded by a numeral. This message tells the number of records marked for deletion.

3. Use the List command to make sure the correct records are marked. An asterisk appears next to records marked for deletion.

4. To remove a deletion mark, use the Recall For command. For example, to recall the record marked in step 1, type

`RECALL FOR LNAME="MEAD"`

Note: You can use the Recall For command only before you use Pack.

5. Type PACK and press Enter. The marked records are deleted from the file.

Using the Assistant menu:
To use the Browse command:

1. Select Update from the main menu and Browse from the Update menu.

2. Move the cursor to the record you wish to delete and press Ctrl-U. The word "Del" appears in the lower-right corner of the screen. (To remove the deletion mark, press Ctrl-U again.) If you want to delete more than one record, repeat this step until all the records you want to remove are marked for deletion.

3. Exit the BROWSE mode by pressing Ctrl-End.

4. Use the List command to make sure the correct records are marked. An asterisk appears next to records marked for deletion.

5. Select Update from the main menu and Pack from the update menu. The marked records are deleted from the file.

continued ▶

Changing a Database (continued)

To use the Delete command:

1. Select the Update menu from the main menu and then Delete from the Update menu.

2. Select the Build a Search option from the Delete menu. Select a field name from the list that appears, then select the = Equal To option. Next type in the field whose value identifies the record you want to delete and press Enter. For example, to delete a record that contains the name MEAD in the LNAME field, you would select LNAME and = Equal To, then type in MEAD and press Enter. If you want to delete more than one record, continue to select the Equal To option, type in identifying values, and press Enter until the appropriate records are marked for deletion.

3. Select the No More Conditions option. Then select the Execute the Command option from the Delete menu. dBASE responds with the message "records deleted" preceded by a numeral. This message tells the number of records now marked for deletion.

4. Press any key to return to the main menu.

5. Use the List command to make sure the correct records are marked. An asterisk appears next to records marked for deletion.

6. To remove a deletion mark, select the Recall option from the Update menu. Select the Build a Search option from the Recall menu. Select the appropriate conditions to identify the record you wish to recall. Select the Execute the Command option from the Recall menu. Note: You can use the Recall command only before you use the Pack command.

7. Select the Pack option from the Update menu. The marked records are deleted from the file.

Adding Records with Browse. As we mentioned before, the Browse command displays a number of records at one time. To use this command to add records, Rita types BROWSE and presses Enter. Then she moves the cursor to the last record in the file. Next Rita presses the down cursor key to move beyond the last record (Figure 8-17a). dBASE asks her if she wants to add records. When she types Y for *yes*, a new blank record appears. Rita types in the data on Ted Greenlee (Figure 8-17b). When she is done, she once again presses Ctrl-End to store the data.

Deleting Records

Sometimes a record must be removed—deleted—from a database file. Deleting records from a file is a two-step process. First, the specific records must be marked for deletion by using the Delete command or the Browse command. Second, the record must be permanently removed from the file by using the Pack command. Note that once you remove a record by using the Pack command, the record cannot be recovered.

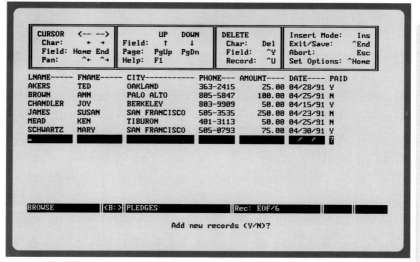

(a)

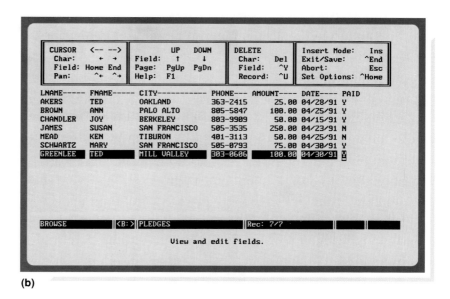

(b)

Figure 8-17 Adding records with Browse. *(a) To add a record by using the Browse command, Rita must move beyond the last record in the file. (b) Then she can type in the new information.*

Deleting with the Browse Command. Suppose Rita receives a note indicating that Joy Chandler has moved and no longer wishes to donate to the station; the Chandler record needs to be deleted from the PLEDGES file. Rita types BROWSE and presses Enter. Then she moves the cursor to Chandler's record and presses Ctrl-U. The word "Del" appears in the lower-right corner of her screen (Figure 8-18a). The Chandler record is now marked for deletion. If Rita accidentally marks the wrong record, she can press Ctrl-U again, and the deletion mark will be removed.

Since Rita wants to delete the Chandler record, she checks to see that the record is properly marked. First she exits the BROWSE mode by pressing Ctrl-End. Then she uses the List command. When the list of records is displayed, dBASE indicates a record marked for deletion with an asterisk in front of the record (Figure 8-18b).

Figure 8-18 Deleting records with Browse. (a) To delete a record, Rita moves the cursor to the record she wants to remove and presses Ctrl-U. Note that the word "Del" appears in the lower highlighted area of the screen. (b) When Rita lists the records, the asterisk next to the Chandler record tells her that the record is marked for deletion.

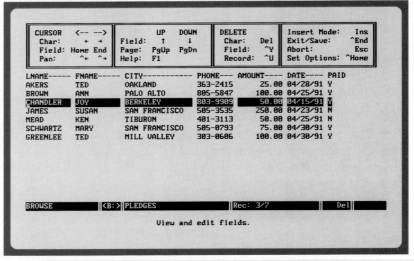

(a)

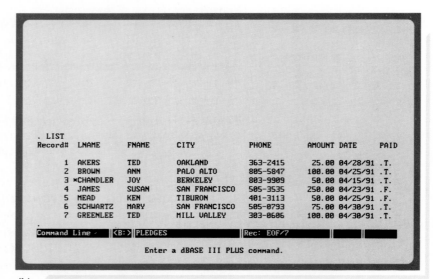

(b)

continued ▶

Figure 8-18 Deleting records with Browse (continued). (c) After Rita uses the Pack command to remove the record, the record is no longer listed.

```
. LIST
Record#  LNAME     FNAME     CITY           PHONE        AMOUNT DATE    PAID

      1  AKERS     TED       OAKLAND        363-2415      25.00 04/28/91 .T.
      2  BROWN     ANN       PALO ALTO      805-5847     100.00 04/25/91 .T.
      3  JAMES     SUSAN     SAN FRANCISCO  505-3535     250.00 04/23/91 .F.
      4  MEAD      KEN       TIBURON        401-3113      50.00 04/25/91 .F.
      5  SCHWARTZ  MARY      SAN FRANCISCO  505-0793      75.00 04/30/91 .T.
      6  GREENLEE  TED       MILL VALLEY    303-0606     100.00 04/30/91 .T.
.
Command Line    <B:> PLEDGES              Rec: EOF/6

              Enter a dBASE III PLUS command.
```

(c)

To actually delete the record, Rita uses the Pack command. At the dot prompt, she types in PACK and presses Enter. The dBASE displays the message, "6 records copied." This tells Rita that there are now only six records in the PLEDGES file—the Chandler record is not one of them. Rita can verify this by using the List command again (Figure 8-18c).

Deleting with the Delete Command. The Delete command is useful for deleting a specific record from a file when the record number is unknown. As with the Browse command, Rita must first mark the record for deletion. To mark Ken Mead's record, for example, Rita types

```
DELETE FOR LNAME = "MEAD"
```

Then she presses Enter. Notice the use of the relational operator in this command. This tells dBASE to search for the record in which the last name field contains the name MEAD. The quotation marks around MEAD indicate that MEAD is a character field. The program indicates the number of records marked for deletion—in this case, one record. As before, Rita uses the List command to check that the proper record has been marked for deletion.

If Rita makes a mistake, she can use the Recall command to unmark the record she has marked. She would type

```
RECALL FOR LNAME = "MEAD"
```

and press Enter. When she uses the List command, the asterisk would no longer be next to the record. Recall is a useful command, but only if used *before* the Pack command is issued.

Now Rita is ready to delete the record. As before, she types PACK and presses Enter. And as before, the program responds with the number of records copied.

When Rita has finished with her editing, she types QUIT to close the file and exit the program.

Just a Start

We have only scratched the surface of database management. But this first database chapter shows you how simple yet powerful a database can be. In the next chapter you will learn more about how to use database management systems: how to select certain records from a file, how to organize data, and much more.

Exercises

8-1

1. Load your database program and insert a formatted disk in drive B.
2. Using the appropriate commands, create the file structure shown in Figure 8-19a. The name of the file should be EX8-1. The NAME field should have a width of 30 characters and the NUMBER field should have a width of 12 characters. Make corrections, as needed, as you type.
3. Use your program to view the structure of the file. How many records are in the database file at this point?
4. Using the appropriate commands, enter the records shown in Figure 8-19b into the EX8-1 file.

Figure 8-19

Field	Field Name	Type	Width	Dec
1	NAME	Character	30	
2	NUMBER	Character	12	

(a)

Record#	NAME	NUMBER
1	SUSAN MILLER	411-234-1900
2	FREDERICK ASTER	555-311-1234
3	JORGE AMADO	611-114-1923
4	VICTORIA COWEN	411-555-9087
5	ISAAC ADLER	611-465-0089

(b)

5. Use your program to list the records in the file. Are all the records you entered shown on the screen?
6. Close the database file and exit the program.

8-2

1. Reload the database program and place your data disk in drive B.
2. Using the appropriate commands, create the file structure shown in Figure 8-20a. The name of the file should be EX8-2.
3. Enter the data shown in Figure 8-20b into the database file.
4. List the data on your screen.
5. Close the file.

Figure 8-20

Field	Field Name	Type	Width	Dec
1	PNUMBER	Character	3	
2	NAME	Character	10	
3	COST	Numeric	5	2
4	QUANTITY	Numeric	8	
5	ORDERED	Date	8	

(a)

Record#	PNUMBER	NAME	COST	QUANTITY	ORDERED
1	238	RAM CHIP	1.50	10	02/14/90
2	117	PROBE	15.00	5	03/17/90
3	874	L.E. PIN	2.00	7	04/02/90
4	692	RIBBON	0.89	1	02/13/90
5	799	CABLE	5.00	14	04/20/90

(b)

8-3

1. Use the database program to create a personal address file. Include the following fields:
   - LNAME
   - FNAME
   - STREET
   - CITY
   - STATE
   - ZIPCODE
   - PHONE

   Name the file EX8-3.
2. Enter information about at least five of your friends.

3. Close the file. Then list the contents of your database. What is displayed on your screen?

4. Retrieve the EX8-3 file. Now list the contents of your database. What is displayed on your screen? What determines the order in which the database records are displayed?

5. Use the appropriate command to list only the LNAME, FNAME, and PHONE fields, in that order.

6. Use the appropriate command to list only the FNAME, PHONE, and CITY fields, in that order.

7. Close the file.

8-4

Assume that you are going to use your database program to maintain a record of the books you have loaned to your friends.

1. Create the file structure shown in Figure 8-21a. Name the file EX8-4.

2. Enter the records shown in Figure 8-21b.

3. Use the appropriate command to add the following record to the database:

   WELLINGTON 08/09/90 NORM YARROW 09/15/90

4. List the records in the database. Where is the new record placed in the database file?

5. Add the following two records to the file:

   THE TAO OF PHYSICS 08/10/90 KATHLYN
      DUGAN 09/30/90
   THE STRANGER 08/15/90 GELAREH
      ASAYESH 09/30/90

6. List the records to check your entries.

Figure 8-21

Field	Field Name	Type	Width	Dec
1	BOOK	Character	25	
2	DATE_OUT	Date	8	
3	LOANED_TO	Character	15	
4	RETURN_ON	Date	8	

(a)

Record#	BOOK	DATE_OUT	LOANED_TO	RETURN_ON
1	HEART OF DARKNESS	07/10/90	ED GRAYSON	08/10/90
2	LEAVEN OF MIRTH	07/12/90	NORM YARROW	07/30/90
3	TIME CAPSULE	07/20/90	LOUISA POTTER	08/20/90
4	ROBERTSON DAVIES	07/25/90	KATHLYN DUGAN	09/15/90
5	THE MESSAGE MERCHANTS	07/30/90	MAURICE SAATCHI	08/05/90
6	THE GILMAN TRAIL	08/07/90	JOHN ANDRILLA	08/30/90

(b)

7. Use the appropriate command to list only the titles of the books borrowed and the date on which they should be returned.
8. Close the file.

8-5

1. Retrieve EX8-4. List all the records in the file. Are all of the records there?
2. Use your program's editing feature to make the following changes:
    ■   Change the name of the book in Record 4 to ROBERTSON JEFFERS.
    ■   Change Louisa Potter's RETURN_ON date to 08/25/90.
    ■   Change the name of the book in Record 2 to LEAVEN OF MALICE.
    ■   Change the name in the LOANED_TO field of Record 2 to MICHAEL CHABON.
3. If your program has a Browse feature, use it to view the records. If not, use the appropriate command to list the records. Check to make sure the changes have been made correctly. Make any additional changes you need to make.
4. Close the file.

8-6

1. Retrieve EX8-4. List the contents of the file. Does the file reflect the changes you made in Exercise 8-5?
2. Delete Record 1 and Record 6. List the file to make sure the records have been deleted. How many records are now in the database file?
3. Delete the record that contains the title TIME CAPSULE.
4. Mark Kathlyn Dugan's records for deletion. View the records to verify that the records have been marked. Then use your program's Recall feature to remove the deletion mark. (Note: Some database programs have a one-step deletion process. If this is the case with your program, simply skip this step.)
5. If your program has a Browse feature, use it to make the changes that follow. If not, use the appropriate commands to make the changes.
    ■   Add the following record to the file:
        GROWING ROSES   08/15/90   LIA ILLGEN   09/01/90
    ■   Change the spelling of Maurice Saatchi to Maurice Satchi.
    ■   For Record 3, change the date in the DATE field to 07/31/90.
6. View the records to make sure your changes are correct.
7. Close the file.

8-7

Assume you are working for a temporary employment service. You are asked to create the database shown in Figure 8-22. Each employee has listed the office position(s) that he or she wishes to obtain on a temporary basis. These positions are listed in the fields SKILL1 and SKILL2. Notice that some employees will accept temporary employment in only one position. If the employee is currently seeking work, the contents of the ACTIVE field is .T. If the employee has been listed previously but is not available now, an .F. appears in the ACTIVE field.

1. Create a database that contains the data shown in Figure 8-22. Name the file EX8-5.
2. Check to see that the contents of all the fields are correct. Because each record in the database has more fields than will fit on the screen at one time, you will need to use the cursor movement keys to move to the fields that do not appear on your screen. Use the appropriate command to make any changes you need to make.
3. Use the appropriate command to list only the FNAME, LNAME, ACTIVE, SSN, and RATE fields, in that order.
4. Use the appropriate command to list only the LNAME, CITY, and PHONE fields, in that order.
5. Use the appropriate command to list only the LNAME, ACTIVE, SKILL1, and SKILL2 fields, in that order.
6. Use the appropriate commands to update the file as follows.

   - Solomon Bridgeto wishes to be listed as active.
   - Ashley Shillito will also accept a temporary position as an editor.
   - Dinah Bell has married. Her last name is now Ritter.
   - Lawrence Hoppt has moved to Europe. His record should be deleted from the file.
   - Elizabeth Smith is changing her rate of pay to $12.75.
   - We have accepted a new client who is currently seeking work. Please add the following information to the file: Last name: Elliott, First name: Susan, Social Security number:

Figure 8-22

LNAME	FNAME	ACTIVE	SSN	RATE	CITY	PHONE	SKILL1	SKILL2
SMITH	ELIZABETH	.T.	001-34-7661	10.00	REDWOOD	789-8303	WORD PROCESSING	BOOKKEEPING
HOPPT	LAWRENCE	.F.	231-56-0823	15.00	CLARION	211-0963	ACCOUNTING	
REMBRANT	VERONICA	.T.	318-00-5223	20.00	MARKHAM	634-1967	PROOFREADING	EDITING
RIDLEY	HOWARD	.T.	954-87-1234	10.00	CLARION	692-2231	MAINTENANCE	LANDSCAPING
BRIDGETO	SOLOMON	.F.	562-34-9758	12.00	MARKHAM	112-3529	RECEPTION	FILING
GREEN	JANE	.T.	911-00-4286	15.00	SALTERTON	311-7398	EDITING	
FAIRMONT	ELDON	.T.	673-56-4401	15.00	STATE COLLEGE	567-0408	WINDOW WASHING	MAINTENANCE
SHILLITO	ASHLEY	.F.	088-34-3624	10.00	CLARION	566-0075	PROOFREADING	
BELL	DINAH	.T.	455-28-4582	10.00	VESTAL	864-0098	RECEPTION	WORD PROCESSING
MUNSON	MATTHEW	.F.	633-98-1185	15.00	SALTERTON	411-2323	FILING	

551–88–1071, Desired rate of pay: $20.00, no address yet, Phone: 624–1867. Susan desires employment as an editor or a proofreader.

7. List the records to check your changes.
8. Close the file and exit the program.

Summary and Key Terms

- A **database** is an organized collection of related data. A **database management system (DBMS)** is software that creates, manages, protects, and provides access to a database.

- A database can store data relationships so that files can be integrated. The way the database organizes data depends on the type, or **model,** of database. There are three database models— hierarchical, network, and relational.

- In a **relational database** data is organized logically in a table called a **relation,** or **file.** Each box in the file contains a piece of data known as a **data item.** Each column of the table represents an **attribute,** or **field.** All the data in any given row is called a **tuple,** or **record.**

- There are two steps to creating a file: designing the structure of the file and entering the data. When a file structure is defined, many database programs require the user to identify the **field names,** the **field types,** and the **field widths.** There are four commonly used types of fields: **character fields, numeric fields, date fields,** and **logical**

fields. The field width determines the maximum number of letters, digits, or symbols to be contained in the field.

- dBASE III PLUS gives you two means of entering commands: the Assistant menu and the COMMAND mode. The **Assistant menu** has a number of options on the top line of the menu. Each option has an associated **selection bar** that appears when the main selection is highlighted by the cursor. When you are in the **COMMAND mode,** the menu screen disappears and a **dot prompt** appears.

- At times, a **relational operator** is needed when making comparisons or when entering instructions. Some commands generally used as operators include $=$, $<$, and $>$.

- Like most database programs, dBASE III PLUS has a number of commands that let you create a file structure, enter records, update records, delete records, edit records, and list records. These commands include the Create command, the List Structure command, the Append command, the List command, the Edit command, the Browse command, the Append command, the Delete Command, the Use command, and the Pack command.

- If you need help when using the database program, you can press F1 to access a help screen.

- At times you may have to **pan**—move sidways across the screen—to view all the fields in a database.

- Deleting records from a file is a two-step process. The specific records must be marked for deletion by using one command. Then the record is removed from the file by using another command.

Review Questions

1. What is a database?

2. What is a database management system?

3. Explain how a database management system benefits users.

4. Explain how a relational database organizes data.

5. Define the following database terms: *field, record, file.*

6. Describe the difference between the Assistance menu and the COMMAND mode.

7. What is the database prompt that tells you that you are in COMMAND mode?

8. What does the Create command let you do?

9. List the four types of information that the database program needs to have to create a file structure.

10. List the four most common types of fields.

11. Suppose you have created a database file named ADDRESS. The file contains NAME, ADDRESS, and PHONE fields. What does each of the commands that follow do?

   a. LIST
   b. LIST NAME, PHONE
   c. LIST PHONE, NAME
   d. LIST STRUCTURE

12. What command(s) could you use to edit data in a database record?

13. What command(s) could you use to add a record to a database file?

14. What steps are needed to delete a record from a file by using the Browse command? By using the Delete command?

FROM THE REAL WORLD

Football to Fashion

Storing data has never been a problem for computer users. Businesses have used database management software in some very imaginative ways. Here are a few specific examples.

A scout for the New England Patriots football team enters data from college scouting reports into a database. Coaches can then retrieve that data in several ways. For example, they can list all of the players available for a particular position, such as quarterback or fullback, and then use the data to draft or trade a player.

The U.S. Patent & Trademark Office keeps 600,000 trademarks and 5 million patents in a database that can be used by patent attorneys, inventors, and businesses seeking a new trademark or studying competitors.

The Travelers Corporation of Hartford, Connecticut, advertises itself as a staid insurance company, but there is nothing conservative about its approach to personal computers. The company's goal, well on its way to actuality, is to have a personal computer on the desk of every employee. Data about customers, policies, and investments is entered into databases; that data can then be retrieved as needed by other employees.

Interior designers at Holiday Corporation struggle to keep up with the design and remodeling of some 2000 hotels, including Holiday Inns, Embassy Suites, and Harrah's. The company headquarters in Memphis includes an elaborate showroom with full-scale mock-ups of each style of hotel room. Designers use personal computers and database management software to enter information from product catalogs: model, style number, price, type and color of upholstery, and so forth. When hotel owners view the mock-ups and select furniture and fixtures, designers can pull all the needed specifications from the database and put it directly onto order forms.

Neiman Marcus, the fashionable Dallas store whose glossy catalog once offered a pair of matched polo ponies for $37,000, is eager to keep close track of its trendy customers. NM uses a fleet of microcomputers to access its mainframe database, where records of its customers' purchasing habits are kept. Armed with this information, the store can alert customers of upcoming events of interest.

9

Advanced Database Management Systems

Chapter Objectives

After reading this chapter you should be able to

- Design a database that contains link fields

- Build a condition for subsequent action to the database

- Locate specific data in a database file by using a condition

- Sort and index files

- Use the Seek command to search large files

- Explain how to open several database files at once

- Explain how to link several database files

- Explain how to join two database files together to create a new file

- Print database reports

In the previous chapter you were introduced to the concept of a database management system. You learned how to use dBASE III PLUS to create a database file. You also learned how to input data records in the database file and how to modify those records. But there is more, much more. In this chapter you will learn to use the database in practical ways—how to locate very specific pieces of information, how to organize the data in your database, and how to combine several different files. Your tool will again be the popular database management software dBASE III PLUS.

A Case of Insufficient Information

Gerry Russell's business was suffering growing pains. From a small health-food wholesale business that she ran herself, Russell Organics had really grown in the past ten years. Now she has more than 150 customers in three states and a staff of 11 full-time employees.

When Gerry was the sole employee of her fledgling company, she kept in her head or in card files the information she needed to run her business. As her business grew, she tackled the problems piecemeal and ended up with three separate file systems—one to keep track of orders and sales, one to keep track of customers, and one to keep track of employees and payroll.

Gerry received regular reports on her company's performance from these systems. But a nagging doubt was forming in Gerry's mind. The data about her company and her customers—her most valuable asset—was scattered about in fragments. There was no way to get an overview of her company's information.

Furthermore, her staff told her that some kinds of information were not available. Gerry knew that the data she needed on customers, orders, staff, and so forth had been "put in the computers" by using the various programs she had purchased. But there was no easy way to merge the necessary data together to give her the information she needed.

Consider some typical requests that Gerry and her staff make.

- "What is the name of the sales representative for customer Fiorini Natural Foods?" (To answer this, Gerry has to look up Fiorini in the customer file; the Fiorini record gives a sales representative identification number, number 13. Then she looks up the identification number in the sales rep file to find the name of the sales representative.)

- "List customer name and address for customers who ordered more than 50 bottles of Superplus Vitamin A." (She must look in the order file and then extract the customer number for all the records of Superplus Vitamin A sales for amounts greater than 50. Gerry uses those customer numbers to look up customer name and address in the customer file.)

- "List quantity on hand for all the products listed on customer order 71286." (Gerry finds order 71286 in the order file. For each product number in the order, she must look in the product file for that product's quantity on hand.)

As you can see, each of these requests calls for some sort of cross-referencing between files. The nature of these requests underscores the need for integrated files, as opposed to the current segregated files. Gerry and businesspeople like her need speedy access to data and answers. A database system can provide it.

RANDOM BITS

Computers Play Ball

Baseball statistics have traditionally been kept by hand or in someone's head. And baseball managers are among the most hide-bound traditionalists around. But now managers are finally entering the computer age and crediting the computer with some wins.

The secret of the computer's success, you see, lies in those years of accumulated records, now stored in a database and quickly accessible to a manager who is right in the ballpark. The manager matches the player to the situation at hand—park, pitcher, inning, and

score—based on the player's past performance. Even the weather is factored in so the manager can know how the current conditions will affect curveball or fastball pitchers.

Consider this example of computer coaching. A particular left-handed batter was usually replaced with a pinch hitter in the lineup against left-handed pitchers. When the computer revealed that he actually hit pitches thrown by lefty pitchers better than those thrown by righties, he was no longer automatically benched.

Since Gerry Russell's business is so complex, she decides to hire a consultant to help her design the database. Gerry needs many database files; however, we are going to look at only four simplified files in this chapter—the customer file, the sales representative file, the orders file, and the products file. Since designing the database is so important, let us take another look at how it is done.

Creating Relations in a Database

As we mentioned in Chapter 8, a database management program can handle relationships between files. But how is this done? In a relational database, a common field called a **link field** links data in one file to data in other files. For example, Figure 9-1 shows two of Gerry's files—her ORDERS file and her SALESREP file. Notice that they have a field in common—the REPNO field. So the link field between these two files is the REPNO field. You can link two or more data files together as long as at least one common field exists in

Figure 9-1 Link fields. In a relational database common fields called link fields can link data in one file to data in other files. In this example the link field between these two files is the REPNO field.

Orders file

ORDERNO	PRODNO	CUSTNO	REPNO	DATE	AMOUNT	TOTAL
B0790	34	31573	13	11/24/89	15	104.25
B0790	35	31573	13	11/24/89	25	123.75
B0791	67	10774	11	11/24/89	10	59.90
B0792	44	11501	11	11/24/89	20	19.00
B0792	67	11501	11	11/24/89	10	59.90
B0793	25	11092	12	11/24/89	20	39.00
B0794	25	20751	11	11/24/89	20	39.00
B0794	44	20751	11	11/24/89	5	4.75
B0795	34	24441	14	11/24/89	50	347.50
B0795	35	24441	14	11/24/89	25	123.75

—— Link Field

Salesrep file

REPNAME	REPNO	SSN	PHONE	COMMISSION
KEN BECKER	11	177-34-1626	634-4436	.T.
WENDY SANCHEZ	12	521-11-2768	634-4405	.F.
JOYCE NAKAMURA	13	985-44-1077	634-4405	.T.
PAT MITCHEL	14	084-12-9526	634-4470	.T.
MICHAL CONFORD	15	577-45-7248	634-3367	.F.

each file. The advantage to this system is that because the files are related, you can refer to a second file when requesting information on a field in the first file. For example, Gerry can use the link field to find out a sales representative's name when she uses the ORDERS file. Later in the chapter we will describe exactly how to do this.

Designing the Database

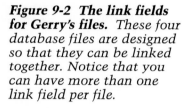

Figure 9-2 The link fields for Gerry's files. *These four database files are designed so that they can be linked together. Notice that you can have more than one link field per file.*

To design an effective database, the database designer must consider both the data to be stored *and* the ways in which the data will be needed. After talking with Gerry Russell, the consultant presents the database design shown in Figure 9-2 for the four files. Notice that the consultant has not placed all the information in one big file. Such a design would be unnecessarily complex and clumsy. Instead, there is a separate file for each major aspect of the business.

The arrows between the files in Figure 9-2 indicate the link fields between each file. Sales representative number (REPNO),

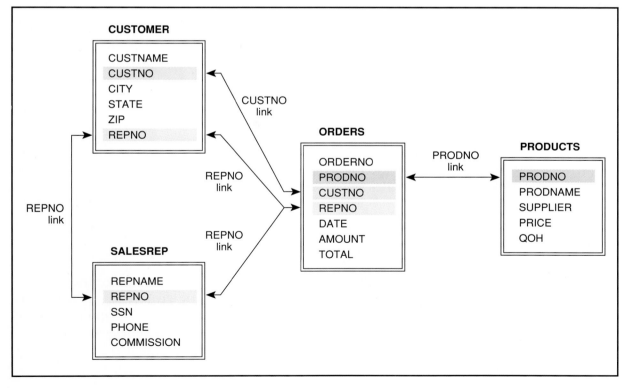

Figure 9-3 The file structures for Gerry's files. *This figure shows the file structures for (a) the PRODUCTS file, (b) the ORDERS file, (c) the SALESREP file, and (d) the CUSTOMER file. Recall that the file structures are produced by using the Create command.*

Field	Field Name	Type	Width	Dec
1	PRODNO	Character	2	
2	PRODNAME	Character	25	
3	SUPPLIER	Character	25	
4	PRICE	Numeric	6	2
5	QOH	Numeric	3	

(a) PRODUCTS file

Field	Field Name	Type	Width	Dec
1	ORDERNO	Character	5	
2	PRODNO	Character	2	
3	CUSTNO	Character	5	
4	REPNO	Character	2	
5	DATE	Date	8	
6	AMOUNT	Numeric	3	
7	TOTAL	Numeric	6	
				2

(b) ORDERS file

Field	Field Name	Type	Width	Dec
1	REPNAME	Character	25	
2	REPNO	Character	2	
3	SSN	Character	11	
4	PHONE	Character	8	
5	COMMISSION	Logical	1	

(c) SALESREP file

Field	Field Name	Type	Width	Dec
1	CUSTNAME	Character	30	
2	CUSTNO	Character	5	
3	CITY	Character	10	
4	STATE	Character	2	
5	ZIP	Character	5	
6	REPNO	Character	2	

(d) CUSTOMER file

for example, is the link field between the SALESREP and CUS-TOMER files. That is, REPNO is the only common field in the sales representative file and the customer file.

Designing the File Structures

The consultant also presents the structure for each of the files, shown in Figure 9-3. These file structures are set up by using the Create command, as you saw in Chapter 8. Recall that the Create command is used to define the name and structure of each of the files.

Record#	PRODNO	PRODNAME	SUPPLIER	PRICE	QOH
1	34	SUPERPLUS VITAMIN A	SUPERPLUS VITAMINS INC.	6.95	100
2	67	BOTANICS NATURAL SOAP	BOTANICAL SOAPS CO.	5.99	39
3	44	WHEATGRASS JUICE	MRS. A'S JUICES	0.95	30
4	25	KEN'S SALT-FREE CHIPS	EASTBAY NATURAL, INC.	1.95	75
5	35	SUPERPLUS VITAMIN C	SUPERPLUS VITAMINS INC.	4.95	45

(a) PRODUCTS file

Record#	ORDERNO	PRODNO	CUSTNO	REPNO	DATE	AMOUNT	TOTAL
1	B0790	34	31573	13	11/24/89	15	104.25
2	B0790	35	31573	13	11/24/89	25	123.75
3	B0791	67	10774	11	11/24/89	10	59.90
4	B0792	44	11501	11	11/24/89	20	19.00
5	B0792	67	11501	11	11/24/89	10	59.90
6	B0793	25	11092	12	11/24/89	20	39.00
7	B0794	25	20751	11	11/24/89	20	39.00
8	B0794	44	20751	11	11/24/89	5	4.75
9	B0795	34	24441	14	11/24/89	50	347.50
10	B0795	35	24441	14	11/24/89	25	123.75

(b) ORDERS file

Record#	REPNAME	REPNO	SSN	PHONE	COMMISSION
1	KEN BECKER	11	177-34-1626	634-4436	.T.
2	WENDY SANCHEZ	12	521-11-2768	634-4405	.F.
3	JOYCE NAKAMURA	13	985-44-1077	634-4405	.T.
4	PAT MITCHEL	14	084-12-9526	634-4470	.T.
5	MICHAL CONFORD	15	557-45-7248	634-3367	.F.

(c) SALESREP file

Record#	CUSTNAME	CUSTNO	CITY	STATE	ZIP	REPNO
1	FIORINI NATURAL FOODS	31573	LODI	CA	94010	13
2	ROSS SUPERNATURAL FOODS	10774	BENTWOOD	OR	95101	11
3	NATURAL LIGHT VITAMINS	24441	SEATTLE	WA	98103	14
4	YREKA HEALTH	11501	VIRGIL	OR	95000	11
5	BACK-TO-NATURE	20751	OXNARD	CA	94111	11
6	BURTON'S NATURAL FOOD STORE	11092	NAPA	CA	94200	12

(d) CUSTOMER file

Figure 9-4 Sample records for Gerry's files. *This figure shows sample records for (a) the PRODUCTS file, (b) the ORDERS file, (c) the SALESREP file, and (d) the CUSTOMER file. Recall that the records are entered by using the Append command.*

Inputting the Data Records

After the file structure has been designed and entered, the data records can be entered into the file. For the purpose of the example, we will assume that the data has already been entered into the database. Figure 9-4 shows sample records for each of the files. The examples in the chapter use this data. If you need to enter this data yourself, review the input process in Chapter 8.

Since this is a complicated example, we will look at it in bite-sized pieces. First we will look at manipulating and using data in a single file. Later, we will get to see the power of using linked files and joined files.

Locating Specific Information

Now that the database has been entered in the computer, Gerry Russell can use it to find and manipulate particular pieces of information. When Gerry needs information on a sales representative, for example, she can instruct her computer to search through her data files. dBASE has several commands that can be used for searches—List, Display, Locate, and Seek. Let us take a look at how the List command can be used to find specific information. (An abbreviated version of the discussions that follow can be found in the box called "Keystrokes Only: The Russell Organics Example.")

Listing Using a Condition

Gerry is interested in finding out the quantity on hand (the QOH field) of Wheatgrass Juice. She knows this information is stored somewhere in the PRODUCTS file. She could simply list the file and scan through the records to find the appropriate record. However, there is a more direct method for finding this information—using another variation of the List command.

Figure 9-5 Listing using a condition. *Gerry can use the List For command to find a specific record or records. In this case she uses the command to find the PRODUCTS record that contains the product name* Wheatgrass Juice.

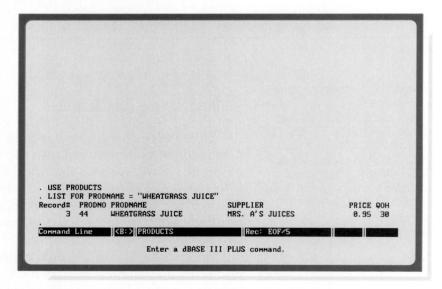

**DOW JONES
NEWS/RETRIEVAL**
A personal computer and
a modem let you access
on-line database services.
Hundreds of these are
available, offering information on everything
from airline reservations
to medical diagnoses to
astrological profiles.

People in business use
financial and business
news services, such as
the Dow Jones News/
Retrieval, to keep tabs on
our quickly changing
world. The Dow Jones
News/Retrieval service
uses database technology
to provide electronic
access to *The Wall Street
Journal*. It also provides
up-to-the-minute news
on the world, govern-
ment, industry, and com-
panies. Items such as
interest and exchange
rates are constantly
updated, and stock mar-
ket quotations are avail-
able in real time. The
fact that this data is
stored in databases per-
mits rapid and accurate
updating of the data. It
also lets people access
vast quantities of data
quickly and easily.

Gerry starts by opening the PRODUCTS file. To do this, she accesses the dot prompt mode by pressing Esc. Then she types

```
USE B:PRODUCTS
```

and presses Enter. Next Gerry needs to type in a command that tells the database program what she wants to search for. She types

```
LIST FOR PRODNAME = "WHEATGRASS JUICE"
```

This command tells dBASE to look through the PRODNAME field and find all the records that contain the name *Wheatgrass Juice* in that field. The equals sign (=) establishes the condition for the search—that is, search until the data item in the PRODNAME field is Wheatgrass Juice. The quotation marks around Wheatgrass Juice tell dBASE that Wheatgrass Juice is a character field. When Gerry presses Enter, dBASE lists the record—and Gerry finds out that there are 30 containers of Wheatgrass Juice in stock (Figure 9-5).

Listing Using Multiple Conditions

If Gerry wants to see only the products supplied by Super-plus Vitamins Inc. whose price is greater than $5.00, she can again use the List command. This time, however, she must specify two selection conditions, one for supplier Superplus Vitamins Inc. and one for price greater than $5.00. The fields in the PRODUCTS file that will be helpful are SUPPLIER and PRICE (see Figure 9-3, on page 300). Gerry will use these fields to build her search conditions. As before, Gerry starts by opening the PRODUCTS file. Gerry then types (on one line)

```
LIST FOR SUPPLIER = "SUPERPLUS VITAMINS INC." .AND.
   PRICE > 5.00
```

and presses Enter. This tells the program to search for all records that contain SUPERPLUS VITAMINS INC. in the SUP-PLIER field *and* to search through these records to find all the records that also contain a price over $5.00 in the PRICE field. Figure 9-6a (on the next page) shows the result. Notice that only the record that contains both of the conditions is displayed.

The .AND. in this command is known as a logical operator. It is used in a command to combine conditions of a search. When .AND. is used, the search is narrowed because *all* the conditions must be met before the program can locate the correct data. Another commonly used logical operator is the

Figure 9-6 Listing using multiple conditions. *Gerry can use the logical operators to search for specific records. (a) The .AND. operator narrows the search to data that meets the two conditions SUPERPLUS VITAMINS INC. and 5.00. (b) The .OR. operator broadens the search by searching for data that meets either one of the two conditions (or both).*

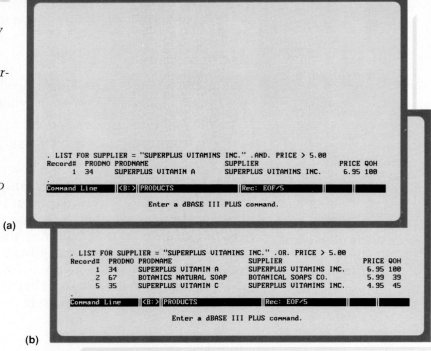

(a)

(b)

.OR. operator. The .OR. operator also combines conditions, but with .OR. only one *or* the other search condition must be true for the combined condition to be true. Therefore, using .OR. broadens the scope of the search. If Gerry had typed (on one line)

```
LIST FOR SUPPLIER = "SUPERPLUS VITAMINS INC." .OR.
    PRICE > 5.00
```

and pressed Enter, she would have gotten a list of records that contained all the records showing SUPPLIER = "SUPERPLUS VITAMINS INC." and all the records showing PRICE > 5.00 (Figure 9-6b).

Sorting and Indexing Records

In Chapter 8 we added records to a database file by using two different commands: Append and Browse. In each case dBASE stored the records in the order in which they were entered. When you list the records in a database file, you can see that the first record you entered is Record 1 and the last record you entered is the last record in the file. (To be completely accurate, it is possible to enter records mid-file by using the Insert command, but this is not commonly done and we do not plan to discuss it in this book.)

In business it is often useful to rearrange the records into some meaningful order. For example, Gerry might like to see an alphabetical list of employees, a numerical list of account numbers, and a chronological list of purchase dates. dBASE provides two commands, Sort and Index, to help users reorder data.

The Sort Command

The Sort command sorts a database file in an order based on the field or fields the user indicates. The command also stores the sorted database file as a new file. When a file is sorted by the Sort command, the record sequence changes in the new file. However, the original database file remains unchanged.

Gerry decides she wants to sort the ORDERS records by product number. First she opens the ORDERS file and lists the contents (Figure 9-7a). Next she must instruct the program to sort *on* a particular field *to* a specific file. To sort the ORDERS records by product number, Gerry types in the command

```
SORT ON PRODNO TO ORDERS1
```

and presses Enter. This tells the program to organize the ORDERS file by sequencing the records using the product numbers and to save the sorted file as ORDERS1. The program responds with the message "100% sorted 10 records sorted."

Figure 9-7 Sorting a database file. *To sort (a) the original ORDERS file, Gerry uses the Sort command to create sorted files: (b) the ORDERS1 file, which is sorted by product number in ascending order, and (c) the ORDERS1 file, which is sorted by product number in descending order.*

```
. USE B:ORDERS
. LIST
Record#  ORDERNO  PRODNO  CUSTNO  REPNO  DATE       AMOUNT   TOTAL
      1  B0790    34      31573   13     11/24/89       15  104.25
      2  B0790    35      31573   13     11/24/89       25  123.75
      3  B0791    67      10774   11     11/24/89       10   59.90
      4  B0792    44      11501   11     11/24/89       20   19.00
      5  B0792    67      11501   11     11/24/89       10   59.90
      6  B0793    25      11092   12     11/24/89       20   39.00
      7  B0794    25      20751   11     11/24/89       20   39.00
      8  B0794    44      20751   11     11/24/89        5    4.75
      9  B0795    34      24441   14     11/24/89       50  347.50
     10  B0795    35      24441   14     11/24/89       25  123.75
.
Command Line      <B:>ORDERS                    Rec: EOF/10
                 Enter a dBASE III PLUS command.
```

(a)

continued ▶

Figure 9-7 Sorting a database file (continued). Note that the records numbers in both (b) and (c) are different from those in (a).

(b)

(c)

dBASE automatically sorts the numbers in ascending order (small to large), as shown in Figure 9-7b. To sort the numbers in descending order (large to small), Gerry would type

```
SORT ON PRODNO/D TO ORDERS1
```

The D after PRODNO stands for *descending*. The result is shown in Figure 9-7c.

Gerry can see the result of her sort by making ORDERS1 the active file and by using the List command to display the records.

The Index Command

A more efficient means of sorting records is the Index command. The Index command is similar to the Sort command, but the approach is different. Like the Sort command, the Index command instructs the program to sort data according to a field specified by the user. However, instead of sorting to a database file, the Index command creates a special kind of file called an **index file.** An index file can be recognized in a directory by the extension NDX. (All regular database files have the extension DBF, which is automatically added by dBASE.) An index file contains **pointers** that "point" to the location of records within a data file. These pointers let dBASE display the records in a particular order. Usually, a database program allows you to create up to seven indexes per file; each must given a separate name.

When you index a file, the original file remains untouched. The program simply uses a list of rearranged record numbers in memory. So when you view an indexed file, the records are displayed in the rearranged order, but each record is still identified by the record number it had when you originally entered the record. For example, an index created on the product number field lets the ORDERS file records be listed in ascending product number order. But if you look at the record numbers in Figure 9-8, you see that the numbers are not in order. That is, the records retain the number assigned by dBASE when originally entered.

Figure 9-8 An indexed database file. When Gerry indexes the ORDERS file numerically by product number, the original—and actual—order of the records is indicated by the record numbers at the left of the screen listing.

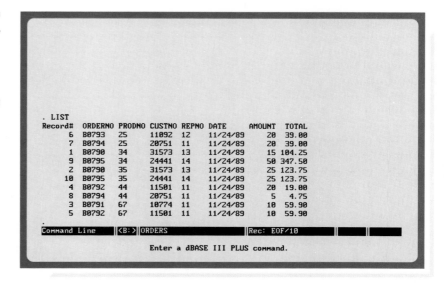

```
. LIST
Record#  ORDERNO PRODNO CUSTNO REPNO DATE      AMOUNT  TOTAL
      6  B0793   25     11092  12    11/24/89      20   39.00
      7  B0794   25     20751  11    11/24/89      20   39.00
      1  B0790   34     31573  13    11/24/89      15  104.25
      9  B0795   34     24441  14    11/24/89      50  347.50
      2  B0790   35     31573  13    11/24/89      25  123.75
     10  B0795   35     24441  14    11/24/89      25  123.75
      4  B0792   44     11501  11    11/24/89      20   19.00
      8  B0794   44     20751  11    11/24/89       5    4.75
      3  B0791   67     10774  11    11/24/89      10   59.90
      5  B0792   67     11501  11    11/24/89      10   59.90
.
Command Line    ||<B:>||ORDERS              ||Rec: EOF/10    ||    ||    ||

          Enter a dBASE III PLUS command.
```

Gerry wants to use the Index command to enable her to access the PRODUCTS file alphabetically by product name. Gerry begins by typing

`USE PRODUCTS`

and pressing Enter to open the PRODUCTS file. Next Gerry types in the Index command:

`INDEX ON PRODNAME TO PNAMEI`

and presses Enter. (She chooses an index file name ending in the letter *I* to remind her that it is an index file.) The program automatically sorts the PRODUCTS file alphabetically by product name and creates an index file in a new file named B:PNAMEI.NDX. Now Gerry double-checks to see that the PRODUCTS file is ordered properly. She uses the List command to list the records in the PRODUCTS database file on her screen and can see that they are now in alphabetical order by product name (Figure 9-9). The original—and actual—order of the records in the PRODUCTS file is indicated by the record numbers at the left of the screen listing.

Gerry can now view the PRODUCTS file in its original state (as the data was entered) or in product name order. She can choose which way she wants to see the file when she opens the PRODUCTS file. To access the PRODUCTS file in order by product name, she types

`USE PRODUCTS INDEX PNAMEI`

and then presses Enter. This tells the program to open the PRODUCTS database file and use the index with the name

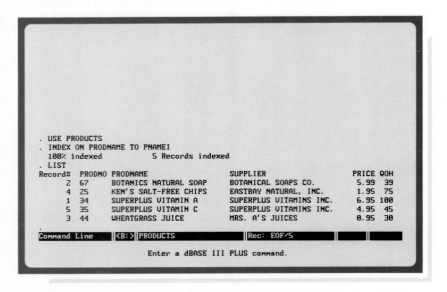

Figure 9-9 Indexing the PRODUCTS file. *Gerry uses the Index command to organize the PRODUCTS file alphabetically by product name.*

PNAMEI. Then Gerry can use any of the commands we have already discussed. When Gerry wants the original order of the PRODUCTS file, she types

```
USE PRODUCTS
```

Sorted versus Indexed Files

The Sort command is useful but has several drawbacks. First, a new database file is created each time the original file is sorted. Gerry, for example, wants to view the ORDERS file by customer number order and also by product number order. If she uses the Sort command, she will have three copies of the same file: one file sorted by customer number, another by product number, and, of course, the original file. Second, each sorted database file uses the same amount of disk space as the original file. If the original file is quite large, sorting the files in several different ways takes up a lot of disk space. Finally, it is easy to lose track of multiple files, and you must update each file separately. In the confusion, users can be left wondering which file actually has the correct data. Usually, sorting is useful only if the database file is a reference file that seldom changes.

However, if indexed files are used, only one database file—the original file—needs to be maintained. When changes are made to this main file, the indexes are automatically updated, provided that the index names are listed when the database file is opened. For example, suppose Gerry has two index files (PNAMEI, PNUMI) associated with the PRODUCTS database file. Whenever she wants to make modifications to the PRODUCTS database file, she opens the PRODUCTS file by typing

```
USE PRODUCTS INDEX PNAMEI, PNUMI
```

The advantages of indexing over sorting seem clear, but there is still another: Indexes permit the use of the Seek command.

Using the Seek Command

The List command can be used to search for a record in a database. This works well with small files. But if a database file contains thousands of records, the List command can take several minutes to locate just one record.

If, however, a file has been indexed, a specific piece of data can be quickly located using the Seek command. To use the Seek command, each record must have a unique identifier—that is, a field whose value is different for each record in the database file. Such fields are called **key fields.** For example, a customer account number would be a key field in a customer file because no two customers have the same customer number. To find information with the Seek command, the database file must contain a key field and the database file must be indexed on the key field. When the database file is opened, the index file that was created by using the key field must also be opened.

Let us look at an example. Suppose a customer calls Gerry Russell to ask about the cost of a product called Botanics Natural Soap; Gerry needs to be able to find information about that product quickly. Gerry has already indexed the PRODUCTS file alphabetically by product name (the PRODNAME field). The index is stored in an index file called PNAMEI. Therefore, Gerry can use the Seek command to locate the record that contains the information on Botanics Natural Soap.

First she opens the PRODUCTS file and the PNAMEI file by typing

```
USE PRODUCTS INDEX PNAMEI
```

and pressing Enter. Then she types

```
SEEK "BOTANICS NATURAL SOAP"
```

and presses Enter.

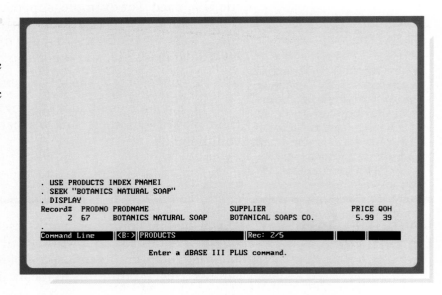

Figure 9-10 Using the Seek command. *After Gerry indexes a file on a field, she can use the Seek command to find records with specific data in that field. Then she can use the Display command to view that record.*

In several seconds dBASE locates (but does not yet display) the record that contains the product name BOTANICS NATURAL SOAP. If no such record is found, dBASE displays "No find" in the lower-left corner of the screen.

If the record is found, Gerry can display it on the screen by using the Display command. To do this, she types DISPLAY and presses Enter. The contents of the record are displayed on the screen (Figure 9-10).

Remember that to use the Seek command, the index must have been created on the field that contains a value that uniquely identifies a record. The identifying value from that field is used in the search condition of the Seek command.

Using Commands That Calculate

Like spreadsheet programs, database programs offer a variety of commands that perform numeric and mathematical calculations, including commands for counting, summing, and averaging. These commands let you extract new information from an existing database file.

The Count Command

The Count command counts, or tallies, the number of records in an active data file and displays the results. Using this command is an efficient way to determine the number of records that meet certain criteria.

For example, Gerry wants to know how many of the orders in the ORDERS file were taken by Joyce Nakamura, whose identification number is 13. To answer the question, Gerry opens the ORDERS file. Then she types

```
COUNT FOR REPNO = "13"
```

and presses Enter. dBASE responds by displaying the number of records that contain Joyce Nakamura's identification number (Figure 9-11, on the next page).

The Sum Command

The Sum command totals (adds up) a column of one or more numeric fields and displays the total. If Gerry wants to know the total dollar amount from the sale of Superplus Vita-

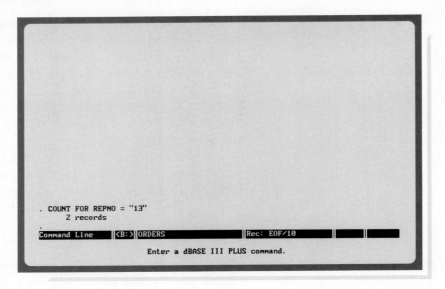

```
. COUNT FOR REPNO = "13"
        2 records
.
Command Line    ||<B:>||ORDERS              ||Rec: EOF/10    ||      ||      ||
                        Enter a dBASE III PLUS command.
```

Figure 9-11 The Count command. *The Count command can be used to find the total number of records that meet certain criteria.*

min C (product number 35), for example, she uses the Sum command to compute this amount. First she opens the ORDERS file. Then she types

SUM TOTAL FOR PRODNO = "35"

and presses Enter. The Sum command tells dBASE to add the amounts in the TOTAL field of every record whose product number field contains 35. dBASE responds by displaying the total dollar amount of Superplus Vitamin C sales (Figure 9-12a).

To get the complete sales for all orders placed, Gerry types

SUM TOTAL

and presses Enter. This tells the program to sum the contents of the TOTAL field for every record in the file. The result is shown in Figure 9-12b.

Remember that to use the Sum command, you must specify a numeric field.

The Average Command

The Average command calculates the arithmetic average of a numeric field in a data file. If Gerry wants to know the

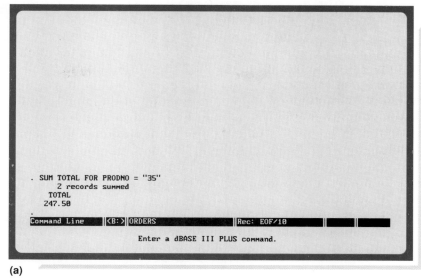

```
. SUM TOTAL FOR PRODNO = "35"
      2 records summed
    TOTAL
  247.50
.
Command Line   ||<B:>||ORDERS              ||Rec: EOF/10
              Enter a dBASE III PLUS command.
```

(a)

```
. SUM TOTAL
     10 records summed
    TOTAL
  920.80
.
Command Line   ||<B:>||ORDERS              ||Rec: EOF/10
              Enter a dBASE III PLUS command.
```

(b)

Figure 9-12 The Sum command. *The Sum command can be used to find the total value of one or more numeric fields. (a) In this example, the Sum command is used to find the total price for all records containing the product number 35. (b) In this example, the Sum command is used to find the total price for all the records in the file.*

average dollar amount sold by Ken Becker (identification number 11), for example, she opens the ORDERS file and types

```
AVERAGE TOTAL FOR REPNO = "11"
```

and presses Enter. The program then displays the result (Figure 9-13, on the next page).

Figure 9-13 The Average command. *The Average command can be used to find the arithmetic average of a numeric field. As shown, you can also find the average for selected records in the file.*

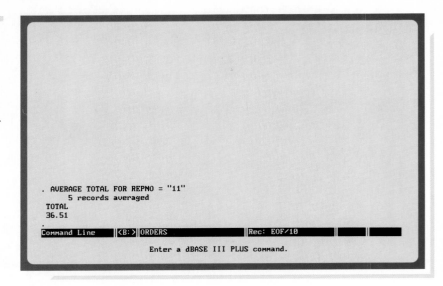

```
. AVERAGE TOTAL FOR REPNO = "11"
     5 records averaged
  TOTAL
  36.51
```
```
Command Line    <B:>ORDERS              Rec: EOF/10
              Enter a dBASE III PLUS command.
```

Using Multiple Files

As we mentioned earlier in this chapter, Gerry often needs to retrieve information about data stored in separate files. The true power of database management software lies in its ability to locate and retrieve information from several different database files at one time. dBASE provides several commands that let you combine data from different files. In this section we will look at two of these commands—the Set Relation command, which temporarily links two files together, and the Join command, which is used to combine two different databases to create a new, third, database. The two files that are being linked or joined together must each contain the same field—the key field or link field. However, these fields need not have the same name in both files.

Recall from the beginning of the chapter that Gerry wanted to be able to find the name of the sales representative for a given customer, Fiorini Natural Foods. To do this with her old file system, she needed to look up Fiorini in the CUSTOMER file to find the representative number of the sales rep to that company. Then she needed to look in the SALESREP file to find the name of the sales rep with that number. With the database program Gerry can simply link these two files together and then access the information she wants with a single command.

To link the two files, Gerry must first identify the link field in the files. If no link field has been included in the design of the files, the two files cannot be linked. Gerry's files, however, have been designed to be linked. Recall that in Figure 9-2 (on page 299) the link field that connects the SALESREP file and the CUSTOMER file is the REPNO field.

If she wishes to use the Set Relation command, Gerry must index one of the files by the REPNO field. To index the SALESREP file by the REPNO field, Gerry types

```
INDEX ON REPNO TO SALEREPI
```

and presses Enter. This tells dBASE to create an index called SALEREPI that allows the SALESREP file to be ordered according to representative's numbers. Next Gerry must open all the files she wants to use at the same time. Let us take a closer look at how she does this.

Opening Several Files Simultaneously

dBASE allows up to ten database files to be open at any given time. To open several files at once, each file must be assigned to its own work area in the computer's memory. The command that lets you do this is the **Select command,** which activates the various work areas. Each work area is referred to by a number (1 through 10) or a letter (A through J). Work Area 1 (also called Area A) is the area that the program automatically starts using, unless the user instructs it otherwise. The area the program is currently using is known as the **selected area,** or the **active area,** and the file stored in that area is known as the **selected file,** or **active file.** To see which files and indexes are in various work areas, press the F6 key.

When using the Select command, Gerry must decide which file will be the active file. She needs to open both the CUSTOMER and SALESREP files; she decides that CUSTOMER will be the active file.

Gerry begins by assigning the SALESREP file, with the SALEREPI index, to Work Area 2 (also called Area B). To do this, she types the following commands, pressing the Enter key at the end of each command.

```
SELECT 2
USE SALESREP INDEX SALEREPI
```

As the screen message reports, now SALESREP is "open in Area 2."

Next Gerry opens the CUSTOMER file by typing

```
SELECT 1
USE CUSTOMER
```

Now that the files are open and CUSTOMER is the active file, Gerry is ready to link the two files.

Linking Files

To combine the CUSTOMER file and the SALESREP file, Gerry must set up a relationship between two files based on the common link field—in this case, the REPNO field. To establish the relationship, Gerry uses the Set Relation command, which instructs the program to connect the files together. To use this command, Gerry types

```
SET RELATION TO REPNO INTO SALESREP
```

and presses Enter. Translated, this tells dBASE to set up a relationship on the REPNO field from the CUSTOMER file in Work Area 1 to the SALESREP file in Work Area 2.

If she types LIST, Gerry would still see only the contents of the active file, the CUSTOMER file, on the screen. However, now she can access information contained in both the SALESREP file, open in Area B, and in the CUSTOMER file. Gerry can tell dBASE to read data from a particular field in a nonactive file by using the $->$ symbol. This symbol "points to" a field in an open file that is not currently the active file. If, for example, an item of data is to be taken from a field in Area 2, then place B$->$ (the B is followed by a dash and then $>$) before the name of the field. Say Gerry wanted to access information in the REPNAME field, which is in the nonactive file in Area 2. She would identify that field by using the name B$->$REPNAME (Figure 9-14a). Fields in the currently active file need no prefix.

To find the name of the sales representative to Fiorini Natural Foods, Gerry types the command

```
LIST B->REPNAME FOR CUSTNAME = "FIORINI NATURAL FOODS"
```

This command tells dBASE to find the associated REPNAME field whenever the CUSTNAME field in the CUSTOMER file is FIORINI NATURAL FOODS. Remember that the B$->$ symbol indicates that the REPNAME field is in Work Area 2. The result of this command is shown in Figure 9-14b.

Joining Files

Suppose that Gerry decides to combine the SALESREP file and the CUSTOMER file. If she wants to make a new file that combines these two files, she must use the Join command. Since she has already opened the SALESREP and CUSTOMER

Figure 9-14 Searching for data in two concurrently open linked files. *To obtain information from a non-active linked file, Gerry must use the B − > indicator. (a) In this example Gerry wants to list the REPNAME field for the records in the SALESREP file, which is in Work Area 2. (b) Gerry finds the name of the sales representative for the Fiorini Natural Foods account.*

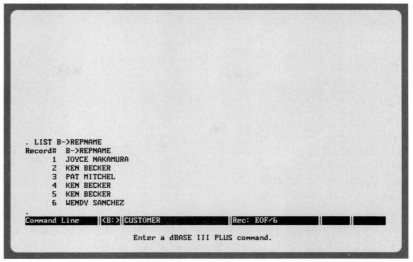

```
. LIST B->REPNAME
Record#  B->REPNAME
      1  JOYCE NAKAMURA
      2  KEN BECKER
      3  PAT MITCHEL
      4  KEN BECKER
      5  KEN BECKER
      6  WENDY SANCHEZ
.
Command Line    ||<B:>||CUSTOMER          ||Rec: EOF/6       ||    ||    ||
                  Enter a dBASE III PLUS command.
```

(a)

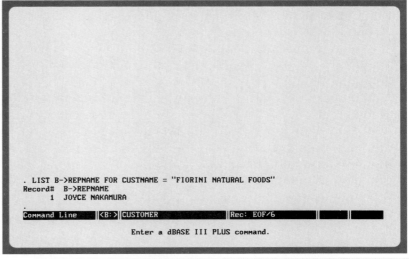

```
. LIST B->REPNAME FOR CUSTNAME = "FIORINI NATURAL FOODS"
Record#  B->REPNAME
      1  JOYCE NAKAMURA
.
Command Line    ||<B:>||CUSTOMER          ||Rec: EOF/6       ||    ||    ||
                  Enter a dBASE III PLUS command.
```

(b)

files, now she can join then. To do so, Gerry must tell dBASE several pieces of information: the name of the file she wants to join with the active file, the name of the resulting new file, and the link field between the two files she is joining.

To use the Join command, Gerry types

```
JOIN WITH SALESREP TO CUSTREP FOR REPNO = B->REPNO
```

and presses Enter. A direct translation of this command: Join the SALESREP file with the CUSTOMER file to create a record in the new file named CUSTREP in every case where the REPNO field in a record in Area 1 equals the REPNO field in

Figure 9-15 Joined files. *Gerry uses the Join command to combine the CUSTOMER file and the SALESREP file into a new file named CUSTREP.*
(a) This figure shows the structure for the new file.
(b) This figure shows the records in CUSTREP. Because there are so many fields in the new file, the data for each record is printed on more than one line, making it look jumbled and unattractive.

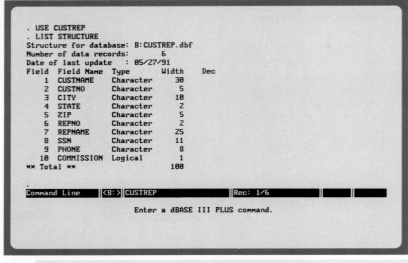

```
. USE CUSTREP
. LIST STRUCTURE
Structure for database: B:CUSTREP.dbf
Number of data records:      6
Date of last update   : 05/27/91
Field  Field Name Type         Width      Dec
    1  CUSTNAME   Character       30
    2  CUSTNO     Character        5
    3  CITY       Character       10
    4  STATE      Character        2
    5  ZIP        Character        5
    6  REPNO      Character        2
    7  REPNAME    Character       25
    8  SSN        Character       11
    9  PHONE      Character        8
   10  COMMISSION Logical          1
** Total **                      100
```
| Command Line | ‹B:› CUSTREP | Rec: 1/6 | | |

Enter a dBASE III PLUS command.

(a)

```
. LIST
Record#  CUSTNAME                    CUSTNO CITY      STATE ZIP   REPNO REPN
AME                  SSN        PHONE     COMMISSION
      1  FIORINI NATURAL FOODS        31573 LODI      CA    94010 13    JOYC
E NAKAMURA           985-44-1077 634-4405 .T.
      2  ROSS SUPERNATURAL FOODS      10774 BENTWOOD  OR    95101 11    KEN
BECKER               177-34-1626 634-4436 .T.
      3  NATURAL LIGHT VITAMINS       24441 SEATTLE   WA    98103 14    PAT
MITCHEL              084-12-9526 634-4470 .T.
      4  YREKA HEALTH                 11501 VIRGIL    OR    95000 11    KEN
BECKER               177-34-1626 634-4436 .T.
      5  BACK-TO-NATURE               20751 OXNARD    CA    94111 11    KEN
BECKER               177-34-1626 634-4436 .T.
      6  BURTON'S NATURAL FOOD STORE  11092 NAPA      CA    94200 12    WEND
Y SANCHEZ            521-11-2768 634-4405 .F.
.
```
| Command Line | ‹B:› CUSTREP | Rec: EOF/6 | | |

Enter a dBASE III PLUS command.

(b)

a record in Area 2. Notice that the CUSTOMER file is not mentioned in the command; because it is the active file, it is assumed to be the file being joined with SALESREP. Also, the REPNO field from the CUSTOMER file needs no prefix since it is contained in the active file.

Figure 9-15a shows the structure of the new file, CUST-REP. Notice that it contains the combined information from both files. Figure 9-15b shows a list of the records in CUSTREP. However, the listing is rather jumbled and unattractive since it contains all the fields in both the SALESREP file and the CUSTOMER file. If Gerry wants to show only the names of

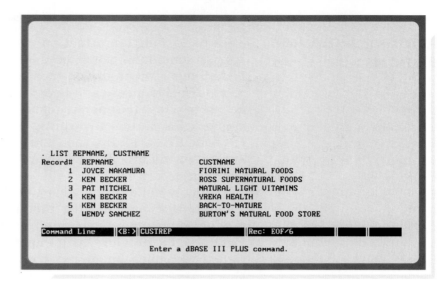

```
. LIST REPNAME, CUSTNAME
Record#  REPNAME                CUSTNAME
      1  JOYCE NAKAMURA         FIORINI NATURAL FOODS
      2  KEN BECKER             ROSS SUPERNATURAL FOODS
      3  PAT MITCHEL            NATURAL LIGHT VITAMINS
      4  KEN BECKER             YREKA HEALTH
      5  KEN BECKER             BACK-TO-NATURE
      6  WENDY SANCHEZ          BURTON'S NATURAL FOOD STORE
.
Command Line    ||<B:>||CUSTREP              ||Rec: EOF/6       ||       ||     ||
                    Enter a dBASE III PLUS command.
```

Figure 9-16 Listing specific data in joined files. *Gerry lists the REPNAME and CUSTNAME fields contained in the CUSTREP file. Notice that CUSTREP has been made the active file.*

the sales representatives and customers, for example, she can make CUSTREP the active file and type

LIST REPNAME, CUSTNAME

and then press Enter. Figure 9-16 shows the result. It is not necessary that files that are joined be indexed, but both files must be open concurrently in two different work areas.

Closing Multiple Files

Once Gerry has finished working with her files, she can close the selected files by using the Clear All command. To use this command, she simply types

CLEAR ALL

and presses Enter. dBASE closes all the files and returns her to the dot prompt.

As you can see, combined database files can be very useful. Since the commands discussed here are powerful, they require more thinking and set-up steps than simpler commands such as Create and List. Although acquiring the skills to manage several database files and more complex commands takes some practice, the ease of data manipulation that you get in return makes it all worthwhile.

Printing Database Reports

Displaying information on the screen is useful, but sometimes people need information in a printed report. dBASE has a menu-driven report generator. That is, the program displays a series of screens that lead you through the necessary steps to generate reports. Creating a report is a two-step process, similar to creating a database file. First you have to create a report form, then you print the report. The program automatically fills in the information in the report when you print the report.

Suppose, for example, that Gerry Russell wants to generate a report that presents the product number, product name, product price, and quantity on hand for each product in her PRODUCTS file. Gerry also wants a total for quantity on hand for each product. She draws a rough sketch on paper of how she wants the report to look (Figure 9-17). Then she opens the PRODUCTS file by typing the Use command.

Creating the Report Form

After Gerry opens the PRODUCTS file, she begins by creating the report form. To do this, she types CREATE REPORT and presses Enter. dBASE then prompts her for a name for the report form file, and Gerry chooses B:STOCKRPT. The program automatically adds the extension FRM to the file name to indicate that the file is a report form file. Next dBASE displays the first screen of the report-generating program (Figure 9-18). There are a number of selections available:

- The Options menu, which is used to define the format of the report

- The Groups menu, which is used to generate subtotals

- The Columns menu, which is used to tell the program what data you want to appear in the report

- The Locate menu, which allows you to locate a specific column in your report and return to the column menu to modify that data

- The Exit menu, which is used to exit the report-generating program

Because her report is simple, Gerry will be using only the Options, Columns, and Exit menus.

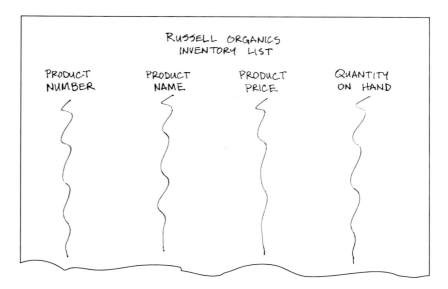

Figure 9-17 Designing a database report. *To help herself visualize the report she wants, Gerry quickly sketches her printed report.*

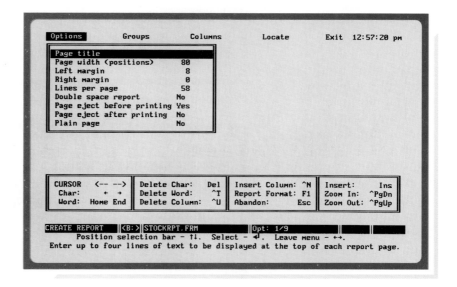

Figure 9-18 The Option menu. *dBASE uses a series of menus to help Gerry generate her report. The first menu she sees is the Option menu. Gerry can use the cursor movement keys to choose from the options listed at the top of the screen. The box toward the bottom of the screen lists other commands she can use. As with the other database screens, the bottom two lines of the screen list information about the currently highlighted option. The database file from which the report is created must be the active file.*

Entering the Report Title. Gerry's report needs a title, so she chooses the Page title option in the Options menu by moving the cursor to highlight Page title. Then she presses Enter, which causes an arrow symbol to appear next to Page title and a highlighted area to appear on the screen (Figure 9-19a). Gerry can type up to four title lines in the highlighted area; she types RUSSELL ORGANICS in the first line and INVENTORY LIST in the second line (Figure 9-19b). Then she presses the Ctrl and End keys together to move out of the box.

Figure 9-19 Entering the report title. To create a title for her report, Gerry (a) presses Enter to choose the Page title option. An arrow appears after the option to remind Gerry that she has chosen this option, and a highlighted area appears on the screen. (b) Gerry types the title in the highlighted areas.

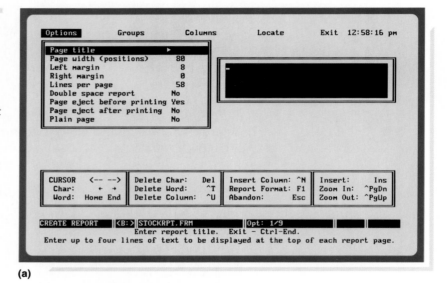

(a)

(b)

continued ▶

Figure 9-19 Entering the report title (continued).
(c) When she pressed Ctrl-End to enter the title, the first word of the title appears next to the Page Title option.

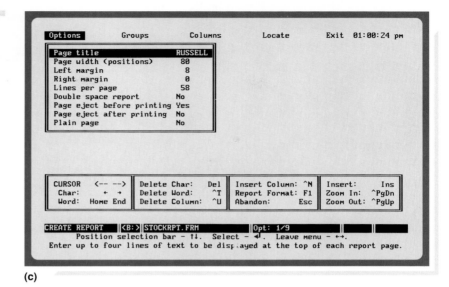

(c)

The first word of the title now appears next to the Page Title option (Figure 9-19c).

Setting the Margins. Next Gerry sets the page margins. First she moves the cursor to the Left margin option and presses Enter. Then she types 15 and presses Enter. Next Gerry selects the Right margin option, types in 15 again, and presses Enter. The Options box now contains the new margin numbers (Figure 9-20).

Figure 9-20 Setting the margins. *Gerry selects Left margin and enters the new margin width. Then she does the same with the Right margin option.*

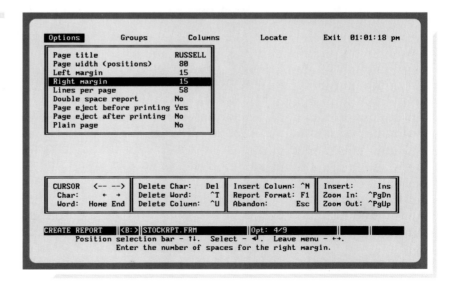

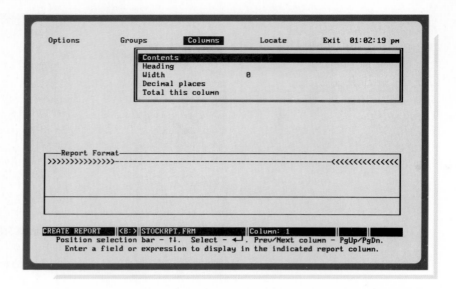

Figure 9-21 The Columns menu. When Gerry moves the cursor to the Columns option, a new menu appears on the screen. Notice the Report Format box at the bottom of the screen. As Gerry enters information about the contents of the report, the format of the report appears in the box. The > and < symbols indicate the number of spaces in the left and right margins. The - symbols show the amount of space remaining in the line.

Entering the Column Information. Gerry uses the right cursor key to move the cursor to the Columns menu (Figure 9-21). The Columns menu lets you input information that tells the program what field to print, where to place it on the page, and what it should look like. Gerry must select each field she wants to use. She starts by selecting Contents, then she types PRODNO—the first database field in the report—and presses Enter. Now she needs to choose a column heading, so she selects the Heading option (Figure 9-22a). Each column heading can be up to four lines, so she types PRODUCT (Enter) and NUMBER (Enter), and then presses Enter twice to leave the box (Figure 9-22b). Notice that at the bottom of the screen in Figure 9-22b, there is a Report Format Box. As Gerry enters the format she wants, a representation of the report appears in the box.

The width of the column is automatically calculated by the program, which sets the width as the size of the database field or the heading, whichever is larger. Since the contents of the field are characters, the last two options in the Columns menu do not apply. Therefore, Gerry moves on to enter the

Figure 9-22 Entering the column information. *Gerry types in the name of the field she wants to use in the Contents line. (a) Then she selects the Heading option—a highlighted box appears. Gerry types in the column heading and presses Enter. (b) The information appears next to the Heading option, and the width of the column is automatically calculated to reflect the active database file. The Xs in the Report Format box show the width of the column in the report.*

```
  Options        Groups       Columns        Locate      Exit  01:03:55 pm

                         Contents      ▶ PRODNO
                         Heading
                         Width             2
                         Decimal places
                         Total this column



              ┌Report Format─────────────────────────────────────────
              >>>>>>>>>>>>>> ------------------------------------<<<<<<<<<<<<<<



                      XX

  CREATE REPORT   <B:> STOCKRPT.FRM          Column: 1
                    Enter column heading.  Exit - Ctrl-End.
              Enter up to four lines of text to display above the indicated column.
```
(a)

```
  Options        Groups       Columns        Locate      Exit  01:05:36 pm

                         Contents        PRODNO
                         Heading         PRODUCT;NUMBER
                         Width             7
                         Decimal places
                         Total this column



              ┌Report Format─────────────────────────────────────────
              >>>>>>>>>>>>>>PRODUCT --------------------------------<<<<<<<<<<<<<<
                            NUMBER


                      XX

  CREATE REPORT   <B:> STOCKRPT.FRM          Column: 1
              Position selection bar - ↑↓.  Select - ↵.  Prev/Next column - PgUp/PgDn.
              Enter up to four lines of text to display above the indicated column.
```
(b)

next field by pressing the PgDn key to complete the column and get a new column definition on the screen.

Gerry proceeds as before to choose the formats for the product name, price, and quantity on hand fields. The last two fields are numeric fields, so she needs to provide definitions for the last two menu options, Decimal places and Total this column, for both fields. dBASE automatically calculates subtotals and overall totals on numeric fields in reports unless Gerry specifies No for the Total this column option. Gerry selects Yes or No by pressing the Enter key. She selects No for the PRICE field and Yes for the QOH field. Figure 9-23 shows the entered formats for all the fields.

Exiting the Report Program. Now that the report form is defined, Gerry saves it by selecting the Exit option from the create report Option menu and then the Save option from the Exit menu. Her report form (not the report itself) is stored in a file named STOCKRPT.FRM, the name Gerry chose earlier.

Figure 9-23 The PRODNAME, PRICE, and QOH fields. *(a) The PRODNAME field. (b) The PRICE field.*

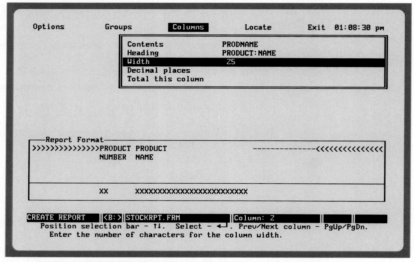

(a)

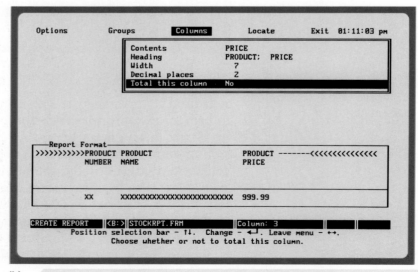

(b)

continued ▶

Figure 9-23 The PROD-NAME, PRICE, and QOH fields (continued). *(c) The QOH field. Notice in the Report Format box that column width for character fields is represented with Xs, and the width of numeric fields is represented with 9s or # symbols.*

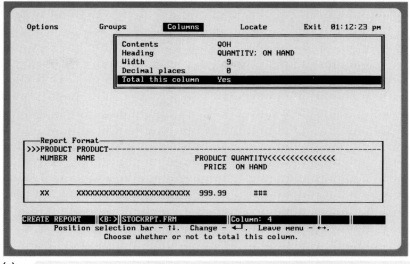

(c)

Printing the Report

Before Gerry prints her report form, she wants to double-check and make sure she entered everything correctly. To do this, she types

```
REPORT FORM STOCKRPT
```

The report appears on the screen (Figure 9-24).

Figure 9-24 Viewing the completed report form. *Gerry uses the Report Form command to see how her final report will look once it is printed. She also checks to see if she needs to make any corrections.*

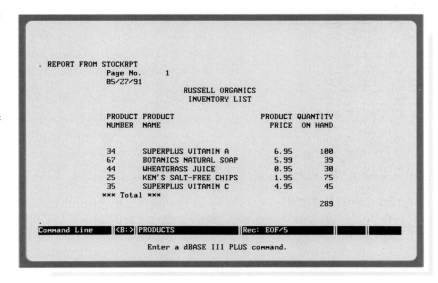

Figure 9-25 The printed report. Gerry's report in printed form. Notice that the program totaled the QOH field.

```
Page No.        1
05/27/91
                        RUSSELL ORGANICS
                        INVENTORY LIST

PRODUCT PRODUCT                        PRODUCT QUANTITY
NUMBER  NAME                             PRICE  ON HAND


34         SURPERPLUS VITAMIN A          6.95      100
67         BOTANICS NATURAL SOAP         5.99       39
44         WHEATGRASS JUICE              0.95       30
25         KEN'S SALT-FREE CHIPS         1.95       75
35         SUPERPLUS VITAMIN C           4.95       45
*** Total ***

                                                  289
```

To print the report, Gerry makes sure that the PRODUCTS file is open and her printer is on. Then she types

```
REPORT FORM STOCKRPT.FRM TO PRINT
```

and presses Enter. dBASE prints the report (Figure 9-25).

On to Graphics

In the first six applications chapters, we have moved from words to numbers to data. The upcoming change to drawings and pictures may be a refreshing variation. But graphics used in business are not a toy. In fact, graphics can show words and numbers and data in ways that are meaningful and quickly understood; this is the key reason they are valuable.

KEYSTROKES ONLY

The Russell Organics Example

These instructions are for using Gerry Russell's database, as described in the text. The dBASE III PLUS keystrokes that follow can also be used when you create your own databases. (Note: Material introduced in Chapter 8 is not covered in this discussion.)

Listing Using a Condition

1. To open the appropriate file at the dot prompt, type USE followed by the name of the file you wish to open. Then press Enter.

2. To list using a condition, you must use the LIST FOR command in the following format:

```
LIST FOR (field name)
(relational operator)
(value contained in
field)
```

For example, in the command (entered all on one line)

```
LIST FOR PRODNAME =
"WHEATGRASS JUICE"
```

PRODNAME is the field name, the equals sign is the relational operator, and WHEATGRASS JUICE is the value contained in the PRODNAME field. Values in character fields must be contained in quotation marks.

3. After typing in the command, press Enter to execute the command.

Listing Using Multiple Conditions

1. To list using multiple conditions, you must use the List For command in the following format (the command would be typed in one continuous line; you only press the Enter key at the end of the command):

```
LIST FOR (field name
1) (relational
operator 1) (value
contained in field 1)
(logical operator)
(field name 2)
(relational operator
2) (value contained in
field 2)
```

For example (this would be entered on a single line),

```
LIST FOR SUPPLIER =
"SUPERPLUS VITAMINS
INC." .AND. PRICE >
5.00
```

2. After typing in the command, press Enter to execute the command.

Sorting a File

1. To sort a file in ascending order, you must use the Sort command in the following format:

```
SORT ON (field name)
TO (new file name)
```

For example (this would be typed on a single line),

```
SORT ON PRODNO TO
ORDERS1
```

2. After typing in the command, press Enter to execute the command.

3. To sort a file in descending order, you must use the Sort command in the following format:

```
SORT ON (field name)/D
TO (new file name)
```

For example (type this on one line),

```
SORT ON PRODNO/D TO
ORDERS1
```

4. After typing in the command, press Enter to execute the command.

5. To access a sorted file, type USE followed by the name of the sorted file and then press Enter.

Indexing a File

1. To index a file, you must use the Index command in the following format:

```
INDEX ON (field name)
TO (index file name)
```

For example (again, this would be typed in one continuous line),

```
INDEX ON PRODNAME TO
PNAMEI
```

2. After typing in the command, press Enter to execute the command.

3. To access an indexed file, use the Use command in the following format:

```
USE (file name) INDEX
(index file name)
```

For example (again, this would be typed in one continuous line),

```
USE PRODUCTS INDEX
PNAMEI
```

continued ▶

The Russell Organics Example (continued)

4. After typing in the command, press Enter to execute the command.

Using the Seek Command

Note: You can only seek a record using fields on which an (open) index file has been created.

1. Type SEEK followed by the value you wish to locate. Values in character fields must be contained in quotation marks.

2. Press Enter to execute the command.

3. To display the located record, type DISPLAY and press Enter. The contents of the record are displayed on the screen.

Using the Count Command

To count all the records in the database file:

1. Type COUNT and press Enter. The total number of records in the file is displayed on the screen.

To count records meeting certain criteria:

1. Use the Count command in the following format:

```
COUNT FOR (field name)
(relational operator)
(value contained in
the field)
```

For example,

```
COUNT FOR REPNO = "13"
```

2. After you type in the command, press Enter to execute the command. The result is displayed on the screen.

Using the Sum Command

To sum all the values in a given field:

1. Type SUM (field name) and press Enter. The result is displayed on the screen.

To sum the values in fields meeting certain criteria:

1. Use the Sum command in the following format:

```
SUM FOR (field name
you wish to sum) FOR
(conditional field
name) (relational
operator) (value
contained in
conditional field
name)
```

For example (you would type the command on one line),

```
SUM TOTAL FOR PRODNO =
"35"
```

2. After you type in the command, press Enter to execute the command. The result is displayed on the screen.

Using the Average Command

To average all the values in a given field:

1. Type AVERAGE (field name) and press Enter. The result is displayed on the screen.

To average the values in

fields meeting certain criteria:

1. Use the Average command in the following format:

```
AVERAGE (field name
you wish to average)
FOR (conditional field
name) (relational
operator) (value
contained in
conditional field
name)
```

For example (you would type the command on one line),

```
AVERAGE TOTAL FOR
PRODNO = "35"
```

2. After you type in the command, press Enter to execute the command. The result is displayed on the screen.

Opening Several Files Simultaneously

1. To activate a specific work area, use the following format:

```
SELECT (work area
number) (Enter)
USE (file name)
(Enter)
```

See the examples on page 315.

Linking Files

1. Simultaneously open the two files you want to link.

2. To link the two files, use the Set Relation command in the following format:

```
SET RELATION TO (link
field) INTO (file name
of file open in Work
Area 2)
```

For example (this would be typed on one continuous line),

```
SET RELATION TO REPNO
INTO SALESREP
```

In this example, REPNO is the link field, the common field between SALESREP and the file in Work Area 1. SALESREP is open in Work Area 2. SALESREP must be indexed on REPNO and the index must be active (use SALESREP Index REPNOI).

3. After typing the command, press Enter to execute the command.

Joining Files

1. Simultaneously open the two files you want to join.

2. To join the two files, use the Join command in the following format:

```
JOIN WITH (file name
of file open in Work
Area 2) TO (file name
of new joined file)
FOR (link field in
area 1) = B->(link
field in area 2)
```

For example (this would be typed on one continuous line),

```
JOIN WITH SALESREP TO
CUSTREP FOR REPNO =
B->REPNO
```

3. After typing the command, press Enter to execute the command.

Closing Multiple Files

1. Type CLEAR ALL and press Enter. dBASE closes all the files and returns to the dot prompt.

Creating the Report Form

Note: To generate a report form, you must open the already created database file on which you want the report to be based.

To enter the report form:

1. Type CREATE REPORT and press Enter. Type in the name you want to use for the report form. The first menu of the report-generating program appears on the screen.

To enter the report title:

1. Select Options from the main Create Report menu.

2. Select the Page title option from the Options menu. A highlighted box appears on the screen.

3. Type in the title you wish to use.

4. After typing in your title, press Ctrl-End to move out of the box.

To change the margin settings:

1. Select the Left margin or Right margin option from the Options menu.

2. Type in number of spaces in the new margin and press Enter.

To enter the column information:

1. Select the Columns option from the Option menu.

2. Select and enter the appropriate data for the Contents, Heading, Width, Decimal places, and Total this column options.

3. When you have completed a column definition, move to the next column by pressing PgDn.

4. When you have finished entering all the data, store the data by pressing Ctrl-End.

To exit the report program:

1. Select the Exit option from the Option menu.

2. Select the Save option from the Exit menu. You return to the regular dBASE menu.

Viewing the Report Form

1. To view the report form, type REPORT FORM followed by the name of the form. Then press Enter.

Printing the Report

1. Make sure the file on which the report is based is open and the printer is on.

2. Type

```
REPORT FORM (report
form name) TO PRINT
```

and then press Enter. For example (type on one line),

```
REPORT FORM
STOCKRPT.FRM TO PRINT
```

Exercises

9-1

1. Load your database program and insert a formatted disk in drive B.

Figure 9-26

```
Field    Field Name      Type         Width       Dec
  1      CUSTNAME        Character      20
  2      CUSTNO          Character       4
  3      STATE           Character       2
  4      REPNO           Character       3


Record#   CUSTNAME                CUSTNO   STATE   REPNO
  1       STEREO STORE              3846     LA     246
  2       WONG'S                    3841     DE     247
  3       NORTHWEST STEREO          3839     AK     248
  4       BOSTON ELECTRONICS        3875     VA     246
  5       UNCLE SAM'S               3856     TX     249
```

(a)　CUSTOMER file

```
Field    Field Name      Type         Width       Dec
  1      REPNAME         Character      20
  2      REPNO           Character       3
  3      SSN             Character      11
  4      PHONE           Character       8


Record#   REPNAME              REPNO      SSN            PHONE
  1       TARA WALTERS          246    177-34-1626    411-3314
  2       JOSEPH GUARDINO       247    521-11-2768    634-7272
  3       ROOSEVELT CLIFTON     248    985-44-1077    555-0010
  4       MARINA MCNALLY        249    557-45-7248    411-8910
```

(b)　SALESREP file

```
Field    Field Name      Type         Width       Dec
  1      PRODNAME        Character      20
  2      PRODNO          Character       3
  3      PRICE           Numeric         6          2
  4      QOH             Numeric         4


Record#   PRODNAME             PRODNO    PRICE    QOH
  1       ADVENT SPEAKERS        110     249.00   100
  2       FISHER VCRS            111     348.00   225
  3       TECHNICS TURNTABLES    112     200.00   150
  4       MITSUBISHI TVS         113     368.00    75
  5       YAMAHA RECEIVERS       114     275.00   225
```

(c)　PRODUCTS file

continued ▶

Figure 9-26 (continued)

Field	Field Name	Type	Width	Dec
1	ORDERNO	Character	5	
2	PRODNO	Character	3	
3	CUSTNO	Character	4	
4	DATE	Date	8	
5	QUANTITY	Numeric	3	
6	TOTAL	Numeric	8	2

Record#	ORDERNO	PRODNO	CUSTNO	DATE	QUANTITY	TOTAL
1	48201	111	3486	07/24/91	10	3480.00
2	48202	113	3841	07/24/91	20	7360.00
3	48202	114	3841	07/24/91	20	5500.00
4	48203	110	3839	07/25/91	30	7470.00
5	48203	112	3839	07/25/91	25	5000.00
6	48203	114	3839	07/25/91	10	2750.00
7	48204	113	3875	07/25/91	10	3680.00
8	48205	111	3486	07/26/91	15	5220.00
9	48205	113	3486	07/26/91	25	9200.00

(d) ORDERS file

2. Using the appropriate commands, create the four database files shown in Figure 9-26. Be sure to view each file, check your file structure and entries, and make corrections as needed.
3. Open (activate) the PRODUCTS file. Use the appropriate commands to find the record number for each of the following:

   ■ Yamaha Receivers
   ■ Product Number 112
   ■ The product that costs $249

   Close the file.
4. Open the ORDERS file. Use the appropriate commands to find the record numbers for each of the following:

   ■ Orders placed by customer number 3846
   ■ Orders for product number 113 for amounts greater than 10
   ■ Orders for amounts greater than 5000.00

   Close the file.

9-2

1. Open the PRODUCTS file you created in Exercise 9-1.
2. Sort the PRODUCTS file in alphabetical order by product name, and store the sorted records in a file named PROD1.
3. View the records in the PRODUCTS file. Has their order changed? View the records in the PROD1 file. Are the records in the correct order?
4. Sort the PRODUCTS file in order of decreasing price, and store the sorted records in a file named PROD2.
5. View the records in the PROD2 file. Are the records in the correct order?

6. Close all the files, then open the PRODUCTS file. Change the price of the Technics Turntables to 250.00.
7. Open the PROD1 file. Has the price for the turntables been adjusted in this file?
8. Open the PROD2 file. Has the price for the turntables been adjusted in this file? If you changed the price of the turntables in the PROD1 file, would the price change in this file? Why or why not?
9. Close the PRODUCTS file.

9-3

1. Open the CUSTOMER file you created in Exercise 9-1.
2. Index the file on the CUSTNO field. Name the index CUSTNOI.
3. View the records in the CUSTOMER file, using CUSTNOI as the active index. How are they ordered?
4. Index the CUSTOMER file on the STATE field. Name the index STATEI.
5. View the records in the CUSTOMER file by using STATEI as the active index. How are they ordered? Is the order different from that of the CUSTNOI index?
6. Close all the files. Then make CUSTOMER the active file—do not open either index. View the records in the file. Has their order changed?
7. Change the customer name in Record 2 to Wong's Video. Close the CUSTOMER file and then reopen it with CUSTNOI as the active index.
8. View the records in CUSTOMER with CUSTNOI as the active index. Has the customer name for Record 2 changed? Are the records still in order by customer number? Close all the files.
9. Open the CUSTOMER file with STATEI as the active index. List the records; are they in the proper order? Has the information in Record 2 changed?
10. Change the state in the Northwest Stereo record to VA.
11. View the records with the STATEI index as the active index. What has happened to the order of the records?
12. Close all the files.

9-4

1. Use the appropriate command to open the CUSTOMER file so the CUSTNOI index is active.
2. Use your program's Seek command to locate the record with the customer number 3875. Use the appropriate command to display this record on the screen.

3. Use your program's Seek command to locate the record with the customer number 3856. Display the record on the screen.

4. List the CUSTOMER file and make a note of the number of records with the value VA in the STATE field. Then use your program's Seek command to locate the records that have VA in the STATE field. Be sure to use the index file that enables you to Seek using the STATE field. Display the record(s) on the screen. Are all the records for STATE = "VA" displayed? Why or why not?

5. Use the appropriate command to close the files.

9-5

Tyrone Franklin, a prospering public artist, wants to use a database to record information about the work he has done for his clients. He asks you to create the database shown in Figure 9-27.

1. Using the information in the figure, enter the database structure and records. The file should be named PROJECTS.

2. Use the appropriate commands to find the following information:

   - The total number of records in which the number of hours worked is greater than 100
   - The total number of contracts completed for Scotts Terrace
   - The total amount that Tyrone has earned working for Scotts Terrace
   - The average number of hours that Tyrone has worked
   - The total amount that Tyrone has earned

3. Tyrone also wants you to list the following record(s) for him:

   - The records of all the projects he has worked on
   - The record(s) of the projects he has done for Danville Plaza

Figure 9-27

Field	Field Name	Type	Width	Dec
1	PROJECT	Character	30	
2	START_DATE	Date	8	
3	END_DATE	Date	8	
4	HOURS	Numeric	4	
5	MATERIALS	Numeric	6	2
6	AMT_EARNED	Numeric	8	2

Record#	PROJECT	START_DATE	END_DATE	HOURS	MATERIALS	AMT_EARNED
1	BAKERSFIELD HALL	04/10/90	04/29/90	60	260.00	1500.00
2	SCOTTS TERRACE	05/13/90	05/25/90	130	458.65	3200.00
3	DANVILLE PLAZA	05/17/90	05/24/90	20	162.37	1000.00
4	JACKSONVILLE HEIGHTS	06/20/90	07/28/90	450	855.00	6500.00
5	PRENTICE TOWERS	07/10/90	08/15/90	250	625.75	4000.00
6	SCOTTS TERRACE	08/20/90	09/01/90	50	340.00	2250.00

- The record(s) of projects on which he spent less than 100 hours working, but earned more than $2000.00
- The records of projects for which the materials cost more than $300.00 or the hours worked were greater than or equal to 100 hours

4. Using the PROJECTS file, index the file on the PROJECT field. Name the index PROJECTI. View the indexed file. In what order are the records displayed?

5. Close all the files.

9-6

For this exercise use the files created in Exercise 9-1.

1. Using the appropriate commands, open the CUSTOMER file in Work Area 2 and the ORDERS file in Work Area 1. Which file is the active file?

2. Using the appropriate commands, try to set up a relation between the two files by using a common field. Are you successful? Why or why not?

3. Index the CUSTOMER file on the CUSTNO field. Now try to set up a relation between the two files. Are you successful this time?

4. After you have set up the relation, use the appropriate command to list the following:

- The name of the customer who placed order number 48203
- The names of the customers who placed orders for quantities greater than 10
- The order numbers for the Stereo Store's orders
- The names of the customers who placed orders for product number 113
- The date on which Northwest Stereo placed its order

9-7

1. Join the two files you opened in Exercise 9-6. Store the combined records in a file named CUSTORD.

2. Open the CUSTORD file. Use the appropriate command to list the structure of the file.

3. Use the appropriate command to list the records in the file.

4. Using the appropriate commands, list the following fields in the order given:

- CUSTNAME ORDERNO
- CUSTNAME DATE
- ORDERNO, CUSTNO, CUSTNAME
- ORDERNO, PRODNO, CUSTNAME, REPNO

5. Using the appropriate commands, find the following information:
   - The total number of orders placed by customer Boston Electronics
   - The average cost of the orders placed by the customer in Louisiana
   - The date of the order placed by Wong's Video
   - The name of the customer who placed order 48203
6. Using the appropriate commands, close all the files.

9-8

1. Use the PROJECTS file you created in Exercise 9-5 to create a report. The title of the report should be PROJECTS COMPLETED. The left margin and right margins should be set at 10. The report should contain the PROJECT, END_DATE, HOURS, and AMT_EARNED fields. You should total the AMT_EARNED field on the report.
2. Use the appropriate commands to print the report.
3. Close the file.

9-9

1. Use the CUSTORD file you created in Exercise 9-7 to create a report. The title of the report should be CUSTOMER ORDERS. The left and right margins should be set at 15. The report should contain the ORDERNO, PRODNO, CUSTNAME, DATE, AMOUNT, and TOTAL fields. The AMOUNT and TOTAL fields should be totaled at the bottom of the report.
2. Use the appropriate commands to print the report.
3. Close all the files.
4. Exit the program.

Summary and Key Terms

- In a relational database a field common to more than one database file is called a **link field.** A link field links data in one file to data in other files. You can link two or more data files together as long as at least one common field exists in each file.

- When you design a database, you must consider both the data to be stored and the ways in which the data will be needed.

- Various types of searches can be performed on a data file. You can specify one condition or multiple conditions. The FOR statement is used to identify the criteria the program is to use during a search. Logical operators, such as .AND. and .OR., are placed in database commands to develop more complex criteria.

- The Sort command sorts a database in an order based

on the field or fields indicated and stores the sorted database as a new file. Data may be sorted in either ascending or descending order, alphabetically or numerically.

■ The Index command instructs the program to sort data according to a specified field; however, instead of sorting to a database file, the Index command creates a special kind of file called an **index file.** In an index file **pointers** "point" to the location of records within a data file. When you index a file, the original file remains unaltered.

■ In dBASE III PLUS the Seek command can be used to search an indexed database file that contains many records. However, each record must have a field whose value is different for each record in the database file; such fields are called **key fields.**

■ Like spreadsheet programs, database programs offer a variety of commands that perform numeric and mathematical calculations, including summing, counting, and averaging. The Count command tallies the number of records in an active data file. The Sum command totals a column of one or more numeric fields. The Average command calculates the arithmetic average of a numeric field.

■ The power of relational database management software lies in its ability to locate and retrieve information from several different database files at one time. The Set Relation command and the Join command are two dBASE III PLUS commands that let you combine data from different files.

■ To open several files at once, each file must be assigned to its own work area in the computer's memory. The Select command activates the various work areas. Each work area is referred to by a number. The work area the program is currently using is known as the **selected area,** or the **active area,** and the file stored in that area is known as the **selected file,** or **active file.**

■ To create a database report, you must first create the report form and then print the report. The program automatically fills in the information in the report when you print the report.

Review Questions

1. Suppose you had a database file that included a STATE field. How would you write the command that would list all the records in which OREGON appears in the STATE field?

2. Using the database file mentioned in question 1, how would you write the command that would list all the records in which OREGON appears in the STATE field and PORTLAND appears in the CITY field?

3. What is a logical operator?

4. What is the difference between the .AND. operator and the .OR. operator?

5. What does the Sort command do?

6. What does the Index command do?

7. List several of the advantages of using the Index command rather than the Sort command.

8. What is the Seek command used for?

9. What must you do to a file before you can use the Seek command?

10. What is the function of the Count command? The Sum command? The Average command?

11. What are two commands you can use to relate database files? How are the two commands different?

12. What do the files have to have in common before they can be combined?

13. What is the effect of the following two commands?

   ```
   SELECT 2
   USE EMPLOYEE
   ```

14. Describe the steps you would take to create a report in dBASE.

FROM THE REAL WORLD

Getting Data at Quaker Oats

In addition to its flagship product, Old Fashioned Quaker Oats, the Quaker Oats Company makes Cap'n Crunch and Life cereals, Aunt Jemima pancakes, Quaker Rice Cakes, Gatorade, and more. Quaker Oats CEO William Smithburg often needed to get information quickly, such as statistics about the sale of hot cereals. However, like other managers before him, he was told that the information he wanted *was* in the company computers, but it was stored in several different places. His requests were not simple, and the answers he received were not fast.

Furthermore, other company executives would sometimes come to meetings with different statistics—from different company files—on the same subject. It seemed clear that a central source was needed. The solution? A database system.

Quaker personnel designed a system, called

Executive Information System, that used company personal computers to access a mainframe database management system. The menu-driven system is so user friendly that executives are given only a half hour of training. But perhaps the key to convincing executives to use the system is the one-on-one training; without an audience they do not feel embarrassed to ask questions.

As soon as they turn on the computer, executives

see the main menu, which offers five options: Financial database, Dow Jones News/Retrieval, Financial spreadsheets, Daily sales, or Exit. The database can provide information such as sales, gross margin, and advertising expenses for each product Quaker produces. This information is particularly important because Quaker monitors each product closely, abandoning those that are weak and promoting those that are strong.

Executives give the system high praise. Even those who were not "raised on computers" and thus showed some initial reluctance, champion the system. At first, they were won over by the system's user friendliness; now they have come to value the system because of the timely information it can provide. As one executive noted, it now takes two minutes to do what used to take two days.

10 Business Graphics

Chapter Objectives

After reading this chapter you should be able to

- Describe the advantages of using graphics

- Explain the difference between analytical and presentation graphics

- List and describe different types of graphs

- Create a simple graph by using Lotus 1-2-3

- Use Lotus 1-2-3 to view a graph, add titles and legends to the graph, save the graph, and print the graph

- Describe the hardware associated with graphics and explain when it is needed

For centuries, people have used graphic arts to convey information. Now, computer-generated graphics have come into their own in a major—and sometimes spectacular—way. Current graphics programs let people produce many different visual images, from simple black-and-white line drawings to elaborate multicolored, three-dimensional illustrations. Computer-animated graphics have developed beyond the stick figures found on the screens of video games to the floating cars, shining logos, and realistic cartoons seen in TV commercials and movies. Computer graphics are also used in education,

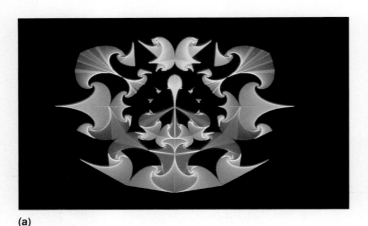

(a)

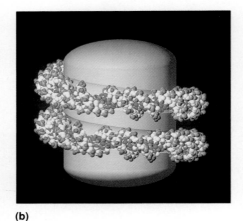

(b)

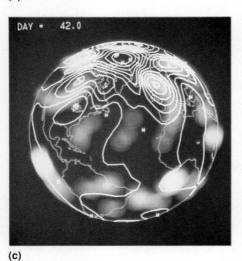

(c)

Figure 10-1 Computer graphics. *These sophisticated color graphics show the combined power of creative imaging and new technology. (a) A colorful abstract computer graphic. (b) An image of a DNA molecule wrapped around another molecule. (c) One image from a computerized global weather model.*

computer art, science, sports, and other areas (Figure 10-1). But perhaps the most prevalent use of graphics today is in business.

Business Graphics

Personal computers give people the capability to store and use data about their businesses. These same users, however, sometimes find it difficult to convey this information to others—managers or clients—in a meaningful way. **Business graphics**—graphics that represent data in a visual, easily understood format—provide an answer to this problem.

Why Use Graphics?

Graphics generate and sustain the interest of an audience by brightening up any lesson, report, or business document. In addition, graphics can help get a point across by distilling an overwhelming amount of data into one simple, clear graph (Figure 10-2, on the next page). What is more, that simple graph can reveal a trend that could be lost if buried in long columns of numbers. To sum up, most people use business graphics software for one of two reasons: (1) to view and analyze data and (2) to make a positive impression during a presentation. To satisfy these different needs, two types of business graphics programs have been developed: analytical graphics and presentation graphics.

Analytical Graphics

Analytical graphics programs are designed to help users analyze and understand specific data. Sometimes called analysis-oriented graphics programs, these programs let you use already entered spreadsheet or database data to construct and view line, bar, and pie-chart graphs (Figure 10-3, on the next page). Later in this chapter we will show you how to create analytical graphics by using the graphics program included in Lotus 1-2-3.

Although analytical graphics programs do a good job of producing simple graphs, these programs are too limited and inflexible for a user who needs to prepare elaborate presentations. Lotus 1-2-3, for example, lets you choose from only a

Figure 10-2 Business graphics. *In business (a) a large amount of data can be translated into (b) one simple, clear graph.*

Material	Cost	Units Sold Each Month			
		Jan.	Feb.	Mar.	Apr.
Copper	85	6	10	13	22
Bronze	235	18	28	36	60
Iron	123	9	15	19	32
Gold	420	32	52	64	110
Silver	260	20	32	40	68
Totals:	1123	85	137	172	292

(a)

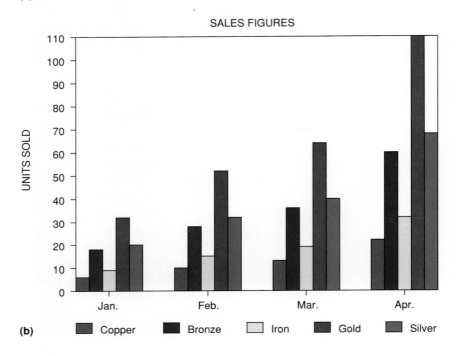

(b)

Figure 10-3 Analytical graphics. *Analytical graphics programs let you produce simple line graphs, bar graphs, and pie charts.*

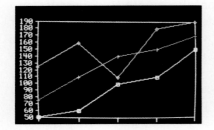
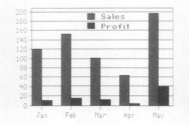
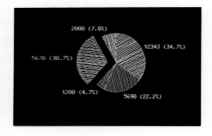

small number of graph types, and the program's formatting features—that can produce different graph sizes, different colors, and different types of lettering—are limited. These limitations may be of little concern to some users. But those who require sophisticated graphics will want to consider presentation graphics.

Presentation Graphics

Presentation graphics programs are also called **business-quality graphics** or presentation-oriented desktop graphics programs. These programs let you produce charts, graphs, and other visual aids that look as if they were prepared by a professional graphics artist (Figure 10-4). However, you can control the appearance of the product when you do it yourself, and you can produce graphics faster and make last-minute changes if necessary.

Most presentation graphics programs help you do three kinds of tasks:

- Edit and enhance charts created by other programs, such as the analytical graphics produced by Lotus 1-2-3

- Create charts, diagrams, drawings, and text slides from scratch

- Use a library of symbols, drawings, and pictures—called **clip art**—that comes with the graphics program. Because the computer produces the "drawings" and manipulates them, even a nonartist can create professional-looking illustrations (Figure 10-5, on the next page).

Figure 10-4 Presentation graphics. These colorful, professional-looking graphs are produced by using a presentation graphics program. Compare these graphics with those in Figure 10-3.

Figure 10-5 Enhancing graphics with clip art. Presentation graphics programs provide a library of symbols that users can choose from.

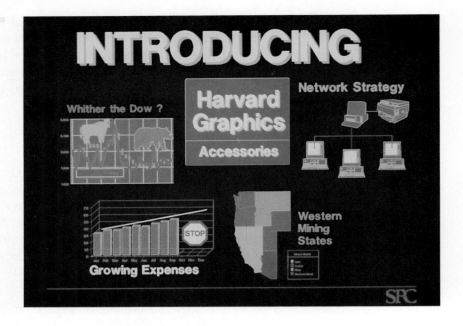

Presentation graphics increase the impact of your message. They make the information you are presenting visually appealing, meaningful, and comprehensible. High-quality graphics have been shown to increase both the amount that a listener learns in a presentation and the length of time that the information is retained by the listener. Also, an audience perceives you as more professional and knowledgeable when you include overhead graphics and slides in your presentation.

You can produce high-quality output on a variety of media: CRT screens, printers, plotters, overhead transparencies, or slides for projection. Some presentation graphics programs let you store pictures, text slides, charts, and graphs on disk. This means you can use the computer to present a series of text or graphic images, one after the other, on your display. When you make a presentation, you can either run the display manually or have the screens presented by the computer automatically, in time increments ranging from four seconds to four minutes per image. A few programs let you animate your images. For example, graph bars might grow as product sales increase.

Some Graphics Terminology

To use a graphics program successfully, you should know some basic concepts and design principles. Let us begin by exploring the types of graphs you can create.

RANDOM BITS

Presentation Graphics Programs

Many presentation graphics programs produce good-looking graphics on a personal computer with a minimum of fuss. These programs let you change such characteristics as type size; color; and position of titles, subtitles, and legends—all with just a few keystrokes. Several programs also feature "slide-show" options that allow you to create, select, and present a slide show of graphics right on the personal computer screen. The two programs described in this box are just a sample of the many presentation graphics programs available.

Harvard Graphics Harvard Graphics, from Software Publishing Corporation, is a complete presentation graphics package. With it you can produce your own graphs and charts and also enhance graphs, from simple to complex, and even make three-dimensional bar graphs. On top of

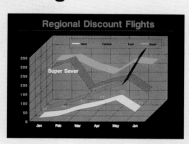

that, you can produce organization charts and project-scheduling charts. The program also includes features such as macros, a library of 92 symbols that can be incorporated in the graphs, and a free-lance drawing option that lets you annotate a chart with arrows, circles, and polygons or draw a chart from scratch. Harvard Graphics slide-show feature comes complete with zoom, fade, and wipe options.

Chart-Master From software publisher Ashton-Tate, Chart-Master lets you translate data from popular spreadsheet programs like Lotus 1-2-3 into pie charts

and line, bar, area, and scatter graphs. The package includes more than 40 options, so you can dramatically improve the way your graphs look. For example, you can size and draw a chart anywhere on a screen, graphics printer, or plotter.

This is useful when you want to reserve the top or bottom of a chart for text created with a word processing program. A large library of standard symbols that you can include in graphs and charts is also available. The images produced by Chart-Master can be reproduced on screen, on graphics printers, on plotters, on slides, or as color prints.

Line Graphs

One of the most useful ways of showing trends or cycles over the same period of time is to use a **line graph.** For example, the graph in Figure 10-6 (on the next page) shows company costs for supplies, utilities, and travel during a five-month period. Line graphs are appropriate when there are many values or complex data. In the business section of the newspaper, line graphs are used to show complex trends in gross national product, stock prices, or employment changes over a period of time.

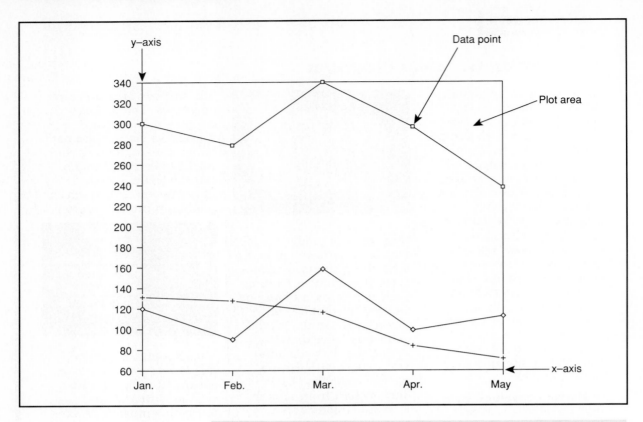

Figure 10-6 A line graph. *Line graphs are useful for showing trends over a period of time. In many analytical programs different symbols are used to show the different types of data being plotted.*

Also, corporate profits and losses are often illustrated by line graphs.

Notice the two solid lines in Figure 10-6—one that runs vertically and one that runs horizontally. Each line is called an **axis.** (The plural of *axis* is *axes.*) The horizontal line, called the **x-axis,** normally represents units of time, such as days, months, or years. The vertical line, called the **y-axis,** usually shows measured values or amounts, such as dollars, staffing levels, units sold, and so on. The area inside the axes is called the **plot area**—the space in which the graph is plotted, or drawn.

Graphics programs automatically scale (arrange the units or numbers on) the x-axis and y-axis so that the graph of your data is nicely proportioned and easy to read. When you become proficient with a graphics program, you can select your own scaling for the x- and y-axes.

Each dot or symbol on a line graph represents a single numerical quantity called a **data point.** You must specify the data to be plotted on the graph. This data is usually referred to as the *values.* The items that the data points describe are called **variables.** Most graphs are produced from the data stored in the rows and columns of spreadsheet files. Recall from the spreadsheet chapters that you can refer to particular rows or columns of a spreadsheet as a *range.* A graph that plots the values of only one variable is sometimes referred to as a **single-range graph** (Figure 10-7a). If more than one variable is plotted on the same graph, it is referred to as a **multiple-range graph** (Figure 10-7b).

To make the graph easier to read and understand, **labels** are used to identify the categories along the x-axis and the units along the y-axis. **Titles** summarize the information in the graphic and are used to increase comprehension.

Figure 10-7 Types of line graphs. *(a) Single-range graphs show only one variable or line. (b) Multiple-range graphs show several different variables or lines.*

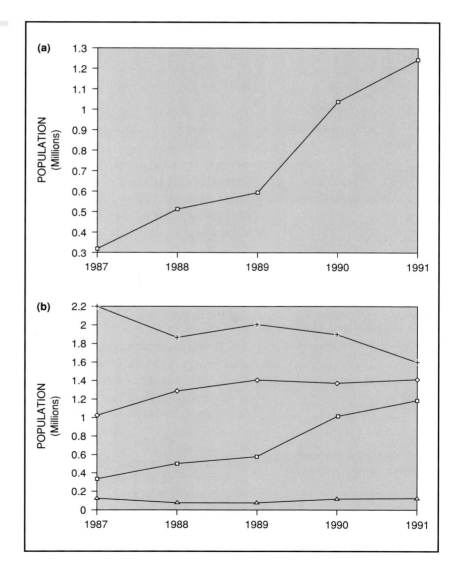

Bar Graphs

Bar graphs are used for graphing the same kinds of data that line graphs represent. Notice in Figure 10-8 that **bar graphs** shade an area up to the height of the point being plotted, creating a bar. These graphs can be striking and informative when they are simple. They are often used to illustrate multiple comparisons such as sales, expenses, and production activities. Bar graphs are useful for presentations, since the comparisons are easy to absorb. However, if there is a lot of data for several variables, the bars on the graph become narrow and crowded, making a confusing and busy graph; in such a case a line graph is preferable.

In Figure 10-8, there are three different types of bar graphs. The first is a **single-range bar graph,** in which only one variable is involved; in this example the single variable is monthly expenses. The second type of bar graph is a multiple-range bar graph called a **clustered-bar graph.** In this type of graph, data values for three different variables—supplies, utilities, and travel—are plotted next to each other along the x-axis. Because clustered-bar graphs contain so much information, it is important to label each cluster clearly. You can also create a **legend,** or list, that explains different colors, shadings, or symbols in the graph. A legend is used at the bottom of Figure 10-8b. The third type of bar graph, the **stacked-bar graph,** is also a multiple-range bar graph. In this graph however, the different variables are stacked on top of one another. All the data common to a given row or column appears in one bar.

Pie Charts

Representing just a single variable, a **pie chart** shows how various values make up a whole. These charts really look like pies; the whole amount is represented by a circle, and each wedge of the pie represents a value. Figure 10-9a (on page 352) shows a pie chart.

Pie charts can show only the data for one variable, January in this example. However, this pie chart does the best job of showing the proportion of the "pie" dollar that goes for rent, supplies, and so forth during that one month. Notice that pie charts often have the written percentage shown by each separate wedge of the pie. It is best to keep pie charts simple; if the pie contains more than eight wedges, you might consider using a bar graph or line graph instead.

BIOTECHNICAL SLIDE PRESENTATION

San Francisco research scientist Dr. Howard Urnovitz uses his personal computer to design slides that show the interaction of antibodies and pathogens and to show how cell fusion takes place in the creation of hybrid cells. If all that sounds a bit complex, consider the first question he is invariably asked after he makes a presentation to his highly skilled scientific audiences: "How did you do your slides?" Urnovitz attributes his success to a Commodore Amiga 1000 computer. Sometimes pictures are worth more than a thousand words.

Figure 10-8 Types of bar graphs. *(a) A single-range bar graph shows only one variable—in this case, monthly expenses. Multiple-range bar graphs show several variables. The other two graphs in this figure show the two basic types of multiple-range bar graphs: (b) A clustered bar graph shows several variables. (c) A stacked-bar graph shows the different variables stacked on top of one another.*

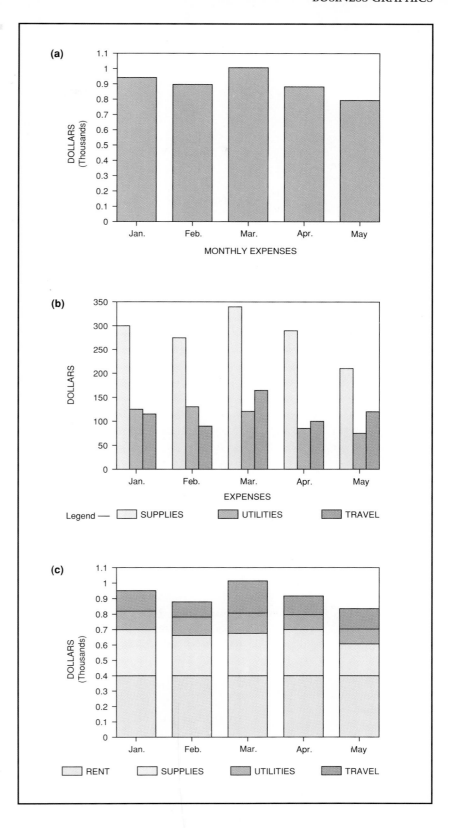

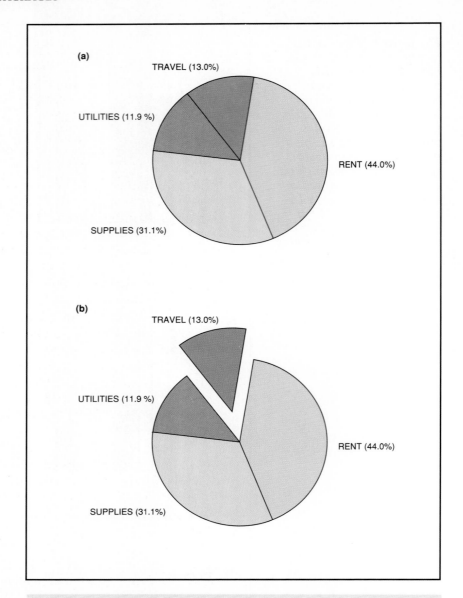

Figure 10-9 Types of pie charts. *Pie charts are used to show how various values make up a whole. (a) A regular pie chart. (b) An exploded pie chart.*

Figure 10-9b shows one of the wedges pulled slightly away from the pie, for emphasis. This type of pie chart is called an **exploded pie chart.** This technique loses its effectiveness if more than one or two "slices" are separated. Not all graphics programs have the ability to produce an exploded pie chart.

Creating Simple Graphs

In this section you will learn how to create, view, and save graphs by using Lotus 1-2-3. As you recall, Lotus stores values and labels in an electronic spreadsheet. Lotus uses the data stored in a worksheet to produce different types of analytical graphics.

The Music Center Example

Mike Berkeley manages Eichner's Music Center. Although primarily a compact-disc store, Eichner's also sells audio tapes, record albums, and videos. Mike knows that any range of numbers, such as a row or column of a spreadsheet, can be displayed in graphic form. He currently has the sales figures for each department set up as a worksheet on Lotus 1-2-3, as shown in Figure 10-10. (To review how to enter data into a worksheet, see Chapter 6.) He decides to turn this information into a bar graph so he can monitor the performance of the different departments. Mike loads the program and retrieves his worksheet with the file name SALES. Now Mike is ready to create his graph. (For an abbreviated version of the discussion that follows, see the box called "Keystrokes Only: The Music Center Example.")

Figure 10-10 Mike's SALES worksheet. *Mike can use the information stored in this worksheet to create different types of graphs.*

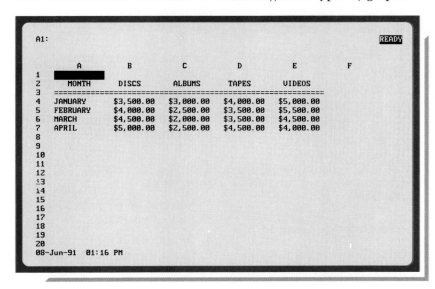

The Music Center Example

These instructions are for creating Mike Berkeley's graphs, as described in the text. The Lotus 1-2-3 keystrokes that follow can also be used to create your own graphs. (Note: Material introduced in Chapters 6 and 7 is not covered in this discussion.)

Selecting the Type of Graph

Note: Before you can create a graph, the data on which the graph will be based must be entered into a spreadsheet.

1. Press the Backslash (/) key to enter the MENU mode.

2. Select the Graph command from the main menu.

3. Select the Type option.

4. Select the type of graph you wish to create.

Choosing the Data Ranges to Graph

1. Select A from the Graph menu.

2. When prompted, type in the first range you wish to graph. Then press Enter.

3. Repeat the process selecting the options B through F that coincide with the ranges you wish to graph.

Viewing the Graph

Note: To view graphs, you must have a graphics adap-ter board in your computer.

To view a graph in black and white:

1. Select the View command from the Graph menu.

2. To return to the Graph menu, press Enter.

To view a graph in color:

1. Select the Options command from the Graph menu.

2. Select the Color option.

3. Select Quit to return to the Graph menu.

4. Select the View command.

5. To return to the Graph menu, press Enter.

Entering the X Range

1. Select the X option from the Graph menu.

2. When prompted, type in the range you wish to use and press Enter.

Adding Legends and Titles

To add legends:

1. Select the Options command from the Graph menu.

2. Select the Legend command.

3. Select A to provide a legend for the A Range.

4. When prompted, type in the legend you wish to use, then press Enter.

5. Repeat the process, selecting the options B through F that coincide with the ranges on your graph.

6. Select Quit to return to the Graph menu.

To add titles:

1. Select the Options command from the Graph menu.

2. Select Titles from the submenu.

3. Select the appropriate title option.

4. When prompted, type in the title you wish to use. Then press Enter.

5. Select Quit to return to the Graph menu.

Saving the Graph

To save the graph as a picture file:

1. Select the Save option from the Graph menu.

2. When prompted, type in the name of the graph you wish to save. Then press Enter.

To save the graph settings in a worksheet file:

1. Return to the main Command menu from the Graph menu by pressing the Esc key.

2. Select the File command.

3. Select the Save command.

4. Type in the name of the worksheet file you wish to save. Then press Enter.

To save the graph settings as a named graph:

1. Select the Name command from the Graph menu.

2. Select the Create command.

3. When prompted, type in the name of the graph settings you wish to save. Then press Enter.

Retrieving the Graph

Note: To retrieve a picture file you must use the PrintGraph utility.

To retrieve the graph settings in a worksheet file:

1. Access the main Command menu.

2. Select the File option.

3. Select the Retrieve option.

4. When prompted, type in the name of the worksheet file you wish to retrieve and then press Enter. The graph settings saved with the file are retrieved with the file.

To retrieve the graph settings in a named graph:

1. Retrieve the worksheet file in which the named graph settings are stored.

2. Select the Name option from the Graph menu.

3. Select the Use option.

4. When prompted, type in the name of the graph you wish to retrieve. Then press Enter.

Setting Up the Graph

To access the Lotus 1-2-3 graphics program, Mike enters the MENU mode by pressing the Backslash (/) key. Then he selects the Graph command from the menu by moving the cursor to the option and pressing Enter. The command tree for the Graph command is shown in Figure 10-11. Lotus displays

Figure 10-11 The Graph command tree. *This command tree shows the different Graph command options available in Lotus 1-2-3. You do not need to use all of these options when you create most graphs.*

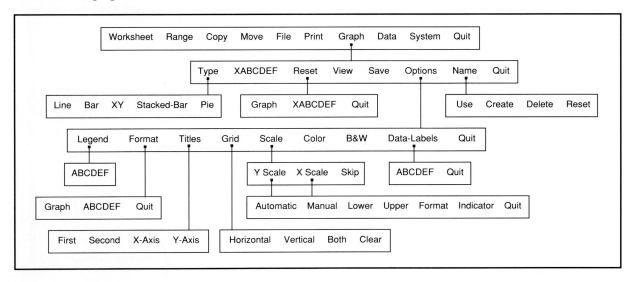

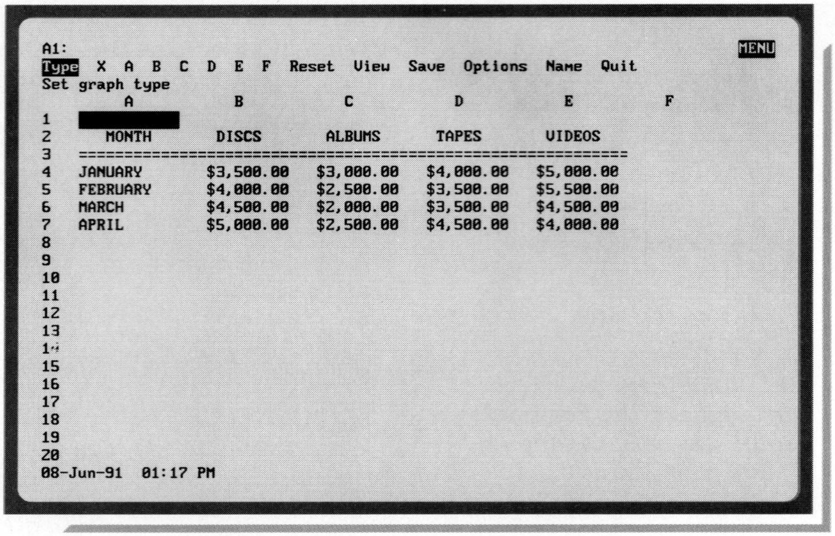

Figure 10-12 The Graph submenu. When Mike selects the Graph option, Lotus presents the submenu shown here.

the first submenu under the Graph command (Figure 10-12). First Mike selects the type of graph he wants. He does this by selecting Type from the graph submenu, and then—from the choices Line, Bar, XY, Stacked-Bar, and Pie—he selects Bar because he wants a bar graph (Figure 10-13). After he presses Enter, Lotus returns him to the Graph submenu.

Next Mike must tell Lotus the data ranges he wants to graph. Recall that Lotus calls a set of values a *range.* The graphics program identifies ranges with the letters A through F. The first range to graph is referred to as the **A Range,** the second is the **B Range,** and so on. The A through F selections on the graph menu let Mike identify these ranges on the worksheet.

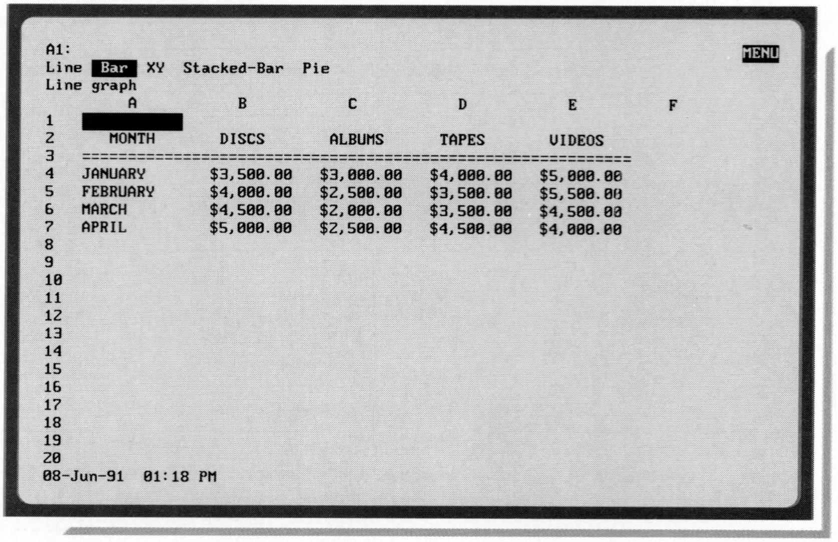

Figure 10-13 Selecting the type of graph. When Mike selects the Type option from the Graph submenu, he is given the option of choosing a line graph, a bar graph, an xy graph, a stacked-bar graph, or a pie chart. He selects the Bar option and presses Enter.

Notice that Lotus can graph up to six different ranges of values on the same graph—one range for each letter. However, Mike needs to graph only four ranges of values: those in columns B, C, D, and E of his worksheet.

To identify the first of his four data ranges (DISCS), Mike moves the cursor over the A option in the menu. Notice in Figure 10-14a that a message on the third line of the command menu explains the option. Mike presses Enter to select the A option. Then Lotus prompts him for the first data range. Since the values in the DISCS column are in Cells B4 through B7, Mike types B4.B7 (Figure 10-14b). Do not be confused by the fact that the A Range consists of cells from column B of the

Figure 10-14 Choosing the data ranges. *To enter the first range of data to be graphed, (a) Mike moves the cursor to the A option and presses Enter. (b) Then Mike enters the appropriate data range.*

```
A1:                                                              MENU
Type  X  A  B  C  D  E  F  Reset  View  Save  Options  Name  Quit
Set first data range
          A          B          C          D          E        F
 1
 2     MONTH       DISCS      ALBUMS      TAPES      VIDEOS
 3    ==================================================================
 4   JANUARY     $3,500.00   $3,000.00  $4,000.00  $5,000.00
 5   FEBRUARY    $4,000.00   $2,500.00  $3,500.00  $5,500.00
 6   MARCH       $4,500.00   $2,000.00  $3,500.00  $4,500.00
 7   APRIL       $5,000.00   $2,500.00  $4,500.00  $4,000.00
 8
 9
10
11
12
13
14
15
16
17
18
19
20
08-Jun-91  01:19 PM
```

(a)

```
A1:                                                              EDIT
Enter first data range: B4.B7_
          A          B          C          D          E        F
 1
 2     MONTH       DISCS      ALBUMS      TAPES      VIDEOS
 3    ==================================================================
 4   JANUARY     $3,500.00   $3,000.00  $4,000.00  $5,000.00
 5   FEBRUARY    $4,000.00   $2,500.00  $3,500.00  $5,500.00
 6   MARCH       $4,500.00   $2,000.00  $3,500.00  $4,500.00
 7   APRIL       $5,000.00   $2,500.00  $4,500.00  $4,000.00
 8
 9
10
11
12
13
14
15
16
17
18
19
20
08-Jun-91  01:20 PM
```

(b)

Figure 10-15 The A Range. *This figure shows what Mike's bar graph looks like with only the A Range graphed.*

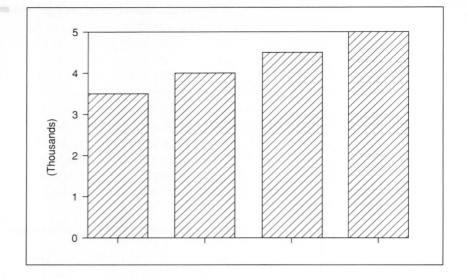

worksheet—the A Range is simply the first range you want to graph; it does not matter which row or column this data comes from. After Mike presses Enter, Lotus returns him to the Graph submenu. Figure 10-15 shows what Mike's graph looks like at this point.

To identify the second range on his graph, Mike selects the B option from the submenu. When Lotus asks for the data range, Mike enters C4.C7—the values from the ALBUMS column. He repeats the procedure, choosing the C and D options for the TAPES and VIDEOS ranges.

Viewing the Graph

Mike decides he wants to see what his graph looks like so far. To see the graph on the screen, he *must* have built-in graphics capability or a *graphics adaptor board* in his computer—if he does not, the graph will not be displayed. Since Mike does have a graphics adaptor board, he selects the View command from the Graph menu. The graph appears on the screen (Figure 10-16a). If Mike has a color monitor and a color graphics card, he can view his graph in color if he wishes. To do this, he selects Options from the Graph menu and then Color from the Options menu. Then he selects Quit to leave the Options menu and selects View to see the graph in color (Figure 10-16b).

Mike can see that he is not done yet—the months are not identified, and he cannot tell which bar represents which item. So he returns to the Graph menu by pressing Enter.

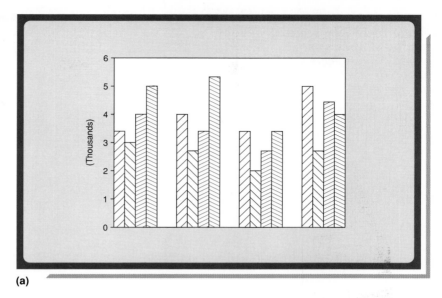

(a)

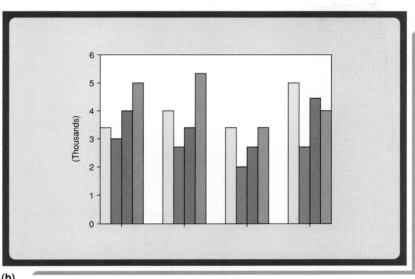

(b)

Figure 10-16 The first version of Mike's bar graph. *Mike uses the View command to see his graph. (a) Notice how Lotus 1-2-3 automatically shades the different bars. (b) Mike can also view his graph in color.*

Entering the X Range

To have the months identified along the x-axis, Mike must select the X option from the Graph menu. This option defines the **X Range**—the data to be displayed as labels on the x-axis. Mike selects the X option, and, as before, Lotus 1-2-3 prompts

Figure 10-17 The second version of Mike's bar graph. Mike selects the X option to label the X Range, the variables along the x-axis.

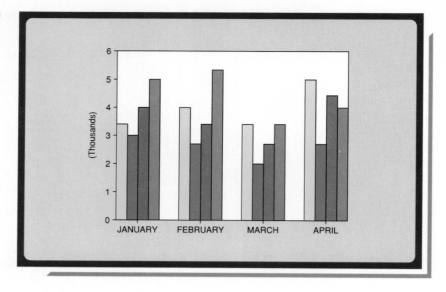

him for the range. In Mike's worksheet the months are in Cells A4 through A7. So Mike types A4.A7 and presses Enter. The result of this command is shown in Figure 10-17.

Adding Titles and Legends

Now Mike wants to add a legend to his graph, since he knows that it will make the graph easier to understand. To provide a legend, Mike first selects the Options command and

Figure 10-18 Adding a legend. (a) Mike selects the Legend option from the Options menu.

```
A1:                                                                    MENU
Legend Format Titles Grid Scale Color B&W Data-Labels Quit
Specify data-range legends
        A            B           C           D           E          F
 1
 2    MONTH        DISCS       ALBUMS      TAPES       VIDEOS
 3    ======================================================
 4   JANUARY     $3,500.00   $3,000.00   $4,000.00   $5,000.00
 5   FEBRUARY    $4,000.00   $2,500.00   $3,500.00   $5,500.00
 6   MARCH       $4,500.00   $2,000.00   $3,500.00   $4,500.00
 7   APRIL       $5,000.00   $2,500.00   $4,500.00   $4,000.00
 8
 9
10
11
12
13
14
15
16
17
18
19
20
08-Jun-91  01:22 PM
```

(a)

continued ▶

Figure 10-18 Adding a legend (continued). *(b) Then he selects the A option to set the legend for the A Range. He types in the legend and presses Enter.*

```
A1:                                                              MENU
A  B  C  D  E  F
Set legend for A range
       A            B           C           D          E        F
 1
 2     MONTH        DISCS       ALBUMS      TAPES      VIDEOS
 3     ==========================================================
 4     JANUARY      $3,500.00   $3,000.00   $4,000.00  $5,000.00
 5     FEBRUARY     $4,000.00   $2,500.00   $3,500.00  $5,500.00
 6     MARCH        $4,500.00   $2,000.00   $3,500.00  $4,500.00
 7     APRIL        $5,000.00   $2,500.00   $4,500.00  $4,000.00
 8
 9
10
11
12
13
14
15
16
17
18
19
20
08-Jun-91  01:23 PM
```

(b)

then the Legend command from the Options menu (Figure 10-18a). The Legend submenu appears on the screen (Figure 10-18b). Mike selects the A option to provide the legend for the A Range of the graph. Lotus 1-2-3 responds with the prompt "Enter legend for A Range." Since the A Range on the graph is the DISCS information, Mike types DISCS and presses Enter. He repeats this process to identify each data range: B, C, and D. To check his work, Mike selects Quit and then View. His graph now appears as shown in Figure 10-19.

Figure 10-19 The third version of Mike's bar graph. *With the added legend, Mike can clearly see which bar represents which variable.*

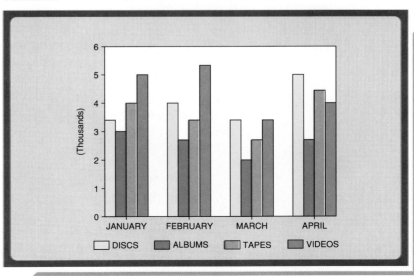

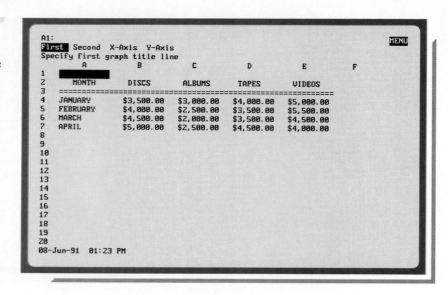

Figure 10-20 Adding titles. When Mike selects Options and then Titles, he is given the choice of creating four types of titles.

Finally, Mike wants titles for his graph. To produce these, he selects the Options command and then the Titles command. Notice that in Figure 10-20 there are four options in the Titles submenu. Lotus can produce two lines of titles for the graph itself and also titles for the x-axis and the y-axis. To enter the first of the two title lines that will go at the top of his graph, Mike selects First from the Titles submenu. When Lotus prompts with "Specify first graph title line," Mike types EICHNER'S MUSIC CENTER and presses Enter. To enter the second line in the title, Mike selects Titles again and then selects Second from the Titles submenu. When Lotus prompts "Enter second graph title line," Mike types MONTHLY SALES and presses Enter.

Mike does not need to title the x-axis, since the units—months—are clearly labeled. However, he does want to title the y-axis information. To do this, he selects Titles and then y-axis. Then he types DOLLARS OF SALES and presses Enter. To view his completed graph, Mike selects Quit to leave the Options menu and return to the main graph menu, then he selects View. The graph is shown in Figure 10-21.

Saving the Graph

Saving a graphics file is not quite as simple as saving a worksheet file or a database file. Mike probably will want to save the graph as two files: a picture file, which lets him save

Figure 10-21 The final version of Mike's bar graph. *Mike uses the View command to see the final version of his graph. Notice how easy it is to understand the information being presented.*

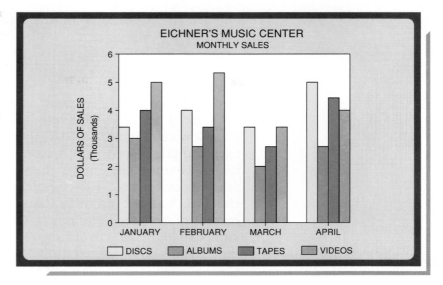

a "picture" of the graph to print later, and a worksheet file, which lets him view and modify the graph.

Saving the Graph as a Picture File. To print his graph, Mike must first save the graph as a picture file on his disk. **Picture files** keep "pictures" of graphs so they can be printed later. A picture file has the extension PIC instead of the extension WKE or WK1 given to regular worksheet files.

Mike can save his graphs in color; however, his printer can print only black and white. Although a graph marked for color can be printed on a black-and-white printer, the result is usually unsatisfactory. That is, on a printer that does not print color, graphs saved as black-and-white graphs are printed more clearly than graphs saved as color graphs. For this reason, Mike decides to save his graph in black and white. To return to a black-and-white setting, he selects Options, B&W, and then Quit.

To save his graph in a picture file, Mike selects the Save option from the Graph menu. Lotus 1-2-3 responds with the message "Enter graph file name." Mike wants to name the file SALES. He types in B:SALES and presses Enter; Lotus saves the file SALES.PIC on his data disk in drive B. Like all PIC files, this file is used to print the graph, and it cannot be retrieved into a Lotus spreadsheet. The Graph-Save command is used only for graphs to be printed.

Saving the Graph as a Worksheet File. Saving the graph for future viewing is as simple as saving a worksheet. Mike returns to the main Command menu by pressing the Esc key. He selects the File option and then the Save command. Later, when Mike wants to retrieve his worksheet again by using the File and Retrieve commands, the data and the graph settings that produce the graph will be loaded with the worksheet. To see the graph, Mike just has to press the Backslash key to enter the MENU mode and select Graph, then View.

Here is an important point to remember. When you use the View command, you see the graph that results from the data and graph settings—ranges, types, titles, legends, and so forth—that are current for that worksheet. If you change the data or the settings, the graph that you view will show these changes. Your picture files, however, are like snapshots. The picture of the graph stored in a PIC file stays the same even if you change the data or settings in the spreadsheet from which that graph was produced. In fact, you could delete the spreadsheet on which the graph in the PIC file was based and you would still be able to print the graph stored in the PIC file. Therefore, if you make changes to your graph, be sure to save it as a new PIC file.

Creating Other Kinds of Graphics

Mike wants to see how his sales information would look as a line graph and a pie chart. He produces these graphs by using the same spreadsheet data he used to produce the bar graph. That is, he does not need to re-enter the sales data for the four Music Center departments into the worksheet.

Creating a Line Graph

To change his graph into a line graph, Mike retrieves his SALES worksheet. Recall that this worksheet was saved with the graph settings for the bar graph. Now Mike simply has to change the *type* of graph he wants to see. To do this, he selects Graph and then Type. Then he selects Line because he wants a line graph. Now he can select View to see the new graph (Figure 10-22). Notice that the line graph contains the same information as Mike's bar graph; the only difference is that the data is plotted with symbols and lines connecting the symbols for each data range. To change back to a bar graph, Mike selects Type and Bar from the Lotus 1-2-3 menu.

Mike wants to keep the graph as both a bar graph and a line graph. However, if there is more than one set of graph settings in a worksheet, then each set must have a unique

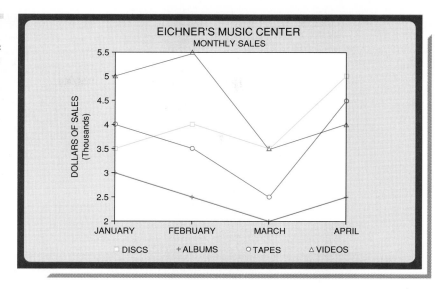

Figure 10-22 Mike's line graph. *Mike can change the type of graph and then keep the rest of the settings that he used for his bar graph to produce a line graph. The different variables are represented by different symbols.*

name. First, Mike must provide a name for the particular graph settings that produce the existing bar graph; that is, he makes the bar graph a **named graph.** The settings of a named graph remain unchanged when Mike enters new settings to create another graph. Second, Mike needs to enter the settings for the new graph and save that graph as a named graph.

To name and save the bar graph settings, Mike selects Name from the Graph menu and then Create from the Name menu (Figure 10-23). When prompted to enter a graph name, Mike types BAR (so that he will remember the type of graph these particular settings produce) and then presses Enter. Now he

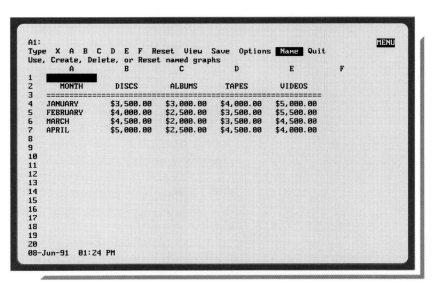

Figure 10-23 Saving a graph as a named graph. *To create a named graph, Mike (a) selects the Name option from the Graph menu.*

(a)

continued ▶

Figure 10-23 Saving a graph as a named graph (continued). (b) Mike then selects the Create option from the Name menu. Then he enters the name he wants to use.

```
A1:                                                                 MENU
Use  Create  Delete  Reset
Save the current graph as a named graph
         A           B           C           D           E          F
 1
 2    MONTH       DISCS       ALBUMS      TAPES       VIDEOS
 3  =======================================================================
 4  JANUARY     $3,500.00   $3,000.00   $4,000.00   $5,000.00
 5  FEBRUARY    $4,000.00   $2,500.00   $3,500.00   $5,500.00
 6  MARCH       $4,500.00   $2,000.00   $3,500.00   $4,500.00
 7  APRIL       $5,000.00   $2,500.00   $4,500.00   $4,000.00
 8
 9
10
11
12
13
14
15
16
17
18
19
20
08-Jun-91  01:25 PM
```

(b)

can produce a new graph without affecting the settings that produce the bar graph. As before, he selects Type and then Line. Then he uses the Name command to name this new graph LINE. Mike also saves both graphs as picture files, since he may want to print the graphs at some later date.

Since the graphs now have names associated with them, the graph name must be entered when it is viewed. To view the bar graph, Mike selects Name and Use from the menu and then enters BAR. Lotus then displays the bar graph. To see the line graph, he again selects Name and Use but enters LINE. Lotus displays the line graph.

Creating a Pie Chart

Recall that only one variable can be used for a pie chart; the existing bar graph cannot be converted directly to a pie chart since it has four variables—one for each department. Mike decides to make a pie chart for just the compact-disc department. But to do this, he must first clear out (reset) the current graph settings so that he can set up the pie chart settings.

To clear out the current graph settings, Mike selects Reset and Graph from the menu. If Mike were to select View now, nothing would appear on the screen because he just erased all the graph settings.

Next Mike constructs the pie chart. He selects Type and Pie from the menu. As before, Mike needs to tell Lotus 1-2-3 which data range he wants to graph. Mike selects A to create the A range; then he enters B4.B7, since the values for the compact discs are in Cells B4 through B7. Mike now wants to add the month names to his graph. Unlike bar and line graphs, pie charts do not use an x-axis. However, Lotus uses the X-Range labels to label each slice of the pie chart. So Mike selects the X option and enters A4.A7 for the X Range. The result is shown in Figure 10-24a.

To create a title for the pie chart, Mike can use the Options and Title commands as before. He enters COMPACT DISCS for the first title line and MONTHLY SALES for the second title line. When he selects View, he sees the graph shown in Figure 10-24b. To store the settings that produced this pie chart

Figure 10-24 Mike's pie chart. *Mike can use Lotus 1-2-3 to produce pie charts. (a) The first version of the chart. (b) The final version. In both cases Lotus automatically calculates the percentages next to the pie slices.*

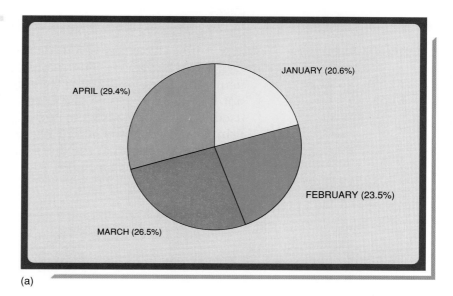

(a)

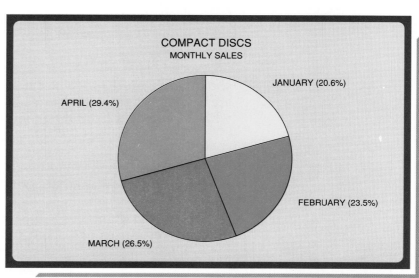

(b)

in the spreadsheet, he selects the Name and Create options. When prompted for a graph name, he enters CDPIE. He selects this name because he will recognize it as the compact-disc pie chart when Lotus lists this name as one of the named graphs. Mike also saves the graph as a picture file.

It is important to note that, like other graph settings, named graph settings are stored as part of the worksheet. Mike makes sure that he saves the worksheet by using the File and Save commands, since he does not want to go through the steps of building the graphs again.

Printing Graphs

Since Mike has saved his graphs in PIC files, those files can be printed. The graphs stored in PIC files are printed using the Lotus 1-2-3 **PrintGraph** program. This program is not on the same disk—the Lotus 1-2-3 System Disk—that is used to make spreadsheets and graphs, so Mike must load the PrintGraph program before he can print his graphs. (For an abbreviated version of the discussion that follows, see the box called "Keystrokes Only: Printing Graphs.")

Loading the PrintGraph Program

If Mike has the full-function version of Lotus 1-2-3, he selects the PrintGraph from the opening menu; he will then be instructed to change disks. If he has the student version, he must exit Lotus 1-2-3. When he sees the A> prompt, he inserts the PrintGraph disk in drive A, types PGRAPH and presses Enter.

Once loaded, the PrintGraph program displays the menu shown in Figure 10-25. The details of the PrintGraph program are beyond the scope of this chapter. However, we will discuss what Mike needs from the menu to print his graphs.

Checking the Hardware Setting

To use the PrintGraph program, Mike needs to tell the program certain things about his computer system. Notice

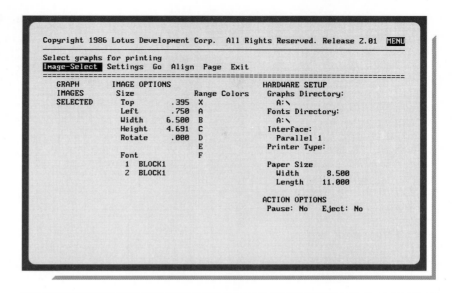

```
Copyright 1986 Lotus Development Corp.  All Rights Reserved. Release 2.01  MENU

Select graphs for printing
Image-Select  Settings  Go  Align  Page  Exit
==========================================================================
    GRAPH      IMAGE OPTIONS                    HARDWARE SETUP
    IMAGES     Size             Range Colors    Graphs Directory:
    SELECTED   Top       .395   X                  A:\
               Left      .750   A               Fonts Directory:
               Width    6.500   B                  A:\
               Height   4.691   C               Interface:
               Rotate    .000   D                  Parallel 1
                                E               Printer Type:
               Font             F
                 1  BLOCK1                       Paper Size
                 2  BLOCK1                          Width      8.500
                                                    Length    11.000

                                                ACTION OPTIONS
                                                  Pause: No    Eject: No
```

Figure 10-25 The PrintGraph menu. *To print graphs, Mike must use the PrintGraph program. When loaded, the program displays the menu shown here.*

"HARDWARE SETUP" at the right of the screen in Figure 10-25; this area contains information about the current default drive, the type of printer being used, and other system characteristics. The Graphs Directory line under HARDWARE SETUP should show the disk drive that contains the PIC files to be printed, and the Printer Type line should display the type of printer currently being used. (Note: The actions described in this section are necessary only if the disk drive and/or printer are not shown correctly on the main PrintGraph menu.)

If the Graphs Directory is not set to the correct drive, Mike needs to select Settings from the PrintGraph menu, Hardware from the first submenu, and then Graphs Directory from the second submenu (Figure 10-26, on the next page). Then he types

B:\

to specify the B drive and presses Enter. Lotus then returns him to the Hardware Setup menu.

If the Printer Type is not displayed or does not correspond to the printer he intends to use, Mike must select Printer from the menu and follow the directions that appear on the screen. He can return to the main PrintGraph menu by selecting Quit twice.

Figure 10-26 Changing the Graphs Directory setting. *Mike needs to tell the program the disk drive where his PIC files are stored. To do this, he (a) selects the Settings option from the main menu. (b) Then he selects the Hardware option from the submenu and (c) the Graphs Directory option from the Hardware submenu. Finally, when prompted, he types in the appropriate disk drive.*

```
Copyright 1986 Lotus Development Corp.  All Rights Reserved. Release 2.01  MENU

Define Hardware and Graph Settinggs
Image-Select Settings Go  Align  Page  Exit
===============================================================================
   GRAPH       IMAGE OPTIONS                      HARDWARE SETUP
   IMAGES      Size                Range Colors   Graphs Directory:
   SELECTED    Top        .395     X                A:\
               Left       .750     A              Fonts Directory:
               Width     6.500     B                A:\
               Height    4.691     C              Interface:
               Rotate     .000     D                Parallel 1
                                   E              Printer Type:
               Font                F
               1  BLOCK1                          Paper Size
               2  BLOCK1                             Width      8.500
                                                     Length    11.000

                                                  ACTION OPTIONS
                                                  Pause: No   Eject: No
```
(a)

```
Copyright 1986 Lotus Development Corp.  All Rights Reserved. Release 2.01  MENU

Specify Hardware Setup
Image Hardware Action  Save  Reset  Quit
===============================================================================
   GRAPH       IMAGE OPTIONS                      HARDWARE SETUP
   IMAGES      Size                Range Colors   Graphs Directory:
   SELECTED    Top        .395     X                A:\
               Left       .750     A              Fonts Directory:
               Width     6.500     B                A:\
               Height    4.691     C              Interface:
               Rotate     .000     D                Parallel 1
                                   E              Printer Type:
               Font                F
               1  BLOCK1                          Paper Size
               2  BLOCK1                             Width      8.500
                                                     Length    11.000

                                                  ACTION OPTIONS
                                                  Pause: No   Eject: No
```
(b)

```
Copyright 1986 Lotus Development Corp. All Rights Reserved. Release 2.01  MENU

Set directory containing graphs
Graphs-Directory Fonts-Directory  Interface  Printer  Size-Paper  Quit
===============================================================================
   GRAPH       IMAGE OPTIONS                      HARDWARE SETUP
   IMAGES      Size                Range Colors   Graphs Directory:
   SELECTED    Top        .395     X                B:\
               Left       .750     A              Fonts Directory:
               Width     6.500     B                A:\
               Height    4.691     C              Interface:
               Rotate     .000     D                Parallel 1
                                   E              Printer Type:
               Font                F                Proprinter
               1  BLOCK1                          Paper Size
               2  BLOCK1                             Width      8.500
                                                     Length    11.000

                                                  ACTION OPTIONS
                                                  Pause: No   Eject: No
```
(c)

Figure 10-27 The Image-Select menu. *When Mike chooses the Image-Select option from the main menu, he sees the menu shown here. He follows the directions on the screen to select the images he wants to print. Then he returns to the main menu to print his graphs.*

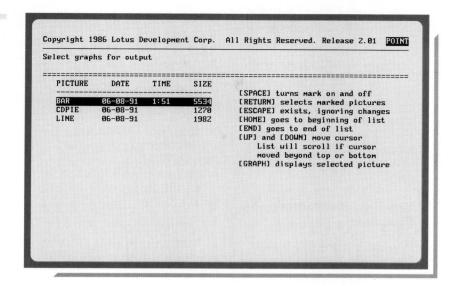

Selecting the Files to Be Printed

Next PrintGraph needs to know the names of the PIC files to be printed. Mike supplies the names by selecting Image-Select from the PrintGraph menu. This command displays the menu shown in Figure 10-27. The names of all the PIC files on the data disk are displayed on the left. The directions for selecting the files to print are on the right side of the screen.

If Mike wants to check the contents of a PIC file, he places the cursor on the name of the file and presses the F10 key. The PrintGraph utility displays the graph on the screen. Mike can press any key to return to the Image-Select menu. Mike decides to print his BAR and his CDPIE graphs, so he follows the directions to mark those files. Once Mike has marked all the PIC files that he wants to print, he presses Enter to return to the PrintGraph menu.

Printing the Graphs

Before Mike prints his graphs, he turns on the printer and checks to see that the print head is at the top of a new page. Then he selects Go from the menu to print the graph. (Note: Lotus 1-2-3 prints graphs very slowly; be prepared to spend some time waiting.) When the graphs are printed, Mike leaves the PrintGraph utility by selecting Exit.

Now that we have explored how to create graphs, let us take a closer look at the type of hardware used with graphics programs.

Printing Graphs

These instructions are for printing Mike Berkeley's graphs, as described in the text. The Lotus 1-2-3 keystrokes that follow can also be used to print your own graphs.

Loading the PrintGraph Program

If you are using the full-function version of Lotus:

1. Select PrintGraph from the main Command menu.

2. Follow the instructions displayed on the screen. The PrintGraph program has been loaded when you see the PrintGraph menu on the screen.

If you are using the student version of Lotus:

1. Exit Lotus 1-2-3.

2. When you see A>, place the PrintGraph disk in drive A and your data disk with the stored PIC files in drive B.

3. Type PGRAPH and press Enter. The PrintGraph program has been loaded when you see the PrintGraph menu on the screen.

Checking the Hardware Settings

Note: These instructions are necessary only if your disk drive directory and/or printer are not shown correctly on the main PrintGraph menu.

To change the disk drive:

1. Select the Settings option from the PrintGraph menu.

2. Select the Hardware option.

3. Select the Graphs Directory option.

4. Type in the appropriate drive followed by a colon and a backslash. Press Enter. To return to the main PrintGraph menu, select Quit twice.

To change the printer information:

1. Select the Settings option from the main PrintGraph menu.

2. Select the Hardware option.

3. Select the Printer option.

4. Follow the directions that appear on the screen to input the correct information.

5. To return to the main PrintGraph menu, select Quit twice.

Selecting the Files to be Printed

1. Select the Image-Select option from the main PrintGraph menu. The Image-Select menu appears on the screen.

2. To view the images before selection, place the cursor on the name of the graph you wish to view and press F10. Press any key to return to the Image-Select menu.

3. Follow the instructions on the screen to select the images you wish to print. Then return to the main PrintGraph menu.

Printing the Graphs

1. Turn on the printer and make sure the print head is at the top of the page.

2. Select the Go option from the main menu to print the selected graphs.

Exiting the PrintGraph Program

Select the Exit command from the main PrintGraph menu. You are returned to DOS.

Graphics Hardware

There are several pieces of hardware, such as a monitor and a keyboard, that you must have to create and print graphics on a personal computer. Other graphics hardware is not necessary but can be useful if you are focusing on graphics. Most of the components that follow were discussed in Chapter 2, so we will only touch on them here.

Input Devices

Normally, all you need to input data for graphics is a keyboard. Some programs let you use other input devices—mice, joy sticks, light pens, and so on—that give you more control over the shapes and lines in free-form graphics, such as illustrations.

Although they are not required for either analytical or presentation graphics, digitizers and scanners are often used with computers employed primarily for graphics. As we described in Chapter 2, digitizers let you input existing images into the computer. Scanners are usually more versatile than digitizers; you can use a scanner to input both images and text (Figure 10-28). Digitizers and scanners are both useful because they

Figure 10-28 A digitizer. *Digitizers can be used to change both graphic and text images into digitized information the computer can store.*

let you convert a printed graph, chart, or picture to computerized data that can be used by a presentation graphics program. If you see an illustration that you like or a really useful graph, you can store it on your computer and use it in your own presentations.

Monitors

As we mentioned in Chapter 2, most monitors can be used to view graphics. Different types of monitors produce different graphic images. If you are using a black-and-white or a monochrome monitor, you cannot display color graphics. However, if you have a **color monitor,** you can view your graphics in color.

If you are using graphics a great deal in your work, you might consider a graphics monitor. These monitors are capable of producing high-resolution graphics in black and white. Color graphics monitors can display more than 4000 colors. When you purchase a monitor, remember that the higher the resolution, the better the picture quality.

Graphics Boards

Many personal computers can display text—letters and numbers—but they may not have the built-in ability to display graphics. Some computers can display graphics, but only very crude ones. To view graphics created with analytic and presentation graphics software, you must have a computer that can display graphics on the screen. If your computer does not come with this capability, you will need to add a **graphics adapter board** to your computer. A graphics adapter board, also called a *graphics card*, is hardware that gives your computer graphics capability. The board is inserted inside your computer and then connected to your screen display. This is a simple operation that requires only a few minutes.

If you want color graphics, and your screen is a color monitor, you need a color graphics board. (Color graphics, by the way, have been shown to be up to 80% more effective in getting a message across to the viewer.) Otherwise, you will need to use a monochrome graphics board.

Currently, there are two standards for high-resolution graphics. The first is the IBM Enhanced Graphics Adapter (EGA).

JUMPSUITS FOR SKYDIVERS

How can you design jumpsuits so when people jump out of airplanes, "fat guys will fall at the same rate as skinny guys?" Use a personal computer. At least that is what Gary Carter, who owns Flite Suit in Pope Valley, California, does. Carter also uses computer graphics to plan color-coordinated looks for skydivers who jump en masse. As many as 100 people may be involved in a free-fall formation, and Carter can give them all a preview of the visual impact their costumes and descent will make.

This graphics board can display 16 colors at 640 × 200 resolution on a standard color monitor. With optional added memory and the IBM Enhanced Color Display monitor, the EGA can display 16 colors from a palette (selection) of 64 colors, at a resolution of 640 × 350 pixels. The second standard is the IBM Video Graphics Array (VGA), at 640 × 480 resolution for use with IBM analog monitors. The VGA is used in several models of the IBM PS/2 personal computers. It can also display 16 colors on one graph and has a palette of 262,144 colors.

Before you purchase a graphics board, verify that the graphics software you plan to purchase is compatible with the board. Also make sure that the graphics board, through its interface with the monitor, can display the text characters needed by your other software, such as word processing, spreadsheets, and database management systems.

Output Devices

Any dot-matrix printer can produce a graphic image; however, usually the number of pixels on the screen is far greater than the number of dots an ordinary printer can produce. So the better printers, such as high-resolution dot-matrix printers or laser printers, can produce better graphics. Ink-jet printers and plotters can also produce graphic images. Printers that can produce a hard copy of the graphics you produce on your screen are called **graphics printers.** Some graphics printers can print on both paper and overhead transparency sheets.

Most computer systems allow you to create and print color graphics even when colors cannot be displayed on the monitor.

Color dot-matrix printers use a ribbon with horizontal ink bands in black, red, blue, and yellow. The colors in an image are printed when the print head strikes against one of the horizontal bands—or two bands together—to reproduce the colors on the screen.

Many *ink-jet printers* contain nozzles for black, red, blue, and yellow inks. To create the image, the printer sprays particles of ink on paper or on the acetate sheets used for overhead transparencies. Most ink-jet printers provide high resolution.

Using laser technology, *laser printers* produce graphics output of very high quality. Laser printers are available in models that print only black and white and in models that print colors. A good laser printer is fast and capable of reproducing graphics images at the high resolution of 300 dots per inch.

Named after the graphs they plot, *plotters* use colored pens to produce images and to letter text on graphs and charts. Some plotters can produce output on both paper and on acetate overhead transparency sheets. Plotters are not as versatile as graphics printers because they cannot be used to print word processing documents. However, a high-quality plotter can produce beautiful graphs and charts.

Communications among Computers

In these past seven chapters, you have studied the key applications that make personal computers useful: word processing, spreadsheets, database management, and graphics. The picture will be enhanced still further when you discover how computer users pass this information around. The ability to communicate from computer to computer is significant. This is the subject of the next chapter.

Exercises

10-1

1. Load your graphics program and place a formatted disk in drive B.
2. Enter the data shown in Figure 10-29. You will want to change some of the default column width settings.
3. Use the data in columns B and C to create a bar graph. You may make up any titles and legends you need.
4. View the graph. Is this a single-range graph or a multiple-range graph?
5. Save the worksheet with the graph settings as EX10-1.
6. Clear the screen.

Figure 10-29

	A	B	C
1		BASEBALL	FOOTBALL
2			
3	1988	2,250,000	4,000,000
4	1989	2,325,000	3,750,000
5	1990	2,300,500	3,525,000
6	1991	2,175,000	3,850,000

10-2

1. Retrieve EX10-1.
2. View your graph. Has it changed?
3. Change the contents of Cell B4 to 2,400,000.
4. View the resulting graph. Has it changed from the one you saw in Exercise 10-1?
5. To make the graph understandable, use the appropriate commands to do the following:
   - Identify the years along the x-axis.
   - Create a title for the graph. It should read

     YEARLY STADIUM ATTENDANCE
     For Baseball and Football Games

   - Create a title for the y-axis. It should read

     Number of Persons Attending

   - Create legends for the graph that identify the contents of the two data ranges you are graphing.
6. View the graph.
7. Name the graph settings BAR1.
8. Save the worksheet with the revised settings as EX10-2.

10-3

1. Retrieve EX10-2 if necessary. Then change the graph settings you entered in Exercise 10-2 to create a line graph. The line graph should have the same X Range, titles, and legends as BAR1.
2. View the graph.
3. Name the graph settings LINE1.
4. Save the graph itself as a picture file named LINE1.PIC.
5. Use the BAR1 graph settings. View the graph. Has it changed?
6. Save the graph as a picture file named BAR1.PIC.
7. Save the worksheet as EX10-3.
8. If necessary, load the PrintGraph program. Print BAR1.PIC and LINE1.PIC. (Remember, printing graphs may tie up your printer for a while.)

10-4

1. Retrieve the EX10-3 worksheet.
2. Reset the graph settings. Can you still retrieve and view the bar and line graphs you created?
3. Use the appropriate commands to create a pie chart that shows the attendance for baseball games. Then view the graph. Are the "slices" of the pie labeled?

4. Use the appropriate commands to label each slice of the pie. View the graph again to check your work.

5. Create the following title for the pie chart:

```
YEARLY STADIUM ATTENDANCE
For Baseball Games (1988-1991)
```

6. Name the graph settings PIE1 and save the graph as a picture file named PIE1.PIC.

7. Create a similar pie graph for the football game data. The title for this graph should read:

```
YEARLY STADIUM ATTENDANCE
For Football Games (1988-1991)
```

8. Name the graph settings PIE2 and save the graph as a picture file named PIE2.PIC.

9. Save the worksheet as EX10-4.

10. Issue the appropriate commands to view BAR1, LINE1, PIE1, and PIE2.

11. Print PIE1.PIC and PIE2.PIC.

10-5

1. Create the worksheet shown in Figure 10-30a.

2. Use this worksheet to create the graph shown in Figure 10-30b. Include all the labels, titles, and legends shown.

3. Name the graph settings BAR2 and save BAR2 as a picture file named BAR2.PIC.

4. Save the worksheet with the current settings as EX10-5.

5. Change the following information in the worksheet:

   ■ Change the $24,000.00 in Cell B3 to $27,000.00
   ■ Change the $4,100.00 in Cell C5 to $4,600.00
   ■ Change the $4,150.00 in Cell E5 to $4,800.00

6. View the graph now produced from the BAR2 settings. Does it reflect the changes to the worksheet?

7. Print BAR2.PIC. Does the printed graph reflect the changes to the worksheet? Why or why not?

10-6

1. Use the EX10-5 worksheet to create the graph shown in Figure 10-31a. Remember to include all the labels, titles, and legends shown in the figure.

2. Name the graph settings LINE2.

3. Use the worksheet to create the chart shown in Figure 10-31b (on page 380). Include all the labels, titles, and legends shown in the figure.

4. Name the graph settings PIE3.

5. Use the worksheet to create the graph shown in Figure 10-31c (on page 380). Include all the labels, titles, and legends shown in the figure.

6. Name the graph settings BAR3.

Figure 10-30

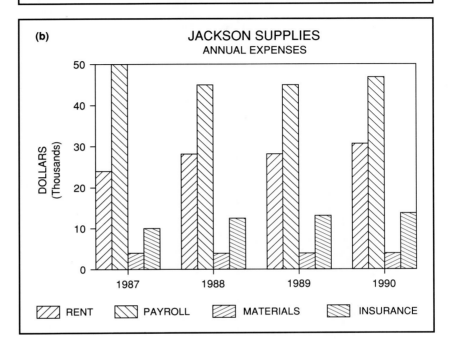

(a)	1987	1988	1989	1990
RENT	$24,000.00	$28,880.00	$28,880.00	$31,020.00
PAYROLL	$50,000.00	$45,000.00	$45,000.00	$47,000.00
MATERIALS	$4,500.00	$4,100.00	$4,700.00	$4,150.00
INSURANCE	$10,000.00	$12,000.00	$13,500.00	$15,000.00

Figure 10-31

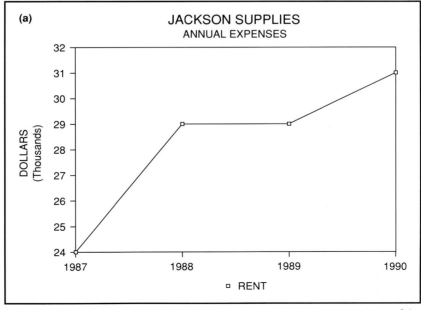

continued ▶

Figure 10-31 (continued)

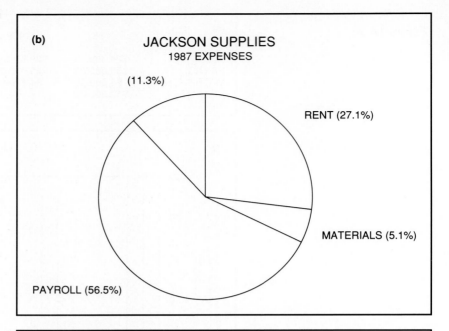

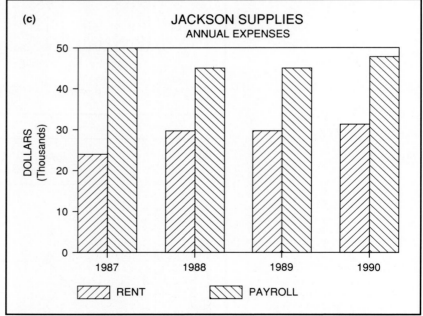

Assume you are in charge of sales for Able Security. You have compiled the sales information shown in Figure 10-32. Your manager is interested in presenting this material in graphs at a coming meeting.

Figure 10-32

	HALLS, A.	BENKE, J.	GLIDE, C.	ALBEE, W.	TOTAL
JAN SALES	46	65	52	48	211
FEB SALES	55	78	48	50	231
MAR SALES	52	80	55	65	252
QUARTER TOTAL =	153	223	155	163	

1. Use your graphics program to produce the following graphs:
    -   A bar graph showing total sales for each month (save this graph as a picture file named BAR4.PIC).
    -   A stacked-bar graph showing each salesperson's sales by month (save this graph as a picture file named SBAR1.PIC).
    -   A pie chart showing total quarter sales for each salesperson (save this graph as a picture file named PIE4.PIC).

    The graphs should include labels, titles, and legends when appropriate.
2. Save the worksheet as EX10-6.
3. What graphs can you view on your screen at this point? Why?
4. Print the three graphs.
5. Exit the program.

Summary and Key Terms

-   **Business graphics** represent business data in a visual, easily understood format. They help clients and managers analyze data, and they help make business reports more interesting.

-   Two types of software have been developed for business graphics. **Analytical graphics** programs help users analyze and understand specific data. **Presentation graphics** programs, or **business-quality graphics** programs, produce more sophisticated graphics that are appropriate for formal presentations. Presentation graphics programs also contain a library of symbols and drawings called **clip art.**

-   There are three main types of graphs: line graphs, bar graphs, and pie charts.

-   A **line graph** has vertical reference lines. Each line is called an **axis.** The horizontal line is called the **x-axis,** and the vertical line is called the **y-axis.** The area inside the x-axis and y-axis is the **plot area.** Each dot or symbol on a line graph is a **data point.** Each data point represents a **value.** The items that the data points describe are called **variables.**

-   Graphs that plot the values of only one variable are called **single-range graphs.** A **multiple-range graph** plots more than one variable.

-   With **bar graphs,** comparisons are shown by the lengths or heights of bars in columns or rows. In a **single-range bar graph,** only one variable is involved. A **clustered-bar graph** shows more than one variable. A **stacked-bar graph** also shows multiple variables, but the bars are stacked on top of one another. You can create a **legend** to explain the colors or symbols on a complex graph. **Labels** identify the categories along the x-axis and the units along the y-axis. **Titles** summarize the information in the graph.

-   A **pie chart** represents a single variable and shows how different values make up a whole. Each wedge of the pie represents a value. On an **exploded pie chart,** a wedge is pulled slightly away from the pie for emphasis.

■ After accessing the graphics program and selecting the type of graph, you must specify the data ranges you wish to graph. The first range, or set of values, to graph is referred to as the **A Range,** the second is the **B Range.** The **X Range** is the data to be displayed as labels on the x-axis.

■ **Picture files** keep "pictures" of graphs so they can be printed later. Saving the graph as a worksheet file allows you to view and modify the graph. If you wish to save more than one type of graph based on the same worksheet data, you must make each graph a **named graph.**

■ **PrintGraph** is the Lotus 1-2-3 program that prints graphs.

■ Most monitors can be used to view graphics. A **graphics monitor** is capable of producing high-resolution graphics. To use graphics software, you must have a computer that can display graphics on the screen. A **graphics adapter board** can be added to a computer that does not have this capability. Printers that can produce a hard copy of the graphics you produce on screen are called **graphics printers.**

Review Questions

1. Why are personal computer graphics used in business?

2. Explain the difference between analytical and presentation graphics.

3. Describe the similarities and differences between a single-range bar graph, a clustered-bar graph, and a stacked-bar graph.

4. What is an exploded pie chart?

5. Where does Lotus 1-2-3 get the data it needs to make a graph?

6. How many different sets of data can Lotus 1-2-3 plot on a single graph?

7. What is the X Range used for in a Lotus graph?

8. What is meant by the B Range in a Lotus graph?

9. What types of titles can you include in a Lotus graph?

10. What is a named graph?

11. What is the difference between a picture file and a regular worksheet file?

12. Briefly describe the steps you need to take to print a graph using Lotus 1-2-3.

13. What is the difference between a digitizer and a scanner?

14. What is a graphics adapter board? When is it needed?

15. What are the two standards for high-resolution graphics on the personal computer? How are these standards different?

FROM THE REAL WORLD

Using Graphics to Design Fabrics

We have described the uses of business graphics at length, but some personal computer users go beyond the basics. Designers at Burlington Industries use personal computer graphics to create fabrics of many patterns and colors. Designers can design and preview a pattern on the screen and then transfer the design to a handloom. But things have not always been that simple.

Since 1924, Burlington Industries mills have cranked out more miles of fabric than any other company. But as recently as ten years ago, Burlington was still using manual, labor-intensive methods to design fabrics. Even the first, most simple phase—sketching and weaving fabric samples to show prospective customers—could take an intolerable five weeks. The process was costly, especially when compared with the cost of the competition in other countries with lower labor costs.

Designers began by hand-drawing patterns on grids, where a ¼-inch square denoted a stitch; coloring the squares took about a week per sample. This was followed by setting up the loom and weaving samples. But even experienced designers sometimes found that their finished samples held unpleasant surprises. If they did not like it, they had to reweave it.

To tackle these problems, Burlington turned to automation, investing in personal computers. Now the designer can preview what the fabric will look like on the computer screen. If necessary, design changes can be made; this process continues until the designer is satisfied and decides to weave the loom sample. Although designers do not expect to eliminate mistakes, they know that by the time a sample is actually woven, there is a high probability that it will be what the customer wants.

Each time a designer devises a pattern, he or she is confronted with nearly 10,000 combinations of threads in various colors. Using the computer, designers can modify original selections by selecting alternative colors or textures; the fabric is then redrawn on the screen. Some designers work closely with the customer, showing them printed versions of a pattern as it develops, softening a shade or perhaps widening a stripe.

And how do the designers feel about all this? They are in step with the computers and, in fact, have suggested improvements. They would like to be able to see two fabric samples side by side on the screen. They would also like all of their computers to show the colors exactly the same way.

Will computers take over the whole process? It seems unlikely, since customers still want to know what the finished fabric feels like. Computers cannot replace touch.

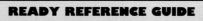
Keystrokes for WordPerfect, Lotus 1-2-3, and dBASE III PLUS

Learning to use a new applications program can be difficult at first. This guide contains alphabetical listings of some of the different commands and the corresponding keystrokes in WordPerfect, Lotus 1-2-3, and dBASE III PLUS. If you forget how to do something—for example, boldface a word—simply look up the command in the appropriate section.

Some WordPerfect Keystrokes

The descriptions that follow summarize some of the most commonly used WordPerfect commands and the related keystrokes. Most of these commands are discussed in Chapters 4 and 5.

The keys you should press are enclosed in brackets ([]). Keystrokes separated by a dash indicate that those keys should be pressed together. For example, for centering, [Shift-F6] means hold the Shift key down while you press the F6 key.

For most of these commands, you need to use the function keys on the left side or top of the keyboard. The plastic template that fits over the function keys is a helpful reminder of what each key does.

Boldface [F6] Press the F6 key and then type the word(s) to be emphasized.

After you have finished, press F6 again to signal the end of boldface. If you want to boldface words that are already typed, mark them first as a block, then press F6.

Cancel [F1] The Cancel command cancels—or undoes—the most recent command you issued. For example, if you inadvertently delete some text, the Cancel command gives you the opportunity to restore the text.

Center [Shift-F6] This command centers a line of type between the left and right margins. It is easiest to press the keys before you type the line to be centered. If the line to be centered is already typed, then first mark it as a block and then use the keystrokes to center it.

Copy Block After a block has been marked, press Ctrl-F4, then select option 2. Move the cursor to the new location. Press Ctrl-F4 again, then select option 5. The duplicate block is inserted.

Cursor Control The cursor movement keys move the cursor a character at a time; you can use combinations of these keys to move the cursor greater distances. To move the cursor a word to the right, use Ctrl-right arrow. To move the cursor a word to the left, use Ctrl-left arrow. To return to the beginning of a document, press (in order, not together) Home, Home, up arrow. Press Home, Home, down arrow to move the cursor to the end of the document.

Date [Shift-F5] Begin by pressing Shift-F5. If you then choose option 1, the date appears in your document at the current cursor location. Option 2 lets you experiment with the format of the date; the default format is month-day-comma-year: July 10, 1992. (Caution: This command only retrieves the date. The date must be set correctly first, probably by the DATE command in the operating system.)

Delete A few of the common ways to delete characters follow. Press the Del key to delete the current character. Press the Backspace key to delete the previous character. Use Ctrl-Backspace to delete the word the cursor is under. Use Ctrl-End to delete from the cursor to the end of the line.

Delete Block After a block has been marked, press Ctrl-F4, then select option 1. This deletes the marked block.

Delete File [F5 Enter] Press F5 and then press Enter. Move the cursor to highlight the file you want to delete, then select option 2.

Double Space [Shift-F8 4] Begin by pressing Shift-F8, and then select option 4. When you see "Spacing set," select option 2 and press Enter. Text will be double spaced from that point forward in the document. Use the same command, but

select option 1 to revert to single spacing later in the document. You can also use Reveal Codes to remove the double spacing altogether.

Exit WordPerfect [F7] Press F7. When WordPerfect asks if you want to save the document, type N if you do not. You will usually type Y. After you type Y the file name is displayed if the file already exists. Simply press Enter to verify the name. If it is a new file, you must supply a file name. Note: If you are saving a file that already exists, you are asked if you want to replace the existing version of that file; usually, you do want to replace the existing file with a new version, so type Y. Next WordPerfect asks if you want to exit the program. Type Y to return to DOS, or type N to open a new Word-Perfect file, or press F1 to return to the same document you just saved.

Help [F3] If you need help with something, press F3, then press any key to see a list of functions. Choose the function you wish to learn more about.

Indent [Shift-F4] Pressing Shift-F4 indents every line of a paragraph. However, to indent just the first line of a paragraph, press the Tab key (just to the right of the F4 key on most keyboards).

Justification In WordPerfect, right justification is the default. However, the text does not appear justified until it is printed. To switch to ragged right, press Ctrl-F8, and then select option 3. To return to right justification, press Ctrl-F8, then select option 4.

List Files [F5 Enter] Press F5 and then press Enter to list the files on your data disk while you are using the word processing program.

Margin Settings [Shift-F8 3] Press Shift-F8 and then select option 3. When you see "Left margin =," key in the new left margin number and press Enter. Then key in the new right margin number followed by Enter.

Mark Block [Alt-F4] Place the cursor at the beginning of the block you want to mark. Press Alt-F4, then move the cursor to the end of the block.

Move Block After a block is marked, press Ctrl-F4, then select option 1. The block disappears. Now move the cursor where you want to insert the block. Press Ctrl-F4, then select option 5. The block is inserted.

Page Numbers [Alt-F8 1] Press Alt-F8 and then select option 1. Then choose the appropriate page-number position.

Print [Shift-F7] Press Shift-F7 and several options appear. You will usually want to select option 1 to print the full document.

Retrieve [Shift-F10] After you press Shift-F10 WordPerfect asks for the name of the file to retrieve. This is the name you gave the file when you originally saved it.

Reveal Codes [Alt-F3] Each time you use a special feature, such as boldface or line spacing, WordPerfect places a hidden code within the text. The Reveal Codes command lets you view and/or delete the hidden codes (with the Backspace key). To hide the codes again, press any key that does not affect the cursor—the Spacebar is handy.

Save [F10] Press F10 and WordPerfect asks for the name of the file you want to save. If a file by that name already exists, you are asked if you want to replace the existing file with your new file. If you have just revised the existing document, you probably want to type Y. If you type N, the old file will not be replaced, and you will have to create a different file name for your new document.

Save Block Mark the text block you wish to save. Then press F10. When asked, type the block name, then press Enter.

Search [F2] This key produces the message "Srch:." Type in a word, phrase, or character, then press F2 once more. The search progresses from the cursor to the end of the document. To search backwards from the cursor to the beginning of the document, press Shift-F2.

Search and Replace [Alt-F2] After you press Alt-F2, the message "w/Confirm?(Y/N) N" appears. Type Y to verify each replacement individually. When you see

"Srch:," type in the word or characters you wish to replace, then press F2. The message "Replace with:," appears. Type in the substitution and then press F2 again. WordPerfect asks you to confirm the replacement each time it finds the word you wish to replace.

Spelling Checker [Ctrl-F2] After pressing Ctrl-F2, select option 3 if you want to check the entire document.

Superscripts/Subscripts [Shift-F1] To mark a superscript or subscript, press Shift-F1 just before the character you want to mark. Then select from the options offered on the screen. The superscript or subscript appears above or below the line only when printed.

Thesaurus [Alt-F1] To use the thesaurus, place the cursor under the word you want to look up. Then press Alt-F1.

Typeover [Ins] To change from the INSERT mode to the TYPEOVER mode, press the Ins key. To return to the INSERT mode, press the Ins key again.

Underline [F8] Press the F8 key, then type the words to be underlined. After you have finished typing, press the F8 key again to stop the underlining. If you want to underline words that are already typed, mark them as a block, then press F8.

Vertical Centering [Alt-F8 3] Press Alt-F8, then select option 3 to center text vertically on a page.

Some Lotus 1-2-3 Keystrokes

The descriptions that follow summarize some of the most commonly used Lotus 1-2-3 commands and the related keystrokes. Most of these commands are discussed in chapters 6, 7, and 10.

The keys you should press are enclosed in brackets ([]). When a command requires that you supply the beginning and ending cells in a group of contiguous cells (a range), the notation <range> is included with the keystrokes.

Change Cell Entry To change an already entered cell entry, move the cursor to that cell. Then type in the correct contents and press Enter.

Change Column Width of One Column [/WCS] Place the cursor in the column whose width you wish to change. Type /WCS and then type the new width (1 to 240 characters) and press Enter.

Change Directories [/FD] This command replaces the current directory (see Appendix A of this text) with a new one. Type /FD and type in the correct directory. Press Enter.

Change Width of All Columns [/WGC] Type /WGC and type the new width (1 to 240 characters) and press Enter. Note: The /Worksheet Column Set command (/WCS) overrides the setting you define with the /Worksheet Global Column (/WGC) command.

Choose Graph Type [/GT] When you enter this command, a menu of options appears. Select the type of graph you wish to create from this menu.

Choose Graph Data Range [/G] Six different sets of values can be graphed on the same graph. Each set of values is identified by a letter A through F. To choose the A range, for example, type /GA and then enter the first range you wish to graph. To choose the B range, type /GB and enter the second range you wish to graph, and so on through the F range.

Choose Graph X Range [/GX <range>] Use this command to indicate the cells in the worksheet that contain the information used to label the x axis of the graph.

Copy Cell Contents [/C <FROM range> <TO range>] To create a copy of existing cell entries, type /C. When prompted for the *copy from* range, enter the range of cells you want to copy. Then press Enter. When prompted for the *copy to* range, enter the range of cells in which you want the copies to appear. Then press Enter. When you copy labels and numbers, Lotus 1-2-3 makes exact duplicates of the original entries in another location. When you copy formulas, Lotus adjusts cell addresses in the formula unless the cell addresses are absolute or mixed.

Delete Column [/WDC] Place the cursor in the column you wish to delete, type /WDC and press Enter.

Delete Row [/WDR] Place the cursor in the row you wish to delete, type /WDR and press Enter.

Edit Cell Entries [F2] Place the cursor on the cell whose contents you wish to edit and press the F2 key. You are placed in the EDIT mode and can use the cursor movement keys to move to the position in the current cell contents where you want to insert or delete characters. Use the Del or Backspace key to delete characters. Press Enter when you are through editing.

Erase Cell Entry [/RE] Place the cursor on the cell whose contents you want to erase. Type /RE and press Enter.

Erase Range of Cells [/RE <range>] Type /RE and the range of cells you want to erase (for example, A10.F10) and press Enter. You can point to the range of cells by moving the cursor to the first cell in the range, typing in a period, and moving the cursor to the last cell in the range. Then press Enter.

Erase Worksheet [/WEY] If you type this command, the worksheet in memory is erased and you see an empty worksheet on your screen. This command does not erase worksheets stored on disk. If you want to keep a worksheet, remember to save it on disk before you erase it.

Erase Worksheet File [/FE] Type /FE and tell Lotus the type of file you want to erase by selecting Worksheet. Select the name of the file from the menu of file names by using the cursor movement keys and pressing Enter. Then select Yes from the menu. Notice that you can use the /FE command to erase any Lotus file on your disk.

Format Labels Globally [/WGL] This command sets the format of labels for the entire worksheet. All labels entered into the worksheet without a label-prefix character are aligned according to the alignment set with this command. This command does not affect labels already entered in the worksheet. The possible formats are left, right, and centered.

Format Labels in Ranges [/RL] This command formats *existing* labels in a range of cells. The possible formats are left, right, and centered in the cell. Range formats override global default formats. This command has no effect on values.

Format Values Globally [/WGF] This command sets the way numeric values appear for all cells in the worksheet that have not been formatted by the /RF command. If a value's formatted display does not fit within its cell width, asterisks are displayed in the cell.

Format Values in Ranges [/RF] This command sets the numeric format used to display numbers in a range of cells; it does not affect the actual value of the numbers stored in the cells. You can change the format of a range of cells either before or after entering numbers in the range. Range formats override global default formats. If a value's formatted display does not fit within the width of its cell, asterisks are displayed in the cell.

Exit Current Menu [Esc] If you find yourself lost in the Lotus 1-2-3 menu system, you can return to familiar territory by pressing the Esc key. Each time you press the Esc key, you move up a level in the menu system. If you continue to press Esc, you eventually leave the MENU mode and return to the READY mode.

Function Keys

Key	Description
F1	Displays the Help screen.
F2	Switches to the EDIT mode.
F3	Displays range names.
F4	Makes or unmakes a cell address absolute.
F5	GO TO key: Moves cursor to a specified cell address.
F6	Moves cursor between windows.
F7	Repeats most recent Data Query.
F8	Repeats most recent Data Table operation.
F9	Recalculates formulas when using Manual recalculation.
F10	Draws graph using current graph settings.

Help [F1] Display information on a topic by pressing the F1 key. The Help Index displays the major topics. Select a topic by using the cursor movement keys to place the cursor on a topic and pressing Enter. Leave the help screens by pressing the Esc key.

Insert Column [/WIC] Place the cursor in the column just to the right of where you want the new blank column to appear. Type /WIC and press Enter.

Insert Row [/WIR] Place the cursor in the row just below where you want the new blank row to appear. Type /WIR and press Enter.

List Files [/FL] To display the names of all files of a particular type stored in the current directory on your disk, type /FL and choose the file type you want to list. Then press Enter.

Move Cell Entries [/M <FROM range> <TO range>] The Move command moves entries from one range to another, replacing the contents of those cells. The contents of the cells in the *move from* range are erased. Formulas in the worksheet are adjusted to reflect the new locations of the cells.

Print Graph To print a graph, you must use the Lotus 1-2-3 PrintGraph program. Once you have loaded the program, select Image-Select from the menu, select the image (PIC file) you wish to print, then select Go.

Print Worksheet [/PPR <range> G] This command prints the contents of the cells in the range on your printer. For example, to print the worksheet in cells A1 through F20, first place your cursor in the upper-left cell of the range to print (A1, in this example). Then type /PPR and enter the range you wish to print (in this case, A1.F20). Press Enter and then type G to start the printing.

Quit Lotus 1-2-3 [/QY] To exit Lotus and return to the DOS prompt, type /Q. When prompted, type Y and press Enter.

Reset Graph Settings [/GR] Use this command to reset or cancel some or all of the current graph settings.

Retrieve Named Graph [/GNU] This command retrieves named graph settings that you have previously created. These settings are stored by Lotus in the worksheet. When prompted, type in the name of the graph settings you wish to retrieve.

Retrieving Worksheet Files [/FR] This command erases any worksheet in memory and replaces it with the worksheet you retrieve from disk. Type /FR and select the file you want from the menu by using the cursor movement keys and then pressing Enter.

Save Graph in a Picture File [/GS] Save a "picture" of a graph you have created to your disk in a PIC file. You can view or print the contents of this file only by using the Lotus 1-2-3 PrintGraph program.

Save Graph as a Named Graph [/GNC] Use this command to create a name for graph settings in your worksheet. When prompted, type in the name of the graph settings you wish to save in the worksheet and press Enter.

Save Worksheet Files [/FS] Type /FS to save a worksheet in memory to your disk. If it is a new worksheet, type the name of the worksheet and press Enter. If you are modifying a worksheet that you previously retrieved from disk, Lotus displays the name of the current worksheet when it prompts you for a file name. Save the new worksheet in the existing file by pressing Enter and then typing R to replace the previous contents of the file with the new worksheet.

View Graph [/GV] Use the graph settings you have entered to display a graph on your display screen.

Some dBASE III PLUS Keystrokes

The descriptions that follow summarize the most commonly used dBASE commands and the related keystrokes. Most of these commands are discussed in chapters 8 and 9.

The commands you should enter are enclosed in brackets ([]). These commands are entered at the dot prompt. You must press Enter at the end of each command. Most of these commands require that a database file be active (in USE); and the commands refer to that active database file. When a command requires that you supply the a specific piece of information, such as a file name, the information you need to enter is enclosed in angle brackets (<>).

Add Records [APPEND] or [BROWSE] APPEND displays the data-entry form for one record. Data is entered into a new blank record at the end of the database file that is in use. The Browse command displays up to 17 records on a screen. With Browse you must move to the last record in the file, then press the down cursor key to move beyond the last record. When dBASE asks if you wish to add records, type Y. A blank record appears. With both Append and Browse, press Ctrl-End to save your entries and changes.

Close Active File [USE] If you are currently using a database file, typing USE and pressing Enter will close the file.

Close Multiple Files [CLEAR ALL] If you are using several files at once or a single file with indexes, entering CLEAR ALL closes all currently open files and their respective indexes.

Create File Structure [CREATE] After you enter the Create command, dBASE prompts you to type in the name of the database file you wish to create. Type the name and press Enter. The file structure form appears on the screen. Type in the necessary information for each field. Press Enter to move to the next field. When you have completed the structure, press Ctrl-End and then Enter to save the structure.

Create Report Form [CREATE REPORT] After you enter the Create Report command, dBASE prompts you to type in the name of the report file you wish to create. Type the name and press Enter. The report structure form appears on the screen. Use the cursor and the menu to select the options you wish to use. Type in the necessary information for each field and additional feature you want on your report, such as title, margin size, and so on. When you have completed the structure, select Exit, then Save to save the structure and return to the dot prompt. Note: To create a report, the database file that provides the data for the report must be open.

Delete Records Deleting records is a two-step process. First mark the records for deletion by using the Delete command or the Browse command and Ctrl-U. Then you delete the marked records by using the Pack command. When listed, records marked for deletion are preceded by an asterisk. To restore records marked for deletion, use the Recall command. Note: Once Pack has been used, you can no longer recall a record. Always double-check before using the Pack command.

Edit Records [EDIT <record number>] or [BROWSE] Use the Edit command to modify records in an open database file. Type Edit followed by the number of the record you want to modify. For example, to edit record 5, type Edit 5 and press the Enter key. The requested record will appear on the screen and you can make your changes. Press PgUp or PgDn to move to other records in the file. After making the necessary changes, press Ctrl-End to save the changes. The Browse command allows access to all the records in a database file. Use the cursor movement keys to move to the field(s) you wish to change. Make the necessary changes, then press Ctrl-End to save the changes.

Exit dBASE [QUIT] The Quit command closes all currently open files and returns you to the DOS prompt.

Function Keys

F1	Displays dBASE's help screen.
F2	Activates the Assist Menu facility.
F3	Lists the records in the active database file.
F4	Lists the names of all database (DBF) files on the default disk.
F5	Displays the structure of the active database file.
F6	Displays the current status (names of all open files, work areas, and settings) of dBASE.
F7	Displays information on memory variables (these are used in dBASE's programming language).
F8	Displays the current record in the active database file.
F9	Signals dBASE that you wish to append records to the active database file.
F10	Signals dBASE that you wish to edit records in the active database file.

Index Files [INDEX ON <key field> TO <index file name>] The Index command creates a new index file with the extension NDX. Index files order database files in a logical sequence (alphabetical, numerical, and so on) based on a character, numeric, or date field.

Join Multiple Files [JOIN WITH <file name 2> TO <new file name> FOR <link field> = B → <link field>] The Join command creates a new database file by combining two open database files, using a field that is common to both. The database files must have previously been opened in two separate work areas (see Open Multiple Files).

Link Multiple Files [SET RELATION TO <link field> INTO <file name of file in Work Area 2>] The Set Relation To command links two open database files using a field that is common to both. The database files must have previously been opened in two separate work areas (see Open Multiple Files) and the file open in area 2 must be indexed on the link field and the index must also be active (open). Note: The Set Relation To command links the two files only temporarily and does not create a new database file.

List File Structure [LIST STRUCTURE] or [DISPLAY STRUCTURE] Use the List Structure command or the Display Structure command to display the structure of the active database file.

List Records [LIST] The List command is used to show the contents of the active database file. All records are displayed unless a selection condition is specified.

List Specific Fields [LIST <field name 1>, <field name 2>, <etc.>] To list specific fields, enter LIST followed by the fields you wish to view in the order you wish to view them. The requested fields for all the records in the file are displayed.

List Using One Condition [LIST FOR <field name 1> = <selection condition>] To find a record or records containing a specific piece of information, enter the List For command. The equals sign in the command may be replaced with other relational operators: >, <, >=, or <=. Character values must be contained in quotation marks. The record(s) are displayed on your screen.

List Using Two Conditions [LIST FOR <field name 1> = <selection condition one> .AND. <field name 2> = <selection condition two>] The equals sign in either part of the command may be replaced with another relational operator: <, >, >=, or <=. The logical operator .AND. narrows the range of the search. If you wish to widen the range, replace .AND. with .OR. Character values must be contained in quotation marks. The record(s) are displayed on your screen.

Modify File Structure [MODIFY STRUCTURE] To change the structure of your file, enter the Modify Structure command. The file structure is displayed on the screen. Enter your changes, then press Ctrl-End to save them.

Open Multiple Files To open several files at one time, you must use the Select command in conjunction with the Use command. For example, to open two files concurrently, one in Work Area 1 and one in Work Area 2, type the following commands, pressing the Enter key at the end of each command line.

```
SELECT 2
USE <file name 2>
SELECT 1
USE <file name 1>
```

Unless otherwise specified, database files will always be opened in Area 1. You may also use the Select command to switch back and forth between open files. For example, if you type SELECT 2 and press Enter, the file in Work Area 2 becomes the active file.

Print Report [REPORT FORM <report file name> TO PRINT] Make sure your printer is on and the database file on which the report is based is open. Then enter the Report Form command.

Seek Records [SEEK <data to be found>] The Seek command can be used only with open, indexed database files. The associated Index file must also be open. The command searches for the first record in the file that matches the criteria you enter. Character values must be contained in quotation marks. To display a record found by the Seek command, type Display and press Enter.

Sort Files [SORT ON <key field> TO <sorted file name>] The Sort command creates and saves a new sorted database file that contains all of the data in the original file. Sorted files can be ordered in a logical sequence (alphabetical, numeric, and so on) based on character, numeric, or date fields.

Use File [USE <file name>] To open, or use, a database file, enter the Use command and the name of the file you wish to use. The name of the open database file appears in the highlighted bar near the bottom of the screen. If the database file has been indexed, list the names of the index files following the name of the database file. For example: —USE PHONE INDEX LNAMEI.

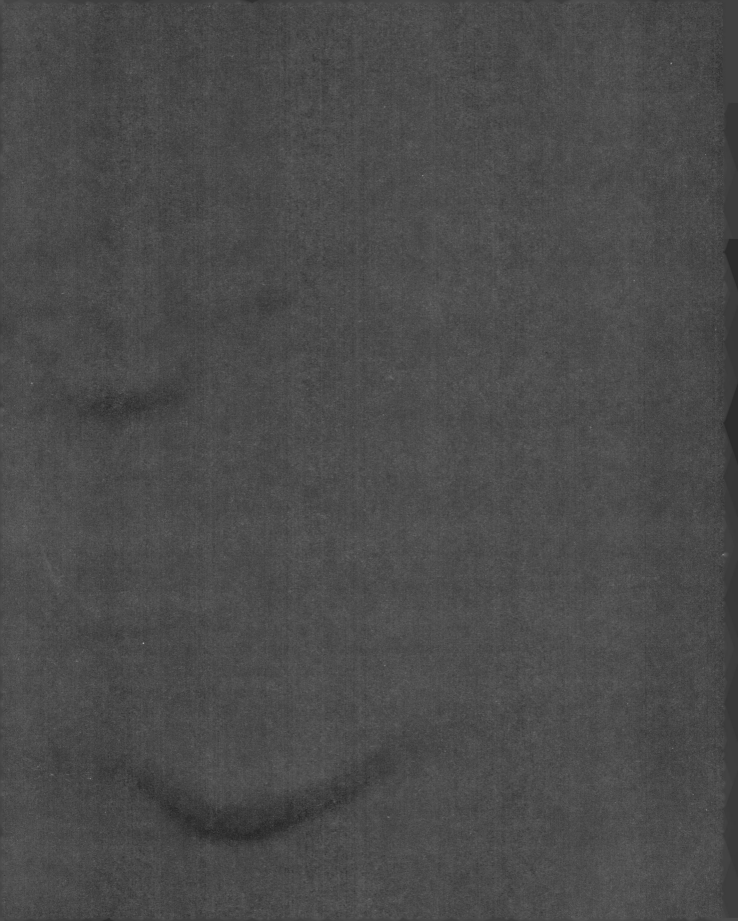

Beyond the Basic Applications

You have seen the camera enthusiast who begins with a simple camera and film but eventually adds extras such as filters and fancy lenses. The story is the same for personal computer users.

The heart of this book contains the basic applications. But there is much more. Now we will explore some of the other important applications that users usually want after they understand the basics.

At the top of the list is a data communications package; for some users this package is even more important than the basic applications. Next is desktop publishing, software whose attractions include convenience and economy. Finally, there is a variety of software packages that offer file recovery programs, desktop managers, and expert systems.

Data Communications

Chapter Objectives

After reading this chapter you should be able to

- List the advantages of data communications

- Describe the components of a data communications system

- Explain how data is transmitted over communications links and list the different kinds of communications links

- Distinguish wide area from local area networks and describe different configurations

- List the parts and types of local area networks

- Describe the way users interact with communications software

- Explain the importance of data communications standards

The applications we have discussed so far—word processing, spreadsheets, database management, and graphics—all involve a single user interacting with one personal computer. But many users need to share data and information. Today, sharing information often means that data is sent directly—electronically—from one computer to another. **Data communications systems** are computer systems that transmit data over communications lines, such as telephone lines.

You can use these systems to send and receive information quickly and fairly cheaply, since the data is transmitted electronically in the form of signals. Plus, the transmission of data over communications lines lets different pieces of electronic equipment communicate with each other.

Thus, when considering personal computers (especially in business) a key point is **connectivity**—a computer's potential to communicate with other computers. In a small business, data might be shared among only two or three personal computers in the same office. In a large company, however, there may be hundreds—or even thousands—of personal computers in offices, warehouses, and factories. For workers to work effectively, their computers need to communicate electronically.

Consider, for example, the computing needs of a national fast-food chain. In each restaurant in the chain, the manager uses spreadsheet software on a personal computer to monitor the daily costs and income for the restaurant. At the end of each business day, the data stored in these spreadsheet files is sent over the phone lines to the minicomputer in the district office. For example, the personal computer in a restaurant in Palo Alto transmits data to the district office in San Francisco. During the evening the minicomputer in the San Francisco office produces reports using the combined data from the chain's restaurants in northern California. The district manager uses these reports to analyze the profitability of each restaurant and to plan advertising and special promotions. At the end of each week, the district data is sent via satellite to the mainframe computer at the national headquarters in Chicago (Figure 11-1). The combined data from all districts nationwide is used as a factor in long-range corporate planning.

Each restaurant and each office of the organization has a computer powerful enough to meet its computing needs. Furthermore, these computers can communicate with each other. This arrangement is an example of **distributed processing.** The company's operations are more effective because data is not isolated in individual computers. This example demonstrates some of the advantages of computer communications; there are many more.

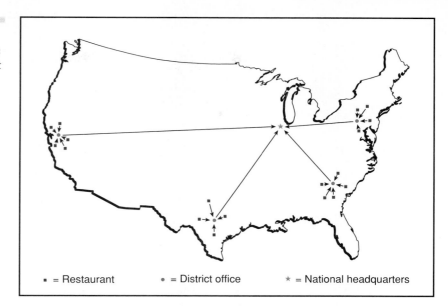

Figure 11-1 Distributed processing. *In this example each restaurant and district office as well as the network headquarters has a computer powerful enough to meet its computing needs. Futhermore, a data communications system allows data to be sent to and from the various offices.*

■ = Restaurant   ● = District office   ★ = National headquarters

A Data Communications System: The Basic Components

S pecial hardware and special software are needed for a data communications system. As a user, your direct involvement is through the data communications software. We will describe that software later in the chapter, but first you need to have some understanding of data communications hardware and how data is transmitted from computer to computer.

The basic configuration of a data communications system—how the components are put together—is fairly straightforward. Although there are many choices for each component, all data communications systems consist of three basic physical components. These components are (1) the sending device, (2) a communications link, and (3) the receiving device. Another component that is often used with this basic configuration is a modem.

Sending and Receiving Devices

Sending devices are used to send data to another location, where it is accepted by a receiving device. Suppose, for example, that you want to send a message to a friend who works in another area. If you have a computer and your friend has a computer and you send information over the telephone lines,

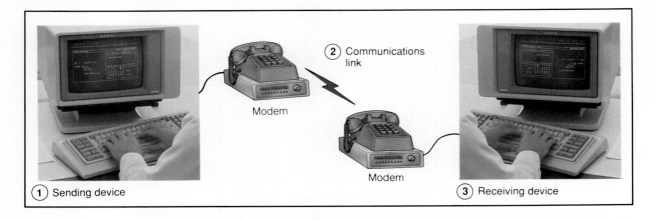

① Sending device   ② Communications link   Modem   Modem   ③ Receiving device

Figure 11-2 Sending and receiving devices. *A sending device, such as a personal computer, is used to send data via a communications link to a receiving device, in this case another personal computer. The sending and receiving devices can also be minicomputers or mainframes.*

your computer is the sending device, your friend's computer is the receiving device, and the telephone lines are the communications link (Figure 11-2). Sending and receiving devices can also be minicomputers or mainframes.

Communications Links

Since a computer transmits data as electrical impulses, it needs a medium, or conductor, to get the data from one place to another. A **communications link** is the physical medium used for transmission. These media vary according to their information capacity and susceptibility to electrical interference. Let us take a look at some of the most common communications media.

Wire Pairs. Among the most common communications media are **wire pairs,** also known as **twisted pairs.** Wire pairs are wires twisted together to form a cable, which is then insulated (Figure 11-3). Wire pairs are inexpensive and frequently used to transmit information over short distances. However, they are sometimes susceptible to electrical interference, or noise. **Noise** is anything that causes distortion in the signal.

Coaxial Cables. Known for their high capacity and resistance to noise, **coaxial cables** are insulated wires within a shield enclosure (Figure 11-4), which can be laid underground

Figure 11-3 Wire pairs.
Among the most common communications media, wire pairs are wires twisted together to form a cable. The cable is then insulated.

Figure 11-4 A coaxial cable.
This type of coaxial cable is designed for use with monitors.

Figure 11-5 Fiber optic cable.
These delicate, light-conducting glass strands transmit data faster than any other medium.

or undersea. These cables can transmit data at rates much higher than those of wire pairs.

Fiber Optics. Instead of using electricity to send data, **fiber optics** uses light. Fiber optic cables are made of glass fibers, thinner than a human hair, that can guide light beams for miles (Figure 11-5). Fiber optics can transmit data faster than other media and are less susceptible to noise than wire. In addition, the optical fibers are lighter and less expensive than wire cables.

Microwave Transmission. Another popular medium is **microwave transmission** (Figure 11-6), which transmits data signals through the atmosphere. Since microwave signals cannot bend around the curvature of the earth, relay stations—

Figure 11-6 Microwave transmission. *Microwave signals can follow only a line-of-sight path, so stations must relay this signal at regular intervals to avoid interference from the earth's curvature.*

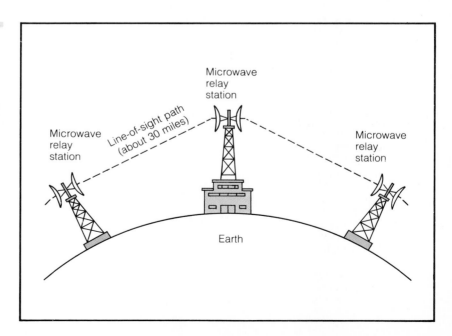

Figure 11-7 Satellite transmission. *A signal is sent from a earth station to the relay satellite in the sky, which changes the signal frequency before transmitting to the next earth station.*

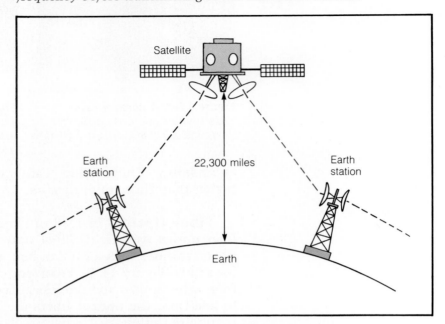

usually antennas in high places such as the tops of mountains and buildings—are positioned at points approximately 30 miles apart to continue the transmission. Microwave transmission offers speed, cost-effectiveness, and ease of implementation.

Satellite Transmission. Communications satellites (Figure 11-7) are suspended in space 22,300 miles above the earth. The basic components of **satellite transmission** are earth stations, which send and receive signals, and a satellite component called a transponder. The **transponder** receives the transmission from an earth station, then transmits the data to a second earth station. Like fiber optics, satellite transmission is not prone to noise and electrical interference, thus the chance of error is reduced.

Modems

As we mentioned in Chapter 2, a *modem* converts computer data to signals that can be carried by the communications link and vice versa. Notice in Figure 11-8a that modems are used in pairs; one at either end of the transmission.

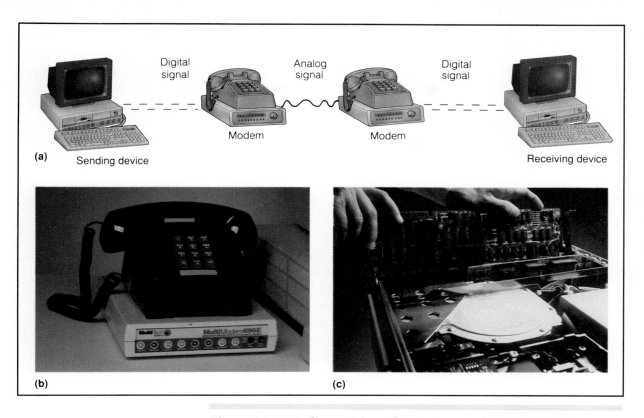

Figure 11-8 Modems. (a) Modems convert digital signals to analog signals for traveling over communications links and then reverse the process at the other end. (b) This external direct-connect modem is connected to the telephone line by means of a telephone jack. (c) An internal modem board can be placed in an expansion slot inside the computer by the user.

Modems vary in the way they connect to the telephone line. There are two main types: direct-connect modems and acoustic coupler modems.

A **direct-connect modem** is directly connected to the telephone line by means of a telephone jack. An **external direct-connect modem** is separate from the computer (Figure 11-8b). Its main advantage is that it can be used with a variety of computers. If you buy a new personal computer, for example, you can probably keep the same modem. Personal computer users who regard a modem as one more item taking up desk space can buy a modem that is out of sight, literally. Most major microcomputer manufacturers now offer **internal modem boards** that can be inserted by users (Figure 11-8c). Some microcomputers even have an internal modem built in as part of the standard equipment.

An **acoustic coupler modem** is connected to a telephone receiver rather than directly to a telephone line. Some acoustic couplers are connected to the computer by a cable, but others are built-in. The advantage of acoustic couplers is that they can be connected to a phone, but signal quality suffers since the connection is not made directly to the telephone line.

Most modems have a built-in speaker that lets you monitor your call as it is being placed by your data communications software. You can hear the dial tone first and then the tones the modem generates to represent the phone number of the receiving computer. If your call is answered, the next sound will be the high-pitched beep from the receiving modem. This signal is known as a **carrier signal.** If someone is already using the phone line, you will hear a busy signal. With a modem and the proper data communications program, you can dial local, long-distance, and international calls to communicate with computers in other countries.

Now that we have discussed the basic components of a data communications system, let us see how these components work together, beginning with how data is transmitted.

Data Transmission

Data is transmitted from one computer to another along the communications link. The data is transmitted at various speeds, depending on the selected mode of transmission. At times, the data may also need to be translated from one form of code to another, so it can be accepted by the receiving device. In this section we will discuss the different forms of data and the different ways in which it is transmitted.

Digital versus Analog Transmission

A computer produces digital signals, which are simply the presence or absence of an electronic pulse. Thus, **digital transmission** sends data as distinct pulses—on or off—in much the same way that data travels through the computer (Figure 11-9a). However, communications links such as telephone lines were designed for transmitting voices. Telephone lines use **analog transmission,** which sends data as a continuous signal (Figure 11-9b). A computer's digital signal must be converted to an analog signal before the data can be transmitted via analog communications links.

Figure 11-9 Digital versus analog signals. *(a) Digital signals are discrete electronic signals. (b) Analog signals are continuous electronic signals.*

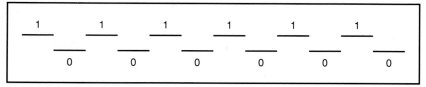

(a)

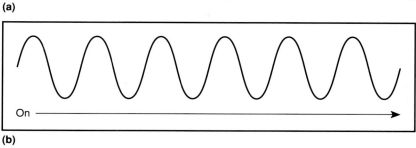

(b)

Analog signals are continuous electronic signals in the form of a wave. This wave form has three characteristics, as shown in Figure 11-10.

- **Amplitude** is the height of the wave, which indicates the strength of the signal.

- **Phase** is the relative position in time of one complete cycle of the wave.

- **Frequency** is the number of times the wave is repeated during a specific time interval.

Converting digital signals to analog signals is called **modulation** and the reverse process—reconstructing the original digital message at the other end of the transmission—is called **demodulation.** These conversions are made by a modem (short for *modulate/demodulate*). Note that a modem is not needed if you are transmitting data on a communications link that accepts digital transmission.

Figure 11-10 An analog wave pattern. *In this figure an analog wave is labeled with its characteristics: amplitude, phase, and frequency.*

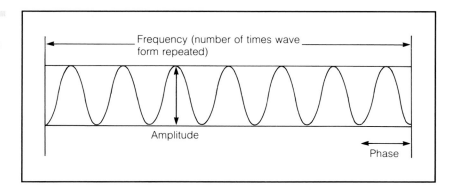

Asynchronous versus Synchronous Transmission

Sending data to another computer works only if the receiving device is ready to accept the data. By "ready," we mean more than just available; the timing of the computers must be compatible. The receiving device must be able to keep in step with the sending device. Two techniques commonly used to keep the data moving smoothly from sender to receiver are asynchronous and synchronous transmission.

When the **asynchronous transmission** method (also called the **start/stop** method) is used, a *start* bit is transmitted at the beginning of each group of bits. Likewise, a *stop* bit is sent at the end of the group of bits. When the receiving device gets the start bit, it sets up a timing mechanism to accept the group of bits. Most transmission involving personal computers is asynchronous.

Synchronous transmission sends characters together in a continuous stream. The sending and receiving devices are synchronized by having their internal clocks put in time with each other by a bit pattern transmitted at the beginning of the message.

Synchronous transmission equipment is more complex and more expensive than equipment required for asynchronous transmission. The payoff, however, is speedier transmission, free from the bonds of the start/stop characters.

Half-Duplex versus Full-Duplex Transmission

As Figure 11-11 shows, personal computer data transmission can be characterized as half-duplex transmission or full-duplex transmission, depending on the permissible directions of data flow.

Half-duplex transmission allows transmission in either direction, but only one way at a time. A computer can send data and, after it is received, accept a message in return. **Full-duplex transmission** allows transmission in both directions at once. Systems supporting computer-to-computer communications often are full-duplex to avoid bottlenecks.

Transmission Speed

The speed at which data travels through the communications links is measured in **bits per second (bps),** sometimes

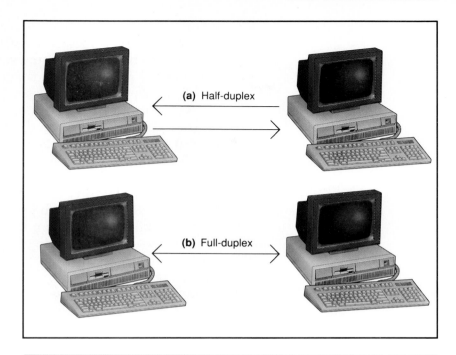

Figure 11-11 Half-duplex versus full-duplex transmission.
*(a) Half-duplex transmission can send data in either direction,
but only one way at a time. (b) Full-duplex transmission can
send data in both directions at once.*

called the **bit rate** or **baud rate.** For example, a rate of 300 bps
means that 300 data bits can be transmitted in each second.
Typical rates for microcomputers are 300, 1200, 2400, 4800,
and 9600 bps.

Protocol

Communication between computers is a complicated
process. To exchange information, two computers must use
the same communications standards. Like the signals that a
baseball catcher and pitcher exchange for pitches, **protocols**
represent an agreement among different parts of the networks
about how the data is to be transferred. For example, the speed
at which data is transmitted needs to be determined. The duplex
setting of your computer must match that of the computer
with which you want to communicate, either half-duplex (HDX)
or full-duplex (FDX). You also need to establish whether you
will be sending 7 or 8 data bits per character, what the parity
setting is, and the number of stop bits associated with each
character that you send and receive.

If you are using a modem, you must also make sure your modem settings are compatible with the remote modem's settings. If you do not use the same settings, the modem places the call, but the response from the remote computer produces strange symbols or meaningless combinations of letters and numbers, sometimes referred to as *garbage,* on the screen. If this is the case, check the speed, data bit, parity, and stop bit settings to see that they are correct. If you are able to establish the connection but occasionally see strange symbols on the screen, you probably have a bad phone line. If you have the call waiting phone feature, you may also run the risk of garbage on the screen. Some people like the call waiting feature for voice phone calls—it lets them know that someone is trying to get through—but call waiting interferes with the operation of a modem.

There are several steps that you should follow to ensure that your computer will use the correct protocol when you want to communicate with another computer. To determine the characteristics of both your computer and the remote computer, read the instruction manual that came with your modem, talk to the owner of the remote computer, and/or talk to a computer specialist in your area. If you are making a connection with an established organization, there are often toll-free phone numbers to call so you can get the information you need. When you are using data communications software, you will often be choosing the protocol parameters through a series of menus (Figure 11-12).

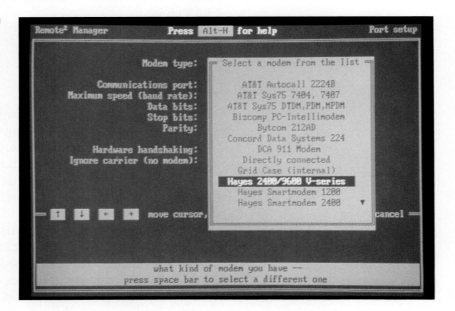

Figure 11-12 Setting protocol parameters. Data communications programs such as CROSSTALK, shown here, help you set protocol parameters by presenting a series of menus one menu at a time.

Now that we have looked at how data is transmitted, let us take a look at the software that makes data communications possible.

Communications Software

Computers can communicate directly with relatively simple devices like printers and monitors. To communicate with another computer, however, personal computers need to use a **communications program.** You interact with this software, which presents options in menu form. There are several different kinds of communications programs, which perform different functions. In the sections that follow, we will examine the software packages for each type.

RANDOM BITS

Network Heartaches and How to Avoid Them

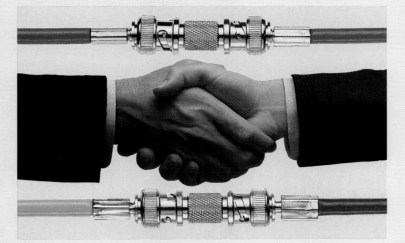

Although the concept of networking is straightforward, many things can go wrong. In fact, networking is never quite as simple as manufacturers would have us believe. Here are some factors that you should be aware of:

- Make sure that new hardware added to the network is using an operating system that is compatible with the network.

- Remember that you are not alone on the network and, consequently, your actions may affect others. In particular, do not run untested software that may bring the system down unless the network manager is on hand to undo the mess or it is after hours.

- Do not turn off a shared device. Although it seems to make no sense, there have been examples of one user on a LAN receiving a file from a distant database, only to have another LAN user switch the modem off.

- Agree on policies for use of the common printer. Otherwise, you may find that your report prints on someone else's letterhead.

- Be alert: The hard disk associated with the network server can crash, just like any other disk. Make sure you make backup copies of your files.

Terminal Emulation Software

A **terminal** is simply a device that lets you communicate with a computer. One type of communications program is called **terminal emulation software** because your personal computer emulates—imitates—a terminal. The other computer, called the **host** computer, accepts the keystrokes you type as input and sends characters that the communications program displays on the personal computer screen. However, since your personal computer acts like a terminal, which has no storage capacity, you cannot store or send files while communicating with the host computer.

In most cases, you can simply use terminal emulation software and a modem for this type of communication. In some cases, you may also need to purchase a terminal emulation expansion card or board to insert into your computer. By talking to an operator of the host computer, you can find out what kind of terminal your computer must emulate to communicate with the host.

Terminal emulation software is the minimum software needed to communicate with a remote computer. If you want to transfer files from your computer to another computer, then you need to run a file transfer program.

File Transfer Software

To transfer files between two computers, you must use **file transfer software.** With file transfer programs you can **download** files—retrieve a file from another computer and store it in your computer memory—or **upload** files—send a file from your computer to another computer. To transfer a file from one personal computer to another, both computers must be running file transfer programs. Since a file sent from one computer to another travels through a physical communications link, the link itself may introduce problems. For example, electrical conditions on a telephone line can cause parts of files that are being transferred to be scrambled or lost. These problems are addressed in the data communications software by **file transfer protocols,** which ensure that an error-free file is delivered to the receiving computer.

Both computers involved in the file transfer must use the same file transfer protocol. Two excellent file transfer protocols are XMODEM and Kermit. These protocols are usually included in most file transfer programs. When you signal the data communications program that you want to send or receive a file, it asks you to select (usually from a menu) a file transfer protocol. Be sure that you select the protocol that is being used by the computer at the other end of the phone line.

Full-Function Software

Data communications programs that enable your computer to emulate a variety of standard types of terminals and to communicate by using several standard file transfer protocols are called **full-function data communications software.** With this type of software, your computer has the ability to emulate a terminal and also to transfer files. Some full-function software packages have additional capabilities. As with other data communications programs, both computers must be using the same type of program and have the same protocol.

Setting up your data communications program may seem to be somewhat complicated. However, these programs are very easy to use. The built-in default settings usually do what you want, so changes are not needed. Most data communications programs use well-designed menus that make setting up and using the program easy. Furthermore, if you are going to use the program on the job, a computer professional will often set up the program correctly for you.

Networks

Computers that are connected so they can communicate among themselves are said to form a **network.** There are two kinds of networks: wide area networks and local area networks. A **wide area network** (**WAN**) sends data over long distances by using the telephone system. In business, personal computers are often used to send data over a WAN to a larger computer. However, minicomputers and mainframe computers are set up so that they can be accessed by terminals. When a personal computer is used as a terminal, special terminal emulation software—previously discussed in this chapter—is needed.

An alternative to WANs are local area networks. A **local area network** (**LAN**) sends data among computers linked together in one building or in buildings that are close together. Since most networked personal computers are used in LANs, we need to examine this subject in more detail.

Local Area Networks

A local area network is a collection of personal computers—and sometimes larger computers—that share hardware, software, and information. In simple terms, LANs hook personal computers together through communications media so that each personal computer can share the resources of the others. Personal computers attached to a LAN are often referred to as **workstations.** All of the devices—personal computers and other hardware—attached to the LAN are called **nodes** on the LAN. As the name implies, LANs cover short distances, usually one office or building.

Here are some typical tasks for which LANs are especially suited:

- A personal computer can read data from a hard disk belonging to another personal computer as if it were its own. This allows users who are working on the same projects to share word processing, spreadsheet, and database data.

- A personal computer may print one of its files on the printer of another personal computer. (Since few people need a letter-quality printer all the time, this more expensive type of printer could be hooked to only a few computers.)

- One copy of an applications program, when purchased with the proper license from the vendor of the program, can be used by all the personal computers on the LAN. This is less expensive than purchasing a copy of the program for each user.

As any or all of these activities are going on, the personal computer whose resource is being accessed by another can continue doing its own work.

These advantages go beyond simple convenience; some applications require that the same data be shared by coworkers. For example, consider a company that sends catalogs to customers, who can then place orders over the telephone. Waiting at the other end of the phone line are customer service representatives, who key the order data into the computer system as they are talking to the customer (Figure 11-13).

Each representative has a personal computer on which to enter orders, but all representatives share common computer files that provide information on product availability and pricing. It is not practical to provide a separate set of files for each representative because then one representative would not know

***Figure 11-13 Using a
LAN.*** *Customer sales representatives share order
data through a series of
connected personal
computers.*

what the others had sold. That is, an individual representative's file would reflect only the sales made by that particular
representative. One representative, for example, could accept
an order for 20 flannel shirts when there are only 5 shirts in
stock because other representatives had already accepted orders
for that product.

In this kind of application, workers must have access to
one central master file that will reflect the activities of other
workers. Then, when a representative checks the file to see
whether there is enough of a product available to accept an
order, he or she can be confident that the quantity on hand has
been updated and is correct.

Local Area Network Components

There are many different LAN devices; however, all LANs
require certain components. The following are some of these
standard components:

■ The nodes on some LANs are connected by a shared **network cable.** Low-cost LANs are connected with twisted
wire pairs like those used to connect the telephones in a
building. However, many LANs use coaxial cables or
fiber optic cables. These types of cables are more expensive but allow faster transmission speeds.

- LANs use a hardware device called a **cable interface unit,** a set of electronic components in a box outside the computer, to send and receive signals on the network cable. Cable interface units vary with the type of LAN.

- A **network interface card,** inserted in one of the personal computer's internal expansion slots, contains the electronic components needed to send and receive messages on the LAN. A short cable connects the network interface card to the cable interface unit.

- A **gateway** is a hardware device—sometimes even a separate computer—that connects two dissimilar networks. A gateway, for example, can connect a WAN to a LAN. Users on both networks can share devices and exchange information.

- A **bridge,** sometimes called a **router,** connects two LANs of the same type so that messages can be sent from a node on one LAN to a node on a different LAN.

Local Area Network Topology

The physical layout of a LAN is called a **topology.** LANS come in three basic topologies: star, ring, and bus networks. A **star network** has a central computer that is responsible for managing the LAN. It is to this central computer—sometimes called a **server**—that the shared disks and printers are usually

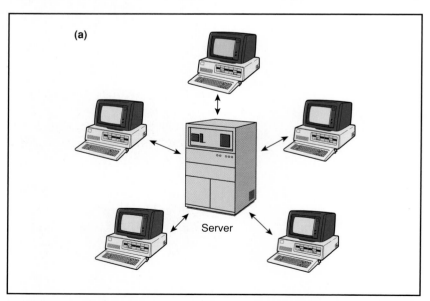

Figure 11-14 LAN topologies. (a) The star topology has a central host computer that runs the LAN.

(a)

Server

continued ▶

attached (Figure 11-14a). All messages are routed through the server. A **ring network** links all nodes together in a circular manner, without benefit of a server (Figure 11-14b). In ring networks, if one computer goes down, the network goes down. Disks and printers are scattered throughout the system. All the nodes in a **bus network** are linked to a main cable. Each node is assigned a portion of network management. However the system is preserved if one component fails (**Figure** 11-14c). The majority of LANs are bus-structured.

Figure 11-14 LAN topologies (continued). *(b) The ring topology connects computers in a circular fashion. (c) The bus topology has different nodes attached to a main cable.*

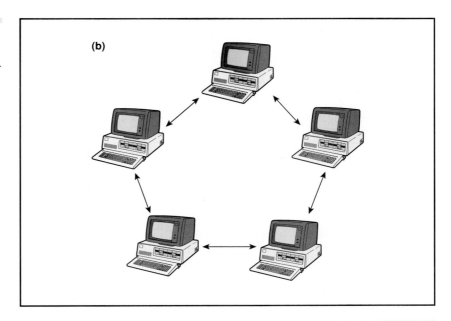

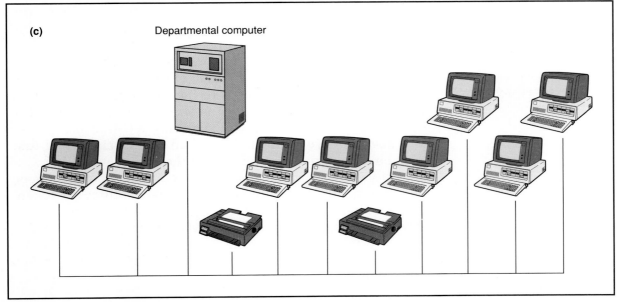

CABLED CADETS

Each cadet at the Air Force Academy owns his or her own personal computer, and the computers are all linked together. The system, using approximately 200 miles of cable, is one of the largest local area networks in the nation. Each cadet's room includes a built-in computer screen. The cadets use their computers for a variety of purposes, particularly word processing for term papers. It is also popular for electronic mail, since the network links together cadet rooms, faculty, staff, the gym, field house, and dining hall. A cadet can send a message from his or her room to someone in any of those locations. Each cadet receives several hours of training on microcomputer operation and software. The payoff is an expected savings of an hour per day on academic work.

Types of Local Area Networks

The two most common types of LANs are popularly known as Ethernet and the IBM Token Ring Network.

Ethernet is the most popular type of LAN. Ethernet uses a high-speed network cable. Since all the nodes in a LAN use the same cable to transmit and receive data, they must follow a set of rules; otherwise, two or more nodes could transmit at the same time, causing garbled or lost messages. To control access to this single shared cable, a protocol called **Carrier Sense Multiple Access with Collision Detection (CSMA/CD)** is used. Since CSMA/CD is a commonly used access protocol, let us examine it more closely.

Before a node can transmit data, CSMA/CD requires that the node check the cable to see whether it is being used. The node "listens" for the carrier signal on the cable; if the carrier signal indicates that the cable is in use, the node must wait. When the carrier signal indicates that the cable is free from other transmissions, the node can begin transmitting immediately. This is the CSMA part of CSMA/CD and can be summarized as *Listen before transmitting and do not transmit until the line is not being used by another node.* This part of the protocol prevents most problems.

However, in spite of these precautions, a message collision can occur on the network cable if two or more nodes happen to begin transmission at exactly the same instant. The collision is detected by the collision detection portion of CSMA/CD. The transmissions are stopped immediately, and only one of the nodes is allowed to begin transmission again. When the transmission of that node's message is complete, the cable becomes free for use by the other nodes.

The IBM **Token Ring Network** connects nodes in a ring topology by using a network cable of twisted wire pairs. The protocol for controlling access to the shared network cable is called **token passing.** The idea is similar to that used in the New York City subway: If you want to ride—transmit data—you have to have a token. The token is a special signal that circulates from node to node along the ring-shaped LAN.

Only one token is available on the network. When a node on the network wishes to transmit, it first captures the token; then it can transmit data. When the node has sent its message, it releases the token back to the network (Figure 11-15). Since only one token is circulating around the network, only one device is able to access the network at a time, and problems are avoided.

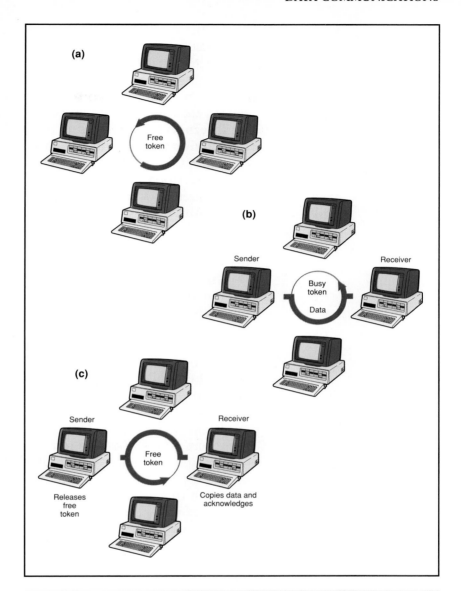

Figure 11-15 IBM Token Ring Network. *This type of network connects nodes in a ring. An electronic signal, or token, circles the ring. (a) The sender waits for the token to pass by, and then (b) captures the token to transmit data. (c) The receiver retrieves the data and sends the token back to the sender.*

Data Communications Standards

S tandards are important in the computer industry; money is saved if everyone can coordinate effectively. Nowhere is this more obvious than in data communications systems, where so many components—from different manufacturers or even different countries—must come together. A detailed discussion of data communications standards is beyond the scope of this text. However, it is important for you to be aware of these standards when you purchase computer equipment.

The two international organizations that are most important in establishing standards are the **Consultative Committee on International Telegraphy and Telephone (CCITT)** and the **International Standards Organization (ISO)**.

The CCITT is part of the United Nations. It publishes recommendations that cover hardware and communications techniques. If you need to communicate internationally, you may find it necessary to use a modem that complies with one of the CCITT standards, such as the X.25 standard for access to public data networks or the X.400 standard for electronic mail.

The ISO developed the **Open Systems Interconnection (OSI)** reference model, sometimes called the ISO/OSI model. This model is a description of the standards needed to allow international communications. Manufacturers and software vendors use the ISO/OSI model to guide their product development. For example, the Ethernet standard for LANs is part of the OSI model.

A third data communications standard, developed by IBM, is **System Network Architecture (SNA).** To access IBM networks, you must comply with the SNA standard. Since IBM was there first, SNA does not strictly follow the OSI model.

If you need to access a network that uses one of the above standards, your data communications program may provide you with this capability. If not, you may need to connect your computer to an electronic device called a **protocol converter,** which lets you communicate by using a protocol different from that provided by your data communications software. An alternative to a protocol converter is a gateway. Gateways, you recall, are used in LANs to access networks that use different communications standards. If you are not attached to a LAN that provides a gateway, you may be able to access a gateway over the phone by using your modem.

Using Networks to Access Data

The merger of communications and computers is helping businesspeople get full value from each technology. Let us consider some of the important applications of data communications systems in the business world.

Electronic Mail

Releasing people from the tyranny of the telephone, **electronic mail** is the process of sending messages directly from one terminal or computer to another. A user can send messages to his or her supervisor downstairs; a query across town to someone who never seems to be able to come to the phone; and the same memo simultaneously to regional sales managers in Cleveland, Raleigh, and San Antonio. The beauty of electronic mail, or **e-mail,** is that a user can send a message to someone and be assured that the person will receive it. Furthermore, electronic mail is delivered in seconds, eliminating most of the delays involved in getting a message or document from one person to another.

Of course, electronic mail works only if the intended receiver has the electronic mail facility to which the sender is connected. There are several electronic mail options. A user can enlist a third-party service bureau that provides electronic mail service for its customers. A second popular option is to use a public data network, such as CompuServe. Another possibility is that a user may purchase an electronic mail software package for a microcomputer or for a large computer system. E-mail service can usually inform you when you receive mail and then lets you read, discard, save to disk, or print the messages.

Voice Mail

With **voice mail,** a user tries to complete a call the usual way but, if the recipient does not answer, the caller can then dictate a message into the system. The voice mail computer system then translates the message into digital pulses and stores it for the recipient. Later, when the recipient checks the system, the message will be delivered in audio form.

Figure 11-16 Faxing it.
Facsimile technology can send documents requiring fast attention to remote locations within seconds. The image shown being withdrawn from the machine was input into a different machine in another location just moments before.

Facsimile Machines

Something like a copy machine connected to a telephone, a **facsimile machine** can send quality graphics, charts, text, and even signatures to other offices almost anywhere in the world (Figure 11-16). Called **fax** for short, facsimile machines have been used in business for years. Now the circuitry for transmitting and receiving fax transmission has been placed on circuit boards that can be inserted in an expansion slot inside a personal computer. If your computer has a fax board, you can send documents and drawings to a fax machine or to another personal computer with a fax board. Your computer can also save the messages and documents you receive as files.

Teleconferencing

Teleconferencing is a way to bring people together despite geographic barriers. The simplest type of teleconferencing is called **computer conferencing,** which is a method of sending, receiving, and storing typed messages as part of a network of users. Add cameras and wall-sized screens and you have another form of teleconferencing, called **videoconferencing** (Figure 11-17). Although these conferences are not inexpensive, the price seems low when compared to the airfare and accommodations costs for in-person meetings of scattered participants.

Electronic Banking

In place of using checks, many businesses already handle some financial transactions electronically. In **electronic fund transfers** (**EFTs**), people pay for goods and services by having

Figure 11-17 Video-conferencing. *These businesspeople have rented a teleconferencing room with the necessary equipment in place—including a large wall screen to see colleagues in another city.*

funds transferred from accounts electronically, using computer technology. One of the most visible manifestations of EFT is the ATM, the automated teller machine, which is often found on a bank's outer wall.

Information Services

Users can connect their personal computers to commercial consumer-oriented communications systems via telephone lines. These services—known as **information utilities**—are widely used by business customers. Two major networks are The Source and CompuServe Information Service. These networks offer a broad range of services, including national news wires, stock index, encyclopedia references, travel reservations, banking, weather reports, and even medical and legal advice. Of particular interest to business users are investment information, world news, and professional forums.

Videotex Shopping

One of the newest forms of retailing is interactive, two-way cable **videotex**—data communications merchandising. Consumers shop at home for a variety of products and services. Using a video display catalog, they order products from a participating retailer (Figure 11-18). When the order is received in

Figure 11-18 Videotex. The menus on this page and the next page provide a representative sample of videotex sales options available on your home computer.

(a)

continued ▶

Figure 11-18 Videotex (continued). *The menus on this page and the previous page provide a representative sample of videotex sales options available on your home computer.*

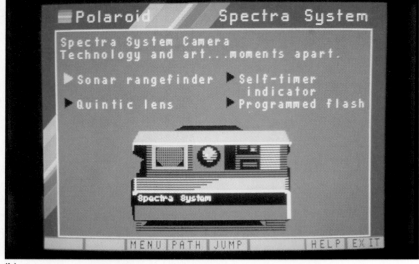

(b)

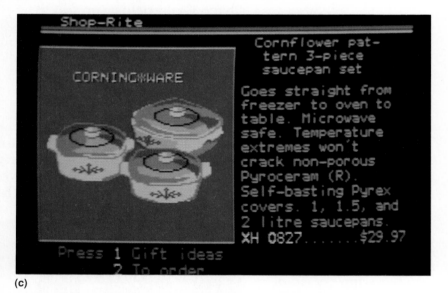

(c)

the computer, the retailer assembles the goods from a fully automated warehouse. Simultaneously, funds are transferred from the customer's to the retailer's bank account. Customers choose between picking up the order at a nearby distribution point or having it delivered to the door.

Bulletin Boards

Telephone-linked personal computers that provide public-access message systems are called **bulletin board systems** (BBSs).

Bulletin boards operate on a principle similar to bulletin boards in laundromats or student lounges: Someone leaves a message, but the person who picks it up does not have to know the person who left it. To access another computer, all you need to know is the bulletin board's phone number.

When your modem calls the number of the BBS, its modem automatically answers your call. You will be asked to identify yourself and, perhaps, to supply a password. Then, you can view messages from other callers to the bulletin board. You can also leave your own messages to be posted—stored—on the bulletin board. Some BBSs store programs that you can retrieve and store in your own files.

Anyone who has a personal computer can set up a bulletin board. It takes a computer, a phone line, a modem, a couple of disk drives, and some software that costs about $50. There are over 10,000 BBSs in the United States. Some are used by technical people who share information. Many businesses maintain their own bulletin boards that offer such services as product information, free software, and information for buyers and sellers. However, many BBSs resemble a social electronic mail service used to help friends stay in touch.

The Need to Communicate on Paper

This chapter has addressed the need to communicate directly from computer to computer. However, we are still a long way from the fabled "paperless office." In fact, the need to communicate on paper remains strong. But the computer can take a major role in that process as well. The new, and perhaps best, way to use computers with paper is called desktop publishing, and it is the subject of the next chapter.

Summary and Key Terms

- **Data communications systems** are computer systems that transmit data over communications lines.

- **Connectivity** is a computer's potential to communicate with other computers. Businesses with many locations or offices often use distributed processing, which allows both remote access and remote processing. Processing can be done by both the central computer and the other computers that are hooked up to it.

- The basic configuration of a data communications system consists of a sending device, a communications link, and a receiving device. Sending and receiving devices can be personal computers, minicomputers, or mainframes.

- A **communications link** is the physical medium used for transmission. Common communications links include **wire pairs,** or **twisted pairs; coaxial cables; fiber optics; microwave transmission;** and **satellite transmission.** In satellite transmission, a **transponder** receives and transmits data from and to earth stations.

■ **Noise** is electrical interference that causes distortion when a signal is being sent over a communications link.

■ A **modem** converts computer data to transmittable signals and vice versa. The **signal** coming to a receiving modem is known as a **carrier signal.** A **direct-connect modem** is directly connected to the telephone line by a telephone jack. An **external direct-connect modem** is not built into the computer and therefore can be used with a variety of computers. An **internal modem** is on a board that fits inside a microcomputer. An **acoustic coupler modem** is connected to a telephone receiver rather than the telephone line.

■ **Digital transmission** sends data as distinct pulses. **Analog transmission** sends data in a continuous signal in the form of a wave. The wave has three characteristics—**amplitude, phase,** and **frequency.** Converting signals from digital to analog is called **modulation;** the reverse process is called **demodulation.** Both conversions are made by a modem.

■ Two common methods of coordinating the sending and receiving of data are **asynchronous transmission** and **synchronous transmission.** Most transmission involving personal computers is asynchronous; this method, also known as the **start/stop** method, keeps groups of bits in step by including signals at the beginning and end of each group of bits. Synchronous transmission transmits

groups of bits in a continuous stream, which allows faster transmission.

■ **Half-duplex transmission** allows data to be transmitted in either direction, but only one way at a time. **Full-duplex transmission** allows transmission in both directions at once.

■ The speed at which data travels through communications links is measured in **bits per second,** or **bps.** This measurement is also known as the **bit rate,** or **baud rate.**

■ Any two computers exchanging information must be configured to follow the same data communications protocol. A **protocol** is a set of rules for exchanging information between a terminal and a computer or between two computers.

■ To communicate with each other, personal computers need to use a **communications program.** One type of communications program is **terminal emulation software,** which enables a personal computer to imitate a terminal. A **terminal** is a device used for communication with a computer. The **host** computer accepts as input the keystrokes you type on the "terminal." **File transfer software** programs enable you to **download** files from or **upload** files to another computer. **File transfer protocols** in the data communications software ensure that files are delivered error-free. Data communications programs that enable a computer to emulate a variety of standard types of terminals and to communicate using several standard file transfer

protocols is called **full-function data communications software.**

■ Computers that are connected so they can communicate among themselves are said to form a **network.** A **wide area network (WAN)** sends data over long distances by using the telephone system. A **local area network (LAN)** links computers in close proximity.

■ Personal computers attached to a LAN are often referred to as **workstations.** Each device in the network is known as a **node.**

■ The nodes on some LANs are connected by a shared **network cable.** A **cable interface unit** sends and receives signals on the network cable. A **network interface card** contains the electronic components needed to send and receive messages on the LAN. A **gateway** connects two dissimilar networks. A **bridge,** sometimes called a **router,** connects two LANs of the same type.

■ The physical layout of a LAN is called a **topology.** In a **star network,** the central computer—sometimes called a **server**—manages the LAN. Two other topologies are a **ring network** (in which the nodes are arranged in a ring) and a **bus network** (in which the nodes are connected to a main cable and each shares in network management).

■ **Ethernet** is one common type of LAN. A protocol called **Carrier Sense Multiple Access with Collision Detection (CSMA/CD)** controls access to Ethernet's network cable. IBM's **Token Ring Network** is another common type of LAN. The protocol for controlling access to the shared network cable is called **token passing.**

■ Two organizations that establish data communications standards are the **Consultative Committee on International Telegraphy and Telephone (CCITT)** and the **International Standards Organization (ISO).** The ISO developed the **Open Systems Interconnection (OSI)** reference model. Another communications standard is the **System Network Architecture (SNA)** developed by IBM.

■ A **protocol converter** lets you access a network that uses standards different from those used by your data communications program.

■ Some applications of data communications systems include **electronic mail,** or **e-mail; voice mail; computer conferencing; videoconferencing; teleconferencing; electronic fund transfers,** or **EFTs; information utilities; videotex;** and **bulletin board systems,** or **BBSs.**

■ A computer with a fax board can send documents and drawings to a **facsimile machine—fax—**or other personal computer with a fax board.

Review Questions

1. What are data communications systems?

2. What is distributed processing?

3. What hardware is needed to establish communications between geographically separated computers?

4. In addition to phone lines, what are some other common communications links?

5. What is the difference between a direct-connect modem and an acoustic coupler modem?

6. Define the following types of transmission: digital, analog, asynchronous, synchronous, half-duplex, full-duplex.

7. What is protocol, and why are protocol standards important?

8. What is terminal emulation software?

9. How does full-function data communications software differ from terminal emulation software?

10. Differentiate a WAN from a LAN.

11. List several advantages of a LAN.

12. What is a gateway? How is it different from a bridge?

13. Describe three common LAN topologies.

14. What are the two most common types of LANs?

15. How does token passing work?

16. Describe some practical applications of data communications systems.

17. What are some of the kinds of information available through information utilities?

18. Describe how a bulletin board works.

Networks to Train Olympic Athletes

The United States Olympic Committee (USOC) has always been eager to use technology in the ongoing attempt to trim seconds, add inches, bolster strength, and improve the techniques of America's athletes. The latest approach is a computer network to link USOC training centers with major universities. The network provides coaches with the latest developments in sports science and medicine all over the country.

Coaches and their athletes benefit from this computer network strategy in two ways: access to programs and access to information.

Consider the programs first. These programs are developed by researchers at the USOC Sports Science Program. Sport-specific computer programs can help analyze an athlete's performance. For example, one computer program analyzes body chemistry during practice or competition. The athlete wears what appears to be an oversized digital watch. This device is not, in fact, a watch, but a tiny radio receiver recording signals about metabolic activity from an electronic monitor taped to the athlete's chest. After a performance the wrist-receiver is removed and its data downloaded to a nearby laptop computer. In minutes the computer can produce a printout of the athlete's metabolism throughout the performance, including heart rate and blood pressure.

Other programs focus on psychological profiles to provide a summary of an athlete's mental skills in his or her sport. These programs can provide information about how athletes handle stress as they contemplate competition and then during competition. Information gathered from physiological studies can be combined with psychological data to provide a more thorough understanding of the relationship between mental and physical factors.

The other important aspect of the network is information sharing.

Coaches have 24-hours-a-day access to a national sports-science network that provides the results of nationwide research in sports science. Trainers can share all sorts of information, such as how to lie most aerodynamically during a downhill luge ride. Furthermore, they have access to a central database of leading-edge research in sports medicine. This research can have a measurable effect on an athlete's performance. For example, scientific testing and analysis of a runner of the 100-meter dash might help shave a tenth of a second off the runner's race time—enough to make the difference between a gold or a silver medal.

12 Desktop Publishing

Chapter Objectives

After reading this chapter you should be able to

- List the advantages of desktop publishing over word processing

- List the advantages of desktop publishing over traditional publishing methods

- Explain some fundamental publishing concepts and use the appropriate terms

- Describe how desktop publishing software works

- Describe the hardware needed to support desktop publishing

Would you like to be able to produce well-designed pages that combine elaborate charts and graphics with text and headlines in a variety of typefaces? Would you like to be able to do all this at your desk, without a ruler, pen, or paste? The technology that lets you do all this is here today, and it is called **desktop publishing,** or, sometimes, **electronic publishing.** With desktop publishing software, you can design sophisticated pages and, with a high-quality printer, print a professional-looking final document (Figure 12-1).

Until recently, people who wanted to publish had just two alternatives—the traditional publishing process or word processing. Both processes have significant disadvantages. Some recent versions of word processing packages offer desktop publishing features; however, serious desktop publishers prefer

Figure 12-1 Desktop publishing. *With desktop publishing software and a high-quality laser printer, you can create professional-looking newsletters and documents.*

WASHINGTON
NEWS & EDITORIAL

Insulock Comes To Market— Revolutionary Building Material

Canadian Insulock Corporation, whose stock symbol is CIK, started trading on the Vancouver stock exchange in March of this year. This company has acquired the international manufacturing and marketing rights to the polyurethane interlocking building block developed by the Insulock Corporation of Seattle. This block has been described by the builder of the first insulock house "as the biggest advance in the building industry in many years." It has also been predicted by Gordon Vary, past chairman of Architectural Department of University of Washington "as having the potential of revolutionizing the method of building throughout the civilized world."

A combination of expended resources, high interest rates and a U.S. building recession prevented the development of a market for the block. They joined forces with Canadian Insulock Corporation, which was incorporated on October 19, 1984, under the Companies Act of the Province of British Columbia.

The success of Canadian Insulock in developing a worldwide market for this product will benefit the shareholders of Insulock Corporation (USA), who own 32% of the Canadian company and receive a 5% royalty of net profits generated by the Canadian company. In an agreement signed

(Continued on page 10)

Mr. Market Timer— Flexible Money Management

Paul A. Merriman, recognizing the individual's need to provide for his or her own retirement in these critical times, organized Paul A. Merriman and Associates in 1983. This firm has devised a unique money management program that allows the small accounts to receive the same level of service as the large accounts. His program is adaptable to the needs of the aggressive investor as well as the very conservative one.

Clients' funds are invested in no-load mutual funds and money market funds. His market timing procedure, switching between equity and income funds, should greatly reduce risk on invested capital. Since he utilizes no-load funds, investments are not depleted by commissions. His management fees are modest even for the small investor, running only $25 per quarter or 2% per annum on the invested capital, and decrease when invested capital amounts to $100,000 or more to a low of 1% when the funds reach $500,000 plus. Organized in 1983, his business has grown to 2500 clients and money under management exceeds $30 million.

Mr. Merriman, a personable young man, after graduation from college in 1966 became the youngest broker ever approved to trade with a member of the New York Stock Ex-

(Continued on page 11)

SCW WASHINGTON NEWS & EDITORIAL is dedicated to being a unifying voice for local business and individual investors. Freedom and private enterprise are closely intertwined. Small business and personal initiative of the individual are the seeds of the free enterprise system that made our country great. We appreciate the support of those who share our goals.

In This Issue					
1	Insulock	8	Lumalure	14	Interesting People
1	Market Timer	10	S.B.C. Technologies	17	Speakeasy
3	News Briefs	12	Arsenic Process	22	Market Quotes
5	Akcho	13	Public Relations	23	Trading Post

the power of separate desktop publishing software. The development of desktop publishing offers a solution to the publishing problems of both large companies and individuals.

Consider the case of Kyle King, who works for a marketing communications company and wants to send a newsletter to his clients. He wants to use the newsletter to promote products, report company news, and let customers communicate. In the past Kyle tried to publish a newsletter by hiring conventional publishing services. But timing was a problem: By the time the newsletter was printed, the information was out of date. Futhermore, using outside help to produce the newsletter was expensive. Kyle also tried to produce the newsletter himself, using word processing software; but the result was an unprofessional-looking flyer.

With desktop publishing Kyle can produce a newsletter by himself that looks professional, without the cost and delay of going to outside services. Unlike word processing, desktop publishing gives the personal computer user the ability to do **page composition.** That is, Kyle can decide where he wants text and pictures on a page, what typefaces he wants to use, and what other design elements he wants to include. He can also insert graphics into the text. Desktop publishing fills the gap between word processing and professional typesetting (Figure 12-2, on the next page).

In this chapter we will present some publishing terminology and then discuss desktop publishing software and the hardware needed to support it.

The Publishing Process

Sometimes we take the quality appearance of the publications we read for granted. A great deal of activity goes on behind the scenes to prepare a document for publication. Writers, editors, designers, typesetters, and printers all contribute their knowledge and experience to complete a finished document. When you begin to plan your own publications, the many roles you must play and the amount of work involved in producing a publication will become apparent.

Figure 12-3 (on page 421) shows the main steps involved in publishing a newsletter. Desktop publishing makes it possible for the user to complete the editing, design, and production cycles by using a personal computer. Desktop publishing also eliminates the time-consuming measuring and cutting and pasting involved in traditional production techniques.

Figure 12-2 Word processing versus desktop publishing. A bland newsletter was changed into this interesting page with desktop publishing software.

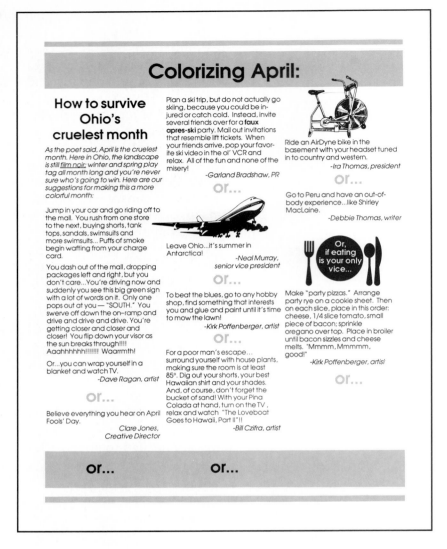

PRINCIPLES OF GOOD DESIGN

Desktop publishing programs put many different fonts and images at your disposal, but you can overwhelm a document if you crowd all of these onto a page. The guidelines that follow will help get favorable reviews for you and your document.

■ Do not use more than two or three typefaces in a document.

■ Be conservative: Limit the use of decorative or unusual typefaces.

■ Use different sizes and styles of one typeface to distinguish between different heading levels, rather than several different typefaces.

■ Avoid cluttering a document with fancy borders and symbols.

■ In your effort to fit everything on one page, do not use type that is too small to read easily.

The Art of Design

Word processors can generate lines of text that look like a typed page, but if you are producing a brochure or newsletter, a more sophisticated design is expected. One part of the design is **page layout**—how the text and pictures are arranged on the page. For example, magazine publishers have found that text organized in columns and separated by a solid vertical line is an effective page layout. If pictures are used, they must be inserted into the text. Their size might need to be adjusted so they will fit the page properly. In addition to page layout, designers must take into account such factors as headings,

Figure 12-3 The publishing process. Desktop publishing users can complete the editing, design, and production cycles with the help of their personal computers.

WRITING CYCLE

1. Write manuscript
2. Make preliminary illustration suggestions

EDITING CYCLE

1. Edit manuscript
2. Suggest illustrations
3. Copyedit manuscript
4. Prepare manuscript for production and design

DESIGN CYCLE

1. Estimate total length of manuscript
2. Design pages
3. Choose type
4. Design other page elements
5. Choose colors
6. Produce samples pages
7. Generate illustrations

PRODUCTION CYCLE

1. Typeset text
2. Proofread text
3. Place text on pages
4. Place illustrations on pages
5. Add finishing touches to prepare for printing

PRINTING CYCLE

1. Strip in halftones and four color separations
2. Make plates
3. Print documents
4. Bind document if necessary

type size, and typefaces. Are general headings used? Do separate sections or articles need their own subheadings? Does the size of the type need to be increased or decreased to fit a story into a predetermined space? What is the best typeface to use? Should there be more than one kind of typeface used on a page?

To help you understand how some of the decisions are made, we need to discuss some of the publishing terminology involved.

Typefaces: Sizes and Styles

The type that a printer uses is described by its size, typeface, weight, and style. **Type size** is measured by a standard system that uses points. A **point** equals about $\frac{1}{72}$ inch. Figure 12-4 shows type in different sizes.

The shape of the letters and numbers in a published document is determined by the typeface selected. A **typeface** is a set of characters—letters, numbers, and symbols—of the same design. Some common typefaces are shown in Figure 12-5. Notice that a typeface can be printed in a specific **weight**—

Helvetica (12 pt)

Helvetica (18 pt)

Helvetica (24 pt)

Helvetica (36 pt)

Helvetica (48 pt)

Figure 12-4 Different point sizes. *This figure shows a variety of different point sizes in the typeface called Helvetica.*

Helvetica:
ABCDEFGHIJKLMNOPQRSTUVWXYZ
abcdefghijklmnopqrstuvwxyz
abcdefghijklmnopqrstuvwxyz
abcdefghijklmnopqrstuvwxyz

Bodoni:
ABCDEFGHIJKLMNOPQRSTUVWXYZ
abcdefghijklmnopqrstuvwxyz
abcdefghijklmnopqrstuvwxyz
abcdefghijklmnopqrstuvwxyz

ITC Korinna:
ABCDEFGHIJKLMNOPQRSTUVWXYZ
abcdefghijklmnopqrstuvwxyz
abcdefghijklmnopqrstuvwxyz
abcdefghijklmnopqrstuvwxyz

Garamond:
ABCDEFGHIJKLMNOPQRSTUVWXYZ
abcdefghijklmnopqrstuvwxyz
abcdefghijklmnopqrstuvwxyz
abcdefghijklmnopqrstuvwxyz

Zapf Chancery Light:
ABCDEFGHIJKLMNOPQRSTUVWXYZ
abcdefghijklmnopqrstuvwxyz
abcdefghijklmnopqrstuvwxyz
abcdefghijklmnopqrstuvwxyz

Euro-stile:
ABCDEFGHIJKLMNOPQRSTUVWXYZ
abcdefghijklmnopqrstuvwxyz
abcdefghijklmnopqrstuvwxyz
abcdefghijklmnopqrstuvwxyz

Figure 12-5 Samples of typefaces. *Shown here are different weights and styles of typefaces. Notice that changing the weight or the style of a typeface can change its appearance.*

such as boldface, which is extra dark—or in a specific **style**—such as italic. These changes in typeface provide emphasis and variety. A **font** is a complete set of characters in a particular size, typeface, weight, and style.

As shown in Figure 12-6a, varying the size and style of the type used in a publication can improve the appearance of a page and draw attention to the most important sections. However, using too many different fonts or using clashing fonts can create a page that is unattractive and hard to read (Figure 12-6b). Use different fonts with discretion.

Most printers used in desktop publishing store a selection of fonts in a ROM chip in the printer. These are called the printer's **internal fonts.** Also, most desktop publishing programs provide a **font library** on disk. A font library contains a wide selection of type fonts called **soft fonts.** A soft font can be sent—downloaded—from the library disk in the computer's disk drive to the printer. Then the printer can print type in the new font.

Figure 12-6 Sample designs. *(a) This example uses complementary typefaces to produce a professional-looking document. (b) The same page created with clashing typefaces.*

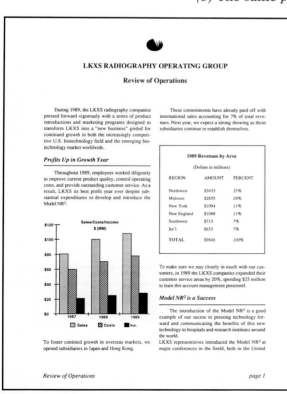

(a)

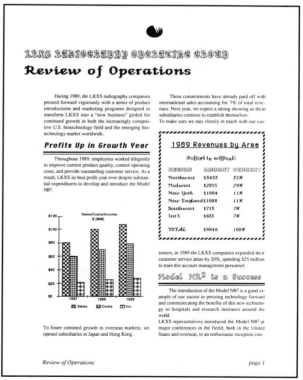

(b)

Leading and Kerning

Two terms you will encounter when you begin desktop-publishing are *leading* and *kerning*. **Leading** (pronounced "ledding") refers to the spacing between the lines of type on a page. Leading is measured vertically from the base of one line of type to the base of the line above it (Figure 12-7). Leading—just like type size—is measured in points. **Kerning** refers to adjusting the space between the characters in a line. In desktop software each font has a default kerning. Occasionally, you might want to change the kerning to improve the appearance of the final typeset work. An example of kerning is shown in Figure 12-8.

Figure 12-7 Leading.
Increasing the amount of leading between lines of type increases the amount of white space between lines.

Solid leading (9/9)

When I wrote the following pages, or rather the bulk of them, I lived alone, in the woods, a mile from any neighbor, in a house which I had built myself, on the shore of Walden Pond, in Concord, Massachusetts, and earned my living by the labor of my hands only.
—Henry David Thoreau

+1-point leading (9/10)

When I wrote the following pages, or rather the bulk of them, I lived alone, in the woods, a mile from any neighbor, in a house which I had built myself, on the shore of Walden Pond, in Concord, Massachusetts, and earned my living by the labor of my hands only.
—Henry David Thoreau

+2-point leading (9/11)

When I wrote the following pages, or rather the bulk of them, I lived alone, in the woods, a mile from any neighbor, in a house which I had built myself, on the shore of Walden Pond, in Concord, Massachusetts, and earned my living by the labor of my hands only.
—Henry David Thoreau

Figure 12-8 Kerning. (a) In this example, the space between the characters is not altered. (b) Kerning, or adjusting the space between the characters, can improve the overall appearance of the characters.

(a) Unkerned   AVANT GARDE

(b) Kerned   AVANT GARDE

Figure 12-9 Halftones.
Halftones consist of a series of dots. Reducing the size of the dots makes the resulting halftone clearer.

Halftones

Halftones, which resemble photographs, appear in newspapers, magazines, books, and desktop publishing documents. Halftones are representations made up of black dots printed on white paper. Different numbers and sizes of dots in a given space produce shades of gray. As you can see in Figure 12-9, the smaller the dot pattern used, the clearer the halftone. Most printers used in desktop publishing can produce halftones that meet professional standards.

Now let us put this publishing background to work by examining desktop publishing in more detail.

Desktop Publishing Software

Desktop publishing systems let users (1) create text and graphic images, (2) design the layout for each page of a publication and choose the fonts for the text, (3) move the text and images into the layout, and (4) print the result. You have already studied how to create text with a word processing program and how to create graphic images with a graphics program. The third and fourth steps are straightforward once you become familiar with the desktop publishing software package. It is the second step, the design of the pages, that is the heart of desktop publishing.

Imagine planning headlines not just in terms of what they say, but in terms of the size of the typeface and the spacing between the letters. Now try to decide just where a certain drawing should go, and how large it should be. Should the text be in columns? If so, how many columns and how wide? These are only some of the design issues to consider. But addressing these issues is easy with desktop publishing software; it lets you plan and change the page—right on your computer screen.

The software requirements for desktop publishing are

- A word processing program to create the text to be used in the publication

- A graphics program to create and use graphics for the publication

- A page composition program

The page composition program is the key ingredient of a desktop publishing system. Let us consider this program's design capabilities.

RANDOM BITS

The Macintosh Forever

The Apple Macintosh computer started out as a clever toy, overpriced and underpowered. Its superb graphics interface and ease of use, however, marked it as a machine that was user friendly. The Mac won instant friends in the home market and in some educational markets.

Business was another matter. Apple tried to promote the Macintosh as a serious contender in offices, but many corporations resisted the machine in favor of IBMs and IBM-compatible machines. But now the Mac is making inroads in such heavyweight companies as The Bank of America; Hughes Aircraft;

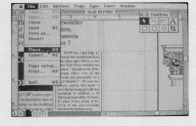

and the accounting firm of Peat, Marwick, Mitchell & Company.

Why the turnaround? There are several reasons, including expanded software selection, a versatile network to hook the Macs together, price cuts, and—finally—the option of compatibility with IBM. Another major incentive was low training costs; the

Mac is so easy to use that savings are substantial.

However, one of the most compelling reasons for the improvement in the Mac's fortunes is its particular suitability for desktop publishing. Using the Macintosh, desktop publishing software, and a laser printer, users could—for the first time—produce professional-looking, inexpensive documents with ease. Although other personal computers also offer desktop publishing, the Macintosh was first and, some say, the best. Desktop publishing is certain to remain a key factor in the continued success of the Macintosh.

Page composition programs, also called **page makeup programs** or **desktop publishing programs,** make it possible for you to design the layout of each page of a publication on the computer screen. Using these programs, you can determine the number and the width of the columns of text to be printed on the page. You can also indicate where pictures, charts, graphs, and headlines should be placed.

Page composition programs provide menus, as shown in Figure 12-10, that let you specify the fonts you want to use in your publication. These programs also let you adjust the default leading, if necessary, to fit a block of text that is a little too long or too short into a column of your page layout.

Once you have created the design for each page, the page composition program takes the text files created by your word processing program and the graphics you produced with your graphics program and inserts them into the page design that you have laid out. Page composition programs also let you move blocks of text and pictures around on your page. If you are not satisfied with the way the page looks, you can change the size of the type or the pictures or edit them.

Once the document is infused with words and graphics and in final design form, printing can be done in a variety of ways.

- If only a few copies of the finished work are needed, they can be printed on the computer's attached printer.

- To create several copies, a high-speed copier can be used to reproduce the original hard copy from the computer's printer.

Figure 12-10 A desktop publishing menu. Most desktop publishing software lets you choose typefaces, typestyles, and type sizes from a menu.

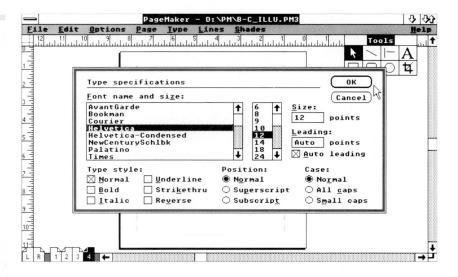

- If the highest-quality copies are required, the file created by the desktop system can be stored on disk and taken to a sophisticated typesetting system to produce typeset copy. This can then be professionally printed if a large number of copies are needed.

PageMaker from Aldus Corporation is a popular page composition program (Figure 12-11). PageMaker, like other page composition programs, pulls together information from files created by different programs, such as word processing or graphics programs, and places this information on one page. For this reason, PageMaker is usually used with a program from Microsoft Corporation called Windows. Windows lets the user integrate information stored in different types of files. Windows also contains its own word processor and graphics programs. Another powerful page composition program is Ventura Publisher from Xerox Corporation.

Some page composition programs offer **desktop publishing templates,** which are prepared page layouts stored on disk. Templates provide predesigned outlines that are then filled in with text and graphics. Designed by experienced professional designers to guide the novice desktop publisher, templates suggest page design elements such as headline placement, the number and width of text columns, the best fonts to use, and image placement.

Figure 12-11 Desktop publishing programs. *There are several popular desktop publishing programs on the market today. PageMaker is shown here.*

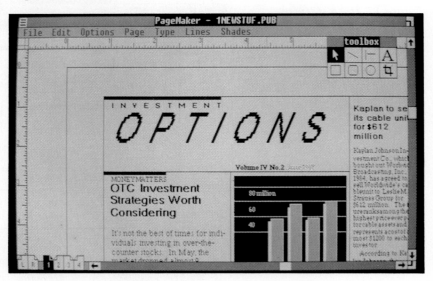

Figure 12-12 Clip art. *A variety of clip art software can be purchased and used to improve the appearance of a document.*

Page composition programs can also integrate *clip art*— images already produced by professional artists for public use— into your publication to enliven your text. You can purchase disks that contain various kinds of clip art. Figure 12-12 shows examples of the kinds of illustrations included in a clip art library.

Hardware for Desktop Publishing

Computer hardware in general was described in detail in prior chapters. The discussion that follows focuses on the special needs of desktop publishing.

Input Devices

The input devices used in desktop publishing are the keyboard and the mouse. A scanner may also be used for inputting. Text is entered by using the keyboard. A mouse is often used to make menu selections and to manipulate blocks of text and graphics on the screen. Existing text and graphics can be entered in the desktop publishing system by using a scanner.

Figure 12-13 A two-page display monitor. With a two-page display monitor, you can see two full pages side by side on a screen.
This can be very helpful if you are working on multiple-page
documents.

Monitors

For desktop publishing, the quality of the monitor is particularly important. The pages displayed on the screen must
be very clear, so you need a high-resolution monitor. Since
images are usually included in publications, you also need
graphics capability. If you use color in your publications, then
you need a color monitor. Some documents show an illustration across two pages; magazine advertisements are often laid
out in this way. A special monitor is needed for this type of
work so both pages can be seen side by side on the screen.
Figure 12-13 shows a two-page display monitor.

Printers

The quality of the printer is one of the most important
aspects of desktop publishing. Although most desktop publishing systems include either a laser printer or a high-quality

dot-matrix printer, the best desktop publishing printers must be capable of producing text that closely resembles the quality of professional typesetting. If you need clearer, sharper text, an alternative is to send the disk file produced by a page composition program to a typesetter designed with a special interface so it can print your file. In either case, you can get a printout that is **camera-ready**—that is, it can be photographed to make a plate for printing.

Printer Resolution. The characters and pictures that you are reading in this book (which was typeset) and other publications are actually made up of thousands of tiny dots. The smaller the dots that a device can print, the higher the *resolution.* The size and density of the dots is measured in dots per inch (dpi). The more dots per inch, the clearer and sharper the characters and graphics produced by the printer (Figure 12-14).

Typesetters can produce camera-ready originals at resolutions of 1200 to 2540 dots per inch. This level of resolution is called **typeset quality.** To approximate typeset quality, printers used in desktop publishing must be able to print text and graphics at resolutions of at least 300 dots per inch. Some laser printers can print at resolutions of 1200 dots per inch. The quality of resolution is a factor to consider, since research has shown that text printed at a higher resolution is more readable and understandable than text printed at a lower resolution.

Page Description Languages. Printers used for desktop publishing must have a **page description language (PDL)** embedded in a ROM chip. PDLs let a page composition program (such as PageMaker) tell the printer exactly how to use

Figure 12-14 Comparing dots per inch. *The higher the number of dots per inch (dpi), the greater the resolution of the text. Most laser printers have between 300 and 1200 dpi output.*

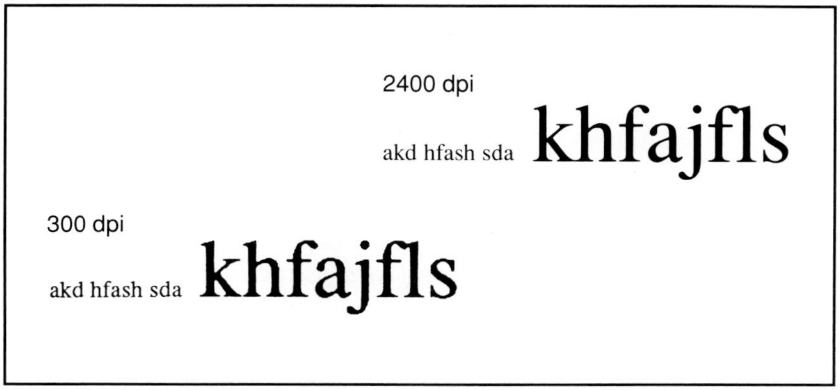

2400 dpi

akd hfash sda   khfajfls

300 dpi

akd hfash sda   khfajfls

NEWFONT 140

NEWFONT 144

NEWFONT 155

CREATE YOUR OWN FONTS

If you are using a page description language (PDL) such as PostScript, you can purchase programs that will let you create variations on the PDL fonts without spending months learning how to be a PDL programmer.

One such program, NewFont from Corel Systems, takes PostScript fonts and lets you add shadows or outlines. Using the simple menu, you can also change the proportion and density of the fonts and slant individual letters or make a line of type slope diagonally up or down the page.

fonts, type sizes, text, and graphics. That is, after you compose a page on the computer, the page composition program sends the correct instructions to the printer's PDL. Since your page composition program is what gives the PDL its instructions, you do not need to worry about learning the PDL yourself.

PostScript, a product of Adobe Systems, is the most common PDL used in printers for desktop publishing. PostScript is also the most common PDL used in typesetting machines. If a page designed with a page composition program is produced on a printer that uses PostScript, it can also be sent via disk to a typesetting machine that uses PostScript if typeset-quality resolution is desired.

Printer Speeds and Duty Cycles. In addition to the resolution of a printer and the PDL, the speed of the printer and its duty cycle are important for desktop publishing. For business use, desktop printers should have a print speed of at least eight pages a minute. The **duty cycle** is a measurement of ruggedness. To designate the recommended level of use for a printer, duty cycle is usually expressed in pages printed per month. A printer used for desktop publishing in most businesses should have a duty cycle of at least 4000 pages per month.

Desktop Publishing: The Payoff

The design, typesetting, and printing costs incurred by company publications are a major business expense. In fact, in American businesses, the cost of publications is second only to personnel costs. Many companies spend hundreds of thousands of dollars annually on publishing. Publications are a major expense for nonprofit organizations as well.

Most newsletters, advertising leaflets, technical manuals, and in-house business publications do not have to be of the finest quality. They can be designed, produced, and printed with desktop publishing. Even in cases where a large quantity of copies is needed and it is more practical to employ a professional printer, desktop publishing can still be used to design and produce the publication.

Because of their speed, flexibility, and output quality, desktop publishing systems can rapidly produce not only newsletters, forms, and technical documents but also letterheads with company logos and manuals with magazine-style layouts. Users value the time and money savings, but what they value even more is the control—the ability to see exactly how a change

in the type size or layout looks by observing the results immediately on a computer screen and to decide if the change is
appropriate. No more company newsletters filled with typos
and amateurish drawings—most offices are moving to the
greener pastures of desktop publishing.

More Software Coming Up

T hus far, each applications software chapter has featured a particular category of software. However, there are many other types of packages worth mentioning. We will examine an assortment of such software in the next chapter.

Summary and Key Terms

- Desktop publishing, or **electronic publishing,** helps people produce professional-looking, high-quality documents containing both text and graphics. Desktop publishing can save time and money and can give people better control over the final product.

- The publishing process includes editing, designing, producing, and printing.

- One part of the overall design of a document is **page layout**—how the text and pictures are arranged on the page. Adding type to a layout is called **page composition.**

- Printers offer a variety of type. Type is described by **type size, typeface, weight, and style.** Type size is measured by a standard system based on the **point.** A **font** is a complete set of characters in a particular size, typeface, weight, and style.

- Most printers used in desktop publishing contain

internal fonts stored in a ROM chip. Most desktop publishing programs provide a **font library** on disk. The font library contains a selection of type fonts called **soft fonts.**

- **Leading** refers to the spacing between the lines of type on a page. **Kerning** refers to adjusting the space between the characters in a line.

- A **halftone**—representations made up of dots—can be produced by desktop publishing printers.

- The software requirements for desktop publishing include a word processing program, a graphics program, and a page composition program. **Page composition programs,** also called **page makeup programs** or **desktop publishing programs,** enable the user to design the page layout.

- Some page composition programs offer **desktop publishing templates**—prepared page layouts stored on disk. Page composition programs may also let a user integrate clip art—prepared drawings—stored on disk.

- Input devices used in desktop publishing are the keyboard and the mouse. Scanners can also be used to input text and graphics.

- For the highest-quality publications, high-resolution monitors and printers should be used. Printer quality is particularly important if the user wishes to produce **camera-ready** printout.

- Printed characters and pictures are actually made up tiny dots. The smaller the dots printed, the higher the resolution. The size and density of the dots is measured in dots per inch (dpi). Resolutions of 1200 to 2540 dpi are called **typeset quality.**

- Printers used for desktop publishing must have a **page description language** (**PDL**) embedded in a ROM chip.

- In addition to the resolution of a printer and the PDL, the speed of the printer and its duty cycle are important. **Duty cycle** is expressed in pages printed per month.

Review Questions

1. What is desktop publishing?

2. What advantages does desktop publishing have over word processing?

3. What advantages does desktop publishing have over traditional publishing methods?

4. How is the size of type specified?

5. What is a typeface?

6. What is a font?

7. What are a printer's internal fonts? What are soft fonts?

8. What is meant by the term *leading*?

9. What is meant by the term *kerning*?

10. What are halftones?

11. What is a page composition program?

12. What are desktop publishing templates?

13. What is clip art?

14. What input and output hardware are needed for desktop publishing?

15. What is meant by the resolution of a printer?

16. What is the function of a page description language?

FROM THE REAL WORLD

Ten Desktop Publishing Projects

These brief portraits show the variety of applications for desktop publishing.

Annual reports Colorful charts and diagrams for the annual report of Great Northern Nekoosa Corporation, a paper manufacturer, are designed with Page-Maker software on the Macintosh computer.

Civic newsletters The Orange County Trust newsletter is produced with PageWriter software. One issue of the four-page newsletter takes the designer just four hours to create.

Consumer guidebooks *The Complete Car Cost Guide* is a guidebook exploring costs for new and used cars. The designer uses PageMaker to lay out the text and Adobe Illustrator to create icons. The graphs that make up much of the guide are created separately and then imported into the design.

Consumer pamphlets D.I.N. Publications creates an assortment of brochures, flyers, and posters on health-linked topics. The publications are created with PageMaker software. Various font styles and headline sizes are included in each brochure, along with eye-catching boldface and underlining techniques.

Corporate magazines The inside pages of *IN Magazine*, a publication for a

design and marketing communications firm, are designed with a desktop publishing package called XPress. This particular package was chosen for its ability to print around picture images: The expected image area is blocked out, and the text runs around the edges of the image.

Economic newsletters Metlife Capital Credit's *ECONOMIC Quarterly* is produced by using a combination of Excel, a spreadsheet package, and the desktop publishing software XPress.

Industry newspapers The American Electronics Association's trade association newspaper, *Update*, is produced with PageMaker.

Literary magazines Published in New York City, the magazine *Contemporaries* is created with the software package called Ventura Publisher. The magazine's publishers chose Ventura because it supports PostScript, a page description language that lets them produce fonts of various sizes.

Video tape catalogues The *Captain Video Catalog*, which lists 14,000 movies available from Captain Video, is produced with Ventura Publisher.

Viewer's updates The "Insider" section of *TV Guide* is produced with Superpage. This colorful section displays text, photographs, and illustrations.

13 Other Important Software Packages

Chapter Objectives

After reading this chapter you should be able to

- Describe the variety of personal computer software available

- Describe utility programs, desktop organizers, and keyboard enhancer programs

- Differentiate between integrated and stand-alone software

- Define the function of project management software

- Explain vertical market software

- Describe what an expert system is

Many personal computer users learn typical software applications. That is, they acquire skill with word processing software and probably some skill with spreadsheets, database management, and graphics software. The typical end-user may not need to know more. But for those who wish to explore further, a rich and varied software collection is in store.

This chapter is an introduction to some of the additional software you may wish to investigate. In most cases, no attempt is made to demonstrate how the software works. If you are interested in more detailed information, talk with vendors, explore your college computer lab, interview knowledgeable people at your workplace, or study product reviews in computer magazines.

Disk Utility Programs

D OS is a powerful operating system. However, some users need functions that are not included in DOS. **Disk utility programs** are designed to perform some of the tasks that DOS cannot.

There are a number of different types of disk utility programs. Let us begin by examining the software that might save your job or at least your files—file recovery software.

File Recovery Programs

Suppose you absentmindedly delete a file from a disk and then realize that you need it. DOS cannot *undelete* a file, but **file recovery software** can. When you delete a file from a disk, the file is not actually erased from the disk. Instead, DOS places a special mark in front of the name of the file in the disk's directory. This mark lets DOS know that it can store another file over the deleted file. Thus, if you delete a file but have not yet stored more files on the disk, the deleted file is removed from the directory but is still on the disk. A file recovery program removes the mark from the file name and makes it possible for you to access your file again.

Another type of file recovery program, called an **unformatting program,** lets you reconstruct the files on a hard disk even after the disk has been mistakenly reformatted.

File Consolidation Programs

If there are many files on a disk and you add and delete records in the files, parts of a file may be written in separate locations on the disk. This **file scattering** slows down your applications programs because they cannot read data quickly from the disk. A **file consolidation program** identifies scattered files and then groups these fragments into areas that can be read efficiently from the disk.

Hard-Disk Management Programs

Hard disks can hold hundreds of files, so programs that help DOS manage a hard disk are very useful. Although DOS lets you organize files into separate groupings called subdirectories, **hard-disk managers** make this organization apparent (Figure 13-1). For example, suppose that you have your word processing program and document files stored in one subdirectory, your spreadsheet program and its associated data files stored in a second subdirectory, and your database program and database files stored in a third subdirectory. When you start up your computer, the hard-disk manager displays a menu

Figure 13-1 Hard-disk manager. *Hard-disk manager programs, such as the one shown here, help you keep your files in order.*

showing these subdirectories. To access your spreadsheet program, you just select from the menu. Then when you list your spreadsheet files, you see only the files stored in that subdirectory. This feature is especially useful when you are searching for a file on a hard disk that holds thousands of files.

Other Utility Programs

Print spoolers are programs that let you print files without tying up the computer. They set aside an area of memory as a **buffer**—a temporary storage area—between the computer and the printer. When you issue a print command from an applications program, the data to be printed is stored in the buffer. Control of the computer is transferred back to you and your keyboard immediately. The print spooler works in the background to send the data stored in the buffer to the printer while you work on other projects.

RAM disks are programs that set aside an area of the computer's memory and treat it as a disk drive. This area of memory is assigned a disk drive name, such as drive D. The advantage of a RAM disk over an actual disk drive is that data can be read from and written to it much faster. Applications programs that read and write data to a disk frequently, such as a database management system, run much faster when used in conjunction with a RAM disk program. However, you need to remember to copy any information stored in the RAM disk to an actual disk if you want to store it permanently, since the RAM disk's contents are erased when the computer is turned off.

Keyboard Enhancement Programs

Keyboard **enhancement programs,** sometimes called **macro generators** or **keyboard processors,** can be used to modify some of the capabilities and functions of the keyboard. For example, if you think it is more convenient to use the Alt key as a Shift key, you can use a keyboard enhancement program to make the change.

The big payoff of keyboard enhancement programs is that you can use them to create keystroke macros, which are similar to the macros discussed in Chapter 7. By pressing a key or two, you can activate an entire series of previously stored keystrokes. For example, suppose you have to enter a long sequence of keystrokes to print an applications program file. By using a keyboard enhancer program to store the keystroke sequence, you can execute the keystrokes by pressing one key, such as the Num Lock key. Storing several such keystroke sequences eliminates much repetitive work.

Desktop Organizer Programs

If you work in an office, you probably have a set of tools on your desk that you use regularly: a calculator, a note-pad, a telephone directory, a calendar, a daily appointment schedule, and assorted scraps of paper with important notes. Furthermore, you may use the calculator, and then the note-book, and then the telephone—all in quick succession. In fact, you may even interrupt your work with one tool to switch to another.

Desktop organizer programs are designed to bring order out of the chaos of most desktops. Most desktop organizers include a calculator, a notepad (a mini word processor), a calendar and daily appointment book, a phone directory and dialer, and an alarm that you can set to remind you of important meetings during the day (Figure 13-2). Some of these programs also include a feature called a **clipboard,** which lets you transfer data between two different applications programs. Desktop organizers are

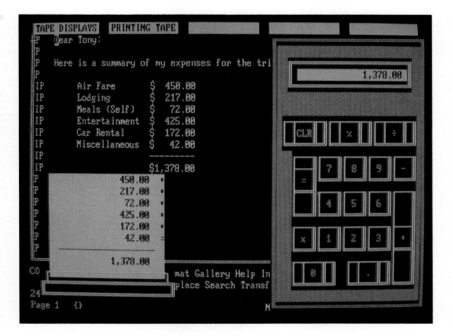

Figure 13-2 A desktop organizer. With a desktop organizer you can quickly access and use items such as calculators, address files, clocks, and calendars.

quite inexpensive, a factor that also contributes to their attractiveness to users. What is more, desktop organizer programs let you use these tools on your computer without leaving the application you are currently using. That is, you can use your desktop tools on an "interrupt basis," just as you might do without the computer.

Suppose you are working on a spreadsheet in Lotus 1-2-3 and receive a phone call to attend a meeting Thursday at 2:00 P.M. Press the keys to access the desktop organizer program, select the calendar option from the menu that appears on your screen (Figure 13-3), and enter the day and time of the meeting. Then, press the keys that instantly return you to the spreadsheet program. Similarly, if you are typing a report by using a word processing program and need to make a short calculation, access the desktop calculator to make the calculation and return instantly to the report.

Usually, desktop organizers are **memory-resident,** or **RAM-resident.** A memory-resident program is usually loaded into the computer's memory before you load an applications program such as Lotus 1-2-3 or WordPerfect. Used only on demand, the memory-resident program lurks in the background and is activated only when triggered by certain keystrokes. When activated, the program appears in a window on your screen, superimposed over the program you are currently using. In fact, it is said to pop up on the screen, an action that leads to the nickname **pop-up programs.**

Figure 13-3 A desktop calendar. You can take notes with this desktop organizer calendar without having to leave the applications program you are currently using. When you want to return to your project, simply press the appropriate keys.

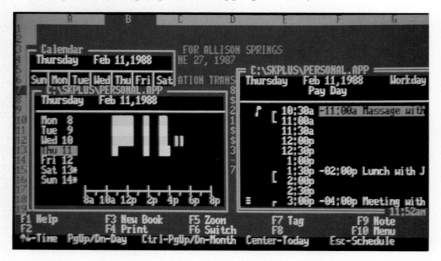

RANDOM BITS

Choosing a Software Package

We have said a lot about who is using what kind of software and even why they are using it. But exactly *what* are they using and how did they decide on that particular package? Some software brand names seem to be well established. But software is changing too frequently to be listed anywhere but in a weekly or monthly periodical.

For any given applications category there are literally dozens or even hundreds of products for sale. Which way should you turn? The following are some things you should keep in mind when making a selection:

Hardware If you already have a computer, hardware is your first limitation. That is, you can use only software that works on your machine. If you have an uncommon brand of computer, your software choices are significantly narrowed. If you have a popular brand, chances are there is a wide selection of software available.

Standards If you will be working with others, say, sending word-processed documents for their perusal, then your choice of a word processing package is constrained by their choice. You must choose to agree. Sometimes the process is even more straightforward: If you work for an organization with established software standards, you use the

package the organization has selected.

Recommendations Everyone has an opinion. In particular, trade journals make it their business to have opinions, offering elaborate rating systems and survey results. Salespeople in retail software stores also have opinions and are usually happy to share them. And do not forget your friends and colleagues.

Join the crowd Sometimes it is worth going with the most "popular" package just because at least you will share common ground with the majority of users. Many entrenched software packages stay that way, even when superior technology comes along. An established base, if it works adequately, is expensive to replace.

Integrated Programs

Most programs are **stand-alone programs**—that is, they perform only one task: word processing programs are used only for word processing, spreadsheet programs are used only for spreadsheets, and so on. People who need to switch back and forth between several types of programs waste time juggling disks and loading programs. In addition, most of the commands used to store, retrieve, and print data vary from program to program. Each time a new stand-alone program is used, the user must remember a new set of commands.

Thus, the concept of **integrated software,** an all-in-one package of programs, is very appealing. If your word processing, spreadsheet, database, graphics, and data communications programs are available in one common package, you can use menus to move from one application to another without having to exit one program, switch disks, and load the new program. Also, you do not have to learn five different commands for each basic task because the commands for each task are the same throughout the package.

Another advantage of integrated packages is that data transfer between programs in the package is fast and easy. For example, if you use an integrated package, a table of spreadsheet numbers can easily be moved into a word processing report. Similarly, graphs can be prepared by using the graphics program and then inserted into text prepared by using the word processing program. In contrast, if you use three stand-alone programs—a word processing program, a spreadsheet program, and a graphics program—you will find that moving data from one program to another ranges from complicated to impossible.

The advantages of integrated packages have created a user demand for these programs. Two different approaches have been taken by software developers to meet the demand:

- Include word processing, spreadsheet, graphics, and database capabilities in one program package (Figure 13-4).

- Offer a program that coordinates separate programs— that is, a program that integrates stand-alone programs by presenting a common interface to the user and handling data transfer between the programs. These coordinating programs are called **window managers.**

Despite their many advantages, sales of integrated packages have not skyrocketed. There are several reasons for this.

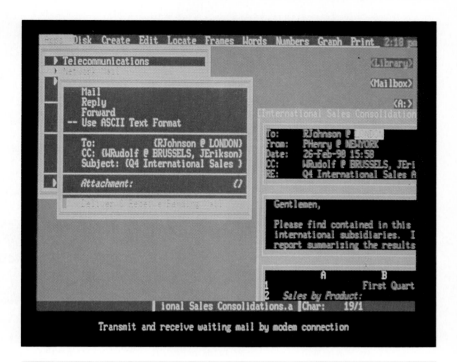

Figure 13-4 An integrated program. The integrated program shown here, Framework, has word processing, spreadsheet, database, graphics, and data communications capabilities in one package.

First, the individual functions (such as word processing or graphics) within an all-in-one package are usually not as strong as those in stand-alone packages. Integrated programs are similar to Swiss army knives that include can openers, saws, screwdrivers, and drills. The tools work, but they perform less well than a tool designed specifically for one job. Second, integrated packages are rather expensive, and you pay for all the functions in the package even if you really need only two or three. Finally, integrated packages require more computer memory and more disk space than one stand-alone program.

Window Manager Programs

As we have already noted, window managers integrate stand-alone applications programs. Also, they make it possible for users to display several different applications programs concurrently. Each application appears in a separate **window**—a rectangular area of the screen. Most window pro-

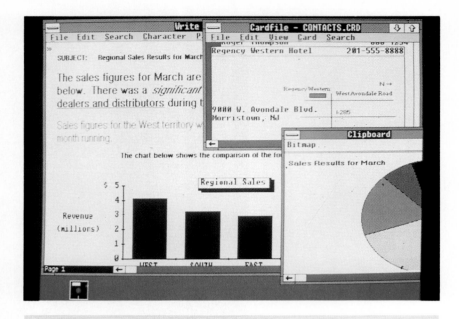

Figure 13-5 Window managers. *When you use window manager programs, each application appears in a separate rectangle on the screen. You can use the different programs by activating the appropriate window.*

grams actually execute only one applications program at a time. The window that contains the applications program currently being used is called the **active window,** or **current window.** When the user leaves a window, the program execution in that window stops and the execution in the next window selected begins (Figure 13-5).

By providing a standard visual interface between the user, DOS, and the applications program, window managers reduce the difficulties some people experience when using DOS or a new applications program. With many window managers, the mouse can be used to interface with the screen. Window managers also eliminate data file incompatibility between stand-alone programs. You can easily transfer data between an application such as Lotus 1-2-3 in one window and WordPerfect in another window.

Another feature of window managers is that they provide an extra layer between DOS and the applications program (Figure 13-6) by managing the execution of the individual applications programs. The applications programs use the same commands and function in the same way whether they are running in a window environment or running as a stand-alone program.

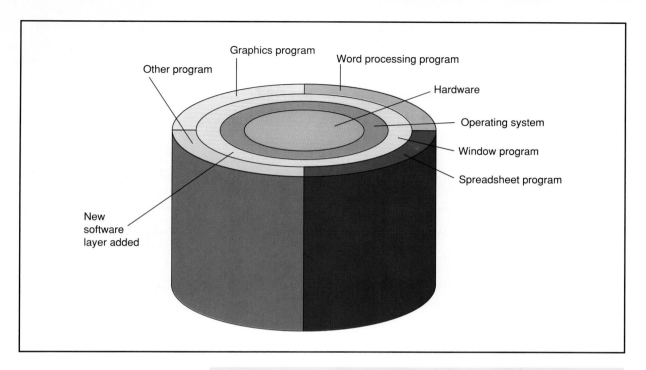

Figure 13-6 A conceptual diagram of a window program. *On the outside, closest to the user, are the applications programs. The window program acts as an extra layer between the applications programs and the operating system.*

Window managers usually come with built-in desktop organizer features, such as a notepad, calculator, and appointment book. Since window managers place an additional processing load on your computer, they work well only on personal computers with a lot of memory and hard-disk storage. Also, because the technology for window managers is relatively new, they can integrate only some of the many word processing, spreadsheet, and database programs that are available. Discuss the minimum recommended memory, disk storage, and compatibility with the vendor before purchasing a window program.

Project Management Software

Managing a project so it is completed on time and within budget is a difficult job that requires the coordination of many separate tasks. **Project management software** helps you schedule and track the progress of large projects.

Project management packages let you quickly and easily enter information on a project. You can then see when various portions of the job will be completed and which resources are being used on different tasks. These outputs can be seen graphically or in tables (Figure 13-7).

Figure 13-7 Project management software. *This type of software helps people plan projects by providing a graphic representation of a project's stages and schedule.*

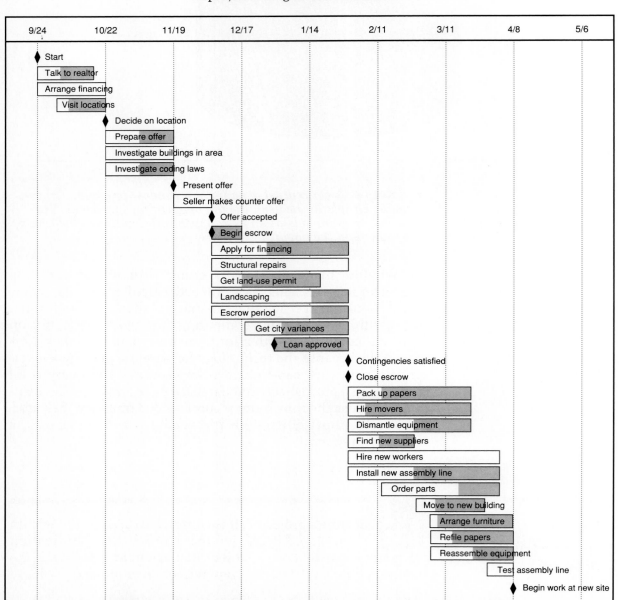

Like spreadsheets, project management software can also be used as a "What if . . ." tool to project the impact of delays or revisions or to try out plans on screen before implementing them. For example, you can determine how much overtime will be necessary to meet a deadline if one stage of the project slips by a week.

There are already over 300 project management packages available, ranging from inexpensive programs that display only the length of time each project task will take to programs that offer complex project planning and scheduling tools. Project management software has become a fundamental business tool. Any type of project—from construction, to manufacturing, to moving to new facilities—can be managed using this type of software.

Basic Project Management

Part of the success of a project depends on making optimal use of time and resources. Project management software helps you oversee complex projects effectively by

- Dividing the overall project into manageable tasks.

- Assigning resources (people, machines, materials) to each task. Many packages let you define resources in a table before assigning them to tasks (Figure 13-8).

- Reassigning resources to tasks as a situation changes.

Figure 13-8 Project management resource lists.
Many project management programs let you enter the necessary data in the form of a list or a table.

	Resource	Capacity	Unit Cost	Per	Days to Complete	Cost to Complete
1	Forecaster	No limit	0.00	Day	35.0	0.00
2	Production mngr.	No limit	0.00	Day	25.0	0.00
3	Recruiter	No limit	0.00	Day	17.0	0.00
4	WP operator	No limit	0.00	Day	7.5	0.00
5	WP equipment	No limit	0.00	Day	5.0	0.00
6	Production VP	No limit	0.00	Day	15.0	0.00
7	Prototype artist	No limit	0.00	Day	30.0	0.00
8	Graphic artist	No limit	0.00	Day	30.0	0.00
9						
10						
11						
12						
13						
14						
15						

Cost to Complete: 0.00   Total cost of project: 0.00

COMMAND: Activity Calendar Delete Edit Goto Help
                      Options Print Quit Transfer View
Select option or type command letter
RESOURCE   Microsoft Project: Spencer.RES

All resource capacities set to "No limit." Microsoft Project assumes resources are unlimited until you specify a limit.

For example, for a project designed to select an accounting software package, some of the tasks might be interviewing users, writing requirements, locating vendors, preparing a request for proposals, reviewing proposals, evaluating vendors, selecting a vendor, testing the system, and training the users. You can use the software to enter descriptions of the tasks and resources. Then the program creates graphics that represent project status and the flow of work. The graphics could be bar charts on a time line or PERT charts. **PERT charts** (PERT stands for program evaluation review technique) are excellent devices for visually depicting dependent relationships. For example, if a task cannot be accomplished until several earlier tasks are finished, each of those tasks is linked by a line to the subsequent task (Figure 13-9).

Once the project is underway, you might discover that one of the tasks cannot be completed on time or that certain resources cost more than originally expected. For example, perhaps a particular system will be available for testing only after a certain date. Or perhaps the person interviewing users gets sick and misses work for a week. You need to know how these changes will affect the rest of the schedule, and if the project can still be completed on time and within budget. Project management software lets you make these and other changes. Then it automatically recalculates the schedule and budget so you can view the resulting project status.

Figure 13-9 A PERT chart. PERT charts show the dependent relationships in a project. In this example the first script, set design, and shooting must be done before the story can be made. However, the set design and shooting can and should be done at the same time to maintain the most efficient schedule.

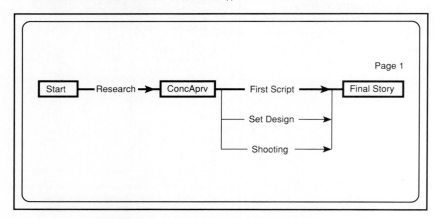

Time and Cost Projections

Most project management packages let you monitor both time and cost projections. You can use the software to display graphs to show completed, partially completed, and incomplete tasks. You can also try different scenarios to see which is the most efficient and least costly. For example, you might evaluate the effect of hiring more help during critical stages of the project, compare the costs and scheduling advantages of speeding up one phase of the project versus adding overtime later, or consider the advantages of doing jobs in-house as opposed to contracting them out.

Managing a project calendar is critical. You provide the starting date of the project or the end date when the project must be completed. Then the software uses calendars to monitor the time it takes to complete each task and creates a time line based on those projections. You can define a project calendar to account for normal workdays, vacations, and holidays (Figure 13-10). Some types of software even let you change the length of the workday.

Costs are also an important consideration. Many project management programs let you transfer project files to spreadsheets for a more detailed cost analysis. In addition, you can display or print project costs, usually with the help of graphics, and the printed summary can be especially useful. Typical costs include the cost of resources, cumulative costs over the life of a project, and a comparison of budgeted and actual expenses.

Figure 13-10 Creating a project calendar. *Many project management packages let you define a project calendar to account for normal workdays, vacations, and holidays. The calendar days can be turned "on" to indicate working days, or left blank to indicate nonworkdays.*

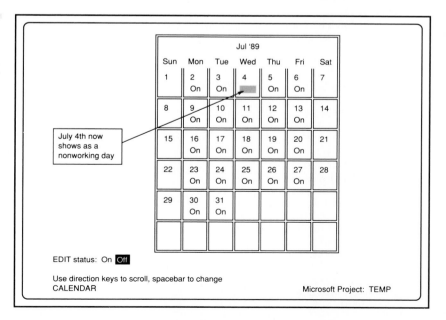

A successful project is usually the result of good planning based on solid information. With project management software you can increase the quality, quantity, and timeliness of the information you use to make decisions.

Vertical Market Software

SOFTWARE FOR THE BIG EIGHT

The Big Eight, as the primary accounting firms are known, provide excellent customer service. That means, of course, taking the client's software into account. Some samples:

Arthur Andersen & Company trains its consultants to be experts with the accounting, financial, and human resource software that their clients may wish to install. The training goes beyond learning to run the programs; consultants learn how to apply the software to a business setting. The company expects such service to improve the overall quality of consultant-client relationships.

Price Waterhouse has produced its own microcomputer software to help the firm's 10,000 auditors perform "What if . . ." analysis, lease accounting, and income tax calculations at client sites.

Peat, Marwick, Mitchell & Company developed its own microcomputer software for evaluating productivity at client sites. Typical clients are banks, insurance companies, and the government.

Throughout this book we have focused on general-purpose programs. For example, a database program can store any data, and a word processing program can create text about any subject. However, many businesses need software specifically designed for their type of work.

Much as a doctor may specialize in pediatrics or a lawyer in criminal law, software manufacturers may specialize in a particular industry or application. A group of similar customers, such as bankers or dentists or tax preparers, is called a **vertical market.** Many entrepreneurs have reaped rewards by creating software for vertical markets (Figure 13-11). Professionals are a particularly fertile market: There is software for accountants, dentists, doctors, and lawyers and even packages that combine professional interests, such as accounting software for doctors. Some specialists concentrate on the banking or insurance business. Others concentrate on small busi-

Figure 13-11 Vertical market software. *Software designed specifically for vertical markets—such as accountants, engineers, lawyers, and real estate agents—is becoming increasingly popular.*

nesses, writing programs to help service stations, travel agents, or cleaning services. Since these markets are specialized, users can expect to pay more for these programs. But the payoff is often hours of time saved on the job.

Statistical Packages

Statistics is the science of collecting, analyzing, and interpreting numerical data. In business, statistical analysis is a vital part of marketing research, economic forecasting, product research and development, and quality-control programs. Statistics are also widely used in engineering and in scientific research. **Statistical programs** are used to perform sophisticated statistical analyses on data and then to produce reports that organize the results of the analyses (Figure 13-12).

Statistical programs available on personal computers are usually scaled-down versions of programs originally written for large computers. If a corporation's mainframe computer is running the same statistical program as a personal computer, then portions of the corporate data can be downloaded for analysis on the personal computer. Thus, using personal computers makes the analyzed data more readily available to users.

Figure 13-12 Statistical packages. *Statistical programs are used to perform sophisticated statistical analyses and then to produce reports that organize the results of the analyses.*

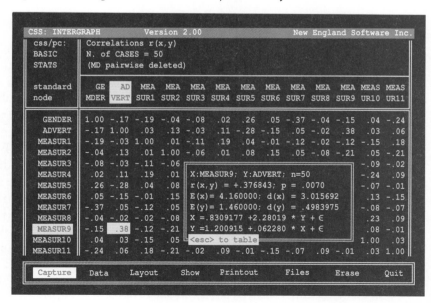

Expert Systems

An **expert system** is a software package containing an extensive set of organized data that permits the computer to serve as an expert on some topic. The user is the knowledge seeker, usually asking questions in a natural (English-like) language format. The expert system is the knowledge holder, responding to an inquiry about a problem with both an answer and an explanation of the answer. For example, presented with the legal question, "What will happen if the bill of particulars is not received before the adjourned deadline?" the expert system might respond, "Prepare a motion to dismiss the case." The expert system works by figuring out what the question means and then matching it against the facts and rules that it "knows." These facts and rules, which reside on disk, are originally generated by a human expert.

For years, expert systems were no more than a bold experiment, the exclusive property of the medical and scientific communities. Special programs could offer medical diagnoses, search for mineral deposits, or examine chemical compounds. But in the early 1980s these systems began to make their way into commercial applications.

Like any other business tool, an expert system is valuable only if it earns its keep. The high cost of an expert system can usually be justified in situations where there are few experts but great demand for knowledge. First, however, the expertise must be obtained from the expert, which is not an easy task.

Building an Expert System

Experts in a field often seem to have intuitive knowledge. They cannot explain why a particular course is right; they just "know" it. Consider the case of a clothing retailer who uses human credit experts to decide whether a customer's credit line can be extended to include the desired purchase. While the sales clerk waits on the phone, the credit expert keys in the customer's account number. By the time the customer's credit history prints out, the credit expert has reviewed the information and has made a yes/no decision. This is not a computer expert system—it is a human expert using customer information stored on computer files. The person who tries to figure out how human experts know what they know is sometimes called a **knowledge engineer.** A knowledge engineer gives

EXPERT SHOPPERS

Want to be an expert shopper and get the most for your money? Some people use an expert shopper's guide such as *Consumer Reports*, a magazine that compares and rates products. But now consumer experts have taken that approach one step further: Instead of scanning rows and columns of product ratings, you can use an expert system on a personal computer to narrow your choices.

An expert shopping system typically asks a variety of questions to determine your needs. For example, if you are in the market for running shoes, you might be asked questions about the anatomy of your feet, the terrain you run on, how long and how often you run, and your price range. The expert system then recommends products that meet your needs.

Some software manufacturers expect these systems to be in use in stores soon, but others caution that most consumers are not ready for electronic advice.

human experts progressively more difficult problems and reviews their responses to analyze the experts' decision-making processes.

Over the years knowledge engineers have found that an expert's intuitive knowledge is usually based on a set of rules. Once these rules are established, they can be included in an expert system program. However, other issues complicate the problem of building an expert system. Who is the expert? If there are several experts, do they agree? If not, whose information is used? How much expertise can be given to the computer, and at what point is human intervention appropriate?

Businesses may choose to build their own expert systems to perform well-focused tasks that can be crystallized into rules. However, very few people are capable of building an expert system from scratch. The sensible alternative is to buy an **expert shell**—software that has the basic structure to find answers to questions. Then, the buyer fills in information on the chosen subject.

The Expert Systems Market

Expert systems will eventually become commonplace in companies, just as personal computers did before them. Some expert systems are now available for personal computers. Currently, the main factor limiting the use of expert systems on personal computers is that the programs require a substantial amount of internal memory. A large amount of data—in the form of rules, facts, and source codes—must also be stored. Thus, hard disks must be used. Despite these obstacles, it seems likely that more expert systems designed for personal computers will appear in the near future.

We noted earlier that expert systems are often in a natural-language format. Some industry analysts feel that expert systems are beginning to mimic the analytic processes of humans—that is, coming close to artificial intelligence. For a computer to have **artificial intelligence,** it must be able to understand the facts it knows, create new thoughts, and engage in wide-ranging coherent conversations. By these standards expert systems today are very limited, since they have "intelligence" on only one given topic. However, in the future we may see expert systems that can communicate on many different levels.

File under Miscellaneous

We have presented people solving problems with conventional types of software. There are, however, many other software packages on the market. To complete the picture, here is a sampler of software that could be used in a business setting.

Begin with a handy software package that makes it easy to create mailing labels. Then add another type of software package that lets you create your own professional-looking office forms, without help from the company artist. Another program lets you design fancy fonts for everything from calendars to the invitation to the holiday office party. Still another helps you organize all your files on disk by name and type. Another software package lets you add temporary electronic notes to any computer file—the same sort of notes you write on yellow flags that stick to papers. A disk optimizer program takes your unseen disk files and rearranges them in an orderly, efficient fashion. Backup programs make extra copies of your disk files for safekeeping. A drafting program lets you make a floor plan of the office and rearrange it as you wish.

And, finally (if all else fails . . .), a job-search assistance program assembles your answers to questions into a resume, complete with a chronological list of accomplishments and career objectives.

Looking at the Big Picture

This book has been devoted to personal computer software. However, there are broader issues. Who is in charge of all the computers in a company? How is purchasing done? Is training available? Is there some master plan so that computer users can communicate with each other? There are many questions like these, and many answers. We will tackle both in the upcoming chapter.

Summary and Key Terms

- **Disk utility programs** perform some tasks that DOS cannot. **File recovery software** enables users to recover files they have deleted inadvertently. An **unformatting program** allows users to reconstruct hard-disk files that have been reformatted inadvertently.

- **File scattering** slows down applications programs. A **file consolidation program** finds scattered files and then groups the files more efficiently.

- **Hard-disk managers** are utility programs that clarify the organization of files on the hard disk.

- **Print spoolers** are programs that let you print files without tying up the computer. They set aside an area of memory as a **buffer** between the computer and the printer.

- **RAM disks** are programs that set aside an area of the computer's memory and treat it as a disk drive.

- **Keyboard enhancement programs,** also called **macro generators** or **keyboard processors,** can be used to modify some of the keyboard assignments and to save keystrokes.

- Most **desktop organizer programs** include a calculator, a notepad, a calendar and daily appointment schedule, a phone directory and dialer, and an alarm. Some of these programs also include a **clipboard,** which allows you to transfer data between two different applications programs. Desktop organizers are usually **memory-resident,** or **RAM-resident.** Memory-resident programs are often called **pop-up programs.**

- Most programs are **stand-alone programs,** performing only one task. **Integrated software** packages provide users with different programs that work together by using the same set of commands.

- **Window manager programs** integrate and coordinate stand-alone programs. They allow users to display several different applications programs at the same time, displaying each application in a separate **window.** The window containing the application currently being used is the **active window,** or **current window.**

- **Project management software** helps users schedule and track the progress of large projects. The program creates graphs to show project status and flow of work and **PERT charts** to depict the dependent relationships between tasks.

- **Vertical market software** focuses on the needs of a particular industry or application or group of similar customers.

- With **statistical programs,** users can perform statistical data analyses and produce reports that organize the results of the analyses.

- An **expert system** is a software package that presents the computer as an expert on a particular topic. A **knowledge engineer** analyzes the knowledge of a human expert to build an expert system. If a business wants to build its own expert system, it may buy an **expert shell.**

- **Artificial intelligence** is a computer's ability to understand known facts, create new thoughts, and engage in wide-ranging coherent conversations.

Review Questions

1. What is a disk utility program?

2. Describe some of the different types of disk utility programs.

3. What does a keyboard enhancement program let you do?

4. What functions are typically found in desktop organizer packages?

5. What is meant by the term *pop-up program*?

6. What is an integrated program?

7. How is an integrated program different from a stand-alone program?

8. Describe some of the features of window manager programs.

9. What is meant by the term *active window*?

10. Describe how project management software helps a user oversee a project more effectively.

11. What are PERT charts?

12. What is meant by the term *vertical market software*?

13. What are statistical programs used for?

14. What is an expert system?

15. What does a knowledge engineer do?

Egghead Software

Where will you buy your software? Through a consultant? A local software distributor? A retail personal computer store? A retail software store? Mail order? There are numerous possibilities. The most dazzling software-selling success, however, is Egghead Software, a retail chain established in 1984 "for people who don't know a microchip from a potato chip." As its zany name suggests, Egghead does not do anything in the usual way.

The "usual way" was to refuse demonstrations of software packages that were for sale. In fact, this approach is exactly what propelled Egghead founder Victor Alhadeff to action. As a computer novice, he had tried to purchase some software for his son's computer. He was surprised that he could not give the software a test drive and even more surprised that the salespeople seemed to speak only computer jargon.

Alhadeff changed all that. Each Egghead store, whether in Chicago or San Francisco, has four personal computers in the store for demonstration purposes. In addition, a try-before-you-buy slogan encourages customers to browse through manuals and then sit down and plink at the keyboard while considering a software purchase. Egghead personnel are required to learn at least one new software package per week, a fact that makes them knowl-

edgeable demonstrators. The ongoing training for employees includes encouragement to speak straightforward English to customers. Egghead's knowledgeable staff has a genuine interest in helping customers.

Egghead bills itself as a discount software store, offering 10–50% discounts on all their merchandise. But the key to success has proved to be not price but service. Service begins with a huge inventory for users to peruse. Furthermore, Egghead is willing to special-order software at a customer's request. A customer can return a software package within two weeks for a complete refund, no questions asked. Other service options include training (Egghead University for Eggsecutives), a newsletter, a 1-800-EGGHEAD order

desk, and exhibitions (Eggzibitions) in convention halls so that users can talk directly to vendors about the software they manufacture.

The complete formula, in summary, is demonstrations, knowledgeable salespeople, discount prices, and a large inventory. The formula has paid off. Egghead now has more than 100 stores and is opening about six new stores per month. Furthermore, Egghead now has a sales force that sells directly to such big-ticket customers as Boeing and IBM.

Egghead was founded to serve software customers, but it also serves another constituency: software makers. Producers from Microsoft to the lone software entrepreneur want their software in an Egghead store.

14 Personal Computer Issues

Chapter Objectives

After reading this chapter you should be able to

- Explain the significance of personal computing

- Describe the broad issues related to the use of personal computers in business, including the management of personal computers and related resources

- State the reasons why training is needed on personal computers—especially hands-on training

- Define the term *ergonomics*

- Explain why computer security is important

Consider the beginning of Joanna Tripp's workday. Joanna is construction coordinator for Wilhite Construction. When she arrives at work, she turns on her microcomputer, which is part of a network of office computers. Her screen lists a menu of options (Figure 14-1). Joanna selects Today's calendar, and the screen displays the message "10:30 AM—Fremont project, materials shortages meeting." She needs to ask the supplier to bring recent materials lists to this meeting, so she uses her word processing program to compose a quick memo. Then she sends it to the supplier via electronic mail.

Next, Joanna chooses Read mail from the menu. The screen displays a list of three memos, two letters, and a report—all sent to her electronically. Joanna scans the mail list and decides that a memo from Tony Palmer about a possible labor strike of masonry workers needs immediate attention. She displays the memo on the screen and stores the other mail to read later. Joanna uses her voice mail system to try to contact Tony. When he does not answer, she dictates a voice mail message for him (Figure 14-2).

Then Joanna turns to the computer files for the Fremont project. First, she uses a spreadsheet to see how the materials shortage—and the possible high replacement prices—may impact the project costs. Next she uses another spreadsheet to predict the effect of a potential strike on the project's schedule.

Figure 14-1 An office network system. *When Joanna Tripp arrives at work each morning, she can use her personal computer, which is linked to other computers in the office, to choose from a variety of tasks.*

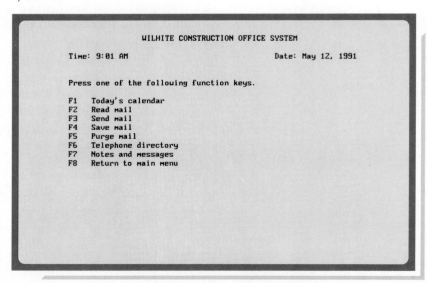

```
              WILHITE CONSTRUCTION OFFICE SYSTEM

    Time: 9:01 AM                        Date: May 12, 1991


    Press one of the following function keys.

    F1    Today's calendar
    F2    Read mail
    F3    Send mail
    F4    Save mail
    F5    Purge mail
    F6    Telephone directory
    F7    Notes and messages
    F8    Return to main menu
```

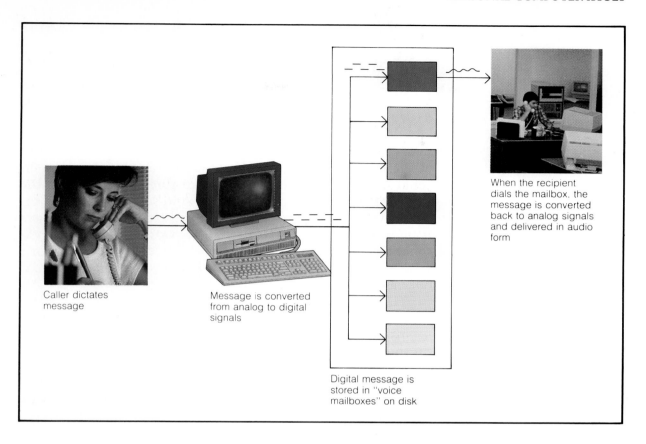

Caller dictates
message

Message is converted
from analog to digital
signals

Digital message is
stored in "voice
mailboxes" on disk

When the recipient
dials the mailbox, the
message is converted
back to analog signals
and delivered in audio
form

Figure 14-2 A voice mail system. *Joanna's message is stored in Tony's voice mailbox on disk. Later, Tony can check his mailbox and get the message.*

Less than an hour has passed since Joanna walked into her office, but she has already accomplished work that might have required an entire morning if done manually. She uses the computer as casually as she does the phone or copy machine. Joanna's workday is not atypical. You can also expect to use a personal computer and its related software if you work in an office.

Personal computing has become a significant force in business computing. We have already noted the many uses for a personal computer in the office, ranging from word processing to desktop publishing. However, we have not yet examined the issues involved in incorporating personal computers into a business. In this chapter we will address some of the issues involved, from buying personal computers to training employees to use them.

Managing Personal Computers

When personal computers burst on the business scene in the early 1980s, there was little warning and less planning. The experience of the company Joanna Tripp works for is typical. One day a personal computer appeared on the desk of an engineer who had brought his computer in from home. Then two company accountants bought a pair of machines; they had squeezed the money for the purchase out of the overhead budget. The personnel manager bought personal computers for herself and her three assistants in the company's far-flung branch offices. And so it went, with personal computers popping up all over the company. Managers realized that the reason for runaway purchases was that personal computers were so affordable. Since most departments could pay for them out of existing budgets, the purchasers did not have to ask anyone's permission.

There were no provisions for managing the purchase or use of personal computers. On the other hand, there were no rules *against* them. Pioneer users, noting increased productivity, had no trouble justifying their purchases. As users mastered personal computer software, they felt self-reliant, free from the computer professionals on whom they had long been dependent.

Managers, however, soon were faced with several problems. The first was incompatibility. The new computers came in an assortment of brands and models. Software that worked on one machine did not necessarily work on another. Second, users were not as independent of the computer professionals as they had thought; they needed assistance in a variety of ways. Finally, no one person was in charge of the headlong plunge into personal computers. Many organizations solved these management problems in the following ways:

- The compatibility problem was addressed by acquisition policies.

- The assistance problem was handled through information centers.

- The problem of lack of management was solved by creating a new position—the microcomputer manager.

Let us examine each of these solutions.

Microcomputer Acquisition

In a business environment managers know they must control the acquisition and use of personal computers. As we have noted, workers purchased personal computers before any company or office policies had been set. The resulting compatibility problems meant that employees could not communicate easily or share data between computers. Consider this example: A user's budget process may need certain data that resides in the files of another worker's personal computer, or perhaps the required data is the output yielded by combining figures from the second and third computers. If the software and hardware these people use do not mesh, compatibility becomes a major problem.

In many companies the computer professionals, often in the **Management Information Systems** (**MIS**) department (Figure 14-3), have taken control of personal computer acquisition. Their methods vary but often include the following:

- **Standards.** Most companies now have established standards for personal computers, for the software that will run on them, and for data communications. Users can still buy what they want, but they must conform to the standards if they want to tie into corporate resources. For

Figure 14-3 MIS function. *In some companies the Management Information Systems (MIS) department monitors the use of personal computers in the company.*

example, if IBM PC architecture is the standard, then any IBM PC-compatible machine is acceptable.

- **Limited vendors.** Some companies limit the number of hardware and software vendors (sellers) from whom they allow purchases. It is usually impossible to prevent multiple-vendor situations, but MIS managers have discovered that users are satisfied with a small number of vendors from which to select.

- **Limited support.** MIS departments generally control a company's purchases by specifying which hardware and software they will support in the form of technical assistance and training.

As you can see, these methods overlap. But all of them, in one form or another, give the MIS department control. In other words, users are being told, "If you want to do it some other way, then you're on your own."

The Information Center

If personal computer users compared notes, they would probably find that their experiences are similar. Budget Analyst Gwen Price is typical. She convinced her boss to let her have her own personal computer so she could analyze financial data. She purchased a popular spreadsheet program and, with some help from her colleagues, learned to use it. Soon she thought about branching out in other areas. She wanted a statistics software package but was not sure which one was appropriate. She thought it would be useful to have a modem but did not feel she was equipped to make a hardware decision. Most of all, she felt her productivity would increase significantly if she could get her hands on the data in the corporate data files.

The company information center is the MIS solution to these kinds of needs. A typical **information center** gives users support for the user's own equipment. The information center is devoted exclusively to giving immediate user assistance, with little or no red tape.

Information center services often include the following:

- **Software selection.** Members of the information center staff help users determine which software packages suit their needs.

Figure 14-4 Computer information centers. Information centers often provide training. Shown here, employees learn how to create reports by using an integrated program.

- **Data access.** If appropriate, the staff members help users get data from the large corporate computer systems to be used on the users' own computers.

- **Training.** Education is a principal reason for an information center. Classes are usually small, frequent, and on a variety of topics (Figure 14-4).

- **Technical assistance.** Information center staff members stand ready to assist in any way possible, short of actually doing the users' work for them. Their help includes advising on hardware purchases, assisting with the selection and use of software, finding errors, helping users submit formal requests to the MIS department, and so forth.

To be successful, the information center must be placed in an easily accessible location. The center should be equipped with personal computers and terminals, a stockpile of software packages, and perhaps a library. It should be staffed with people who have a technical background but who can explain topics in plain English. Their mandate is "The user comes first."

The Microcomputer Manager

The more personal computers move into the general worker population, the more corporate accountability becomes a factor. When a large company starts spending millions of dollars on personal computers, its top-level managers want to know where all this money is going. The company's auditors begin worrying about data security. The company's legal department begins worrying about workers illegally copying software. Soon, everyone is involved, and it is clear that someone must be responsible for personal computer use throughout the company. That person is the **microcomputer manager.**

There are four key areas that need the attention of the microcomputer manager:

- **Technology overload.** The microcomputer manager must maintain a clear vision of the company goals, so that users are not overwhelmed by the massive and conflicting claims of aggressive vendors plying their wares. Users overwhelmed by phrases like "network topologies" or "file gateways" or served a jumble of acronyms can turn to the micro manager for guidance with their purchases.

- **Cost control.** Many people who work with personal computers believe the initial costs are paid back rapidly and that this "fact" should satisfy managers who hound them about expenses. However, the real costs of a personal computer entail training, support, hardware and software extras, and communication networks—much more than just the initial hardware. The micro manager's role includes monitoring these expenses.

RANDOM BITS

A Glossary for Computer Crooks

Although the chapter emphasizes helping you keep your hardware, software, and data safe, it is useful to understand the terms associated with computer criminals. Many of these words or phrases have made their way into the general vocabulary.

Data diddling Changing data before or as it enters the computer system.

Data leakage Removing copies of data from the system without a trace.

Logic bomb Sabotage delivered in a program that will trigger damage based on certain conditions; usually set for a later date—perhaps after the perpetrator has left the company.

Piggybacking Using another person's identification code or using that person's data files before he or she has logged off.

Salami technique Using a financial system to squirrel away small "slices" of money that may never be missed.

Scavenging Physically searching trash cans for printouts and carbons containing not-for-distribution information.

Trap door An illicit program left within a completed program, allowing unauthorized—and unknown—entry.

Trojan horse Covert illegal instructions placed in the middle of a legitimate program.

Zapping Bypassing all security systems with an illicitly acquired software package.

- **Data security and integrity.** Access to corporate data is a touchy issue. Many personal computer users find they want to download data from the corporate mainframe to their own computers and this presents an array of problems. Are they entitled to see the data? Might they manipulate the data in new ways and then present it as the official version? Might they expect MIS to take the data back after they have toyed with it? The answers to these perplexing questions are not always clear, but at least the microcomputer manager will be aware of the issues.

- **Computer junkies.** And what about employees who are feverish with the new power and freedom of the computer? In school, these user-abusers are called hackers, but on the job they are often called computer junkies because of the addictive nature of their fascination with the computer. Unable to resist the allure of the machine, they overuse it, neglecting their other work. Microcomputer managers usually respond to this problem by establishing guidelines for computer use.

The person selected to be the microcomputer manager is usually from the MIS department. Ideally, this person has a broad technical background, understands both the potential and the limitations of personal computers, and works well with a diverse group of users.

Training was mentioned briefly in the discussion on the information center. This topic is of keen interest to both managers and users and deserves its own section.

Training

Users do need training. Consider this example: An employee at a boat company came across an unattended personal computer that had been "left on." Thinking perhaps of an unwatched television set wasting electricity, he turned it off. This was a serious mistake, because the computer was in the middle of updating the company's accounts receivable files. The files were in disarray for almost two weeks, and it took a computer professional to untangle the mess. Although we often think of training as learning how to use the computer, training also includes learning not to leave an active computer unattended and learning how to avoid interfering with computer processing.

SOFTWARE FOR THE REST OF US

User friendly. Easy to use. As easy to use as a toaster. These are some of the phrases—and exaggerations—used about personal computer software. But software manufacturers know better. They hire ordinary people—nontechies—to test their software.

One famous story features a confused woman who did not know how to use the mouse that came with the software. She tried running it across the screen and then down the leg of the table. In desperation, she turned the computer off and started over. Experiences like this remind software manufacturers how complicated it all is.

In response to such "usability" tests with consumers, software manufacturers have simplified and expanded software manuals and offered improved tutorial diskettes with the software.

A more significant problem, however, is the investment that companies make for hardware and software that remain unused—or, at least, not used to their full potential—because employees have not been trained to use them.

Who will do the training? In-house training is fairly common and often works out well, especially if sponsored by an established organization such as the information center. Another approach is to use vendor training. Sometimes this training is included in the price of the software. Another option is setting up classes for employees at a local community college that offers training on a variety of software packages for a nominal fee (Figure 14-5). If the number of user trainees is very large, it may be appropriate to train a group of people who will then instruct their colleagues on the job in their own office environment.

The traditional training tool is user documentation (Figure 14-6). But documentation is only the beginning. A company may have its own training center equipped with terminals, modems, personal computers, printers, and other equipment. The final training ingredient is software, either the actual software or a tutorial. Personal computer software often comes with a **tutorial,** a training package on disk that can be used interactively right on the computer.

If personal computer users are to gain skills and confidence, then their training must give them practice in the skills

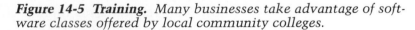

Figure 14-5 Training. *Many businesses take advantage of software classes offered by local community colleges.*

Figure 14-6 Documentation.
Clear, easy-to-follow documentation is an essential training tool.

that build their confidence. Documentation for users is important but not sufficient by itself. People need lots of practice.

What do users need to know? First, they need to know how to do some very basic tasks. For example, if someone is using word processing software, he or she first needs to know how to enter, save, and print a document. The next task is making simple changes to the document. Later, the user can attempt more complex tasks such as searching and replacing and moving blocks of text. Eventually, users who need more unusual tools, such as outline programs, can add these to their repertoire.

When people are first learning how to use a computer, they need a series of achievable goals to build their confidence. Eventually, users can reach the final goal—that of knowledgeably using new software.

In addition, users need to know how to install the software on their own systems. Furthermore, they need to understand the differences between versions of the software and to have a clear understanding of copy protection as it relates to the software they are using. Finally, they need to know how to get assistance when they need it.

Next let us consider the physical comfort of personal computer users. The subject, often touted in the press, is called ergonomics.

Ergonomics: The Person/Computer Connection

Ergonomics is the study of human factors, primarily physical, in the design of workplaces. The human body is not designed for repetitive work; eventually, physical problems may arise from it—headaches, dizziness, back problems, a stiff neck, blurred vision, and aching wrists. To minimize these ill effects, workstations and jobs should be designed ergonomically—that is, to fit the person rather than the environment.

Companies can apply ergonomic principles to computer workstations in numerous ways: They can minimize monitor glare by providing high-resolution screens, glare guards, and tilting monitor stands; they can provide chairs that have greater back support; they can place computers at a level that increases wrist support; and they can allow users to alternate computing with other duties (Figure 14-7, on the next page).

If ergonomic concerns are addressed, job satisfaction and productivity should increase, while fatigue and errors should decrease. Managers are very interested in ergonomically designed machines, and many manufacturers are careful to use

Figure 14-7 An ergonomically designed work area. Ergonomically *designed work areas, such as the one shown here, help reduce physical problems workers may develop on the job.*

the word *ergonomic* in their advertisements because it suggests a personal computer that is desirable.

Most people are too busy using their personal computers to worry about the computer's security. But the issue is important. In the next section we will discuss computer security.

Security

One summer evening, two men wearing coveralls with company logos backed a truck up to a building that housed a university computer lab. They showed the lab assistant, a part-time student, authorization to move 23 personal computers to another lab on campus. The assistant was surprised but reasoned that the move was probably justified since

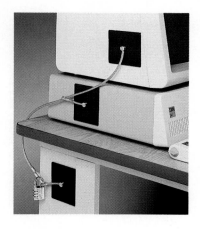

Figure 14-8 Hardware security. *Locking up disk drives, keyboards, and other pieces of computer hardware can help minimize theft.*

lab use was light during the summer quarter. The computers were moved, but not to another lab. After this incident, all the computers on campus were locked in place (Figure 14-8).

As this example indicates, personal computer security breaches can be pretty basic. There is a large and active market for stolen personal computers and their internal components. However, the loss of hardware, though not insignificant, is not a major problem in itself, since hardware loss is usually covered by insurance and the hardware can be replaced. The more significant problems involve damage to software and data.

Software Security

Software security has been an industry concern for years. Many questions have been raised, such as the ownership of programs. What is to prevent a programmer from taking listings of programs from one job to another? Is the owner the person who wrote the program or the company for which the program was written? And what can we do to protect software from being stolen or copied?

Unfortunately, very little can be done to prevent the stealing of microcomputer software. There are some legitimate reasons for copying software: After paying several hundred dollars for a program, you definitely want to make a backup copy in case of disk failure or accident; you might want to copy the program onto a hard-disk drive and use it more conveniently from there, or you might want to have one copy at the office and another to use at home. Software publishers have no quarrel with any of these reasons for copying software. But, thousands of computer users copy software for another reason—to get the program without paying for it.

And therein lies the problem. For years, software publishers placed copy protection on their software—a software or hardware roadblock to prevent pirated copies. But legitimate owners argued that it is unfair to restrict customers who pay just to outsmart a few thieves. As a result, many owners boycott programs with copy protection. Recently, many manufacturers have omitted copy protection, but they have still sued culprits, especially large companies, for copyright infringement. Despite all the manufacturer's efforts and despite copyright laws, software continues to be copied as blatantly as music from tape to tape. However, as a software user, you should remember that copying software *is* stealing, and you should respect the rights of software publishers.

RANDOM BITS

Computer Viruses and Vaccines

A computer with a disease? No, not really. A computer "virus" is actually a computer program that can destroy programs and data or interfere with processing. In addition, a virus is contagious; that is, it can be transmitted from disk to disk and computer to computer. Many viruses reside on popular public domain or shareware programs offered on public bulletin boards. These viruses, a form of computer crime, represent a clear and present danger to the programs and data stored on your computer's disks.

How Computer Viruses Work

Virus programs have taken many forms; however, the following is a typical example: A programmer secretly inserts a few unauthorized instructions in a personal computer program. When the program is downloaded from a bulletin board, the illicit instructions lie dormant until the disk with the infected program is used. Then the virus inserts the instructions into hidden files of the operating system. When a command, such as COPY or DIR, is used, the virus copies itself onto other disks in the system. Since the virus is hidden from the user, it can spread from disk to disk and the process can be repeated again and again. In fact, each newly infected disk becomes a virus carrier.

With the most debilitating viruses, the virus instructions increment a counter each time the virus is copied to another disk. When the counter reaches a certain number, such as 4, the virus erases all data files. But this is not the end of the destruction, of course; three other disks already have been infected. Other viruses reformat hard disks, corrupt data files, or cause constant annoying small problems. Although most viruses are destructive, some are quite benign; one displayed a peace message on the screen on a given date.

Luckily, you can avoid some viruses by using write-protected disks, and others by using computer "vaccines."

How Computer Vaccines Work

Most computer vaccines are designed to prevent the changes to the system files that a virus tries to make. The vaccines also flash warnings to tell you that the active program is trying to make such changes—a sign that you should erase the program immediately. Other vaccines can locate viruses on a disk and write over that part of the disk to prevent the virus from doing damage. Still other vaccines prevent viruses from replicating if they do get in your system or block the viruses' malicious tricks.

Common-sense prevention helps prevent viruses: Do not load public domain software from unknown sources, write-protect your disks if possible, and consider installing a computer vaccine.

Data Security

In these days of computer hackers, viruses, and Trojan horses (see the "Random Bits" boxes in this chapter), protecting data is becoming increasingly difficult and important. Several steps can be taken to protect data, however. These include the following:

BULLETIN BOARDS UNDER ATTACK

Bulletin boards provide wonderful advantages to users calling in from across town or across the country. Participants give software hints, exchange news, sell wares, and share a variety of information. But this is one bit of sharing that authorities think goes beyond mischief: sharing the phone numbers and passwords—that is, access—to computer systems. Some bulletin boards carry such information as casually as they post the time of the next club meeting. Information that is supposed to be a closely guarded secret is on view for the bulletin board public. One government official noted that you might as well have a billboard on the street that says "Here is the combination to the bank vault in case you want to use it." In some states legislation has been introduced to curb such practices.

- Discard printouts, printer ribbons, and the like that might be sources of information to unauthorized persons.

- Use passwords—secret words or numbers that must be typed on the keyboard to gain access to the system. Change passwords often and compartmentalize information by passwords.

- Use internal computer controls and auditor checks to keep track of all accesses or attempted accesses to certain data.

- Scramble—that is, code—data messages sent over communications lines.

- Use built-in software protection to restrict access to the computer system.

Personal computer users need to be concerned about the computer's environment as well as about theft. Most personal computer data is stored on diskettes, which are vulnerable to sunlight, heaters, cigarettes, magnets, hard objects, and dirty fingers. Hard disks used with personal computers are subject to special problems too, such as electrical surges. The data, consequently, is vulnerable as well.

To protect against data loss, most manufacturers discourage eating and smoking near computers and recommend some specific cleaning techniques, such as vacuuming the keyboard and cleaning the disk-drive heads. You can also use **surge protectors**—devices that prevent electrical problems from affecting data files. The computer is plugged into the surge protector, which is plugged into an outlet (Figure 14-9). Finally, you should always make backup copies of all your data files. If you do not, the risk is considerable.

Awareness of personal computer security is gradually rising. However, security measures and the money to implement

Figure 14-9 Surge protectors. *A loss or sudden surge of power can erase valuable data. Surge protectors protect your system from unpredictable electrical problems.*

them should be directly related to the amount of the expected loss. Since the dollar value of personal computer losses is often relatively low, personal computer security may be less vigorous in many companies.

The End of the Beginning

You are nearing the end of the book. At this point, you should have acquired a little knowledge about what you can do with personal computer software. The computer industry will veer onto unknown paths, and software will surely change. In addition, your career will progress in unimagined directions. But basic understanding about computers remains the same. And in the future, you can build on the basic knowledge you have gained here.

Summary and Key Terms

- When microcomputers first became popular in the business world, most businesses did not have general policies regarding them, and this situation led to several problems. Many businesses developed acquisition policies to solve the compatibility problem, established information centers to provide assistance to users, and created the position of the microcomputer manager to ensure coordination of microcomputer use.

- Microcomputer acquisition policies may include establishing standards for hardware and software, limiting the number of vendors, and limiting the hardware and software the **Management Information System (MIS)** department will support.

- An **information center** typically offers employees classes on a variety of computer topics, helps in getting data from corporate computer systems, and gives technical assistance on such matters as hardware purchases and requests to the MIS department.

- Typically, the **microcomputer manager** guides the company's purchases of computers, monitors costs for computer-related expenses, manages or advises on the issue of data security and integrity, and establishes guidelines for computer use.

- Computer training is an important process in businesses—it helps users use the software and hardware more efficiently and reduces costly mistakes.

- **Ergonomics** is the study of human factors, primarily physical, in the design of workplaces.

- Computer security consists of a system of safeguards designed to protect a computer system and data from deliberate or accidental damage or access by unauthorized persons. Common threats include theft, vandalism, illegal software copying, and various means of damaging data.

- Personal computer and data security includes such measures as locking hardware in place, providing an appropriate physical environment, and using a **surge protector,** which prevents electrical problems from affecting data files.

Review Questions

1. Describe some of the ways that personal computers have changed the way people work.

2. Describe the three main microcomputer management problems.

3. Describe three common methods through which managers control microcomputer acquisition.

4. What are some of the functions of an information center?

5. Describe four ways in which a microcomputer manager can help a company.

6. List some reasons why training is important to users.

7. What is ergonomics, and how does it relate to the workplace?

8. List some of major hazards to the security of hardware, software, and data.

9. Why do some software companies place copy protection on their software?

10. Why is loss of data a more serious problem than loss of software or hardware?

11. List some of the methods used to protect data.

FROM THE REAL WORLD

Hands-On at Kaiser Aluminum

Some companies provide training after the fact. That is, an employee is presented with a ready-to-use computer and then sent to training classes, probably in a formal classroom setting. Kaiser Aluminum has been that route, but the company did not find it satisfactory. Kaiser found that, even after a lot of hand-holding, many employees were too frightened to even touch the machine and took a month or longer to feel comfortable with the new tool.

Kaiser decided to take a radically different approach: Make the employees do it themselves. The legal department seemed a prime candidate for experimentation. Employees in that department were given a choice—to compute or not to compute. Only two said a flat-out "No." Two others said they might be interested at some later time. The remaining 35 formed the volunteer group. These employees were taken to a conference room where their new computers were awaiting them—in boxes. The employees were shown how to unpack and assemble their own machines. The conference room soon looked like a computer store.

Then they learned to format their hard disks and install their own software, piece by piece. That was the first day. The employees started getting excited and had to be forced to leave their computers and go home. The second day the employees received hands-on training in using the operating system and software they had installed: word processing, spreadsheets, database management, and various other packages.

The difference between the legal personnel and the employees who had everything done for them was, according to one trainer, astronomical. The legal employees finished their training on a Friday and many of them came in and worked on Saturday. They could not wait until Monday to start using their new computers. There is a side note to this tale: The legal department employees who did not want to get involved with computers changed their minds in a hurry and insisted on being included in the next phase.

The lesson here is not new and is, in fact, as old as education itself: People learn best by doing.

Appendixes

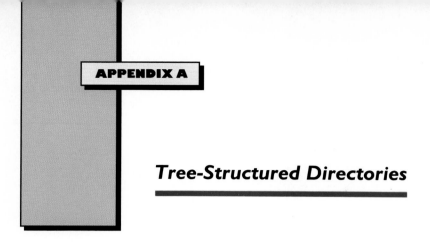

Tree-Structured Directories

One of the qualities of computers that makes them so useful is their ability to store data on disks so that it can be easily accessed. Managing this data is one of the major responsibilities of the operating system. As personal computers have become more powerful, they have been able to store increasingly large amounts of data on disks. Although computers have no trouble remembering where data is stored and how to find the data on their disks, humans sometimes do become confused. The solution is to use a tree-structured directory system.

This organizing technique is often used with hard disks and high-capacity $3\frac{1}{2}$-inch disks. Even if you do not organize your files in this manner, many experienced users do, so you may need to know how to access data stored by another user in a tree-structured directory.

Tree-Structured Directories

As we explained in Chapter 3, when a disk is formatted using the FORMAT command, the operating system creates a directory for the disk. As files are stored on the disk, their names and locations are placed in the directory. The DIR command lets you see a listing of the names of the files contained in the directory. This main (or primary) directory is sometimes referred to as the *root directory*. With a tree-structured system any (or all) the files in the root directory may themselves be directories known as *subdirectories*. Subdirectories can contain additional files or still other subdirectories.

Suppose, for example, that you have a hard disk and that you often create files by using Lotus 1-2-3, WordPerfect, and dBASE III PLUS. A

Figure A-1 A tree-structured directory. In this figure, there are three subdirectories—LOTUS, WP, and DBASE—under the main root directory.

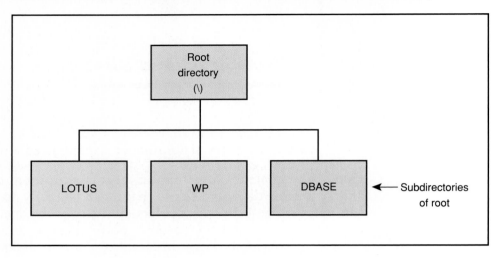

Figure A-2 Using the DIR command. When you use the DIR command, you see a listing of the main subdirectories. The C:\ on the screen indicates the root directory. Any subdirectories under the root have <DIR> after their names.

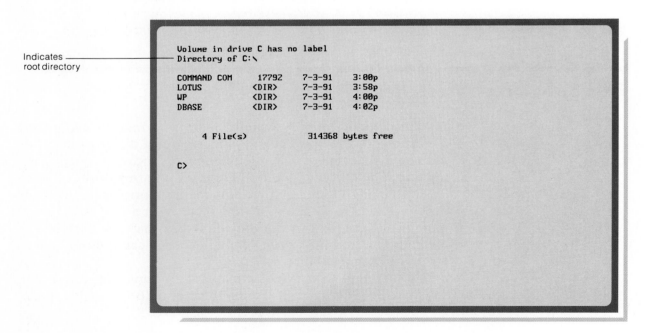

possible tree-structured organization for your disks is shown in Figure A-1. Notice that the figure looks something like an upside-down tree with the root directory at the top and the Lotus, WordPerfect, and dBASE subdirectories forming the branches.

If you use the DIR command, you will see a listing similar to Figure A-2. The root directory is always indicated with a backslash (\). Any subdirectories under the root have <DIR> after their names. You are not able to see a listing of the files in the subdirectories, however—the DIR command lists only the files in the currently active directory. Later in this appendix we will describe how to make a subdirectory the currently active directory so that you can access the files it contains.

The are three types of commands usually used with tree-structured directories: Make Directory (MD), Change Directory (CD), and Remove Directory (RD). In addition, tree-structured directories may require the use of paths, the COPY command, and a TREE command. Let us take a look at each one of these.

Creating Subdirectories

So how do you structure your disk to create a tree-structured directory? You let your operating system, DOS or OS/2, do it for you. The procedure you follow to structure a disk is the same regardless of the name of the drive. But let us assume that the disk you are going to structure is in drive C.

Remember that the root directory on the disk is created automatically by the operating system when you format the disk. When you first access a disk drive, the root directory is the current (active) directory. To create subdirectories under the root, use the Make Directory command (MD). This command is the same whether you use DOS or OS/2. For example, to create a subdirectory for Lotus 1-2-3 files under the root directory, make sure that the screen displays the operating system prompt and that you are in the root directory. Then type

```
MD \LOTUS
```

and press Enter. This creates the subdirectory with the name LOTUS.

You need only use the MD command once to create a subdirectory. If you have created a subdirectory, it will always be available to use unless you delete it or reformat your disk. You can treat a subdirectory as if it were a separate disk within a larger disk.

APPENDIXES

If you wish to add the subdirectory DATA to the subdirectory LOTUS, type

```
MD \LOTUS\DATA
```

and press Enter. This creates an additional subdirectory under the LOTUS subdirectory.

You can follow the same procedure to create more subdirectories—such as the WP and DBASE subdirectories—under the root directory. If you type DIR and press Enter, you will see that you now have three subdirectories. The DATA directory under the LOTUS directory is not shown. To see this directory, you must make LOTUS the active directory. Let us see how this is done.

Changing Directories

To make a subdirectory the active directory, you must change directories from the root directory to the subdirectory. To do this, use the Change Directory command (CD). This command allows you to move from one directory to another associated directory. Recall that in Figure A-1 the paths (or branches) lead from the root to each of the three subdirectories. There are, however, no direct connections between the subdirectories themselves. This means that if the LOTUS subdirectory is the current directory, you must first move back to the root to make WP or DBASE the current directories.

To illustrate the use of the Change Directory command, assume that the root directory is the current directory and that you want to move into the LOTUS subdirectory. To do this, type

```
CD \LOTUS
```

and press Enter. Notice that you follow the CD command with the name of the subdirectory.

At this point if you type DIR and press Enter, you see that you are now in the LOTUS subdirectory. To return to the root directory, simply type

```
CD \
```

and press Enter. Now you are back in the root directory and can access another subdirectory such as WP.

Deleting Subdirectories

The Del and Erase commands do not delete subdirectories. DOS and OS/2 have a special command, the Remove Directory command (RD) for this purpose. However, the subdirectory you wish to remove must be empty—that is, contain no files—before the command can be executed successfully. If the subdirectory contains any files, you must first delete them before you can delete the subdirectory. To delete all the files in a subdirectory, make sure the subdirectory is the current directory and then type

```
DEL *.*
```

and press Enter. Then type Y when the operating system asks for confirmation of the command. This command deletes all the files in your directory. Caution: If you use this command when the root directory is the active directory, all the files on the disk will be deleted. Make sure you change directories first.

Once the subdirectory is empty, you can delete it by using the RD command. For example, to remove the WP subdirectory, you move to the root directory and type

```
RD WP
```

and press Enter.

Using Paths

Once a subdirectory is the active directory, use it just as you use the root directory. You can save, retrieve, and delete your files. It is also possible to retrieve files from other directories by specifying a path to those files. A *path* to a file is a listing of the directory names that tells the operating system how to reach the file you want to use. The operating system can locate the file you are requesting by following the path to the file.

To illustrate the concept of a path, let us assume that you do a lot of word processing for your company's Marketing and the Production departments. To keep each department's documents separate, you create on your hard disk two subdirectories under a WP subdirectory, as illustrated in Figure A-3. You store the documents for the Marketing department in the subdirectory MKT. The documents for the Production department are stored in the subdirectory PROD. If you are working with WordPerfect in the WP subdirectory and you need a document file named BUDGET from the MKT subdirectory, you type

```
C:\WP\MKT\BUDGET
```

and press Enter. The directory names \ (for root directory), WP, and MKT tell the operating system where to find the file that you are requesting. Notice that the directory names are separated by the \ character.

Figure A-3 Subdirectories. *Each subdirectory can contain other subdirectories and files. In this example, the WP subdirectory has two subdirectories—the MKT subdirectory and the PROD subdirectory. In addition, the MKT subdirectory contains the BUDGET file.*

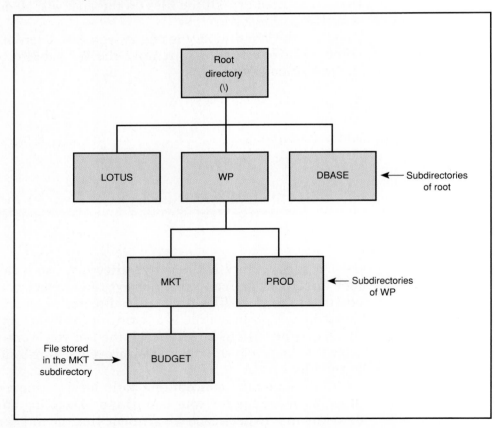

An alternative way to specify the path to the BUDGET file is to type

```
MKT\BUDGET
```

and press Enter. You can leave out the root directory and the WP sub-directory because you are already in the WP directory. DOS or OS/2 searches in the current subdirectory—the WP subdirectory—to find MKT and then the file.

If you do not specify a path to the file you want to retrieve, the operating system searches only the current directory of your default disk drive. For example, if you are running WordPerfect in the WP sub-directory and you ask WordPerfect to retrieve the file BUDGET, WordPerfect displays the message "ERROR: File not found." This means that WordPerfect asked the operating system to search the current direc-tory (WP) for the file named BUDGET, but since BUDGET is stored in the MKT subdirectory, the requested file is not in the current directory.

Moving files around in a complicated tree structure can become tricky. To avoid complexity, the simplest technique is to have one sub-directory for each of your applications programs and to store the files that you use with the application in the same subdirectory. Create more subdirectories only if the number of files in a directory becomes too large to keep track of.

Copying Files into Subdirectories

To copy a file from the root directory into a subdirectory, you must specify the subdirectory. For example, if you want to copy all Lotus 1-2-3 spreadsheet files (that is, all files with the extension WKE) from the root directory of a disk in drive A to the LOTUS subdirectory on drive C, type

```
COPY A:\*.WKE C:\LOTUS
```

and press Enter. To copy all the database files (that is, all files with the extension DBF) from a subdirectory named DBASE on drive C into a subdirectory named DBASE on drive A, type

```
COPY C:\DBASE\*.DBF A:\DBASE
```

and press Enter.

Using the TREE Command

There is a command available in PC-DOS and OS/2 that is used to display the contents of a tree-structured disk. This command—the TREE command—lets you see the contents of the root directory and all the subdirectories and file names on a disk. The TREE program file is not loaded automatically when PC-DOS or OS/2 is booted. This means that if TREE.COM is not in the current directory, the TREE command is not available to you; you must load TREE.COM from the PC-DOS or OS/2 disk(s).

To use the TREE command, make sure TREE.COM is in your current directory. (In this example the current directory is on drive C.) Then type

```
TREE C:/F
```

and press Enter. All the directory and file names on drive C are displayed on your screen. If the display scrolls up the screen before you can read it, press the Pause key to freeze the display and then press the Spacebar to start the listing again. If your keyboard does not contain a Pause key, press Ctrl-S. To start the listing again, press Ctrl-Q.

We have introduced some new concepts in this appendix that you will find useful as you continue your work with applications packages. There are some additional commands we have not covered that relate to the organization of large amounts of data in disk files. If you would like to dig deeper into the topic of file structures, check the manual supplied with your operating system.

Lotus 1-2-3 as a Database

Lotus 1-2-3 is a program that provides three functions. As you have seen, it is a very powerful spreadsheet and graphics program. In this appendix we will examine the database capabilities of Lotus. Although Lotus is not a true database management system like dBASE III PLUS (because Lotus cannot easily extract related information from two related files), Lotus can manage data stored in a single worksheet.

In Lotus a database is one worksheet (Figure B-1). A record is a row of data in the worksheet. No blank rows are allowed in the area of the worksheet that contains the data records. Fields are the columns, and field names are always stored as a one-line heading in the first row of each column.

Figure B-1 A Lotus 1-2-3 database. *Data for a Lotus 1-2-3 database is entered into a regular Lotus spreadsheet. Each row is one record, each column is a field. The field names must be in the first row of the database. Note that there are no blank rows.*

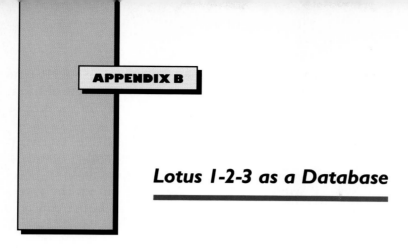

	A	B	C	D	E	F	G	H
1	LAST NAME	FIRST NAME	1ST QTR	2ND QTR	3RD QTR	4TH QTR	TOTAL	REGION
2	GONZALES	JOSE	$10,000	$9,000	$15,000	$12,000	$46,000	EAST
3	NEY	MICHELLE	$5,000	$4,500	$6,000	$5,000	$20,500	MIDWEST
4	WELLSLY	ART	$20,000	$18,000	$19,000	$20,000	$77,000	EAST
5	KEMPT	JAMES	$15,000	$14,000	$15,000	$13,000	$57,000	PACIFIC
6	JEROME	BETTY	$19,000	$18,000	$19,000	$17,000	$73,000	EAST
7	BYNG	JOHN	$9,000	$7,000	$10,000	$8,000	$34,000	MIDWEST
8	HALKETT	COLIN	$12,000	$14,000	$11,000	$12,000	$49,000	MIDWEST
9	PACK	MARTHA	$10,000	$11,000	$8,000	$9,000	$38,000	PACIFIC
10	BACHELU	SALLY	$8,000	$5,000	$6,000	$9,000	$28,000	PACIFIC
11	REILLE	BARBARA	$17,000	$18,000	$19,000	$18,000	$72,000	MIDWEST
12	MORTIER	ANN	$12,000	$1,000	$13,000	$11,000	$37,000	EAST
13	PHAM	THUY	$17,000	$19,000	$14,000	$15,000	$65,000	PACIFIC
14	SUN	GRACE	$19,000	$18,000	$19,000	$17,000	$73,000	MIDWEST
15	PACK	DENNIS	$16,000	$10,000	$13,000	$15,000	$54,000	EAST
16	BLUCHER	ROBERT	$10,000	$12,000	$11,000	$13,000	$46,000	MIDWEST
17	MURAT	JOAN	$18,000	$16,000	$14,000	$11,000	$59,000	PACIFIC

Field name

Record

Field

A Lotus database has the capacity to store up to 8191 records and 256 different fields in a record. However, the amount of internal memory in your computer may impose a lower limit on the size of the database you can store.

A database like the one shown in Figure B-1 is constructed using the Lotus commands discussed in chapters 6 and 7, just as you would set up any worksheet using Lotus. In fact, a database in Lotus is really a special type of worksheet. Once you have set up the worksheet and entered the data, the Data commands (/D) in Lotus can be used with the worksheet.

The Data commands are especially useful when you have many records in your database. However, we will use only the 16 records in the database shown in Figure B-1 to illustrate the principles of using a Lotus database. We will illustrate the use of two of the most important commands, Sort and Query.

The Sort Command

The Sort command, available in the Data submenu, has several options, as Figure B-2 shows. Lotus can sort both numeric fields and label fields. When Lotus sorts a label field—for instance, the LAST NAME field— it sorts the records in alphabetical order. If Lotus sorts a numeric field, such as the TOTAL field, it sorts the records in numerical order.

To sort the data in a database, Lotus needs to know three things:

1. Where in the worksheet the data to be sorted is found

2. The field or fields (Lotus can sort on either one field or a combination of two fields) in the data range that contain the values or labels that will be used to rearrange the records

3. Whether the sorted values (or labels) should appear in ascending (lowest to highest) or descending (highest to lowest) order

So, to sort the database shown in Figure B-1 in order of decreasing value in the TOTAL field, type

```
/DS
```

to select the Data command and then the Sort command. Then, to enter

Figure B-2 The Sort menu. *After selecting Data from the main menu and Sort from the Data menu, you see this menu.*

```
A1: 'LAST NAME
Data-Range  Primary-Key  Secondary-Key  Reset  Go  Quit
Specify records to be sorted
        A           B          C         D         E         F
 1   LAST NAME   FIRST NAME  1ST QTR   2ND QTR   3RD QTR   4TH QTR
 2   GONZALES    JOSE        $10,000    $9,000   $15,000   $12,000
 3   NEY         MICHELLE     $5,000    $4,500    $6,000    $5,000
 4   WELLSLY     ART         $20,000   $18,000   $19,000   $20,000
 5   KEMPT       JAMES       $15,000   $14,000   $15,000   $13,000
 6   JEROME      BETTY       $19,000   $18,000   $19,000   $17,000
 7   BYNG        JOHN         $9,000    $7,000   $10,000    $8,000
 8   HALKETT     COLIN       $12,000   $14,000   $11,000   $12,000
 9   PACK        MARTHA      $10,000   $11,000    $8,000    $9,000
10   BACHELU     SALLY        $8,000    $5,000    $6,000    $9,000
11   REILLE      BARBARA     $17,000   $18,000   $19,000   $18,000
12   MORTIER     ANN         $12,000    $1,000   $13,000   $11,000
13   PHAM        THUY        $17,000   $19,000   $14,000   $15,000
14   SUN         GRACE       $19,000   $18,000   $19,000   $17,000
15   PACK        DENNIS      $16,000   $10,000   $13,000   $15,000
16   BLUCHER     ROBERT      $10,000   $12,000   $11,000   $13,000
17   MURAT       JOAN        $18,000   $16,000   $14,000   $11,000
18
19
20
19-Jun-92  02:13 PM
```

the range that contains the data you wish to sort, select Data-Range from the menu and enter the range of the worksheet that contains the database. You must include all the records in the database and all the fields in the database. However, do not include the row of field names. In our example, select Data-Range from the Sort submenu and, when prompted for the data range, type

A2.H17

and press Enter. Next, indicate that you want the data sorted using the TOTAL field by selecting Primary-Key from the menu. The primary key is the field that Lotus uses to sort the data in the specified range. When you select the Primary-Key option, you are prompted to enter the column in the data range that contains the primary key. Since column G contains the TOTAL field in the example, type G1 and press Enter. Notice that you enter the cell containing the field name, not the field itself. Lotus then asks whether you want the data in ascending (A) or descending (D) order. Type D and press Enter to choose descending order.

Now you have given Lotus the information it needs to perform the sort. To actually sort the records in your database, select Go from the

Sort menu. When Lotus has completed the sort, the database is displayed on your screen as shown in Figure B-3. Notice that all the fields in a record have been moved as a unit during the sort. It is not just the values in column G that move, it is the whole record that is moved to a new place in the database. Now a sales manager can find at a glance the names of the top sales reps.

Sometimes sorting requires that you sort on more than just one field. For example, if the data in the database needs to be arranged alphabetically by sales rep name, you need to sort using both the LAST NAME and the FIRST NAME fields. For example, you might want the records to be sorted alphabetically on last name and, if any records contain the same value for LAST NAME (as is the case of Dennis and Martha Pack), you might want the computer to include FIRST NAME when alphabetizing. To let Lotus know this, select Primary-Key from the Sort menu, type A1 (because column A contains the LAST NAME field), and press Enter. Then type A (to specify ascending order) and press Enter again. Next select Secondary-Key, type B1 (because column B contains the FIRST NAME field), and press Enter. Then select A to specify ascending order and press Enter. The secondary key specifies the additional field that the data will be sorted on. That is, first the data will be sorted by LAST NAME, and then, keeping the LAST NAME order as it is, the records will be sorted by FIRST NAME. To actually sort the records, select

Figure B-3 Data sorted on the TOTAL field. *When you sort the data on the TOTAL field in descending order, the records in the database appear as shown.*

	A	B	C	D	E	F	G	H
1	LAST NAME	FIRST NAME	1ST QTR	2ND QTR	3RD QTR	4TH QTR	TOTAL	REGION
2	WELLSLY	ART	$20,000	$18,000	$19,000	$20,000	$77,000	EAST
3	JEROME	BETTY	$19,000	$18,000	$19,000	$17,000	$73,000	EAST
4	SUN	GRACE	$19,000	$18,000	$19,000	$17,000	$73,000	MIDWEST
5	REILLE	BARBARA	$17,000	$18,000	$19,000	$18,000	$72,000	MIDWEST
6	PHAM	THUY	$17,000	$19,000	$14,000	$15,000	$65,000	PACIFIC
7	MURAT	JOAN	$18,000	$16,000	$14,000	$11,000	$59,000	PACIFIC
8	KEMPT	JAMES	$15,000	$14,000	$15,000	$13,000	$57,000	PACIFIC
9	PACK	DENNIS	$16,000	$10,000	$13,000	$15,000	$54,000	EAST
10	HALKETT	COLIN	$12,000	$14,000	$11,000	$12,000	$49,000	MIDWEST
11	GONZALES	JOSE	$10,000	$9,000	$15,000	$12,000	$46,000	EAST
12	BLUCHER	ROBERT	$10,000	$12,000	$11,000	$13,000	$46,000	MIDWEST
13	PACK	MARTHA	$10,000	$11,000	$8,000	$9,000	$38,000	PACIFIC
14	MORTIER	ANN	$12,000	$1,000	$13,000	$11,000	$37,000	EAST
15	BYNG	JOHN	$9,000	$7,000	$10,000	$8,000	$34,000	MIDWEST
16	BACHELU	SALLY	$8,000	$5,000	$6,000	$9,000	$28,000	PACIFIC
17	NEY	MICHELLE	$5,000	$4,500	$6,000	$5,000	$20,500	MIDWEST
18								
19								
20								

Go. When the sorting is finished, the database appears as shown in Figure B-4.

The Reset option in the Sort menu cancels current Data-Range, Primary-Key, and Secondary-Key settings. The Quit option returns you to the READY mode. Your most recently specified data-range, primary-key, and secondary-key are retained in the worksheet. If you will perform the same sort again, be sure to save your worksheet by typing /FS and pressing Enter.

When you sorted the database on the TOTAL field, you were sorting the records on a field that contained a formula. That formula summed the values in the four QTR fields of the same record (for example, @SUM(C5..F5)). In the example this creates no problems when you sort because Lotus adjusts the cell addresses in the formula as it is sorting the records. When the sort is finished, the formulas in all the records are adjusted for changes in the row position of the record in the database. However, when a field contains formulas that include cell references to cells in a different row or cells outside the data range, Lotus does not adjust the formulas as the records in the data range are moved around. This means that if you sort records containing such formulas, the data you want is no longer in the cell address used in the formulas; your worksheet displays erroneous results. Be careful when you sort ranges containing formulas. Always check to see whether the formulas in the worksheet have been adjusted properly so that they reflect the new position of the record in the database.

Figure B-4 Data sorted on the LAST NAME field and the FIRST NAME field. *This figure shows the use of the LAST NAME field as the primary key and the FIRST NAME field as the secondary key.*

	A	B	C	D	E	F	G	H
1	LAST NAME	FIRST NAME	1ST QTR	2ND QTR	3RD QTR	4TH QTR	TOTAL	REGION
2	BACHELU	SALLY	$8,000	$5,000	$6,000	$9,000	$28,000	PACIFIC
3	BLUCHER	ROBERT	$10,000	$12,000	$11,000	$13,000	$46,000	MIDWEST
4	BYNG	JOHN	$9,000	$7,000	$10,000	$8,000	$34,000	MIDWEST
5	GONZALES	JOSE	$10,000	$9,000	$15,000	$12,000	$46,000	EAST
6	HALKETT	COLIN	$12,000	$14,000	$11,000	$12,000	$49,000	MIDWEST
7	JEROME	BETTY	$19,000	$18,000	$19,000	$17,000	$73,000	EAST
8	KEMPT	JAMES	$15,000	$14,000	$15,000	$13,000	$57,000	PACIFIC
9	MORTIER	ANN	$12,000	$1,000	$13,000	$11,000	$37,000	EAST
10	MURAT	JOAN	$18,000	$16,000	$14,000	$11,000	$59,000	PACIFIC
11	NEY	MICHELLE	$5,000	$4,500	$6,000	$5,000	$20,500	MIDWEST
12	PACK	DENNIS	$16,000	$10,000	$13,000	$15,000	$54,000	EAST
13	PACK	MARTHA	$10,000	$11,000	$8,000	$9,000	$38,000	PACIFIC
14	PHAM	THUY	$17,000	$19,000	$14,000	$15,000	$65,000	PACIFIC
15	REILLE	BARBARA	$17,000	$18,000	$19,000	$18,000	$72,000	MIDWEST
16	SUN	GRACE	$19,000	$18,000	$19,000	$17,000	$73,000	MIDWEST
17	WELLSLY	ART	$20,000	$18,000	$19,000	$20,000	$77,000	EAST

The Query Command

Finding individual records in a database that contains hundreds or thousands of records is time-consuming. However, the Lotus 1-2-3 Query command (Figure B-5) lets you selectively view data records quickly and fairly easily. When you select Query from the Data submenu, the menu shown in Figure B-5 appears. This menu permits you to specify the conditions under which a record is to be selected for viewing. It also lets you specify which information in the record is to be displayed.

In this section we will look at one of the Query commands—the Find command. The Find command locates records that match the criteria, or conditions, that you specify. Lotus highlights—one at a time—those records in the database that meet the conditions. If no records are found, Lotus sounds a "beep" to signal that no records in the database meet your selection criteria.

Before you can use the Find command, however, you must specify two pieces of information for Lotus to use. First, Lotus needs to know the range of the database it should search. This range is referred to as the **Input Range.** Second, Lotus needs to know the selection criteria— that is, what it is trying to find. The conditions used in the search are placed in a separate area of the worksheet known as the **Criterion Range.** For example, suppose you want Lotus to find all the records that have

Figure B-5 The Query menu. *When you select Query from the Data submenu, you see this menu.*

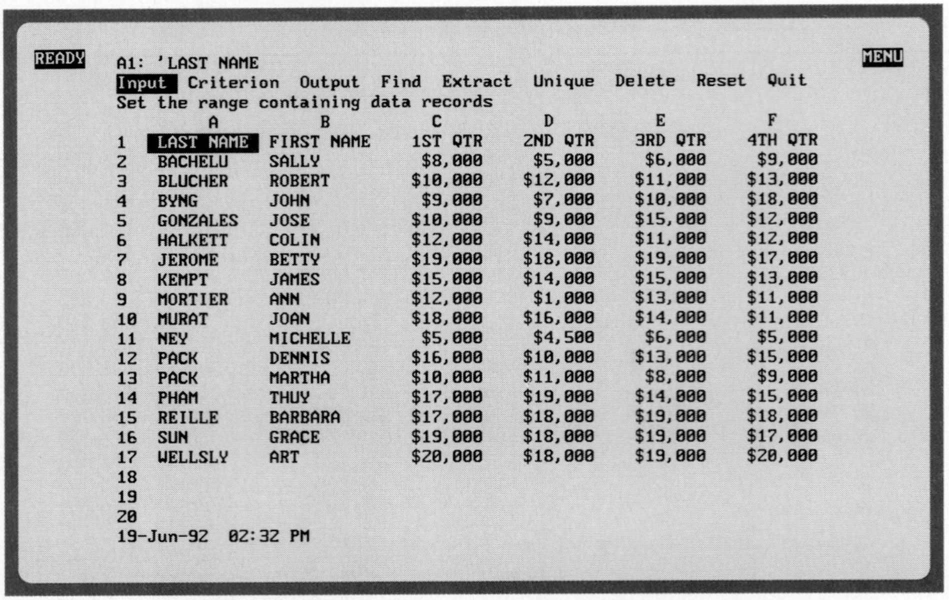

```
READY   A1: 'LAST NAME                                              MENU
        Input  Criterion  Output  Find  Extract  Unique  Delete  Reset  Quit
        Set the range containing data records
             A          B           C          D          E          F
        1   LAST NAME  FIRST NAME  1ST QTR    2ND QTR    3RD QTR    4TH QTR
        2   BACHELU    SALLY        $8,000     $5,000     $6,000     $9,000
        3   BLUCHER    ROBERT      $10,000    $12,000    $11,000    $13,000
        4   BYNG       JOHN         $9,000     $7,000    $10,000    $18,000
        5   GONZALES   JOSE        $10,000     $9,000    $15,000    $12,000
        6   HALKETT    COLIN       $12,000    $14,000    $11,000    $12,000
        7   JEROME     BETTY       $19,000    $18,000    $19,000    $17,000
        8   KEMPT      JAMES       $15,000    $14,000    $15,000    $13,000
        9   MORTIER    ANN         $12,000     $1,000    $13,000    $11,000
       10   MURAT      JOAN        $18,000    $16,000    $14,000    $11,000
       11   NEY        MICHELLE     $5,000     $4,500     $6,000     $5,000
       12   PACK       DENNIS      $16,000    $10,000    $13,000    $15,000
       13   PACK       MARTHA      $10,000    $11,000     $8,000     $9,000
       14   PHAM       THUY        $17,000    $19,000    $14,000    $15,000
       15   REILLE     BARBARA     $17,000    $18,000    $19,000    $18,000
       16   SUN        GRACE       $19,000    $18,000    $19,000    $17,000
       17   WELLSLY    ART         $20,000    $18,000    $19,000    $20,000
       18
       19
       20
       19-Jun-92  02:32 PM
```

TOTAL values greater than 50,000. The input range is the complete database and the condition for the search is a value in the TOTAL field greater than 50,000.

Setting Up the Input Range

The input range must include all the data field names and all the records you want to search. To enter the input range, select Input from the Query menu. Then type the range and press Enter. In our example the field names are contained in row 1 and the data records are in rows 2 through 17, so when prompted, type A1.H17 and press Enter.

Once you have specified an input range, Lotus continues to use that range unless you indicate a new range. If you save your worksheet to your disk with the /FS command, Lotus stores the input range you have selected when it saves your worksheet.

Setting Up the Criterion Range

Now that you have specified the input range, your next step is to set up the criterion range. Setting up the criterion range is a two-step process. First, choose a blank area of your worksheet in which to store the selection conditions you define. Usually, this area is to the right or below the database. Then copy the field names you wish to use from the database into the blank area you have chosen. Also enter the specific criteria for those fields into the range. Second, choose the Criteria option from the Query menu. When prompted to enter the criterion range, enter the range in the separate area of your worksheet that contains the field names and conditions you wish to use.

Let us take a look at an example, using the sample database. Suppose that you wish to find the records of all the sales reps that have a value in the TOTAL field greater than 50,000. First, select Input from the Query menu. Then enter the data range—A1.H17—and press Enter. This establishes the input range.

Next, to set up the criterion range, move the cursor to an unused portion of the worksheet—for example, Cell J1. The criterion range will have at least two rows—one for the field names you wish to use and one for the criteria (selection condiitons). You can use up to 32 fields to establish the criteria. The field names you enter must be entered exactly as they appear in the input range; therefore, always use the Copy command to copy the field names from the database into the criterion range.

In this example you need only one field, TOTAL. To enter the field name in the criterion range, copy the field name in Cell G1 to Cell J1. Next, in Cell J2, enter the actual selection criterion. To do this, type the equation $+G2 > 50000$ in Cell J2 and press Enter. This tells Lotus that you want to find all records in which the TOTAL field (which is in column G) contains a value greater than 50000. The worksheet now appears as shown in Figure B-6a. Although Cell J2 contains the formula $+G2 > 50000$, 0 is displayed in that cell in the worksheet. This is because

Figure B-6 Searching for a single condition. *(a) Cell J1 and Cell J2 make up the criterion range. (b) When you use Find, Lotus 1-2-3 highlights the records that meet the criterion.*

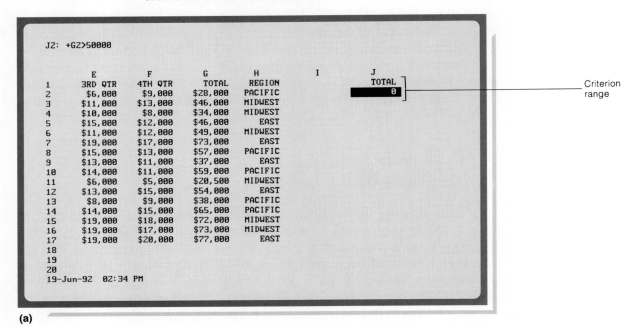

	E	F	G	H	I	J
	3RD QTR	4TH QTR	TOTAL	REGION		TOTAL
2	$6,000	$9,000	$28,000	PACIFIC		0
3	$11,000	$13,000	$46,000	MIDWEST		
4	$10,000	$8,000	$34,000	MIDWEST		
5	$15,000	$12,000	$46,000	EAST		
6	$11,000	$12,000	$49,000	MIDWEST		
7	$19,000	$17,000	$73,000	EAST		
8	$15,000	$13,000	$57,000	PACIFIC		
9	$13,000	$11,000	$37,000	EAST		
10	$14,000	$11,000	$59,000	PACIFIC		
11	$6,000	$5,000	$20,500	MIDWEST		
12	$13,000	$15,000	$54,000	EAST		
13	$8,000	$9,000	$38,000	PACIFIC		
14	$14,000	$15,000	$65,000	PACIFIC		
15	$19,000	$18,000	$72,000	MIDWEST		
16	$19,000	$17,000	$73,000	MIDWEST		
17	$19,000	$20,000	$77,000	EAST		

J2: +G2>50000

19-Jun-92 02:34 PM

Criterion range

(a)

	A	B	C	D	E	F	G	H
1	LAST NAME	FIRST NAME	1ST QTR	2ND QTR	3RD QTR	4TH QTR	TOTAL	REGION
2	BACHELU	SALLY	$8,000	$5,000	$6,000	$9,000	$28,000	PACIFIC
3	BLUCHER	ROBERT	$10,000	$12,000	$11,000	$13,000	$46,000	MIDWEST
4	BYNG	JOHN	$9,000	$7,000	$10,000	$8,000	$34,000	MIDWEST
5	GONZALES	JOSE	$10,000	$9,000	$15,000	$12,000	$46,000	EAST
6	HALKETT	COLIN	$12,000	$14,000	$11,000	$12,000	$49,000	MIDWEST
7	JEROME	BETTY	$19,000	$18,000	$19,000	$17,000	$73,000	EAST
8	KEMPT	JAMES	$15,000	$14,000	$15,000	$13,000	$57,000	PACIFIC
9	MORTIER	ANN	$12,000	$1,000	$13,000	$11,000	$37,000	EAST
10	MURAT	JOAN	$18,000	$16,000	$14,000	$11,000	$59,000	PACIFIC
11	NEY	MICHELLE	$5,000	$4,500	$6,000	$5,000	$20,500	MIDWEST
12	PACK	DENNIS	$16,000	$10,000	$13,000	$15,000	$54,000	EAST
13	PACK	MARTHA	$10,000	$11,000	$8,000	$9,000	$38,000	PACIFIC
14	PHAM	THUY	$17,000	$19,000	$14,000	$15,000	$65,000	PACIFIC
15	REILLE	BARBARA	$17,000	$18,000	$19,000	$18,000	$72,000	MIDWEST
16	SUN	GRACE	$19,000	$18,000	$19,000	$17,000	$73,000	MIDWEST
17	WELLSLY	ART	$20,000	$18,000	$19,000	$20,000	$77,000	EAST

(b)

the first record in the input range does not have a TOTAL value greater than 50000. If the first record in the input range met the selection criterion, then a 1 would be displayed in the cell.

Now you that you have entered the criterion, you need to tell Lotus that the criterion is to be found in Cell J1 and Cell J2. To do this, select the Criterion command from the Query menu. When prompted for the criterion range, type J1.J2 and press Enter.

Executing the Find Command

Now you are ready to use the Find command. To start the search for the records in the database that match the selection criterion, select Find from the Query submenu. If Lotus 1-2-3 finds no records that match the selection criterion, the computer beeps and returns to the Query menu. Note: The computer also beeps if you make a mistake when using the Find command. So always check to see that your criteria, criterion range, and input range are properly entered before assuming that no records in your database match the selection criterion.

When you execute the Find command, Lotus highlights the first record that meets the criterion (Betty Jerome's). To see any other records that match the criterion, press the down arrow cursor movement key. Lotus highlights the next record with a total value of more than $50,000. To see all the records that match the criterion, keep pressing the down arrow key. When Lotus finds the last record that meets the selection criterion, the computer beeps when you press the down arrow again. Figure B-6b shows all the highlighted records. When you want to leave the FIND mode, press Enter or the Esc key to end the search and return to the Query menu. To leave the Query menu and return to the READY mode, select Quit on the Query Menu.

Searching for Values in the Database

When you are looking for records that have a particular value in the database—for example, records with a TOTAL field value of 50,000—you can simply enter the value in the criterion range. However, when you are looking for records that fall in a spread of values—like TOTAL less than 40,000—you need to enter the first cell address (preceded by a plus sign to signal Lotus 1-2-3 that you are entering a formula) and use a logical operator ($<$, $<=$, $>$, $>=$, $<>$) to state the criterion, as we did in Cell J2 in the previous example.

Searching for Labels in the Database

Suppose a sales manager needs to know which sales reps work in the Pacific sales region. In the READY mode he copies the field name that will be used in the selection criterion (REGION, in Cell H1) to the first row of the criterion range (Cell J1). Then he copies the label he was looking for (PACIFIC) into Cell J2. He selects the Data Query Find command, and Lotus 1-2-3 searches the database and highlights the records of sales reps from the Pacific region.

Use the Copy command when entering field names or labels into the criterion range. Labels can be stored left-justified, right-justified, or centered; the Copy command will duplicate the positioning—you will not have to think about it. Labels can contain blank spaces to the left that are not obvious when you glance at the worksheet. Field names and labels entered in the criterion range must exactly match the field name and labels in the input range, or the Find command will not work properly. By using Copy, you ensure the match.

Using Multiple Criteria

What if the sales manager wants to know which sales reps in the EAST region have total sales of $60,000 or more? In this case, two different database fields are used as selection criteria. You need to include both database field names in the first row of the criterion range. To do this, copy TOTAL from Cell G1 into Cell J1. Then type $+G2 >= 60000$ into Cell J2. Copy REGION into Cell K1 and the condition, EAST, into Cell K2, as shown in Figure B-7a.

Now select Criterion from the Query menu and type J1.K2 when prompted for the range. Then press Enter. Finally, select Find from the submenu. Notice, as shown in Figure B-7b, that two records match the selection criteria. Note that only those records that match both of the criteria in the second row of the criterion range are selected. Lotus finds the records of the sales reps who are in the EAST region AND who have total sales of $60,000.00 or more.

As another example of using multiple selection criteria, suppose that the sales manager needs to know the names of sales reps who work in the EAST region with sales of at least $60,000.00 OR sales reps from the PACIFIC region who had sales less than $40,000.00. When conditions are in an OR relationship, then they are placed in separate rows

Figure B-7 Searching for multiple conditions by using AND. *(a) If you want Lotus 1-2-3 to find all the records that are true for two or more conditions, place the conditions in separate columns in the criterion range. (b) When you use Find, Lotus highlights the records that meet the criterion.*

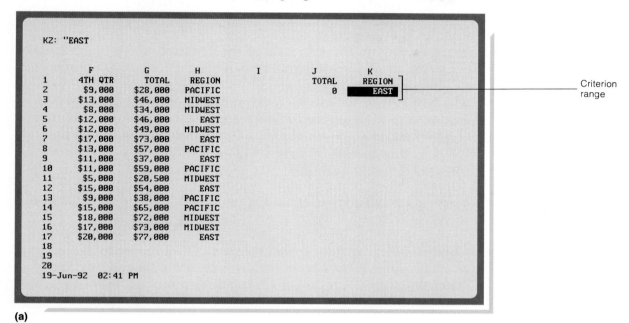

(a)

(b)

in the criterion range, as shown in Figure B-8a. Notice that Cell J3 displays a 1, since the first record in the input range (Sally Bachelu's) indicates total sales of less than $40,000. Remember to redefine the criterion range to J1 . . . K3 before using the Find command. Lotus highlights the records shown in Figure B-8b. Notice that a record is found if it matches *either* the criterion in row 2 of the criterion range OR the criterion in row 3 of the criterion range.

Since setting up the criteria and the criterion range is the hardest part of using the Find command, remember the following points:

- The first row of the criterion range must consist of one or more field names copied from the database. The remaining rows (under the field name row) contain the actual criteria. A criterion that refers to a particular field in the database must be placed under the field name of that field.

- Selection conditions in the same row must all be satisfied before a record is selected.

- Conditions in different rows are in an OR relationship. Lotus selects records if they meet the criteria in the second row of the criterion range OR if they meet the criterion in another row of the criterion range.

- The criterion range should include all the columns (fields) and all the rows used to state the selection criteria. Otherwise, any criteria entered but not included in the criterion range will not be used by Lotus. Be careful not to include a blank row in the criterion range. If you do this, Lotus finds and highlights *all* the records in the database. The reason for this is that Lotus assumes that each row in the criterion range expresses a valid selection criterion. If a cell in the criterion range is blank, Lotus assumes that you have no selection criteria for that cell. If all the cells in a row are empty, then (since the criterion in different rows are in an OR relationship) Lotus assumes that you have *no* restrictions on the records that are found.

- You must be in the READY mode to make entries in the criterion range.

Figure B-8 Searching for multiple conditions by using OR. *(a) If you want Lotus 1-2-3 to find all the records that are either true for one condition or true for another condition, place the conditions in separate rows in the criterion range. (b) When you use Find, Lotus highlights the records.*

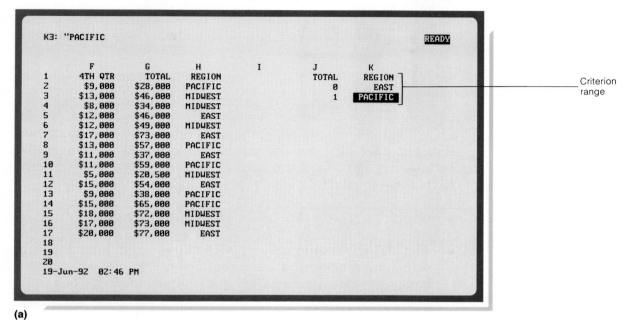

(a)

Criterion range

	A	B	C	D	E	F	G	H
1	LAST NAME	FIRST NAME	1ST QTR	2ND QTR	3RD QTR	4TH QTR	TOTAL	REGION
2	BACHELU	SALLY	$8,000	$5,000	$6,000	$9,000	$28,000	PACIFIC
3	BLUCHER	ROBERT	$10,000	$12,000	$11,000	$13,000	$46,000	MIDWEST
4	BYNG	JOHN	$9,000	$7,000	$10,000	$8,000	$34,000	MIDWEST
5	GONZALES	JOSE	$10,000	$9,000	$15,000	$12,000	$46,000	EAST
6	HALKETT	COLIN	$12,000	$14,000	$11,000	$12,000	$49,000	MIDWEST
7	JEROME	BETTY	$19,000	$18,000	$19,000	$17,000	$73,000	EAST
8	KEMPT	JAMES	$15,000	$14,000	$15,000	$13,000	$57,000	PACIFIC
9	MORTIER	ANN	$12,000	$1,000	$13,000	$11,000	$37,000	EAST
10	MURAT	JOAN	$18,000	$16,000	$14,000	$11,000	$59,000	PACIFIC
11	NEY	MICHELLE	$5,000	$4,500	$6,000	$5,000	$20,500	MIDWEST
12	PACK	DENNIS	$16,000	$10,000	$13,000	$15,000	$54,000	EAST
13	PACK	MARTHA	$10,000	$11,000	$8,000	$9,000	$38,000	PACIFIC
14	PHAM	THUY	$17,000	$19,000	$14,000	$15,000	$65,000	PACIFIC
15	REILLE	BARBARA	$17,000	$18,000	$19,000	$18,000	$72,000	MIDWEST
16	SUN	GRACE	$19,000	$18,000	$19,000	$17,000	$73,000	MIDWEST
17	WELLSLY	ART	$20,000	$18,000	$19,000	$20,000	$77,000	EAST
18								
19								
20								

(b)

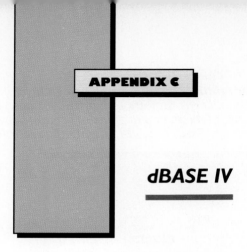

dBASE IV

As users have explored the capabilities of database management programs, they have seen the need for some improvements. Many users have asked for the following types of changes:

- Overall, a greater ease of use and a more friendly user interface.

- The ability to communicate with databases on mainframes and minicomputers so that an authorized user can download data from large corporate databases to a personal computer's database.

- A more complete implementation of the relational database model.

- Compliance with an existing language that meets international standards for database definition, data storage, and data retrieval. This standard language, developed in the 1970s by IBM, is called Structured Query Language (SQL).

- The ability to generate better reports by using simpler, easier-to-learn methods.

- Data-sharing capabilities for personal computer users that match the data-sharing capabilities of a database management system (DBMS) on a mainframe or minicomputer.

In response to user requests, Ashton-Tate created a new DBMS program—dBASE IV. dBASE IV surpasses the capabilities of dBASE III PLUS and establishes a new high standard for personal computer DBMS. In this appendix we will describe some of the features of dBASE IV and the ways in which it is the same as or different from dBASE III PLUS. We will also give you an overview of SQL and explain why so many people feel that it is *the* language to use to manage your data.

dBASE IV

dBASE IV was designed so that users of dBASE III PLUS could immediately use the new program without a lot of training. All of the commands that you learned and used as you worked through chapters 8 and 9 of this text work in exactly the same way in dBASE IV. And dBASE III PLUS data files and indexes can be used by dBASE IV without any modification. dBASE IV also includes an improved help function that is like the help screen available in dBASE III PLUS—but better. In addition, dBASE IV has a new user interface, over 200 new or improved features, and works much faster than dBASE III PLUS.

Separate dBASE IV versions have been written to run with DOS and with OS/2. (For a discussion of OS/2 see Appendix D.) The DOS version runs on the IBM PC, XT, AT, and PS/2 systems. A hard disk and 640K of RAM are required. The OS/2 version requires an IBM PC-AT or PS/2 with 2M of RAM, a hard disk, and a 80286 or 80386 microprocessor.

Using the dBASE IV Menus

In dBASE IV the dBASE III PLUS Assistant menu has been replaced by a superior system of menus called *work surfaces.* These menus let you edit, display, and manage your data.

The most important new menu is called the *Control Center.* This is the first menu you see after loading dBASE IV. (You can reach it from the dot prompt by typing ASSIST and pressing Enter.) Unlike the Assistant in dBASE III PLUS, the Control Center provides access to nearly all of the features of dBASE IV and is much simpler to use. As shown in Figure C-1 (on the next page), the Control Center menu consists of six panels. As you can see, the six panels (moving from left to right across the screen) display the options dFILES (which means data files), Queries, Forms, Reports, Labels, and Applications. Most users will do most of their work by using the Control Center. This menu system uses the same selection technique (called point and shoot) that was used with the dBASE III PLUS menus. First you move a pointer to a menu item by

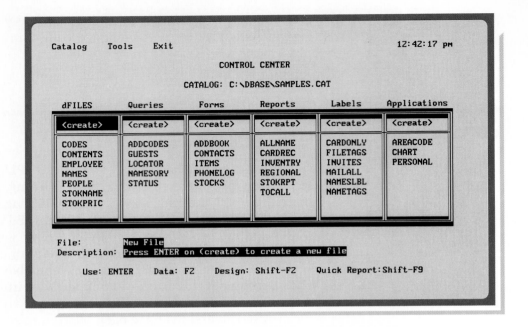

Figure C-1 dBASE IV Control Center screen. The dBASE IV Control Center screen lets you access nearly all of the features included in dBASE IV.

using your cursor movement keys. Then you select the item by pressing Enter.

Let us take a closer look at the panels of the Control Center menu.

The Data Panel

In the leftmost panel—the dFILES panel—you see the names of existing database files. In dBASE IV you can create new database files and modify existing files just as you did in dBASE III PLUS. Database files are accessed and manipulated using what dBASE IV calls the *Database File Design* screen (Figure C-2). This important screen lets you create and modify database file structures, add and delete groups of records, and sort and index database files.

If you are using the Control Center menu, you create a new database file by selecting the <create> option in the dFILES panel. The Database File Design screen appears on the screen. To modify the structure of an existing database from the Control Center, move your cursor to the name of that database file (remember, all existing database file names are displayed in the dFILES panel). Then press Shift-F2. When you release the keys, type DESIGN and press Enter. You will now see the Database

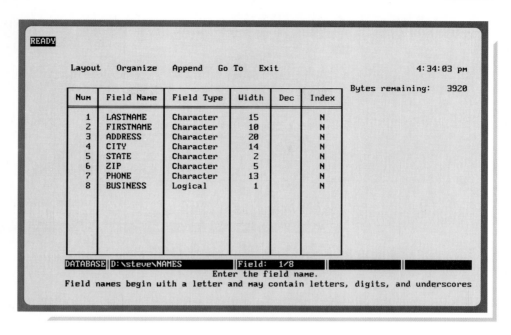

Figure C-2 dBASE IV Database File Design screen. *The menu included on this screen lets you create and modify database file structures and files.*

File Design screen and can modify the file. To reach the Database File Design screen from the dot prompt, use the Create or Modify Structure commands.

This may seem complicated at first, but the dBASE IV menus and screens prompt and help you each step of the way. After you have used the Control Center a few times, you should feel very confident with it. And, as we mentioned, dBASE IV has excellent help screens available for every command.

The Queries Panel

From the Queries panel of the Control Center, you can invoke the *Query By Example (QBE)* processor—a feature not available in dBASE III PLUS. The name *Query By Example* comes from the fact that you can specify record selection criteria by entering an example of the data you want below the names of the field(s) that you select. Database experts have found that with the QBE method, users can become very capable very quickly. The technique is similar to that used by Lotus in the Criterion Range of a Lotus database.

The Queries screen is shown in Figure C-3 (on the next page). Using the Queries menu, you can open and link databases, choose indexes,

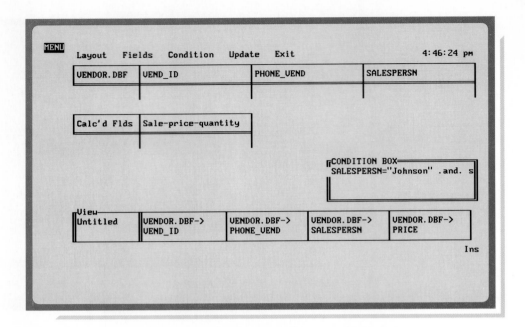

Figure C-3 dBASE IV Queries screen. *You can use the Queries screen menu to open and link databases, choose indexes, and select fields to display. The view table at the bottom of the screen temporarily displays the relations you create.*

and select fields to display. You can also specify record selection criteria that create a temporary data table called a *view,* which is not physically stored in the database. On this screen dBASE displays the fields from each of the databases you open and the resulting view. You select fields and define links between databases by selecting them with your cursor.

The Other Control Center Panels

The Forms panel lets you create special data-entry forms for your computer's screen. As you know, dBASE Create and Append commands supply simple data-entry screens for a database. With these screens, you enter data into a database from the keyboard. The Forms panel, however, lets you create data-entry forms that help you enter data rapidly and more accurately than the simple screens used with the Create and Append commands. This panel gives you control over the placement of fields and descriptive text. It also lets you specify editing and validation criteria to help you avoid entering incorrect data into the database.

You can use the Reports panel to create report forms similar to those you created with dBASE III PLUS. The dBASE IV report generator is much easier to use and lets you produce far more sophisticated reports than the dBASE III PLUS generator.

The Applications panel lets you write programs in the dBASE IV programming language and execute these programs. We did not discuss programming in chapters 8 and 9, but both dBASE III PLUS and dBASE IV have built-in programming languages. These are used to extend the power and usefulness of the dBASE program. Ashton-Tate claims that dBASE IV programs run much faster than the same programs in dBASE III PLUS.

The Labels panel allows you to create printed labels. For example, you could use the Labels Panel to print onto mailing labels the names, addresses, and zip codes stored in a database.

To understand the usefulness of the Control Center, you must actually sit down and use dBASE IV. In this section we hope we have been able to give you some insight into the functioning of the Control Center and its importance as a user interface to dBASE IV.

The dBASE IV Structured Query Language

One of the biggest improvements made in dBASE IV is the addition of a structured query language. Structured Query Language, usually abbreviated SQL (pronounced "sequel"), is a very powerful relational database management language developed by IBM and released to customers in 1979. It is used with a variety of DBMSs on mainframes, minicomputers, and—increasingly—on personal computers. SQL is not an applications package like dBASE. Rather, it is a language that works with databases in the same way that BASIC works with data files; it is used by many DBMSs as a standard way for users to define a database, load it with data, and then use the database.

SQL is much easier to use than BASIC (you do not have to be a programmer) and is rapidly becoming a universal database language with which different programs and even different computer systems can communicate and share data stored in databases. Actually, there are several versions of SQL that vary in small ways. But most vendors of DBMSs are beginning to follow the IBM standard of SQL as used in the mainframe DBMS called DB2.

Why SQL Appeals to Users

SQL appeals to database users for several reasons. First, SQL is a nonprocedural language—in other words, it is smart. You do not have to tell it exactly how to store, retrieve, modify, or delete data; you just tell it what you want and SQL figures out how to do it. To make the power of a nonprocedural language clear, compare it with dBASE III

PLUS, which uses a procedural language. When you make a dBASE III PLUS query, you must tell what database files and indexes are needed and exactly how to get the data you want—step by step (Figure C-4a). SQL however, knows all about where the data is, what indexes to use, the possible sequences of operations when retrieving data from your database, and which is the most efficient way to get the data that you want. You do not have to specify a lot of procedural details when you query a database by using SQL (Figure C-4b).

A second reason for the popularity of SQL is its ability to draw data from many databases in different locations. These databases are called *distributed databases.* This ability allows a user in a company to prepare a report by using data stored in different locations throughout the country or the world.

A third reason for SQL's user appeal is that SQL is well established as an international standard language on mainframes, minis, and micros. A user can learn one database language and use it on a variety of computers. Furthermore, with SQL, users can use their personal computers to easily retrieve data stored on other computers, including mainframes and minis.

To enter the SQL mode, you type SET SQL ON from the dBASE IV dot prompt and press Enter. The dot prompt becomes a SQL prompt (the letters SQL are displayed as the prompt rather than a dot). When you

Figure C-4 dBASE III PLUS versus SQL commands. *(a) These dBASE III PLUS commands are used to generate the same information as (b) this single SQL command. Both queries may seem complicated at first, but the SQL query is actually much more straightforward and executes more quickly.*

```
(a)     . USE GRADES INDEX GINDX
        . SELECT 2
        . USE STUDENTS INDEX STUINDX
        . SELECT 3
        . USE CLASSES INDEX CINDX
        . SELECT 1
        . SET RELATION TO STDNUMB INTO B
        . SELECT 2
        . SET RELATION TO S_NUM INTO C
        . SELECT 1
        . DISPLAY ALL STDNUMB, B->LNAME, B->FNAME, C->YEAR, GRADE


(b)

SQL SELECT STDNUMB, LNAME, FNAME, YEAR, GRADE
      FROM GRADES, STUDENTS, CLASSES
      WHERE STUDENTS.STUDNUMB = GRADES.STUDNUMB AND STUDENTS.S_NUM =
            CLASSES.S_NUM
      ORDER BY STDNUMB
```

issue SQL commands, the results are immediately displayed on your screen. When you are using SQL, the dBASE files you use are converted to SQL tables, and SQL tables can likewise be converted to dBASE files. Many dBASE IV commands that have no direct SQL counterparts can be used in the SQL mode. To leave SQL and return to the dot prompt, the command SET SQL OFF and press Enter.

The Most Important SQL Commands

For all its power, SQL is a simple language; it uses only 14 commands. The table that follows lists the most frequently used SQL commands.

COMMAND	ACTION
Create Table	Given field names and data types, creates a new SQL database table. It is similar to the dBASE Create command.
Create Index	Creates an index by using fields in a database table. Like the dBASE Index command.
Create View	Creates a temporary table that is not stored in the database but is of temporary use to the user. This table consists of fields from database tables already stored in the database. Like the Create View command in dBASE.
Insert	Inserts new data records into an existing database. It functions like the dBASE Append command.
Delete	Deletes one or more records from a database table. Equivalent to the combination of Delete and Pack in dBASE.
Update	Enables a user to modify field values in records. Similar to the Replace command in dBASE.
Select	Specifies the data a user wants to retrieve from one or more SQL databases. This is the most often used SQL command. It is somewhat like the dBASE List command. Most other database languages require many separate statements to retrieve the data that SQL can retrieve with one Select statement.
Drop Table	Deletes a specified database table. Like the dBASE Delete File command.
Drop Index	Deletes a specified index. Like the dBASE Delete File command.
Alter Table	Allows a user to add new fields to an existing database table. Available in the DB2 version of SQL but not in some other versions. Like the dBASE Modify Structure command.

The Future of SQL

At this point in its development, SQL by itself is not a complete database programming language, so it is often used with languages like COBOL on mainframes and minis. On personal computers, it is usually used in conjunction with DBMS applications packages like dBASE IV, but it can also be used with some high-level programming languages like COBOL.

In the future, however, SQL will probably be enhanced to become a more complete language. Although predictions in the area of data processing are never sure things, it is a safe bet that SQL will be in use and evolving for at least the next decade and probably on into the twenty-first century.

Using dBASE IV with Local Area Networks

With dBASE IV Ashton-Tate has greatly improved the ability of users to share data on local area networks (LANs). Networks of computers are becoming commonplace in offices because users need to share programs, data, and peripheral devices. The sharing of data demands that a data management program enforce security provisions like passwords to protect sensitive data. Data sharing also requires that the problems that arise when two users attempt to retrieve or to modify the same record at the same time be resolved systematically with no loss of data. And, when all of an organization's data is in one database, the DBMS program must provide some way to recover from serious user errors or computer system failures.

dBASE III PLUS was designed to function on a LAN, but dBASE IV far surpasses the limited data-sharing capacity of dBASE III PLUS. dBASE IV also includes new security and disaster-recovery procedures. With dBASE IV personal computer users now have a data-sharing capacity previously available only on mainframe and minicomputers.

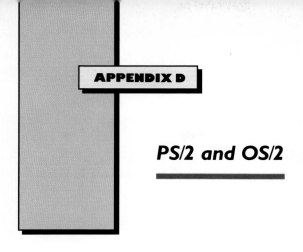

APPENDIX D

PS/2 and OS/2

In the previous chapters of this book, our discussion focused on the IBM PC and the MS-DOS (or PC-DOS) operating system. The applications programs we described, like Lotus 1-2-3 and WordPerfect, were designed to be used with DOS and the IBM PC. In April 1987 IBM announced a new family of computers called the Personal System/2, or PS/2 for short. IBM also announced a powerful new operating system, Operating System/2 (OS/2) from Microsoft Corporation, that is designed to be used with several of the PS/2 models. In this appendix we will give you background information on both the PS/2 and OS/2. We will also explain how to use applications programs like Lotus 1-2-3 with the PS/2 and OS/2.

The IBM PS/2 Computers

The PS/2 family of computers consists of several basic models (Figure D-1, on the next page). For you to understand some of the distinctions between the different models, we must first describe some of the new technologies that IBM has incorporated in the PS/2.

- The PS/2 uses $3\frac{1}{2}$-inch disks rather than the $5\frac{1}{4}$-inch disks found in the IBM PC. The $3\frac{1}{2}$-inch disk's greater storage capacity, smaller size, and built-in protection against dirt and damage make it clearly superior to the old $5\frac{1}{4}$-inch disk. Unfortunately, there are two different $3\frac{1}{2}$-inch storage standards, 720K and 1.44M (1.44 million bytes). We will discuss the implications of these two standards later in this appendix.

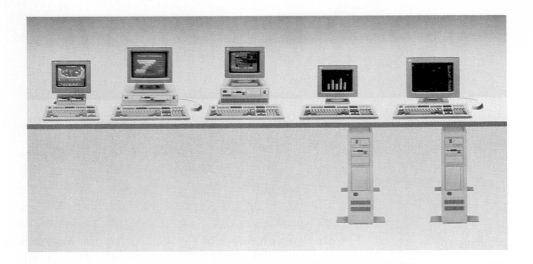

Figure D-1 The IBM PS/2 family. *The IBM PS/2 comes in a variety of different models.*

- With the PS/2, IBM introduced two improved graphics display standards that produce much clearer displays than the standard IBM-PC:

  1. The Multicolor Graphics Array (MCGA) that supports modes of 640 × 480 pixel resolution on a monochrome display or 320 × 200 pixels with four displayed colors.

  2. The Video Graphics Array (VGA) that offers a graphics mode with 640 × 480 pixel resolution and 16 displayed colors plus a text mode with 720 × 400 pixels and 16 colors.

- The models of the PS/2 use one of three new microprocessor chips: the 8086, the 80286, and the 80386. As in the PC, only one of these microprocessors is used in the CPU of each PS/2. All three of the new microprocessor chips work faster than the 8088 chip used in the standard IBM PC. The 80286 and 80386 chips give you the option of using the new OS/2 operating system; the 8086 does not.

- IBM introduced a new bus (the data movement path inside the computer) called the Micro Channel, which moves data inside the PS/2 faster than it could be moved inside the standard PC. Only some of the PS/2 models use this bus—the ones that do can run your programs faster, but they will not accept the add-on cards and boards that you may have purchased for your PC.

- A new keyboard has been added to the PS/2. The keyboard has been expanded and some keys have been relocated. The function keys that were at the left of the standard PC keyboard are now arranged along the top. There are 12 function keys on the PS/2, but keys F1 through F10 work exactly the same way with an applications program as they did on the PC. Many applications programs do not yet have a use for keys F11 and F12.

Another difference in the keyboard is that the PS/2 keyboard has a set of cursor movement keys just to the right of the Enter key. These keys are in addition to the cursor movement keys associated with the number keys at the far right of the keyboard. PS/2 users who want to continue to use the cursor movement keys in the number pad (as they did with the PC) must remember to press the Num Lock key before they try to use the cursor movement keys in the number pad. This is necessary because, when you turn on the PS/2, Num Lock is on. Pressing the right cursor key, for example, generates the number 6 rather than moving your cursor. To avoid headaches, it is a good idea to teach yourself to use the dedicated cursor movement keys on the new keyboard.

Using Applications with DOS on the PS/2

If you want to use your PS/2 and DOS to run applications like Lotus 1-2-3 or WordPerfect or to program in BASIC, there is little difference between using the PC and the PS/2. Everything that you have learned about these programs using the PC works in exactly the same way on the PS/2. The programs just work faster on your PS/2. However, some of the DOS commands you use may change because of the new disk drives and the new drive storage standards. Let us take a closer look at these changes.

Using DOS with $3\frac{1}{2}$-inch Disks

Although the new $3\frac{1}{2}$-inch disks are easier to use and can store more data than the old $5\frac{1}{4}$-inch disks, the size difference creates a problem if you need to exchange programs or data between the two types. The common solution is to attach an extra $5\frac{1}{4}$-inch disk drive to the PS/2. This disk drive is usually configured as the B drive. The COPY command can then be used to transfer data and programs between the two disks. However, you cannot use the DISKCOPY command to copy files between $5\frac{1}{4}$- and $3\frac{1}{2}$-inch disks because the data storage formats are different on the two types of disks.

Using DOS with the New Storage Standards

Another problem with the $3\frac{1}{2}$-inch disks is that there are, as we mentioned, two standards for storage: the 720K and 1.44M standards. If a $3\frac{1}{2}$-inch disk drive is a 1.44M drive, then it can read $3\frac{1}{2}$-inch disks written on a 720K drive. However, a 720K drive *cannot* read disks that have been recorded at a density of 1.44M. If you need to move programs or data from a PS/2 model with the 1.44M drives over to a model with the 720K drives, use the following technique:

1. Insert a $3\frac{1}{2}$-inch disk in the A drive—this should be the 1.44M drive. Format the disk by using the following command rather than the usual FORMAT command:

   ```
   FORMAT A:/N:9/T:80
   ```

   This will cause the 1.44M drive to format the disk by using the 720K format. Remember that formatting a disk erases whatever is already stored on it, so use a new disk or a disk whose contents are no longer needed.

2. Copy the files you want to transfer onto the newly formatted disk. Now you can use this disk in the 720K drives.

Using DOS with Hard-Disk Drives

Most of the PS/2 systems are sold with built-in (fixed) hard-disk drives. In a computer lab for student use, you will often find that the applications programs you want to use have already been stored on the hard disk. This will require that you become familiar with using a hard disk. Some of the procedures change when you are using a hard disk. For example:

- You usually need to start your system without a disk in the A drive. The computer boots from the hard disk, which is referred to as drive C. When DOS is loaded, instead of the A> prompt, either a C> or a C:\ prompt is displayed on your screen. Any commands you type are interpreted by the computer as referring to files stored on drive C.

- You will usually store your own data files on a data disk in drive A or drive B. To switch to the A drive from the C drive, type A: and press Enter. To switch to the B drive from the C drive, type B: and press Enter.

- Hard disks can store so many files that hard disks are usually partitioned into several subdirectories. For information regarding the use of subdirectories, see Appendix A.

The OS/2 Operating System

Operating System/2 from Microsoft Corporation is a powerful new operating system with many features that go far beyond the functions that DOS can perform. There are two editions of OS/2—the Standard Edition and the Extended Edition. The Extended Edition includes a database manager and a data communications manager. The database manager is a DBMS; it performs the same kinds of functions that dBASE III PLUS performs and complies with the standards used by an IBM mainframe DBMS. The data communications manager performs many of the functions that a data communications program performs. One of the advantages of the Extended Edition of OS/2 is that it will facilitate both the connection of the PS/2 to computer networks and the exchange of data between the PS/2 and IBM mainframes and minicomputers.

OS/2 is designed for the IBM PC AT and those models of the PS/2 that use the 80286 or 80386 microprocessor. Microsoft recommends that your system contain at least 2M of memory and a hard-disk drive if you wish to use OS/2.

Whole books have been written about OS/2 and a complete consideration of OS/2 is beyond the scope of this appendix. What we will do here is give you a overview of the OS/2 features and describe how you can use OS/2 with your applications programs.

OS/2 Features

Once you have learned to use a program such as WordPerfect with the DOS operating system, using the program with OS/2 will be a breeze. You are not going to have to learn a whole new set of commands. In fact, you can think of OS/2 as an operating system with a dual personality. OS/2 contains the familiar DOS commands, but it also includes a whole set of additional commands. If you want to use OS/2 just to run the DOS versions of Lotus 1-2-3, WordPerfect, or dBASE III PLUS, then you can use OS/2 just as if you were using DOS.

Perhaps an analogy is in order. OS/2 is like a car with a very powerful turbocharger that you can switch on or off. OS/2 has two modes—the REAL mode and the PROTECTED mode. With its turbocharger off, OS/2 is in what is termed the *REAL mode* (its DOS mode) and it works like DOS. If you switch OS/2 into its *PROTECTED mode* (its OS/2 mode), it is like switching on the turbocharger. You will have a lot more power and capability at your command. Applications programs written to run in the OS/2 REAL mode are usually not very different from the programs that you used with DOS. However, applications written to run in the OS/2 PROTECTED mode are able to make use of the increased capabilities of OS/2. Most of the people who use OS/2 do so to have access to these more sophisticated applications.

When the PROTECTED mode is used, OS/2 is a *multitasking* operating system. This means that you can run several applications programs at the same time—you do not need to wait for your computer to finish one task before you start work on another. For example, you can work on a spreadsheet in Lotus 1-2-3 or enter data in a dBASE database file at the same time that your computer is printing out a letter you wrote using WordPerfect. You do not need to save your work and exit from one applications program before loading the next. In the PROTECTED mode you can switch back and forth between different programs and easily move data from one program to another.

Another advantage of using OS/2 in the PROTECTED mode is that each applications program can use up to 16M of memory, about 25 times the memory that an application could use with DOS. Even if your computer does not have this much RAM storage, an applications program can still access huge amounts of memory because OS/2 uses *virtual memory* (sometimes referred to as *virtual storage*). This means that if OS/2 needs more main memory than your computer has, OS/2 will temporarily use disk space for memory.

When OS/2 runs multiple programs in PROTECTED mode, it protects all the memory space used by one applications program from any attempted use by another applications program. This means that you can start or stop a program without affecting the work of any other programs that are running concurrently. In contrast, if you run OS/2 in REAL mode, OS/2 becomes a *singletasking* (one program at a time) operating system like DOS and does not protect memory space.

Another new feature of OS/2 is the way in which you can interact with the program. OS/2 version 1.0 interacts with the user via what is called the *Session Manager*. When you start your computer, the Session Manager appears on your screen. The Session Manager displays a menu of the programs that are currently running and lets you switch between the different programs.

OS/2 version 1.1 and higher interact with the user via the *Presentation Manager*. The Presentation Manager is like the graphic user interface used in the Apple Macintosh and by the Microsoft program called Windows. It is designed to be used with a mouse, although one is not required. You communicate with OS/2 by selecting icons or choices from a menu, checking off boxes, and filling in boxes called dialogue boxes (Figure D-2).

The features discussed in this section are not the only new features introduced by OS/2, but they are probably the most important ones for users of applications programs. Now that we have touched on some of the characteristics of OS/2, let us see how we can use it to execute applications programs like Lotus 1-2-3 and WordPerfect.

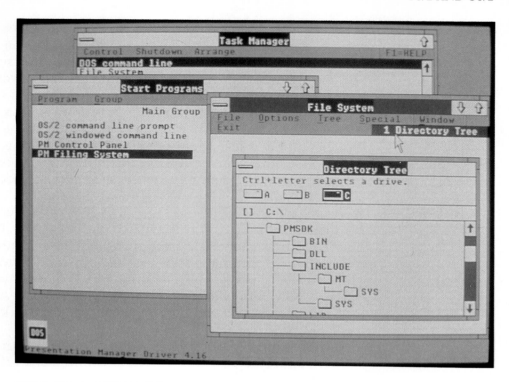

Figure D-2 The OS/2 Presentation Manager. *The Presentation Manager appears as the opening screen on OS/2 versions 1.1 and higher.*

Using Applications with OS/2 on the PS/2

One aspect of the current versions of OS/2 that does not differ from DOS is the file system used by OS/2. The data files that are created and read using OS/2 are exactly the same as DOS files. This is important because it means that the files that you created using DOS, such as reports written using WordPerfect or Lotus 1-2-3 spreadsheets, can be accessed by these same programs when they are run using the OS/2 operating system. This means that you will not have to re-enter all your data if you want to switch to OS/2.

Most of you who are using OS/2 now will be using the Session Manager or Presentation Manager and running versions of applications programs that were written to run with DOS. Therefore, in this section we will restrict our discussion to using OS/2 in the REAL mode. This is sometimes referred to as using the *DOS Compatibility Box* of OS/2 because you are using OS/2 as if it were DOS.

As we mentioned earlier, when you start up OS/2 version 1.0, you will see the opening screen displayed by the Session Manager. If you have booted your computer and you do not see this screen, press Ctrl-Esc. The Session Manager screen should appear on your screen if your hardware and software are functioning properly.

When you see the Session Manager opening screen, use your mouse or the cursor movement keys to move the cursor to the *DOS Command Prompt* entry and select it by pressing Enter or your mouse button. This signals OS/2 that you want to use the REAL mode of OS/2 and want the DOS prompt. You should see the following prompt on your screen:

```
[Real C:\]
```

The "Real" next to the C:\ prompt indicates that you are in REAL mode. (When OS/2 is running in PROTECTED mode, the prompt displayed is [C:\].) [Real C:\] is like the C> prompt in DOS, and you can enter the familiar DOS commands when you see it. Figure D-3 shows a list of the DOS commands that can be used when you are working in the REAL mode of OS/2.

If you want to load an applications program—for example, Word-Perfect—simply type the appropriate command, in this case WP. You should see the program's opening screens. You can now start using the program, and it will function for you exactly as it does when you use

Figure D-3 DOS commands available in OS/2. *These DOS commands may be used in the same way when using OS/2.*

APPEND	KEYB
ASSIGN	LABEL
ATTRIB	MKDIR (MD)
BACKUP	MODE
BREAK	MORE
CHCP	PATH
CHDIR (CD)	PRINT
CHKDSK	PROMPT
CLS	RECOVER
COMMAND	RENAME (REN)
COMP	REPLACE
COPY	RESTORE
DATE	RMDIR (RD)
DEL	SET
DIR	SORT
DISKCOMP	SUBST
DISKCOPY	SYS
EDLIN	TIME
ERASE	TREE
EXIT	TYPE
FDISK	VER
FIND	VERIFY
FORMAT	VOL
GRAFTABL	XCOPY
JOIN	

DOS. When you exit from the program you will be returned to the Session Manager screen. If you are finished using your computer, you can turn it off when the Session Manager screen is displayed.

If you want to run another program, such as Lotus 1-2-3 or dBASE III PLUS, then again select the DOS Command Prompt entry from the Session Manager screen. Next type 123 or DBASE and press Enter to start the program.

If you are using a version of OS/2 that uses the Presentation Manager, then the concepts in the previous discussion still apply. However, when you are using the Presentation Manager, much of your interaction with the computer will be via the Presentation Manager's graphic interface.

Remember that although OS/2 is a multitasking operating system, it is running in the singletasking mode when you are using the REAL mode. This means that you have to save your data files before you exit from a program. It also means that you must exit from one program (for example, dBASE) before you can start using another program like WordPerfect.

OS/2 is a complex operating system and, as we mentioned, there are several versions and editions. In this supplement we cannot explore all the various ways in which OS/2 can be set up to run your applications programs. You will probably have to do some more reading about the particular way in which OS/2 is used at your facility. But we hope that we have given you some of the flavor of OS/2. Remember that OS/2 is simply there to support your use of applications programs, and these programs are essentially the same programs that you used when you were using DOS.

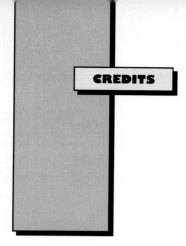

CREDITS

We are indebted to the many people and organizations who contributed excerpts, illustrations, and photos to this book. In particular, we would like to thank Egghead Discount Software, Inc. for allowing us to photograph in-store settings and software packaging.

Text Credits

Portions of the Real World page entitled "Computers Make Computers at IBM" based on an article by Ken Greenberg, *PC World*, December, 1986.

Portions of the Real World page entitled "Generation Gap at the Office" based on "Battling the 'Quill-Pen' Mentality," *PC Week*, December, 1987.

Real World page entitled "All the Gold in California" based on "Gold Fever on a Spreadsheet," *Computerland Magazine*, January/February, 1988.

Portions of the Real World page entitled "Getting Data at Quaker Oats" based on "A New Information System Serves Up Instant Statistics for Top Executives," *PC Week*.

Portions of the Real World page entitled "Using Graphics to Design Fabrics" based on "Designing Fabric with Custom CAD Program," *PC Week*.

Real World page entitled "Networks to Train Olympic Athletes" based on "A New Way of Training Olympians," *PC Week*, February 9, 1988.

Illustration Credits

F4-4   Figure adapted from WordPerfect template for the IBM PC, PC/XT, AT. Copyright © WordPerfect Corporation, Orem, UT.

F6-17   Redrawn from Timothy J. O'Leary, *The Student Edition of Lotus 1-2-3 User's Manual*, © l987, Addison-Wesley Publishing Company, Inc., Reading, MA.

F6-18   Redrawn from Timothy J. O'Leary, *The Student Edition of Lotus 1-2-3 User's Manual*, © 1987, Addison-Wesley Publishing Company, Inc., Reading, MA.

F6-21   Redrawn from Timothy J. O'Leary, *The Student Edition of Lotus 1-2-3 User's Manual*, © 1987, Addison-Wesley Publishing Company, Inc., Reading, MA.

F7-11   Marilyn Popyk, *Up and Running*, © 1987, Addison-Wesley Publishing Company, Inc., Reading, MA. Figure 6.17 on p 287. Reprinted with permission.

F10-7a,b   Redrawn from Timothy J. O'Leary, *The Student Edition of Lotus 1-2-3 User's Manual*, © 1987, Addison-Wesley Publishing Company, Inc., Reading, MA.

F10-11 Redrawn from Timothy J. O'Leary, *The Student Edition of Lotus 1-2-3 User's Manual*, © 1987, Addison-Wesley Publishing Company, Inc., Reading, MA.

F10-12 This copyrighted © material has been provided by Dynamic Graphics, Inc., 6000 N. Forest Park Drive, Peoria, IL 61614, and may not be reproduced in any way without express written permission of Dynamic Graphics, Inc.

F13-8   © copyright Microsoft Corporation, 1984–1987. Reprinted with permission from Microsoft Corporation.

F13-10 © copyright Microsoft Corporation, 1984–1987. Reprinted with permission from Microsoft Corporation.

Text Photo Credits

BG-4 Both Courtesy of International Business Machines Corporation

BG-5 Left Uarco, Inc.

Right Photo Courtesy of INMAC, Santa Clara, CA

BG-6 Top Courtesy of International Business Machines Corporation

Middle Courtesy of BASF Corporation/Information Systems

Bottom Microscience International Corporation

BG-7 Top Courtesy of Epson-America
Middle, bottom Photo Courtesy of Hewlett-Packard Company

BG-8 Bottom Photo Courtesy of INMAC, Santa Clara, CA

BG-9 Photo Courtesy of Toshiba America Inc., Information Systems Division

BG-10 Top Reproduced by permission of Hayes Microcomputer Products, Inc.

Bottom Polaroid

BG-11 Jerry Spagnoli

BG-12 Jerry Spagnoli/Egghead Discount Software

BG-13 Courtesy of International Business Machines Corporation

BG-14 Jerry Spagnoli

BG-15 Courtesy Heald Colleges of California

BG-17 Both Jerry Spagnoli

Chapter 4

136 Left Copyright Steven Borns 1988
Right Dow Jones & Co., Inc., publisher of the Wall Street Journal

Chapter 5

149 F5-8 Jerry Spagnoli

152 Hal Lewis

154 F5-12 Courtesy of Misco, Inc.

174 Four by Five

Chapter 6

201 Courtesy of Software Publishing Corporation

210 Courtesy of the United States Mint

Chapter 7

234 Copyright Paul Ambrose 1984

256 The Bettmann Archive

Chapter 8

293 Copyright David Smart 1988

Chapter 9

297 Courtesy of the Oakland Athletics Baseball Company

303 Photo Courtesy of Dow Jones & Co., Inc.

339 Courtesy of the Quaker Oats Company

Chapter 10

342 F10-1(a) Melvin R. Prueitt, © Los Alamos National Laboratory

F10-1(b) The Graphics Systems Research Group at the IBM U.K. Scientific Centre

F10-1(c) National Centre for Atomospheric Research/National Science Foundation

344 F10-3 Left, right © Lotus Development Corporation 1986. Used with permission. Middle Mouse Systems

345 F10-4 Left Polaroid
Middle, right Produced with 35mm Express TM from BPS

346 F10-5 Courtesy of Software Publishing Company

347 Left Courtesy of Software Publishing Company
Right Provided by Ashton-Tate Corporation

350 Copyright Ed Kashi

373 F10-28 Courtesy of the Houston Instrument Division Ametek, Inc.

375 Copyright Ed Kashi

383 Courtesy of Burlington Industries, Inc.

Chapter 11

390 F11-2 Photo Courtesy of Unisys Corporation

F11-3 Courtesy of National Wire and Cable Corporation

391 F11-4 Photo Courtesy of INMAC, Santa Clara, CA

F11-5 Courtesy of Optical Cable Corporation, Salem, VA

393 F11-8(b) Courtesy of Multi-Tech Systems, Inc.

F11-8(c) Courtesy of NCR Corporation

398 F11-12 Courtesy of Crosstalk Communications

399 Roberto Brosan, Copyright 1988 all rights reserved.

403 F11-13 Courtesy of International Business Machines Corporation

406 Courtesy of the United States Air Force Academy

409 F11-16 Courtesy of AT&T

411, 412 F11-18(a-c) Courtesy of Prodigy Services Company

416 Four by Five

Chapter 12

418 F12-1 Courtesy of Synthesis Concepts, Inc. and *Publish!* Magazine

420 F12-2 Copyright 1988 Aldus Corporation

423 F12-6 Adam Zakin

425 F12-9 Adam Zakin

426 Courtesy of Apple Computer, Inc.

428 F12-11 Copyright 1988 Aldus Corporation

430 F12-13 Courtesy of Western Digital Imaging

432 Courtesy of Corel Systems Corporation

435 Middle IN™ The Magazine for the Information Age, published by MCI Corporation. Designed and produced by Frankfurt Gips Balkind.

Right Reprinted with permission from TV Guide magazine, Copyright 1987 by Triangle Publications Inc., Radnor, PA.

Chapter 13

439 F13-1 Courtesy of Individual Software Corporation, Inc.

441 F13-2 Courtesy of Polytron Corporation

442 F13-3 Sidekick Plus is a product of Borland International

443 Jerry Spagnoli/Egghead Discount Software

445 F13-4 Provided by Ashton-Tate Corporation

446 F13-5 Microsoft® Windows copyright Microsoft Corporation, 1985–1988. Reprinted with permission from Microsoft Corporation.

452 F13-11 Jerry Spagnoli

453 F13-12 Courtesy of StatSoft, Inc., Tulsa, OK

458 Photo Courtesy of Egghead Discount Software

Chapter 14

461 F14-2 Left Copyright 1987 Robert Holmgren

F14-2 Right Courtesy of Texas Instruments

463 F14-3 Copyright Joel Gordon 1984

465 F14-4 Courtesy of International Business Machines Corporation

468 F14-4 Courtesy of Cromemco, Inc.

469 F14-6 Wayland Lee

470 F14-7 Courtesy of Misco, Inc.

471 F14-8 Courtesy of Misco, Inc.

473 F14-9 Courtesy of Misco, Inc.

476 Courtesy of Kaiser Aluminum & Chemical Corporation

Appendix D

510 Courtesy of International Business Machines Corporation

515 Microsoft® Windows/screen images copyright Microsoft Corporation, 1985–1988. Reprinted with permission from Microsoft Corporation.

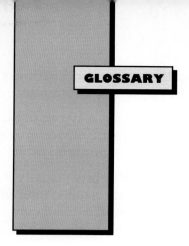

GLOSSARY

absolute address A spreadsheet cell address that does not change when a formula is copied from one location to another.

access arm A mechanical device that can access all the tracks of one cylinder in a disk storage unit.

acoustic coupler modem A modem that connects to a telephone receiver rather than directly to a telephone line.

active area In a database, the work area currently being used; also called the selected area.

active cell The cell available for current use on a spreadsheet, also called the current cell.

active file In a database, the file currently being used; also called the selected file.

active window The window in which the user is currently working.

ALU See *arithmetic/logic unit.*

amplitude The height of the carrier wave form in analog transmission.

analog transmission The transmission of computer data as a continuous electric signal in the form of a wave.

analytical graphics Traditional line graphs, bar charts, and pie charts used to illustrate and analyze data.

applications software Programs designed to perform specific tasks and functions.

arithmetic/logic unit (ALU) In a computer, the electronic circuitry that executes all arithmetic and logical operations.

artificial intelligence The field of study that explores computer involvement in tasks requiring intelligence, imagination, and intuition.

ASCII (American Standard Code for Information Interchange) A coding scheme using 7 bits to represent a data character.

asynchronous transmission Data transmission in which each group of message bits that represents a character is preceded by a start signal and ended with a stop signal.

attribute In a relational database, a column or field of a table.

audio-response unit See *voice synthesizer.*

axis A reference line of a graph. The horizontal axis is the x-axis. The vertical axis is the y-axis.

backup A duplicate of a disk or file.

bar graph A graph made up of filled-in columns or rows that represent the changing nature of data over time.

baud rate A term used to describe the rate at which electronic signals are transmitted.

BBS See *bulletin board system.*

binary system A system in which data is represented by combinations of 0s and 1s, which correspond to the two states off and on, respectively.

bit A binary digit, either a 0 or a 1.

bits per second (bps) A measure of the rate at which data is transmitted.

block See *text block.*

boilerplate Text stored in a separate file to be used later in other documents.

boldface Printing of characters or words in type darker than the surrounding characters or words.

booting the system The process of copying the operating system into memory.

bridge A device that connects networks of the same type, allowing equipment on one LAN to communicate with devices on another. Also called a router.

buffer A temporary area of computer memory in which documents or other data can be stored before being released to the printer or another device.

bulletin board system (BBS) Telephone-accessible personal computers that provide public message systems.

business graphics Graphics that represent data in a visual, easy-to-understand format.

business-quality graphics See *presentation graphics.*

bus lines Electrical pathways connecting the parts of a computer.

bus network A network formed when each hardware device or computer is connected to a common cable.

byte String of bits (usually 7 or 8) used to represent one character of data; a letter, digit, or special character.

cable interface unit An electronic component used to send and receive signals on a network cable.

camera-ready In publishing, final copy that is photographed to create printing plates.

cell The intersection of a row and a column in a spreadsheet. Entries in a spreadsheet are stored in individual cells.

cell address In a spreadsheet, the column and row coordinates of a cell.

cell contents The label or value contained in a spreadsheet cell.

central processing unit (CPU) Electronic circuitry that executes stored program instructions. It consists of two parts: the control unit and the arithmetic/logic unit.

character A letter, number, or special character (such as $).

character printers Impact printers that print one character at a time.

chip See *integrated circuit.*

clip art Illustrations stored on disk that are used to enhance a graph or document.

closed architecture Personal computer design that limits add-ons to those that can be plugged into the back of the machine.

clustered-bar graph Bar graph comparing several different but related sets of data.

coaxial cable Bundles of insulated wire within a shield enclosure; can transmit electronic signals very rapidly.

cold boot Loading the operating system into memory when the system is not already running; usually accomplished by turning on the power switch.

command-driven program Applications program that requires the user to use (and remember) commands, rather than to make selections from a menu.

command menu A set of command choices in an applications software program such as Lotus 1-2-3.

command tree A hierarchical diagram that shows all the choices from a main command menu and the associated submenus.

communications link A medium for carrying data communications signals between two places.

computer A machine that accepts data (input) and processes it into useful information (output).

computer conferencing A method of sending, reviewing, and storing typed messages within a network of users.

computer programmer A person who designs, writes, tests, and implements programs.

conditional replace A word processing function that queries the user whether or not to replace a particular item each time it is found in a document.

configuration The components of a computer hardware system.

connectivity A computer's potential to communicate with other computers.

context sensitivity Software feature that allows a user to access information about the application or command the user is currently using.

control panel The upper portion of a spreadsheet screen; consists of status, entry, and prompt lines.

control unit The circuitry that directs and coordinates the computer system in executing stored program instructions.

copy-protection A software or hardware block that makes it difficult or impossible to make unauthorized copies of software.

CPU See *central processing unit.*

current cell See *active cell.*

current drive The disk drive currently being used by the computer system; also called the default drive.

current window See *active window.*

cursor A flashing indicator on the screen; indicates where the next typed character will be inserted.

cursor movement keys Keys on the keyboard that allow the user to move the cursor on the screen.

daisy wheel printer A letter-quality character printer that has a removable wheel with a set of spokes, each containing a raised character.

data Raw material to be processed by a computer.

database A collection of related data files.

database management system (DBMS) A set of programs that creates, manages, protects, and provides access to a database.

data buses See *bus lines.*

data communications The process of exchanging data over communications facilities.

data communications program Software that links a personal computer to another computer system.

data disk A disk used to store files created by the user.

data point A single value represented by a bar or symbol in a graph.

DBMS See *database management system.*

default drive The disk drive to which commands refer in the absence of any specified drive. Unless instructed otherwise, an applications program stores files on the default drive.

default settings Settings automatically used by a program unless the user specifies otherwise.

demodulation Reconstruction of a digital signal after analog transmission.

desktop organizer program Software that allows the user to perform several small tasks, such as calculations or note taking, without exiting from an applications program.

desktop publishing Use of a personal computer, special software, and a laser printer to produce high-quality documents that combine text and graphics.

desktop publishing program Software package for designing and producing professional-looking documents.

digital transmission The transmission of data as distinct pulses.

digitizer A graphics input device that allows the user to create images. It often has a stylus that can be used to draw or trace images, which are then converted to digital data that can be processed by the computer.

direct-connect modem A modem connected directly to a telephone line.

disk directory A list of the names and characteristics of the files currently stored on a disk.

disk drive A device that allows data to be read from a disk and written onto a disk.

diskette A disk on which data is recorded magnetically.

disk operating system (DOS) A set of programs designed to manage a computer's resources.

disk utility program Software that performs tasks related to computer and disk management.

displayed value The calculated result of a formula or function in a spreadsheet cell. The number in a cell displayed according to a user-specified format.

distributed processing A system of connected computers in various locations.

document Any written communication that conveys information.

documentation A written description of how a program works. Also refers to the instruction manual for packaged software.

DOS See *disk operating system.*

dot-matrix printer A printer that activates a matrix of pins to produce a character on paper.

dot prompt In dBASE, the prompt that tells the user that the program is ready for a command.

downloading Retrieving data from another computer.

duty cycle Used to describe a of4printer in terms of the number of pages printed per month. The higher the duty cycle, the more rugged the printer.

EDIT mode Spreadsheet mode that allows the user to edit the contents of a cell.

electronic fund transfer (EFT) Paying for goods and services by transferring funds between accounts electronically.

electronic mail (e-mail) The process of sending messages directly from one terminal or computer to another. The messages may be stored for later retrieval.

electronic publishing See *desktop publishing.*

electronic spreadsheet An electronic worksheet that organizes data into rows and columns; produced using a spreadsheet program such as Lotus 1-2-3.

e-mail See *electronic mail.*

ENTRY mode Spreadsheet mode that lets the user enter data.

ergonomics The study of human factors, primarily physical, in the design of workplaces.

expansion slots The slots inside a computer that allow a user to insert additional circuit boards.

expert shell Software having the structure to find answers to questions; the questions can be added by the user.

expert system A software package that presents the computer as an expert on some topic.

exploded pie chart A pie chart with a "slice" that is separated from the rest of the chart.

external direct-connect modem A modem that is separate from the computer.

external DOS commands Commands that access DOS programs residing on the DOS disk as program files. The programs must be read from the disk before they can be executed. These program files are not automatically loaded into the computer when it is booted. See *internal DOS commands.*

facsimile machine (fax machine) A device used to transmit documents or pictures electronically via telephone lines.

fax machine See *facsimile machine.*

fiber optics Transmitting data as light along glass fibers.

field A set of related characters; a column of data in a database.

field name In a database, the unique name describing the data in a field.

field width The maximum number of characters or digits that can be contained in a field.

file A collection of related records.

file consolidation program Software that finds files that are scattered in fragments on disk and groups these fragments in a single location so that the file can be read efficiently from the disk.

file extension Up to three characters that follow the dot in a file name; used to identify the type of file.

file name The unique sequence of characters used by DOS to identify a file.

file recovery software Program that makes it possible to access accidentally deleted files.

file specification The complete file name. Consists of the disk drive on which the file is stored, the file name, a dot, and the file extension.

file transfer software Data communications software that lets the user transfer files between connected computers.

firmware Read-only memory storing special programs.

floppy disk A flexible disk on which data is recorded magnetically.

font A complete set of characters in a particular size, typeface, weight, and style.

font library A variety of type fonts stored on disk.

format The specifications that determine the way a document or worksheet is displayed on the screen or printer.

formatting Magnetically marking the boundaries of tracks and sectors on a disk and creating a disk directory; also called initializing.

form letter program A program used with word processing programs to produce "personalized" letters.

formula In a spreadsheet, an instruction to calculate a value.

frequency The number of times an analog signal cycles during a second.

full-duplex transmission Data transmission in both directions at the same time.

full-function software Data communications software that lets a computer emulate a variety of terminals and communicate using different file transfer protocols.

function A built-in spreadsheet formula.

function keys Special keys that execute commonly used commands; the commands vary with the software being used.

gateway Device that connects two dissimilar networks, allowing machines in one network to communicate with those in the other.

global character A special character, such as *, that is used to represent any string of characters; often used in DOS commands.

grammar and style program A program that identifies unnecessary words and wordy phrases in a word-processed document.

graphics Pictures or graphs.

graphics adapter board See *graphics card*.

graphics card A circuit board that lets a computer display pictures or graphs as well as text.

graphics monitor Monitor capable of displaying high-resolution graphics.

graphics printer A printer—such as a dot-matrix, ink-jet, or laser printer—that can produce graphic output.

half-duplex transmission Data transmission in either direction, but only one way at a time.

halftone Reproduction of a black-and-white photograph; made up of tiny dots.

hard copy Printed paper output.

hard disk A metal platter coated with magnetic oxide and used by the computer for data storage.

hard-disk manager Program that helps the user organize files.

hardware The physical components of a computer system.

host computer The central computer in a network.

icon A small figure on the computer screen that represents a computer activity.

impact printer A printer that forms characters by physically striking the paper.

index file A file that allows data in a database file to be presented in a different order. It also allows the user to quickly search a database file for a record.

index generator program A program that permits marking important terms in word-processed text and can automatically generate an index when the document is complete.

information Processed data; data that is organized, meaningful, and useful.

information center A company center that offers employees computer-related training, help in getting data from other computer systems, and technical assistance.

information utility Commercial consumer-oriented communications system, such as The Source and CompuServe.

initializing See *formatting*.

ink-jet printer A printer that sprays ink from nozzles onto the paper to create characters or pictures.

input Data that is input to the computer system for processing.

input devices Devices that put data in machine-readable form and send it to the computer's processing unit.

insert mode In word processing, a text input mode in which text is inserted at the current cursor position without overwriting any text already in the document.

integrated circuit One or more complete electronic circuits embedded on a small silicon wafer.

integrated software An all-in-one package of several different applications programs, such as word processing, spreadsheet, and database management programs. Data can be passed readily from one program to another.

internal DOS commands Commands that access DOS programs that are loaded into the computer when the system is booted.

internal font Font built into the read-only memory of a printer.

internal modem A modem on a circuit board that can be installed inside a computer.

joy stick An input device that allows control of figures on a CRT screen.

justification Aligning of text along left and/or right margins.

K See *kilobyte*.

kerning Adjusting the space between characters to create wider or tighter spacing.

keyboard A common computer input device similar to the keyboard of a typewriter.

keyboard enhancement program Software that lets the user modify some of the capabilities and functions of the keyboard.

key field In a database, a field whose value is different for each record in the database file. The key field is used to identify a record.

kilobyte (K) 1024 bytes.

knowledge engineer A computer professional who gathers information from human experts; this expertise can be used in an expert system program.

label In a spreadsheet, data consisting of a string of text characters.

label prefix In a spreadsheet, a special character that identifies an entry as a label and tells the program how to display the label in a cell.

LAN See *local area network*.

laptop computer A small, portable computer.

laser printer A nonimpact printer that uses a light beam to transfer images to paper.

leading The vertical spacing between lines of type.

legend Text beneath a graph that explains the colors, shading, or symbols used to label the data points.

letter-quality printer A printer, such as a daisy wheel, that produces high-quality output.

light pen An input device that allows the user to interact directly with the computer screen.

line graph Graph made by connecting data points with a line.

link field A common field included in database files that allows related records to be retrieved from separate files.

local area network (LAN) A network designed to share data and resources among several computers that are (usually) within the same building.

macro A stored sequence of keystrokes that can be executed using only one or two keystrokes.

macro generator See *keyboard enhancement program*.

mainframe A large computer that has access to billions of characters of data and is capable of processing data very quickly.

Management Information Systems (MIS) A set of formal business computer systems designed to provide information for an organization.

megabyte 1 million bytes.

memory The electronic circuitry that temporarily holds data and program instructions needed by the CPU.

menu An on-screen list of command choices.

menu-driven program Applications programs that allow the user to issue commands by choosing from a list.

MENU mode Spreadsheet mode that allows the user access to command menus.

microcomputer The smallest and least expensive class of computer.

microcomputer manager The manager in charge of personal computer acquisition and use.

microprocessor A general-purpose processor on a chip.

microwave transmission Transmission of data signals through the atmosphere via high-frequency radio signals.

minicomputer A computer smaller than a mainframe and usually larger than a microcomputer in storage capacity.

MIS See *Management Information Systems.*

mixed cell reference A spreadsheet cell reference in a formula that is part absolute and part relative.

mode indicator Message displayed on the screen by a spreadsheet program; tells the user the program's current mode of operation.

modem A device that converts a digital signal to an analog signal or vice versa. Used to transfer data or programs between computers over analog telephone lines.

modulation The process of converting a signal from digital to analog.

monitor Microcomputer display screen.

monochrome A computer screen that displays information in one color on a background of another color.

monospace printing A method of printing in which all characters occupy the same amount of horizontal space.

motherboard The main circuit board of a microcomputer.

mouse A hand-held computer input device whose rolling movement on a flat surface causes corresponding movement of the cursor on the screen.

MS-DOS (Microsoft Disk Operating System) See *disk operating system.*

multiple-range graph A graph that plots the values of more than one variable.

named graph The user-defined settings stored in a worksheet that create a particular graph from data in the worksheet.

near–letter-quality printer A 24-pin dot-matrix printer or a printer that prints each letter twice; a high-quality printer.

network A computer system that uses communications equipment to connect two or more computers and their resources.

network interface card A card inserted into a computer; contains many of the electronic components needed to send and receive messages on a LAN.

node A device—such as a personal computer, hard disk, printer, or another peripheral—that is connected to a network.

noise Electrical interference that causes distortion when a signal is being transmitted.

nonimpact printer A printer that produces output without physically striking the paper.

nonvolatile Refers to memory that retains data even after electrical power is interrupted or turned off.

numeric keypad A group of keys on the computer keyboard; used for entering numbers.

open architecture Personal computer design that allows additional circuit boards to be inserted in expansion slots inside the computer.

operating system A set of programs that manage a computer's resources.

output Raw data that has been processed into useful information.

output devices Devices, such as printers, that make processed information available for use.

packaged software Software that is ready for use by nonprogrammers and sold in stores.

page composition program See *desktop publishing program.*

page description language (PDL) A language built into printers used in desktop publishing. Used by desktop publishing program to control the way a printer prints a page.

page footers Information printed consistently at the bottom of each page of a multipage document.

page headers Information printed consistently at the top of each page of a multipage document.

page layout In publishing, the process of arranging text and graphics on a page.

pan To move the cursor between fields on a record.

parallel printer A printer to which a computer can send the bits in a character over separate wires; must be located within a few feet of a computer.

PDL See *page description language.*

personal computer See *microcomputer.*

PERT chart A project management tool showing the relationships among a project's tasks, as well as their timing.

phase The relative position in time of a cycle of an analog signal.

picture file A file used to print graphs; contains a "picture" of a graph. Has the extension PIC.

pie chart Pie-shaped graph used to compare values that represent parts of a whole.

pitch Number of characters per inch across a page.

pixel Picture element on a computer display screen.

plot area Area in which a graph is drawn.

point Typographic measurement equaling approximately $\frac{1}{72}$ inch.

pointer In a database, the connector, or link, to a particular record in a database file.

pop-up program Program that can be accessed temporarily while another program is running.

presentation graphics Graphics that are used to communicate, illustrate, and emphasize a message to an audience.

printer A device for generating output on paper.

processor The central processing unit (CPU) of a computer.

program A set of step-by-step instructions that direct the computer to perform specific tasks and produce certain results; also called software.

project management software A program used to schedule and monitor projects consisting of many tasks.

proportional printing A method of printing in which different characters occupy different horizontal widths; also called proportional spacing.

proportional spacing See *proportional printing.*

protocol A set of rules for the exchange of data between a terminal and a computer or between two computers.

ragged-right margin An uneven right edge of the text in a document.

RAM See *memory.*

RAM disk A program that sets aside part of the computer's memory and treats it as an extra disk drive.

RAM resident Refers to a program that stays in memory, ready to be activated when needed.

random-access memory (RAM) See *memory.*

range A group of one or more cells, arranged in a rectangle, that a spreadsheet program treats as a unit.

read-only memory (ROM) Memory that can only be read; it cannot be used for storage by the user. The contents of ROM are not lost after the power is turned off.

read/write head A device that reads the magnetized areas on a storage medium, such as a disk, and converts them into the electrical impulses that are sent to the processor.

READY mode Spreadsheet mode indicating that the program is ready for whatever action the user indicates.

record A collection of related fields; for example, data about a person or thing.

relation A table in a relational database.

relational database A database in which the data is organized in a table format consisting of columns and rows.

relational operator An operator—such as $<$, $>$, or $=$—that allows a user to make comparisons and selections.

relative address A spreadsheet cell reference that is adjusted when it is copied to a new location.

resolution Clarity of a monitor display screen.

ring network A computer network in which the devices are connected to one another in the form of a ring.

ROM See *read-only memory.*

router See *bridge.*

satellite transmission Data transmission from earth station to earth station via communications satellite.

scrolling A word processing feature that allows the user to move to and view any part of a document on the screen in 24-line chunks.

search and replace A word processing feature that finds and changes each instance of a repeated item.

secondary storage devices Auxiliary units, typically disk storage, outside the CPU; can store additional data and programs.

selected area See *active area*.

selected file See *active file*.

serial printer A printer to which the computer transmits bits one at a time in sequence.

server A controlling device that performs specific functions (such as allowing access to a modem) for other devices in a network.

single-range graph A graph that plots the values of only one variable.

soft font Font that can be downloaded from a personal computer into a printer from files stored on disk.

soft-sectored diskette A diskette whose sectors are determined by DOS.

software See *program*.

source disk The diskette that is being copied.

speech recognition device See *voice input device*.

speech synthesis The process of enabling machines to simulate voice output.

spelling checker program A program that checks the spelling in a word-processed document.

spreadsheet A worksheet divided into rows and columns that can be used to organize and present data. Spreadsheet programs create an electronic spreadsheet for the user.

stacked-bar graph Bar graph in which all data common to a given row or column appear stacked in one bar.

stand-alone program Individual program that performs a single function, such as a word processing program.

star network A network consisting of one or more smaller computers connected to a central host computer.

statistical program Software used to perform sophisticated statistical analyses on data.

status line In word processing, the on-screen line that tells the name of the document, the current document page, the line on which the cursor rests, and the horizontal cursor position.

submenu An additional set of options related to a prior menu selection.

subscript A character printed one-half line below the surrounding type.

supercomputer The largest and most powerful category of computers.

superscript A character printed one-half line above the surrounding type.

surge protector Device that protects the computer and its data from being lost or damaged by electrical problems.

synchronous transmission Data transmission in which characters of data are sent in groups (blocks), allowing high-speed transmission.

system disk A disk containing the files that hold the internal part of DOS.

system prompt A signal displayed on the screen that tells the user that DOS has been loaded into memory and is ready to accept commands or execute an applications program.

system reset See *warm boot*.

table of contents program With a word processing program, this program allows the user to mark chapter headings in a document and automatically generate a table of contents when the document is completed. This feature is often included in a word processing program.

tab stops Position settings that indicate where the cursor will move when the Tab key is pressed.

target disk The receiving diskette during a Copy command.

teleconferencing A system of holding conferences by linking different locations through computer terminals or personal computers.

template (a) Plastic sheet placed over the function keys to help the user remember tasks performed by each key. (b) In a spreadsheet program, the same term is used to mean a worksheet that has already been designed for the solution of a specific problem.

terminal A device that consists of an input device, an output device, and a link to the main computer.

terminal emulation software Data communications software that makes a personal computer act like a terminal that communicates with a larger computer.

text block A continuous section of text in a document.

thermal printer A printer that produces characters by using heat in the pins in the print head.

thesaurus program With a word processing program, this program provides a list of synonyms and antonyms for a word in a document. This feature is often included in a word processing program.

toggle switch A keystroke that turns a function of a program on or off.

topology The physical layout of a LAN.

tracks The concentric circles in which data is stored on a disk.

tuple A record (row) in a relation .

twisted pair Cable consisting of two insulated wires that have been twisted around each other to reduce electrical noise during transmission.

typeface Set of characters of the same design.

typeover mode A text-entry mode in which each character typed overwrites the character at the cursor position.

type size The size, in points, of a typeface.

user friendly Refers to software that is easy for novices to use.

uploading Sending a file from one computer to a larger computer.

value In a spreadsheet, data consisting of a number representing an amount, a formula, or a function.

variable On a graph, the items that the data points describe.

vertical market Market consisting of groups of similar customers, for example, lawyers, doctors, or farmers.

videoconferencing A technique for holding conferences by using computers, cameras, and wall-size screens.

videotex Data communications merchandising.

voice input device A device that accepts the spoken word through a microphone and converts it into digital code that can be understood by the computer.

voice mail A system in which the user can dictate and receive messages that are stored by a computer. These messages may be sent between computers over a network.

voice output device See *voice synthesizer*.

voice synthesizer A device that converts data in main storage to vocalized sounds understandable to humans.

volatile Refers to data that is lost from memory when the electrical power is interrupted or turned off.

volume label A disk label stored by the user on the disk; seen when the DOS command DIR is used.

WAN See *wide area network*.

warm boot The action of rebooting a computer system that is already running.

wide area network (WAN) A network that lets users send data over long distances via the telephone system.

window A separate area on the computer display screen.

window manager Software that coordinates and integrates separate stand-alone programs.

wire pair See *twisted pair*.

word processing Computer-based creation, editing, formatting, storing, and printing of text.

word wrap A word processing feature that automatically starts a word at the left margin of the next line if there is not enough room on the line.

worksheet An electronic spreadsheet produced by a user and stored on disk by using a spreadsheet application program.

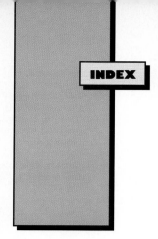

INDEX

NOTE: Page numbers that appear in italics indicate illustrations. BG stands for Buyer's Guide and RR stands for Ready Reference.

Licensing Agreements and Disclaimers

WordPerfect®

A version of this textbook contains an educational version of WordPerfect 4.2. Using the diskette(s) accompanying the book indicates your acceptance of the terms and conditions outlined below:

The Software is protected by copyright laws, and no unauthorized copying, distribution of, or any other act with respect to the Software is allowed that would violate those laws. You may not modify, reverse engineer, decompile, or disassemble the software and may not deliver copies to, or sell, rent, lease, or sublicense the Software to anyone else.

Benjamin/Cummings warrants that the diskette(s) delivered are free from defects in materials and faulty workmanship under normal use during the period of 90 days from the date of original delivery. If a defect in a diskette appears during this 90-day period, the defective item may be returned to Benjamin/Cummings, postage prepaid, addressed to Information Resources Group, Benjamin/Cummings Publishing, 390 Bridge Parkway, Redwood City, CA 94065. Benjamin/Cummings will replace the defective item without charge. This warranty applies only to diskettes packaged with this textbook, and does not cover items damaged, modified, or misused after delivery.

This warranty is in lieu of all other express warranties on the diskette(s). The software itself is licensed "as is," without any express or implied warranties whatsoever. The owners, their distributors, and dealers shall in no event be liable for indirect, incidental, or consequential damages, whether resulting from defects in the diskette(s) or from any defect in the software itself or documentation thereof.

Any implied warranties that are found to exist are hereby limited in duration to the 90-day life of the express warranties on the diskette(s) given above. Some states do not allow the exclusion or limitation of incidental or consequential damages, or any limitation on how long implied warranties last, so these exclusions or limitations may not apply to you. This warranty gives you specific legal rights and you may also have other rights, which vary from state to state.

dBASE III PLUS™

A copy of the student edition of dBASE III PLUS accompanies one version of this textbook. If you are using this version, please read this agreement before using the dBASE III PLUS program. By using the dBASE III PLUS program, you show your agreement to the terms of this license.

Exclusions of Warranties and Limitations of Liability

The copy of the dBASE III PLUS program made available for the use with this textbook is a limited functionality version of dBASE III PLUS, and is intended solely for educational, training and demonstration purposes. Accordingly, this copy of dBASE III PLUS is provided "as is," without warranty of any kind from Ashton-Tate or (licensee). Ashton-Tate and (licensee) hereby disclaim all warranties of any kind with respect to this limited functionality copy of dBASE III PLUS, including without limitation the implied warranties of merchantability and fitness for a particular purpose. Neither Ashton-Tate nor (licensee) shall be liable under any circumstances for consequential, incidental, special or exemplary damages arising out of the use of this limited functionality copy of dBASE III PLUS, even if Ashton-Tate or (licensee) has been apprised of the likelihood of such damages occurring. In no event will Ashton-Tate's or (licensee's) liability (whether based on an action or claim in contract, tort or otherwise) arising out of the use of this limited functionality copy of dBASE III PLUS exceed the amount paid for this textbook.

Limited Use Software License Agreement

Definitions

The term "Software" as used in this agreement means the limited use version of dBASE III PLUS which is made available for use in conjunction with this Textbook solely for educational, training and/or demonstration purposes. The term "Software Copies" means the actual copies of all or any portion of the Software, including back-ups, updates, merged or partial copies permitted hereunder.

Permitted Uses

You may:

- Load into RAM and use the Software on a single terminal or a single workstation of a computer (or its replacement).
- Install the Software onto a permanent storage device (a hard disk drive).
- Make and maintain up to three back-up copies provided they are used only for back-up purposes, and you keep possession of the back-ups. In addition, all the information appearing on the original disk labels (including copyright notice) must be copied onto the back-up labels.

This license give you certain limited rights to use the Software and Software Copies for educational, training and/or demonstration purposes. You do not become the owner of and Ashton-Tate retains title to, all the Software and Software Copies. In addition, you agree to use reasonable efforts to protect the Software from unauthorized use, reproduction, distribution or publication.

All rights not specifically granted in this license are reserved by Ashton-Tate.

Uses Not Permitted

You may not:

- Make copies of the Software, except as permitted above.
- Rent, lease, sublicense, time-share, lend or transfer the Software, Software Copies or your rights under this license except that transfers may be made with Ashton-Tate's prior written authorization.
- Alter, decompile, disassemble, or reverse-engineer the Software.
- Remove or obscure the Ashton-Tate copyright and trademark notices.
- Use the Software or Software Copies outside the United States or Canada.

Duration

This agreement is effective from the day you first use the Software. Your license continues for fifty years or until you return to Ashton-Tate the original disks and any back-up copies, whichever comes first.

If you breach this agreement, Ashton-Tate can terminate this license upon notifying you in writing. You will be required to return all Software Copies. Ashton-Tate can also enforce our other legal rights.

General

This agreement represents the entire understanding and agreement regarding the Software Copies and supersedes any prior purchase order, communication, advertising or representation.

This license may only be modified in a written amendment signed by an authorized Ashton-Tate officer. If any provision of this agreement shall be unlawful, void, or for any reason unenforceable, it shall be deemed severable from, and shall in no way affect the validity or enforceability of the remaining provisions of this agreement. This agreement will be governed by California law.